# THE LIFE AND POETRY
# OF FRANK STANFORD

James McWilliams

# The Life and Poetry of Frank Stanford

THE UNIVERSITY OF ARKANSAS PRESS
FAYETTEVILLE * 2025

Copyright © 2025 by the University of Arkansas Press. All rights reserved. No part of this book should be used or reproduced in any manner without prior permission in writing from the University of Arkansas Press or as expressly permitted by law.

978-1-68226-272-6 (cloth)
978-1-68226-279-5 (paperback)
978-1-61075-837-6 (electronic)

29 28 27 26 25   5 4 3 2 1


Designed by William Clift



LIBRARY OF CONGRESS CATALOGING-IN-PUBLICATION DATA
Names: McWilliams, James E., author.
Title: The life and poetry of Frank Stanford / James McWilliams.
Description: Fayetteville : The University of Arkansas Press, 2025.
Identifiers: LCCN 2024045147 (print) | LCCN 2024045148 (ebook) |
  ISBN 9781682262726 (cloth) | ISBN 9781610758376 (ebook)
Subjects: LCSH: Stanford, Frank, 1948–1978. | Poets, American—20th
  century—Biography. | LCGFT: Biographies.
Classification: LCC PS3569.T3316 Z76 2025  (print) | LCC PS3569.T3316  (ebook) |
  DDC 811/.54—dc23/eng/20241007
LC record available at https://lccn.loc.gov/2024045147
LC ebook record available at https://lccn.loc.gov/2024045148

*For Ralph Adamo,
saint of New Orleans*

*Nobody knows you. No. But I sing of you.
For posterity I sing of your profile and grace.
Of the signal maturity of your understanding.
Of your appetite for death and the taste of its mouth.
Of the sadness of your once valiant gaiety.*
    —FEDERICO GARCÍA LORCA

# Contents

*Prelude* ix

*Introduction* xv

ONE
A "Grade A" Baby 3

TWO
Life on the Levees: 1953–1956 23

THREE
"Frankie was the Star": Memphis, 1956–1961 49

FOUR
"Motley Boy on the Loose": 1961–1964 85

FIVE
"Subiaco's Unofficial Poet Laureate": 1964–1966 121

SIX
College, Part One: 1966–1968 153

SEVEN
College, Part Two: 1968–1971 189

EIGHT
"A Remarkable Chaos": 1970 to Early 1972 225

## NINE
"I Am Ready to Rise from My Ashes": 1972 — 263

## TEN
"A Syntax of Images": 1973 — 305

## ELEVEN
"The Untold Days of the Poet": 1974–1975 — 355

## TWELVE
"My Wife Is Painting Alot": 1974–1975 — 401

## THIRTEEN
Lost Roads: 1976–1977 — 441

## FOURTEEN
"I Wandered I Sang": 1978 — 483

*Coda* — 505

*Bibliographical Note* — 507

*Acknowledgments* — 511

*Notes* — 515

*Index* — 613

# *Prelude*

> Death doesn't fuck around.
> —FRANK STANFORD, "LOST DOG AND A WILD HAIR"

*E*ARLY MORNING, JUNE 3, 1978, an Uptown New Orleans house at 519 Webster Street. Frank Stanford got out of bed, went into the bathroom, and wrote in black ink a message on the wall, just above a tacked-up poster of Michelangelo's The Last Judgment.
"What is Frank looking for?"¹
He got dressed and took ten dollars and an old suitcase that belonged to his friend and fellow poet Ralph Adamo, in whose house he had just slept. After packing his clothes, Frank went to meet the writer Ellen Gilchrist for breakfast. They ate on Magazine Street—possibly at Tranchina's. "This is good-bye," Frank said to her after breakfast. "This is really good-bye."²
Then Kay DuVernet, a poet and photographer with whom Frank had spent the night, picked him up and drove him to the airport to fly home to Fayetteville, Arkansas.³
What was Frank Stanford looking for? Impossible question. Nobody will ever fully know. But on that morning at least, he wanted an escape. Typically, escaping was something he did well. Frank escaped having to ask his friend Ralph for money. He escaped whatever expectations DuVernet, a woman whom Frank had known for many years, might have

entertained about the poet she had loved through the night.[4] But most notably, Stanford, by sojourning in New Orleans for over two weeks, had escaped facing in person the anger of his wife Ginny Crouch Stanford and his lover C. D. Wright.

Because the jig was up. A day or two after Frank left for his trip to New Orleans on May 18, the two women had discovered that they'd been deceived by the handsome and charismatic poet. Frank had told Ginny that his relationship with C. D. was a working relationship; and he had told C. D. that his marriage with Ginny was one of convenience. But the facts were otherwise: He was in love with and sleeping with both women. And now these women were letting him know that they knew. They were also making it clear that he would suffer consequences. When C. D. and Ginny met at a mutual friend's house in Fayetteville to discuss the matter, they were, according to this friend, "holding each other up for support, and they were really angry."[5] Frank Stanford was not eager to head back home, whatever that word now meant to him, into a maelstrom of emotion.

He must have known the discovery was going to happen. Ginny had evidently found love letters he'd written, presumably to Wright, in a file of his poems to which she had ready access. "It felt," Ginny later recalled, "like the end of the world."[6] Almost twenty years later Wright remembered Ginny's immediate response to her discovery of the evidence: "Within two hours she was at my door."[7] Frank had kept these two talented and intelligent women in the dark about each other—or at least about the nature of his relationship with them—for nearly two and a half years.

Ginny and C. D. bonded in their pain and desire for retribution. "There was a lot of tenderness between them," recalls the friend whose kitchen they met in.[8] "We talked for the next two weeks and there was a lot of driving back and forth," Wright said about her meetings with Ginny, who was living in southern Missouri. As they waited for Stanford to return, the two women planned a reckoning. Once the legendary poet returned to Fayetteville, mustering whatever it took to come through the door at 705 Jackson Drive, he would face that with which he had always had a complicated relationship: reality.[9]

So, on this morning of June 3, 1978, standing in Ralph Adamo's bathroom, Stanford was in an unprecedented position: The poet was trapped. Reality—something he'd long eluded or at least kept at bay—now had him in a vice. No artifice, much less art, could free him. For perhaps the first time, Stanford finally knew the answer to the question he had written on the wall that morning. He may have even penned those words as his epitaph.

IN THE LEAD-UP TO THIS moment, Stanford had twice delayed his flight home. On May 31, he had written to his mother, "I'm fine and having a very good time. This [New Orleans] is a wonderful city full of wonderful people."[10] Frank had gone to the coast with friends—to a town called Pass Christian and possibly others. On June 2, back in New Orleans, he'd spent the night at Adamo's house, with DuVernet, who thought Frank "was full of holy water."[11] At some point on June 2, Frank had arranged to have flowers sent to Lucinda Williams, a woman he had only known for a few months but who notes, in a draft of her memoir, "I was enamored of him. I was in love with him."[12]

On June 3, after breakfast with Gilchrist, Stanford took an 8:45 a.m. flight to Little Rock, where he transferred to a 1:00 p.m. flight to the Northwest Arkansas Regional Airport. He opted for window seats. It was most likely on this plane where he wrote on a white legal pad: "I would not be honest if I said I was just totally free of fear and sadness. There is sadness and there is fear."[13] After being picked up at the airport by his friend Sherman Morgan, he arrived home at 705 Jackson Drive in the midafternoon. The rental was a small ranch house at one end of a quiet street. Honeysuckle vines threaded through a chain-link fence.[14] The lawn was freshly cut and manicured.[15] In the covered garage stood the bulky hardware of the literary press—White River Printers—that he and Wright ran together. Between the garage and the house stretched a laundry line to which the pages of poetry books were pinned to dry before being bound into volumes that launched the careers of other young poets, many of whom Frank had selflessly nurtured into maturity.[16]

As Frank approached the front door, he saw in his white 1977 Datsun pickup truck a foreboding tableau of objects: From the rearview mirror hung a pair of women's underwear and cut-up pieces of his father's Stetson hat; below it was a cover of a Lightnin' Hopkins album.[17] This was a dark shrine designed to haunt and mock the man for his infidelities, his uncontrollable passions, his lies. It was to presage the "spite and rage"—as Ginny put it—he was about to face.[18]

When he entered the house, Stanford encountered two deeply pained women. Ginny later recalled that he had on a new white shirt and khaki pants and was tan from his beach venture. His face looked thin, and "he had the distant air of a man just back from war."[19] Frank tried to hug Ginny, but she refused him. He told her he loved her, but for the first time, she did not respond. His belongings had been shoved into boxes. Ginny affirmed that she had filed for divorce. From home and marriage, Stanford was now estranged. Then came the fight. "We had this verbal showdown, the three of us for hours," Wright recalled.[20] Soon she was vomiting in the bathroom and Ginny was sobbing in the kitchen. The emotions continued to mount. "I wanted to put him through a wall," says Ginny in a written account of that day.[21] Then, as she later put it, "We proceeded to slice and dice him."[22]

At this point, around 6:00 p.m., Frank, who had spent his entire life avoiding confrontation, said he needed to go to his office at the surveying company where he worked. In his absence, paperwork had piled up, and he needed to check in, he said. They made the two-mile drive to the office at 118 West Center Street. C. D. Wright said it was just her and Frank in his truck; Ginny said it was the three of them. Either way, both women agreed how strange it was for Frank to later leave the office wearing a red hoodie sweatshirt, his head down and his hands jammed in the big front pocket.[23]

Not long after they returned to 705 Jackson Drive, Frank said he needed to rest for a while and went into the bedroom right off the kitchen, shut the door, and lay down on the bed he had shared with C. D. for nearly two years, a bed that had once belonged to her grandmother.[24]

Minutes later the phone rang in a hallway about five blocks away. Jim Whitehead, a former teacher of Frank's and a founder of the MFA program at the University of Arkansas, walked from his home office—the very spot where Frank and C. D. had met less than three years earlier—to answer it. His daughter was in the house at the time and remembers her dad picking up the phone, pausing, and yelling as loud as she ever heard the big man yell, "God dammit!" before rushing out of the house.[25]

What Ginny had heard from the bedroom, around 7:00 p.m., sounded like Frank was hitting something with a piece of wood. She later described what Frank did to himself with the .22 revolver he'd taken from his boss's desk and hidden in his hoodie: "In the span of the longest five or six seconds I have ever lived through, Frank fired three shots into his chest. Three pops, three cries ... After the third cry I knew he was dead."[26] Ginny ran across the street for help while C. D., standing over Frank's body, screamed and screamed. When Ginny came back, she straddled him, pumping his chest while C. D. breathed into his lifeless lungs.[27] Ginny recalled that his eyes turned "from hazel to porcelain green." She remembered thinking, "This is real. This is real this is real."[28]

## Coda

He died like the last note of Neil Young's guitar, he died like the first breeze off the ocean in the morning, he died like the water trickling out of an old *clay pot, he died like my black cat howling at the window, he died like the drunks at Sixth and Mission, he died like the smoke filled rooms that choked me last night, he died like the sad harmonica player, he died like the hands of the clock I couldn't see moving.*

—GINNY STANFORD, CA. 1993[29]

Frank Stanford with his Saint Francis necklace, ca. 1976–77.
*Photo by Ginny Crouch Stanford.*

# *Introduction*

"EVERYONE FORGETS THAT ICARUS ALSO flew." The words of poet Jack Gilbert—whom Frank never knew but should have—remind us that a death does not define a life. At least it shouldn't, especially a life as actively lived as Frank Stanford's. Stanford shot himself three times in or near his heart at the age of twenty-nine. Like so much about his life the final act seems almost impossible. His was a dramatic exit, and those who know Stanford cannot avoid speculating about why it happened. But those are motives only one man will ever know. For all his obsession with death, this book is not an attempt to analyze, or even understand, Frank Stanford's suicide. As one of Frank's friends put it, "Of his death we should have little to say."[1] With this I agree.

Stanford's nearly thirty years were full of life. He was an orphan who never met his biological parents; a summertime resident of Mississippi levee camps staffed by Black laborers; the educational product of Benedictine monks and an autodidactic reading habit; a teenager who lived a comfortable bourgeois life in a lakefront house; a prodigious and promiscuous lover; a student of cultures local and global and high and low; a child prodigy; a land surveyor; a muse with a near-photographic memory; a devotee of jazz, blues, film, and classical music; a barfly; a karate and judo expert; a publisher; the founder of a small press; an exacting gardener; a savvy editor. And when it was time to tell the big lie, he was astonishing. So yeah, Icarus flew.

Stanford was a chameleon. As a kid he fashioned himself into a southern aristocrat with Mississippi heritage and roots dating back to England (to Earl of Sandwich peerage, no less).² Later, he became a periodically reclusive and often brooding artist from Northwest Arkansas, a charismatic and well-read Ozarkian hillbilly who wrote poetry that proved irresistible to the nation's leading journals (the elite "little magazines" especially); toward the end, he buttoned down, cut back on his drinking, and acted as a professional editor of his own small publishing company, Lost Roads Publishers, where he ushered young and underrecognized talent toward future success in a spirit of wisdom and guidance. Finally, ending the journey with what his friend the poet Thomas Lux called an "irreversible cliche,"³ he became a writer whose reputation has been overly defined by a striking, self-inflicted, and fatal act.

But there was and always will be the poetry. From a very young age, it was a constant in Frank's life. Accolades from contemporaries never wavered. Allen Ginsberg praised Stanford's writing and urged him to send more poems to him.⁴ Alan Dugan labeled Stanford "a genius" and "a true poet."⁵ Thomas Lux admired his correspondent's "rare talent," deeming his poems "goddam terrific."⁶ Franz Wright called Stanford's poems "staggering for their courage and beauty."⁷ Eileen Myles said that his poetry was "lurid" and "mythical."⁸ John Berryman, Terrance Hayes, and Lawrence Ferlinghetti ("I do dig many of your poems"⁹) have all praised Stanford's work. Richard Howard, whose own poetry could not have been more unlike Stanford's, taught Stanford's poems in his Columbia University classes.¹⁰ C. D. Wright noted that "everybody who met him stirred to his vision."¹¹ Ellen Gilchrist summed up the poetry world's feelings for Stanford when she said that "everybody worshiped him," adding that "he was a genius, a true, complete, and total genius."¹²

Such affirmation might go to anyone's head, and Stanford was hardly immune to the allure of praise. His personal struggles were one thing, and they were reliably mercurial and intense. But his faith in his own poetry, even before he began to publish it, remained steadfast. In the early 1970s he typed out the claim that "my feet will fit sweet William Faulkner's boots like a glove," noting how he planned to "whip every poet under thirty." In this same typed note (seemingly written to himself), he flexed even more, saying, "I'm going to be Jean Cocteau and William Faulkner at the same time."¹³ In 1970 he bragged to a fellow young poet that "Pablo Neruda spit me into the ear of Jules Renard."¹⁴ A few years later Stanford wrote to his publisher that "poets of all persuasions, so far, have liked my work—that means I'm writing poetry."¹⁵ His feelings were unequivocal: "I like being accepted by all phases of the literary scene."¹⁶

Egotistical, yes, but not necessarily wrong. Frank Stanford was writing bold and original poetry, and few readers knew about it. He was writing poetry that led Jim Whitehead, his teacher at the University of Arkansas, to call him "the most brilliant poet of his generation."[17] It was poetry that led poet and Frank's friend John McKernan to tell Frank Stanford scholar A. P. Walton that "he is the best poet of his generation. Period."[18] Poets so disparate in style, background, and artistic temperament as those listed above universally shared high admiration for Frank Stanford. This kind of admiration affirms his broad and undervalued influence on the modern American literary tradition. Stanford has had important fans, but he still lacks a wider readership.

And there's a great deal to read. To say that Stanford was prolific is an understatement—he produced in a decade what would comprise a career's worth of writing for most poets. "He left an astonishingly large body of finished poetry," his friend Ralph Adamo writes in a 2000 issue of the *Asheville Poetry Review*.[19] "He was so prolific," according to an editor he worked with, "that, for all I know, there might be whole drawers full of secret treasures."[20] In fact, much as with the poet Fernando Pessoa, there were. In addition to poetry, Stanford wrote short fiction, novels, screenplays, plays, and essays, leaving many of these manuscripts unpublished, some of them inaccessible and many of them, as we'll see, burned to ashes. But he wrote all the time. Even the work that is easily available—thanks in part to Copper Canyon Press's 2015 publication of *What about This: Collected Poems of Frank Stanford*—astonishes in its volume.[21]

The bulk of Stanford's output consisted of relatively short lyric poems. Many hundreds, and likely thousands, of them. The themes in these poems vary, but in significant ways, they collectively track Stanford's evolving persona and disposition throughout his brief adult life. Across eight published chapbooks, there was a burst of youthful vibrancy in the beginning (*The Singing Knives*), the heavy onset of darkness at the end (*Crib Death*), and an autobiographical continuum of emotions in between.[22] Throughout it all Stanford, like one of his idols, William Faulkner, created a fictional universe where familiar characters experienced themselves in the flow of southern time and place. His poems integrate figures familiar and exotic into the same Delta landscape that preoccupied Faulkner. His entire creative process rejected sophisticated urbanity in favor of common and countrified voices—voices that reflected in Stanford's work what John Stuart Mill had called "utterance overheard."[23] The lowbrow backcountry registers thrive on language, music, humor, and violence that achieve a kind of unforced southern sublimity. For all their wonderful strangeness and sympathy for the grotesque, Stanford's poems are so accessible they can find you before you're aware of it. Bill Willett, Frank's lifelong and best friend, said that, while he himself was never a formal student of poetry, Frank always "wrote about things that almost anyone could find some familiarity with, something that was real down to earth."[24] One of Frank's many girlfriends recalled how she "loved . . . how he could find simple words to get his point across."[25]

But as A. P. Walton has observed, while Stanford "spent nearly his entire brief life in the relatively finite radius of the Mississippi Delta, Memphis, and northern Arkansas," he "is a world poet."[26] Stanford's wildman-from-the-backwoods persona—fueled by his comments such as "I'd rather have knocked out Sonny Liston than written *The Waste Land*"— should never obscure the fact that his curiosity and attention focused heavily on literature, art, film, and music from Europe, South America, and Japan.[27] This "redneck surrealist" immersed himself in the foreign venues of international writers, poets, and movies—especially those from France, Spain, and Italy.[28] He was familiar with ancient Greek and Latin works (all translated), mythologies (Norse, Irish, Greek, Native American), and medieval epics. He knew the Old Testament like a biblical scholar. His interest in foreign themes and images was driven by an insatiable desire to hear new voices, as well as an occasional sense that, as he complained to an editor about being stuck in a writing seminar in Northwest Arkansas, "I feel like I'm living in occupied territory!"[29] While he could be quite comfortable being occupied in that territory, he constantly broke out of it, if only in his mind, to experience worlds beyond the South and, in ways that affirm his bold experimental impulse, to bring those worlds back to Arkansas.

Frank's free-ranging Romanticism further prevented him from simply being labeled a regional voice with a cult following. As with two of his idols, Byron and Keats, the theme of death, hardly limited to the South, was his lodestar. In Stanford's work, a vast collection of characters comes and goes, scenes shift from Mississippi to Memphis to Arkansas, and throughout it all the small dramas of otherwise unnoticed lives dance in the moon shadow of death. Calling Stanford's verse her "first living poetry," C. D. Wright admired "his beautiful sepulchral language."[30] The poet Franz Wright called him "one of the great voices of death."[31] These death-obsessed poems, most of them published between 1974 and 1977, allowed Stanford to nourish his muse, one sustained by his inherent awareness of life's ephemerality in its becoming, its being, its ending. He did this while creating a poetic world he owned, even dominated, through a polyphonic, southern, global, and wildly inclusive language marked by limitless space and unshakable faith in the power of youthful genius.

Stanford's lyric poems, which appeared in the nation's little magazines in the early and mid-1970s, stand on their own terms as an impressive literary achievement. But they emerged alongside and conversed with a single and far more defining literary accomplishment. While Melville had *Moby-Dick*, Whitman had *Leaves of Grass*, and Ginsberg had *Howl*—and Frank knew each of these works well—Frank Stanford had *The Battlefield Where the Moon Says I Love You*. No artist, especially not one as productive and wide-ranging as Stanford, should have their career defined by a single poem. But because it was so thoroughly preoccupying and epic, so heavy and self-referential and autobiographical, *The Battlefield*, a poem that he worked on for nearly half his life, can rightly be called the touchstone of Frank Stanford's career.

IT IS ONE THE LONGEST published poems in the history of American literature.[32] *The Battlefield* has earned Stanford comparisons to literary figures such as Rimbaud (Lorenzo Thomas called him "a swamp-rat Rimbaud"[33]), Melville, and Whitman. Some critics, not implausibly, believe his work exceeded the ambition of some canonized writers. There is a "cult of Stanford"—a cohort of obsessed fans who have known and read and studied and searched and *believed* in Stanford from the moment they encountered him. These acolytes tend to find each other and thrill in their shared discovery. The poet Leon Stokesbury calls them "devoted disciples not / to be denied."[34] They argue that *The Battlefield* should elevate Frank Stanford to the status of one of the twentieth century's most important poets. They insist we are missing out when we overlook him. The poet Lee Upton recalled "the jolt I experienced when first reading him." Writing to me in 2020, she said, "Looking at his poems tonight, the jolt recurs."[35] Thinking back on when she started reading *The Battlefield*, Lucinda Williams recalled, "Nobody had ever read anything like it." It was, she added, "feral and on fire."[36]

Stanford's adult life was, most of the time, deeply troubled. Perhaps because of this, he was prone to being mythologized. The provenance of *The Battlefield* is, like a lot of Stanford's life, shrouded in mystery and myth. Some legends insist he began writing an early version of it, as Frank himself sometimes suggested, before he was even a teenager. On its face, the assertion seems absurd. But C. D. Wright, for one, did not dismiss the idea.[37] Whether it's true or not—and I'll explore the question in the pages ahead—the youthful energy that runs throughout the poem helps explain what Frank thought the poem would do to those who heard, consumed, and experienced it. In a 1974 letter he described his ever-evolving creation: "In a different mail you will find 375 pages of a 500 page ms. The original was over a 1000 pages, but I got rid of half of it.... The other 125 pages are lost somewhere in the mail. The poem, which at one time extended over 40,000 lines, is called 'the battlefield where the moon says I love you.'" He then suggested how to read it: "This long poem will obliterate your eyes, so don't read over 10 pages a day."[38] It's not the worst advice he ever gave.

The poem is, in its first published edition (1977), 542 pages of small print. Its first stanza is its last. It is unpunctuated. It is marked by erratic line length and (at least on the surface) seems to lack narrative cohesion. Reading it for the first time is not unlike getting mired in the thornier patches of *Ulysses*—and there are, indeed, many similarities with Joyce's masterpiece (such as the fact that nobody in the epic is worth more than their last paycheck). Thematically and geographically, *The Battlefield* ricochets across a South so rural and carnivalesque it might even feel alien to southerners. The protagonist, Francis Gildart (an obvious stand-in for Francis "Frank" Gildart Stanford), explores dreamscapes conveyed in a shifting babel of sounds. The poem thrives on a mostly North Mississippi idiom that samples liberally from everything from Shakespearean tones to clipped, countrified expressions to risqué levee-camp slang to standard dozens-like banter. "His imitation of all dialects was uncanny," C. D. Wright said.[39] "He was," she noted, "a major listener."[40] A "moving picture" becomes a "moom pitchu"; a lunatic becomes a "looney tick"; and Saturday becomes "Saddy." Frank listened intently to how people spoke words. When young Francis gets uppity in the classroom, he does not declare to his teacher, "I need to use the bathroom." That would be boring. He says instead, "Miss Fulgum this chevalier needs to piss" (2625).[41] Those of us who fall under the spell of such arch-irreverence, achieved by tinkering so boldly with the simplest language, a tinkering generally done without irony, cannot help but fall, often hard, for this kind of poetic playfulness.

Language and music and noises blend and dance and sometimes clash and reverberate. Careful readers will hear a South pulsing with the undertones of gospel music, medieval troubadour marches, blues riffs, jags of jazz, and backwoods slang. Describing the poem to a friend, C. D. Wright wrote, "I see it ... thoroughly under the influence of *Beowulf* and *Sir Gawain*, also by Chaucer, the Arthurian romances, all but the metaphysical writers, also by all the English romantics, the French and Spanish surrealists, Whitman, the Bible, and by very very few contemporary Americans though he read them all." That was only the beginning of his influences. Also to be considered, Wright continued, were "European filmmakers and jazz musicians and anyone who talked to him or said something within his earshot; Japanese and Chinese literature was hardly foreign to him by the time he wrote the *Battlefield*."[42] Whatever the mélange of cultural genres, the lyricism intrinsic to the language, as well as speaker Francis's innocently brilliant ability to tap it, turns the poem into something that seems more unimaginable with every reading.

On numerous occasions, Francis, a precocious wordsmith, fixates on and almost fetishizes a single term, letting it clang into a scene like a hammer on a gong. In this case it's the word "cavalry."

> Jimmy circled his hand and pointed straight ahead like a charge
> called by a calvary officer doggonit there I go again
> tripping up on that word I mean cavalvalry I mean cavalry I know it like
>     my name
> ever since I missed it at the city spelling B
> when the teacher called it out I spelt the wrong word I tell you I
> know them both like the back of my hand I knew them then
> it was bad elecution on his part I say it was the way he pronounced it
>     (8382–88)

More is happening here than immediately hits the ear. Frank addresses his protagonist's humorously fraught relationship with the word "cavalry" by having Francis stumble over its pronunciation ("doggonit there I go again") and then exploring the source of the confusion. After several attempts to say the word correctly—"calvary," "cavalvalry," and finally "cavalry"—he determines that the origin of the problem was an elementary school spelling bee where the teacher's accent made the word sound different than the way it was spelled. Adding to the confusion was whether the teacher was asking about Golgotha (Calvary) or soldiers on horseback (cavalry). To further drive home the complicated relationship among the heard word, the spoken word, and the written word, Francis criticizes the teacher for "bad elecution," which might seem ironic were it not for the likelihood that Frank Stanford is spelling the word the wrong way only because that is how Francis heard it as it came out his mouth. Thus the misunderstanding comes full circle, leaving Francis so befuddled he never gets back to the story of Jimmy pointing ahead and gesturing "charge." We are, in short, dealing with a very different kind of literary experience, one where the sounds and meanings and even the sight of words get wonderfully stewed into a verbal gumbo that gets richer over time.

While tackling *The Battlefield* requires readers to make an adjustment, the poem is not as obliterating as Stanford described it to be. With a little practice, it can be fluidly readable. Those who persist often discover an accessible flow that eases the poem's ostensible difficulties. This process of discovery, because the poem requires the reader to do the work of punctuation to find the interior rhythm, fosters a satisfying intimacy with the text, a closeness coming from direct involvement in the shared quest for poetic understanding. Whereas Joyce's *Ulysses* asks the reader to examine from the outside in, *The Battlefield* says to the reader, *Come in. Welcome.* A literary scholar who did significant research on Stanford shortly after he died writes, "The realization of intensity or monotony in the battlefield depends in part on the spirit the reader brings to it."[43] Stanford, who once said, "I can be completely seduced by just a voice,"[44] invites us into the excitement of that seduction and asks us to work with him to make his words transcend the reality we are too accustomed to accepting as all there is.[45]

The tenacious reader is soon warmed by language that teems with originality, humor, insight, and pathos. "I have never met a student of poetry," the poet Ralph Adamo has written, "who did not immediately and even ravenously respond to the words of one or another of many Stanford poems."[46] *The Battlefield* is a poem that, rather than limiting the reader to ten pages at a time, grows into a literary addiction. As one editor put it, *The Battlefield* "sticks like glue," and it "can really possess a soul."[47] The appeal derives in part from sensibilities honed far outside academia. Stanford disliked formal education and intellectual posturing and would not have lasted a long morning as a college professor. The formality of language alone would have spun his head off. Some of the most entertaining scenes in *The Battlefield* involve Francis throwing tantrums in the classroom. Accordingly, and perhaps empathetically, the reader's initial response to the poem tends to be more emotional than intellectual. C. D. Wright recalled that on reading a draft of *The Battlefield* for the first time, "I felt absolutely helpless to so much wildness of heart, so much fury and hilarity."[48] The poet Alan Dugan, who celebrated Stanford's "amplitude," wrote in response to excerpts from the poem, "You do my heart good."[49] (Trust me, as someone who reads the poem aloud two Saturdays a month with friends, when I say Dugan was right.)

This emotion that the text inspires evokes what Whitman called "the blab of the pave."[50] Varied habits of speech among characters in constant and often chaotic dialogue root Stanford's poem in both the patterns of southern life and the expressions of European, Latin American, and even Japanese literature. Stanford's "blab" enriches common experience in the rural South with both raw native expressions and avant-garde foreign registers. His "pave" was more a muddy two-track road than a smooth, hard top, but it barreled across the rural landscape with the assurance that wherever it went, it defied the old slogan that you "can't get there from here."[51] Francis Gildart covers expansive territory in the poem; Stanford's language moves like a locomotive on the tracks but maybe not for long. Tongues are country and dirty and urbane, delivered in multiple languages, sometimes through dead sign languages and arcane rebuses. Settle in, the thing says. Be willing to wander through the fun house, but rest assured: No matter where you are, you're there. And then you'll keep going, deeper and deeper into there.

Stanford's finely tuned ear missed nothing. It was, according to C. D. Wright, "virtually infallible."[52] He was enthralled by "people's talk."[53] The blended lingua franca of hollers and levee-camp shouts, circus tents and juke joints, Italian peddlers and French chevaliers, bar talk—all of it effectively replaces Whitman's New York sidewalk chatter with something even more linguistically tangled. The Whitmanesque spirit of inclusion thickens; Stanford declares in one poem, "I intend to sing here," permeating the text with an ineffable charm and tenderness confirming the South's overlooked tolerance for outcasts and outliers, weirdos and misfits, freaks and outlaws.[54] Foreigners. Migrants. Dwarfs. Gypsies. One-legged peddlers. Stanford's language choices—or those of his characters—will sometimes hit the contemporary reader's ear as crude and insensitive, if not plain offensive (the N-word is common in the poem). But Stanford wrote with arms wide open. Few artistic expressions, in the South or elsewhere, have harbored so much love for Flannery O'Connor's "grotesques," traveling carnival freaks, mad-dog-bitten gypsies. It's fun. But something deeper lurks. *The Battlefield*, a poem that C. D. Wright called "historical and experiential," highlights the South's potential to seek more merciful forms of beauty and justice.[55] "One day," Alan Dugan predicted, "it will explode."[56]

THAT ONE DUGAN GOT WRONG. *The Battlefield* has largely fizzled. The world knows little about Frank Stanford and his work, about Francis Gildart and his epic ventures. A. P. Walton, in his landmark Stanford thesis, explained that "rarely does such a gaping bifurcation exist—nor last for upwards of half a century—between prolific talent and relative obscurity."⁵⁷ It's a strange fate to experience for a writer whom Leon Stokesbury once called "the best young poet in America under the age of thirty-five."⁵⁸ Those who have already discovered Stanford's work will easily relate to poet James Wright's reaction when he first encountered it: "It is astounding to me that I was not even aware of this superbly accomplished and moving poet."⁵⁹ Ralph Adamo puts the matter of Stanford's reputation more matter-of-factly: "Frank's work is neglected. Frank's work is great.... You don't need to read much of Frank's work to be hooked."⁶⁰

Right after Stanford died, Michael Cuddihy, a publisher and editor who celebrated Frank's poems, noted how "Frank's work was often overlooked, despite its appearance in some of our finest little magazines. There is no point in speculating why."⁶¹ But nearly fifty years after his death, there is. Reasons for this neglect need to be considered in some detail, if only to gain insight into the poet's elusive and shape-shifting, if not self-subverting, character. The neglect also reminds us how and why exceptional art can slip through the cracks and languish as oblong pieces hard to fit into boxes made by well-connected tastemakers, relegated to obscurity by forces and factors the gatekeepers notice but for whatever reason shut out.

Stanford did not play the game. He did not hobnob in the New York scene. The poetry business, despite the frequency with which he submitted poems, meant little to him. "I don't give a shit about a lot of the literary goings on I hear about," he wrote a friend.⁶² "I think New York is strange," he told his publisher Irving Broughton. Speaking of his poetry, he said, "I can't conceive of myself sitting on a stage and reading it," adding, "I sure wouldn't like to be on a stage looking at five hundred New Yorkers or somebody."⁶³ In a letter to the poet Richard Eberhart, Stanford noted that "I haven't kept that much eastern literary company," referring to poets based in New York and Boston.⁶⁴ "New York and my blood mixed like swamp water and whiskey," he wrote to Dugan after his first and only trip there.⁶⁵

The artist residency circuit was also one he avoided, and not necessarily out of spite or disdain. He admitted his lack of interest in Bread Loaf or Yaddo, reiterating that his indifference to the insider literary community "makes me feel, maybe, like something is wrong with me." He worried, "Is it pretentious, or puerile, to feel this way?"⁶⁶ When he began to seek a publisher for *The Battlefield* in 1972, he asked Dugan if "that Yale place" might look at it. He also wondered about "one of those Guggenheim things."[67] The language itself seems to distance him from ambition, emphasizing the cultural gap between Fayetteville and the Northeast. Stanford might have been a rebel as a poet, but it would be a mistake to see his reclusiveness as a petulant affectation of defiance. He understood that joining a literary scene might improve his exposure, but he was hesitant to do that because—especially after a year in an MFA poetry workshop—he suspected it would do nothing to improve the quality of his writing. About that he may have been right.

Frank preferred to stay put in Arkansas. He liked being secluded with his first wife Linda in a small cabin on a big hill in Fayetteville called Mount Sequoyah. He was comfortable while holed up with a girlfriend in a tiny studio in a house undergoing renovation in town by the university. Later, with his second wife, Ginny, he isolated himself on their four-acre plot on the edge of Rogers, Arkansas, and, after that—off and on—in Liberal, Missouri. He enjoyed these nooks off the grid, holes to hide in while he cut his own wood to stay warm, grew some of his own food to eat, and wrote without distraction. In these quiet spaces he had access to books, his typewriters, a garden, two cats, ample alcohol, a brilliant woman with whom to read aloud and share his creativity, and, only when he wanted, visiting friends. It was in these secluded places that Stanford wrote most productively. And if productivity and an honest commitment to art came at the expense of exposure or lost social capital in a literary scene, so be it; he saw this trade-off as worth it. As he writes in the poem "The Mind Reader," "blessed are the composers nobody will listen to."[68] At times he was so confident in the inherent quality of his work that he saw lack of recognition as a badge of honor, as if his poetry was such an exotic but undiscovered species of writing that anything as token-like as an award would only diminish it.

Stanford also needed to be close to the landscape of images and sounds so necessary for his work to thrive. "I hear the sounds of trees, the making of homes, books, boats, and coffins," he writes in an unpublished prose fragment, one that evokes Flannery O'Connor's claim that "The Southern writer's greatest tie with the South is through his ear."[69] The floral and faunal wildlife of the countryside, including its fair share of human animals, was a subject always close to his experience and, as such, near the tip of his pen. Stanford, who was famous among Fayetteville artists, was something of a homebody, a loyal inhabitant of the South, a voracious, hardworking, and brainy country kid happy to tap into the establishment so long as he could do so from the security of his porch or, as he phrases it in *The Battlefield*, "the balcony / of the delta" (7998–99). C. D. Wright noted that "he was not a player." Had he been in a fancy literary scene, she surmised, "he would have thumbed his nose at it."[70]

Geographically speaking, Stanford rarely ventured far from the Delta's balcony. He grew up as a rich boy with a world of privilege under his thumb. But cutting his ties to his blue-blood heritage, he spent his brief adulthood as a poet bitching over "the God Fucking Buck."[71] He was almost always broke, and his paltry finances if nothing else kept him rooted in Northwest Arkansas. Only once in his life did he visit New York and on only two occasions Washington, DC. Back home, he attended a poetry workshop in the MFA program at the University of Arkansas for two semesters (even though he was an undergraduate), dropped out of school, and gained employment as a land surveyor, a job that kept him roaming in the rugged Ozarkian landscape for nearly a decade.[72]

Stanford stuck to the Ozarks much in the way that Faulkner stuck to Oxford, Mississippi. Northwest Arkansas was no place to hit the big time, much less get noticed by a big readership. More to the point, while Fayetteville was alive with poetic talent in the 1970s—"There are too many writers in this town," C. D. once complained about the place[73]—it was not necessarily a town with a long-standing or well-connected literary community. Reflecting on his time in the Arkansas MFA program with Frank, poet R. S. Gwynn said, "There was nowhere in Fayetteville to get guidelines when it came to publishing."[74] Regarding this claim, one is reminded of what Malcolm Cowley has said of Faulkner: "Although Oxford, Mississippi, is the seat of a university, it is even less of a literary center than was Salem, Massachusetts, during Hawthorne's early years as a writer; and Faulkner himself has shown an even greater dislike than Hawthorne of literary society. His novels are the books of a man who broods about literature but doesn't always discuss it with friends; there is no ease about them, no feeling that they come from a background of taste refined by argument and of opinions held in common."[75]

Fayetteville was Stanford's Oxford and Salem, a remote enclave of creativity unburdened by the pressure of "opinions held in common." But still, lonely in its own way. On more than one occasion Stanford did lament, "I do think I need to leave this place."[76] But he never did, and it's tempting to say he couldn't. When his friend and first publisher, Irv Broughton, asked him a question about "filmmakers in America now," he said he had no idea how to answer because—and he was speaking geographically—"I'm a million miles from nowhere."⁷⁷ And as far as he was concerned, this was not a problem.

Stanford's publishing choices reflected the self-imposed provinciality of a poet whose "experience," as C.D. Wright noted, "was kept within the borders of four contiguous states: Mississippi, Tennessee, Louisiana, and Arkansas."⁷⁸ He had obvious opportunities to take his early work in an explicitly commercial direction. Had he done so, he might have been a wild success. But he resisted these opportunities, opting to publish his books in one of the more obscure presses in the country: Mill Mountain Press. Mill Mountain, run by Irv Broughton, was a one-man show with a shoestring budget founded in Roanoke, Virginia, and, for most of its duration, based in the literary hinterlands of Washington State. Before Broughton published Stanford's first book in 1972 (*The Singing Knives*), his operation had a single title to its credit.⁷⁹ Broughton became heroically loyal to Stanford and a dogged advocate of his work. There would be no "Frank Stanford" without Irv. But he was also perpetually out of money, often because he was lending it to Frank, and therefore always behind schedule.⁸⁰ Mill Mountain's distribution was sporadic and its exposure largely driven by word of mouth. Six of Frank's nine books went out of print in the 1970s, all within a few years of being published. Still, Stanford stuck with Broughton until the end. He did so, as we'll see, for complex reasons, most of them having to do with an abiding need for creative control and loyalty, both of which Frank desperately needed and Irv reliably provided.

When Stanford entered poetry contests, which was rare, he sabotaged himself (or stuck to his ideals, depending on your view), bombarding committees with manuscripts three times the specified length. Rules annoyed him, so he ignored them. He pursued an aesthetic mission whether his aesthetics were in favor or not. He aimed to complete a grand poetic ambition he seems to have mapped out for himself as a teenager at Subiaco Academy, the Arkansas boarding school he attended for his last two years of high school. Accomplishing that goal seemed far more important to Frank than landing the big book contracts, going to a writers' retreat, getting university teaching positions, or scoring Guggenheim Fellowships, as many of the poets with whom he corresponded were doing. Such accomplishments and accolades never seemed to have impressed or interested him. When he needed to find outside work, he was more likely to contemplate working on his uncle Jimmy's farm in Greenville, Mississippi, which he sometimes did, or finding more work as a surveyor than finishing school and getting a teaching job, which would have likely been a disaster.[81]

For all these reasons, his poems have rarely been anthologized and his reputation has remained equally stellar and regional.[82] As one critic puts it, "Stanford's poems have stayed in circulation by word of mouth."[83] Another wryly refers to the Stanford cult as "an ever growing few."[84] C. D. Wright recalled that, except for a fourth-grade award for poetry, "he went unhonored."[85] Dugan's prediction—"It will explode"—has thus far not happened. There have been no fireworks over *The Battlefield* beyond the cult. Instead, there were Stanford's three tragic bangs and a big poem that sneaked out the door with all the force of a whimper.

THIS BIOGRAPHY AIMS TO BRIDGE the chasm between Stanford's influence within the poetry world and his place in the larger canon of American literature. At the same time, it wants to create a link between a few cultish acolytes and a broader audience of readers. But before getting to the life and work, some related questions need to be addressed, if only for context: What exactly do we mean by Stanford's place in the canon? And what about that canon—what kind of canon are we talking about? And, most importantly, how does placing Frank in that canon alter our understanding of southern literature, race, and our ever-evolving notion of the American South or even the American souths? And, last, how might answering these questions help nudge Frank Stanford from obscurity to, if not popularity, something maybe a little less than obscurity?

It is a testament to Stanford's significance to American letters that his work is central to all these questions. Once his "place" becomes clearer, the "canon" of southern writing might very well have to adjust to accommodate him. C. D. Wright, in an essay on *The Battlefield*, notes how it "fulfills the poet's offhandedly stated, immoderate intention to reclaim the landscape of American poetry."[86] And in a way, evaluating Stanford's impact on American letters requires rethinking the entire notion of southern literature altogether—and, eventually, what "the South" means to itself and the United States. The life and work of Frank Stanford, once presented and appreciated in its fullness, calls for a new and more inclusive narrative for the art and expression of the American South, one that extends to many souths and beyond and one that demands that we rethink the fall of the Old South as the defining benchmark of a regional literature.

This claim hinges on what ultimately defines Stanford's work: his unwavering attention to marginalized voices. "I take to / people that are all fucked up," says Stanford's alter ego Francis Gildart (466–67). Later, he notes, "The help is always better than the ones in the bow ties" (6472). And near the end, "I call to the downtrodden" (12328). This impulse is as true for Francis Gildart as it was for Francis Gildart Stanford and for Frank's heroes Walt Whitman and Pier Paolo Pasolini. To his friend and editor Michael Cuddihy, Stanford explained, "I like to be around the monks, the poor— black and white—and alone with myself."[87] As with the blues, which was Frank's music, his poetic ear was finely tuned to the experiences of multiracial and multiethnic misfits and outcasts. Those who lived under the weighty thumb of the powerful interested him the most. "The American rural South of his poems," writes Leon Stokesbury, "is full of defeat and the aimless wanderings and grotesques that accompany defeat."[88] C. D. Wright notes that "injustice . . . was an intense preoccupation."[89] Stanford agreed with his spiritual counterpart Walt Whitman, who insisted we "stand up for the stupid and crazy."[90] Indeed, themes of dispossession, diminishment, marginalization, and, most notably, racial prejudice pervade not only *The Battlefield* but also much of the rest of Stanford's work. "Good men," remarks Francis toward the end of *The Battlefield*, "have not been given their due" (11878). *The Battlefield* is in part an epic expression of revenge and retribution—and cultural reassessment—in honor of the overlooked poor, weak, overworked, abused, and forgotten.

Stanford could squeeze a sprawling epic of oppression through a medicine dropper. In fact, he believed he could condense history into a single line just as powerfully as it existed in the history books or collective memories of its descendants. "I run," he writes in the poem "The Mind Reader," "with the convicts and gypsies . . . I dream about helping convicts make a break."[91] The convicts and gypsies and freaks were the ones who were most exposed, vulnerable, expressive, and with the least to hide when they spoke. Their experiences in his poems come off as the culmination of long historical processes marked by social friction, struggle, and redemption. Any person of power in the corpus of Stanford's work reliably, and often hilariously, gets taken down a notch or two. Those on the outskirts, by contrast, revel magisterially in their fleeting moments of unschooled wisdom. These moments exceed the carnivalesque to achieve a sort of literary grace, the kind that can perhaps be glimpsed elsewhere only in Flannery O'Connor's, Cormac McCarthy's, and Mark Twain's finest moments.

In the Delta region, with its ever-present legacy of slavery and Jim Crow and white trash and Lost Cause, not to mention its entrenched plantocracy of deplorables, this ambition persistently commands our attention. Stanford not only included but also validated those whom the power elite ignored, mocked, lashed, and lynched. *The Battlefield*, if only by looking at and *listening* to the South's blues tradition, is a literary work of profound social justice and not the social justice that calls for political reform but the social justice that calls for us to acknowledge the deeper humanity of people long ignored. It sits squarely in what one historian has called "the third tradition"—a populist attempt by poor whites, Native Americans, Black Americans, scrappy foreigners, and other overlooked ethnic groups to smash the plantation oligopoly and regain some control over basic human dignity.[92]

This general concern for the oppressed notwithstanding, it is race that usually comes to the fore for Stanford in *The Battlefield*. C. D. Wright goes to the core of Stanford's poetic mission when she writes of the poem, "Compressed by a single issue, the civil rights in the South, it addresses a particular historical period and concerns a defining point in the persona's budding life."[93] Another critic describes *The Battlefield as* "an epic freedom ride."[94] Yet another has insightfully noted that "the world of Stanford's poems roughly parallels C. Vann Woodward's *The Burden of Southern History*."[95] The poet Eileen Myles writes of Stanford that "there's voodoo in his work . . . so much African influence his narrator seems black *and* white."[96] A feature in *American Poetry Review* calls *The Battlefield* "one of the most ambitious political poems of our time: an unequivocal quest for racial justice."[97] This is all true. But Stanford himself, wary of ever reducing his work to a lecture, was quick to temper any definitive assessments: "I don't think I could be accused of being didactic. . . . I don't preach to anybody."[98]

Still, it is for a good reason that the Black poet Ishmael Reed, after reading Stanford's work, honestly thought he was a fellow Black poet and, no doubt on that basis, posthumously granted him the first Zora Neale Hurston Award for excellence in literature.[99] A funny mistake, perhaps, but an easy one to make. In *The Battlefield* and elsewhere in Stanford's work, the voices of the dispossessed, as Stanford conveyed them, ring with the clarity of angels, or, as Frank called his closest Black friends in Fayetteville, those "emeritus professors of the dark heart."[100]

F RANK STANFORD'S SUCCESS AS A poet hinged on a unique understanding of landscape, language, and race in the American South. Throughout his work, language is cumulative and voracious. It can move like a tornado across the page. Its idioms, tropes, and vernacular expressions encompass the landscape's historical and aesthetic character without closing it off to continental expressions. Critically, Stanford grasped a hidden paradox about the inner chaos animating southern life: Blacks and whites were divided by racism, *but their vernacular was shared.* They spoke the same patois, a patois as special and powerful as a secret handshake.

Stanford's poems imagine a world where this patois is recognized and embraced by Blacks and whites and, through the slow drama of everyday dialogue, turned into the lingua franca of friendship and liberation. When Francis, the protagonist of *The Battlefield*, remembers his friend Sylvester, a Black man lynched for a rape he did not commit, he says:

> when my mind is clear I think of Sylvester
> with his talk like a steamboat of jive of magic we would sit on the
>     bench and
> spit and whittle we was some kind of friends just like that
>     (3526–28)

It was that "steamboat of jive" that thrilled Stanford to the center of his being and brought him deeper and deeper into the vernacular of the American South. Later Francis explains how "I was filled with the spirit of brotherhood the community of language" (11770). It's the kind of recognition—"spirit of brotherhood the community of language"— that the South deserves, a recognition with the power to alter virtually every stereotype marking its troubled history. And while there will always be an impulse to charge Stanford with the sin of appropriation, close readers of his work know best that his interest in the dialogue of Blacks reflected curiosity, respect, and even envy for what he saw to be, ultimately, a shared language of expressive amplitude.

Stanford's well-honed ear for the language of Black people and poor whites and so many others, reflected his unusual personal history. Starting at the age of three, he spent several summers living in Arkansas and Mississippi levee-camp communities. He did so because his adoptive father, Albert Franklin Stanford ("Frank Sr."), was an engineer who built and maintained levees throughout the Arkansas and Mississippi Delta. Frank and his adopted sister Ruth, in addition to their (similarly aged) adoptive niece and nephew, were the only white children who lived in the camps. They stood out as obvious minorities among Black workers and their children. For at least three summers the Stanford family— Frank, Frank Sr., Frank's mother Dorothy, and his sister Ruth—lived in temporary homes that stood among mobile canvas tents, many of which could be collapsed and repitched as the laboring party moved down the levee line over the course of the summer. The famous Flood of 1927, which washed out the Delta, might have been a distant memory for the South in the 1950s, but it remained spectral in the minds of those who maintained the levees in the hopes of avoiding such future disasters. As a boy, Stanford lived in this world perpetually concerned with the prospect of raging floods and collapsing levees. Hovering over it all was his father, the man who held back the floods, a man he admired with something like awe. It is no mystery why so much of *The Battlefield* takes place in and around levee camps, with a young, white Francis testing authority alongside older Black characters, outraged at the injustice Jim Crow imposes on his friends, seeking to rebel in the spirit of a Huckleberry Robin Hood. It was what Frank knew as a child.

Such a rare experience—a white kid being socialized and acculturated into an otherwise segregated Black workplace (before *Brown v. Board of Education* no less)—influenced more than Stanford's social views. It infused his poetry and the imaginative landscape where his verse found heft and form. Stanford was not a "political poet" in the traditional sense of the term. He did not explicitly preoccupy himself with the overt themes of race or integration or civil rights or Vietnam, railing away in politically rancorous tones. He was no preacher. Even if they lurk on the periphery, current events, including the politics of racial injustice, are largely absent in his work. Commonplace political discourse neither encompassed enough cultures nor reveled in an interesting enough language for Frank to answer its call to action.

Still, the justice that the civil rights movement addressed remains paramount in *The Battlefield* and beyond. Stanford's approach to the marginalized Southerners, and the injustices they endured, was more literary than political, more psychologically imaginative than expository, and—most critically—more attuned to the blab of the pave than the pontification of the pulpit.[101] Stanford tapped memories, and imaginings and embellishments of memories, of his own experience living from Mississippi to Memphis to Arkansas to attend to language that bound Blacks and virtuous white hillbillies and gypsies and French dwarfs into the same social space. In so doing, he placed a big billowy tent over a poetic landscape that, while inevitably evoking Faulkner's fictional Yoknapatawpha, exceeds it in social complexity and originality. It does so because the experiences of characters on the periphery of history are transmuted from past to present through a common dialogue, as opposed to one race serving as a set piece to mark the decline of another (a standard critique of Faulkner). In this respect Stanford's work harbors tremendous hope.

Put differently, Stanford grasped the social intricacies of southern life in an intuitive rather than a studied way. The writer Ernest J. Gaines once said of Faulkner that, while he included Black characters in his novels, he did not round them out, primarily because he did not understand them well enough to do so. Not so for Stanford. "He identified," poet Ralph Adamo writes of Stanford and the cast of outcasts who populate his poems, "from the inside out."[102] His characters—Black people, white people, Italians, carnies, hicks, vagrants, sapsuckers, hillbillies, what have you—are fleshed out into figures endowed with deep interiority, speaking with authentic and plausible voices, voices connected to a history and reflective of Stanford's own experience in the larger Black social milieu of the camps, juke joints, dive bars, and lilting shacks across the rural South. They are made genuine because, to Stanford, they were genuine. They were as real as anything and anyone he knew. His accomplishment as a poet was to have these people and their landscape come alive on the page through their weird and gorgeous language and the stories they wrought from it.

The understated but sincere respect Stanford pays these men and women fuses with a scarred rural southern geography that's as open as it can be to global vernaculars and voices. Readers of Faulkner will see similarities. But unlike Faulkner's Yoknapatawpha, Frank's imagined world, which is childlike in the best way, became more real for him than the reality in which he lived. This transformation was essential to Stanford's art and its underlying social mission. With passion that recalled Lord Byron—"what I really wanted to be was Lord Byron" (13167)—he lost himself in his dreams, dreams that spun a kaleidoscope of local and global images and voices, and then turned them into an unreal reality where he preferred to live.

IF THE "PLACE" OF STANFORD'S work was an enchanting southern geography filled with a diversity of pariahs seeking to achieve a measure of racial redemption through language and landscape, then what of the canon into which such an artistic ambition should fit? Answering this question requires a brief overview of how southern history and literature have intersected throughout the second half of the twentieth century.

In 1958, when Frank Stanford was turning ten years old, the great historian of the American South, C. Vann Woodward, published a seminal essay in the *Virginia Quarterly Review*.[103] (He updated the article twice, last in 1993.) In it, the Yale professor and proud Alabaman addressed the issue of southern exceptionalism. In a country increasingly defined by rapid economic growth, industrialization, and demographic change, how would the South fare under what he called America's "Bulldozer Revolution"? As the "American Way of Life" overwhelmed regional cultures and as the "urge to conformity" flattened diversity into a homogenized, modernized whole, how could the South maintain its unique nature?[104] Given the obvious black mark on its past, not to mention the long shadow the legacy of slavery cast on the present, there was a bigger question at stake: Should it even want to preserve its heritage?

Woodward, who was no romantic, said yes. He knew that the South's process of immersion into mainstream America was well underway. He wrote in the early 1990s that "the South is going through economic expansion and reorganization that the North and East completed a generation or more ago."[105] But he still longed for the preservation of his regional culture, one that genuinely reckoned with race while honoring the southern values that transcended its awful legacy. His famous essay hinged on a single factor yet to be swallowed by the forces of modernization: "the collective experience of the southern people." In this collective, the South nurtured a seed of cultural continuity. He explained, "It is in just this respect that the South remains the most distinctive region of the country. In their unique historic experience as Americans the Southerners should not only be able to find the basis for continuity of their heritage but also make contributions that balance and complement the experience of the rest of the nation."[106]

Phrases such as "collective experience of the southern people" and "continuity of their heritage" are obviously clear red flags for anyone attuned to the corrosive rhetoric of southern pride. But Woodward, even back in 1958, was in no mood to revive the cynical shibboleth of the Lost Cause. His pride was of a different stripe. Rather than calling for the return of a "morally discredited" racial heritage, he advocated for a South that, more than any other region, faced "the somber realities of hardship and defeat and evil and"—as Faulkner puts it—"the problems of the human heart in conflict with itself." This necessary confrontation was underway, Woodward suggested, and it was happening in a realm most critics and historians of the South were failing to notice: southern literature.[107]

Recognizing Stanford's significance as a poet of the American South who broke the mold of a poet of the American South requires stepping back and looking at the literary trends preceding his work. In 1930 a group of heritage-proud southern writers calling themselves the Agrarians (or, in an earlier iteration, the Fugitives)—including Allen Tate, John Crowe Ransom, Andrew Lytle, and Donald Davidson—published *I'll Take My Stand*. In this saber-rattling volume they declared their fierce commitment to southern exceptionalism, articulating the sacredness of a static and rural culture unique to the American South. No apologies softened their defiance. In the book's opening essay, Ransom writes, "About the only American given to [looking backward] is some unreconstructed Southerner, who persists in his regard for a certain terrain, a certain history, and a certain inherited way of living." And what of this unreconstructed southerner? Ransom explains, "I wish that the whole force of my own generation in the South would get behind his principles and make them an ideal which the nation at large would have to reckon with." *Here* was a red flag.[108]

Stanford, who loathed provincial characterizations of regional identity, seized on it. In a letter to Dugan, he was clear about his assessment of such movements: "I say piss on the neo-Fugitives." To one of his editors he wrote, "The last thing in the world I care about is the Fugitives." On a scrap of paper, he referred disapprovingly to "this neo-fugitive school of redneck scalawags."[109] Stanford rejected these writers as his literary ancestors for good reason. They undertook their mission to save the South from industrial homogenization without regard for the legacy of race and the vernacular language that marked the region so deeply. The Agrarians' inattention to slavery, slave culture, Jim Crow, racial oppression, the blues, or any of the prejudicial legacies that silenced the South's underclass contradicted the entire notion of Woodward's "collective experience of the southern people." The fact, as Stanford saw it, was that the Agrarians, in this singular oversight, were no better than racists and xenophobes. Genteel perhaps, but not enough so to hide their true stripes.

Stanford's work accordingly thrives on the very paradox that the Agrarians ignored: the history and people, and thus the language, that made the South exceptional. The social experience of the lowly, his work insisted, ensured the southern exceptionalism that the Agrarians so desperately needed. Blinkered by hoary racial attitudes, these southern gentlemen never looked beyond their own circle to discover the wealth of cultural expression with origins in the slave quarters and hollers and levee camps, a wealth that exceeded in originality the stilted productions coming out of the antebellum mansions. This is a distinction that Stanford not only understood but also based his life and art on revealing.

Woodward, for his part, also distanced himself from the Agrarians. Nonetheless, he highlighted southern qualities that, as the Agrarians would have agreed, removed the South from the rest of the nation. What kept the South grounded in an identity all its own, Woodward argued, were realities such as a simple rurality, a failure to embrace the gospel of progress, a rejection of "the legend of American innocence," and a general intolerance for a growing habit of abstraction that fostered disconnectedness from "the concreteness of life."[110]

Writers whom Woodward praised for having best understood these distinctions were responsible for the Southern Renaissance in American literature. They included Robert Penn Warren, Eudora Welty, Thomas Wolfe, and William Faulkner (one might also add to this list Flannery O'Connor and Carson McCullers). To ignore these writers, Woodward insisted, would be "to deny to America participation in a heritage that is far more closely in line with the common lot of mankind than the national legends of opulence, and success, and innocence."[111] In their work, he suggested, rested the hope of identifying and preserving a South that was both in touch with its racial heritage and, *because of that connection*, exceptional. Within these stories, the values that might preserve southern exceptionalism could thrive.

Looking back at this assessment, it is hard not to sigh, to lament even: If only Woodward had known of Frank Stanford! To be clear, Stanford never understood himself to be part of any genre or group of writers. He was never comfortable as a member of a writing workshop for two semesters. As a poet and person, he was radically individualistic, often to the point of being a loner. But it comes as no surprise that, of all the writers mentioned by Woodward, the one whose vision Stanford characterized as most consistent with his own was William Faulkner. To the extent that we might link Stanford to the Southern Renaissance, it would have to be through the bard of Oxford. In a letter to a friend Stanford explained, "Dugan and a couple of others put it better than I could when they said I had more in common with Faulkner than the New Critics."[112] This seems right.

But it's also an undersell. In at least one area, Frank Stanford attempted something far more ambitious than Faulkner and Faulkner's contemporaries ever knew to undertake. When it came to portraying an exceptional South, these writers certainly confronted race. But (with few exceptions) they kept Black Americans at an emotional and psychological distance. Stanford—by recentering the focus of southern literature squarely on the marginalized, by seeing them inside-out through the patterns of their own speech and through their endured struggles, by befriending them and eating and drinking with them—ensured that Woodward's "collective experience of the southern people" not only included but also *delved into* the expressions and mentalities of Black southerners, seeing the South through their eyes, hearing it through their voices. Black culture, as every true southerner knows, is inseparable from southern culture. Although his family may have wished otherwise, Stanford came to know that reality intuitively.

No cultural expression honors this idea and this awareness more directly than the blues. In a brilliant move, Stanford sidestepped the Agrarians to situate his work in a blues tradition. It was a tradition that, while the Agrarians were busy taking their stand, was taking shape as a literary genre through the works of Langston Hughes, Sterling Brown, Zora Neale Hurston, Richard Wright, Ralph Ellison, and Albert Murray. These writers, whose work coalesced in LeRoi Jones's Black Arts Movement in the 1960s, examined literature from the perspective of what historian and folklorist Clyde Woods calls a "blues epistemology." This was a worldview that captured the individual and collective suffering of Black Americans while instilling pride and resilience in the face of denigration. The blue note is a note played just under the traditional Western note, and it became the subterranean place from which an oral literature emerged. Woods has called its home "a poetically subversive core."[113] Stanford was nothing if not poetically subversive, and his attentiveness in *The Battlefield* to folk wisdom, hoodoo, work chants, the moral corruptibility of power, and humor—lots of humor—confirms his place in this essentially southern literary heritage. In many ways, his life from the time he was a young boy in Mississippi and Memphis to when he was a college student in Fayetteville was a journey from the most distant periphery to the very center of the blues tradition—and thus to the cultural core of the American South.

For Stanford, the result of this literary orientation was unprecedented poetic expression that thrived on the tall tale, the trickster, the Delta blues, secular and religious slave songs, North Mississippi banter, levee-camp hollers, hillbilly yells, and the code of carnival. Stanford sensed and absorbed the richest and most resonant sounds of southern life and literature, all the tropes and characters and themes and idioms that made the region unique, while simultaneously presenting them through lowly characters and experiences that southern literature had not yet confronted or conveyed with such honesty, humor, boldness, and awareness of suffering. Whatever this was, it was new. And it blossomed from the blues.

Stanford thereby embraced a southern heritage worth not only recovering but also celebrating. It is a heritage with roots that go back to slave experience, do a bypass around the Fugitives and Agrarians, flirt with the authors of the Southern Renaissance, and then cede authority to a rising generation of Black artists including Jesmyn Ward, Natasha Trethewey, T. Geronimo Johnson, Kevin Young, Tayari Jones, Nikky Finney, Randall Kenan, and others. These writers—who are also joined by painters and photographers such as Endia Beal, Chandra McCormick, and RaMell Ross—are now in the process of authoring a new Southern Renaissance, one with a lineage connecting the runaway slave narrative to the contemporary struggles of mass incarceration.

The idea that the bridge between this past and such a thrilling and dynamic present and future is a huge but largely unknown poem, a poem that not only the South but also the country has yet to experience in its fullness, might sound like a ridiculous tall tale, if not totally absurd. And that, I think, is exactly how Stanford would want it to sound. Ridiculous, tall, true.

AFTER FRANK'S DEATH, C.D. WRIGHT WAS unfailingly generous when it came to helping anyone trying to put him on the map of American literature. In 1997, she wrote a letter to a potential early biographer of Frank Stanford, warning him that Stanford, while "funny, profound, mythic, sexual," was also a liar. "At lying, as well as writing," she warned, "he knew no match." Her hope, therefore, was that this writer would "just address the work—that is, evaluate the poetry without trying to reconstruct the ever-shifting and dodging life behind it."[114]

One can imagine many good reasons Wright may have had for offering this advice. Topping that list might be the challenge of weaving a narrative into a life that desperately sought to control its own legacy. I can only guess what Frank Stanford would think of the endeavor of writing about his life, and I can only guess he'd resist it or at least have a love-hate relationship with it and possibly leave behind bread-crumb trails toward multiple false narratives. Perhaps he has already done that. Perhaps I've been hoodwinked. I certainly can't rule it out. Nonetheless, as Wright indicated in the same letter, she was not averse to the pursuit of a proper biography. But do not attempt it, she advised, "unless you are really prepared to interview everyone closest to him in detail and try to sort out the life you believe he lived, as opposed to the life we all wish he had lived."[115]

After hundreds of interviews, in addition to a close reading of every archival (and nonarchival) document available (to my knowledge) on Frank Stanford, I am confident, modestly and humbly so, in having done what Wright (whom I never met, as she died just before I started this book) advised. Yet on every page and in every sentence, my confidence is checked by the kind of doubt that Stanford demands of anyone trying to make sense of him and his work. In the conclusion of her letter, Wright wrote something that explains why my caution, my doubt, is apt: "The biography does not belong to one person alone."[116] For a figure who shifts, hides, and shines as Frank Stanford does, that's exactly as it should be. That said, what follows is the first biography of what I hope is many more.

# THE LIFE AND POETRY
OF FRANK STANFORD

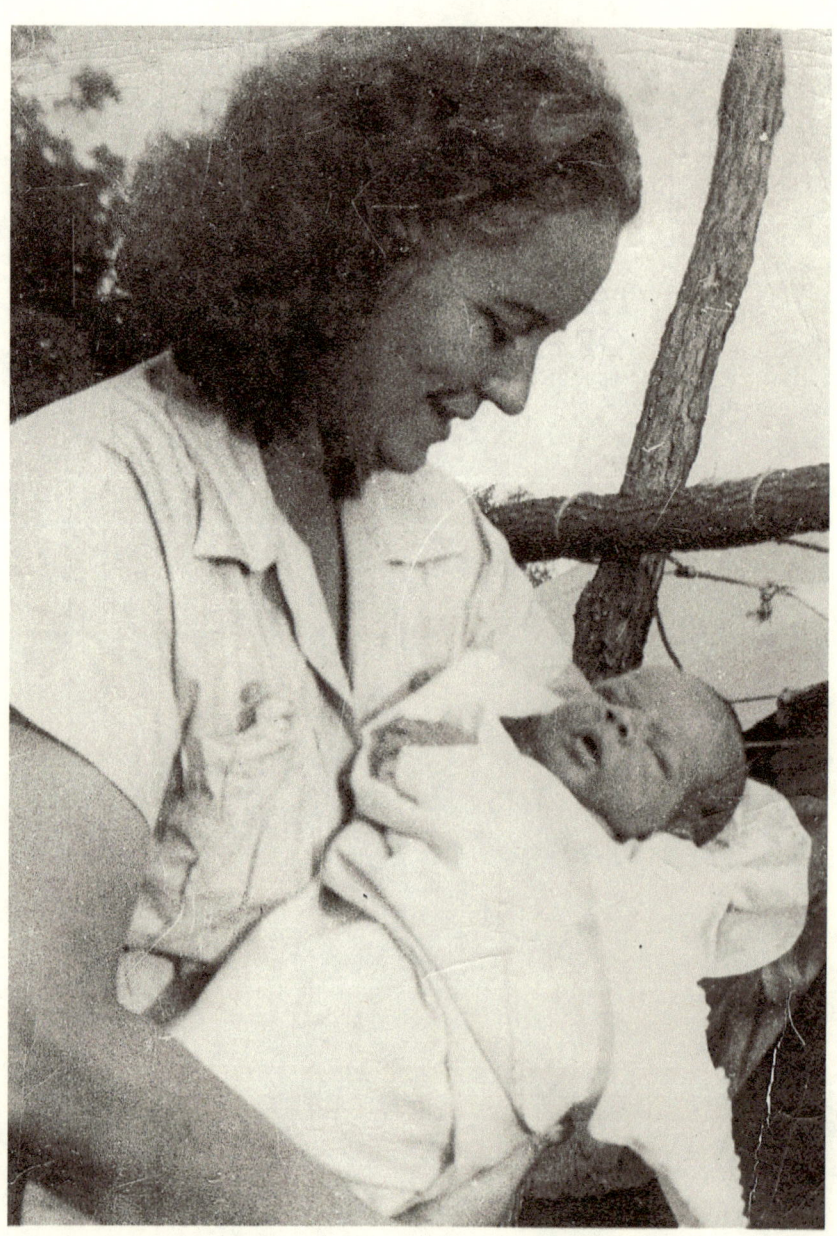

Dorothy and Frank, 1948. *Photo courtesy of Irv Broughton.*

## ONE

# A "Grade A" Baby

THE POET WAS SOUTHERN, DISTINGUISHED, and broken from day one. Dorothy Gilbert Alter—thirty-six years old and divorced—adopted him on the day of his birth, on August 1, 1948, at the Emery Memorial Home in Richton, Mississippi. A woman of faith, she wrote on that day in her son's baby book: "May God be within you to refresh you, around you to protect you, above you to bless you, beneath you to hold you up."[1]

Emery was a Christian retreat for unmarried pregnant mothers founded by a local lumber magnate. It was managed by one Reverend Mabel Cooper, a nurse and missionary worker from Kansas.[2] The baby's biological mother likely used an alias (Dorothy Margaret Smith) and, after giving birth, left Emery like a ghost in the night. Emery Memorial Home itself disappeared in a more conspicuous manner, burning to the ground under ambiguous circumstances and taking vital records with it in 1964.[3] The land on which it once stood became a cattle ranch.[4] Because of this fire, Frank Stanford would never be able to easily research his biological parents. This absence became a defining preoccupation for him, a concern he used, and sometimes manipulated, to shape his future persona and poetry.

Stanford's adoptive mother was by all accounts an exceptional woman. Dorothy Gilbert Alter's application for her son's adoption was the first ever granted to a single woman in Mississippi.[5] When she decided to adopt, she vowed to approach the Department of Child Services only when she was able to raise the child *properly*. To her, properly meant *southern*. She would bring up her child on property she owned in

Greenville, Mississippi, where she'd been raised, where her family had roots, and where she was enmeshed in a social scene she idealized as quintessentially Dixie.[6] Frankie, no matter what his actual origins were, would be, as far as Dorothy was concerned, a well-bred and well-mannered son of the South.

Acquiring a child as a single woman demanded from Dorothy habits her son would later demonstrate in abundance: hard work, keen intelligence, a penchant for mythmaking, and some subterfuge. To earn money for a farm, Dorothy did something that might seem remarkably un-southern, given how much the culture of the South valued gendered hierarchy. She went to work managing a Firestone store. This was another milestone, as she was the first woman in the United States to do so. "I sold tires," she said in a 1997 interview. "I did everything to run the store."[7] A local newspaper praised her as "a born executive" who thrived in an all-male environment. She became, according to the article, "a leader who has contributed greatly to the advancement of Greenville."[8] Beginning in the 1940s during the war, it was not unusual for southern white women to take professional jobs, supported as they often were by Black domestic workers who managed their homes.[9] Even so, Dorothy's leadership position in a male-dominated industry was, wartime circumstances notwithstanding, unusual for a woman in 1940s Mississippi.

Dorothy served the Delta's economic interests by supplying and certifying industrial tires for the bulldozers and backhoes operated by the region's many levee-repair companies—companies that maintained the structures that paralleled rivers to prevent flooding. Delta levee camps were slow to mechanize; some companies used nothing but mule teams until 1945. But Dorothy helped foster the region's transition to mechanization and a stronger levee system by equipping the machines that built the region's infrastructure. She provided an essential product, one that, in helping to control the Mississippi River and its tributaries, sustained cotton plantations while protecting residents from the region's notoriously fierce flooding.

Dorothy also enjoyed the loyal patronage of the region's levee men, many of them well-educated and influential engineers and contractors. "If you need tires, get them from Dorothy Alter. She knows how to get them," said one prominent male member of the business community who seemed to come to the Firestone shop more than he needed to. "I did know," she recalled with pride.[10] Dorothy also gave back to her community. A newspaper reporter remarked that "her philanthropic deeds cannot be counted."[11] She was not above deception, if that's what it took to get ahead. Her methods were consistent with the shortcuts employed by the region's cotton planters and levee builders, from whom she undoubtedly learned some tricks of the trade. Since the Great Depression, the Delta had benefited substantially from federal expenditures. Most of this money went to sustain the region's integrated cotton, levee, and railroad systems. Inevitably, the savviest Delta businessmen, planters included, learned how to monopolize federal aid, usually shunting limited resources to the wealthiest and largest operators.[12]

Dorothy learned how to do the same but on a smaller scale. She admitted to tapping a friend's influence in state government to secure limited federal permits for her tires—no easy task during the war—and she used those permits to certify *all* tires, whether they were for government work or not. The whole arrangement was a little shady, and knowingly so. "I knew a way to get the tickets, but nobody else knew it," she said, "and I didn't tell them, of course."[13] Proud of her role as a female business leader, she later hung a photo of herself surrounded by her all-male staff on the walls of the homes where she lived throughout her life.

By 1945, Dorothy had saved enough money to buy the "little farm," as she called it, where she would bring baby Frank a few years later. The property she purchased was just outside of downtown Greenville. It came with cleared pastures and a grove of over one hundred pecan trees, which she would harvest "with the help of one Negro man."[14] According to an article in the *Delta Democrat-Times*, "She [had] purchased the O. B. Bates Farm . . . two miles east of Greenville." The property was located on Old Leland Road, a main thoroughfare into town. Dorothy, perhaps to enhance the property's plantation aura, named it Green Acres.[15] Expansive and bucolic, Green Acres, she reasoned, was a fit place to raise a child. After Frank was born, she bred collies, rabbits, and chickens, turning the farm where Frank would live until he was three into something like a petting zoo. Dorothy recalled how, when Frank started to talk, which she said he did before he was five months old, "he'd want to know about the birds and the trees and animals."[16] That was primarily what he saw every day.

In 1948, when Dorothy was ready to adopt, she met with the head of the state adoption agency, who had been alerted to Dorothy's application by Dorothy's friend Zelma Price. Mrs. Price was a valuable contact to have for any person hoping to adopt a child in Mississippi. According to a 1953 *Delta Democrat-Times* editorial, she was "a courageous and progressive woman." Childhood issues were her legal specialty. She had served for many years as a state representative, a position that enabled her to write several important pieces of legislation reforming the state's Youth

Court. Price's appointment as a Washington County judge reflected her merit as an attorney and legislator, but the editorial noted how "she has never avoided civic obligations."[17] Helping her friend Dorothy, a single woman in a southern state, legally adopt a child was one such obligation. Dorothy was wise to get Price's support, much as she was wise to hide the fact that she was divorced, claiming widowhood because the fact of a divorce might hinder her adoption application.

Dorothy recalled that the woman agent who came to evaluate whether Green Acres was a suitable place for raising a child was "very masculine, wearing a black suit and stern face." But, undeterred by the woman's hard exterior, Dorothy gave her spiel: "I told her all about my life, that I was a businesswoman, managing the Greenville Firestone." The agent proved to be more interested in the sheep grazing the pasture than Dorothy's adoption plans. She said, "I can get you a 'grade A' baby if you let me have a pair of those sheep." Dorothy looked at her and said, "You may have them all." Two board meetings later, the agency's director called Dorothy and told her that, as Dorothy put it, "she'd rather have me as a mother of one of her children than anyone she knew."[18]

With that green light, Dorothy contacted her lawyer, signed an adoption decree in Greenville, and after getting a call that a child was about to be born, drove the 230 miles to Richton, Mississippi, 22 miles east of Hattiesburg, to pick up her son.[19] Francis was born at 10:14 a.m. on August 1, 1948, weighing in at a solid nine pounds, two ounces. "The treasure was put into my arms," Dorothy remembered. Then, accompanied by attorney Price and Greenville Bible Club leader Hazel Scully, Dorothy drove with baby Frankie, as she called him, home to Greenville.[20] It was only when Dorothy put him to bed that night at Green Acres that she discovered that her son, who had been quiet as a mouse on the car ride to his first home, had entered the world with a broken collarbone.[21]

## Greenville in Black and White (1948)

Frankie's official name underwent its own journey. Initially he was named Francis Gildart Smith, Smith being the last name his anonymous biological mother registered with the Emery Memorial Home. When the adoption paperwork cleared on August 20, he was Francis Gildart Alter.[22] "Alter" reflected the fact that Dorothy was still using the last name of her ex-husband, Carl Alter, even though she had written off her marriage to him as a youthful indiscretion. But to her it was "Gildart" that mattered. Gildart came from, as Dorothy put it, "five grandfathers on my mother's side of the family."²³ In the opening of *The Battlefield*, Frank reiterates the point, writing, "I know my great grandfather was Francis Gildart" (421). The depth of this lineage, as Dorothy would remind her son throughout his life, stretched from Mississippi to Georgia and to soil literally scorched by Sherman.

"Stanford" was added to Francis Gildart in 1952, when Dorothy married Albert Franklin Stanford, a levee engineer almost thirty years her senior who moved the family to his home in Memphis. But until then, "Greenville" and "Gildart" were what Dorothy wanted Frankie to know as essential to his origins. When it was time, in the fourth grade, to turn Frank's baby book over to him for his own safekeeping, she scratched out "Richton" as his place of birth and wrote over it, in bold blue letters: "Greenville."²⁴ In the opening pages of *The Battlefield*, Frank has his alter ego, Francis, state, "I know the old legends mother told me" (403). They were legends Dorothy hoped her son would accept with pride and, ideally, without asking too many questions.

Not only did "Gildart" matter to Dorothy, but so did Greenville. Located in the Mississippi Delta, Greenville in the 1940s was a combination of genteel patrician order and bluesy melodic chaos. This balance was sustained by the demand for cotton and white control of Black labor. In this respect it was, as historian James C. Cobb has put it, "the most southern place on earth."²⁵ A study from the Works Progress Administration said of racial violence in the Delta that "it is a way of life."²⁶ Dorothy's romantic description of the Delta obscured this way of life while glorifying the perceived virtues of planter aristocracy, noblesse oblige, paternalistic authority, and the static racial order she intended her son to assume his place in.

In Greenville, Frank was ushered into a small world of established writerly talent. The area's leading lights at the time were literary-minded business and cultural figures such as Shelby Foote, Hodding Carter, and William Alexander Percy (for whom the local library is still named). These writers were regional and national icons, and Dorothy knew them well.²⁷ Her respect for them inevitably trickled down to her son over the years. Two pages into *The Battlefield* we discover "my grandmother riding sidesaddle through the lowlands to meet Percy" (52). A bit later we read how "at Will Percy's grave I saw the men coming back from the First World War and falling in love with bourbon and french" (3481–82). (In a poem from Frank's 1975 chapbook *Shade*, we find "books that smelled of Will Percy's stables.")²⁸ These lines suggest that young Frank grew up hearing news and gossip about the prominent families with whom his mother and her parents socialized. Dorothy even noted how many Greenville citizens often confused the accomplishments of her family with those of the Percy family, accomplishments such as ridding Greenville of the Klan and ensuring the availability of tractable Black labor while minimizing the violence required to do so.[29]

Percy, Foote, and Carter were Greenville's town fathers. They shaped the region's adherence to, if not quite the Lost Cause version of southern history, then at least a South where the traditional racial order prevailed under quiet paternalistic authority. They officially despised any organization as ignorant as the Klan, but their sense of refined heritage had little tolerance for equality. Speaking specifically of Hodding Carter and his ilk, historian Neil R. McMillen highlights the connection between Greenville's genteel elite and the more ignorant racist citizenry. The white elite "knew that when rednecks played their roles as heavies in the lynching tragedy they often did so with the tacit consent, sometimes the active participation, and nearly always the close observation of their social betters."[30] This line was fine. Blacks should certainly not be lynched for their transgressions of the social order. Such an act could threaten federal largesse. Still, they had to know their place, and that place was in the supposedly benevolent employment of white men. If it took an occasional lynching to reinforce this lesson, so be it. The elite were content to let the Klan do the dirty work, even if it remained a solution best avoided.

Dorothy's views on race were forged in this environment. They evidently solidified there as well. Later in life, when she traveled to Richmond, the capital of the Confederacy, she visited the house where Robert E. Lee officially took charge of the Southern armies. "I stood there," Dorothy later recalled, "with tears falling down my cheeks."[31] These tears of joy honored her mythologized heritage. The late Ruth Rogers, the daughter Dorothy would adopt a year after adopting Frank (and call Ruthie), remembered how racial slurs were, as they were for most Deltans speaking in the privacy of their parlors, common in her house (including "nigger this, nigger that").[32] In *The Battlefield*, Frank touches on the complexity of this heritage when young Francis mentions:

> a threnody a tragedy of unknown blood and General Lee's men
> spoke of themselves
> as Les Miserables
> the war of the theatres
> at the age of ten I had memorized every battle and cavalry tactic of
>     the civil
> no the war to the states so I could forget it
> this stinking bird wasn't going to bend my back my whole life

as the credentials of the family that took me in are excellent...
(11564–71)

His midsentence correction—"war to the states" rather than Civil War—shows Francis instinctively remembering to honor the views of his mother, her literary neighbors, and the general ethos of white Greenville. "I would fight for the Confederacy today," Dorothy's friend, the writer Shelby Foote, told the *Paris Review*. "The Confederacy fought for some substantially good things."[33] Although the comment sounds like it might have been uttered in 1899, Foote said it in 1999. "Our plantation system," Percy wrote in his memoir *Lanterns on the Levee* (1941), "seems to me to offer as humane, just, self-respecting, and cheerful a method of earning a living as human beings are likely to devise."[34] Such reactionary nostalgia dripped less heavily from Hodding Carter's pen. But he, too, with his opposition to anti-lynching laws and desegregation busing, joined the club of proud southerners taking a stand for an agrarian ideal rooted in racial distinction. As he wrote to his friend Will Percy about *Lanterns*, "I want only to get back to Greenville and do my best to preserve there the pattern you uphold."[35] Dorothy's Greenville respected these men and adhered to their views.

As a single, working, independent, and landowning mother of an adopted child, Dorothy Gilbert Alter might have seemed an odd fit for this brand of Delta plantocracy. However, she blended right in, dutifully playing the role of the charming, God-fearing, racially conscious southerner committed to the Delta's traditional hierarchy.[36] In addition to her stellar reputation with the region's professional class, there was Green Acres, with its stately native pecans and manicured pastures. She frequently put her handsome farm to social use by hosting events that allowed her to display, if not an actual plantation, then at least a strong aesthetic commitment to southern pride.

In May of 1946, as the regional paper reported, Dorothy held an "informal garden party" for Greenville High School's graduating seniors. Although the event was billed in the social pages as an "informal" affair, guests confronted a hired hostess who ushered them down a garlanded receiving line. Honorees wore "costumes of pastel cotton." The reporter assigned to the event wrote: "Games and dancing were enjoyed. The picnic tea was served from a long damask covered table which held arrangements of mixed summer flowers."[37] The most dedicated southern belle would have felt right at home on the manicured lawn of Green Acres. Whether it was tears for Lee in Virginia or tea for the belles in Greenville, Dorothy cast her lot with the Percys and the Carters. She was ensconced, through heritage and hard work, in what the paper's society column called her "legion of friends."³⁸ This was the social world Frankie came home to in August 1948.

## From the Plantation to Parchman (1911–27)

One of the more noteworthy facts about Dorothy and her adopted children is that she never formally told them they were adopted. I'll return to this later, but it must be noted here that this was a decision that only makes sense when we understand Dorothy's life before Green Acres, the values to which she ascribed, and the deep pride she invested in them. She considered her lineage too southern and privileged to place her children outside of it. Instead, she followed a time-honored ritual that went something like this: Lay claim to a heritage, ignore the reality of the role of race in preserving it, do whatever it takes to stay afloat financially, and maintain appearances at all costs. This last requirement demanded that she downplay the adoptions and Frank and Ruth. Writers from Langston Hughes to Ralph Ellison to Kevin Young have shown how Black Americans wore proverbial masks to negotiate the turbulent racial atmosphere of the American South. But whites like Dorothy wore their own masks as they came of age in a segregated South where the purity of lineage for whites was sacred. Dorothy's life before adopting her son in 1948 reveals the way she donned the mask of southern privilege, a mask she intended her children to inherit and wear without question as a birthright. She never wanted the fact of adoption to interfere with the myth she so effortlessly lived out.

There was a long tradition among members of the Delta's white middle class of claiming aristocratic heritage.³⁹ Dorothy Gilbert, born in Greenville in 1911, was not immune to this habit. In a 1998 interview, she presented her father, Judson "Judd" Malcolm Gilbert, as coming from "southern Mississippi Blue Blood."⁴⁰ She was proud that he "was a plantation man" who owned "a cotton plantation near Greenville where I was born."⁴¹ Her mother, Carolyn Beatrice Gildart,⁴² was described as an even more socially prominent figure, "the one who always led the first dance at the Governor's Ball." She "dressed every day as if she had company coming over."⁴³ Dorothy came from a family that, by her own assessment, "traced its roots back many generations to English aristocrats." She recalled that her days growing up on the plantation were, because of this history, "the happiest time of my life."⁴⁴

If only because it goes unmentioned in her own account, it would be easy to miss the ever-present influence of race in her story. Such absence is precisely what the southern racial order was designed to achieve for white citizens in the American South: a sense that their position, real or mythologized, was as natural as the moon and magnolias. The Gilbert family—Dorothy was one of six children—employed a staff of Black servants. Dorothy's recollection of her family's help reminds us how unthinkingly whites assimilated the South's racial hierarchy, doing so as if it were the great chain of being. Race was an absence that Dorothy internalized and never felt the need to question.

This could at times make her seem blissfully oblivious. She later said that she became especially close with one of the younger sisters of her family's servants, a Black girl named Mattie. "She and I fished together, we rode horses together, we did everything together," she recalled. "Mattie was a real friend, and I loved her for everything we did together." But it was a qualified friendship. Dorothy's more revealing recollection comes when she adds about Mattie, "Her sister was a maid. Her aunt was the housekeeper. Her aunt's husband was the cook."[45] They did "everything" together, in other words, except live together, formally dine together, go to school together, and worship together.

Jim Crow segregation was the actual framework within which Dorothy befriended Mattie. In 1997 Dorothy surmised that her relationship with Mattie "made my whole life different from other southern women about colored people."[46] But again, Dorothy's experience as a privileged white girl with a Black friend whose status was marked by her family's servitude to the Gilberts was hardly unusual. Having Black friends was fine, perhaps even admirable for white elites who could advertise their magnanimity. But the implicit message was that those Black friends had to know their place. Mattie's status on the plantation certainly ensured that she did. The imprint of this dynamic on the identity of a white girl growing up on a Delta cotton plantation was indelible, deep, and in Dorothy's case, immutable.

But as the Gilberts' servants knew, there was more to the Mississippi Delta than cotton plantations and the patrician order the plantocracy demanded. There was violence, incarceration, racial oppression, horrific labor conditions, and, emerging from this darkness, raw lyrical expressions seductive in their beauty and power. Few places embodied these qualities as thoroughly as Parchman Farm. Although this moment in Dorothy's personal narrative warranted only a single sentence in her life narrative, her family in the mid-1920s moved sixty miles down the road to the largest and most notorious prison farm in the country. Frank

Stanford, who later learned about this episode in his family's history, had his protagonist, Francis, declare about his grandfather:

> I saw Governor Vardaman show him
> where to sign his name when he named him warden of Parchman
> Penitentiary
> (3476–77)[47]

And then: "I saw the convicts with their axes raised and ringing like the battle swords" (3478).

Dorothy's father, Judd Gilbert, suffered a small stroke in the mid-1920s and, at least in the immediate aftermath, could no longer run his Greenville plantation. To avoid selling the farm while he recovered, he took a position as manager of Camp Six at the Parchman Farm plantation. Parchman was a twenty-four-thousand-acre racially segregated prison camp associated with the Mississippi State Penitentiary. Judd Gilbert oversaw about 150 men who grew cotton and corn and slaughtered pigs for the state to sell at market value. Dorothy and her family moved into a cramped house across the way from the camp's largest dormitory, called "the cage," which held the prison's most hardened convicts. Apart from other managers and their families, virtually all their neighbors were Black men and women who lived in cheap housing on the prison's periphery to be near their loved ones and, in some cases, benefit from the supplies the prisoners stole from the prison. It was not uncommon for prisoners to funnel food and clothing supplied by the prison to their families on the other side of the plantation's fence to feed and clothe them.[48]

Parchman teemed with men, most of them Black. After decades of struggling, and often failing, to keep Black workers locked into unfair sharecropping and tenant contracts, planters had devised other ways to secure their labor. Incarceration proved quite effective. Minor infractions, such as "loitering," could land a Black man in Parchman, and if racism was genteel in Greenville, it was brutal at Parchman. Few institutions embodied the fierce racial disparities in law, justice, and society more severely than such farms, where convicts toiled under the threat of the lash. For at least two years, as a teenager, Dorothy experienced the Delta not as a refined plantation but as a harsh penitentiary.

Moving to Parchman was an obvious demotion for the Gilberts. But it was one that Dorothy, as she reconstructed her past, easily wove into her otherwise charmed southern narrative. White southern families, especially elite ones, understood what it was like to experience a fall. For all their social capital, Delta planters had known since the 1820s that nobody's fortune was secure, particularly if it depended on cotton and Black labor. Economic ruin lurked with the next boll weevil outbreak or levee collapse. Or war. For example, Dorothy's father's family had once owned a plantation outside Atlanta, but they had had to head for the hills of Mississippi and scratch their way back to economic security after William Tecumseh Sherman, in Dorothy's terms, "destroyed the area."[49]

The lore of this identity-defining fall from grace lingered for Dorothy, as it did for many southerners. Frank absorbed the story enough to tell his editor in 1973 that his ancestors "were burned out and somehow they tracked and got on a flatboat and came somewhere to Arkansas."[50] Yankees, Dorothy said more pointedly, "came down here to pound the life out of us." Every southern Stanford patriarch had been anxious ever since, and it was an anxiety that Dorothy, who despised "Yankees," never outgrew. "As a child I grew up with the people who suffered so bitterly during and after the Civil War," she said, adding, "the war has been in me always and I despise Lincoln."[51]

White southerners, as the story went, had suffered, and a proud resilience was the only way to survive. If a stint at Parchman was what the family had to do to recover, then they would do it. But the culture shock there was severe. While the Parchman experience was a phase in life that Dorothy chose not to dwell on, other than to say, "I had a terribly hard life there,"[52] horrific Parchman stories proliferated in the local and national media. Prisoners often mutinied, as they did in the early 1930s when "the group of convicts, many of them desperate characters, refused to leave the barred quarters and go into the field to work." They were finally convinced to do so "under stern measures"—which is to say, the threat of "tear gas, bombs, and ammunition."[53] In 1930, a visiting engineer was found shot dead under mysterious circumstances on the sleeping porch of Camp Five.[54] Dorothy's family had a direct brush with danger. The details of this incident are vague, but they were evidently held hostage for several hours by an escaped inmate.[55] Although nobody was physically injured,[56] the story was passed down enough for Frank to recall as an adult that his grandmother "was kidnapped when she was pregnant along with two of her children by some convicts when my grandaddy was warden."[57]

Camp Six, Judson Gilbert's charge, came in for especially severe scrutiny. Abuse was rampant in this camp, at least enough to raise the specter of "grand jury action." Nearly a third of the camp's men had refused to work, exercising their right to appeal for an investigation because of poor labor conditions. Convicts cited being denied water in the sweltering heat. One man testified, "Last September, with the sun bearing down as hard it ever gets, we were picking cotton in yonder field and had not had a drink of water since 1 o'clock. It was then 5 in the afternoon. Our tongues were parched to the roofs of our mouths." Another recalled how, after a group of men filed complaints, "we were taken right there on the turn row and the strap put on us 15 times."[58] Nowhere does this news coverage directly implicate Judd Gilbert by name. Still, these stories highlight the coercive authority that prevailed at the camp, an authority more severe than anything the family knew back in Greenville, where they were eager to return and forget this chapter of their lives.

## The Blues (1920s)

If Parchman in the mid-1920s introduced the Gilbert family to a more violent brand of racial disparity, it was also the very time and place where, in response to that violence, a counterlanguage of resistance was born: the Delta blues. The Gilbert family lived, if only briefly, at the vital epicenter of a significant cultural moment sustained by Black men armed with guitars and backed by ad hoc field choirs. Folklorist Alan Lomax called the blues that came out of Parchman "poetry that rings like a hammer on an anvil."[59] Lomax, who joined his father John Lomax (along with the blues legend Leadbelly) in a quest to document the songs sung by Parchman prisoners in the late 1920s and 1930s, visited the prison shortly after Judd Gilbert was hired to run Camp Six.

If these men crossed paths in the Parchman fields, which they likely did—Alan Lomax would have been a hard man to miss dragging around three hundred pounds of recording equipment—they would have discovered that their views differed. Lomax would have seen Gilbert as an operative in an institution akin to a concentration camp. He complained that "conditions in these state pens perpetuated the worst aspects of plantation slavery."[60] Lomax likewise characterized Parchman as a place where "southern penologists joyously and self-righteously humiliated, bullied, beat, often tortured, and sometimes murdered their charges."[61]

The flip side of this suffering was the raw power of the music that Parchman produced. It was a depth of lyrical expression unprecedented in southern history. The emotional roots of that music date back to the antebellum South and the slave experience. In the 1920s and 1930s, the musical link to that past was especially palpable. "It's not only what happened to you," John Lee Hooker said of the blues, "it's what happened to your foreparents and other people."[62] Through this generational connection, Hooker reminds us of Richard Mizelle's claim, in his study of the Flood of 1927: "Blues emerged as a sophisticated social and cultural interpretation and counter-movement to the oppression, violence, and surveillance blacks experienced for centuries under slavery, post-slavery, and peonage in the South."[63] Dorothy and her family witnessed this reality firsthand, but they ignored it. The Lomaxes listened to it first-hand, and they recorded it.

The Lomaxes have been justifiably accused of exploiting the talent they recorded. To some degree, they did. But there is little doubt that the blues they heard and preserved at Parchman moved them to genuine empathy for both the underlying suffering and the music that captured it. "These songs and others I heard that day I shall carry in my heart forever," John Lomax wrote. "The reaction from a high pitch of emotional excitement gave me a sleepless night." He was touched by "more than two thousand voices of black men singing in reverential tones the spiritual songs of a race."[64] It was, as he wrote to a friend, "music of mystery and wistful sadness."[65]

Alan's ears pricked up to more scintillating melodies, but they too left him awed in an otherworldly way. Sitting on a woodpile among men named Bull, Bama, Dobie Red, Tangle Eye, and 22, he became transfixed as "choruses rolled across the field." The songs he most admired were the ones laced with sexually crude lyrics such as "I ain't been to Georgia, but I been told / Women in Georgia got the sweet jelly roll." Lomax relished the "playful eroticism of Africa" and the way "work-song leaders were always rhyming about the jelly in the biscuit." The lyrics he recorded spoke of lust, labor, and longing in language that was far more expressive than anything the Lomaxes had ever heard. These words simply pulsed with sex:

> Big-Leg Rosie, with her big-leg drawers
> Got me wearin these striped overalls.
> When she walks, she reels and rocks behind.
> Ain't that enough to worry a po convict's mind.

Or:

> Oh my baby, my honey gal—
> Driving Hard, huh [This "huh" follows each line.]
> Hard to please, never done—
> Just one inch was the bargain—
> Wants another and another—
> I told her, "Bargain's a bargain"—
> Done no good, not a bit—
> Change her mind, right away—
> Want a yard, foot ain't enough

Wants my hammer, handle too
Says "be a man, like your old dad"—
Drive her home, my honey boy.[66]

This was language unheard in the Greenville mansions. By tuning in, the Lomaxes preserved and perpetuated a fundamental form of folk communication, the kind Frank would later absorb like a sponge. As a mode of expression that captured the complex emotions of Blacks toiling under white power, this evolving vernacular, although developing right in front of them, was lost on Dorothy and her family. It was language sung and chanted by Blacks for Blacks, and if it kept them to the hoe, whites reasoned, then let them carry on with their strange noise.[67] For the Gilberts, Parchman was nothing more than a hell on earth, a cacophony of chaos that you could only hope to escape, which they soon did.

In the early 1930s, the Gilbert family moved back to Greenville to revive as best they could their former life on their old plantation, which had been washed out by flooding in their absence. "We lost so much in the great flood of 1927," Dorothy recalled.[68] But the blues went nowhere except, after decades, into college campuses. After he went to college, Frank Stanford would become deeply enmeshed in the world that such music preserved. The Black language and culture of the Deep South, as well as the Black people who lived it then and historically, reached him, wrenched him from his past, and invited him in. There is therefore something apt, even prophetic, about this brief overlap between Frank's ancestors and the birth of the blues at Parchman. It's a coincidence highlighting not only how two oppositional languages coexisted in the Deep South but also how they echoed forward, offering future white generations an opportunity to reject traditions they were bred to uphold.

In an insightful description of how the blues accomplished what it did, how it offered someone like Stanford the sound of rebellion, historian Clyde Woods writes, "The blues offers a multi-ethnic working class vision of a flawed United States haunted by its own practices of racial oppression and enforced poverty." The blues are, he adds, "an unapologetic celebration of life, resistance, spiritual affirmation, community."[69] It is worth noting here that this description applies uncannily to Frank's future magnum opus, *The Battlefield*, a poem that channels the language of the blues born at Parchman to imagine a community that celebrates racial equality through "an unapologetic celebration of life."

But back in Dorothy's day, when the blues were just emerging, every white child of the South knew what language they were to speak. Dorothy would inevitably socialize Frank into the racial ideology of Greenville through the paternalistic ethos of the Percys and the Gilberts. This acculturation into the conservative racial order of the Old South would become the foundation of Frank's childhood years, shaping him into the young man his mother wanted him to be. Frank would, of course, rebel. He would open his ears to what was happening on the other side. And he would do so through a language, maskless and beautiful, that his mother wanted nothing to do with.

## Dorothy's Road Back to Greenville (1930-48)

Frank's mother was eighteen when her family left the prison plantation. For about ten years she shifted into early adulthood and worked a series of jobs before making her way back to Greenville and thriving at Firestone, buying Green Acres, and adopting her two children. "I had to go to work" was all she could say about a future looking into the face of a global depression.[70] She found work in New Orleans and then Greenville before moving to Memphis.[71] There she got a job at Sears, where she stayed, living in a small studio at 579 East Street, until 1939. Her experience at Sears taught her how the company worked "from top to bottom."[72] Even though she did not want to be there, she was happy to have a job during the Depression and did her work more than diligently. The family's pastor in Greenville wrote her an encouraging note to say that "we are also very much delighted to know of your own success in your work. With the start you have there is no knowing how high you may go in commercial lines."[73] The pastor identified something inherent in Dorothy's character: Every job she took, she took seriously.

Shortly after moving to Memphis, Dorothy married Carl Alter.[74] Seven years later, childless, they divorced. It was, she recalled, "a broken marriage and I was in a terrible condition."[75] During their time together, they nurtured each other's interest in writing. Carl published in local newspapers doggerels that glorified the Old South.[76] Dorothy wrote overwrought essays that probed her favorite themes at the time, "love and pain." She wrote passages such as "He who loves must suffer—it is writ true large upon the canvas of the earth, and up the holy sky" and "Every fruit of love must come to birth in hands of travail, else the dawn is lit with wailing and with reaching forth of hands, with bitter agony and mighty strain."[77] Dorothy concluded late in life, "I should have been a writer."[78]

Dorothy and Carl responded to their failing marriage with anxious literary expressions of woeful gloom. Dorothy:

> For though I know he loves me
> Tonight my heart is sad
> His kiss was not so wonderful
> As all the dreams I had.

After they divorced, Dorothy quit her job at Sears and went to California. Carl wrote:

> You hitched your wagon to a star
> Now I wonder where you are?
> "Here I am," she softly said
> In Reno wishing I was dead
> I wish I'd hitched it to a horse
> and thus avoided this remorse.

A few years later, Dorothy was still penning her anger on the page, using a phrase she repeated often: "he who loves must suffer!"[79] In fact she did not go to Reno in the wake of her divorce but rather went to Los Angeles. "I had been through hell," she said, remembering her arrival in California. Nonetheless, in Los Angeles she played on her managerial talent to get another job at Sears. "I got my own desk," she recalled, "and in two weeks I had four departments to take care of."[80] She oversaw the production and mailing of the company's catalogs. She complained of the tedium but performed, as always, exceedingly well.

Dorothy moved back to Greenville after America entered World War II, reuniting with her family and reentering the social milieu of the Delta, this time as an adult. She was warmly welcomed at Bible meetings and other community gatherings. After taking some business classes at night, she began her work at Firestone, where she was popular and well liked. A local newspaper took note, valorizing Dorothy as one of the heroic "women on the homefront." It noted that the Firestone Corporation "saw that she was a born executive and sent her to school to learn about selling tires and other unfeminine things like that." Another article noted how "she has earned the love and respect of her associates."[81]

Dorothy continued to write, and if her poetry was any indication, her faith in finding love was rekindled by the familiar comfort of Greenville's social scene. Expressions of pain and suffering yielded to notions such as "For all they know of tenderness and worth / Aye every fruit of love must come to birth."[82] She excelled at her job, bought Green Acres, kept her heart open, adopted a son in the late summer of 1948, and brought him home to Green Acres.

As a single mother, Dorothy had a lot to juggle. She decided to leave Firestone, pursuing instead a series of odd jobs that allowed her to balance raising Frank—and, a year later, her adopted daughter, Ruthie—with the necessity of earning money to support them. In 1949, she opened a day-care center at 230 North Shelby Street, right in town. An advertisement in the local paper read, "Opening Day Nursery and Boarding Home for Children . . . Phone Mrs. Dorothy Alter."[83] By August 1949 she was breeding and selling collie puppies, "perfectly marked," to supplement her income.[84] All the while she became increasingly active in the local First Baptist Women's meetings.[85] In 1949 an aunt and uncle of Dorothy's moved in with her. Her uncle, from her mother's side of the family, was a retired planter named Richard P. Davis. He died of a heart attack in March 1950, leaving his wife to care for Frank while Dorothy was off working her odd jobs.

In March of 1950 Dorothy started managing a restaurant near Greenville's city hall, at 133 South Shelby Street, called the Hide-Away. It featured a large family-style table that was often decorated with "mixed summer flowers." She hosted luncheons for bridesmaids, Red Cross volunteers, and meetings of the Daughters of the American Revolution.[86] The restaurant, which only served lunch and breakfast, offered menu items such as "home baked pastries" and "creole shrimp with hot breads and pies."[87] But Dorothy and her business partner gave it a twist. An advertisement extolled the opening of a new and improved Hide-Away with "good food" and "good books." It was billed as "not just another place to eat but another KIND of place."[88] It did not last long. Hide-Away closed in 1951 after the owner became ill.[89]

Through these endeavors Dorothy was making a favorable impression on Greenville as an affable, God-fearing, and hardworking member of the community. But she was most remembered years after she left for something that almost everyone who knew her mentioned: her culinary skills. A 1965 recollection of "old stuff" in the Greenville paper recalled, "Dorothy now . . . lives in Mountain Home, AR," but "no less an epicurean than Mrs. Rosalea Raphael assures us that [she] was famous for many more pieces de resistance than [her] fried rabbit." Raphael remembered practically begging for the proprietor's cheese pie recipe.[90] Whatever Dorothy cooked, it was, as with virtually everything else related to her persona, southern. "Frankie," she recalled, "liked southern food." As if he had a choice. When Frank was married to his second wife, Ginny, Dorothy bristled at the idea that Ginny thought Frank ate too much meat. "They never had meat," Dorothy lamented.[91] This was an omission she rectified by cooking for her son fried pork and gravy and sixteen-ounce steaks whenever he came home to Mom.

Albert Franklin Stanford (center) with business associates, ca. 1945.
*Photo courtesy of Carole Hess.*

## "A Father for the Children"

For all of Dorothy's hustle, Green Acres proved too much to handle. In late 1951 she sold it and downsized, moving with the kids into town. But this transition did not last long, as Dorothy had another move in the works. One of the levee engineers to whom she'd sold tires at Firestone—that man who declared, "If you need tires, get them from Dorothy Alter"—was a tall, thin, chisel-faced man named Albert Franklin Stanford. He was described by one friend of Dorothy's as a "spare, silver-haired and soft-spoken gentleman" who had "a face sculpted like the Indian on a Buffalo Head nickel."[92] He was professionally successful, a Memphis gentleman well respected in the lobby of the Peabody hotel and widely known throughout the Delta as one of the region's finest engineers. There were drawbacks to him as a romantic partner. Albert Franklin Stanford was twenty-seven years older than Dorothy Alter, a contemporary and friend of her parents, and still married. But none of it prevented him from falling hard for his personal tire saleswoman. They began attending social events together as early as 1944, whenever he visited Greenville on business, which he started to do with increasing regularity.

And it seems they did more than go to parties. As Albert Franklin Stanford's granddaughter Carole remarked, "I think that you can count on the fact that [Albert and Dorothy] were together" before his wife died. Indeed, as the granddaughter pondered the notion, she added, "He and Dorothy were definitely together before our birth grandmother ever passed away."[93] They were intimate enough in 1948 for Albert Franklin Stanford to sponsor Frank at his baptism. Whenever he and Dorothy first became romantic partners, seven months after Albert Franklin Stanford's wife Edna died of stomach cancer in August 1951, Dorothy Alter became Dorothy Stanford, and Francis Gildart Alter became Francis Gildart Stanford.[94] Decades later, a close friend of the Stanford family said that "Dorothy married Albert Franklin Stanford because she wanted a father for the children she adopted."[95] Even so, as Dorothy's friend, the writer Joan Williams, recalled, Dorothy "gave Mister Frank a love and warmth he had not had before."[96]

Albert Franklin Stanford, a levee engineer born in Arkansas and raised in Memphis, would take Dorothy and her two adopted kids out of Greenville and the culture she knew so well there. He would also adopt the children. Frank Sr. knew exactly on which side of the language divide he stood. Not with the blues. If nothing else, Albert Franklin only intensified Dorothy's commitment to the values of the Old South. Indeed, the Stanfords' life in Memphis reenforced the same racial attitudes as those that had defined Dorothy's upbringing.

But there was a catch—and an important one. "Frank Sr.," as the family would call him, had to take his new family to levee camps every summer so he could oversee levee repairs. These camps were pitched on what Frank Stanford would call in *The Battlefield* "the balcony of the Delta" (7998–99)—in Snow Lake, Arkansas—and they situated Frank in an entirely more fascinating reality than the one he knew at home. Here was a place defined by new people speaking a new language, a place with a whirl of blues-driven sound and voices, and a place where a young Frank Stanford would, by just living life as a kid, unknowingly find material for a lifetime of poetry.

Frank Stanford (*opposite end of table*) on his fifth birthday; his sister, Ruth, is in the foreground. Snow Lake, Arkansas, 1953. *Photo by Dorothy Stanford. Photo courtesy of Carrie Prysock.*

TWO

# Life on the Levees

## 1953–1956

"THE MISSISSIPPI DELTA," WROTE THE Greenville-born writer David Cohn in 1935, "begins in the lobby of the Peabody Hotel in Memphis and ends on Catfish row in Vicksburg."[1] First opened in 1869 and famous for the ducks shepherded daily to a fountain in the lobby, the Peabody was where Albert Franklin Stanford kept an office with the Cotton Exchange.[2] The hotel appears often in *The Battlefield* and elsewhere in Stanford's work. There's "the peg-legged man / who knocks a pigeon wing in the Lobby of the Peabody" (728–29). There's "the mustachioed alcoholic in a white suit playing pitch at the Peabody" (7216). There's the poor guy who cleans duck shit off the Peabody's red carpets for a living (724). "I can dream in the Peabody Hotel," Stanford writes in a poem called "The Dreams."[3] These references are mostly easygoing and lighthearted, the mood as whimsical as mallards waddling to the fountain for a bath.

But near the end of *The Battlefield*, after young Francis has witnessed and confronted the injustices that his Black friends have endured, he evokes the Peabody in a different way. Francis explodes:

> like I told you I've had enough I can't take it anymore
> from that duck fountain in the lobby of my daddy's well he ain't a for
>     real one
> but from there clear to where my sister goes to school with them
>     episcopalians
> in Vicksburg from there on into infinity I reckon ever sapsucking
>     son-of-a-bitch

with a lowdown tongue has got it all sewed up
   (11676–80)

These lines, which pulse with emotion, reflect a conversion. The white-bread Delta traditions that once ushered Francis, and Frank, into adolescence have here been jettisoned in favor of another purpose. Gone is the reverence for the grand, all-white-serving hotel (Francis won't even say its name); acknowledged is the fact that his father is not his biological father ("ain't a for real one"); explicit is the rejection of proper diction ("ever" instead of "every"); and scorned is the silence in the face of Jim Crow oppression ("lowdown tongue . . . all sewed up"). These sentiments confirm Francis's growing allegiance to a new language, one that he experiences after taking up with a small community of Black folks in Memphis. About the tradition he is abandoning, he says:

I could go back
and kiss all their asses and play like a fool like they want or win the
   spelling
B or win the essay why I am a good American contest and they'd all
   forgive me but
to hell with it I'll just go my own way . . .
   (1392–95)

Frank Stanford would do nothing if not go his own way. His choice to cut ties with the Old South and hear a wider range of voices began with his childhood experiences on the levees along the Mississippi River. As an adult, Frank well understood the historical significance of the levees in the Delta. He saw them as the foundation of a society where, as historian Clyde Woods once wrote, "White settlers had been developing . . . since the Trail of Tears, displacing Native Americans in order to plant native cotton." He knew that, again in Woods's words, "the levees of the 1930s, constructed in the wake of the Flood of 1927, were arguably the last big act of that century-long drama of relocation, allocation, and distribution of wealth."[4] Frank told Irv Broughton in 1973 that "the levee, the moving of dirt, affected every white man as well as every Black man in the South, whether you lived in a shack or worked in a farm or whether you were a millionaire or a senator."[5]

What young Frank saw daily at the levee camp in Snow Lake, Arkansas, was Black men working. Most Black levee workers toiled under three-month summer contracts—during the "slack season," when their labor was less needed on cotton plantations.[6] Notably, these levees became—because of Frank Sr.'s supervisory role as a levee engineer—the venue where Frank would directly experience for the first time the Black culture of the Deep South. The camp was a microculture marked by racism and poverty. But it was also marked by the language, characters, and relationships to the land that defined the Delta's patterns of life. It all left a permanent impression on Frank, a boy who had the privilege to experience this culture directly while he was young and highly impressionable.

Frank's time at the Snow Lake levee camp was relatively brief but enormously formative. For many weeks over several summers, the camp was all he knew when it came to summer vacation. His experience there informed his observation, years later, about "how shitty white people were" to the Blacks whom he would befriend.[7] But it was also an experience that allowed him to blur racial lines with a Black community that would help turn *The Battlefield* into an epic poem with a deeper mission. Just as critically, the levee-camp summers ensured that Stanford's poetry always held close the liberated spirit of childhood. "Childhood," according to Leon Stokesbury, "was always his major source of poetic inspiration."[8] The levees that A. F. Stanford constructed and fortified in Snow Lake, Arkansas, protected more than King Cotton. For his adopted son, they preserved as if in amber the innocence and freedom of a kid being a kid—outdoors, with little oversight, free to explore unknown worlds that would change the way he saw his own.

## Levee Life

This experience was made possible by Stanford's adoptive father. The elder Stanford was born on September 24, 1884, in Waldron, Arkansas. His lineage went back to colonial Georgia, to a time when the Creeks and Cherokees populated the Blue Ridge Mountains before the Indian Removal Act of 1830. The Stanfords owned plantations in Columbia and Warren Counties until the Civil War forced them out.[9] Frank Sr.'s parents—James Cosby Stanford and Sarah Evaline Taff—moved from Pine Log, Georgia, to Waldron, Arkansas, in 1869. Dorothy, speaking about her much older husband, sounded a familiar theme, saying, "His parents had been wealthy but were ruined by Sherman when he destroyed Atlanta. They took what belongings they could and fled." Once settled in Arkansas, James Stanford worked as a farmer and merchant.[10]

The Stanford family valued education and hard work. Out of eight brothers and sisters, only four survived to adulthood. Two became medical doctors and another an attorney.[11] Later in life, Frank Stanford, although shaky on the details, recalled what he'd heard about this commitment to education. Of his father he said, "His daddy took him in a wagon, took all seven of them to the University of Arkansas, and all seven of them got their degrees. Some of them went on to be veterinarians, physicians, and some of them, PhDs. He was an engineer."[12] Frank Sr. earned a degree in civil engineering at the University of Arkansas in 1904, putting himself through college by working—as his son later would—as a land surveyor.[13] He began work as an independent levee contractor in Driver, Arkansas, in 1911 and married Edna Alexander in 1917. After joining with a few other contractors, he developed the Driver Contracting Co. into a viable business.[14]

The Great Flood of 1913 was a boon for Frank Sr.'s fledgling firm. The demand for sturdier levees in Arkansas and Mississippi skyrocketed. Stanford moved to Memphis sometime in the early 1920s to oversee the expansion of the Driver business, but by 1925 the company bought him out. With the payout, Albert Franklin founded the Stanford Contracting Company, which joined with several other contracting companies to establish the Mississippi Valley Branch of the Associated General Contractors.[15]

There Stanford distinguished himself as a highly talented businessman and engineer. He was known, according to a colleague, "as one of the most outstanding authorities on levee construction in the Lower Mississippi Valley."[16] This was the right reputation to have on the eve of the big Flood of 1927. When that elemental disaster hit, it destroyed more than 120 major levees throughout the Delta. Amid this historic destruction, Stanford became president of the Mississippi Valley Flood Control Branch, a perch from which he would oversee the reconstruction and maintenance of the region's levees for thirty years. It was a position in which he would prosper financially, ushering his second family into an elegant standard of living.

Central to Frank Sr.'s success was securing cheap labor. The Flood of 1927 put a premium on exploitable Black labor and, in turn, fostered especially brutal levee-camp discipline. It was paramount that the region's white leaders not only acquire Black labor but also—as was the case for cotton plantation owners—keep it from joining the Great Migration north. Landowners and politicians knew that, as Alan Lomax noted of the men who worked the levees, laborers "enjoyed the freedom of roaming from job to job."[17] This challenge—keeping Blacks in the Delta and tied to the levees—inspired the methods that whites used to secure the labor necessary to rebuild and maintain a levee system that would protect the region's cotton, as well as the plantocracy that thrived on it.

Tactics varied. In the immediate wake of the 1927 flood, Blacks often pursued their tasks at gunpoint—whether on the levees or unloading Red Cross supplies.[18] In a less extreme approach, white leaders forced Blacks to obtain food and shelter exclusively at Red Cross field sites to create dependency on federal provisions. William Alexander Percy, who led the effort to keep Black labor localized and dependent, bluntly remarked, "None of us was influenced by what the Negroes themselves wanted: they had no capacity to plan for their own welfare; planning for them was another one of our burdens."[19] Delta Blacks who refused to consign themselves to the levee camps were subjected to "vagrancy" charges. The *Chicago Defender* reported on one notice that was posted throughout the Delta: "All Negroes in Greenville outside of the levee camp who are able to work should work. If work is offered them and they refuse to work they should be arrested as vagrants."[20] This legal fiction was no idle threat but rather an effective way to undermine labor autonomy.

Low and inconsistent pay, endless work hours, and a rigged commissary system locked most laborers into debt peonage. Blacks collected half of what whites did—about one dollar a day in the early 1930s—and were then gouged at the "robissary," the only place where they could find safe drinking water, food, and tent rentals. These expenses consumed 50 percent of a worker's paycheck, one that, if he was Black, he would not even reliably receive.[21] It was in this context that the sociologist Rupert Vance deemed racial relations in 1935 akin to slavery. "Nowhere but in the Mississippi Delta," he wrote, "are antebellum conditions so nearly preserved."[22] The Work Progress Administration expressed the same idea a bit differently, describing the Delta as having "a degrading mode of life."[23] More recently, the poet Kevin Young has put his own twist on this idea, calling the Delta of this era "Death's cousin / once removed."[24]

This was the environment in which Albert Franklin Stanford was schooled to his trade. Notably, he learned his skills under the mentorship of the notorious Charles Lowrence.[25] Lowrence's brutality was legendary. Among folklorists and levee workers, Lowrence remains the most likely contender for the source of the moniker "Mr. Cholly," the eponym for levee-camp abuse that Black workers lyricized in numerous levee-camp moans.[26] Frank Stanford later recalled, "There's a phrase now that is pretty common where the white man is called Charlie. I guess you would spell it Cholley. The first time this was used was with my daddy's boss." He added, "He was a mean man, this Charley Lawrence."[27] Lowrence's cruelty may have been prevalent enough to single-handedly inspire a unique form of protest music. Perhaps the most popular example of that genre is this stanza:

> I axed Mister Charley
> What time of day.
> He looked at me
> Threw his watch away.[28]

As the levee worker F. M. McCoy told Alan Lomax about the Black workers with whom he labored, "They're always singing 'Mister Cholly, Mister Cholly.'" In an environment of "pistol whippings and the ever-present threat of lynching," Lowrence was meaner than most—"meanness ran in his family," according to Lomax.[29] As late as the early 1950s, levee workers shuddered in song and story over the horrors evoked by "Mister Charley Loren."[30] In 1941, Son House, the great bluesman from Lyon, Mississippi, recorded "Camp Hollars" with Fiddlin' Joe Martin, in which he sings, "Oh, oh, Mr. Charlie . . . I done decided . . . I won't work no more."[31] Charles Lowrance and his harsh labor discipline ensured that such a choice—working no more—was more fantasized in song than acted on.

In 1929, the percentage of levee camp workers who were Black was 63 percent. In Lowrence's camps it was 92 percent.[32] One reason for this disparity is that Lowrence could save on sanitation when he hired a Black workforce. His camps were filthy. "At many of the negro tent camps," reported the US Public Health Service after an investigation that included Lowrence's camps, "no excreta disposal facilities were provided with a result that probably requires no elaboration." The report added that the foremen had "no desire to consider sanitation as essential to the camp."[33]

Despite Lowrence's reputation, Dorothy spoke highly of him and was proud of her husband's association with a man of such prominence. She called him "Old Man Charley" and noted how Frank Sr. "went into partnership" with him and benefited from his guidance. Lowrence ended up buying out Frank Sr., but the men continued to develop a lifelong friendship.[34] The brutal conditions the NAACP and AFL uncovered when they undertook their investigations of Delta levee camps in the early 1930s, while certainly precipitated by the intense labor demands of the 1927 flood, dated back to the tactics pioneered by Lowrence earlier in the century, at the very time when he joined forces with Frank Sr. to reshape the way the region managed labor to build levees. Charley Lowrence provided the mold into which Albert Franklin Stanford poured his career.

## Snow Lake, Arkansas

In the small world of Stanford scholarship, a great deal is made of Frank Stanford's experience as a kid growing up in levee camps—and rightly so. This experience was essential, encouraging Frank to do as Rainer Maria Rilke advised and "write about what your everyday life offers you."[35] That everyday life began in May 1953, when Frank Sr. and Dorothy loaded Frank and Ruth—ages four and three—into the back of the family's black Cadillac for their first summer adventure to Snow Lake, Arkansas. Their driver was a sinewy wisp of a Black man named Charlie Bolivar Lemon. Known throughout *The Battlefield* as "Charlie B.," he becomes in *The Battlefield* a close confidant of Francis. In real life, Lemon was born in 1927 to a fifteen-year-old mother with a fourth-grade education who, at least in 1940, made less than fifty dollars a year.[36] He grew into a wiry adult who worked at St. Joseph Hospital in Memphis, possibly as a janitor. By 1948, the year Frank was born, he was listed in city records as a "laborer." It is unclear how Lemon met Frank Sr., but he is later listed in the *Memphis City Directory* as working as "a machine operator" for the "Stanford Co.," a job he kept until the Stanfords left Memphis in 1961.[37] "Charlie B. Lemon is one, real character," Frank Stanford wrote to an editor in 1974, "too tough and lean and good to be drowned out by any of the poet's spices."[38]

Also sitting in the Cadillac on the way to Snow Lake was Emma Spriggs, a Black woman who worked for Frank Sr. for nearly thirty years and at this point served his family as a full-time cook at the levee camp. "We loved the food she prepared," said Dorothy, "especially her 'levee camp chicken,' thin slices of pork soaked in molasses, dipped in flour, and fried."[39] Frank Stanford gives Emma a couple of moments in *The Battlefield* as well, such as when Francis says to a cousin who is visiting the camp: "want me to fix you some pancakes and salt pork Emma showed me how to do it" (5015). In the poem "Lap," the speaker says about Emma, "She pours sweetmilk over me before the sun comes up" and that "Emma is a humming."[40] And in less happy times, again in *The Battlefield*, "big mama Emma whupped us with a hickory stick" (448). Emma and Charlie B., as real-life characters, offered Frank at a tender age access to the Black community in Snow Lake in a way his parents never could.

As Charlie B. chauffeured the extended family to Snow Lake in the late spring of 1953, in a car that supposedly could hold fifteen people, Frank talked.[41] He talked a lot. Dorothy remembered well the way Frank would ask questions for the entire 120-mile trip. "Frankie always talked," she said. "He had to know about the world and everything in it."[42] Frank enjoyed talking so much that he acted as his sister Ruth's mouthpiece for a couple years. She would tell him what she wanted to say, and he would say it for her.[43] Frank Sr. would interrupt Frank's back-seat soliloquies and offer a shiny quarter to "the one who goes the longest without a word." But Frank would sustain the chatter, mostly posing unanswerable questions about "the people who lived along the highway."[44]

Upon reaching Snow Lake, the family set up camp among the Black levee hands and their families. "[D]addy makes us live like the crew in a shack or a tent," says Francis only 237 lines into *The Battlefield*. This was true to a point. Frank Sr. was the boss, the "Charley" of the operation, as it were, so the Stanfords stayed either in an especially large canvas tent connected to a trailer with air-conditioning or—after a couple of summers, because of "the fights in camp"[45]—just outside the campgrounds in a rented house. Frank Stanford later recalled the early accommodations as "huge tents with wooden floors and wooden screen, and a roof and sides with flaps that rolled down, and then a wood stove or a kerosene stove inside." He also remembered hearing gunshots and people fighting and kicking dogs. "It was," he remembered more than anything else, "hot as hell."[46]

By the early 1950s, some contractors had come to realize that greater productivity resulted from fairer labor practices and that integration between whites and Blacks improved living conditions for labor and management alike. This was true at Snow Lake. "We ate with them," recalled Frank Coleman about the Black tenants. Frank Coleman was Frank Sr.'s grandson and was roughly the age of Frank and Ruth (who were technically his uncle and aunt). Frank Coleman accompanied his grandfather and his grandfather's new family to the camps on several summers. Frank Stanford, his sister Ruth, and Frank Coleman played with the Black kids all day everyday: "They were kids of the workers, you know, Black kids, and you were not separated from them." Coleman said about race, "I don't think at that age we felt like there was a difference." The Black workers, he insisted, "were treated well by my grandfather."[47] There is some evidence, such as a few existing payroll accounts, that Frank Sr. had evolved beyond his Mr. Cholly days.[48]

Dorothy also recalled some racial integration in the camps. "There were many Black children in the levee camp, but there were white children in camp too," she said. "The whites lived at one end, and the Blacks lived at the other, and we were in the middle."[49] Ruth remembered how Dorothy "wouldn't mind us playing with little Black kids, but at the end of the day, they went home and we went home."[50] At mealtime, though, they were back together, and it was Dorothy's job to ensure that the hired cooks, led by Emma, fed not only the levee workers and their families but also the community at large. Frank Coleman remembered, "People would come from all over and eat with them. Salespeople who were traveling in the area and whoever would come over and eat at the food tent." Of Dorothy, he added, "She had gumption."[51] By all accounts, she ran the show much as she had at Sears and Firestone.

None of this should suggest that Snow Lake was any sort of paradise—racially, culinarily, or otherwise. Far from it. Conditions at the camp were harsh. "At the levee camp," Coleman remembered, "it was what you'd think." That is to say, "while the Black people were treated very well by my grandfather, yet again they were Black"—they "lived lives of poverty, in tents.... It's so foreign to think about, that people lived like that." He added that he "didn't like it."[52] Frank Stanford later noted how men would pour into Snow Lake from Memphis, Clarksville, New Orleans, and "set up these tents, usually along a bayou or something."[53] The memories of the camp's physical layout stayed with Frank over the years, serving as maps for many scenes in *The Battlefield*, becoming that "treasure house" of memory that Rilke, in his masterful *Letters to a Young Poet*, insisted poets should raid.[54]

Dorothy did not see Snow Lake as much of a treasure house. She was bothered by what she and her kids were exposed to. On one occasion she had to threaten a severely intoxicated "white trash cracker" because he was insisting on buying more whiskey from the shop that she ran at the camp. She lunged at the man with an ax, forcing him out of the store. Frank Sr., suffering from a case of kidney stones (for which he needed frequent operations), was forced to sit in a rocking chair and watch the ordeal from a distance, his son at his side. "Young Frankie saw the whole thing," she remembered, "and he was scared to death that I was going to have to beat the man in the head. I was too."[55]

On the first page of *The Battlefield*, a variation of this incident gets embellished by Francis, who manipulates it to transfer power to his father. Francis says:

> a drunk peckerhead pulled a pistol on daddy
> mother had a double bit axe just in case but daddy kicked his teeth in
> (30–31)

As an adult, Frank remembered how the levees could be violent, recalling an accident where a worker was nearly decapitated and noting how bodies were tossed in the levee ditches because murderers "knew they'd be covered over with dirt." When asked what it took to build a levee, Frank Stanford said dirt, sweat, "and sometimes it takes blood."[56] While some of this was certainly exaggeration, which Frank was prone to, there is no question that the prospect of violence in the camp was an ever-present concern.

Prostitution was also rampant in the camps. Dorothy recalled how, on paydays, "every slut from Memphis, or wherever, came into camp to take the money away."[57] This was a predictable practice, which Gene Campbell, in his "Levee Camp Man Blues," captured musically in 1930:

> Men on the levee hollerin', "Whoa and gee"
> Men on the levee hollerin', "Whoa and gee"
> And the women on the levee camp, hollerin', "Who wants me?"[58]

Emma, who according to Dorothy made ice cream to sell to the working women, had to guard the cash she earned with a pistol.[59] In *The Battlefield*, Francis adds intrigue to Emma's weapon, noting how "Emma got the pistol back the same one she got took away from her for shooting / a man" (6393). Stanford also notes in the poem "Lay" that "She buries her pay in a bucket."[60] There were other dangers. Dorothy recalls having to whack a determined rattlesnake out of the tent she was sharing with Frank—a snake that kept lunging at a bottle of milk she was trying to give him.[61] Frank Coleman remembers his mother almost not letting him go to camp because of all the "fights in the Black tents."[62] Snow Lake was, in short, a chaotic far cry from a tearoom in downtown Greenville, much less life in a comfortable suburb of Memphis. Still, as Dorothy put it, "Frankie knew the levee and the river growing up."[63] At the least, as Francis confirms in *The Battlefield*, "I learned the ways of the cooktent" (14522), a sure indication that Frank and his friends ate well while enduring hot summers at a levee camp in the middle of nowhere.

Located in an elbow-like crook of the Mississippi River, about 15 miles as the crow flies from Rosedale, Mississippi (but 115 miles as the car drives, because of the lack of bridges), Snow Lake was, more than anything else, isolated. Coleman remarked, "I remember how remote it could be."[64] A researcher named Bill Carpenter, who ventured to Snow Lake in the 1980s to see where Frank spent his summers, determined "there is nothing there ... that part of Arkansas is truly forlorn."[65] Frank Sr.'s nephew, John F. Stanford, remarked in an interview, "When you drive to Snow Lake it's the end of the road.... The place was dirty, dingy."[66] Frank later put this way: "The levee camp was off in the wilderness.... There is no road there."[67] A relatively recent article on Snow Lake has the headline

"Town Where the Highway Ends."[68] This was an aspect of the place Frank seemed to appreciate.

Francis reiterates this isolation in *The Battlefield*. He says:

> there ain't no
> real road to where we is you can look on any map and I'll bet you can't
> even find the name of the village we are staying in this summer and I'll
> be damned sure you can't find no road to it unless you got a hold of
> a bootlegger's map . . .
> (7060–64)

Elsewhere in the poem he notes:

> my home part of the years in the weeds in the mud in the shacks
> in the tents in the roads that don't see but a half dozen automobiles
> all year long . . .
> (4445–47)

Beyond levee building, not much else happened in Snow Lake. Nonetheless, for young Frankie and Ruthie, Snow Lake was an unsupervised playground. It was a place where Black and white children lived, ate, jumped, skipped, fished, rode bikes, and celebrated birthdays together. Coleman recalled how he, Frank Stanford, and Ruth would "play with some of the kids of the workers, the Black kids." He added that "we were not separated from them." The kids would "play in the creek all day, catch frogs, just do the things kids do outside."[69]

The Black kids were especially memorable for Frank and Ruth. Ruth recalled hanging out with boys with names unlike the ones their friends had back in Memphis—names such as Baby Gauge, Ray Baby, BoBo, and Six Toes, or Born in the Camp with Six Toes. "We went fishing, ran around in cotton fields with dolls, and played in the levees," she said. "On other days, we just ran up and down dirt roads and threw rocks." She remembered how Frank and Baby Gauge went fishing every day.[70] In *The Battlefield*, Francis highlights how he and Baby Gauge and some other camp kids "have pee wars sometimes / and others we'll circle a snake or come on to a fire in the woods / and all of us will pee" (5179–81). In an undated poem draft Frank writes:

> At the age of eight Born In The Camp With Six Toes
> Baby Gauge and Myself buried one end of a fire ladder
> in the mud on the island[71]

Levee camp, Snow Lake, Arkansas, ca. 1953–55. *Photo by Dorothy Stanford. Photo courtesy of Ginny Crouch Stanford.*

Dorothy once took Ruth on an errand down a wooded road far outside of camp. When Dorothy was startled by a herd of deer, Ruth, who had evidently been to this spot many times, said, "Mother, it's just deer."[72] In *The Battlefield*, Francis remarks:

> a herd of deer crossed the levee
> my sister has all the luck
> (6391–92)

Whatever the case, wherever the venture, these kids rambled. As Frank, referencing levee life in a poem called "Island," writes: "We all did we all were."[73] And it's true. They did, and they were.

Adult oversight was minimal at camp. Dorothy was busy managing her husband's payroll, commissary, mail, and meals. "She was far more hands on than any other woman at the camp," recalls Frank Coleman.[74] Records from the levee payroll confirm her micromanagement, the disparity in the levee workers' tasks and compensation, and possibly Frank's later insistence that his father paid his employees "a good wage"—so much so that "he was always getting in trouble for this."[75] The company employed about seventeen people a week. Between July 14 and July 20, 1958, Charlie B. Lemon's occupation is listed as "rough bulldozer"; he worked seventy hours that week and made $162.45, which would have come out to over $600 a month in 2024 dollars. David McElduff, who becomes "MacCulduff" in a Stanford poem, is listed as an "oiler"; he worked sixty-eight hours and was paid $118.90. Lawrence Gage, Baby Gauge's father, is listed as "motor patrol," worked sixty-one hours, and made $150.15; Raymond Lewis Jr., the father of Ray Baby, made only $43 for thirty hours of labor.[76] With Frank Sr. out in the field checking levees and Dorothy overseeing domestic duties at the camp, Frank, Ruth, and their nephew were free to roam amid the camp's Black community.[77] This community preserved for Frank Stanford real-life characters and experiences that would animate his poems and stories.

Frank and Ruth were looked after by Emma's teenage son, a Memphis teenager named O. Z. Durrett (sometimes pronounced Ozzie by the family). According to Coleman, O. Z. "had to keep a gun to protect the kids in case fights broke out" among the levee workers. Born in 1938, O. Z. was ten years older than Frank; his mother was the family's maid in Memphis.[78] Stanford writes in *The Battlefield* that "O.Z. was the oldest so he ran the show he was the boss" (6374). In an unpublished story called "Those Fools Who Try to Write Books but Not That Russian," he writes, "O.Z. is my brother" and observes how "in those days, on the stretch of river we run on that summer, it wasn't nobody to mess with us and those who run with us."[79] In the poem "Island," from *Shade* (1975), Frank writes, "Me and O.Z. walked everywhere. We had a seine a compass."[80] Referring to his cousin Jimmy, Francis says, with respect to O. Z., "I guess me and him could have told him what to do / since it was we was white but we never thought of it" (6376–77). They were joined in their activities by several children of the Black levee camp workers—again, most often Baby Gauge and Ray Baby. If O. Z. needed to check in with an older figure of authority, there was always Charlie B., the Stanfords' chauffeur, and possibly a man named Mose Jackson, an ex-convict from Parchman who owned a nearby sorghum farm.[81] Both these men were almost certainly armed while on the levee, comprising a kind of de facto security team for this unconventional summer camp.

"He did not make up the Black people who lived in camp," Dorothy said of Frank and his poems.[82] What she did not say—because she likely disagreed with his choice—is that he thoroughly valorized them. The

O. Z. Durrett, 1964. *Photo courtesy of Carrie Prysock.*

opening poem in Frank's first book, *The Singing Knives* (1972), provides a memorable sketch of these characters. The poem, which Frank says he wrote in 1964, with the camp memories fresh in his mind, is called "The Blood Brothers":

> There was Born In The Camp With Six Toes
> He popped the cottonmouth's head off
>
> There was Baby Gauge
> He tied the line to his wrist
> He tied it to the alligator gar
> He rode the fish

There was Ray Baby
He stole the white man's gold tooth
He knocked it out with a two-by-four
He rode the moon-blind horse

There was Charlie B. Lemon
He had four wives and a pair
Of long-toed shoes

There was Mose Jackson
He threw snake eyes in his sleep

There was BoBo Washington
A rat crawled in the bed
And sucked the blood
Out of his baby's head

There was Jimmy
He had the knife like night
He was white

I had the hands like dragonflies
I killed one white man
He was a midget
I did it with a frog gig
It was the summer of the Chinese daughter
I danced on the levee[83]

The poem speaks to the essence, and the characters, of the levee camp days. The violence, the adventure, and the sweet strangeness combine to create a childlike fascination with a foreign place and people. In *The Battlefield*, Francis refers to himself as "I francis gildart knight of the levees" (7028). But the Whitmanesque undercurrent of respect and affection for other characters, all of them unified in an isolated camp culture where all manner of eccentricity prevails, culminates in something wonderful and unexpected: a celebratory levee dance. It's a dance evoking the freedom a child might feel in such displaced circumstances, unencumbered by the bourgeois rules that restricted behavior at home in Memphis, with minimal parental oversight, for long stretches of the summer. And then, of course, one cannot overlook the title—"The Blood Brothers"—as a phrase reflecting the intensity of relationships confirmed by a scene in the book's second poem, "The Singing Knives":

> He took the knife and ran it
> Across his arm
> Then he ran it across mine
> Blood came out like hot soda
>
> He tied our arms together
> With the blue bandana
> And we laid down in the cotton[84]

In *The Battlefield*, Francis again evokes that sacred moment of union:

> I can smell where
> we cut our wrists with a broken wine bottle blood brothers forever
> (2194–95)

These characters find solidarity throughout *The Singing Knives*, a book so rooted in levee-camp life that the last line reads, "sweet Jesus the levees that break in my heart." Cousin Jimmy, who later accepts the stolen gold tooth from Ray Baby and places it in his own mouth (see the poem "Tapsticks"[85]), shows up repeatedly in Stanford's poems:

> I dreamed Jimmy was pouring ice water
> Over my head at noon

And, later:

> Jimmy would go by the house for ice water
> And make the truck backfire.
> Oh, I really liked that.[86]

Based on Frank Stanford's older cousin Jimmy Lee, who was from Greenville, Jimmy in *The Singing Knives* was an eighteen-year-old worth worshipping: He wrung the necks of chickens, listened to Jimmy Reed on the radio, and threw knives with such force that they hummed. Jimmy and Francis join Charlie B. and a host of other Black men on epic ventures in *The Battlefield*, moving through the camps as a biracial squad of troubadours practically daring southern conventions to deny them their pleasure.

All camp denizens, adults and children alike, were somewhat obsessed with the levees themselves. According to Dorothy, her husband "loved

Frank, Ruth, and O. Z. preparing to make their own mini levees, ca. 1954.
*Photo by Dorothy Stanford. Photo courtesy of Ginny Crouch Stanford.*

building levees." Levees, the art of constructing them, and levee quality were ongoing topics of discussion in the supervisors' tents. The kids absorbed the details and took pride in their father's stellar reputation among levee engineers. Dorothy remembered riding with her husband and Ruth to inspect a levee that had just come under contract with her father's company. It was a crumbling berm about to disintegrate. Upon seeing it, Ruth, only four years old, was appalled. "This must be someone else's job," she insisted, "because it's a mess," telling her dad that "it doesn't look like yours." Frank Sr. proudly assured her that, until recently, it hadn't been.[87]

Frank and Ruth joined Baby Gauge and O. Z. in making their own miniature levees around the drainage ditches outside the tent camps. "We imitated them, their work," Frank said of the employees, adding that "I was the boss."[88] The Taylor and Taylor equipment company donated miniature bulldozers to kids living in the camps, but Frank, hoping for a better approximation of the levee building experience, wished for a dragline crane to do the excavating. Dorothy remembered looking out of her tent one afternoon to see Frank and O. Z. turning Frank's bicycle into a mock dragline. "Frankie took his building seriously," Dorothy said. "He wanted to be so much like his daddy, a levee builder."[89] In a poem called "The Dreams," Stanford would later write: "I can dream I've been building levees for fifty years like daddy."[90] In *The Battlefield*, Francis describes his father's levees being so strong that a tornado "probably done bounced off Albert Franklin's levee and gone set down in Spider's bean field" (6518–19). As for the miniature levees Frankie built, they did not fare as well. He remembered when one of the foreman's kids came along and threw some water at one and "it just washed a big gap in the side of the levee."[91]

Frank's direct memories of the levee camps, as relayed in a 1973 interview conducted by his publisher Irv Broughton, were as specific as they were fond. He remembered how Baby Gauge's father, Lawrence, drove a Buick with big rounded wheel wells and "had a little cigarette holder. Real cool." He recalled the way a woman named Sadie chewed gum and that she wanted to get a diamond in her gold teeth to join the clubs, hearts, and spades in the other teeth. But one memory about Sadie really stuck with him. He explained: "She would clean the shit out of her babies' asses with a willow stick. . . . She'd take a willow stick she'd been beating the other kids with, and then she'd break it in two and clean this yellow shit out of these . . . children's asses. . . . I'll always remember that." Also notable were "the commissary with a little soul food and such," and how, when his "folks were gone," he'd sleep over with his Black friends. "It seemed natural to me," he added.[92]

If most of camp life was unconventional by wealthy southern standards, there was at least one attempt by Frank Sr. to acculturate his son to more conventional habits of southern white men. Ruth noted that Frank Sr., especially at the camps, generally paid little attention to her and Frank. Due in part to his advanced age and his declining kidney health, he found it hard to be active in their lives.[93] But Frank Sr., initiating one of the more obvious examples of father-son bonding in the South, bought Frank a shotgun around the age of seven, and they went on occasional hunting adventures in and around Snow Lake. The levees, because they created retention ponds, primed the region for bird hunting. On several occasions Frankie joined his father on expeditions organized by the Neal Hunting Lodge to shoot doves and turkey. Hunting foxes was also a popular sport in Snow Lake, if only because the animals burrowed into the levees, where they were not only easier to find but important to control, as they weakened the structure.[94]

Frank Sr. had hunted his whole life. In an undated and unpublished poem, Frank Stanford wrote:

> There are three reasons why
> my father was the best shot
> in the country.
> He never dreamed of being good
> with a gun, he never practiced.
> It just came to him.[95]

Not so much for Frank. After one hunt, Frank Sr. mentioned to Dorothy that their son had performed more heroically during the prehunt breakfast, downing a half-dozen eggs, sausage, ham, toast, and biscuits—"Have you ever seen him eat like that!"—than on the hunt itself.[96] Francis, in *The Battlefield*, recalling "two years ago when I was ten," describes how "I smelled the strong coffee of the hunting camps / I saw what stuck to my ribs" (6326, 31–32). What Dorothy might not have told her husband was that after Frank shot his first dove, someone told him that the birds "married for life."[97] He eventually vowed to stop hunting. As he explained to Broughton in 1973, "Just for the record, I don't own a gun, and I don't hunt."[98] In his poem "Linger," Stanford suggests that hunting is the barbarous activity of brutish men:

> I'm just waiting for the bow hunters
> So I can run them off [99]

Twenty years after his first hunting experience, he would write in a letter to a friend, "Lately I've seen so many small birds mourning their mates by the side of the road. . . . They look like a flower, a bluegill, a butterfly, beautiful, but squashed and stinking on the road, mate beside them."[100] Frank was no killer of the innocent.

## Dark Journey

These were charmed summers for Frank Stanford, his sister, and their friends. While much is rightly made of his early years at the levee camps, at least two qualifying points should be considered. First, there was nothing especially unusual about whites and Blacks interacting in a rural society sustained by Black labor. Whether your authority on this point was C. Vann Woodward or William Faulkner, you would know that—far more than in the North after the Great Migration—Black and white lives overlapped routinely, whether it was on the levee or in the cotton fields, not to mention the kitchen or the bedroom. You would also know that this interaction did not necessarily translate into interracial empathy or understanding. One of the Delta whites' "genial delusions," David Cohn wrote in 1948, was thinking that "because they live among masses of Negroes, employ Negro cooks, maids, nurses, washerwomen, they intimately understand Negro life." What they missed, Cohn perceptively realized, was the existence of "a vast inner life."[101]

This inner life—and this is the second point—was shaped by the reality of Jim Crow. Sure, young Frankie grew up around Blacks. But Blacks grew up around Frankie too, and they brought to the camps a collective history that the Stanfords did not—and perhaps, given their own history, did not want to—comprehend. Any attempt to understand Frank Stanford and the early world that shaped him, must not ignore why these Black men and their families were sodding and dragging and patching levees, doing work that was brutal, underpaid, dangerous, in the first place. Frank grew up in the Arkansas Delta in the 1950s. He was as perceptive as any kid his age could be; he knew the deal. And he would later, in his poetry, try to let us know.

In *The Battlefield*, Francis talks about how "me and Baby Gauge was intending to go / to school together at last ever since that young colored man come driving / through camp throwing out papers with headlines about the Supreme Court" (8910–11). But *Brown v. Board* might as well have been duck shit in the Peabody lobby as far as daily life in the Delta was concerned. Stanford acknowledges as much in another poem, called "The Mind Reader," where he writes:

> so long Baby Gauge
> we'll never go to school together[102]

Race was everything and everywhere, and the less traditions changed, according to those in power at the Peabody and Snow Lake, the better. The

Black community into which Frankie, Ruthie, and their nephew Frank Coleman were dropped experienced lives of ongoing oppression that, while always maintaining a measure of agency, were defined by decades of disenfranchisement backed by white custom, law, and violence. Their journey to the levees was a dark one.

This is no place for a full exegesis of the decades of injustice that drove Black men and women to work the levees in the 1950s, but a few facts bearing on the comparative opportunities available to whites and Blacks in the midcentury Delta deserve mention. In the 1940s, white teachers in the Delta earned three times what Blacks did, investment in schools was $175 per pupil in white schools but only $11 per pupil in Black schools, and discriminatory funding raised and diverted tax dollars from Blacks to pay for white schools.[103] "Unspoiled by education," Blacks were considered primed for menial labor. They were expected to stay put in rural and often demeaning occupations. In the 1940s, half of Black women in the Delta worked as field hands, mostly picking cotton, while only 15 percent of white women did so. Black men in skilled trades declined precipitously between 1890 and 1940 as whites replaced them at higher wages. Black-owned newspapers and banks nose-dived after World War I, with the offices of many newspapers being bombed and banks being denied credit so Blacks had to borrow "from the private folks." Meanwhile, white-owned newspapers such as Hodding Carter's *Delta Democrat-Times*, founded in 1938, rose from the ashes of the Depression to dominate the region's media coverage while an all-white group of elected bank examiners explicitly determined not to qualify Black-owned banks. Black men seeking justice in a Delta courtroom knew that verdicts were rigged by men who wore black robes during the day and white ones at night.[104] In 1938, as Carter was inking up the presses for his new newspaper, Senator Theodore G. Bilbo assured his constituents that lynching was "an immediate and proper and suitable punishment."[105] The *Delta Democrat-Times* would never contradict him.

The point should be clear: When the Stanfords loaded the Cadillac for the trip back to Memphis in late August, after yet another season at the levees, they did so as passive beneficiaries of this active history. The racism that became especially entrenched in the Delta between the Depression and the Stanfords' Snow Lake days secured a labor force that kept Albert Franklin, the levees, and the cotton economy alive and thriving. To blame a child for not recognizing this reality would be unfair. To marvel at the way that child, when he became a man, returned to it and critiqued it in a way no American poet had is to acknowledge a voice that we still need to hear.

It was typically in late August that the Stanfords, along with Frank Coleman, Charlie B., Emma, and her son O. Z. Durrett, boarded the stretch Cadillac (in some years it was a Lincoln) for the ride back home to Memphis. But one year—likely 1954—they had to stay well into September. During that time Frank Stanford, coming close to the promise offered by *Brown v. Board of Education*, attended the local public school in Snow Lake, which was attended by mostly Black children. As he remembered it, he did something rather unusual there: He taught classes—possibly when he was as young as seven. "I had a job helping to teach," he recalled. "When I was in the first grade, I helped teach grades one through eight in Snow Lake." The young product of private schools and a wealthy Memphis public school, Frank—if only as a testament to the South's educational disparity—was qualified academically to undertake this task. Plus, he added, all his friends were at school, and "I did not want to be alone."[106]

## The Strange Country of Childhood

These summers at Snow Lake planted different seeds for different futures. O. Z. Durrett and his mother eventually moved to Chicago so she could start a day-care center and he could work for the electric company. How did O. Z. recall his days in the levee camp? Did the fact that he named his daughter Ruthie indicate some deeper affiliation with the Stanfords? Perhaps. Perhaps not. It's also possible that Charlie B. Lemon, on his deathbed in 2003, surely proud of his well-educated daughter—a former college administrator (also named Ruth!)—recalled Frank and the Stanfords and their time together at the levees.[107] One also wonders if the real Charlie B. ever read about *The Battlefield*'s Charlie B., a man the real Jimmy Lee called "cool" and "a main man" in an interview almost fifty years after those Snow Lake summers.[108] One can only imagine that Dorothy, for whom the levee camps were reminiscent of her time as a teenager in Parchman, was relieved to head back to Memphis and perhaps overjoyed when her husband retired in 1961, a decision that allowed the family to move to a lakefront home in Mountain Home, Arkansas, leaving behind the levee camps once and for all.

Frank is an easier case to assess. We know for certain that he never left behind Snow Lake. He might have wanted to "get some of my blood / back from the Snow Lake mosquitoes," as he wrote in the poem "Spell," but the time he spent there was golden.[109] When he celebrated his fifth birthday at the camp, Dorothy snapped a photo of the tent where the birthday crowd sat around a table ready to eat cake (see the photo opening this chapter). Frank and Ruth, the only white kids present, are beaming. Toward the end of his life, Frank was planning to film interviews with the characters from the levee days as part of a documentary about Snow Lake and levee building. In an unpublished typescript document, Stanford histrionically registered his objection to leaving camp at the ends of the summers:

> Whenever we broke camp I swallowed rat poison
> Or stuck my hand under the floorboards
> They had to tie me up in the back of a Lincoln
> They gagged me and flew me out by cropduster[110]

In discussion with his editor in the 1970s, he said, "I always identified the city as not what I was about—something opposite. I thought that was artificial and I couldn't wait to get back to the country and build the levees."[111]

As this desire to stay in Snow Lake suggests, the levees were synonymous in Frank's mind with childhood, and childhood, with its innocence and openness to language and experience, became central to his identity as a poet. Again, it seems right to highlight Rilke's advice in *Letters to a Young Poet*: "And even if you found yourself in some prison, whose walls let in none of the world's sounds—wouldn't you still have your childhood, that jewel beyond all price . . . ? Turn your attention to it."[112] Rilke was not alone. Baudelaire said, "Genius is no more than childhood recaptured at will, childhood equipped now with man's physical means to express itself, and with the analytical mind that enabled it to bring order to the sum of experience."[113] William Stafford, a poet who corresponded briefly with Stanford and admired his work, wrote, "When we are kids we make up things, we write, and for me the puzzle is not that some people are still writing, the real question is why did the other people stop?"[114] And as Peter Szondi said of Walter Benjamin: "Almost everything childhood was can be withheld from a person for years, suddenly to be offered him anew as if by chance."[115]

Frank Stanford read these writers—or at least Baudelaire and Stafford—and he embodied their ideas. *The Battlefield* is told from the perspective of a twelve-year-old boy. The poem speaks to the creative wealth and imaginative freedom, and ultimately the liberatory potential, of childhood. Frank always indicated that childhood was critical to his identity as an artist. In a letter to one of his editors, he noted how the poet Donald Justice had read some of his poems and "voiced something to me about my beginning with my voice." Stanford agreed with the assessment but was quick to root the origins of that voice in the experiences of youth. "I wrote," he explained, "constantly, early [in life], to find it."[116] That early voice was the purest, the one that ushered him back into the language of the Mississippi Delta, the vernacular he first encountered as a kid at the levee camps. It's an obvious point but worth noting: Children can be open to experiences, people, and language in ways adults are not. Younger children are especially receptive to the language patterns. Lauding the magic of childhood in a poem called "Children at the Point of Death," Stanford writes:

> they touch birds
> say what they see
> walk fence lines[117]

Which is not a bad summary of what Frankie did in the levee camps run at Snow Lake.

If the levees were synonymous with childhood for Frank, then childhood was intertwined with Albert Franklin Stanford. A lot of Frank's poetry is, in a way, an ongoing ode to a complicated man who Frank always knew was not his biological father and whom he never really knew very well. Frank Sr. died in 1963, when Frank was fifteen. He was, perhaps because of his grandfatherly stance in his son's life, primed to be what Frank later was as well: mythologized. The man appears all over Frank's work. "The book is full of my father's eyelashes," opens "Soybeans" from *Shade* (1975), a poem that ends with the sentence (likely evoking the role of his father in his life) "Anyway the rain / came through like a hitchhiker."[118] And in "A Man Born in the Forest," in the same volume, Frank writes:

> Just like a light skinned woman
> there was a deer
> to come out of the Snow Lake Woods
> and speak to my father[119]

*Arkansas Bench Stone* (1975) is dedicated in part to his father, whom he calls "a legendary figure."[120] Frank even describes the experience of encountering his father for the first time:

> I met my father in a library in Memphis, Tennessee.
> Bees flew out of the sun.
> The strange country of childhood,
> Like a dragonfly on a dog chain.[121]

The strange country of Frank's early childhood was the levee camp of Snow Lake, Arkansas. Like a tethered dragonfly, which is another common motif in Stanford's work, he would spend most of his adult life attached to these memories, sometimes flitting away from them but always returning in his heart. This was a place made possible by his father, a place where, when Frank was a child, the bluesy language of the Delta echoed across the levees that stood like pyramids built by Albert Franklin Stanford.

Frank Stanford, grade four, Sherwood Elementary School yearbook photo, 1958. *Photo courtesy of Carrie Prysock.*

THREE

# "Frankie Was the Star"

## Memphis, 1956–1961

"**[Y]**ou live in the mansions and you live in the shacks," declares Francis in *The Battlefield* (14648). In another part of the poem, he offers the same sentiment: "I don't take / to houses too much less it's a good shack or a mansion nothing in between" (11304–5). This was one way of noting the difference between life in the levee camps and life back in Memphis. When the Stanford family returned home after summers at the levees, they moved from a tented landscape of Black labor to a sheltered enclave of white comfort. As Stanford wrote to a friend in 1971, "After the jobs were over + the levee was done, we'd go back to Memphis to the big house."[1] *The Battlefield*'s Francis does not overlook the disparity of such a transition. Perhaps he even celebrates it, explaining how "the first day we got back from camp / I walked in the Peabody and tipped my hat" (6411–12).

Call it a hat tip of appreciation. There was certainly much to appreciate in a city that was, as Francis puts it in *The Battlefield*, "just full of automatic doors" (10876). Doors indeed opened easily for the Stanfords. From 1952 to 1957, they lived at 1157 Knox Avenue, in the Frayser section of North Memphis. Their home was a three-bedroom, three-thousand-square-foot ranch house located in a solidly middle-class neighborhood. In 1957, when Frank was nine, the family moved from Frayser to a tonier neighborhood known as Audubon Park.[2] Frank Sr.'s grandchildren recall this bigger house at 1118 Oak Ridge Drive with pride. "The house back in Frayser was an older home," one said, but the new one "was a Federal-style house with columns and steps that went way up." Another remembered how "our grandparents' bedroom seemed huge to me in the new house," as did Ruth's room. "It was a very upper-middle-class, affluent home."[3]

Frank had his own bedroom in the attic space, "with two twin beds and I would stay there," Frank Coleman recalled. He said being with Frank "was like having a brother."[4] Ruth, who also noted that the house had six bedrooms and six baths, remembered that Frank's room had a study and bookcases, and on them in a row he kept little white statues of all the US presidents—"He could tell you who every one of them was."[5] Model cars that Frank had glued together decorated the windowsills.[6] Nobody mentioned many books lining the walls of the Memphis home, a point that Dorothy would later angrily dispute. Either way, being back in Memphis was a welcome transition after the sweltering summers on the levee.

## "If It Was It Is Now"

"My poetry has drawn a lot off my life," Frank said in 1973.[7] *The Battlefield*, which Stanford may have started writing in earnest in 1964, is set in the year 1960. Key elements of its drama play out in Memphis, an urban setting still fresh in Stanford's mind as he wrote the poem. Told through the perspective of the protagonist, Francis Gildart, *The Battlefield* provides autobiographical insight into young Frank's life when he was living in the big house in a nice neighborhood in Memphis. Frank Stanford scholar A. P. Walton considers Stanford's biography "virtually inseparable from his poetry."[8] C. D. Wright's preface to the 2000 edition of *The Battlefield* notes the many characters and events that came from Frank Stanford's life. "The poem," in this way, "anchored him to the world," she writes.[9] Stanford himself noted that "there are characters that are closest to my real past" throughout the poem.[10] Like Lord Byron in *Childe Harold's Pilgrimage*, Stanford invested the text with his own experiences.

Stanford's autobiographical focus explores both personal experience and the surrounding events happening simultaneously in Memphis. When the fictional Francis remembers that a song "is the same as Miss Barker played in fourth grade" (2222), it seems significant that Frank's actual "baby book" contains a photograph of a young woman sitting on a bench above which Frankie has written "Miss Barker . . . 4th grade."[11] Likewise, when a man in *The Battlefield* asks Francis "what do you do / besides play catcher play fullback play tennis go fishing collect stamps with little billy phillips" (2842–44), Stanford's baby book not only confirms his participation in all these activities but also reveals that Frank wrote "Billy Phillips" below a photo of a boy with thick glasses and a wry smile yanking a cat off

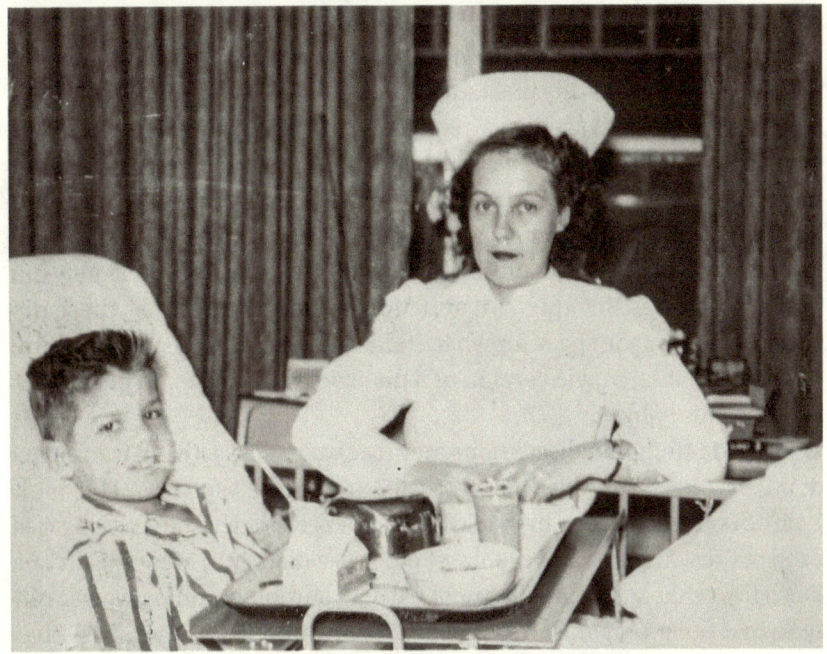

Frank, after an emergency appendectomy in Memphis, ca. 1956.
*Photo by Dorothy Stanford. Photo courtesy of Carrie Prysock.*

the ground by its scruff.[12] Ruth notes, "I remember when his appendix ruptured and he was in the hospital."[13] Not only is there a snapshot of a grinning and bedridden Frank to record the moment,[14] but *The Battlefield*'s Francis confirms it as well, saying:

> what good is my tongue anyhow the doctor oughten took that out when
>     he cut
> the busted appendix out
>     (10512–13)

In these small but significant ways, the poem becomes a repository of autobiography. As an adult, Frank wrote to an editor, "Some times I'm totally lost in the past."[15] Much of that past was accessed as he wrote his big poem.

But Frank's historical consciousness was decidedly public as well. When it comes to Memphis in the late 1950s (*not* the late 1960s), *The Battlefield* presents a sweeping if unconventional history of a unique time and place. It anticipates claims by historians that Memphis was one of the more interesting cities in the country in the way it confronted race in the 1950s. One study reminds us that racial matters in Memphis were more than "the simple battle of white racists against black activists."[16] Memphis, unlike Greenville, was an urban venue marked by a modest measure of racial fluidity due largely to grassroots activism supporting a Black-led civil rights agenda. To some extent, Memphis fostered a "crossover" culture that tempered some of the more reactionary responses to racial issues elsewhere.[17] Discussions over race and discrimination might have simmered in Memphis, as they did throughout the South (and the nation, for that matter), but they rarely boiled over, as they routinely did in places such as Birmingham and Montgomery. Sometimes these discussions even made space for what Stanford later called "a black Socratic stance"—that is, a civic version of a dialogic back-and-forth played out in the public sphere.[18]

In 1950s Memphis, discussions over race were most active in the realms of music, sports, parades and festivals, and the newspapers. The adult Frank Stanford, through his adolescent alter ego, Francis, directly engages each of these themes and events, sketching a history of Memphis in *The Battlefield* that surrounds Francis with an autobiographical verisimilitude that the protagonist negotiates with uncanny skill. Stanford's attentiveness to the past might appear to echo the *Partisan Review*'s call in the 1950s for poets to "speak to history," an imperative that Robert Lowell, John Berryman, and Allen Ginsberg often took to heart.[19] But, as was true for every trend he confronted (including confessional poetry), Stanford sidestepped it or at least shaped it into something more personal, experimental, and idiosyncratic.

Rather than howling at history through politicized poems, he instead collapsed the past into image-driven, dream-infused vignettes packed with racial and autobiographical significance. Not unlike Proust, Stanford ushered the past into the present and forged them into a transcendent and multifaceted reality. Hinting at such a technique, Stanford, according to scholar Murray Shugars, refers in *The Battlefield* to "some youth who had grown old before his time," a kid who "decided to retell" his dreams "in a manner where he made something more than what was there before."[20] This is right on the money, as it's exactly what Stanford does with Francis in *The Battlefield*. In an unpublished fragment of a short story, Frank writes, "The past like an anchor with an infinite length of chain, would descend into the fathoms of the present, and I would wait and wait for it to embed itself in my heart."[21] *The Battlefield*'s historical focus, especially as it concerns race in the South, becomes a lens into an adolescent boy's experience witnessing racial strife and seeking some manner of reckoning.

Stanford's perch on the ledge of the historical present allows *The Battlefield* to offer a philosophy of history that complicates conventional history. As so often happens in the poem, Stanford intervenes and alludes to what is happening in the text or even what he is thinking about what is happening in the text. In one case, he has Francis declare:

> knowledge must include an acquaintance
> with the past but it must do more than that it must be accompanied by an
> imaginative ability to put ourselves in the shoes of long ago and other
> peoples
> (9723–25)

This ambitious form of transhistorical empathy reflects the vision of a philosopher Frank read in high school: the eighteenth-century Italian Jesuit Giambattista Vico. Vico believed, as explained in his book *New Science*, that to understand the past one must understand the meaning people at the time invested in their events and experiences. Francis adds a Proustian twist to Vico, saying:

> I might
> presently I live out my past so presently I can live with the pressure
> like a diver has in his ears . . .
> (8706–8)

It is likely no coincidence that a mysterious and talented figure who appears near the end of the poem, when Francis is on his freedom ride, is a man named Vico. In such ways, Frank left behind a radically unconventional bibliography of intellectual influence.

Of course, the weight of the past does not always sit easily in the present. That ledge can feel especially precarious when the violence of oppression dominates historical consciousness. The Black character Dark, who, pondering the lynching of Francis's friend Sylvester, adds—in an echo of William Faulkner's "the past is never dead, it's not even past"[22]—that "if it was it is now" (9142–43). On the topic of Sylvester's lynching, Francis realizes "it is just the past / which is the present" (9130–31). And yet again, near the end of the poem: "my past is simultaneous with my present" (12295). Frank Stanford insists that history is condensed and *felt* in the life of Francis Gildart. This twelve-year-old protagonist-hero is prepared to cycle the past through the present and, in so doing, experience the burden of historical injustice in the moment of 1960. It is a burden rooted in history, energized by language, and transported to the present through epic poetry.

Stanford's philosophy of history is thus a quest for an archetypical understanding of his world. It is an ambition glimpsed in Francis's remark that "if we can see others as they see themselves we shall / find that primitive beliefs and customs are not based upon ignorance" (9730-31). Accordingly, the adult Stanford believed the poet should seek the widest possible range of voices and images, thinkers and seekers, experiences, ideas, and perspectives. They should integrate these disparate viewpoints—be they from jazz, blues, classical music, Russian literature, Japanese warrior verse, carnival barkers, Black taverns, French surrealists—because they are all living evidence of poetic fruit borne of primordial seeds. Stanford could pursue such combinatory thinking because he was unusually skilled at holding seemingly unrelated expressions in one place, allowing them to cross-pollinate and following the impact of their relationship in other places. In this way, *The Battlefield* offers a kaleidoscopic approach to the past, one that taunts our linear and teleological preoccupations.

With this kind of openness, the poet-philosopher was always on a backward trajectory, trying to discover original meanings. That is, he was seeking the ancient and primitive moment when the first human created the first meaning from the first sound and image and then marveling at the echoes, ideas, and actions that followed. There was a crazy logic to this quixotic process. Like fishermen with lines lodged in the ancient mud of a riverbed, Frank Stanford's poems pull up prehistoric artifacts to examine what their lines gathered during the ascent, what they hauled up from depths mysterious and dark. Moreover, by moving from the primordial sludge through historical layers of thought and experience, through the past and into the present—and then, to top it off, becoming clairvoyant—Francis becomes Stanford's Keatsian hero. By experiencing the mythical process of becoming, ever attentive to what the poet Edward Hirsch calls "the psychic action involved in the making," Frank and Francis together reveal what it was like to experience Memphis in the late 1950s.[23]

## "He Loved His Memphis Home"

Dorothy and Frank Sr. created an idyllic domestic atmosphere for their children in Memphis. They loved their adopted children as much as they did Frank Sr.'s grandkids, and they worked to make childhood as carefree an experience as possible. They did well. "It was a happy house," said Carole Hess, Frank Sr.'s granddaughter. No longer having to work (except over the summers at the levee camps), Dorothy, preoccupied as ever with the idea of an unsullied lineage, spent her time breeding Keeshonds. She kept them in a dogtrot cage to the side of the house. Frank Sr.'s grandkids remember their grandfather sitting on the sofa in the expansive den reading the paper under "sassafras wooden lamps that were kind of twisted." Because of his age and declining health, he could not, Hess said, "roll around on the floor with us."[24] Ruth remembered the same, saying, with a touch of regret, "We didn't do much with him."[25] But Frank Sr. was game to take the kids to his office at the Peabody hotel, where they would run around the lobby, eat lunch at the café, and of course watch the ducks walk to the fountain. When Frank Sr. entered the lobby, his grandson recalled, "it was like 'Here comes the president.'"[26] His kids and grandkids enjoyed the attention conferred on their respective father and grandfather by the Memphis elite.

Frank Sr. handed out shiny coins and crisp bills to the kids. "That was a big thing with him," said his granddaughter. "He always brought us those silver dollars."[27] Ruth recalled that when she and Frank and their friends walked to the local general store to buy candy, the neighborhood kids would produce a handful of loose change while Ruth and Frankie would unfold a five-dollar bill, eliciting amazement from their peers.[28] Holidays, especially Thanksgiving and Christmas, were big family affairs. The Stanfords brought home huge Christmas trees and decorated them with bubble lights and tinsel in the large den. "It was very warm and welcoming," Hess remembered. Dorothy, who did the cooking alongside a Black domestic helper named Laura, routinely sat on the front porch's "bouncy chairs" after supper, rocking the kids on her knees and floating smoke rings into the air.[29] It was no wonder, as Dorothy remembered about her son, Frank, "that he loved his Memphis home."[30] Troubled poets might frequently lay claim to troubled childhoods, but Frank would not have that option.

While the Stanford parents worked hard to make Memphis a place of boundless love and affection, their efforts sometimes floundered. The problem was usually with Ruth. Frank Coleman said that "Frankie was the apple of Dorothy's eye, and Ruth was not," adding that "Ruth did not feel that she was loved."[31] Ruth's daughter has said that her mother "always felt like the black sheep."[32] Ruth's feelings of resentment, over what she said was being neglected and unloved, grew over time. Less than a month before he died, Frank Stanford wrote a note to his mother saying he had heard yet again that she and Ruth "were no longer talking," lamenting how "this just goes on and on."[33] Ruth thought that her mother had adopted her and Frank "to trot us out and show us off to friends."[34] Carole Hess notes how Ruth had a tougher time with nearly everything she attempted.[35]

"Then you had Frankie," Coleman said, "the muscular, athletic one." His "charisma," as Hess called it, was evident at a young age.[36] "Dorothy loved Frank," Stanford's first publisher and longtime friend, Irv Broughton, said. "There was no question she idolized him."[37] Even Frank Sr. may have played favorites with his adopted children. "I think he loved Frankie as much as anybody could have loved Frankie," Coleman said, noting, "I don't feel the same way with Ruth; she didn't compare to Frankie."[38]

Frank, without necessarily intending to, consumed all the attention. But he did not ignore his sister. Ruth remembered her upbringing with considerable bitterness, but she also noted that her brother looked after her.[39] If there was a football game and the older boys were going out afterward, Frank made sure she got home safely before he went back out. Ruth's admiration for her brother began early and never ebbed. When they were in the levee camp, according to Dorothy, "Ruth followed Frankie everywhere he'd go because she adored him."[40] In *The Battlefield*, Francis notes how, at the camp, "my sister lost her new shoes," in response to which Francis declares, "I went barefoot myself so she wouldn't feel bad" (8594). Ruth said of her brother that, when they were growing up, "I idolized him."[41] It is hard to escape the fact that, as Carole Hess put it, everyone did. And that idolization may have come at the expense of Ruth's happiness. "Frankie," Hess added, "was the star."[42]

Sports were critical to his stardom. Frank documented his own athletic commitments in his first ever writing project: the "baby book" his mother gave him to update when he was ten.[43] "At the age of eight," he wrote in a schooled script, "I played for my cub-scout team, 3 base. At 10 I played cather [sic] and 3 base for my church team, all Saints. At 10, 11, I played quater [sic] back and fullback on my football teams. At 11 I play guard at basketball."[44] He started taking karate classes in the fourth grade.[45] Even at this age Frankie was notable for his distinct physical features. He was a good-looking, slightly beefed-up kid with a big smile and stark white teeth. The positions of catcher and fullback both attest to his stocky and strong bearing. These qualities would serve him well when he pursued and excelled in judo in high school and college, all underscored by a physical stamina that would help him in his extensive forays into the Arkansas wilderness as a surveyor.

In *The Battlefield*, Francis, who has been hanging out with Charlie B. and a Black character named Tang (or Tangle Eye) and has started to absorb some of their speech patterns, says, "I was stout fah my age" (8334). Never one to downplay her son's physical accomplishments, Dorothy recalled how "Frankie was the star of the football team." Frank Sr. would fantasize about Frank growing up to play for the University of Arkansas. "He wanted Frankie to be a Razorback," Dorothy said.[46] Whatever sport it was—Frankie did not care much for football, in fact—Stanford took pride in his physicality and prowess at performing it. He would be concerned about his body, always watching his weight, until the end.

Formal schooling never appealed to Frank Stanford, but he attended grade school without much of a fuss. In the late summer 1954, Frank went to Snow Lake Elementary for a brief period because the family had to stay in Snow Lake so Frank Sr. could finish work there. Then, when the family returned to Memphis, he transferred to Our Lady of Sorrows Elementary School, where he stayed through second grade. He did his third-grade year at West Frayser Elementary School. When the family moved to Oak Ridge Drive, he went to Sherwood Elementary and then Sherwood Junior High between 1957 and 1961.[47] He mentions his Sherwood experience in "The Mind Reader"—"the name of my school is Sherwood not the forest"[48]—and in *The Battlefield*, where Francis recalls:

> I entered the Science Fair with my planetarium made of kotex boxes
> I made constellations with a pencil I poked holes in the boxes
> I put the stars on the ceiling of the school
> they named it sherwood...
>   (1177–80)

These shout-outs should not suggest affection. "Schooldays," Francis notes, "was shit" (13237).

Memphis schools were segregated. In May 1954 the US Supreme Court had stated that "in the field of public education the doctrine of 'separate but equal' has no place."[49] As we have seen, *The Battlefield*'s Francis refers to the landmark *Brown v. Board* decision, stating:

> me and Baby Gauge was intending to go
> to school together at least ever since that young colored man come driving through camp throwing out papers with headlines about the Supreme
>   Court
>   (8910–12)

But because this ruling left implementation to local authorities, the Sherwood schools, like all public schools in Memphis at the time (and in Snow Lake too), fought integration well into the 1960s.[50] Still, these transitions from one school to another for Stanford were notable for the range of experiences to which they exposed him—rural, urban, Catholic, nondenominational, wealthy, not so wealthy, and even (in Snow Lake) dirt poor. Add to this diversity the fact of Frank's moving back and forth every summer from a nearly all-Black community to an all-white community, and it seems evident that, even before the fourth grade, he had, despite being raised in a sheltered and privileged southern home, been exposed to an admirable range of cultures and experiences in Tennessee, Arkansas, and Mississippi. He'd seen a lot of the South's souths.

Stanford's lifelong indifference to formal education was something he sometimes had fun with. Early in *The Battlefield*, Francis imagines himself as Caliban throwing a tantrum in the classroom. He says:

> I play a character from The Tempest by William Shakespeare
> I get up on the desks and yell I take off my shoes and break the lights I say
> fuck arithmatic I start turning the people over in their desks . . .
>     (1097–99)

This scene was more wish fulfillment than reality, perhaps reflecting a twenty-year-old Stanford's feelings about classes at the University of Arkansas rather than those of the well-behaved kid he was at Sherwood. Frank's earliest grades are unavailable, but there is every reason to assume he was a solidly good student. He thought well enough of his fourth- and fifth-grade teachers, a Mrs. Barker and a Miss Wallace, to register their names above their snapshots as he updated his baby book in the late 1950s.[51]

It was during the fourth grade—on April 14, 1958—that Frank Stanford first earned the only award he'd ever win (while alive) for his poetry. "Frankie Stanford" earned fourth prize in a poetry contest for a poem called "The Sphinx," not an insignificant achievement given that entrants came from forty-five Memphis schools. When faced with the assignment, he hadn't known what to write about and had told his mother he'd prefer to skip it. But Dorothy, an amateur poet herself, had urged him on, suggesting a poem about a pyramid. The contest was sponsored by the Tennessee Federation of Women's Clubs, and the winners were asked to read their work at the prestigious Nineteenth Century Club.[52] Dorothy recalled how "we had our chauffeur drive us to pick up the teacher and the principal of the school, and Frank, Frankie, and I went to the Executive Club [sic]." She loved the way "Frankie stepped on stage in front of all those people and read that poem so beautifully. It was amazing to me because I thought he was shy." Unfortunately, Dorothy did not keep the poem. "I gave it away," she said. "But it was a beautiful poem."[53]

All Dorothy ever said about Frank as a student was that "he was a genius." She bragged that "when he was in school in Memphis, a friend of mine [on the Board of Education] called me and she said, 'I'm not supposed to tell you this [but] your child has the highest IQ in Memphis.' "[54] In fact, Dorothy was upset by the news. She knew that, as Francis puts it in *The Battlefield*, there was a "fine line / between genius and madness" (13277). Later in his life, Stanford's teachers and friends would marvel at his intellectual talent—namely, his almost photographic memory, the range of his reading habits, and his penchant for quickly processing and condensing mountains of information. Virtually all this learning was done on his own, outside the classroom, the result of a wildly ambitious inner compulsion to consume as many books and accumulate as many cultural references as he could categorize or synthesize. "Schooldays" might have been shit, as Francis claims, but he was, as *The Battlefield* confirms, "able to pass the sixth grade in the city" as if on cruise control (14525).

Handsome, athletic, and—if only according to his mother—the leading genius in Memphis, Frank was popular. "[He] would always have a bunch of guys come over," recalled his nephew Frank Coleman. "There were always kids playing outside."[55] The baby book is loaded with snapshots documenting Frank's active social life. In one, he runs at the camera with a tomahawk cocked behind his head while a friend named Howard (who is holding an alarmingly real-looking toy rifle) pretends to shoot him in an apparent game of cowboys and Indians. Other friends whose pictures are included are Billy Phillips and Gary Fletcher. All the boys are dressed like little James Deans—jeans rolled up and white T-shirts tucked in—as they romp around suburban front yards. Frankie wrote his companions' names beneath their individual pictures. At the very top of the page he added, "Friends."[56]

Frank Coleman remembers enjoying spending time at his grandfather's house because "all the neighborhood boys would come over." Although Coleman was gawky and a bit nervous in temperament, Frankie always warmly included him in their games. Frankie's mood, reliably "happy-go-lucky," was infectious.[57] Ruth confirmed this picture of her brother as the center of an active social life. "Memphis was very neighborly," she said. "Frank loved hanging out with kids in the neighborhood and having sleepovers." She added, "Frankie got along with anybody."[58] Ruth also noted that he "was always the most popular in the neighborhood. He had all the boys running around with him."[59]

When Carole Hess and Frank Coleman—again, Frank's niece and nephew but roughly the same ages as him and Ruth—visited the Stanfords' Oak Ridge Drive home in Memphis, the kids went to the zoo together, the Pink Palace planetarium to look at constellations projected onto the ceiling, and to the Peabody hotel. Two aspects of their regular

Frank, *second from left, front row*. Mrs. Barker's fourth-grade class, Sherwood Elementary, 1959. *Photo courtesy of Carrie Prysock.*

presence in Frank's life are particularly significant. First, the grandchildren knew full well—"It was not even an open secret"—that Frank and Ruth were adopted and not just by their grandfather but by Dorothy as well. "We *always* knew they were adopted," said Frank Coleman. "To this day we do not believe that Frankie did not know." He added, "Where did they [Frank and Ruth] think they came from?"[60] It's a fair question. It's also a loaded one, given how Stanford would later dissimulate on the matter of his adoption and lineage. As we will see, at some point between his senior year in high school and his junior year in college, around 1966 to 1968, Frank Stanford, in a dramatic fit of angst, would announce to his close friends that he had just then learned of his adoption. He grieved over the news; he went dark; he shifted his attention to a new community of friends; and with this realization, he fueled his poetry.

A great deal has been made of this late revelation. It is typically presented as the pivotal moment in his young adult life. Stanford claimed that his discovery of being adopted muddied his identity and darkened his persona, alienating him from a fabled past. It severed biological ties to Greenville, his lineage, his "happy-go-lucky" personality, and even the legendary connection to English nobility. It was easy, and perhaps legitimate, to blame Dorothy for this allegedly all-too-late, passive confession.

She had always told the children that they were "the chosen ones" but never explained to Frank or Ruth that "chosen" actually meant from a home for unwed mothers in Richton, Mississippi.[61] It was as if she was implicitly asking them to accept without question the Delta heritage and Greenville birth so critical to her own identity—and to call her "Mother" rather than "Mama" or "Mom." They were to play along with that fiction because the story conferred so much privilege on them that it would have been foolish to do otherwise.[62]

But too much about Frank's experience in Memphis indicates that he would have suspected that he might have been adopted. His niece and nephew knew full well as kids that Frankie and Ruth came from the Emery Memorial Home, and given the implausibility of Memphis's greatest genius not wondering who his real dad was (he openly knew, after all, that Albert Franklin had adopted him), it is hard not to conclude that, at a young age, Frank Stanford would have sensed that something was up. Stanford physically looked nothing like his mother or father, a fact he alludes to late in *The Battlefield* when Francis says:

> I doubt she was my real mother
> probably someone who had found me and taken me in
>    (10524–25)

As a kid with an easy life and loving family, Frank, as Dorothy had hoped, had no cause to make an issue of it. There was every reason to take the path of least resistance, if only because the comfort of Dorothy's narrative was too seductive to question or turn against her. But still, as Frank later noted in "Will," a poem published in 1975:

> One day in the planetarium
> Word come I was a bastard.[63]

The planetarium was in Memphis, and it was a place Frank often went with Ruth, Frank Coleman, and Carole Hess. People have identified a wide range of moments as the time when Frank Stanford "learned of" his adoption. But Frank's identification of the planetarium as a place where he went when he was around ten years old and where he maybe experienced the first stirrings of recognition that he might have been adopted is likely a valid hint of when he sensed that he was not the biological son of his mother. He just kept it to himself, rendering the most basic foundation of his young life a secret.

The second noteworthy aspect of Stanford's Memphis affiliation with Frank Sr.'s grandkids, another one that he kept to himself, was the sexual experimentation that he and Frank Coleman engaged in in Frankie's attic bedroom. They did so not only with each other but with the neighborhood boys as well. "Frankie and I played around," Coleman said. Frankie initiated it. "I don't know whether it's normal," Coleman said, "but it was like mutual masturbation, and it was always when I'd spend the weekend." On some occasions Frankie invited his friends over to join in, and the boys would take turns fondling one another. "It was my first introduction to something like that," said Coleman. He also noted that, while the activity started off as experimental, it continued for years, even after the family moved to Mountain Home, Arkansas, in 1961. "Frankie had a very deep interest in it," he said. And while Stanford was the instigator, Coleman consented. "I kind of enjoyed being over there on the weekend and knowing that we might play around," he said. "I mean, he was somebody that I enjoyed going to see. I enjoyed Frankie. Yeah, Frankie was very— He's masculine, and I'm not, if you know what I mean. It was something I looked forward to."[64] Such experimentation among young adolescent boys is not uncommon, and while Stanford never actively pursued homosexual partners as an adult, his experience with his nephew could be seen as a harbinger of an open and active sexual life throughout his twenties.

## "The Help"

Concerns about unknown lineage and weekend sexual explorations notwithstanding, daily life in Memphis for the Stanford family was an extension of Dorothy's early adult life back in Greenville. Race helped ensure this continuity, while Frank Sr.'s wealth and status solidified it. Dorothy and Frank Sr. continued to rely on a staff of Black workers to keep domestic affairs in order. Charlie B. Lemon and O. Z. Durrett still worked as chauffeurs for the family. Emma served as the family's maid while Charlie B.'s mother helped with the cooking.[65] Frankie and Ruth were dropped off and picked up at school by Charlie B., who lived in an apartment behind the house.[66] "I made Mama Covoe [who appears on the first page of *The Battlefield*] out of this woman Emma," Frank wrote in the summer of 1972.[67] In *The Battlefield*, Francis takes the commonplace event of being picked up at school by Charlie B. and gives it a twist:

> Charlie B wrote me a note to get out I played a good hooky
> we rode around we shucked and jived
> we went downtown and got a fresh cat we had it fried I swigged a little beer
> (1193–95)

As is often the case, Francis's portrayal of the scene may be less a deviation from Frank's reality than it seems. In an interview Frank later recalled, "I went to Memphis with Charlie B. Lemon. Went to Goldsmith's . . . all these places, and got me some clothes. Seersucker suit and cool-looking shoes. Cuban shoes. Orange like a *Moby-Dick* cover. Whatever the publishing house is, you know, that cover of orange."[68] In this way, *The Battlefield* conflates reportage and poetry.

While Coleman said that the help "were like part of the family," he admitted that there was a perpetual *"Driving Miss Daisy"* feel to the relationship between the Stanfords and their Black employees. Charlie B. and O. Z. "were always there, they were always around." But Coleman agreed that "they sometimes treated me like 'Okay, here we go. We gotta do what we gotta do.' "[69] Ruth was more explicit about the relationship between her mother and the help. "They knew their place," Ruth said. "They came in the back door, and they were assigned to work and wore maid uniforms."[70] Deep down, Coleman knew that "Charlie B. was savvy," or as Frank Stanford would later put it, "He was a bad son-of-a-bitch when he wanted to be," as well as "slick talking, good looking."[71] In *The Battlefield* Charlie B. had "that wounded man look in his eye" (7978), And in "The Mind Reader," Frank writes:

> I know the songs of the jive cat Charlie B. Lemon
> I am a personal friend of his
> my dreams sing in the choir like him
> they pitch curve balls for WDIA like him
> they drive the Cadillac like him[72]

A close friend of Stanford's remembered how "he talked about Charlie B. more than anybody."[73]

Using another movie reference, Coleman said that *"The Help* was going on with us in Memphis."[74] Ruth remembered when, at Christmastime, her parents took the family out to eat and "Charlie B. came over and sprinkled presents in the yard and on the roof like he was Santa Claus." She added that "we both grew up with this, and we did not know how to make a bed, how to cook, how to do laundry."[75] Still, Dorothy and Frank Sr. took their end of the bargain seriously. When O. Z.'s mother decided she and her son would be better off in Chicago, Frank Sr., according to Dorothy, "wrote letters on his behalf to every place he applied, and O. Z. got a wonderful job working for the biggest electrical company in Chicago."[76] In *The Battlefield*, Stanford alludes to this support when he writes how "O.Z. was the oldest so he ran the show . . . daddy was going to send him to college" (6376, 6379).

"The help" was a visible manifestation of the Stanford family's position in Memphis society. Maintaining that position required frequenting that legendary and segregated locus of cotton, status, and power: the Peabody hotel. Dorothy and Albert Franklin used the occasion of the annual big football game between Arkansas and Ole Miss, held in Memphis, to shore up their respective social connections throughout the Mississippi Delta. The local newspaper reported in 1953 that "Mr. and Mrs. A. F. Stanford have invited a large group of friends to be their guests for the Arkansas-Ole Miss football game here tomorrow."[77] As Frank reiterated later in life, his father "was well known in the city."[78] Attendees included members of Dorothy's Greenville circle of friends and family, such as her sister Jacquelyn, her cousin James Lee, and his wife. From Albert Franklin's circle, Charley Lowrance (Mr. Cholly, his first employer and mentor) and his wife came to Memphis from Driver, Arkansas, for the festivities. The elaborate nature of the event was designed in part to highlight the family's significant role in this deeply southern game-going tradition. The report noted, "The guests will gather at the Peabody for cocktails and luncheon. At 1:30 a Memphis Street Railway bus will pick the group up and transport them to Crump stadium."[79] It was not the Kentucky Derby or the St. Botolph's Club, but the social posturing fed the same ambition.

The Stanfords' social connections sometimes intrigued young Frank. Beyond Frank Stanford's parents and teachers, several adults closely acquainted with his family made impressions on him as he grew into early adolescence. Most significant was the presence of novelist Joan Williams. Williams, whose father worked with Frank Sr. on the levees (selling him dynamite), became a close friend of Dorothy's. She spent considerable time, often weeks, at the Stanfords' home in Memphis and, later, in Mountain Home. She tapped her friend Dorothy's expertise about levee camp life, which figured heavily in her 1966 novel *Old Powder Man*. She also used the Stanfords' future lakeside house as a respite and writing retreat. "She started in Memphis asking me to tell her stories of the camp and all," Dorothy recalled.[80] The novel came out in 1966 to rave reviews, propelling Williams's long career as a novelist.

Not incidentally, Williams was once romantically close with William Faulkner, whom she met as a student at Bard in the late 1940s. While Frank did not start reading Faulkner until he was thirteen, he certainly knew about him through his mother's association with Williams, a woman whose career was inevitably boosted by her relationship with the writer down the road in Oxford, Mississippi. Williams's husband, Ezra Bowen, whom she married in 1953, wrote for *Sports Illustrated*.[81] Williams's stature as a novelist, her connection to Faulkner, and Bowen's manly blend of literary and athletic talents made Frank a little bit starry-eyed when the couple visited his parents. Williams recalled how "Frankie had an idealized vision" of her husband.[82] After he began to publish in the 1970s, Frank Stanford tracked down Williams and handed her copies of his chapbooks, noting how, when she was visiting their home when he was a boy, he would be in the next room writing as well. Williams's emphasis on the levee camps resonated with Frank. A few weeks after Frank's death, Williams wrote to Frank's widow to express her condolences and note that she had been meaning "to ask if he might look at something of mine."[83]

Another adult who left his mark on Frank after the family moved to the Oak Ridge Drive address is a critical character referred to in *The Battlefield* as "the astronomer." Possibly based on a professor at Southwestern at Memphis (now Rhodes College) who lived down the street from the Stanfords, the astronomer—whose real name Dorothy could not remember in a 1997 interview—would occasionally come over to the Stanfords' Memphis home and discuss levee construction with Frank Sr. He was also happy to teach Frank how to use his telescope. "He was older than I and younger than my husband," Dorothy said, adding that "he knew the heavens and he knew how to show Frankie."[84] He also evidently knew the machinery that could get people there, as Francis notes in *The Battlefield*:

> all I have to look forward to is the next
> launching of a rocket a Vanguard or a Jupiter C . . .
> (2197–98)

These rockets were built between 1956 and 1959, the very years when Frank was getting to know the astronomer in Memphis. In a typescript document in Stanford's archive, Stanford writes about how, in Memphis, "I took up with an Egyptian mathematician who taught at the local college." In the same document he adds, "I was very fond of telescopes."[85] The astronomer showed Frank the planet Saturn when he was in the fourth grade.[86]

The astronomer appears throughout *The Battlefield*, usually as a humorous foil to Francis's less intellectually inclined exploits. Early in the poem, Francis notes:

> I know the astronomer
> he comes to the house and talks to daddy about physics and floods
> (385–86)

He also mentions how the astronomer "left those books at my father's house" (10084). Charlie B. is less impressed with this man of learning, assuring Francis that the astronomer is nothing more than "an egg head"

(394). The astronomer might be a stuffy mathematician, but he certainly has benefits to offer. Francis says, "I got the idea for my entry in the Science Fair from the astronomer" (1160). But mostly he comes in for some ribbing in *The Battlefield*, especially for his stern commitment to behavioral decorum and more so for his insistence that Francis read the canon of Western literature. He pushes Kant and Hume onto Francis and insists that he also read Werner Jaeger's *Paideia*, an exploration of the ideals of Greek civilization.[87] Francis, amid enjoying the freedom of the Snow Lake levee camps, complains to his Black friends:

> you know that astronomer
> back in Memphis
> he wants me to be well I don't know what he wants me
> to be whatever it is I has to stay inside and read books and talk right and
> wear a tie to supper ain't that a pile of shit you tell me if it ain't
> (1707–10)

In an extended rumination on the astronomer, Francis says:

> for a long time I suspected my family of hiring a headshrinker and
>     having him
> disguise himself as an astronomer
> (10100–10101)

The astronomer offers an urbane contrast to the language and culture Frank absorbed in the Delta at the levee camps. In this respect, he becomes a foil for much of the verbal rebellion at the core of *The Battlefield*. The astronomer offers Francis the lingua franca of professional respectability, a set of rhetorical conventions that elite white people used to mark their status. By experimenting with, and eventually embracing, the language of the levee camps, Francis, as a white kid from a privileged family, threatens to undermine his family's expectation that he "talk right." When he begins to pick up some of Charlie B.'s phrases, it is not to mock Charlie B. but rather to honor, as perhaps only a child can, the intrinsic appeal of his cool style, especially in comparison to that of the stuffy old astronomer. The fact that Francis is adopted, that he is an orphan, further situates him to undertake the subversion of superficially accepting the astronomer's instruction while freely surrendering to the more appealing language of the levee camps.

For all the flack that the astronomer catches from Francis, his character also offers the adult Stanford a way to explain his own cultural curiosity and bookish nature. Stanford would cultivate a lifelong reading habit that would astound teachers and peers. One is reminded of Isaiah Berlin's remark about John Stuart Mill's early education—Latin and Greek and calculus by the age of twelve—being "an appalling success."[88] So it was for Frank, although he never seemed overly put out by the expectations. "Francis what shall we talk about tonight," the astronomer asks, before dropping a litany of cultural references Francis seeks to master, including François Villon, François Rabelais, Dante Alighieri ("it took a year for us to finish Dante Alighieri" [2661]), Robert Johnson, Akutagawa Ryūnosuke, and François Couperin. In a letter that Frank wrote to a fellow poet in 1971, he noted how, when the levee season ended, "we'd go back to Memphis to the big house and my Daddy would teach me elementary phil. + history + geography."[89] The idea of Frank Sr. doing this seems not unlikely, as he was well educated, but it makes even more sense for the astronomer.

"I must devote myself," Francis concedes as he contemplates the astronomer's daunting list (6671–72). Frank Stanford dutifully cultivated a voracious aesthetic curiosity that encompassed medieval French poetry, the country blues, the *Inferno*, Japanese short fiction, and baroque musical composition. Through this learning, the astronomer convinces Francis that he must aim to "be a saga" (2656). At the core of this goal was Stanford's omnivorous intellectual curiosity, his exploration of what Francis calls "the constellation the books" (387), an exploration espoused by the obscure professor down the street, backed by his father, and taken up in nascent form by young Frank Stanford.

If the astronomer showed Frank the literal and literary stars, the biggest star that Frank sought to see was another neighbor who lived less than a half mile away, at 1034 Audubon Drive, and just one degree removed from his mother. A few years into his fame and just about to move into Graceland, Elvis Presley became Frank's first musical obsession. Dorothy, albeit with some consternation, remembered how Frankie and his Snow Lake friends, all Black kids, listened to Elvis obsessively at the levee camps. "I got so tired of it," she complained. Back in Memphis, Frank and Ruth sat in the den with their parents and watched the famous *Ed Sullivan* appearances, which began in 1956.[90]

Frank and Ruth enjoyed unusually easy access to local Elvis concerts because of another one of Dorothy's close friends, the Hollywood actress Louise Fazenda. Fazenda, who starred in dozens of films between 1913 and 1939 (once alongside Bette Davis), later married the producer Hal Wallis, who starred Elvis in some of his movies. "Both Frankie and Ruth listened to Elvis all the time," recalled Dorothy. "I detested the noise." Still, she remembered taking Frank and Ruth to a Memphis charity event where Elvis performed. Fazenda, who frequently visited Dorothy in Memphis, had given her a pile of tickets obtained through her husband. The kids let loose. "During the show," Dorothy said, "I looked down, and Frankie and Ruth were hollering and carrying on like all the teenagers in the place." Dorothy kept the family's phonograph in her personal study at home, and she recalled how she would have to leave her office when "the children would come in to listen to Elvis."[91]

The fact that the King lived close by mattered a lot to Frank. Frank and Ruth (usually joined by their niece and nephew) would often walk down the block in the hopes of sneaking a peek. One of Frank Sr.'s nieces lived across the street from Elvis and, Hess recalled, "We would stand on top of her car so we could look over the fence to try and see Elvis."[92] Ruth remembered how she and Frank climbed the outside of the fence and once caught a glimpse of Elvis soaking in his pool.[93] Not surprisingly, Presley figures periodically in *The Battlefield*. "Elvis lives right up the street," says Francis. And, more fantastically:

> I was asleep and Jimmy and Elvis Presley walked in a little drunk
> Elvis shook me on the shoulder he said can I borrow a comb I ain't
>   famous yet
> (4852–53)

And more specifically, "I know Elvis Presley lives up the street ten houses" (215). Although Frank never got to know Elvis as he did Joan Williams and the astronomer, Elvis left an imprint on Frank that, as for so many young kids in America, was indelible. As an adult, Frank wrote an unpublished poem in which he observed how "Elvis Presley made his knees receive the spirit."[94]

## *The Battlefield*'s Shadow History of Memphis

The fact that Elvis did live up the street about ten houses highlights something critical about *The Battlefield Where the Moon Says I Love You*: The poem is full of verifiable facts about a boy coming of age. Commenting on Stanford's work in general, one critic notes how "so many of Frank Stanford's poems focus on this moment before the awakening from innocence."[95] The core of Frank's prelapsarian life centered on friends and family, sports and school, music and the stars, trips to the Peabody and the Pink Palace. These pursuits are as evident in interviews and archives as in the poem, and in this respect, we can infer that the poem is deeply autobiographical.

But it is not an autobiography. When it comes to exploring the city of Memphis where his experiences transpired—that is, the wider cultural and social circle around Frank's life as a kid—*The Battlefield*'s autobiographical emphasis is more than unconventional: It is revisionist. This is hardly grounds for the poem's dismissal as bad history. To the contrary, understanding the nature of Stanford's revisionism lends rare insight into the adult Stanford's changed perspective on race and the cultural cost of young Frank's privilege as a boy growing up in Memphis, a city with rare opportunities to cross racial lines that, at the time, he rarely crossed. Stanford determined that the remembered experiences of his youth required a context to give those experiences meaning. *The Battlefield* provides that context.[96]

While *The Battlefield* is mostly rural in focus, the scenes set in Memphis offer an important frame around young Frank Stanford's actual life there. They do so in a way that Frank might not have actively recognized when he first started writing as a kid, but the adult Frank Stanford certainly did. They remind us that *The Battlefield* is the chronicle of a life lived roughly eight years earlier, one that blends the personal and political—the public and private—to situate Francis and Memphis on the brink of racial transitions or crossovers that Frank himself, having inherited the Greenville code of racial conduct, would not have seen coming when *he* was a twelve-year-old in Memphis.

When living in Memphis, young Frank Stanford was understandably numb to the habits of privilege. As he was conditioned to do, he experienced race without knowing he was experiencing it. But the older Frank, as he revised *The Battlefield*, was a different person requiring a different past, one that reflected his awakening to a new language, a new manner of understanding and experiencing race, culture, and justice. Frank Stanford thus wrote about Memphis as a grown man aware of the deeply implicit racial assumptions that shaped his upbringing. Hindsight, which unifies all the history we need unified, allowed this. The poem was (among many other things) his way of not only showing himself what had been hidden in plain sight when he lived in Memphis as a boy but also showing how utterly fascinating and transformative that obscured culture was. In this respect, *The Battlefield Where the Moon Says I Love You* offers a kind of shadow biography of Frank Stanford's life in Memphis. Stanford is showing us the history of what he missed and later, as a poet looking back, found.

Frank's attraction to Memphis's biggest star provides the perfect starting point for exploring Stanford's approach to narrating his early life. His fascination with Elvis placed him on the precipice of a burgeoning blues movement unique to Memphis in the late 1950s. Unlike previous peak moments in the blues tradition, such as the one that his mother missed at Parchman, this one captivated a younger generation of white southerners. Elvis was for so many white kids the gateway act to Black music. But Frank Stanford did not know how to cross that line, or even step in that direction. Sam Phillips, founder of the Memphis Recording Service Studio (or Sun Studio as it was later renamed), said of young white kids interested in the blues, "There was something in many of [them] that resisted buying this music. The Southern ones especially felt a resistance that even they probably did not quite understand."[97] So he filtered the Delta blues through white performers such as Carl Perkins, Jerry Lee Lewis, and, of course, Elvis in a way that allowed whites to feel the blues without glorifying the bluesmen. As Robert Gordon, author of the magisterial *It Came from Memphis*, writes, "Black music was still considered trash music by white society."[98] But deep down they knew that the "trash" was treasure.

White singers channeling the blues were safer for whites. "The Negro could not be accepted as an idol; it was a sin," Phillips said. If Dorothy was irritated with her son's attraction to Elvis, one can only imagine her consternation had it been B. B. King to whom Frank danced. And so Frank, as we have seen, got to experience Elvis at the age of ten, little knowing that, down on Beale Street, just down the street from his father's Peabody hotel office, studios were etching into vinyl the Black musicians who made Elvis possible: B. B. King, Rufus Thomas, Albert King, and Bobby Blue Bland.[99] The blues had come a long way from Parchman to Memphis, and Beale Street was, according to Robert Gordon, "the Mississippi Delta's largest plantation."[100] Through autobiographical revisionism, Frank Stanford used music to reveal the melodic history that his own privilege had once denied him. What young Frank missed, Francis, mask off, sees and hears. "I can dream on Beale," Frank writes in a poem called "The Dreams."[101]

Repeatedly, this is what Stanford does with music in *The Battlefield*: He reminds us of how he grew up within earshot of racial thresholds he would later cross. By showing what was happening in the late 1950s, fully visible to others but not yet to him, he presents a history whose calculated inaccuracies say as much as the exacting accuracies. For example, in *The Battlefield* he refers to a scene where he and Charlie B. Lemon drive to downtown Memphis, park the big Cadillac out front of a catfish house, and, as Francis describes it:

> he had me go turn the radio on
> full blast the music drifted in the cafe like smoke it was Bobby Blue Bland
>    (1197–98)

After Francis and the astronomer finish reading Dante, Francis, brilliantly merging the bluesman's Mephistopheles with Alighieri's *Inferno*, alludes to Robert Johnson, saying, "one of my favorites is the one who sold his soul to the devil" (2667). When a racist ticket taker at the drive-in theater declares a personal preference for Hank Williams over Ray Charles and has the gall to suggest that Charles's blindness is a gimmick, Francis erupts from the back seat:

> tell that mother fucker who I am
> and tell that lady Ray Charles is blind as a bat
> and while you're at it tell her she's bat fuck too
>     (7794–96)

Point made.

Elvis might have opened Frank's eyes when he was a boy to the visceral thrill of music moving through the body, but the blues and gospel, under an older Frank's direction, ultimately shook the soul for Francis. He says:

> a man coasted down the road on a bicycle with a mudflap
> he was singing blues before sunrise and tears standing up in my eyes
>     (6358–59)

When Jimmy says, "I don't feel too good I'm down," Francis says, "what you want to hear a little B.B" (5775–76). They continue:

> no he says I feel like a sinner put on some gospel
> who I says
> Dixie Hummingbirds singing I Been Buked and I Been Scorned
> mother lent that one to Sadie I believe
> then I want to hear Mahalia Jackson doing Didn't It Rain
> I see I says you going professional
> go ahead and put on Old Ship of Zion by the Pilgrim Jubilee Singers
>     while you
> are at it I says hey can I put on the Pilgrims' Overture too
> yea I guess so but put it on last
> Jimmy thanks I really like those trombones this time of day . . .
>     (5778–86)

To get at this level of connection between sound and emotion, Francis is able to access Mahalia Jackson, the Pilgrim Jubilee Singers, and Dixie Hummingbirds. But all Frank had back in the day was Elvis.

Still, Elvis was the right place to start, and any doubt that Elvis was the gateway to the blues for Frank Stanford is resolved near the end of the poem, when Francis "walk[s] the block to Elvis's house" and shares thoughts with him on the bluesman Son House, before the two leave together singing "Boom Boom Boom Boom"—"[John Lee] Hooker's tremendous big hit" (14302-4). The fact that Elvis would, in the words of a *Pittsburgh Courier* reporter, "crack Memphis segregation laws" and play on "colored night" (actually Black Community Day) at the Memphis Fairgrounds on June 19, 1956, further portends the crossover that Stanford would soon make as a college student in Fayetteville roughly the same age as the King was when he walked into Sam Phillips's studio, both men discovering a world where language and music merged into something transcendent, something for which they lacked a history, and thus something that renewed life.[102]

The organization most responsible for Presley's crossover into the Black community was the Memphis radio station WDIA, known then as "the Mother Station of the Negroes."[103] WDIA was the first station in the United States to employ a team of all Black disc jockeys.[104] Stanford emphasizes the racialized nature of Memphis's music scene in the specific attention he pays WDIA in *The Battlefield*. In Frank's Memphis, few institutions encouraged more crossover experiences than this historically notable station. "When I first started at WDIA," recalled the great Beale Street bluesman Rufus Thomas, "no black voice had ever been on radio. Everything was white."[105] WDIA changed that. Founded in 1947 and one of only six stations on the Memphis dial, WDIA began as a white-owned station playing bland country records. When listenership stagnated, the station hired black deejays such as Thomas to spin blues and gospel records. By the early 1950s, while still white-owned, WDIA was the top station in the city in terms of listenership. Historian Charles Hughes refers to the station, which also hosted talk shows related to Black life in Memphis, as "a black public sphere" and as "a kind of free space where identities need not be defined" by white Memphis.[106] Instead of stereotyping Black music, white Memphis, if only on the dial, listened to it.

Black programming mattered to Frank. As an adult, in 1973, he would write to a friend that something "drastic" had happened at the longtime Black station WLAC in Nashville: "Alot of white rockshit music. What has happened to my old friends? Surely the gospel still comes through."[107] WDIA makes an important appearance in *The Battlefield*. Francis hears music drifting from a jukebox in a honky-tonk frequented by local rednecks. He says:

> the song that was playing
> was the one that come out by a colored man and a country singer at the same time
> (7209-10)

Although this is speculation, this could be a reference to "Ain't That a Shame," cowritten by Fats Domino and released in April 1955 but covered and made famous by Pat Boone in May 1955. Whatever the case, the crossover nature of Memphis music is evident in what Francis's cousin Jimmy has to say about the song:

> since white people owned the radio station they told them not to play
> the colored version but you could get it from
> WDIA on your dial in Memphis it was a big deal if it ever come on the radio
> turn it up loud in the car and be sure the windows were rolled down
> this pissed the white man off it was their theme song
> and some nigger was singing it but the nigger he wrote it what about that
>     (7211–16)

What about that, indeed. Never one to make a revenge fantasy subtle, Francis recounts how "Jimmy got the chainsaw out of his / truck and commenced doing what he came to do / to saw up the honkey tonk" (7280–82). Again, Francis the kid knows what Frank the kid didn't know, and that knowledge—born of the hindsight that taking over a decade to write this poem provided—allows the reader cultural access to the Black music of Memphis. In such ways Frank Stanford orients his lost past to his found present, merging them in the true music of Memphis.

IN ADDITION TO MUSIC, BASEBALL was intricately entwined with race. As he wrote in his baby book, Frank played baseball in Memphis for his Cub Scout team and the church league, switching between third baseman and catcher.[108] Joan Williams, the writer who often visited the family, remembered his impressive exploits at the plate. She wrote, "One evening I went to a Little League game with the Stanfords and Frankie hit his first home run! Afterward we gathered about him excitedly, and I see that half-smile on the face of a tired, dusty boy, pleased with himself."[109]

Memphis did not have a professional baseball team in the major leagues. But it was home to the Memphis Red Sox, a team affiliated with the Negro Leagues. The Negro Leagues began when Blacks were banned from white professional baseball leagues during Jim Crow. The Red Sox had been a fixture in Memphis since 1923, but in the 1940s, as Blacks returned from the war and began to urbanize the South, the organization's popularity took off. The team played at Martin's Stadium, and its games were well-advertised in white-owned newspapers. The Sox management scored a white publicist who was a strong civil rights advocate from Chicago, and attendance for a typical game soon approached ten thousand fans, many of them white. The Red Sox were in a league with teams such as the Indianapolis Clowns and the Atlanta Black Crackers, monikers that suggested a comedic reputation. But the players were no joke.[110] When Frank Stanford was hitting home runs in the Memphis Little League, the big-league team in his hometown—a team followed by whites and Blacks alike—was all Black.

The depth of talent in the Negro Leagues became evident to talent scouts when teams from the Negro Leagues easily defeated major-league franchises in games played during off-season barnstorming events. In April 1947, Jackie Robinson broke the color barrier, becoming the first Black person to play major-league baseball in the modern era. In July, Larry Doby followed Robinson's example, moving from the Negro Leagues to the Cleveland Indians. Several more Black athletes went to the show that year, including the Memphis Red Sox pitcher Dan Bankhead, who joined the Brooklyn Dodgers as the major league's first black pitcher.[111] Over the next decade, major league scouts raided the Negro Leagues for their finest talent. This profit-driven racial poaching further benefited the majors by bringing more Black spectators to their stadiums. The Dodgers smashed attendance records when Robinson joined the team, leading the *Pittsburgh Courier* to quip, "Jackie's nimble, Jackie's quick, Jackie makes the turnstiles click."[112] While these were milestones of innovation marking progress in racial integration, the migration to the majors effectively gutted the Negro Leagues. Throughout the 1950s, attendance at Red Sox games declined. By 1959, when Frankie was eleven and playing baseball on two teams, the Red Sox—the only show in town—folded.

Stanford makes the intersection of race and baseball a common and often entertaining motif in *The Battlefield*. Although he never refers to the Red Sox by name, it is quite plausibly the team Francis goes to see when he mentions that "Dark is going to come by and pick me up and take me to the / Sunday Baseball Game" (7032–33). As for his own engagement in the sport, Francis joins his cousin Jimmy in a kind of reverse integration, the two off them becoming the only white players on an all-Black baseball team. They call themselves the King Snakes and are not to be confused with the "Crawling Black Snakes they / is convicts and is bad" (7048–49). Francis, as did Frank, plays catcher. His mitt is "made out of old saddle leather," and after catching for nine innings, Francis notes how "my hand is all swole up and red" because the "pitcher can really burn them in" (7038–40).

For all the talent the team possesses, there is one drawback that will send the King Snakes the way of the Memphis Red Sox: They play baseball without a baseball. As Francis explains, "now I say ball but there ain't no ball ... / but we say we got a baseball and it don't really matter" (7043–44). Until it does matter. When a representative from a New Orleans business called Dr. Tichenor's Antiseptic arrives to sponsor the team and pay for their uniforms, which will carry the slogan "The Best Antiseptic in Town," there is considerable excitement among the King Snakes about possibly getting "purple uniforms with black stripes" (7051, 7064). But "when the man saw one of our games and found out we / didn't use no ball he said shit these crazy niggers now I seen it all" (7052–53). He gets in his car and drives off. That's the last we hear about the King Snakes. Much like the Red Sox, they succumb to circumstances beyond their control. Not incidentally, one common form of pregame entertainment in the Negro Leagues was called "shadow ball," an activity where players played with an imaginary ball.[113]

Stanford's treatment in *The Battlefield* of a Black team that plays without the sport's defining white object is significant for reasons beyond the parallel of the team's demise and that of the Memphis Red Sox. The founder of Dr. Tichenor's Antiseptic was a man named George H. Tichenor, a Tennessee doctor and former Confederate officer who concocted alcohol-based antiseptics to clean the wounds of Confederate soldiers and *only* Confederate soldiers. His commitment to the Confederacy was so unyielding that he refused to allow his elixirs to be used on Union men. Well into the twentieth century, his commercial products came in bottles emblazoned with a Confederate flag.[114]

In the way that James Joyce does in *Ulysses*, Stanford makes sure that references such as the one to Tichenor are not random. There are few throwaway details in the poem. Professors could be kept very busy. Obscure references reliably harbor messages that deepen the text's immediate concern, which in this case was a Black baseball team being approached for sponsorship by a white salesman hawking a product that would supposedly purify their bodies (many of Tichenor's products also promised to whiten teeth). Of course, if the company man from New Orleans did not dismiss the boys as "crazy niggers" (7053), the team would have worn jerseys that read "The Best Antiseptic in Town," a cheap insult, literally behind their backs, stitched onto their jerseys. In his study of Memphis baseball, historian Montgomery Kurt McBee observes how "the Memphis Red Sox organization ... provided the African American community with an indirect method of protest against segregation when organized direct protests were forbidden." When more confrontational tactics eventually became acceptable—sit-ins, marches, and boycotts—the team's "central place of importance in Memphis' African American community diminished."[115] Sometimes, as Stanford knew, a baseball game is more than a baseball game.

The team's decline, in short, coincided with the rise of genuine civil rights initiatives in Memphis, and it fostered this transition as well. In yet another telling parallel to his own past, Frank Stanford explicitly links Francis's awakening to the realities of racial injustice to his awakening to the realities of playing baseball without a baseball. When Francis is struggling to make sense of the lynching of his friend Sylvester, his friend Dark tells him:

> they hung him and that's it
> all you can say is it happened and that's it . . .
>     (9239–40)

As they approach the park for the Sunday Baseball Game, Dark insists that Francis see the cold hard truth of racism through an analogy to the hapless, ball-less, uniformless King Snakes. He says:

> I don't even think about tomorrow I don't even think about what's
> up this road I ought to know it's a baseball game you say but I ain't even
> knowing that no suh cause that be like saying we play with a baseball and we
> don't it gone take you a long time to learn that about us but you will you'll
> get up one morning and you'll say I know that . . .
>     (9153–57)

A few scenes later, Francis knows that. With the zeal of a convert, he is off on a freedom ride, clapping and yelling from the back of the bus, "yas-suh Brother" (9379), off to fight the good fight. On the bus he has brought his catcher's mitt.

STANFORD FURTHER CONTINUED TO DEVELOP his shadow history of Memphis through his treatment of the city's most conspicuous annual events: the Cotton Carnival, the Mid-South Fair, and the Cotton Makers' Jubilee. In his poem "The Hearse on the Other Side of the Canvas," from *Shade* (1975), he writes, "The world is a circus I put in my ear."[116] Carnival-like events thrilled Frank, figuring significantly in his life and, accordingly, in *The Battlefield*. "[T]he midsouth fair is a gyp the only thing good is the world's smallest man / who happened to be a personal friend of mine," Francis says early in the poem. He then advises, "don't go on thursday because every hillbilly in Arkansas will be there" (460–62). This was as close to autobiography as Stanford could get without calling the poem one. C. D. Wright remembered that Frank visited the Cotton Carnival and the Mid-South Fair when living in Memphis as a kid. "These were real annual events," she wrote, adding how "the world's smallest man was there every year too."[117] The fact that Frank and C. D. only knew each other for just under three years and that Frank shared these memories with her at the end of his life highlights the ongoing prominence of these carnivals in his mind.

Stanford takes matters to an entertaining extreme in the poem. Francis befriends the world's smallest man, introducing a classic southern grotesque early in the narrative, and the little man dubs Francis "my little outlaw" (490). But the world's smallest man—Count Hugo Pantagruel[118]—ends up losing his temper and murdering Crawling Vine, the carnival's hermaphrodite, before rendering him/her into hamburger meat and serving him/her to members of a local religious revival. Pantagruel goes on the lam and ends up founding a rogue carnival troupe on a ship cruising the Mississippi River. It names itself "The Floating Troupe of the Unnaturals" (922). Pantagruel writes to Francis:

> we have a fat lady that makes good ballast we have a wondering poet
> who draws fierce looks from the husbands . . .
>  (914–15)

Things proceed well until they encounter "the townsfolk," who "stood guard on the banks they never let us put in" (923). Eventually the misfits come under fire for their deviant flamboyance. Pantagruel elaborates in his letter to Francis:

> a local group accused us of bootlegging
> a whole school of little boats rowed out with torches to meet us they
>  boarded
> without permission sacking what they could they said we were running
>  whiskey
> and whores of course it was found and of course upon seeing the
>  chinamen they cut open
> the sacks of opium that the jugglers smoked . . .
>  (935–39)

He signs off with "X Count Hugo Pantagruel the world's smallest man and friend / of the Devil," to which Francis adds, "such were the last words of the freak" (959–60). Francis lets us know early in the poem that "I take to people who are all fucked up" (466–67). Pantagruel is his first case in point, a twenty-two-inch-tall man who walks on a high wire with crutches, a man who comes from the carnival.

The Cotton Carnival originated in 1931 as the marketing brainchild of the cotton industry. It aimed to be an annual Mardi Gras–style pageant designed to ensure that cotton stayed king in an increasingly industrializing South. In time it became nothing short of what one history of the region deemed "a public spectacle" and "the South's principle form of collective public expression."[119] The *Kingsport News* put it this way: "It's a fixture in the lives of everyone in the area—from the families who actually pick the cotton in the hot fields to those who operate the world's largest spot cotton market in Memphis."[120] Frank Sr.'s grandkids remember the Cotton Carnival as the highlight of spring, an event they eagerly attended to see who would be that year's cotton king and queen.[121]

The families who picked the cotton took issue with the carnival's claim to be "a fixture in the lives of everyone." Not them. The Cotton Carnival was in actuality a paean to the Old South. It was as if Confederate monuments came alive and marched in the streets to celebrate the Lost Cause. The Blacks who participated were routinely demeaned by the stereotypes they had to embody. Black men were harnessed to pull floats as if they were draught horses. "All the negroes were horses," one Black teenager complained.[122] Black women, dressed as stereotypical plantation mammies, reenacted washing days on the happy farm.[123] And as far as observing these offensive scenes went, Blacks could not have attended had they wanted to. Memphis authorities refused them admission. When the Memphis bluesman Rufus Thomas performed on Beale Street during one carnival season, he bemoaned that "my people could not come see me."[124] All in all, the Cotton Carnival was a civic ritual through which white Memphis continued to stoke the embers of Dixie.[125]

In response to their denigration by the Cotton Carnival, Black Memphians—noting, "I, too, make cotton; behold how lovely I am"[126]—started their own festival. It was called the Cotton Makers' Jubilee. This countercarnival began in 1935. The first festival drew twenty-five thousand spectators representing Blacks from a range of socioeconomic backgrounds. Nearly all reports commented on the music. In 1937, the *High Point Enterprise*, a North Carolina–based newspaper, reported the "scorching notes of a red hot 'blues' band echoed over Beale Street." It also pointed out how "doctors, lawyers, the insurance men, and the dentists, as well as the loose-jointed men of the cotton fields and the muscle bound laborers of the levee camps became again a care-free people while they joyously opened another cotton makers jubilee."[127] The newspaper succumbed to familiar Black stereotypes in its coverage (the oh-so-carefree Black worker), but the Cotton Makers' Jubilee challenged such caricatures by highlighting the scholarly and professional accomplishments of Blacks beyond the plantation. The event was, according to one critic, "a reply to the one-sided version of history that black people learned throughout their childhood."[128] Indeed, the Cotton Makers' Jubilee was a comprehensive celebration of Black life, one that eventually became so packed with events that it lasted a full week. The annual celebration reached its apogee in the late 1950s, when Frank Stanford was coming of age in Memphis, attending the Cotton Carnival and the Mid-South Fair, staying safely in the lane of his birth.

But in *The Battlefield*, he swerves. Yet again he allows Francis to cross over into the history that eluded Frankie when he lived in Memphis. When a Black kid named Five Spoke walks to Memphis pushing a lawn mower ("he decided that Lula Mississippi wasn't quite / his speed" [5857–58]), he shows up, and "he said to himself now this is what I call / a City because you see it was the first night of the Cotton Carnival" (5866–67). But Five Spoke quickly learns he can't go to the Cotton Carnival because of his race. Although Stanford does not mention the Cotton Makers' Jubilee by name, it is almost certainly the event he has in mind when he writes:

> the first thing he [Five Spoke] saw was the all black drill and precision
> team
> from Melrose High and I can tell you he wore out some soles high stepping
> along with them on the side of the street . . .
> (5868–70)

Melrose High was and still is nearly 100 percent Black and especially well known for its marching band and musical performances.

When Five Spoke finishes the march, "he went up to the top of some / building and looked out the window and seen the white Carnival" (5870–71). Therein he discovers a spectacle of another sort. He sees "the Queen and King float in on a barge" and "all the fireworks and the double ferris wheels that dip you out over the Mississippi" (5872–73). The building he is watching the scene from is almost surely the Peabody hotel. The night janitor finds Five Spoke and tells him to get out, as his kind are not welcome without a white person's accompaniment. At this point Francis steps in:

> I told him to come on look out the window with me
> we shot the shit and decided to go to the white Carnival so I had to be
> his escort
> (5876–77)

They go to "one of these girly shows," but when Francis goes to the bathroom, Five Spoke is booted out ("the barker run him off"), and "that night he slept on a bale of cotton that was on a broken down float that / everyone had forgotten about on account of all the good time and all" (5883–84). Five Spoke wakes up and goes to mow the grass at the local police station.

A FINAL AREA WHERE STANFORD'S *The Battlefield* uncovers the Black side of an otherwise white Memphis in 1960 involves the local press. In the late 1950s and early 1960s one of the more explosive journalistic battles in the country raged between Black Memphians and the *Commercial Appeal*, a white-owned and white-run paper with a circulation in the hundreds of thousands. At stake was the matter of using courtesy titles when writing about Black women. Black Memphians opposed to the paper's refusal to address Black women as "Miss" or "Mrs." voiced their concerns through the Citizens Improvement Committee. Arguing that "a vested interest in bigotry" would harm profits, the committee called on the paper to end its "odious custom" of "using given names when referring to Negroes, and in refusing courtesy titles." The issue mobilized the Black community to initiate a boycott against the paper that drew the attention of Martin Luther King. Eventually the paper conceded.[129]

Stanford declares his support for Black resistance to prejudicial white journalism in yet another seemingly random but deeply Joycean name drop. Referring to the lawn-mowing Five Spoke, who is about to solve a crime, he notes, "he knows it like mule carts like tunes in a water jug like the name Daisy Bates" (6027). Daisy Bates was a pioneering Black journalist from Arkansas who founded and edited the *Arkansas Weekly*, the only Black-owned paper dedicated to covering civil rights in the state. The reference, for Francis, is yet again apt and relevant. Repeatedly in *The Battlefield* he rails against the racist press. Infuriated by the way cops "drive that patrol car down / a back road once a week and tell some nigger on a tractor boy I think / you busted a row" (2803–5). Francis recalls how, when it comes to an innocent Black man minding his own business,

> they get some lay low fixed up
> between them and then ambush him while he's playing the mouth harp
> in the outhouse then they bring him into town over a mule and say
> how they shot it out with him bullet for bullet them that never fired
> but one slug into his head while he was wiping his ass ...
> (2807–11)

And then:

> I tell you
> the man that runs the newspaper he's in with all them on it so he
> lies in a big story so everybody will start getting his paper . . .
>     (2811-13)

Considering the danger he faces when boarding the freedom bus, Francis thinks:

> I'll be lucky to be alive they
> done blowed up eleven of these buses in the last year and nobody will
>     never
> even hear about it cause the mens that owns the papers won't put it in
> and pieces of my body blowed all over that cottonfield's face . . .
>     (9369-72)

The Citizens Improvement Committee would have understood, as would have Daisy Bates, citizens who worried in such terms.

As an addendum to this discussion of Stanford's shadow history, nowhere are race, the history of Memphis, Frank Stanford, and the character Francis Gildart as rooted in actual history more than in the delightfully weird figure of Sputnik Monroe. Monroe, a white man, arrived in Memphis in 1957 and quickly made an impression as a showman wrestler with a fiery attitude that evoked loving jeers from mixed-race audiences. Billing himself as "220 pounds of twisted steel and sex appeal," Monroe recalled how, in Memphis, "rich white kids dug me because I was a rebel."[130] But Black audiences were equally enamored, flocking to his performances, where they were jammed into nosebleed seats. In an unpublished story, Frank Stanford has a Black woman say, "Sputnik Monroe hit that cracker on the head the other day, came up side him with a folding chair. Woo, there was some blood on the screen."[131] And in *The Battlefield* Francis says to a friend: "would you believe Sputnik Monroe got whupped by a gorilla" (4197). Monroe, the white man taking on the dumb crackers, eventually refused to perform until Black audiences were moved into the front section of Ellis Auditorium. Monroe took his act to the next level of theatricality when he worked dwarf wrestlers into his shtick. The most noteworthy of his dwarfs—this one billed as "the World's Most Perfectly Formed Midget Wrestler"—was not a "midget wrestler" at all but Jerry Phillips, the twelve-year-old son of Sun Records' founder, Sam Phillips.

The act was a hit but ended abruptly in 1962 when an angry fan "tried to stab Sputnik Monroe's most inspired area." This attempted unscripted castration was too much for Jerry's parents. Monroe wisely retired the act. But he fought for civil rights to the end.[132]

THE SHADOW HISTORY THAT Frank Stanford wrote to capture the hidden Memphis of his youth—the Memphis of the mid- and late 1950s—highlights the insularity that white privilege and segregation imposed on his early adolescence. But Stanford was doing more than documenting the hidden-in-plain-sight history of Black Memphis. He was also addressing a central question about southern culture and race. The Agrarian advocacy for a South that was immune to the homogenizing forces of northern industry and commerce long insisted on southern exceptionalism through an embrace of Jeffersonian values that supposedly separated the South from the rest of the country. These values included a commitment to leisure, tradition, religion, agrarianism, family, subsistence agriculture, and hierarchical order. The Agrarians' fatal oversight in their doomed effort to restore a gentler Old South was not realizing that the most defining qualities of the American South emerged from slavery and its legacy. "They deliberately avoided the subject," writes Paul Conkin in his overview of the movement.[133] Worse, some of them openly denied the influence of Black culture overall, even spirituals, on the South.[134] But by ignoring or denigrating Blacks in their attempt to define the South as exceptional from the rest of the country, the Agrarians were ignoring and denigrating the very source of the cultural uniqueness so critical to their identity as southerners.

This irony was not lost on Frank Stanford, and *The Battlefield* proves it. His treatment of Memphis speaks powerfully to the Agrarians' omission. It's almost a complete answer to it. As a young adult and quickly maturing poet, Stanford was explicit about his disdain for the Agrarian vision. Referring to an earlier iteration of the Agrarians and their defining publication *I'll Take My Stand*, he wrote to fellow poet and friend Alan Dugan, "I have no stand when I write."[135] One way of showing this disdain was, in a sense, to undermine the mundane southerness of his very Agrarian-value-laden upbringing with the experiences and expressions of Blacks who were all around him but, at the time when he was growing up, unseen by the white establishment—or seen as only "the help."

For this shift in perspective, he could thank his experience crisscrossing from levee life to Memphis life, from the mansions to the shacks and the shacks back to the mansions. As Stanford's friend and fellow poet Sam Gwynn said, "You know, so Frank had a childhood; he had a privileged upper-middle-class, mostly white childhood... except those summers. And that's kind of what he mythologized and kept going back to as a resource."[136] The mansions were fine and all—I mean, who was Stanford to complain? But it was the shacks that would ultimately shape his adult identity, drive his poetic vision, and help him create a childhood and dreamscape that would give deeper meaning to his life and work.

Frank in junior high, Mountain Home, Arkansas. *Photo courtesy of Irv Broughton.*

FOUR

# "Motley Boy on the Loose"

## 1961–1964

"I HAVE BEEN VERY LUCKY IN life and poetry," Stanford wrote to his friend and editor Michael Cuddihy in 1974. He expressed this when he was nearing the height of his publishing success. He then added, "As John Lee Hooker would put it, Born in Mississippi, Raised up in Tennessee—I would add, Come Into My Own in Arkansas." This was an apt and accurate self-assessment. Stanford's voice as an artist, while always connected to his Greenville and Memphis roots, matured in the hills of Arkansas. "The move from the Delta to the Ozarks—by way of Memphis," he concluded, "was pressurized carbon."[1] A metamorphosis, as he saw it, into brilliance.

In the summer of 1961, the Stanford family moved to Mountain Home, Arkansas, a relatively small town located in the southern Ozarks. Frank was twelve. He had visited the region before, noting in his baby book how he and his family "went to the Ozarks, visited the caves" when he was ten.[2] He could not have known that it was on those trips from Memphis, driving down Highway 62, that his parents became enamored with a place called Lake Norfork, a secluded spot on the outskirts of Mountain Home. "Frank [Albert Franklin] had been talking about living outside of the city," Dorothy recalled.[3] He wanted to return to his home state. As they passed lakefront properties, they entertained the idea of leaving Memphis once Frank Sr., nearing the end of his career and in worsening health, retired as a levee engineer.

Dorothy plotted and organized the move. The Memphis papers routinely ran advertisements for lakeside retreats in the Ozarks. When a Lake Norfork ranch house came up for sale in 1960—"six bed, five bath, 40 by 50 living room on the lake"—Dorothy urged her husband to buy it. Frank Sr. loved the region but wasn't sure about the house. He had long wanted to build a hunting retreat near his old Snow Lake haunts.[4] In the mid-1950s he had gone so far as to purchase a nearby abandoned twenty-one-room lodge on a large piece of property but had not been able to develop it, because as Dorothy put it, modern nails were too weak for the ancient wood. But he was also growing too infirm to hunt. Joan Williams recalls that he walked with a slow shuffle, "listing slightly backwards."[5] Still, he was skeptical of retiring to a remote lake house, assuring his wife that, despite the charm of the place, the house was probably damp and full of splinters.[6]

When they went to visit the home, situated on a small but private peninsula called Mallard Point, he changed his mind.[7] Dorothy remembered their mutual admiration for what still stands as an elegant ranch house near the end of Mallard Point Road. It's a place that one visitor described as "more of a multifamily vacation home."[8] "We loved it," Dorothy said.[9] An ad in a local paper noted that any house in that location was highly coveted, referring to the "showcases on Mallard Point . . . on the shore of lovely blue Lake Norfork."[10] This would be the setting—lakeside, relatively isolated, relaxed—where Frank would settle in and write many of his earliest poems.

As was typical for Dorothy, the move happened without much of a warning to the kids or to anyone else for that matter. "Frankie did not know we had purchased a new home," she said. She sent him and Ruth away to Greenville to see Dorothy's older sister Louise and the kids' cousin Jimmy Lee when she and Frank Sr. went to close on it. "I wanted it to be a surprise," she explained, insisting to Louise that she not let the kids know that their parents were in Mountain Home, sealing a new fate for the family. When Frank finally learned that they were leaving Memphis, he was more than surprised. "He was sick," Dorothy recalled. "He was a home-loving person," she said, and at home he was popular, a standout on several sports teams, settled into a municipal school system, and happy to be a wealthy kid in a fine neighborhood with a big house.[11] Even Frank Sr.'s daughter had no foreknowledge about the family's relocation. "I came home and asked my mother if she knew that [the Stanfords] were moving," Frank Sr.'s granddaughter recalled, "and my mother was quite floored by the news."[12]

No one was surprised, however, with how the new lake home spoke to the Stanfords' wealth and privilege. Extravagance seemed to be a constant prerequisite for the Stanfordian image. "It was a huge home," Frank Coleman remembered.[13] It was a home that, according to one frequent visitor, ensured that people knew the Stanfords "were well off and known for it."[14] When the family arrived, their prominence was conspicuous to the understated middle-class community. A Mountain Home Junior High classmate of Frank's recalled how "they drove around in a Lincoln that was like eighty feet long, and here was this kid in really nice clothes, an upper-class rich kid among a bunch of hillbillies."[15] Another classmate agreed: "When they first moved here, people did not know a lot about them, but they sure saw this big black stretch limousine."[16]

Frank Stanford's time in Mountain Home was brief. He would be off to boarding school three years after moving there. But it proved to be a pivotal phase in his life and a significant one for a poet who would never fully abandon the emotional resonance of childhood. Flannery O'Connor's opinion that "anybody who has survived childhood has enough information about life to last him the rest of his days" definitely rang true for Frank.[17] Mountain Home fostered a childhood experience that was at once free ranging and contained by his parents' love for their children. Frank was let loose on Lake Norfork much in the way he was let loose in Snow Lake, and the overall experience coronated his childhood with the laurels of innocence and discovery. "There is," writes the psychoanalyst Adam Phillips, "no rule that people have to grow up."[18] Frank's time in Mountain Home inclined him to such an opinion.

It's easy to see why growing up was never Frank's driving ambition. For much of his young adult life he resisted the snares of adulthood. His reverence for youth and lament for its possible loss is a central theme in his poetry. In *The Battlefield*, Francis dreams that "somewhere the shutter beats during the thunderstorm and that same / fine looking lad is weeping like a silent boat that must be bearing / away his childhood" (12129–31). Mountain Home was an Eden before the fall, a small town where Frank's mind and body were unusually unburdened, a sweet spot on a lake full of fish where an adolescent kid could live as a child in a world he re-created every day.

The southern Ozarks also fostered Frank's lifelong interaction with nature. The Arkansas landscape was a mysterious realm where, as Francis puts it in *The Battlefield*, "you might turn up spines of swindled Indians or plantation letters" (14404) or discover "the haunted ship the tornado set down in the woods a hundred years ago" (47). In a way, his time there presented Frank with an idealized sense of freedom, a quality that's evident throughout *The Battlefield*. His liberation from the tedium of conventional life, something the natural world offered him, became a necessary foundation for his poetry. And poetry for Frank became a purified form of expression that thrived on images, sounds, smells, feelings, and sexual urges, the innocent essence of things that is perhaps most accessible when one is young, brilliant, and, as Frank would find himself becoming, lost in one's own vibrant literary reality.

## "There Weren't Any Black People"

Race still mattered, although in a different way. As we've seen, when the Stanfords moved from Greenville to Memphis in 1953, their social status remained linked to race. The ethic of noblesse oblige and proximity to Black citizens only intensified when the family reached Memphis, where the racialized Peabody hotel was their locus of professional and social life. Summers at the levee camps in Snow Lake, Arkansas, and the fact that "the help" was as just as present in Memphis as it had been in Greenville further normalized for the Stanfords the power imbalance that defined life in the American South. Ruth remembered how "Mother raised us as coming from a southern aristocratic family."[19] This sense of identity anchored the Stanford mindset, rooting it in a hierarchy that would never budge in Dorothy's mind but would later undergo a major transformation in her son's.

This habit of racial differentiation ended in Mountain Home. It ended not because the Stanfords' racial attitudes shifted or because Mountain Home was free of racism. Instead, it was because Blacks did not live in Mountain Home. Period. "The racial politics would have been *none*," said Bill Willett, who became Frank's best friend a few months after the Stanfords moved to town. There was no racial strife "because there weren't any Black people—Germans and Czechoslovakians, yes, but no Black people."[20] Dick House, who lived in Mountain Home and hung out with Bill and Frank, agreed, saying, "We didn't get to see much prejudice, because there weren't any Blacks here."[21] To be sure, white residents had designed it this way. Dorothy said that as you drove into Mountain Home, there was "a great big sign, as big as this little house, that said, 'Come Live With Us: No Skeeters, No Niggers.'" She noted that any Black person bold enough to step foot in Mountain Home "for any reason" could expect trouble.[22] Ruth recalled that "in Mountain Home there were no Blacks within five counties; they wouldn't even stop going through town."[23]

There were exceptions, albeit short-lived ones, primarily because the Stanford family decided to retain their help. The first to give Mountain Home a try was a domestic worker named Laura. As Dorothy recalled, Laura "persuaded her husband [back in Memphis] to let her come stay with me a while" in Mountain Home. "Some Yankee neighbors," Dorothy said, treated Laura just fine.[24] But it was not long before she was headed back to Memphis, having had enough of the local residents. Bill Willett confirms Laura's temporary sojourn, noting with some surprise that the family "actually brought a Black maid with them" in the first place and confirming that her tenure with the family in Mountain Home was necessarily brief.[25]

The other exception was Charlie B. Lemon. According to House, who played football with Frank and Bill at Mountain Home High, Charlie B. would come into town at night to avoid detection and then drive the Stanford family to the team's football games. Referring to the coaches, House said, "They used to let him drive in and park behind the goalpost," away from the regular parking lot, "because they did not want to let people know that it was a Black man driving the car."[26] Frank later remembered how, for Charlie B. to do this, the football coaches had to cut the hog wire fence around the field to let the car through. He added how "a lot of guys would run into the car, you know, trying to intercept a pass." But these visits were anomalies. Charlie B., a man whom Frank later praised as a guy who took shit from nobody, soon stopped coming as well. "I guess in the South," Frank said about the racism Charlie B. endured, "most people are hung up about it."[27]

In March 1963, racial issues intensified when an Illinois-based pharmaceutical company, Baxter Laboratories, spent $2.5 million to build a plant in Mountain Home. The company planned to hire 150 employees, many of them highly skilled Black workers from Chicago.[28] "The locals ganged up and began to threaten the Blacks," Dorothy recalled. White residents intimidated dozens of Black workers, forcing them to seek jobs elsewhere. Dorothy remembered how "one Black man was hired for a big job in the laboratory," but he and his family "only stayed long enough to move into their home and out of their home—it wasn't the place for them." In one case, Frank witnessed a group of angry whites harass a local Black man by yelling at him, "If you don't get out of here, we're going to kill you."[29]

While Memphis is a mainstay in *The Battlefield*, Mountain Home never appears. This makes sense. The racial themes pertinent to *The Battlefield*, themes that echo Frank's actual experiences, were absent in Mountain Home. The small town was an all-white haven where "a growing number of retired persons [were] making their homes," according to the *Blytheville Courier News* in 1963.³⁰ Carl Launius, who undertook the first scholarly study of Stanford, called the place "an arch-conservative Ozark town."³¹ Bill Willett said Mountain Home provided residents with "a nutshell existence."³² In Memphis, as seen in *The Battlefield*, Stanford places his alter ego Francis on the brink of a biracial world. In Snow Lake, also as seen in *The Battlefield*, Stanford puts Francis in the thick of interracial interaction. In the camp he is deeply involved in the lives of Baby Gauge, BoBo Washington, and most notably Charlie B. Lemon. But in Mountain Home, there were no biracial aspects of daily life for Frank to explore. As an autobiographical work preoccupied with Black vernacular and rooted in racial interaction and justice, *The Battlefield Where the Moon Says I Love You*, with the possible exception of some fishing scenes, had little use for Mountain Home.

## "My Chosen Ones"

"Bull"—as Frank's classmates called him, surely because of his stout stature—was not yet an adult. But he had to start thinking about some adult-like issues.³³ His father was quite sick. Frank Sr. was ailing, shuffling around the house and requiring constant attention from Dorothy, who had little time for the kids. Joan Williams, who visited the Stanfords on Mallard Point several times, recalled about Frank "how hard it was for the boy to have a father not only so old but dying before his eyes."³⁴ The related issue of adoption—which intensifies for adolescents—persisted with greater urgency. Frank always expressed deep respect for his father, but he also knew that Frank Sr. was not his biological father. Dorothy's decision not to tell the children that she had adopted them only became more awkward in Mountain Home. "Sometimes," Stanford writes in "The Mind Reader," a poem he said he started in 1959 (and likely revised for many years after), "I feel like a motherless child."³⁵ Dorothy never really helped. "You were my chosen ones," remained her refrain. Nothing more than that. Still, as Joan Williams said, "she thought he [Frank] had always known."³⁶ Frank's friend Bill Willett saw the matter this way: "Dorothy was trying to maintain that southern aristocratic attitude, and any blemish like that would tarnish that image." It was, he added, "foolish pride" that kept her from being fully transparent with her children about their adoption from the Emery Memorial Home.³⁷ Either way, there remained no further clarification on this issue after the move, even as Frank's father was dying.

Being away from Memphis may have had the paradoxical impact of making Frank hold tighter to the fiction that Dorothy promoted. Dorothy's strategy to diminish his inevitable curiosity was to reiterate her family's rootedness in southern traditions and values, to normalize the narrative beyond the impulse to question it. "Dorothy always told him about the Gildart family, which supposedly had lineage all the way back to England, to the Earl of Sandwich," Willett remembered. He also noted how Frank easily warmed to this version of his family history: "I remember Frank telling me about that," Willett noted, adding about this regal background that "he was proud of it."[38] There were advantages, as Frank knew, to coming from privilege, and in the not terribly southern enclave of Mountain Home, there may have been even greater occasions to stress that history, those advantages, that pride of place.

In essence, both Frank and his mother lived a fiction neither of them dared disrupt, at least at this point in life. It remained a secret they shared but did not discuss. She convinced herself that she had given him enough information to know he was adopted. Frank, in turn, pretended that he was part of his mother's elite bloodline enough for her to believe it. Inwardly questioning his origins while outwardly playing the role of the Mississippi-born southern gentleman-to-be, "Bull" not only kept his secret; he may have even thrived on it. Holding the issue close to his chest, he forged ahead, the rich kid from Mississippi via Memphis, into what eventually proved to be a delightfully feral Ozark boyhood, one marked on the surface by constant engagement with lake life, ongoing social popularity, continued athletic success, and sex.

But beneath the surface there was, along with his adoption, a growing habit of secrecy that would define much of Frank's life. Frank quietly pursued a fierce reading habit, an interest in the occult, and the start of a lifetime's worth of poetic output. Willett remembered how this was a time and place "that was a boon to his imagination."[39] Describing their Mountain Home years, Ruth, who saw her brother daily, summed them up in the simplest and most honest terms: "These were good but complicated times."[40]

## "I Am the One Called Fish"

Lake Norfork was created in 1943 by a hydroelectric dam situated in the White River Basin.[41] The lake became the center of Frank's life in Mountain Home, and it happened to be known nationally for its impressive fish stocks. Lake Norfork and Bull Shoals Lake were common sites of record-breaking catches. The early 1960s were especially impressive. Anglers heading out from the Cranfield Boat Dock, down the road from the Stanfords' house on Mallard Point, reported, according to one article at the time, "more large bass taken in the last two weeks than for any similar period in the history of the lake."[42] With trout prevalent in the White River and local accommodations for fishermen widely available (the Silver Maple Resort being an especially popular venue), fishing in the Lake Norfork region was a year-round endeavor.[43]

Frank's previous experience in the great outdoors was minimal. Tooling around the generally barren Snow Lake landscape during the levee days, plus a few hunting trips with his father, was pretty much the extent of it. Memphis was suburbanized and sheltered from anything but the most conventional organized team sports. But Mallard Point was a less structured environment to explore. Lake Norfork offered access to a sprawling outdoors, which was why three million people visited the place every year to fish and hunt. For an athletic and active young teen who was free to stay outside as much as he could and with minimal adult oversight to restrict his explorations, the place was a little wilderness for him to explore. Frank gravitated to the water. "He was up at the crack of dawn out on the lake, and he was out there," Ruth recently remembered, "twenty-four seven."[44]

Frank got a job at the Cranfield Boat Dock, where he sold tackle and bait, taught water-skiing, pumped gas into motorboats, and eventually took seasoned fishermen on lake tours.[45] Frank had not fished since his Snow Lake summers, when he regularly cast lines from the shores of retaining ponds with Baby Gauge, who taught him to fish.[46] The Stanford family kept two motorboats, one of them a regal Chris-Craft at Cranfield and the other a pontoon boat at their private dock.[47] Frank, a twelve-year-old with access to both boats, explored the lake right after they moved into the house in May 1961. He often drove straight into storms. "I enjoyed getting out in my boat when I was younger and heading into them," he later said. "I got a great sense of peace from being in these storms."[48] Everyone who visited the Stanfords at Mallard Point—whether it was family or friends from school—was taken for a ride by Frank. Even Laura, the Black domestic worker whose stay was brief, went fishing with Frank on Lake Norfork.[49]

Frank's angling success on the lake is chronicled in "The Lake Norfork Fishing Letter," a weekly typed-up record of catches made by anglers visiting from around the country. Although the lake was populated with expert adult fishermen, Frank was routinely listed as a top fisherman. On April 17, 1964, he landed the seventh largest fish of the day, a seven-pound, twelve-ounce largemouth bass caught with a "bomber" lure. A week later he was fifth with an eight-pound, four-ounce largemouth caught with a "hog caller." But it was with a "hellbender" in early November 1963 that Stanford topped the charts, beating adult anglers from Illinois, Missouri, Iowa, Kansas, and Oklahoma, with a seven-pound walleye.[50]

These exploits led to him being hired by the local marina to take tourists on fishing ventures. His experience as a guide informs a poem from his chapbook *Shade* (1975) called "Slow Rag of the Yearbook":

> All I get is twelve bucks a day guiding the lost men
> I take them into the waters they want to remember
> . . . . . . . . . . . . . . . . . . . . . . . . . . .
> I give them one chance at the big one . . .[51]

In another poem, "Blue Yodel of Those Who Were Always Telling Me," he offers at least one downside of being a fishing guide. A client instructs him, "Bait my hook . . . that's what I'm paying you for."[52] Ruth remembered that Frank "was really good with these rich folks and they all loved him."[53]

"He took to Norfork Lake," his mother said, "and he won fishing trophies."[54] One such victory came when Frank landed what Dorothy, prone to exaggeration, recalled as a thirty-two-pound bass. Frank convinced his mother to get it taxidermized. Ruth noted how the fishermen whom Frank took out always came back with impressive bounties that got written up in "The Lake Norfork Fishing Letter."[55] When Frank caught an even bigger fish than the prize-winning one, his mother put an end to the taxidermy habit, telling him it was too expensive.[56] But Frank kept the original stuffed fish his whole life. It later burned in a fire at Ruth's house after his death.[57]

Much of Frank Stanford's shorter verse, especially that written between 1964 and 1971, channels fishing imagery. Frank's first book of poetry, *The Singing Knives* (1972),[58] includes the poem "The Blood Brothers," in which we learn that Baby Gauge, with whom a very young Frank routinely fished at Snow Lake, "tied the line to his wrist / He tied it to the alligator gar / He rode the fish." In the volume's next poem, "The Singing Knives," Stanford writes:

> I dreamed the fish bandits stole the hogs
> Off my lines

Later in the same poem:

> I dreamed I was fishing in heaven with Sho Nuff
> and Jesus cleaned the fish

A poem called "The Bass" captures the image of a hooked fish:

> He jumps up high
> against the night,
> rattling his gills
> and the hooks
> in his back.

Another poem called "The Minnow" notes how "If I press / on its head, / the eyes / will come out / like stars. / The ripples / it makes / can move / the moon."[59] In one of the earliest poems Stanford published (in *Chicago Review*, 1971), "The Albino," a character says:

> "I don't know about other things
> But fishing will be good today."[60]

In "The Smoking Mirrors," also published in 1971, he writes, "I am some mother / who baits your hook / some father who cleans your fish" and "I am the one called Fish."[61] Finally, in a line that bears repeating because it so tenderly blends Stanford's love of the outdoors with his ear for language, Francis, in *The Battlefield*, says:

> I want people of twenty seven languages walking back and forth saying
>   to one
> another hello brother how's the fishing
>   (4493–94)

It may be that nothing he wrote was more sincere than that.

Dorothy, who spent her Mountain Home days caring for her elderly husband, left the kids to do generally as they pleased. "The house was fashioned for informality," recalled Joan Williams, who visited Dorothy with her two sons, Matt and Bo, in the summer of 1964. She remembers that Frank was always coming and going but was away most of the time on one adventure or another.[62] Ruth added how he was always on the lake "guiding people or fishing."[63] Williams recalled "a sturdy, muscular boy, busy with a summer job on the lake."[64] In *The Battlefield*, Francis describes Frank during this time aptly: "I motley boy on the loose" (12671).[65]

Water-skiing was a close second to fishing for Frank. "Frank was a wonderful skier," Ruth recalled.[66] He picked it up immediately and became highly skilled at the sport over the course of a single summer, so much so that he was teaching lessons by August 1961, just a few months after moving to the lake. Frank's cousin-in-law, Elise Lee, remembers how "Frank just took us skiing all summer."[67] Frank's niece and nephew remember how theatrical Frank was on the water: "He was an entertainer; believe me," Carole Hess said, adding how "he would take us out on the boat, and he would ski, then he showed us how to ski barefoot."[68] Dorothy said how "he loved to water-ski and he won contests."[69] Frank, while discussing his childhood on Mallard Point, later said, "I love the water. . . . I just love the water. . . . I just like water on me."[70]

Frank's ability to teach skiing opened him up to a chance meeting that would shape his future more than any other encounter. In the summer of 1963 at the end of Frank's second summer on Lake Norfork, he met a handsome, athletic, blue-eyed thirty-two-year-old priest named Father Nicholas Fuhrmann.[71] Fuhrmann was visiting Mountain Home from Subiaco Academy, a Catholic boarding school with a Benedictine abbey located a few hours away on the other side of the Ozark National Forest. He was in town for the summer to serve as the interim pastor at St. Peter the Fisherman, Mountain Home's Catholic church. He'd been asked to teach some kids in his parish how to water-ski but did not know how to do so himself. He'd seen a sign on the boat dock for ski lessons and called for an appointment. When a muscular young kid with perfect hair showed up as the instructor, Fuhrmann laughed. But Frank was all business. He put the priest in the boat and took him out on the lake.[72]

After getting Fuhrmann in the water, Frank yelled to him, as the priest bobbed behind the boat, "Just get your skis on top of the water, and hang on to the rope. I will pull until you stay on, ya hear? Just stay on!" Fuhrmann did as told. When the boat took off, he recalled, "I popped up like a cork coming out of a champagne bottle." But his feet splayed in opposite directions. Seeing the priest nearly split in two, Frank slowed the boat down, gave him a few seconds of slack to recover, and then gunned it at top speed, all the while yelling tips that Fuhrmann couldn't hear over the roaring engine. But he got up as Frank had promised, and having endured "this battle for survival," he was thrilled with the experience. "Okay," Frank said when they returned to the dock, "you learned." Then he demanded a five-dollar tip.[73]

One year later, Frank, with the encouragement of Father Fuhrmann and several other monks who came to know Frank on the lake, left Mountain Home for Subiaco Academy, where the charismatic priest, who was also an impassioned English teacher, would play a central role in shaping the career of the charismatic boy poet.[74]

## "You're a Real Cute Kid"

The Stanfords' large house and direct lake access meant that—despite Frank Sr.'s worsening health—summers were bustling with activities and visitors. Frank Coleman and Carole Hess have warm memories of seeing the Stanford family on Lake Norfork. Frank took them fishing every day. "We would catch something like a hundred brim," Hess recalled, "and do a huge fish fry.... It was a beautiful setting." Frank Coleman added that Frank Stanford was "really a happy, happy child."[75] Frank Stanford's cousin, Jimmy Lee, also visited the Stanfords in the summer of 1964 (and possibly other summers).[76] Lee, who was six years older than Frank, plays a significant role in *The Battlefield*, as well as in many other Stanford poems. Ruth recalled them being quite close.[77] This closeness was further cultivated when Frank later went to Greenville for a couple of summers, primarily to work with Jimmy on his parents' cotton farm.[78] According to C. D. Wright, Jimmy "was the Jerry Lee Lewis of Frank's boyhood"—that is, kind of a delightful goofball. She added how "he was probably a heller in his youth, [but] nothing to the extent *The Battlefield* portrayed, not a felon, not insane."[79]

In "The Blood Brothers"—which Frank stated that he wrote in 1964—Jimmy is the only white person introduced in the opening cast of characters:

> There was Jimmy
> He had the knife like night
> He was white[80]

In the following poem, "The Singing Knives," he appears in its dramatic opening:

> Jimmy ran down the road
> With the knife in his mouth
> He was naked
> And the moon
> Was a dead man floating down the river

Then at its center:

> I dreamed Jimmy was pouring ice water
> Over my head at noon

And toward the end:

> I dreamed Jimmy rowed out the front door
> With a hawk on his shoulder

Eventually Jimmy, with "the bandanna around his neck / And the pilot's cap on," hurls his nicknamed knives into the wall against which the speaker stands:

> he threw Boo Kay Jack at me
> He threw Django at me
> . . . . . . . . . . . . . .
> The bone handled one
> The hawk handled one
> The one with a blade like a skiff

The poem ends with a scene of intense communion between the cousins:

> He took out the knife and ran it
> Across his arm
> Then he ran it across mine
> Blood came out like hot soda
>
> He tied our arms together
> With the blue bandanna
> And we laid down in the cotton
> I wished I was riding a mule somewhere
> Blowing a jug
> With a string full of crappie
> And the cotton making everyday[81]

As these brief excerpts suggest, Stanford, from a young age and with little academic knowledge of literary history, was taking on a deep tradition. He was confronting the old agrarian romance celebrated by poets such as John Crowe Ransom, Allen Tate, and even Robert Penn Warren. And he was doing so with the emotional rawness of a poet such as Jim Harrison, the confessional urgings of Sylvia Plath, and the genre-busting subversion of Robert Altman. In these lines, Stanford begins to imagine an exceptional poetic South where, although the cotton still makes, the air hums with knives named after mangled jazz guitarists, cousins slice and tie themselves together in solidarity, and hawk-shouldering boatmen row the poem to the brink of surrealism. Through imagery and language that seems infinite (if you can open a poem with a naked man running down the road with a knife in his teeth, man, you can do anything), Frank was unhinging the South from its hidebound past, sinking it into the extraordinary ordinariness of life, and opening its future to something much different and, possibly, much better.

Jimmy is central to the *Battlefield* as well. He is called "the Wolfman" or "the Wolf" and acts as Francis's older mentor. He is a bad boy, or at least perpetually mischievous, always a bit crosswise with the law, cuckolding the husbands of local wives and defiant of authority in general. He struts through backwoods Mississippi and Tennessee, full of lust and dreams of conquest; he's a competitive knife thrower; he hates the local "peckerwoods," always sides with the Blacks, with whom he drinks and carouses and from whom he takes fashion tips. He has a truck. Francis totally adores Jimmy. But he also chides him for his frequent lack of self-control. Jimmy more than tolerates Francis but gets impatient with his cousin's elaborate dream sequences, partially because precocious Francis, when recounting these dreams, uses sophisticated vocabulary that Jimmy does not understand.

In one example highlighting Francis's verbal facility, Francis, who is in the middle of spinning a big yarn about Five Spoke, says "he / sauntered up he what Jimmy says he sashayed up" (5934–35). Francis must make these kinds of ad hoc shifts often—in this case replacing "sauntered" with "sashayed" in midsentence when Jimmy says, "he what." Such interruptions eventually lead Jimmy to respond by saying things like "just finish the story" (5944) or "if you / are you trying to give me the run around I'm going to beat your little ass you hear" (6071). This antagonism is always playful. Jimmy actually finds the stories entertaining, and Francis, much like Frank himself, ultimately backs away from conflict rather than diving into it, never forgetting that he and Jimmy remain not only cousins but full-blown *blood brothers*. Plus, Jimmy comes in handy at times. "Jimmy let me watch him screw a girl," Stanford notes in "The Mind Reader." And then "he showed me how to jack off."[82]

In the summer of 1964 on Mallard Point, Joan Williams visited with her two boys—Matt and Bo. "Frankie could well have ignored them as pests," she wrote, but instead he spent a lot of time with them. When one of her kids broke Frank's guitar, he shrugged it off and took them boating and fishing. Williams recalled that "once he had them down on his bed hitting them with a pillow and, swinging it, broke the ceiling light." Williams came over from the next bedroom when she heard the glass shatter only to find Frank "still kneeling, pillow in hand, lightly smiling, and afraid I've come angry because of his roughhousing." When, in the aftermath of the accident, Frank asked Ruth to get a Band-Aid for his cut arm, Williams's kids playfully mocked his thick southern accent.[83]

In the fall of 1961, Frank started the eighth grade at Mountain Home Junior High School. His attitude remained generally lax about formal schooling. "He was an average student, as far as his grades went," said Bill Willett, "but as far as his intellectual abilities, it was way beyond what he did in his academics."[84] In "The Mind Reader" Stanford refers to "the sepulcher of report cards" but follows up on this image with the comment that "I got straight A's."[85] A clear case of wishful revisionism. His transcript confirms he was a solid C student, even in English, although he did get As in biology and civics and a D in algebra.[86] Frank showed (ironically enough) aptitude in math (again, Francis says in *The Battlefield*: "I get up on the desks and yell I take off my shoes and break the lights I say / fuck arithmetic" [1098–99]). He became a member of the "100 Club," which consisted of a handful of students who earned a perfect score on the National Office Management–sponsored math exam.[87] Dorothy always interpreted Frank's math skills, at least as they were confirmed on standardized tests, as evidence that he was fated to follow in the footsteps of Frank Sr. into the respectable field of engineering.

Notes left by classmates in Frank's high school yearbooks from 1962 to 1964 reveal that his peers were well aware of his literary interests. "Bull," one wrote, "it sure has been a great year in English." Another: "It's been a lot of fun going to school with you, especially in English."[88] Classmate Beverly Franklin said, "You could tell he was probably a deep thinker—he was very eloquent." She said that when she later learned he'd become a writer, "that didn't surprise me." She further noted that, while this was not in any way Frank's intention, it was hard not to feel stupid around him. "He was obviously bright."[89] Frank's reputation for intelligence preceded him. One literary-minded Mountain Home girl, a year younger than Frank, brainy and intrigued by what people said about him, remembered how "the Mountain Home kids I hung out with said I should meet him. That I would like him. And I knew he was called Bull. That there was a mystique about him. That he was smart."[90] This girl was Carolyn Doris Wright, the future poet and romantic partner of Stanford who would go by C. D. And while the two only met for a brief moment in 1964, when Frank was sixteen and Carolyn fifteen, about a decade later C. D.'s friend Fred McCuistion handed her a coveted copy of *The Singing Knives*, which at the time was being passed around Fayetteville like an illegal drug.[91] C. D. later said that "I recognized him from the drawing, so I guess I had seen him before, probably at Lake Norfork or somewhere."[92]

Frank's social life was active, and it, too, centered on the lake. Beverly Franklin, who lived near the Stanfords on Mallard Point, said that "the big thing for us teenagers, at that time, was to hang out on the lake, swimming, boating, and all that stuff."[93] The Stanford family held fish fries in their backyard, inviting all the neighbors to join. Mallard Point became a popular spot for Frank's classmates too.[94] One of them wrote as much in his yearbook: "I'll always remember the times you've taken me skiing."[95] Frank had no curfew, and sometimes he stayed out all night. "He liked to party a bit," Franklin remembered, noting there was always "a little alcohol" but never any drugs.[96] "I hope we can have some more wild times next year," a schoolmate wrote in his yearbook, adding, "There is never a dull moment when you're around."[97] Things definitely were not dull the night after the Ali-Liston fight in February 1964, when, Frank recalled, "I was in the tenth grade, fingerfucking Davilee [sic] Nevius."[98] Kenny Willett—Bill's brother who also knew Frank in Mountain Home—said, "Everything happens when Frank is around."[99] His classmates seem to have agreed.

In August of 1961, Frank went out for and made the junior high football team at Mountain Home Junior High, where even junior high football was religion. Frank later confessed, "I didn't give a shit."[100] But his ailing father did and strongly encouraged Frank to play the sport. There was always puffed-up talk in the Stanford household of Frank playing college ball someday. "My husband really wanted Frankie to play football," Dorothy said. "He wanted Frankie to be a Razorback."[101] It was notable that, at the first football practice, as one player recalled, "Frank Sr. was there—he didn't get out much, because of his health, but he'd come to watch the first practice."[102] Frank never really excelled at the sport, rarely attending practice and never being labeled a jock. In a draft of a poem scribbled in a composition notebook, he later wrote:

> you can go out for the longest pass
> in the pasture
> so the coach he says bull
> if I told you once
> I've told you a thousand times
> stay on a pattern.[103]

Frank went off pattern a lot: He dyed his jockstrap blue, called the coach "dumb," and hung out with players who smoked.[104] "He was not into team sports," one classmate said.[105] Frank later scrawled in a random set of notes:

> My father suggested I scrimmage with no uniform
> I made the team but never showed up for practice.[106]

His friends had more to say about his antics on bus rides to the games than the games themselves, much less Frank's talent as a football player. In that same poem scribbled in the composition notebook, Frank wrote about his real motivation for being on the team:

> I get to sit with the studs
> in the back of the bus.[107]

It was at the first practice, with his dad watching from the sidelines, that Frank first met Bill Willett. Their encounter, which would lead to a lifelong friendship, was essentially a sanctioned fight. As Willett tells it, it was "a very hot September afternoon," and there was only one uniform left. He and Frank were pitted against each other to see who would get it. "The idea," Willett said, "was to put the other person on the ground.... We lined up, and the coach blew his whistle, and we went at it. We started throwing forearm shivers and knocking heads, stirring up a lot of dust." Eventually the coach came over, yelling, " 'Whoa, whoa, whoa, stop, stop, stop,' and grabs us both by the shoulder and separates us. He goes over to the little guy, who he'd given the next-to-last uniform, took it from him, and gave both of us uniforms."[108]

Despite his muscular stature, Frank disliked fighting, if not confrontation in general, and would avoid it at most costs throughout his life. But Willett, although compact and wiry, was more prone to brawl. ("I've been doing violent things all my life," he said.)[109] Looking back on this sunbaked afternoon in 1961, Willett had to admit that he'd met his masculine match in this stocky rich kid from the big city: "I guess you could say we came out about even," he concluded.[110] His reaction was all respect, the kind that would foster an abiding friendship. And while he never considered himself Frank's intellectual equal, Willett read his friend's poetry with gut instinct and shrewd insight. "I wasn't any man of the world," he said, "but I knew that it was good stuff, and it would just grip you, it would get a hold of you and wouldn't let you loose."[111]

Not only did Frank avoid fights, but he was, by every account, a thoroughly kind, easygoing, and at times playful kid. One male classmate, who went to Mountain Home Junior High and Mountain Home High School with Stanford, echoed a common assessment when he said that "I can recall nothing negative about him; he was just a real nice guy."[112] "We had a lot of fun on football trips," another classmate wrote in his yearbook. "You're a *wonderful* boy and as cute as can be," said a female classmate. And another: "You're a *GREAT* guy with a darling personality."[113] "He was gentle," said Beverly Franklin.[114] "A prankster—liked to pull tricks," recalled Ruth, who also called him an occasional "cutup."[115] In 2011 Willett recalled, "Once we were at my parents house and Frank decided to show them Jerry Lewis' impression of a chicken with its head cut off. He laid on the floor on his side, and while moving his legs, he rotated his body and spun on his shoulder."[116]

Rounding out this picture of charmed youth, adolescent Frank became particularly attentive to his appearance. He was always impeccably groomed and dressed. As one classmate noted, "He could afford to be." He was routinely admired for these qualities. "His appearance was always very important to him," the classmate added.[117] "He liked to be noticed," said another, commenting that "he always had really nice clothes." Franklin remembered how "Frank had a very magnetic personality," adding, "I think he had beautiful hair."[118] "He was well dressed," Willett said. "He liked nice shirts, Hagar slacks. . . . He knew good clothes and wore good clothes. Very distinguished."[119] From his yearbook: "You're a real cute kid, and pretty nice too." And: "You are one of the cutest boys in the school. . . . Maybe we can get together sometime and go skiing." The Mountain High class of 1966 thought highly enough of Frank's attire to name him, in 1964, the school's best-dressed young man. "Sure am glad you got best dressed," his friend added to a yearbook already brimming with adoration.[120]

## "I Sang Like the Weed in the Sea"

There was something deeper brewing inside Frank during these years, inclinations more serious and secretive, dark and divisive. Beyond the water sports, the fishing, the popularity, the friendships, and the happy-go-lucky disposition was a boy blessed or cursed with an emerging literary obsession, and the mentality to feed it, that he generally kept to himself. Frank recalled walking alone during these years—"at night and in the morning"—and spending time in his mind with Vermeer, Modigliani, Chagall, and Keats. "I would think things," he recalled. "I wouldn't understand it. I wouldn't understand it."[121] Some saw hints of this dreamy and distant disposition. Joan Williams recalled Frank's smile as being "indicative that he was listening already to some other, interior self."[122] She further noted how that "slight smile" was "perhaps saying a great deal."[123] One of Frank's classmates noted how, for all of Frank's affability, he could sometimes be in "far, far away land."[124] Frank would leave the house during full moons because he could not sleep and go lie on the dock behind the house. He would lie there and, as he recalled, imagine that "you could get a tan from the moon."[125]

Whether this habit of secrecy was a response to his indeterminate heritage, a quiet way to craft an identity separate from his adopted family, or just part of a normal adolescent desire for privacy is hard to say. But there is no question that Frank was doing a lot more than having a blast out on the lake. One classmate, who was never quite friends with Frank but knew him from a distance, detected this more intense side, noting how "part of him was a little weirder than the rest of us—really weird in fact."[126] Father Fuhrmann referred to this aspect of Frank as one that fostered a kind of "aloofness" that he never lost.[127] A cousin who visited the Stanfords in 1963 said that Frank was "a really nice guy, but he did not talk a lot about what he did."[128] In *The Battlefield*, in a scene where Stanford channels his own story through Vico, the character modeled after Giambattista Vico, he refers to a time "after I had been found out leading a double existence I believe I was thirteen then" (10775–76).

Part of young Frank's "weirdness" came from something southern Ozarkians did not see a great deal of: an obsession with books. Frank was starting the solitary process of becoming one of the most wide-ranging, self-taught, and well-read poets in American history. Not only did his Mountain Home classmates at the time marvel at the depth of his literary exposure, but when he later got to boarding school in the fall of 1964 as a junior, it was immediately evident that he knew more literature than his teachers. As one of his classmates put it: "He was *light-years* ahead of us—we all kind of acknowledged that."[129] Father Fuhrmann, who taught Frank during his first semester at Subiaco, noted his new student's ability not only to recite sections of Chaucer but also to situate him in the intricate history of English literature. "Were it only so simple," Frank gently chastised his teacher after he delivered an elementary lecture on the transition from medieval to modern literature.[130]

Because he was so lavishly rewarded in Mountain Home for being an enviable and relatively normal teen—well-dressed, athletic, and fun—he may have been extra careful about keeping his bookish interests private. Given the town's "typical Southern small-town bias against scholarliness," one Stanford researcher argues that Frank had to hide his fascination with literature, poetry, and philosophy or at least keep it secret from everyone but his trusted friend Willett, who knew about his friend's dream, at thirteen, "to be the Faulkner of poetry."[131] A friend noted that Mountain Home quickly rewarded a young man for his athletic ability but not for being intelligent, adding how the common opinion there was that "the more intelligent you are, the harder time you have getting on in life."¹³² "A young man's show of learning," another Stanford scholar has argued, "was looked upon with raised eyebrows."¹³³

Stanford alludes to the necessary duplicity required to protect this "show of learning" in *The Battlefield* when he writes:

> I wish every one
> could see what little Francis the rich boy has been getting to
> what he's been stalking like a wolf . . .
> (14594–96)

Later in the poem he observes how "I did so much without any notice" (14604). In a scrap of typescript, written around 1972, Stanford writes:

> when I was twelve I used to lock myself in the outhouse
> and read D.H. Lawrence out loud.¹³⁴

In another, echoing Dylan Thomas's "Fern Hill," he writes:

> in this country the widows die virgins
> I Francois said this
> before I reached the age of twelve
> I said nothing though I sang like the weed in the sea.¹³⁵

Mountain Home might have been a free-for-all for Frank, but it was also the start of what Willett identifies as a time when Frank's literary imagination took flight.¹³⁶

If an obsessive reading habit fueled this imagination, where did the books themselves come from? Williams, in her published account of that summer, wrote, "I do not recall books in the house, unless there were a few in shelves on either side of a stone fireplace in the large main room." She also added, "And I do not recall books in Frankie's room."¹³⁷ These comments later rankled Frank's mother. In her personal copy of the *Ironwood* volume that contained Williams's essay, Dorothy registered a note in a defensive hand. "Frank was reading Faulkner when he was 13–14 years old—we did have a library!" she wrote in the margin.¹³⁸ She also noted six years later that "Joan Williams did not do so well with a little of my experience."¹³⁹ It is also worth noting that, if only to support Dorothy, Willett confirmed that Frank, at the time, was "drenched in Faulkner."¹⁴⁰ When it came to Frank's reading accomplishments, a classmate recalled how, even in ninth grade, "he was way, way above us old country boys; he was real nice about it, but he thought on a higher plateau."¹⁴¹ The books, in short, had to be coming from somewhere.

In a 1974 letter Frank suggests where he might have started his reading regimen. He mentions "a fat lady, about forty-eight, who has her PHD. in English." This woman, a linguistics scholar and later hotel owner named Sara Gragg, had "lived next door to us on the lake" and "always had boxes of fine books and I read them all and she was fine to talk to."¹⁴² In an unpublished poem called "Dreaming with My Friend Mona," Stanford offers what sounds like an interesting twist on this possible scenario:

> She only stays a few days at a time
> Her work in the city is important
>
> She brings a satchel of books
> And papers to grade
>
> I wait for her at the crossroads
> Where the bus lets her off¹⁴³

On a fragment of undated scrap paper, Frank writes:

> I want to quit school
> and have the run of her library.¹⁴⁴

In an unpublished prose fragment, in a passage on his life on the lake, Frank states, "I read the professor's books."¹⁴⁵ Given that Frank was, as Ruth and Joan Williams both observed, more or less on his own all day, the idea of him spending hours at the professor's house with her books seems reasonable. In 1971 Frank suggested another origin of his early reading habits in a letter to Alan Dugan. He explained how his mother introduced him at a young age to "those old d[ar]k blue books with the gold trim" that she kept stored in dynamite boxes taken from the levee camp.¹⁴⁶ A week later, he wrote to an editor that these "blue books with gold trim," which "my mother and I read out of dynamite boxes in the levee camp," were from the Book League of America. "I believe," he added, "they had just about every book written."¹⁴⁷

Wherever the books came from, Frank's first publisher, Irv Broughton, as well as Father Nicholas Fuhrmann, affirmed Dorothy's intellectual influence on her son. Broughton stressed that, while Dorothy did not really understand modernist poetry, "she was a literary person."¹⁴⁸ Fuhrmann said that Dorothy was "the greatest influence on Frank both motherly and as a literary figure herself—she had a classic knowledge of good writing."[149] According to Frank, a steady diet of Melville, Cervantes, Conrad, Kafka, Stevenson, Keats, Turgenev, Marx, Boccaccio, Dickens, and, in Frank's words, "all those fucking Russians" ensured that "by the time I got to high school I had read most of the stuff you have to for masters." He confessed that "some of the authors mother would tell me to read—I wouldn't. I'd read comic books instead."[150] All this reading happened before he went to boarding school in 1964.

People who met Frank at boarding school, in college, and beyond consistently observed a depth of literary immersion well beyond normal expectations. Steve Stern, a novelist who first got to know Frank in 1973, remembered thinking that "he must have read a lot as a kid." Stern observed how, when talking to him, "you began to realize this guy had *read* and just had an encyclopedic sense of literature." Stern says that Stanford's literary interpretations had an almost eerie accuracy. "He had a kind of visceral understanding of whatever literature he was reading, and it always seemed to be astonishingly precise," Stern said.[151] John Biguenet, who became a translator and an English professor after graduating from the University of Arkansas MFA program in the early 1970s, met Stanford at a conference in 1970. Biguenet was astonished by the extent of Stanford's knowledge. He could go deep and speak with professorial fluency about not only English literature but French, Italian, and Spanish as well. The two would talk for hours at the end of the day about films and talks they'd seen.[152] C. D. Wright recalled, "He read the living and the dead. . . . He read the French, the Italians, the Americans. He but lay his hand on a book and inhaled the contents."[153] Sam Gwynn said Stanford "sauntered through his books."[154]

In the early seventies, Frank spoke about his reading habits as a kid to Irv Broughton. He said he read *Lady Chatterley's Lover* "and stuff I wasn't supposed to read." His "big kick" was to take out "aliases at the library so I could check out more books." When it came to books, "I couldn't wait to finish one so I could start another." Describing himself as "a pitcher going against nine batters in a row," he would "just read chapter after chapter." In the summer when he worked at the docks, "when you worked hard, you know, you just dropped right off to sleep," but during the rest of the year he hid under his sheets with the carbide light he usually used for frog gigging and read through the night. He described books as stands of timbers that he would wander through, noting in particular Shelley, Byron, Victor Hugo, Sir Richard Burton, "all the epics," B. A. G. Fuller's *A History of Philosophy*, and books about Saint Francis. "I kept to myself a lot," he said about this reading habit. "I read a lot in boats."[155]

By 1963 or 1964, Frank, barely a teenager, was not only reading literature like a graduate student but also writing poetry more. His sister often said that her brother did very little writing on Mallard Point, insisting that he was rarely "bolted up in his room" scribbling verse. But she did concede how he would occasionally lock himself away and write all night, something he would do for much of his life. As for witnessing her brother in action, however, she said, "I never saw Frankie write a thing."[156]

Dorothy disagreed. She said that "he always did it very secretly." Even back in Memphis, Frank "had a chest at the window of his bedroom that he would sit on and write." Dorothy added that "if I went up and he was writing, he'd cover the page with his arm." If anyone understood secrecy, it was Dorothy. She insisted that "he was writing poems when he was young, but he told nobody."[157] Her remark echoes Francis's claim in *The Battlefield* that "I did so much without any notice" (14666). Bill Willett was unequivocal on this point: "Frank was writing poetry at the house on Mallard Point."[158] C. D. Wright, who would come to know Stanford well in the last three years of his life, said about the "Stanfords in Mountain Home" that "I know his work from that time—he was a prodigious, prolific writer then."[159] She remembered a friend of the Stanford family telling her that, in 1961 or 1962, when they were both in junior high school, Frank gave her poems and that they were "nocturnal," with knives, wolves, and the moon as prominent motifs.[160] Frank himself, in a 1973 letter to his grandmother, told her of his poetry, "I wrote most of it when I was a kid, no one knowing about it."[161]

Later in life, Frank noted how he was, in 1970–72, trying "to make fourteen years of early Huckleberry Rimbaud [manuscripts] readable."[162] In an interview he explained that he wrote "more between twelve and eighteen" than at any other age.[163] A couple of years later he wrote to Alan Dugan, "When I was younger, I wrote all the time."[164] On another occasion, writing again to Dugan, he said, "I had my mind set in being a writer way before I met the likes of these bastards here," a not-so-affectionate reference to his fellow students at the university but yet another piece of evidence that he was finding a poetic voice at an early age, largely in secret.[165]

## "St. Francis and the Wolf" and "Blue Yodel"

Stanford saved, revised, and later typed up hundreds of self-described "fragments" that would later find a home in *The Battlefield*. He worked these into a loosely organized poem, at one point possibly reaching a thousand pages and consisting of many discrete poems, calling it

"St. Francis and the Wolf." "St. Francis" was a reference to himself. His cousin Jimmy was "the Wolf."[166] He dated these fragments "1957–1964." Both the title and dates indicate that Frank was writing much of this poetry while living on Mallard Point in Mountain Home. In 1972 he wrote to a friend, saying that enclosed were "about 300 pages of a (500 page) piece of work I did in 1964, before I was sent off to that monastery for school."[167] In a January 1973 letter he wrote to his "gran-gran," Frank noted (accurately) that he had several chapbooks coming out. But he also acknowledged that they would not really appeal to his grandmother, telling her, "I know most of the things that I've done are what you'd call *épater les bourgeois*." He added that he had written most of it secretly.[168] In *The Battlefield* he explains, "I vanished to sing a blue yodel of that low born bastard / brought up by the finest of families" (11959–60), a line that highlights both his secrecy and his knowledge of his adoption. He adds, "I grew up early" (12392).[169]

The 1957 date might strike anyone as suspect, as he would have been eight or nine years old then. The claim thus requires some context. Recall that Frank did win a fourth-place award in a citywide poetry contest in 1958 in Memphis. His poem about a phoenix might have been an anomaly, "a dubious achievement," as he later called it, but it was, he added, "my first recognition." It surely led him to write more, and even if he did not begin to write with any consistency until many years later, say in 1963 or 1964, there's much to suggest that he wrote poems (or "fragments," as he labeled and numbered them) while in Memphis and before moving to Mountain Home.[170] A compromise answer to this nagging question might rest on the proposition—albeit speculative—that the 1957 date is at least technically true. Frank may have included it to validate something he would always highlight about his poetic persona: its origin in his early virtuosity. By listing the beginning date for so many of his poems as 1957, he was perhaps being at once technically factual and also mythical and enigmatic.

When Frank was twenty-five, he wrote a note to Broughton that says a lot about why dating his poems mattered so much to him: "You have full authority to 'change' anything," he wrote. "My only stipulation, at the bottom, or top, of each poem, or group of poems, the *date* and manuscript title *should* appear. Otherwise, I'll never be able to sleep in peace." These dates mattered to him because "I have to remember the geography, where I've been."[171] He told Broughton that, with his poems, "there has been an assiduous revision going on all the time."[172] To another editor, to whom he had sent a bunch of poems, he explained, "The source of some of my poems are my childhood poems."[173] In a notebook of poems written in

1973, he would write poems and then indicate that they came from "1964 original."[174] In this respect, he would always live with and update evolving work. The May 10, 1972, letter Frank wrote to Dugan offers further insight into how to consider his early virtuosity. After noting that he has enclosed three hundred pages of *The Battlefield*, Frank explains that he has "written some things longer than this, long ago." He recalls how "in 59 I wrote a thing called 'the mind reader' and the following year I did a short version of this; later, I dove into it." He continues, "When copying the manuscript, whenever I spilled something or a word was illegible, I just made something up."[175] By "this" and "it," Stanford is referring to *The Battlefield Where the Moon Says I Love You*. His poetry was, in other words, always in motion, sometimes for a decade or longer, before it settled into print.

It is in this context that we can better consider Frank's frequent claims to having written—or at least started—some of his poems when he was as young as eight, nine, or eleven years old. "The Mind Reader," which Frank dated to 1959, is remarkably sophisticated in its verbal play, imagistic intensity, and sophisticated evocation of place. The poem, perhaps unconsciously reflecting the concomitant emergence of confessional poetics, includes considerable detail from Frank's life between 1959 and 1964, detail that is generally absent from his later poems: "there are women driving Cadillacs to Memphis at tremendous speeds," "I put a blessed rosary on my trout line," "I say my hail marys to the gars," "I take the angels fishing," "I am the samurai kneeling beside the still water," and "I want to lay my head in my mammy's lap so long."[176] Because these images speak to Frank's actual living circumstances in Memphis, Snow Lake, and Mountain Home, it seems reasonable to think that he might have written his earliest drafts at a young age and continued to revise the poem, and deepen its confessional quality, over time. The version of the poem that we read today likely has its roots in impressions and lines that Frank updated repeatedly over many years.

"The Mind Reader" is a poem from "St. Francis and the Wolf," which Frank dated 1957–64. Once again, this timing seems right, as does the sense that the poem was routinely revised. Jimmy Lee, the Wolf, was six years older than Frank and a frequent visitor to the lake. "Jimmy loved Frankie and Ruth," said Lee's wife Elise, adding that "we spent time every summer in Mountain Home."[177] In *The Battlefield* Frank writes, "I not too old not too bad looking omnisexual and sly" (12335)—a pretty good description of himself in 1963 and 1964. Here we can see Stanford's defining poetic conceits identified around the age of fourteen: the adventures of a boy on the verge of young adulthood, a kid rebellious and self-referential, free of parental oversight, exploring a landscape defined by images and themes that Stanford would explore until the end—violence, death, the moon, water, boats, fish, sex, southern misfits, grotesques, wild horses, voices from the hills and highlands, bones fired and charred.

Not surprisingly, the early fragments that made it into *The Battlefield* often exude adolescent exuberance—"I wait for the schoolgirl who waits for me" (12661)—but they exceed juvenilia. At times they grip with nascent Faulknerian force, using familiar Faulknerian imagery, as in the hunting scene from *The Battlefield*:

> the first time I saw you I was hunting wild hogs with a rifle
> with a scope I took out the shell and kept you in the cross-hairs
> until you fell off that bowline you had your daddy string
> across the creek I went crazy right there I had to keep a lookout
> in my drawers one of the old gypsies in your troupe went down
> so the priest came down the river to give her last rites and the wind
> blew the host out of his hands . . .
>
>    (12055-61)

The small dramatic events in this poem, from hunting hogs to crossing streams on a bowline to getting an erection to the administration of last rights by the riverside, could have easily come right out of Yoknapatawpha County, a territory Frank tracked closely in his early poetry.

Or there's this, from another part of *The Battlefield* that was written as a "fragment" in Mountain Home:

> the soldiers on dope with their boots on the throats
> of whores the grandpappy dying at night in another's bed the hunters
> getting their jeep out of the mud are asleep and their dogs are still
> dead to the world and dreaming they are as mad as foxfire again
>
>    (12031-34)

The tenor of these passages reflects Faulkner's "The Bear," *The Reivers*, and *As I Lay Dying*. Still, young Stanford was doing more than echoing the narrative style of his recently deceased literary idol (Faulkner died in 1962). For one, he was exploring, again with confessional overtones, sexual desire. From *The Battlefield* (but originally written as "Fragment 309"): "I exist in the miracles of the nebulous clitoris" (12654). This was adolescent sexual desire, a raw and hormonal phenomenon he certainly was in the midst of experiencing. The fact that he was able to translate these experiences into poetic moments of sensuality means that he left us with a rare poetic insight into adolescent lust. It was a kind of expression uniquely available to an emerging young adult with exceptional verbal power. A recurring topic in *The Battlefield* involves a common theme in Stanford's work as a whole—older women propositioning a younger Frank. This scenario appears with considerable lyric appeal in Fragment 293, which made it into *The Battlefield*:

> in the school teacher's hall she was the only
> one who would take me in to this day I can see her wetting her lips
> with her tongue in my palm I would wake up beside her in the middle
> of the night kissing my fist but that's just another blue
> yodel of young ladies of time past I locked myself in the outhouse
> for her sake ...
> (12005–10)[178]

Of the "ballerina of the high wire," he writes:

> I remember your fingers that smell like honey
> the down on your calves like dust on a guitar which keeps
> a window open the moon through the screen on your belly a comb
> your hair too thick by a soul one strand makes me
> think of an island not on the maps the way you sipped wine
> like a tight ship that never takes in a drop of water and you
> not even sixteen and I was crazy I wanted to ride over a cliff
> the designs of your blouse roads that could lead anywhere
> your fingernails were like pirates coming aboard and my back
> that took a flogging ...
> (12040–49)

These excerpts reveal Stanford's Whitmanesque excitement about the body. Fingers, calves, lips, palm, fist, belly, hair, fingernails, back—they ground these excerpts in a dense corporality inseparable from elemental desire. Phrases such as "I was crazy I wanted to ride over a cliff," "wetting her lips / with her tongue in my palm," and "the moon through the screen on your belly" evoke Whitman's "Song of Myself" and "I Sing the Body Electric" as well as Frank's own erotic encounters along the lake in Mountain Home.

Occasionally in these early excerpts from *The Battlefield* Stanford's sexual accounts become more direct, less lyrical, and perhaps closer to the graphic reality of actual experience. He writes:

> the night before graduation I screwed you in the back of my truck
> and I became wonderful at saying so long now
> (12065–66)

Of this woman, who happens to seek "a bareback rider," he writes with equal beauty and crudeness about "the tuft of your cunt / like moss on the keel of a dark boat"(12061, 12070–71). In an undated, untitled, and unpublished poem he writes, of "the girls I knew in high school":

> They would take off their clothes
> In my truck and blow smoke in my face.

A girl named Beth "pulled my breeches off / As if she were pulling in a net." And there's this:

> Since I was a poet
> They would do things with me
> They wouldn't with anybody else.[179]

Poets.

Frank's actual experience with sex bloomed in Mountain Home. The intimacy with his nephew Frank Coleman continued, but Frank was also getting involved with young women. "Camille was his main girl," Willett remembered, noting that Frank would see her when he went to visit Greenville.[180] In a poem called "My Hands Were Warm," Stanford writes:

> So long Camille of the hills. . . .
> Let's ship out one of these nights . . .
> And yodel
> Fucking it all the way.[181]

In *The Battlefield* he writes, "my lover is Camille the loner" (12170). But there were others in Mountain Home. "Frankie always had girls," said Ruth. "It wasn't just one girl—there were two or three on the side."[182] He didn't need to work too hard. According to Beverly Franklin, "every girl in Mountain Home was after Frankie."[183] In "The Mind Reader" Stanford puts it thusly: "I have eleven girlfriends."[184] Foreshadowing this behavior, Frank independently identified two girls in his baby book as having been "my first girlfriend" when he was four.[185] But he grew up fast. He later told Broughton a story about, in the tenth grade, taking a girl named Adelle out on his boat after a party and how, at least in his version of the evening, "We just fucked, and fucked, and fucked."[186]

If not in a boat, dates typically took place at the Starlight Drive-In or the Baxter Theater. But one exception that both Willett and Stanford recalled with macabre amusement stands out. Willett noted how "one of [the Stanfords'] friends, a local sheriff, was water-skiing, and somehow or other his rope became tangled in the prop, and his leg was cut off."[187] In Broughton's film that he and Stanford cocreated, *It Wasn't a Dream: It Was a Flood*, Stanford notes this incident, recalling "somebody cutting a leg off and me going out and saving him in the water and then going into town and having a date and bringing her out there and swimming around." As for the idea of taking a date swimming to look for a freshly severed human leg, Stanford says, "It's not grotesque. I don't know what it is. . . . It's just strange."[188]

In addition to "St. Francis and the Wolf," Frank also started a collection of poems, many of which he would later publish, under the "Blue Yodel" rubric.[189] He wrote Blue Yodel poems well into the 1970s; many of them are mentioned in *The Battlefield*, and they tended to be quite personal, echoing again the popular confessional spirit of the time. Among Stanford's archived miscellaneous papers, one scrap of a handwritten note describes the Blue Yodel poems as a "series" that he began before 1964.[190] Many images in these poems resonate with Frank's immediate experience in Mountain Home. In "Blue Yodel of Those Who Were Always Telling Me," he lists a series of directives, requests, and feelings that speak to the verbal rhythms of daily life:

Sign my yearbook Don't
write anything like you did in Beth's

You know you can't come in my theatre
unless you got shoes on

Bait my hook that's what I'm paying you for

Why don't you go to Memphis
and buy your clothes

Take it from me
I ever catch you talking like that with my wife
I will kill you you little shit

Frankie I Love you really I do
with all my heart Do you
love me

Quit drinking son

You talk like you work on a boat

You talk like a queer
sometimes

Let me smell your finger

Did you and one Billy Richard Willet
steal the undertaker's pick-up
break into the Junior prom drunk
and thereby commence to dance together
like Russians on the gymnasium floor
boots and cleats and all or not

Can't you run over one measly guard
Put your heart in it

Bull

Do you want me to tell her father
about you two and the Drive Inn

Had enough yet

You're no more eighteen than the man
in the moon

I just felt sorry for you because you didn't have any folks

Go in peace[191]

And so on. Not only are these snippets of realistic dialogue directly related to actual Mountain Home life—girls, alcohol, the movies, the lake, Bill Willett, work as a fishing and boat guide—but the poem's vernacular highlights Stanford's ear for the language of daily life. It is Whitman's street talk, but in this case the high schooler's version. Critics have often called Stanford's poems "visionary," as in way out there. In an interview Frank clarified that while "the visionary life is commonplace for the poet," the elements of that vision have "nothing to do with a necessarily transcendent experience." For the kind of poet he was becoming, being a visionary involved "the hair on his head, the pain in his rotting teeth"[192]—in other words, the ordinary, often unattractive stuff of everyday life made into something extraordinary, which is precisely what Frank is figuring out how to do here as a ninth and tenth grader.

Another Blue Yodel poem, this one untitled, offers other images that confirm the Mountain Home connection, further suggesting that Frank was actively writing poems—or at least embryonic versions of them—in 1963 and 1964. "Thomas Merton has come to my lake to weep to drink," he wrote, referring to a writer he was starting to read and admire. Willett confirmed that he and Frank began to drink alcohol in Mountain Home, a habit echoed in Frank's line, "I partook of cold biscuits and blue Phoenix wine at a very tender age." To see the moon, he noted, "[a]ll you have to do is look out on my lake."[193] And, tellingly given his habit of secrecy, Stanford noted: "I hid books of poetry."[194] Although Stanford would later note that "[e]verything I wrote after '64 is capable of going it alone" but "[t]he earlier stuff can't feign for itself," there seems little doubt that this "earlier stuff" was for real.[195] Stanford was a preternaturally young talent. But, as he confessed in "The Mind Reader," "the truth was kept in a shut mouth."[196]

## "I Practiced the *Katas* of Poetry"

Also noteworthy is the innocence of this early writing. Because his poetic sensibility emerged at such a young age and because he was writing about the most commonplace aspects of everyday existence in Mountain Home, Arkansas, Stanford did not experience the self-awareness of being "a poet." His poetic mentality reflected Rilke's advice that, for the poet to succeed, "he must always remain unconscious, unaware of his best virtues, if he does not want to rob them of their candor and innocence!"[197] Despite becoming well read in the classics, Frank was a stranger to contemporary poetic creeds and schools. During the Mountain Home years, he wrote poetry without a preconceived idea of what a poem written by a contemporary poet was supposed to sound like. A gift of childhood was that he was largely ignorant of trends. Through an extraordinary attentiveness to everyday life, he turned daily experience into poetic expression informed by a sense of place and a grounding less in poetry than classical literature. But, in part because he wrote in secret, there was nothing affected about what he turned out. When he was writing in the late 1960s and early 1970s, when he was more conscious of being a poet, he actively worked to avoid the sense that he was consciously writing poems. He strove to recover that sacred perspective of innocence that had fueled him as a child.

His early poems demonstrate qualities essential to a poetic vision that would mature over the next decade. They seem comfortable with a lack of closure and a sense of infinite possibility—qualities that he would later identify as coming from being in "the flux of things,"[198] a realm swirling with multivalent potential. One reads these fragments and yodels with the sense that had he taken one more step, revised one more turn, added the thinnest sheen of polish, or even just stepped back and thought too much, he'd have ruined them. His best work exists in a balance between the raw and refined. That balance reflects how a person yet to be burdened by the responsibilities of adulthood might exist in the world and, having an ability to articulate the elusive core of that perspective, transform it into poetry.

Besides this instinct, one that was deeply connected to his early experiences as a kid in Mountain Home and his extensive reading habit, a couple of other defining elements of his work appear in nascent form during these Mountain Home years. The physicality of Stanford's early poems is unavoidable, and it reflects his commitment to karate, which he returned to right after moving to Mountain Home in 1961. Father Fuhrmann was exaggerating when he said that Frank arrived at Subiaco in 1964 as a black belt, but there is no doubt that Frank thrived in the sport that he would practice and teach into young adulthood. Willett noted that "he was an absolutely fantastic karate man."[199] Ruth recalled how in Mountain Home "he did karate all the time, and he'd throw up a board and crack it in front of me, you know, scare me half to death."[200]

Frank was explicit about the influence of karate on his poetry. "In my early days," he wrote, "I was a student of all forms. I learned everything and nothing. I practiced the *Katas* of poetry."[201] An undated poem is titled "Kata at Dawn on the Cliff by the Lake."[202] A word of Japanese origin, "kata," meaning "form," refers to a pattern of movement in the martial arts designed to imbue choreographed moves with a naturalistic flow. It is as if you are writing with your body but doing so in a way that seems simultaneously intentional and instinctive. A kata is also meant to be practiced alone, primarily to foster meditation on form. In these ways, it's not a bad metaphor for a Stanford poem. In an interview Stanford touched on the kata of his poetry, albeit with a different metaphor: "What I want to do is use movement and rhythm on different levels. I want it to be like the reader was going into reading the poem as they were going for a boat ride in some swift water, and each layer of the poem was a different thing you had to do. One was the river and one was his use of the paddle."²⁰³

Stanford merges his early interests in karate and poetry in "The Mind Reader." "[T]hey make me train with my Sensei to fight like Bujin," he writes, using a term that refers to a martial god. "I am the samurai kneeling beside the still water," he writes, adding:

> my favorite strangle is the Hadakajime the naked choke
> my favorite throw is Ukigoshi the floating hip
> I'm built for Haraigoshi the sweeping loin
> I dream about Japanese warriors²⁰⁴

At the time Frank had hanging in his bedroom, as his sister recalled, a picture of a judo master.²⁰⁵

Friends recollect Stanford's interest not only in karate (and later judo) per se but also in the sense of mental control the sport nurtured in him. Frank studied karate, according to Willett, "because of the meditative aspects."²⁰⁶ For all his happy-go-lucky moments in Mountain Home, Frank's ability to focus was unnervingly intense. A Mountain Home classmate conveys one example of Frank's trancelike concentration, or at least the macabre result of it. It happened with four boys, Frank and a few friends, out on the lake, in Frank's boat, fishing. When one of them landed a trout, Frank turned to him and, with a hard look on his face, said that he would bite the head off it if his friend would do the same with the next fish they caught. Frank then proceeded to chomp off the fish's head, as coolly as if he were biting into a corn dog. Much to the boy's relief, no more fish were caught that day.²⁰⁷

One might think that such a stunt would require unusual focus, the kind that takes you into an altered state of consciousness. During Frank's time in Mountain Home, he and Willett became interested in pursuing out-of-body experiences. It was a youthful quest for heightened consciousness and an expanded sense of reality that Frank would pursue well into the 1970s. The only mind-altering substance to which he and Willett had access to in Mountain Home was alcohol, which dulled the mind as opposed to heightening it. But interest in the occult brought the men closer to something like astral projection. According to the Stanford scholar Carl Launius, both Frank and Bill "came to believe in the basic concepts of . . . separate planes of existence, the passage of the self from one plane to another, and the self's transcendence of the body manifested in out-of-body experiences."²⁰⁸ In *The Battlefield*, Francis may be experiencing an astral projection when, during one dream sequence, he says, "I glide past it all I forget to ask questions" (1842). He's definitely engaging in some sort of astral phenomenon when he thinks:

> it was like it wasn't even me maybe I was living a part of somebody else's life
> the men at the college told me about how a person even if he's dead can be
> somewhere else that he wants to be I believe this has happened to me before
> (3276–78)

Linking the desire to be "somewhere else" with judo, Willett said, "Frank voyaged into the subconscious.... That's also why he studied karate."[209]

This pursuit might have been as innocent as "light-as-a feather-stiff-as-a-board" levitation experiments, but the quest to cede consciousness to the occult, the desire to exist in a mental state that defied normality, foreshadowed Frank's assessment that "I can sustain my attention too long, thereby being spellbound or overwhelmed."[210] Likewise did it foreshadow a psychiatrist's claim in 1972 that "there is an impression that this patient then concentrates and appears to be in some type of a daydreaming state."[211] Much of Frank's later poetry seems to have been written in a full-on trancelike state. He pursued literature, film, and the occult because of the freedom they offered him to experience reality from other angles than the obvious, default state of consciousness. As one scholar has explained, Frank sought "the poetry of being awake and asleep at the same time."[212] This habit solidified in the nutshell of Mountain Home.

ON AUGUST 29, 1963, Albert Franklin Stanford, Frank's adoptive father and Dorothy's husband of more than a decade, died of kidney failure at seventy-eight.[213] Dorothy, now fifty-one, retained ownership of the house but little else as Frank Sr. had had a previous family to whom he'd left the rest of his estate.[214] Writing to Dorothy the day after Frank Sr.'s death, Sister Louise Joseph, a nun from Kentucky with whom Dorothy corresponded, said, "Please give my love to Ruth and Frank and tell them how sorry I am about their daddy. Even though he had been ill for a long time, they will miss him—especially Frank."[215]

This was true. Frank admired his father. He said in a later interview, "His silence was inspiring, his truth, his word. He hardly ever signed his name on anything.... He didn't have to." Frank remembered Albert

Franklin Stanford standing "six foot two and bone and muscle—sinews ... like an Indian or something."[216] Nearly a decade after his father's death, Frank saw a psychiatrist who reported that "he saw his father die as an invalid after a long sickness and he sometimes has the feeling of a breakdown in his internal organs."[217] Beginning, one suspects, with his heart.

Frank wide awake in class at Subiaco Academy, 1965.
*Photo courtesy of Fr. Jerome Kodell.*

FIVE

# "Subiaco's Unofficial Poet Laureate"

## 1964–1966

WHEN FRANK SR. DIED, FRANK might have been upset, but his mother was totally overwhelmed. "I have," she said, "two children, I have a home to keep, [and now] I have to go to work. . . . I'm not going to be able to take this."[1] But as usual, she composed herself, concocted a plan, and executed it. As was often the case with Dorothy, with certain amount of deception and strategizing, it worked. Her point of contact was the man whom Frank had taught to water-ski about a year earlier, Father Nicholas Fuhrmann, and, beyond him, the institution he represented: Subiaco Academy, a Catholic boarding school located three hours southwest of Mountain Home.

Frank would likely never have gotten into Subiaco on his own merits. His grades at Mountain Home High School were mediocre at best.[2] Subiaco, moreover, almost never accepted students after their sophomore year (preferring a full four years to groom neophytes into real men). Part one of Dorothy's plan thus involved a well-timed religious conversion. Matters of faith were never formally observed in the Stanford household, but back on May 14, 1961, Frank had been confirmed as an Episcopalian at Memphis's All Saints' Episcopal Church.[3] After Frank met Father Fuhrmann, Dorothy had gotten to know him too, as well as several other Subiaco monks. She came to know them because they had benefited from Frank's skiing instruction. (Father Jerome Kodell recalls how "Frank helped some of us make our first efforts at waterskiing.")[4] Impressed with the monks' earnest commitment to education, not to mention their genuine sympathy for her and her family after Frank Sr.'s death, Dorothy—dragging Frank and Ruth into the deal—converted to Catholicism sometime in late 1963 or early 1964. Fuhrmann conceded that Frank became Catholic just "to please his mother."[5] Bill Willett added that the only positive impact Catholicism had on Frank was that it permitted him to eat more fish, his favorite food.[6] Nonetheless, it was a fact: Frank was a Catholic.

Dorothy found genuine comfort in the company of the priests. "She told me that the example of the Subiaco monks took her from the Episcopal to the Catholic," Fuhrmann recalled, noting that two priests especially impressed her: Father Raymond and Father Finton. "They were like Peter and Paul coming through my door," Dorothy told him.[7] In August 1964, with the family officially Catholic, Dorothy signed over Frank's Episcopal confirmation Bible to Joan Williams's kids, writing, "With all my love and prayers—that this will mean as much to you as it did to Frank."[8] The claim that the Bible meant a lot to Frank was, except as it applied to the Old Testament, dubious at best.

Part two was for Ruth and Frank to apply to Catholic boarding schools. Ruth, two years behind Frank in school, was easily accepted at St. Scholastica Monastery, a high school for girls in Fort Smith. Unlike her brother, Ruth was a stellar student, earning almost all As in junior high school and bringing home excellent behavior reports.[9] Still, she and her mother were like fire and gasoline: "Ruth has been simply *awful*," Dorothy wrote to one of the Subiaco priests—so awful that Dorothy did not feel she could handle her adopted daughter on her own.[10] "I think Dorothy wanted to get Ruth into a [boarding] school because she was a little bit wild in the early age," Willett said.[11] Ruth's rebellion was conventional and innocuous, but Dorothy made her quit her evening job at a local restaurant called the Kettle because, after work, she was "riding around town," a euphemism for spending unchaperoned time with boys.[12] A nun in whom Dorothy confided her frustrations assured her that "Ruth must be like most teenagers, just a bit rebellious and feeling that she knows much, when there is still much for her to learn."[13] Under the circumstances, she would soon do her learning on the Arkansas-Oklahoma border at St. Scholastica, where her grades would continue to shine.

Frank's Subiaco application needed a harder sell. After describing her son's status as an all-star Little League baseball player in Memphis and then an ace footballer in Mountain Home—and an accomplished water-skier and fishing guide to boot—she resorted to a further level of hyperbole. In response to the question "Why does the applicant wish to attend the academy?" she wrote, "We are hoping that his recent interest in the priesthood can be intensified." She submitted Frank's application on June 8, 1964.[14] Three weeks later he was accepted.

The third and final step was for Dorothy to get an income and, ideally, stay near her kids, especially Frank. "We are so happy that Francis' application has been approved," she wrote to Father Benno Schluterman three days after receiving the acceptance letter. She was comforted that both Frank and Ruth "will receive the Catholic education they so badly need." Then she made a move that altered the rest of her life: She opened her home to the monks. She continued in her letter to Schluterman, "Frank met Father Nicklas [sic] at Cranfield boat dock last year. We live right on the lake—the last house on Mallard Point—have plenty of room, and the welcome mat will always be out for anyone from Subiaco!" Dorothy was emphatic about this invitation: "Come up for fishing, boating, skiing any time."[15] The brethren came, routinely retreating to Mallard Point for rest and relaxation from the rigors of the abbey, which was attached to the academy.

During these visits, in addition to enjoying Dorothy's first-rate cooking, the monks came to appreciate the difficultly of her domestic situation. She let them know that, after taking her kids to boarding school in late August of 1964, she would return home to an empty house, no job, and a stack of medical bills. She made sure to inform them about her past work experience at Sears and Firestone and as a restaurant manager. She had recently completed a course in hotel management, a fact she also freely advertised. Perhaps channeling Sister Joseph's advice to "ask and you shall receive," Dorothy sold herself to the monks.[16] "She presented herself to the monks as head of a family in flux," recalled a friend of Frank's who got to know Dorothy in 1970, "and they presented to her a solution."[17]

The monks adored Dorothy. "I admired his Southern Belle mother from the beginning," Father Fuhrmann said of her.[18] When she dropped off Frank at school for orientation in the summer of 1964, Father Herbert, a man with whom Dorothy would become very close, offered her a job directing Coury House, the retreat center located on campus. She initially declined, but when she arrived back in Mallard Point and walked into a large empty house and looked at all the medical bills, she changed her mind and was on campus reporting to work a few days later.[19] "Now," she wrote to Father Schluterman, "I am at peace."[20] And she exclaimed: "This is going to be wonderful."[21]

## "We Hit It Off...."

Dorothy and Frank arrived at Subiaco in late August 1964 with the usual Stanfordian flash. Noting how Frank's arrival to campus alongside his mother had the potential to make him seem like a "momma's boy," classmate Leo Lensing remembered how Frank's "stylish clothes" and Dorothy's "cultured demeanor" epitomized "what passed back then for southern refinement." Another fellow student saw Frank arrive and immediately thought: *Mississippi aristocracy*.[22] Here was a young man, as another classmate put it, on his way to becoming "the most authoritative fashion critic on campus." There was no overlooking the careful attention to refinement.[23] The mama's boy image never stuck. Frank, if only by appearance, came off as mysterious and cool.[24] With 265 other boys, he started classes on August 31, 1964.[25]

Frank initially played up his obvious athleticism. "He did not want to be different," Father Fuhrmann said, "he wanted to be part of student life," and sports was an easy way to blend in.[26] Supported by his commanding physical presence, he made the B team in football (he could not play varsity because of an obscure rule of the Arkansas Athletic Association about transfer students).[27] Although his mother remembered him as the perpetual "star on the football team," Frank, praised by his coach as potentially "a superb defensive tackle," was yet again anything but a gridiron standout. "Frank did not care for organized sport," Fuhrmann recalled. "He went out for football to be normal but team sports had no appeal."[28] Fuhrmann added that Frank "wanted to have everything perfect and this was hard to pull off with ten other teammates."[29]

Perhaps because he had gotten to know Frank before he came to Subiaco, and remembered him primarily as an athletic kid, Father Fuhrmann took special interest in Frank's athletic pursuits. "We hit it off together.... He had quite the physique," Fuhrmann said, "and was as strong as he looked."[30] Even before Fuhrmann really got to know Frank, he remembered how "I sensed an exceptional person."[31] Fuhrmann was (at least in 1964) the right monk to have in your corner. He was widely admired by students. One student recalled how he "combined an appreciation in classic literature with outdoors activity."[32] Handsome, popular, rugged, and gregarious, Fuhrmann was deeply involved in every aspect of student life. In addition to being head prefect, dean of men, the faculty advisor for the *Periscope*, and a popular English literature teacher, Fuhrmann was the priest most willing to take kids swimming at nearby Lake Dardanelle, go frog gigging with a few seniors at midnight, haul students to a movie theater in Fort

Smith, purchase a parachute that students could hook behind a car and fly through the sky, or serve as "custodian of the pool." But more than any other activity, Father Fuhrmann was known for serving as Subiaco's legendary boxing coach. It was a distinction that was even acknowledged in a 1966 *Sports Illustrated* article.[33] As early as 1948, when Fuhrmann began at Subiaco as a student, he was committed to boxing, declaring it his life's goal to be "world's heavyweight champ."[34] His classmates nicknamed him "killer."

It did not take long for Fuhrmann, who had taken teams to Golden Gloves competitions throughout Arkansas, Oklahoma, and Missouri, to get Frank into the ring. Frank agreed to attend sparring sessions so long as his new friend Bill Monie (from Greenville, Mississippi) came along. According to Fuhrmann, for whom recruitment was serious business, Stanford and Monie goofed off a bit, "pulling punches and joking with each other."[35] In his study of Stanford's time at Subiaco, Leo A. Lensing recounts what happened next: "Fuhrmann intervened, upbraided Frank for dropping his guard, and then put on the gloves himself. Frank was hesitant to go at the priest he so admired, dropped his guard again, and was laid out with a left hook." Monie, who got his own comeuppance (with an uppercut) a few minutes later, recalled that Frank, after his time in the ring with Fuhrmann, "could see the end of his toes" and that he himself was also soon "on his back looking up." Even from this humbling perspective, they admired Fuhrmann for "teaching pugilism by example."[36] Although not enough to join the boxing team.

## Bushido at Subiaco

Frank had another plan. By his second semester, the catchy phrase "judo at Subiaco" was already synonymous with Frank Stanford. He not only excelled at the sport, which he had been introduced to while learning karate in Memphis, but he built the entire Subiaco program from scratch. Fuhrmann approved the team in the late fall of 1964, giving it practice space, workout mats, and enthusiastic coverage in *The Periscope*, the school paper he headed. But Frank—who was alternatively called by his peers "Coach," "Captain," "Instructor," and "President"—single-handedly got the sport off the ground. Teammate Ron Maggio, who praised Frank's organizational skills, remembers the initial planning meeting, which included Maggio, Stanford, and Monie. After "a very long discussion" late into the evening, the three settled on a plan to popularize judo. Maggio recalled, "Frank did all the requesting for permission from the school, the Judo Society, etc. to

"Coach" Stanford (*top right*) with his team, Spring 1965. *The Pax,* yearbook, 1965, Subiaco Abbey and Academy Collection, Arkansas State Archives, Little Rock, AR. *Photo courtesy of Fr. Jerome Kodell.*

make the club happen. . . . Somehow, he made it all happen."[37] More than fifty years later, Father Kodell, reflecting on Frank's time at "Subi," remembered that he "was best known on campus as head of the judo club."[38]

Stanford's recruitment methods were savvy. Subiaco turned a blind eye to hazing, most of it leveled against terrified freshmen. Emmett Hawkins, a classmate of Frank's, remembered how there was "a whole lot of what we now call harassment and hazing."[39] Freshman Martin Pendergrast got roughed up within a day of his arrival in the fall of 1966.[40] But Frank conspicuously avoided participating in these bullying rituals. Omar Greene, who entered Subiaco as a freshman when Stanford was a senior, said that although Frank was "a formidable person physically" and well known as "captain of the judo team," "he never bullied or hazed underclassmen."[41] Maggio recalls being shocked that Stanford so casually welcomed him into an "upperclassman's room"—a taboo move for most juniors and seniors—and was kind to him.[42] Frank, Greene recalled, was "like a big brother" to many of the underclassmen who were picked on.[43] Pendergrast similarly recalls how, after he got pushed around, Frank, wearing his judo outfit, stopped him in the hall and asked if he wanted to join the judo team. "If he saw somebody bullying someone else, he would in turn bully them," Greene said. In one instance, Frank approached a well-known class bully, asked him for a drag on his cigarette, and, acting as if he were going to smoke it, broke the cigarette in two. As the kid stood there in shock, Frank said in a mocking voice, "Oh, I'm so sorry." Because of Frank's stocky, muscular stature, Pendergrast said, "there was nothing the kid could do."[44]

Frank's defense of hazed underclassmen typically preceded the suggestion that, should they ever want to defend themselves on their own, they could do worse than master a judo throw. Kevin Griesemer, all 108 pounds of him, was persuaded to join the team through Frank's appeal to self-defense.[45] At 180 pounds of pure muscle, Frank exuded the physical confidence his classmates envied. The *Periscope*, in a playful jab at Stanford, joked how when "the captain and instructor of Subi's judo team" was asked if "he could really kill a person with his little finger," he usually responded by "breaking your neck in two or three places."[46] Stanford's appeal to the picked on thus helped bolster enrollment on the judo team, enrollment that the paper accurately predicted was "expected to rise after football season."[47] Greene, who chose boxing instead of judo, remembered that Frank would demonstrate the benefits of judo by randomly "karate chopping several monastery roof tiles with one blow."[48]

Frank did not only all the recruiting but the training as well. "He was a teacher," Father Fuhrmann recalled about Frank's role on the team.[49] And a good one. Before the first season, Stanford, to stoke enthusiasm and instruct his team, arranged for judoists from Fort Smith Northside High School to visit Subiaco and offer demonstrations. A *Periscope* article reported the event, noting how "sports-minded students of Subiaco Academy were given their first taste of judo." Accompanying the article was a picture of a robed judoist torpedoing another one into a mat. Frank stands in the background, arms crossed and head slightly craned to examine the move's execution. The report added that "the club's membership now stands at ten" and that "Coach Stanford hopes to ready the boys for competition with other schools in the near future."[50] The team's first match was in April, just four months after the team formed. To prepare, Frank oversaw three intense workouts a week and conducted a daily randori, a kind of sparring exercise, for anyone interested in additional practice.[51]

The initial judo meet was against the same team that had come to Subiaco to instruct Stanford's newbies back in January. Remarkably, Coach Stanford led his team to victory—two trophies and ten medals—over a much more seasoned squad. It was a clear upset. Frank and Ron Maggio took first in their divisions. After this auspicious start, the *Periscope* reported, "The Subi judokas are hoping to make their team even bigger and better." Not only did the team grow, but, as Bill Monie remembers, they also traveled all over the South during their second year, with Stanford winning nearly every event he entered at the 180-pound level and Monie having occasional success in the 200-pound division. The school paper was somewhat in awe of the fact that "the purpose of the meet was to acquaint new club members with judo techniques," but then they went out and won the thing.[52] Perhaps more than any event during his first year at Subiaco, the stunning defeat of Fort Smith Northside High School shaped Frank's reputation among his peers.

But judo was much more than a physical activity. Frank's commitment to the sport was inseparable from his emerging literary interest in the Japanese warrior tradition. This interest was both an extension and refinement of the poetic katas he'd begun practicing in Mountain Home. In "The Mind Reader," he writes, "I dream about Japanese warriors."[53] It's an influence on Stanford's persona and poetry that's easy to miss, even for those who became closest to him. In a letter C. D. Wright wrote to a friend after Frank's death, she mentioned the obvious influences on his work—European filmmakers, jazz musicians, *Beowulf*, *Sir Gawain*, French and Spanish surrealists, Chaucer, Whitman. But then she remembered how "he was disappointed when he asked me to name off specific influences and I didn't name" a single figure "from Japanese and Chinese literature." These figures were, she added, "hardly foreign to him."[54]

Fellow student Martin Pendergrast recalled Stanford's focus on judo being more philosophical than physical. "He had all kinds of books on the martial arts," he said, "like Tai Chi and ancient Japanese martial arts." And while everyone knew that Stanford "ran the judo team," what stood out the most to his classmates was that he "*studied* karate."[55] Pendergrast noted how Frank taught him "how to do an honor-based vipassana meditation," a Buddhist exercise designed to sharpen insight into an expanded consciousness. Another classmate confirmed that Stanford spent considerable time exploring Zen Buddhism. Yet another recalled a "hefty volume about Buddhism on his bookshelf."[56] The scholar Murray Shugars writes that Stanford was "regularly practicing Zen meditation."[57] He also kept on his shelf a book by Masutatasu Oyama (the founder of full-contact karate) and poetry volumes written by Edo-era samurai warriors.[58]

Grounding Stanford's interest in the martial arts was a more formal commitment to the honor-based samurai code known as Bushido. In "The Mind Reader," which teems with warrior imagery, Stanford refers to "the blessing at sea of the blind warriors the Bushido."[59] It was an interest initiated in Mountain Home and developed at Subiaco but, as Shugars explains, one that would later come to "underli[e] the poetical ethics of *Battlefield*."[60]

According to Inazo Nitobe, author of *Bushido: The Soul of Japan*, Bushido requires a warrior to "face all calamities and adversities with patience and a pure conscience."[61] In *The Battlefield*, Stanford writes early in the poem, "I know there was one Inazo Nitobe" (287). One friend who knew Stanford in the mid-1970s recalls a man who "was absolutely unflappable and knew that everything would pass—nothing seemed to bother him."[62] He was no doubt witnessing a demeanor consciously informed by Frank's focus on Bushido at Subiaco. Bushido is an ethical system demanding the cultivation of courage, self-control, defense of tradition, and fearlessness (or even comfort) in the face of death. In *Zen Buddhism and Its Influence on Japanese Culture* (now published as *Zen and Japanese Culture*), Daisetz Suzuki—a twentieth-century Zen master whom Stanford explicitly cited as shaping his thought—clarifies this last notion, stressing "the samurai's readiness to give his life away at any moment." But again in a reference to a thoroughly Stanfordian quality, he adds that any quest for vengeance in the name of justice (essential to the warrior tradition) requires the warrior "to keep himself away from the public eye."[63]

Moreover, and especially significant given Stanford's reliance on dreams to fuel his poetic vision, the well-trained Bushido warrior attains his superlative qualities by accessing the unconscious. "When the unconscious is tapped," writes Suzuki, "it rises above individual limitations."[64] The master notes how "no great work has ever been accomplished without going mad," an exceptional experience he describes as "breaking through the ordinary level of consciousness and letting loose the hidden powers lying further below."[65] Frank, who would later concede that "it's a delightful situation . . . when you can comprehend and fathom your own madness," had been working to access the subconscious since his Mountain Home days with Bill Willett.[66] Stanford would later reference Suzuki to explain in his only published essay that the quest to access the unconscious "is a good way of sending the poet on a wild goose chase—which he may need from time to time."[67]

In this essay, which came out a year before he died, Stanford leaves little doubt about the role the Japanese warrior tradition played in his poetic sensibilities, especially when it comes to death. Paraphrasing a passage from Suzuki's *Zen Buddhism and Its Influence on Japanese Culture*, he doctors the text to blend the poet and the samurai into the same heroic figure who stares death into submission and seeks vengeance against cravenness and corruption. The original Suzuki sentence reads "When I was still a boy, the thought came upon me that as a samurai I ought to in no circumstances be afraid of death";[68] Stanford's paraphrase of it reads,

"When I was still a boy and writing my poems, the thought came upon me that as a poet I ought to in no circumstances be afraid of death."[69] Thus Bushido and poetry started to merge at Subiaco.

This blend of the Bushido warrior and the crusading poet prevails throughout *The Battlefield*. Sometimes it is explicit ("I know the swordsman Miyamoto Mushashi / . . . / I know the disgrace and death of Lord Asano . . ." [246, 249]) and at other times implicit (as in Francis's honor-based pursuit of vengeance against prejudiced "peckerwoods"). Either way, the judo team that Frank founded at Subiaco became an extension of an ethical foundation that both honored the Bushido tradition and integrated it into his poetic and personal identity, which was maturing in the halls of Subiaco. As if to reiterate the indistinguishability of the poet and poem, Stanford wrote, just after a discussion of katas: "The poem eats when it is hungry, sleeps when it is tired."[70]

## "He Was a Product of the Deep South, Brother"

For all of Stanford's adherence to judo and Bushido, there was no emperor to worship in Arkansas. Frank unfortunately found an easy parallel to the Bushido tradition in another set of obligations and attitudes rooted in soil long tilled by his mother: the Old South. "He had a rebel flag in his dorm room," Mississippian Bill Monie remembered. "He had that thing the whole time we were there."[71] Another classmate confirms that Frank indeed "put a big Confederate flag on the wall of his room."[72] Others recall that he took the big flag down at some point and replaced it with a small one on his desk.[73] Either way, it was a marker of a perceived identity and code, one reiterated by the Confederate soldiers cap he sometimes wore around campus. When Stanford arrived at Subiaco, he was known as the new kid from Mountain Home, but when he left, he did so as a rebel-yelling Mississippian who yearned for the land of cotton. His yearbooks reflect this shift in attitude. In 1965, he noted that he was from Mountain Home, Arkansas. In 1966, he changed it to Greenville, Mississippi. If misleading, this association at least came from an honest admiration for the place. Years later he said of the city, "I love it. . . I love the people of Greenville."[74] But the Greenville label also appealed because it was a bit more way down yonder in the land of cotton. Bill Monie said in 1998, "He was a product of the deep South, brother." A true son of the Confederacy.[75] Frank, in other words, was taking on the Lost Cause his mother had always wanted him to embrace.

Frank Stanford, in a Confederate cap, and Bill Lux, Subiaco Academy, March 1966. *Photo by John Coller. Photo courtesy of John Coller.*

Assuming the Old South trope was an easy and appealing default move for Stanford. It was easy because, as we've seen, he was thoroughly raised to think that way. His mother vocally supported a racial order that Greenville's elite espoused as essential to tradition and honor. Her loyalty to the Lost Cause, fueled by a visceral hatred of Lincoln and Sherman, certainly influenced Frank's defense of southern identity. "He read a lot about the Civil War," Monie later recalled, noting how "we'd swap books between us" about it.[76] That event, or at least his "War of Northern Aggression" version of it, allowed Stanford to see southern history as a decline from a once-noble tradition, one that was infused with codes, expectations, and hierarchies that mirrored the Bushido tradition he valorized.

Classmate Leo Lensing's yearbook, signed by Frank in May 1966, confirms Stanford's conflation of the Bushido and Cavalier mentalities. Lensing, the class valedictorian, from Lake Providence, Louisiana, was off to the University of Notre Dame. This destination piqued Frank's attention, and he advised, with some jest, his fellow southerner to "please retain a bit of your southern heritage as you venture off to Yankee land and join the Irish." His sign-off declared, "Farewell and the ocean of breath is below my navel"—a common phrase used in Zen Buddhist breathing rituals. In another classmate's yearbook Frank further affirmed his loyalty to the Old South, warning the student to "watch out for those lefties in Calif" before signing off with "For a return to the ideals of Robert E. Lee." In such ways Stanford, according to Lensing, "remained infatuated with the South and its misbegotten mythology."[77] Fuhrmann, who tended to be forgiving of Frank's identification with the Confederacy, allowed with an eyeroll that Frank indeed "fancied himself a southern gentleman."[78]

Playing the role of the stalwart Cavalier lurking in a bastion of progressivism further appealed to Frank because, as one classmate put it, he had "a proclivity for baiting folks."[79] The United States was in the middle of the civil rights movement. The monks, for their part, knew which side of history they wanted Subiaco to be on. As Emmett Hawkins, the only Black student in the class of 1966, put it, "They were caught up in the culture of what was going on"—in other words, they were "with it."[80] According to Father Jerome Kodell, Subiaco was ahead of the curve when it came to interpreting the "deliberate speed" of integration, with "the monks having decided during the 1950s to admit black students."[81] Father Fuhrmann was on board as well with Subiaco's integration strategy, especially because it broadened the scope of his football recruitment prospects ("I asked our recruiter to get some colored boarders before Faubus stood in the Central High doorway").[82] Whatever the motive, the monks were adamant that students take racial justice seriously. To further this aim, they updated their Christian Doctrine course to promote civil rights. Following the model of Friendship House, a Catholic group that aimed to improve race relations nationally, the monks initiated a program of "interracial home visits to five negro families in Pine Bluff, and seven in Fort Smith."[83] In many other ways—open debates on the civil rights bill, visits to Little Rock to hear civil rights speakers, and a "States Race Relations Weekend"—the monks stayed attuned to civil rights and racial equality, pushing an unusually progressive agenda, to which most students responded positively.

But not Stanford. "Frank challenged this with his usual vigor," a fellow student recalled.[84] To what extent Frank's offensive declarations were the actions of a provocateur or a racist is not entirely clear and arguably debatable. But when former students later learned about *The Battlefield*'s commitment to racial equality, they noted that this was not the Frank they'd known at Subiaco.[85] Virtually every interviewed classmate of Frank's recalled his racism as being clearly pronounced. Phrases such as "flaming racist" abound.[86] Even Bill Monie, whose immersion in southern norms was so deep that students called him "Colonel," had to admit that Stanford "had a tad of racism in him."[87]

Father Fuhrmann wondered if "his anti-black style" was little more than "a satire," an attempt to mock "what you hear on the redneck circuit."[88] One incident, corroborated by three classmates, suggests that Frank's offensive racial views were no act. It involved a classroom interaction Stanford had with Emmett Hawkins, the one Black student in the class. As one witness remembers it, "Our teacher was doing a very good job discussing race relations. . . . No matter the color of your skin we are all human beings, we are all beautiful in the sight of God, and so on." But in the middle of this lecture, "Frank stood up in class and said, 'Excuse me, Father, let me make a point here.'" Standing next to Hawkins, he said, "How can you say that? Look at the hair. Look at the lips. Look at the color of the skin. Are you saying that we're the same?"[89] Another student who was in the classroom at the time recalls this performance as "excruciating" to observe.[90] Another explained how "we just sat there and listened, and I think most people were shocked at what was happening." In retrospect this student was "horrified" that he did not speak out against such "oratory." But in the moment, "we were all like, *Whoa.*"[91]

Hawkins, for his part, was hardly surprised. He never "batted an eye," students remembered.[92] Racial prejudice was in the air that Hawkins breathed, and he was all too used to it. As a freshman from Memphis, he'd been welcomed to Subiaco by a senior who told him he had no business being there and, for the rest of the year, verbally harassed him for it. On trips to Fort Smith, he often had to wait in the van when the class went into restaurants.[93] Another Black student, a 110-pound freshman named

Freddy Lane, was slammed into a phone booth by all 200 pounds of Bill Monie for no apparent reason other than the obvious. It was, in short, generally not a hospitable environment for Hawkins and Lane. Monie and Stanford did not help. Stanford's "oratory" made overt what was otherwise pervasively implicit.

Hawkins remembered Stanford well. He recalled a student who belonged to a small clique of Mississippians who made zero effort to get to know him or include him in any school activities. Stanford, Monie, and one or two others would sit at their own lunch table, where Frank would regale them with so-called "Tyrone jokes." The group went out of its way to ostracize Hawkins and Lane.[94] By the standards of racism in the Deep South, Hawkins judged Frank to be "just like the normal guys of our era." He said, "I don't think it was cool at the time to associate with Blacks, so of course he didn't."[95] But another student sensed that Stanford's attitudes were so extreme that they "served to increase our sensitivity to what was happening."[96] If there was any direct justice to come for Frank's overt racism in high school, it came hard in late 1969, when Frank went back to Subiaco to referee the Golden Gloves competition for Father Fuhrmann. He asked to take a shot in the ring with a student who was 22–1 as a boxer. In a matter of seconds, Frank, yet again, was on his back looking at his toes.[97]

## "These Men ... Understand What I Say"

Fortunately, there were more beneficial influences on Frank during his Subiaco years. The monks stand out. It is impossible to overstate the lifelong impact that the monks had on Frank, but a scene toward the end of his life illuminates the depth of his connection to them. In May of 1978, just weeks before he died, Frank, sitting with his former teacher on the abbey steps, turned to Father Fuhrmann and said, "I wish I could believe like y'all do."[98] This was fifteen years after Frank had taught Fuhrmann to water-ski on Lake Norfork. Over the years, the two men had become as close as Frank would get to anyone. Fuhrmann remembered how, as they talked that afternoon, Frank stared at a statue of Saint Benedict. "I got convinced," Fuhrmann said, "that he did have death in his heart as we talked on the steps."[99]

Frank was not religious, but he never rejected the notion of an intense inner-directed spiritualism. Fuhrmann remembered thinking, as Frank lamented his inability to believe: *But he already does.*[100] It pained Dorothy

Father Nicholas Fuhrmann, dean of men, ca. 1965.
*Photo courtesy of Fr. Jerome Kodell.*

that Frank rejected Catholicism. Acting as if her children had disowned her, she complained to one of the priests in 1966 that "both Frank and Ruth refuse to go to mass." The topic was so sensitive between Frank and his mother that she added, "I don't dare talk to him about church."[101] But Fuhrmann always saw beyond Frank's refusal to openly worship. "He was just as spiritual as the monks were," Fuhrmann said. "He couldn't write that way if he wasn't."[102] Whereas some Christians adhere to the concept of being "born again," Fuhrmann observed that Catholics have a conversion experience known as the "Baptism of Desire." Frank, he insisted, "had made such a conversion."[103] To the "keen reader" of *The Battlefield*, Fuhrmann also said, "there exists a constant presence of a deeper spiritual presence."[104] Unlike Dorothy, Fuhrmann believed that this presence was ultimately more important to the state of Frank's soul than attending mass.

Frank understood that the monks' faith was radically distinct from his own. When asked if he ever considered becoming a monk, he got right to the point: "Chastity and obedience I can't handle—I wouldn't last long." But he also knew that the monks were fueled by a familiar passion and that they experienced, as he put it, "a longing for the world." Frank, even though he believed that "the muse and the holy spirit are similar," might have had zero interest in such a vocation, but the idea of a calling he understood.[105] His contemplative response to the Benedictine message effectively shaped the poet he would become, one who would later write, with his classmates in mind:

> When the rest of you
> Were being children
> I became a monk
> To my own listing
> Imagination.[106]

Few lines of poetry better capture Stanford's two-year tenure with the monks at Subiaco.

The monks also validated Frank's artistic passion. They did so by instilling in him the particularly Benedictine notion that inspiration derives from inward, prayerlike meditation. Frank's second wife recalled how he "appreciated their devotion to the spiritual path even though he did not share their belief." The monks were "brilliant and eccentric," she said, "so I can see how they would be important influences for him." Their devotion to God and work, she added, reflected Frank's own "devotion to art, which was in many ways quite similar."[107]

The monks also represented what a man could be, offering a stoic model that the fatherless Frank could only admire. The monastery's commitment to "man's need to toil" was evident in the monks growing their own vegetables, brewing their own beer, tending their own dairy, hunting their own game, managing their own swine, building their own workshops, and even operating their own printing press. Their autonomy confirmed a muscular pursuit that appealed to a manly Frank. So did their predilection for sanctioned violence (namely, boxing), more than occasional corporal punishment (smacks to the face, extended time on one's knees), and recreational risk-taking endeavors (parakiting behind a rapidly accelerating Buick!). The monks even left the door open to spiritual recklessness. Students were encouraged to contemplate "the temptations of nihilism and atheism, and the threat of despair."[108]

In his 1975 autobiographical film, *It Wasn't a Dream: It Was a Flood*, Stanford, pondering the monkish disposition, says: "The monks are dreamers and visionaries. Some of them are farmers, and some of them are linguists. Some of them are brilliant. Some of them are passionate, compassionate. Some of them are cruel. All in all, they're men who understand the spiritual life. They understand the vision."[109]

In an undated prose fragment Stanford elaborated on his affection for his teachers: "They all have either a masters degree or a doctorate from secular universities in America or Europe. They eat like pigs, they drink like fish, they work like dogs, they cuss like sailors, they dream like we all do."[110] Father Fuhrmann recalled how Frank got a kick out of the fact that Fuhrmann would climb the water tower on campus "carrying a tube of tools on my back to clean the inside." Stanford was even more taken with Brother Jerry's habit of climbing the tower, sitting on top of it, and playing the harmonica and accordion "to hail the countryside."[111] Such whimsy and eccentricity, Fuhrmann said, "grabbed Frank's imagination."[112] Assessing his relationship with the monks, Frank concluded: "I feel good in the company of these men."[113] He really did. Father Fuhrmann was emphatic that this feeling of comfort "was reciprocated by the monks," men who saw something unique in Frank and loved him deeply for it.[114]

Frank's two years at Subiaco thus offered the ideal environment for a convergence of interests that would allow him to expand the visions and voices that would turn him into a poet. Whereas Mountain Home required Frank to hide his literary ambitions behind more conventional boyhood activities, Subiaco permitted him to own, and even at times flaunt, the brilliant depth and idiosyncrasy of his literary passions. When Frank left Subiaco, he left as an emotionally mercurial but obsessed poet. The monks and the spiritual atmosphere they sustained had much to do with that artistic maturation. "I can relate my experience; I can tell them what I think, what I dream, what I feel," Stanford said. "All kinds of these men ... understand what I say, understand what I say."[115]

## "There Was Something Different about Frank"

If Frank entered Subiaco as a jock and a son of the South, these versions of himself were quickly subsumed by a more honest identity, one that the monks encouraged. It was a literary identity rooted in an eccentric intellectualism that was not only tolerated but, to an extent, even celebrated by his classmates. Within a year Frank was widely known, according to the school paper, as "the unofficial poet laureate of Subiaco."[116] He was also, as a classmate recalled, "an enigma," an offbeat guy who, while indulging in the occasional adolescent stunt, was more likely to stay quiet and retreat into the seclusion of a writing nook than join the crowd.[117] The Benedictine vision, the ambitions of his peers, and the culture of Subiaco in general accommodated the eccentric figure of the holy fool. Frank's was not a persona that lent itself to close friendships. But neither did it foster ostracism. Frank was liked, and at the same time, he had no single friend he could truly call close. Something about his demeanor kept him on the periphery of Subiaco's social circles, a lone wolf lost in a world of words.

Subiaco offered a trove of extracurricular options, but aside from judo, Frank steered clear of them. The "Extracurricular Activities" section on his transcript is largely empty. The two exceptions are an inaugural semester of B-team football and fourth place in a speech contest. His grades were decent but not distinguished. He scored Bs in Geometry, Spanish, and Bookkeeping; Cs in Chemistry; and As in Bible and English. He finished fifteenth out of fifty in his class with an 84.93 average, a clear underachievement given his intellectual aptitude (eighty-ninth to ninety-fourth percentile on the School and College Ability Test—a test that it is hard to imagine him taking seriously). His behavior was generally fine, earning a mark of "Satisfactory" every semester except one, when his transcript suffered an "Unsatisfactory" stamp because, as Father Bartholomew reported, "Frank deliberately broke a cue stick."[118] No doubt a karate move at work.

If Frank was indifferent to classes and extracurriculars, he was otherwise committed to a renewed regimen of reading and writing. The reading was largely in the epic-heroic and romantic genres, with a smattering of modernism in the mix. Subiaco students in the mid-1960s read Beowulf, Chaucer, Shakespeare, Wordsworth, *Sir Gawain and the Green Knight*, *Gilgamesh*, Milton, Coleridge, Keats, Hopkins, and Eliot—basically the classic English canon. Those interested in more modern novels and short stories might be introduced to Flannery O'Connor, Ernest Hemingway, and Graham Greene. Father Fuhrmann later recalled that Frank "read voraciously Faulkner, Steinbeck, and Hemingway."[119] Frank remembered that Father Nicholas "weeded my reading and gave me modern and contemporary works to read."[120] The weeding was sometimes censorious, with acceptable novels marked "OK."[121] *The Catcher in the Rye* did not get an "OK," but Frank not only read it but encouraged underclassmen to do so as well.[122]

Frank devoured literature at Subiaco. He memorized stretches of prose, reciting passages to anyone who'd listen, sometimes even delivering unsolicited recitations out of his dorm room window. He read Thomas Merton and ancient Japanese warrior poetry in the Bushido tradition, choices that influenced the voice and tone of "St. Francis and the Wolf." Father Fuhrmann, thrilled to encounter such a student, actively fostered Frank's literary pursuits.[123] In addition to being an impassioned teacher of literature, he allowed Frank to skip Physical Education and study hall to work on his poems. A roommate remembers how Frank "had a designated place to go to do his writing."[124] Later, Fuhrmann permitted seniors to stay up all night if they were quiet. Frank thus easily found the time to work regularly on his writing, often late into the evening, a habit he would never abandon. "I feel like I'm in a castle or something," he said about working at Subiaco.[125] "He must have done lots of his secret writing then," Fuhrmann recalled. "He was the most independent person I have ever met."[126]

Frank was not only reading intensely at Subiaco but also writing a lot of poetry. In 1972, when reviewing his literary output, Frank mentioned "several epic length prose poems" he did at Subiaco, "all or most of that written during 64–66." He recalled, "In one piece there was a character who found all these Middle Ages manuscripts in the walls of the monastery. He pawned them off on the literary world as his. That was funny."[127] One of Frank's classmates noted how Frank would read his poems aloud—again, often out of his dorm window. "We heard *a lot* of what he wrote," the classmate said, with a hint of exasperation, adding that Frank was at it "all the time."[128] "I did not understand any of it," another student admitted, but he certainly remembered Frank reading it.[129] Bill Monie, whom Frank perhaps spent the most social time with at Subiaco, remembered that "Frank only showed me short poems, stuff that he would write when he was supposed to be doing schoolwork in study hall." When Monie read them, which he did "to accommodate Frank more than anything else," he told him that "this is the goofiest stuff I've ever read in my life," a response to which Frank just laughed.[130] Sometimes, if Frank's reading aloud exhausted the patience of his peers, he'd get pelted with pillows. A classmate recalls: "Frank came by my dorm room in the old building at Subi when I was a senior, paying my roommate, Ron Wachsman (Fr. Nick's nephew) and me a visit. He left us a brief poem, written on the spot, which, damn my eyes, I lost. It was scotch taped to our ceiling for a spell. I remember the first and last line: 'There is spit dripping down the hot pipe. I done it. / I don't know why I do these things, I just do 'em.' "[131]

Roommate Martin Pendergrast remembered how Frank's desk was always piled with manuscripts on which he was working. All Pendergrast could say about the poetry was that it was "not rhymed." He recalled reading some of Frank's "early, goofy poems," noting that one of the last objects Frank removed from his dorm after graduation was "the big poem." He said that Frank took it to his mother's house and kept it on the kitchen table.[132] If nobody else appreciated Frank's poems at the time, at least he could appreciate them himself, which he sometimes did by tacking them to the ceiling of his dorm and reading them in bed.

While Stanford's classmates were excelling in team sports, editing the school paper, or scoring high marks to get on the coveted honor roll, Frank was spending much of his last two years in high school writing poetry that would become the foundation for his writing career. Stanford's classmates and teachers remembered him for a lot of reasons—his controversial racial views, his occasionally bizarre outbursts, his fetish for Mississippi and the Confederacy, his judo, his ability to be engaged and distant at once, his closeness with Father Fuhrmann, and his stratospheric intelligence. Frank himself synthesized these disparate tendencies into a pseudophilosophy he called "Stanfordism." It was an ideology he described in classmate Joe Saunders's yearbook as "a mixture of ultra conservatism, zen buddhism, constitutional liberalism and a bit of American insanity."[133] The self-assessment seems accurate enough.

But the mere freedom to publicly self-assess—to flaunt an eccentric, bookish disposition—was new for Frank, and it must have been extremely liberating. Whereas he had to keep his bibliophilia under wraps in Mountain Home, Subiaco's tolerance for intellectual showmanship allowed him to display, often swaggeringly so, his commitment to literature and writing.[134] "He was intellectually out of my league," said one classmate who would go on to become a professor of geoscience.[135] "He had a huge collection of books," confirmed another, who estimated Stanford's collection to have been in the hundreds. Frank was reading all the time, so much so that "he would walk around with two books in his hands, one in his pocket.... He just churned through all these types of books."[136]

At Subiaco there was no mystery about where the books came from. Frank had access to the school's stellar library. When Frank arrived in the fall of 1964, the *Periscope* ran an article about improvements to the library, noting how a couple of priests had done "a remarkable job in updating" it.[137] Little did the priests know that a transfer student from Mountain Home with a book addiction would soon start pilfering books from its inventory. Stanford was well placed to do so. With his mother living right off campus and working at the school's retreat center full-time, Frank was near campus when most students went home for the holidays and summer break. During these times he would enter the mail room, where books awaited cataloging, and walk off with whatever suited him. "He just filched whatever he wanted," said a classmate.[138] Years later, in a letter to a friend, Frank noted that the book he was reading on Keats had been stolen from Subiaco.[139] In *The Battlefield*, Francis's friend Billy the Jew, a largely undeveloped character based on Bill Willett, has an "idea to break into the Library / and read from the forbidden shelves until dawn" (14305-6).

Stanford was the last person at Subiaco seeking a mentor for his intellectual development. But there is no question that Father Fuhrmann's English classes mattered to Frank. It was Fuhrmann's senior English class, according to a fellow student, "where [Frank] seemed to surrender completely to the creative world that Father Nicholas exposed to us."[140] Fuhrmann was that wonderful anomaly: a brawler who could (and would) knock you on your ass but also grow weepy while reciting from memory Gray's "Elegy Written in a Country Churchyard." His class was where a young man went to fall in love with prose and poetry, if only because the teacher himself had done so and made it all seem so masculine and appealing. A classmate recalled, "Stanford sat next to me in class, but it's like he wouldn't even breathe he was so wrapped up. He was so taken by whatever literary topic we were on. He was so *involved*."[141] He was, in essence, "a Father Nicholas guy."

Fuhrmann lamented that he had to spend so much class time on basic grammar rather than literary interpretation. But he recalled that "when I did spend time on literature, Frank sat up straight and kept his eyes on me with such seeming intensity that I almost grew nervous."[142] Fuhrmann was in a position that would make any teacher anxious—sensing that a student knows much more about a topic than you do. To make matters more unnerving, Frank "*took no notes!*" He just sat and stared. "He never even asked questions," and his comments were worldly and brilliant. Fuhrmann was further intimidated by the way Frank laughed when he recited excerpts.[143] Years later Frank explained how "in one reading [of any classic text], I can come up with some things that a teacher that's been teaching for twenty years hasn't. And I've done it in class."[144] Fuhrmann knew as much.

Fuhrmann also realized that his student had something close to a photographic memory. "I would occasionally assign a poem for memory, usually the opening twelve lines of *The Canterbury Tales*," he said. "Frank had them memorized almost as quickly as they came out of my mouth. He could memorize a poem after one or two readings."[145] Stanford was one of only a handful of students Fuhrmann ever taught who memorized the entirety of T. S. Eliot's "The Love Song of J. Alfred Prufrock."[146] Years later, when the editor Michael Cuddihy failed to send a poem back but asked for a few revisions on what Frank submitted, Frank, who had sent his only copy, rewrote it verbatim from memory and added the suggested changes.[147] "Believe me when I say," Frank wrote when he was twenty-four, "I can remember each moment."[148] When Frank was being interviewed by his publisher at the same age, his publisher opened a question with: "Simone de Beauvoir said, 'Each consciousness seeks the death of the other.'" Frank, who was drinking whiskey, immediately corrected, "No, Hegel said that. I think she prefaced her novel *L'Invitée* with that."[149] He was correct on both counts. While Fuhrmann knew "there was something different about Frank," he was often frustrated that "he did not apply himself" and "had no desire to be on the honor roll."[150] Instead, he seemed to enjoy a position of "detached observation," with his mind taking it all in, rather than active involvement pursuing conventional ambitions such as earning academic awards through good grades.[151] "He was not one to forget, period," C. D. Wright would later say of Frank.[152]

Although grades never mattered to Frank, there was never any question among his peers and teachers about his brilliance. Echoing what Frank's classmates back in Mountain Home said, one Subiaco student who took English with Frank recalled that "he was the foremost authority on just about everything."[153] Another teacher, Father Camillus Cooney, taught Frank during the second semester of his junior year and determined that he was some kind of expert on Keats.[154] Student Joe Saunders said that "he was so much smarter than most of us,"[155] while another student, Omar Greene, said it was immediately obvious that he was "a deep, deep thinker, more than the rest of us."[156]

Fuhrmann was more than just a teacher to Frank. Handsome, athletic, eccentric, literary, and formally committed to an ethical code, he provided Frank a model for the way a man could be, functioning as a kind of father figure. It was a role certainly intensified by the fact that Frank had lost his own father less than two years earlier. Fuhrmann was a relatively young man who was universally respected by the students, so his validation of Frank's commitment to his reading and writing ambitions mattered. "I am still wondering," Fuhrmann wrote decades later, "how much Frank figured I knew about his secret writings." If there was anything he thought he actually taught Frank, he added, "it was the idea that it was quite manly to appreciate poetry."[157] Father Gregory Pilcher, who was a student of Father Fuhrmann's before training to be a monk, noted that Fuhrmann was very popular with the manly crowd, had a "sui generis" teaching style, and could be quick with the one-liners.[158] Frank responded well to all of it.

While Frank felt comfortable embracing his role as "Subiaco's unofficial poet laureate," he also turned inward in a way that distanced him from classmates. "Frank was a classic introvert," Fuhrmann said. "He did not favor focusing on frivolous or petty happenings." Although Frank largely "kept his thoughts to himself," Fuhrmann recalled how he also initiated marathon "night sessions" in the dorm, where students engaged in various free-ranging discussions. Student Bill Lux remembers how "we were a bunch of idiot boys" and how "most things Frank would do would blow past us."[159] On bus trips Frank would sit right behind Fuhrmann and, as the priest drove, free-associate about one his favorite issues: the difference between dreams and reality. Fuhrmann guessed that "his struggle to distinguish between dreams and reality" was his way of avoiding whatever darkness was in him.[160] In any case, he always had Father Fuhrmann's ear. As Leo Lensing put it, Frank was a nice guy who kept himself alive through his intellectual relationship with Father Nicholas.[161]

## "A Very Curious Personality"

For all his introversion and intellectual isolation, Frank wanted to be included in normal social life. His first-rate clothing, most notably, always kept him in the spotlight. Leo Lensing said, "I remember Frank most distinctly as a smart dresser; he was the first person I ever saw in one of those two-toned dress shirts, blue or pink with white collars and cuffs." He alone pulled off a seersucker jacket, and while the rest of the class wore "garish madras jackets" for their senior photo, Frank "was the only boy dressed in white."[162] Then there were the shoes. A student recalled that "whatever bad habits he had were not nearly as indelible as his shined and polished shoes."[163] This quality certainly put Stanford on good terms with the Subiaco dress code, which believed "shined shoes are part of the proper decorum of every student."[164] But for Frank it had nothing to do with decorum. A man's shoes, Stanford said, "were a direct picture window into the psyche."[165] Stanford kept an informal "best-dressed list" and was more than happy to offer his sartorial opinions to anyone willing to listen. "Vain" is what one classmate concluded about Frank's attitude about his appearance.[166]

Other behaviors were more conspicuously overt. "He had these little exhibitionist traits," said Martin Pendergrast, who remembers how

Frank "would stand up in a window with a bunch of people walking under him and throw ancient English books." He would also climb a water tower, yell, and throw more books.[167] One night, during an especially hard thunderstorm, Frank evidently looked at the boys cowering in the dorm and then ran outside holding two metal rods used to hold open dorm windows, yelling into the sky, "Here I am. Come and get me, you bastard!"[168] Two days before the end of senior year, "to celebrate our liberation," Stanford and another student somehow had a bottle of Country Club liquor delivered to the dorm and chugged it (an improvement, for sure, on the "cologne toddies" Frank recalled a classmate making).[169] A drunken Frank ran into the dining hall, tore down the American flag, and went down the aisles holding it, cackling with laughter. After showering one evening, he went into his dorm, picked up a knife, dropped his towel, placed his penis on his desk, and threatened to lop it off. A student who witnessed this act recalls the scene and his thoughts about it: "Oh, my god, don't do that, don't do that. Of course, he did not do that. But none of us thought he was too chicken to do that. Frank was kind of a loose cannon in that respect.... I can still remember the grin on his face and how crazy I thought he was."[170] Such stunts were hard to forget, not to mention notable anomalies for a kid with an otherwise inner-directed temperament.

There was something sad in these vicissitudes between introversion and attention-grabbing outbursts. Back in Mountain Home, Stanford had been seen and appreciated for a range of "normal" extroverted behaviors: He was popular at school, a star on the water-skis, an expert angler, and a decent football player. An all-American kid. His passions—namely, for reading and writing poetry—lived a private life. But at Subiaco, these tendencies flipped. His secrets were liberated; he was free to fly his literary freak flag, and he did. But now it was his extroversion that needed to be cultivated, and the upshot was one awkward outburst after another. Stanford had a gift, and he was respected for it. But respect did not necessarily translate into friendship. Frank seemed to sense this, and he maybe knew that the extroverted act was not fully succeeding. So, on occasion, he attempted these ridiculous attention-grabbing stunts. They would not be his last.

Except for Emmett Hawkins (and even he later said he was happy to see Frank's eventual racial awakening), Frank's classmates universally agreed that nobody *disliked* Frank. But still, the general assessment was that there was just something about him, a kind of odd exceptionalism, that made him seem unrelatable. "He had a very curious personality," said Pendergrast, one wrapped up with his literary eccentricities and an all-knowing demeanor. For better or worse, such is probably the most accurate summation of the popular assessment of Frank at Subiaco: *a curious personality*. Appreciating that personality from a distance was about as close as anyone could get to the unofficial poet laureate of Subiaco. "I don't think he had any really close friends," said classmate Joe Saunders.[171]

Frank's effort to cultivate friendship often went sideways. The judoists were mostly underclassmen, so those relationships were more hierarchical than egalitarian. As for his peers, he could sometimes treat them with a formality that was less off-putting than just plain strange (at least to a regular high school senior). It's not every high school student, for example, who enlists his peers to meditate. After graduation, he told a fellow graduate, "You remind me of Robert Blake. You act tough but have a good heart." What schoolboy says such a thing to another?[172] And while students might have found a feigned performance of self-castration entertaining, it's not exactly an invitation for an enduring friendship ("Crazy and stupid," said one witness). Father Fuhrmann noted how Frank was different in that he "did not go through that rite of passage growing into manhood—I just did not think of him as a youngster."[173] Neither did his peers.

In May of 1965 Stanford tried to overcome some of these social hurdles. Perhaps thinking that if his classmates could see what he was like back in Mountain Home, they might act more familiarly with him, treat him as a regular kid, Frank arranged to take a group of classmates on a trip to his house on Mallard Point in Mountain Home. The *Periscope* reported the event, noting in the headline, "Junior Class Planning Jaunt to Lake Norfork" and explaining that an "activities committee" was busy organizing a weekend of swimming, fishing, and skiing. Good, wholesome fun.[174]

"Wholesome" might not have been the best word. There were discussions of Dorothy and two priests going along as chaperones and taking the crew in a bus, but it seems that Dorothy let an upperclassman drive her car, and the students piled in and went without supervision.[175] One student recalled that when they went out on the lake in the Stanfords' motorboat, everyone on the lake and at the marina knew Frank and was thrilled to see him. Frank, all of sixteen years old, hung coolers of beer around the boat and let them float in the water as he and his friends spent the afternoon drinking and floating around the lake. At one point the Arkansas Coast Guard Auxiliary approached to get a better look at what was happening on Frank's boat. Frank responded by hauling up the coolers, gunning the engines, doing three taunting loops around the

Coast Guard boat, and then racing to the Missouri state line and hiding in a hidden cove that he knew well.[176]

They did a bit of water-skiing on the last day there, but most of their time was spent, according to a follow-up report in the *Periscope*, "loafing around and recuperating." Recuperating for sure. The full story of what happened on Mallard Point stayed on Mallard Point, but one attendee recalled two days marked by absolute drunken mayhem. "We were drunk the whole time we were there," a student recalled.[177] Leo Lensing, who was not on the trip, heard about a student playacting as a rock star with Frank's new guitar and then ending his act by smashing it to bits.[178] Frank only laughed. But in the end, the trip did little to alter the common perception that Frank "didn't have any close friends."[179] According to another visitor, no matter how many trips were made to Mallard Point, "There is no one who would have been able to say that they were Frank's best friend."[180] Fuhrmann perhaps best got to the essence of why, noting that Frank "lived a certain kind of double life."[181]

During Frank's last semester at Subiaco, something began to disturb Frank in a more acute manner. His mother became deeply concerned about her son's increasingly erratic behavior as graduation approached. Evidence of some kind of emotional crisis brewing is circumstantial but not circumstantial enough to ignore. "I am almost at the end of my rope ... worrying about Frank," Dorothy wrote to one of the priests. "He is in real trouble," she continued, "and I do pray that Dr. Snow [the family physician in Mountain Home] can help him."[182] In another letter she chastised the priests for not letting her know about Frank's behavior: "From things he told me last night, I am astounded that no one teacher knew of his conditions. If anyone had noticed, I should have been told." She was concerned about his plans for going to college, admitting that "I seriously doubt that he will be able to go to school next fall," unless the doctor could help him. "I don't know what I'll do," she despaired.[183]

Whatever was going on, Frank recovered enough to leave for college. Dorothy was relieved to report that "Frank came in late last night and we talked—mother, he, and I—until after one. It was like old times. He was jolly, funny, himself again."[184] By late June, she wrote that "Frank is acting much better.... As soon as he realized how he was hurting [his grandmother] he began acting normally again."[185] When Frank said to a doctor several years later, "I am interested in people. I hope what I say and do does not hurt them," this sentiment applied especially well—and it always would—to his mother and grandmother.

## "He Had the Gift"

Throughout all the mood shifts Frank's poetry was always a constant. When he looked back on his Subiaco experience in the early 1970s, that's what he remembered most. "When I was in prep school, when I was in the monastery, the epic form is what I dwelt on," Frank told his publisher Irv Broughton. "I wrote so many lyrics.... I composed some really long—longer than anything you've seen ... I would say several thousand pages."[186] This could possibly have been the "big poem"—some large excerpt from "St. Francis and the Wolf," *possibly The Battlefield*—that Pendergrast saw on Dorothy's kitchen table. Pondering that possibility, Fuhrmann agreed that "he may have already been writing the epic poem" at Subiaco.[187]

Stanford's approach to poetry at this early phase of his career was shaped by a writer, another monk, whom he read intensively, according to Fuhrmann, at Subiaco: Thomas Merton. Merton, a Zen-like Trappist monk, left fingerprints all over Stanford's work. Stanford's book *Shade* opens with a quote from Merton—"I too have slept all night in that stolen Cadillac." Two other Stanford books, *Field Talk* and *Ladies from Hell*, are also marked with Merton epigraphs: "O go home, brother, go home! / The devil's back again, / And magic Hell is swallowing flies," and "The sweet dark warmth of the whole world will have to be my wife."[188] In a 1972 interview with his publisher, Stanford offered a succinct explanation of an important lesson that Merton taught him: "Quite some time ago I read something by Thomas Merton—what he was essentially saying is this: We're unable to let the rose grow. Before there's ever a petal, before we've pricked our finger, or smelled its scent, we're talking about arrangement. No one really looks at a rose growing anymore. There's some fault in us, some lack of faith, which makes us spend endless hours arranging things, when no arrangement is necessary."[189] He ended this description by urging, "Let's don't kill to perform autopsies."

Stanford's commitment to Merton and his watch-the-rose-grow idea illuminates a fundamental tenet of his poetry, one that was developed and preserved in the amber of youth: *Don't consciously build a poem.* Playing with preexisting and complete pieces, he suggested, dooms a poem to sounding like a poem. "Any bright young man can be taught to be artful (they tried it on me)," Frank, pilfering from the poet Kenneth Rexroth, wrote to Irv Broughton. To purposefully arrange—to be artful—was to miss the mysterious, subconscious, dreamy process that ushers the object, feeling, or idea into being, a process that might be more attainable in adolescence than adulthood. Purposeful arrangement, at least as Frank saw it, required too much conventional thought, too many set ideas that muted the magic. Stanford further touched on this idea in some notes he scrawled next to "Strappado," a poem published in *Open Places* in 1972, in a copy of the issue inscribed to the poet Donald Justice. Stanford's notes read, "This poem is, for me, like a dream of a chess game. When you can't, or you don't know how to play or move."[190] While Stanford was indebted mainly to Merton for this notion, the poet George Garrett came in for some credit too. "I believe," Stanford wrote in 1972, "George Garrett has come closer than anyone with his work and ideas about 'informal organization.'"[191]

Stanford's childlike commitment to the embryonic, if not Byronic, phase of creation attuned him to the poetic power of becoming. C. D. Wright wrote to Frank in her notebook after his death, "Do you believe me when I say you don't know what you're missing. If you're not young and crazy it may be too late."[192] When Stanford began to send shorter poems to editors, they routinely noted how his work was unclassifiable. This was because they were reading a poet writing about the rose before the bloom, a poet who, at Subiaco, developed a Mertonesque aesthetic sensibility when he was "young and crazy." Where Stanford looked and listened, nothing sat still—everything was in the exciting vibration of formation. It was all shockingly quivering and at times beautiful in the way things can be in high school. And he got it down in words.

Frank noted that he wrote shorter poems at Subiaco as well. The few complete poems that he highlights from this period reveal what one might expect given his experience there: a blend of Zen idealism, teenage angst, and a sense of the absurd ("American insanity," as he puts it in his yearbook description of "Stanfordism"). It's possible (but unlikely) that Stanford could have backdated old poems, some to as far back as 1957, when he would have been eight or nine years old. This ambiguity should not suggest that Frank was outright lying about the origins of his poems. Not everything he wrote fueled the mythmaking machine, and, again, there is no question that he was writing sophisticated poems at an unusually young age. As C. D. put it, "He was something of a prodigy. He was a guy who had it. He had the gift."[193]

There is every reason to believe that, as Stanford told a friend in 1971, he wrote "The Blood Brothers" in 1964, after having just started at Subiaco. Although we've looked at this seminal poem in the context of Frank's levee-camp experience, it warrants a second look considering what was going on in his life when he wrote it. The poem's opening—"There was

Born In The Camp With Six Toes / He popped the cottonmouth's head off'"[194]—references an actual person from the levee camps who was fresh in Stanford memory (Six Toes did in fact have six toes on one foot, and he wore Frank's hand-me-downs).[195] It also highlights an esoteric form of animal torture not totally unheard of in the more distant corners of the backwoods South. It's quite possible (though not advisable) to snap a snake like a bullwhip and dislodge its head from its body. Pursuing other tricks with animals, the next stanza declares:

> There was Baby Gauge
> He tied the line to his wrist
> He tied it to the alligator gar
> He rode the fish[196]

Baby Gauge, again, was also a real person from Snow Lake. The idea of riding a fish could have been Frank giving a local turn to the story of Arion, the ancient Greek musician and poet who saved himself from drowning by hooking himself to a dolphin and riding it ashore (exactly the kind of story that Frank, unlike many of his Subiaco classmates, would have known). Toward the end of the poem, the speaker turns the spotlight on himself:

> I had the hands like dragonflies
> I killed one white man
> He was a midget
> I did it with a frog gig[197]

The evil-midget motif is a common and curious one in Stanford's work. Stanford might have had in mind the "world's smallest man" he saw at the Cotton Carnival in Memphis several years earlier, an act C. D. Wright remembers him mentioning. Notes he took in the early 1970s mention "that Welsh midget, always in his cuffs."[198] The killing of the midget with a frog gig also echoes the midnight frog gigging expeditions that Fuhrmann—who would pile a few kids on the back of his old army jeep—regularly organized and Frank routinely attended, starting in his first semester at Subiaco. The events of the poem happen during "the summer of the Chinese daughter," and the poem ends with the Francis-like speaker declaring, triumphantly, "I danced on the levee." The fact that Stanford held the typed pages of an early draft of "The Blood Brothers" together with a clip that also held his mother's Mallard Point stationery further supports his claim that he wrote it in or around 1964.[199]

Another poem, "Eleven Nocturnal Koans," he claimed to have written during his senior year at Subiaco. The inclusion of "koan"—a Zen riddle presented to stress the inadequacies of Western logic—is consistent with Frank's growing interest in Buddhism. The subject of the poem, the clitoris, is likewise consistent with the normal curiosities of a sexually precocious seventeen-year-old boy. What is not normal in any of this is much of the unusual and even elegant imagery that Stanford uses to meditate on this mysterious body part.

> The clitoris which swarms like honeybees
> When you touch it
>
> The clitoris of the jellyfish
> With its dose of poison
> . . . . . . . . . . . .
> The clitoris like a footprint in the snow
> Made by a one-legged hermit in the alps
> . . . . . . . . . . . . . . . . . .
> The clitoris of spiced apple yogurt
> No one has stirred[200]

The most impressive part of this poem is that everything that should go wrong doesn't. Even in a poem he wrote at seventeen, Stanford's control of imagery, his masterful juxtaposition of sexual detail, his intuitive discipline, results in the unlikely prospect of a teenager writing a noncringey poem about, of all anatomical geographies, the clitoris. Not incidentally, one descriptive stanza—"The clitoris of lemons on ice with shrimp / In a Chinaman's market / In Mound Bayou Mississippi"[201]—introduces readers to the final destination of the freedom ride that occurs in the second half of *The Battlefield*. Mound Bayou is a real place with a real and serious history; it was the first free Black community in the Deep South, founded in 1887. It seems likely that students might have learned about it as part of Subiaco's educational commitment to Black culture, history, and civil rights, a curriculum Frank challenged. Nonetheless, in poetry, Frank contained the public sphere of Mound Bayou and the most private take on genitalia in the same space, again finding Merton's rose before the bloom.

IN APRIL 1966, SUBIACO SUBMITTED Frank's transcript to the University of Mississippi and the University of Arkansas, his two choices for college. In May he and forty-nine other members of his class graduated. In June, Frank decided he'd attend his father's alma mater.[202] "The Hogs" it would be. One more summer of stealing books from the library, and he was off to Fayetteville and the University of Arkansas. He brought along a deep knowledge of English and American literature, an immersion in the Bushido tradition, a commitment to the Old South, questions about reality and dreams that only deeper investigation into the subconscious could illuminate, and some degree of mental instability. At the center of it all was a pile of writing—a pile of writing encouraged by the monks, the distant admiration of his peers, and a feral poetic voice ready to go its own way.

Bill Willett and Frank Stanford in Fayetteville, Arkansas, ca. 1968.
*Photo courtesy of Bill Willett.*

## SIX

# College, Part One

## 1966–1968

"IT TOOK ME A LONG time to realize . . . the way I wrote was strange," Frank Stanford told his publisher in the early 1970s. "I thought it was just my way of doing something." Frank was learning something critical about his work: It *was* strange, but strange could be good. Strange could be distinguishing. Even if this realization for Frank began with the playful taunts of high school classmates, a strange poem was a poem that got attention. One had to be careful—that is, one had to respect the honest process that ignites a poem. Frank knew as much. He said, "I don't go out and say 'I'm going to hunt down what is strange, then I'm going to put it down on paper'. . . [that] would be like killing and mounting it, and there is enough of that being done." Instead, he said of his poetry: "I just want to let it exist in the flux of things."[1]

When Frank got to the University of Arkansas in the late summer of 1966, he went deeper than ever before into the flux of things. It was where his poetry thrived. It was where the boundaries separating past and present, dream and reality, drunkenness and sobriety, childhood and adulthood, and black and white collapsed, creating space where he could write something unexpected and original. In Frank's personal life, the consequences of dissolved barriers, the result of what one scholar calls Frank's rejection of "a singular identity," could be destabilizing.[2] Father Fuhrmann said that Frank "became a furious, even angry wild beast" when wandering the caverns of negative capability.[3] But when it came to his art, the flux created ample room for endless explorations of language, carnivals of misfits and outcasts, and a global range of cultural expressions. It resulted in, as William Stafford (not necessarily speaking of Stanford per se) put it, "a head in which ideas just roll around like a marble."[4]

During his first three years in Fayetteville, Frank, who was for the first time in his life living away from his mother, distanced himself from his past—or at least the part of his past linked to the Old South. Fayetteville was the most bohemian and intellectually inclined place he had ever been, and it helped him to shed the southern-Cavalier shtick, as well as the personal history that informed it. He escaped from under his mother's dominating narrative, the one that fashioned him into a privileged white son of the South. Neither the Confederate flag nor the rebel cap followed Frank to college. He began listening to his world in a new way, with a fresh openness to vernacular, place, and people that would temper any reactionary tendencies. He developed a genuine interest in Black culture, the ways of poor country folk, and new modes of communication. He made Black friends and hung out in Black venues. Not incidentally, he did so at a time when he also fully embraced the reality of his adoption, a move that fostered his identification with the displaced and the marginalized—many of them Black—who dominate *The Battlefield*, Stanford's magnum opus, which he significantly built out and revised while in Fayetteville.

## "He Was Writing like Crazy...."

Frank's first semester at the University of Arkansas began with Frank following a Dorothy-approved script. He and Bill Willett, who also went to Arkansas, joined a buttoned-down fraternity, Tau Kappa Epsilon, also known as the Tekes, immediately after arriving in Fayetteville for the fall 1966 semester. The decision to rush was consistent with the good old boy mentality that Frank inherited from his family history. Likewise was his decision to declare himself a business major. To be a Teke studying business at Arkansas was, as Frank's sister Ruth suggested, to be something about which Dorothy could boast. "All she cared about was appearances," Ruth said.[5] Willett recalls going through "the little rigamarole you have to do to get into the fraternity" and getting accepted only to find that Frank was already in. Up to this point the two men had not spent much time together since Frank left Mountain Home, and when he had lived there, it had just been bus trips with the football team and occasional weekend séance sessions. But now they were college freshmen together, fellow frat boys, and roommates. "We bonded," Willett remembers. "We had a lot in common."[6]

The most significant thing Willett observed about Frank at the fraternity house was that "he was a poet already."[7] Over the summer of 1966, after graduating from high school, Frank had continued the writing regimen he'd initiated at Subiaco. For a month after graduation, he'd done manual labor for the monks, mostly hauling hay. Fuhrmann remembered how Stanford awed them all by throwing the hefty bales from the barn floor up to the loft. But the work lasted only a few hours a day, and Frank would spend the rest of his time in the school library reading and writing.[8] In July he went to work in Greenville on his uncle Jimmy Lee's farm. Stanford often ended the day there by walking into the Lees' farmhouse and banging out a poem on his typewriter. It was always a poem he had been composing in his head while he worked in the field. One of these poems, as Willett recalls, was about "teenage love, some kind of misgivings, and the heartaches." Greenville had other benefits as well. The "summer of '66," Willett added, was when he "was dating and seeing Camille"—the girl Frank had seen periodically on recent visits. "Camille was his girl."[9]

Frank continued to write regularly after moving into the frat house. However, when he submitted a poem that he wrote for an English class, it was dismissed by the professor as plagiarized. Frank was crushed. Willett recalls coming home to find him "on the verge of tears" and asking to see the poem. He remembers that it was called "Gray Man" and that it "compared bricks, mortar, concrete, buildings, and sidewalks to the people ruling the world." Willett assured Frank that it was terrific and urged him to confront the professor. "Go tell her you wrote this! Show her more poems!" he said.[10] But Frank, averse to conflict, declined, preferring to brood over the matter in silence. According to Willett, Frank "was upset because she would not recognize his abilities." Stanford reacted by writing even more intensely than before. "That's when I understood how committed he was to his work," said Willett.[11] It was also at this time that Willett came to appreciate how accessible Frank's writing was to the nonpoet and the nonscholar, valuing its ability to foster "such an intense feeling that it just puts you there."[12]

A second big thing Willett remembers about Frank when he got to college was his alcohol consumption. "Frank was quite a drinker," he said. He noted how on many occasions "I'd have to come and get him and carry him on my shoulder and flop him in bed." On most occasions he would "handle [alcohol] quite well—he'd get drunk, and the next day he would get up out of bed and was gone." Mixing beer and bourbon, Frank would start drinking late in the day and carry on into the evening, mostly at the frat house and sometimes at the drive-in, where the two men often brought dates. Frank's weight shot up to 220 pounds from about 185. But being particularly concerned with his physical appearance, Frank rectified this situation by eliminating *food* from his diet for days at a time, surely laying a foundation for the intestinal ulcers that would later nag him.[13]

Frank would occasionally frequent the college bars on Dickson Street—sometimes with Willett and sometimes with a new and rebellious Fayetteville acquaintance named Fred McCuistion (a.k.a. Bad Fred). Frank was not one for large groups. One place he started to visit was George's Majestic Lounge, which Willett deemed "the intellectual hangout." But it was at Roger's Rec, which had an edgier vibe, that there was more action, some of it barroom confrontational. One evening, in a dispute over a pool game, a football player approached Frank and taunted him, repeatedly saying, "I'll whoop your ass." Willett, who witnessed the exchange, remembered that Frank's response was to ignore the guy. But the guy persisted, leading Frank to suggest that they fight somewhere private so that they wouldn't end up in jail. The football player continued to mock him, but "Frank didn't say one word; he just waited and waited." Eventually the jock left. In another instance, though, a guy who talked trash to Frank made the mistake of following him into the bar's bathroom, where Frank picked him up and stuffed him into a trough-shaped urinal.[14]

Late in the fall of 1966 Willett walked up to the frat house to find Frank shoving a mattress out the window. He asked for help hauling it over to an apartment he'd rented on Dickson Street. "I'm moving out, and I need a mattress" was his explanation. Willett wasn't surprised. After a couple of months, both men had decided fraternity life was not for them—too many rules, too much decorum expected. One evening Frank and Willett had stayed up late drinking, goofing around, and painting their room, making a racket as they did so. Willett's big brother in the fraternity had scolded them: "You can't be doing that during these hours." Willett had looked at him in disbelief. "We can't be laughing?" he'd asked. This was too much for Willett, who left the Tekes the next morning. Frank followed shortly thereafter, dragging the Teke mattress to a one-room apartment across the street from campus. "We had a good time, and there was nothing wrong with that," said Willett about their brief tenure in Greek life.[15] Dorothy, for one, disapproved, preferring that Frank stay affiliated with the gentlemanly "country club" atmosphere offered by the fraternity.[16]

Stanford's defection from the Tekes initiated a habit of itinerancy that would never end. His first stint on Dickson Street was brief, but in that time period he was paid a visit by a Mountain Home acquaintance named Vernie Harris. Harris remembers a tiny apartment where Frank did little else but "write poetry and sleep."[17] Later, in the spring of 1967, Frank moved to a cottage-type house located behind a two-story residence at 221 Buchanan Street. There he lived with two other recent TKE dropouts—Randy Deaton and Jim Brooks—and, occasionally, Dick House, also from Mountain Home, and, also occasionally, a physics major named Neal Spearmon. Willett lived in the upstairs portion of the front house, and they all shared a small kitchen in the cottage.

Financially, Frank was, for the moment, doing okay. "Dorothy was his resource for a while," said Fuhrmann. And while Fuhrmann thinks Frank went to class for a bit, House insists that he never did. He explained, "He'd go the first day and get his books, and he didn't go back until the test, and then he'd ace everything. It was great."[18] The *Northwest Arkansas Times* indicates that indeed it was great. The paper reported in the early summer after Frank's first year of college that he was one of 205 freshmen to make the honor roll, a feat he'd never accomplished in high school.[19] In a bio that Frank wrote for himself in 1971, he notes that he "lives in Fayetteville, Arkansas, and attends that University of Arkansas, occasionally."[20] The education that the monks gave him, according to Frank, "let me coast through college."[21]

Frank continued to find academic work pointless, preferring lessons learned on the margins from people trained by everyday experience rather than highly degreed scholars. Whereas *The Battlefield*'s astronomer routinely comes in for some ribbing for his fancy learning, characters such as Sylvester, a Black Creole whom Francis likes to banter with (and who is eventually lynched), offer a more appealing answer when it comes to the ideal sources of learning: "motherwit the bible and the Memphis newspaper I know it all he said" (3639). Sylvester razzes Francis, saying, "you is a pen pusher and a book reader," adding that "well now I might not have a etchication in the sense of the word but by the water / of Jerdon I know a hell of a lot mo than you" (3867, 3880–81). As elsewhere, there is nothing ironic or mocking in Stanford's use of vernacular speech in these circumstances. Given that he seems to show some bias toward Sylvester on the issue of book learning versus motherwit, Stanford is in fact highlighting his preference that book learning never smother out the joys of intuition and wit.

Frank's transcript confirms modest academic success. His first semester resulted in a 3.07 grade point average, with As in Principles of Speech and Economics; Bs in Introduction to Philosophy and Reflective Thinking,

Composition, and Introduction to Literature; and Cs in Introduction to Business I (in his declared major) and, oddly enough, Aerospace Studies (one can't help but think that the "astronomer" of *The Battlefield* and the Egyptian mathematician he's modeled after was having an impact). After the second semester his grade point average was up to 3.27—basically a B+—boosted by As in General Sociology, Introduction to Philosophy (honors), and World Literature, with Bs in Aerospace Studies and Honors Composition and just one C, in Economics. Dick House was certainly right about Frank rarely attending class. But he went often enough to know that business was not for him. At the end of the 1966–67 school year, he left the College of Business and joined the College of Arts and Sciences.[22]

With his mother paying the bills and classes little more than an afterthought, Frank had more time than ever before to do what he loved most: write, read, and drink. Willett recalls how "he was writing like crazy when we lived at the Buchanan house." The free time gave free rein to sustained intensity. "He went into his room, he would come out for whiskey, coffee, and go to the restroom," Willett said. This would continue for days, according to both Willett and Dick House. "I just didn't bother him," said Willett.[23] Frank kept up this way of working for years. In an unpublished poem fragment Stanford writes:

> I was always backing out of the picture
> ... I disappeared three days at a time.[24]

The writer Steve Stern got to know Stanford in the mid-1970s and remembers how "we were sitting around his place one night, and Frank said, 'Let's put on a pot of coffee and write all night'—that was writing for him. It was traveling; it was a pure experience."[25] Irv Broughton also remembers how "Frank and I would write all night, sometimes in a marathon of coffee and paper," and he notes that Dorothy would insist to Frank, "You can't live that way!"[26] Looking back on the poems he wrote this way between 1966 and early 1971, Frank noted that "the ratio of *quantity* and *quality* is not impressive, but that makes no difference as long as you can clean up the shit and dispose of it." His friends might have thought him veritably insane, but of his own heroic bouts of shedding, Frank said, "The practice was good."[27]

When Frank emerged from these stints, he was bedraggled—unshaven, bloodshot eyed, and hollow cheeked. "I don't think many people knew a person could do that," said Willett. Willett also remembered an occasion when Frank appeared after several days of isolated writing, as if from hibernation, with a beard, barefooted, and with "hair just as disheveled as hair can get." He stared from crazed eyes, looking at his friend, and said, "Willett, time flies."²⁸ The poet Leon Stokesbury would recall, in a poem that pays tribute to Frank's life:

> When he sat down at a desk
> the juice cracked and came.²⁹

Willett understood the manic behavior, noting that "when you've got something on your mind, while you're working, you don't want anybody to interfere with you."³⁰ Stanford recognized this intensity in himself. In an early-1970s interview conducted by Irv Broughton, he said, "One of my problems is that I can sustain my attention too long, thereby being spellbound or overwhelmed."³¹ He spent much of his freshman year dealing with such a "problem," an affliction his peers might have envied.

Marathon bouts of writing obviously interfered with sleep, but this deprivation had its benefits. Stanford often discussed his ongoing interest in dreams and the subconscious with Willett. Willett said that Frank intentionally altered his sleeping habits to induce visions that allowed reality to slow to a gauzy drift. He took quite literally the French poet René Char's claim that "poetry lives on perpetual sleeplessness" and may well have had Keats's notion of "dim dreams" and "ardent listlessness" in mind as he entered groggy realms of wonderment.³² "Frank was a very short sleeper," Willett said. "He took catnaps that lasted long enough to dream." Willett has noted that "Frank did this often."³³ The intention, also pursued through meditation, was to achieve a dreaminess where he could "leave the body to enter other realms" to achieve what Paul Valéry called a "disorder in the condition of the mind's fertility."³⁴ In a 1972 letter to Willett, Frank wrote, "The poet lives the present through the future by way of the past. He remembers his dreams so he will live them again, dream them again."³⁵ LSD, which was a widely available option in late-1960s Fayetteville, could help. Willett and Frank assumed, in Willett's terms, "that it was able to open up your horizons."³⁶ But Stanford quit the drug before he ever picked it up, preferring to access a dream state through meditation and interrupted sleep habits. Willett and Stanford also knew that LSD, in Willett's terms, would "burn up your brain."³⁷

Stanford elaborated on his manipulation of sleep and dreams in an interview conducted by Broughton. After referencing William Blake, Stanford said: "You can come across things that may be insignificant during the day or maybe not insignificant, and they turn up in that state. But imagine this: that during the day a man is a cartographer for that geography, that terrain, those rivers and waters, and all this land—topography of what he goes through at night. I don't advocate that we should abolish order and accept the chaos of just sleep unless we just want to sleep all the time."[38]

Dreams mixed chaos into the order of waking life and, in so doing, expanded the reality that Frank could explore in his poetry. As for the relationship that Frank saw between dreams and poems, Broughton explained, "I once asked Stanford if he was good at recounting his dreams. He said he believed one dreams his own dream in the poem, that it isn't a matter of recounting; rather it is a matter of actually having the experience in the poem itself. The question of the subconscious, of course, came up. 'The same state,' Stanford ejected [sic]. 'I can deduce [sic] it in myself when I'm awake.' "[39]

Merging the conscious and subconscious, or waking and dreaming realities, defined a core element of Stanford's developing poetics. It was an element that inspired the poet Lee Upton to call his work "hallucinatory and rooted at the same time."[40] Frank, who read Ferdinand Alquié's *The Philosophy of Surrealism*, possibly in 1969, had a nuanced and largely instinctual understanding of surreal notions. But he wanted to be linked with the surrealistic tendencies of César Vallejo and Pablo Neruda rather than those of Robert Bly or James Wright.[41] That is, the pastoral surrealism of Bly and Wright perhaps struck Stanford as too self-conscious, too identifiable, whereas the surrealism of Vallejo and Neruda seemed more baked into the rhythms of themes whose warm connectivity belied the feelings of detachment and isolation in Bly and Wright.

But this preference, maybe because it was a gut feeling more than a clearly articulated ambition, was often lost on editors. When Stanford started submitting his work to the little magazines in the early 1970s, editors would often brand his poems "surreal." Frank generally resisted the term as a way to classify his work.[42] In a 1974 letter to the poet David Walker, Stanford wrote, "I don't mind being called surreal, occasionally, as a few others have said, meaning no harm, when actually they had no better words or ways of understanding reality."[43] In an unpublished prose fragment Frank writes about the Japanese poet Shozaburo Nakayama, "Although his poems may seem to most americans from the city as surreal or dream-like, they are very real. His reality suspends your disbelief into a bridge over a strange river."[44] In this respect Frank echoed Flannery O'Connor, who once wrote about one of her short stories that "this story has been called grotesque, but I prefer to call it literal."[45] O'Connor would have understood Frank's impatience with the generic use of "surreal" to describe his work.

In *The Battlefield*, Stanford repeatedly suggests that reality in the rural South is real in a way that urbanites, especially from outside the South, might not fully appreciate. Francis observes:

> shit I've seen all kinds
> I've seen baptizings at the levee where a big woman will take a
>     preacher down
> why I've seen them get the cross around their neck hung up on a root
> I heard tell of a white deacon who kept up a awful preaching he kept
> stepping back into the river saying come and be drenched in the spirit
> I'll be damned if the fool didn't step off in a blue hole
> and ain't never been seen since
> yea I've seen the one get dunked get snake bit before
> I've been out there a half dozen times myself and I've felt the gars
> brush up against my leg
> I seen a man get religion driving a bulldozer seen him drive the Cat
> in the bayou
>     (6360–71)

The images in this excerpt are exactly the kind that urbanites might dream up as surreal representations of southern exoticism. But to rural southerners—and especially to a kid who spent some of his summers in Snow Lake, Arkansas, and Greenville, Mississippi—it would not be in the least bit bizarre to see a farmer experience the rapture of the Lord while driving a bulldozer or a river baptism resulting in drowning or snakebite. In an important way, this distinction gets to the essence of what Stanford's poetry asks of his readers: Whereas poets are often praised for making the ordinary seem extraordinary, Stanford's attention to backcountry images, sounds, and words can also make the extraordinary seem ordinary.

But, again, this was a difficult message to get across. When Stanford sent an editor a narrative poem about a blind man who works at a factory making mirrors, it was rejected because the editor thought the story's premise was "too surreal." According to Stanford, "I wrote the editor back and told him I'd told my blind friend what he'd said and that the blind man said to tell him that he didn't see it that way."[46] In this respect Stanford echoed a poet he was coming to admire in college: James Dickey, who said that a good dream (as opposed to a nightmare) "has the reality that we can't achieve in reality." Stanford knew that dreams were not surreal but just another version of the real.[47]

*The Battlefield* is accordingly marked by a series of dreams that blur waking life and expand the idea of reality into something that's perpetually shifting. In her preface to the 2000 edition of *The Battlefield*, C. D. Wright notes "the prolific dream sequences" and how they "function transitionally."[48] Dreams and dreaming themselves are explicit themes of the poem. Early on, after mentioning how "one night the moon that molting chicken was scattered all over the woods / just like possum brains on the good road," Francis claims: "mostly I dream." (358–60). Later he mentions how "dreams they are strangers striking matches in the dark," adding that "some of them come and go like flash floods some of them rains that never / let up" (2908–09, 2912). "[M]y dream," he writes, "like a trapdoor like baskets of warm bread" (1777). Francis introduces one dream sequence by stating, "right now I dream" and then declares:

> what I am feeling here and now is got to be nothing but a pipe dream but
> I dream
> all the lawyers and teachers and preachers and government is gagged
> and bound
> on some beach and we is free to do what we want that is how crazy I am
> ha ha
> (3301, 3309–11)

Commenting on these dream phases, Frank's friend and writer Steve Stern said, "I always had the sense that there was no place where his imagination left off and the real world began."[49] Francis, in *The Battlefield*, says as much by channeling Yeats: "the visible / world is no longer a reality and the unseen world is no longer a dream" (14999–15000). Frank's merging of dreams with reality allowed him to connect with what he later called "an inner hush," a place where he could find "that state of the poet's grace."[50]

Still, jags of coffee, whiskey, beer, sleep deprivation, and vision quests hardly hushed the mind. Friends and acquaintances recall how Stanford's compulsive writing habits coincided with eccentric outbursts, much like those that he displayed throughout high school. Frank's Mountain Home friend Dick House remembered how when he was sharing a bedroom with him in the cottage on Buchanan Street, "Frankie would wake up in the middle of the night, and he'd sit up, and he'd laugh like a maniac." House was not especially amused. "He'd laugh for about fifteen minutes or so, then he'd lay back down and go to sleep. I thought, *What the hell?*" It was as if, House said, "he was in another atmosphere."[51] Asked later if he engaged in similar behavior—waking from a dream in the middle of the night and howling—Frank said, "Oh, yes, yes."[52] Willett, who also saw Frank exhibit such behavior, figured it was some kind of "psychological release."[53]

Two other incidents from 1967 confirm Stanford's tendency toward erratic outbursts. When he went home to Subiaco to see his mother, a visit that coincided with the fifth-year reunion of the class of 1962, he sat in a room at the campus retreat center with several old classmates listening to an older student go on about his experiences in Vietnam. While the other students sat around him in a semicircle, respectfully listening to the war stories, Frank, according to one student who was there, "sat off to the side, in a chair, rocking it gently, rhythmically, back and forth against the wall." Suddenly, Frank slammed the front legs of his chair down and, as a classmate recounted it in writing, yelled, "The Egyptians is gonna rule the world!!!!"[54] Huh? Party over. A little nervous laughter and everyone headed to bed. Back in Fayetteville, Willett once found Stanford in the front yard of 221 Buchanan whizzing Bob Dylan records into the street, evidently pissed off that the troubadour was getting famous for qualities not yet recognized in himself.[55] On a page of poetry notes among his miscellaneous papers, Stanford writes, "One boy is throwing old 45 R.P.M. records into the air. We see them gliding like birds."[56]

These performative moments, even more so than at Subiaco, stood in contrast to Frank, who was more often than not withdrawn. Bill Lux, a Subiaco classmate of Frank's who also attended the University of Arkansas, ran into Frank on Dickson Street one afternoon and went up to his apartment for a beer. "Frank was a much different person," Lux recalls. The boisterous guy Lux had known at Subiaco "had metamorphosed into a quiet, reserved demeanor." Frank seemed, Lux recalls, to have totally surrendered himself to his creative world. When Lux left Frank did something Lux did not expect: He gave Lux a bear hug. "I'm thinking that guys don't really do this," said Lux, adding that Frank's behavior seemed to exhibit a lack of confidence in his emotional stability.[57] Father Fuhrmann remembered how Frank, once he got to the university, "lost his extrovert disposition and assumed a more obtuse temperament."[58]

Frank continued to visit Subiaco to see Father Fuhrmann and his mother, who remained concerned about her son's strange behavior. The sleeplessness, alcohol abuse, and outbursts were symptoms that, a year earlier, had convinced her that Frank was not ready for college.[59] In 1967, with these habits still in evidence, she arranged for Frank to see one Dr. Joseph LeBlanc, a general practitioner in Fort Smith. Frank had evidently refused to see a psychiatrist, but he agreed to talk to LeBlanc on a regular basis, the primary concerns being his lack of sleep, obsessiveness over reading and writing, drinking, and—something new—occasional thoughts of suicide.[60] LeBlanc reported to Dorothy that he thought Frank was probably schizophrenic. It's hard to invest this diagnosis with much authority, but Frank's first wife, Linda, in an interview long after their divorce in 1972, conjectured that "the psychiatrist [sic] in Fort Smith who had treated him and diagnosed him as paranoid schizophrenic was not just trying to save him from Vietnam."[61] She sensed that the diagnosis of some sort of mental illness, even if it was not from a psychiatrist, was likely correct. But the fact is we have no professional diagnosis of either schizophrenia or paranoid schizophrenia.

That said, Frank was certainly suffering some kind of psychic distress by 1967. And even if he was not seeking a medical dispensation from military service, Dr. LeBlanc's assessment did in fact get him out of the draft. Bill Willett, traveling on the bus with Frank to Little Rock for preinduction military physicals, remembered how Frank showed him a note from "a Fort Smith psychiatrist" confirming the diagnosis of probable paranoid schizophrenia. Tom Whalen, an Arkansas undergraduate who was along for the bus ride, recalled a similar story: "After the physical and mental tests were over, we asked one another about our classifications. '1Y,' I said, 'and you?' '4F,' Frank said. The word was that he held a black belt in karate and to me he always appeared in great physical shape. 'Damn, how did you manage that?' He leaned toward me, very close, eyes open wide, then leaned back, smiled, and said, 'Paranoid schizophrenic!'"[62]

Willett, who was in the examining room when they were evaluated, remembers how Frank stood against the wall and avoided eye contact with everyone. When the doctors asked him to cooperate, he held up his note from Dr. LeBlanc and said, repeatedly, "I don't participate." The stratagem worked, which was just as well. As Willett aptly noted, "Frank did not need to be in the army."[63]

## "He Was ... Very Introspective"

Frank took four classes in the English Department during his freshman year.[64] To the extent that he attended them, he would have gone to Old Main, the signature building on campus. Next door was the Student Union, a social spot where students often congregated after class. During his first year, Frank continued to dress as he had in high school. Coming from a boarding school so committed to shined shoes that "vigorous brushing sounds could be heard coming from the dorms before lights out," he kept his shoes in order by having them polished in the Union.[65] This is likely how he met a local Black man named Jimbo Reynolds, the Union's lone shoe shiner.[66] A student who knew Frank and Jimbo at Arkansas said of Jimbo: "He was funny and a lot smarter than he let on. He would sort of just smile at people and stuff. If you knew him and talked to him a little bit, he was a really smart guy. I think he had to act a little less smart than he was, up at the school at least."[67] In an unpublished prose piece, Frank, who saw through Jimbo's mask, wrote, "Jimbo is like Zorba. Jimbo used to be a cook. Jimbo has read Kazantzakis, some philosophy, some poetry, but he likes The Tulsa Worl[d]."[68] Frank and Jimbo hit it off. Jimbo was a man about whom Frank would later write:

> I intend to take care of you
> The rest of my life.[69]

Willie E. Reynolds—Jimbo—had come to Fayetteville from Fort Smith, Arkansas, as a twenty-four-year-old in 1935. It was a time, as he put it, "when Black men who did not have a job better not be caught north of Center Street on Dickson." He added, "Twenty years ago I wouldn't have dared to sit down in a restaurant." In addition to his employment as the Union's bootblack, Jimbo worked at the Campus Grill, where he cooked and served burgers and steaks to students.[70] "Frank got to know Jimbo Reynolds well," says Willett, "and he started to affiliate a lot with him."[71] Semon Thompson, a Black law school student at the time and later the first Black professor at Arkansas, recalled that "Frank became Jimbo's big boy."[72] "Big boy" runs deep in the Black literary tradition. Per Sterling Brown's "Odyssey of Big Boy" and Richard Wright's "Big Boy Leaves Home," he's a wanderer, a lover, a worker, a trickster—a charismatic vagabond loyal to the core. Thompson's description was a compliment and a big one. Sam Gwynn, who was an MFA student when Frank was taking graduate writing workshops at Arkansas in his last couple of years as a student, recalled Jimbo as Frank's "Sancho Panza" and noted how Frank even spent time at the house of Jimbo's mother, brought Jimbo along to social events, and began to engage in "Black barbershop talk" with Jimbo.[73] It is hard to find anyone who knew Frank in Fayetteville who did not also know Jimbo Reynolds. "He formed a real close friendship with Jimbo," a fellow student remembered.[74]

In 1968 there were 596 Black people in Fayetteville, comprising just under 2 percent of the city's population. Jimbo ushered Stanford to the center of that community. He did so by inviting Frank to the crucible of social and political life for Fayetteville's Black population: Sherman's Tavern.

Frank Stanford and Jimbo Reynolds hanging out at Sherman's Tavern. *Photo by Ginny Crouch Stanford. Photo courtesy of Ginny Crouch Stanford.*

Sherman's was the first Black-owned business in Fayetteville. It was located at 312 East Rock Street, situated at the bottom of a dip in the road in an all-Black neighborhood between the university and Mount Sequoyah. The area was known by whites as "Tin Cup" and by Blacks as "The Hollow."[75] Others referred to it as "the bottoms."[76] The photographer Deborah Luster, an MFA student at the time and a friend of Frank's, recalled that it "was a funky little bar that almost looked like it had a dirt floor in it. It was low, like a shack."[77] It had a swept dirt floor out front. Semon Thompson called Sherman's "a gathering place" as well as "a study unto itself in consummate racial respect." It was a venue where, to enter, you had to "throw off all trimmings of bigotry."[78] Another former student remembered how, in a town that was so segregated, Sherman's was a place that, for those whites willing to enter with respect, was "just the opposite."[79]

Frank became a regular at Sherman's. The question of why he found the tavern and its Black patrons (and owner) so appealing warrants some reflection. The discrimination that Fayetteville Blacks experienced was of course foreign to Frank. But as an outsider never quite able to find his place in conventional society, Frank might very well have felt at ease in this predominantly Black space, much in the way he felt at ease with the monks, another community with a separate culture that lived on the margins of "normal" life. As we'll see, the stories that patrons told of their racial oppression could easily have appealed to Frank's warrior mentality, embedded as it was in its Manichaean moral code. Considering how the culture at Sherman's—which welcomed him unquestioningly—thrived on language notably distinct from what Frank was hearing at the university or at George's Majestic, it becomes further evident why Frank, whose poetry was already attuned to patterns of everyday speech, took as easily as he did to the tavern.

In so doing, Stanford immersed himself in a world that would powerfully shape his poetry. He spent his time drinking beer, never to excess according to Thompson, and listening to the stories that the men shared.[80] "The only language I like," Frank later wrote to Alan Dugan, "is the mistakes I hear in the taverns, the things said by those who don't know they're saying them."[81] Thompson remembered that Frank "was soulful . . . he was low key, quiet, very introspective." As for the possibility that Stanford was only seeking street cred or visiting the bar in an ironic way, Thompson, with a rise in his voice, said, "No chance. I don't think it was a put on. He liked being around people who did not have any pretensions about them."[82] Others agreed. A former Arkansas poetry student who knew Frank in Fayetteville said that "his heart was in the vernacular as well as with the people" at Sherman's.[83] Ruth Rogers, Frank's sister, recalled, "Jimbo would just tell him all kinds of stories. They'd sit there, and Frank would listen to his stories."[84] Stanford consciously highlights the value of silence amid Black talk in *The Battlefield*. When Francis walks through the bustling all-Black camp in the Arkansas Delta, he thinks, "I learned I could say the most by keeping silent" (14350). At the end of the poem, standing amid the racial utopia he helped create, he reiterates, "I wanted to tell as much as I could so I was silent" (14963). C.D. Wright, whom Frank would bring to Sherman's in the mid-1970s, said of the atmosphere, "The talk by itself inebriated."[85] Frank was hooked.

The men whom Stanford befriended at Sherman's—including the owner, Sherman Morgan—were venerable local citizens committed to civil rights in Fayetteville. Jimbo Reynolds openly and actively condemned racism. Throughout the 1960s "he spoke to many classes [at the university] on the subject [of racism] and was awarded a certificate for his contributions at a workshop on Human Relations." He believed that "the golden rule is colorblind."[86] Sherman Morgan was similarly dedicated to fighting the city's racial disparities. In 1973, the Fayetteville Board of Directors named him head of the city's Housing Authority. This was only the second time in Fayetteville's history that a Black person was appointed to a city commission. Sherman was known informally as "the Black mayor of Fayetteville" and widely admired for his attention to racially equitable urban housing policies. Thompson says that Morgan was so trusted that, when the Fayetteville police got word of conflict in the Black community, they went straight to Sherman and asked him if he could de-escalate the situation. In this way, Thompson added, "Sherman was a linchpin for working through race relations in Fayetteville."[87]

Of those whom Frank came to know especially well at Sherman's, Claude Ricks may have been the most committed to racial integration in Fayetteville. "My dad," said his daughter Deborah, "was deeply concerned with social justice."[88] Ricks moved his family into an all-white neighborhood, where they were not warmly welcomed, in the early 1960s. Bricks were hurled through their windows and shots fired at their house. At Fayetteville High School, Deborah was one of twenty Black kids out of a student body of seven hundred. Claude became, according to the *Northwest Arkansas Times*, "a spokesman for the black community" on race relations in the schools, especially as they related to inclusion in high school sports.[89] In 1955, four Black boys integrated the Fayetteville High School football team, and Ricks, as part of the state Youth Leadership Institute, worked to keep that trend going on all levels.[90] Frank knew Claude's cause well. In an unpublished story, referring to Claude's two sons, he wrote, "It's a long involved story why they don't play on the high school team. None of his people do."[91] Claude was fighting to change that. He also worked with the Youth Leadership Institute to "improve community relations," inspired by the belief, as he put it, "that young people of all races can work together to iron out problems."[92]

Frank Stanford enjoyed being with these civic-minded and engaged Black men. Willett remembers how "Frank was friends with everybody at Sherman's. He was accepted there like everyone else at the bar."[93] These friendships lasted for the rest of Stanford's life. In 1972, when Stanford was visiting New York, he attended a West Indian festival and wrote about it in a letter to Willett, adding that "Jimbo, Sherman, and Claude would have really dug it."[94] He ended a postcard written the same week, "Hello to Jimbo, Claude, Sherman."[95] In 1974 Stanford wrote to an editor and friend, again referencing Jimbo, Claude, and Sherman, that "three old friends are coming over today to go fishing."[96] When Frank and Irv Broughton fantasized about going to Africa someday, Frank said, "Jimbo, the guy that shines shoes in Arkansas, he'd like to go with us. So would Claude."[97] In an unpublished story, Frank writes, "Claude Ricks and I go a long way back" and admires how "he provides for his big family very well."[98]

Stanford came to know the Sherman gang by listening to their stories, many of which were explicit condemnations of the racism they witnessed and endured in Fayetteville. In a letter to a poet friend, Frank, in reference to Claude Ricks, wrote, "Claude's house is shot at again." As for the culprits: " 'Ain't no niggers doing it,' he told me."[99] Frank absorbed these narratives of violence. He believed, as one of Frank's classmates put it, "these people might be poor, they might be forgotten, but there is a lot of wisdom there."[100] He saw how these men confronted the Housing Authority, athletic organizations, neighborhood boards, the university (Semon Thompson helped start a Black Studies program at Arkansas), the police, and the high schools.[101] And he watched them do so with dignity, humor, intelligence, and an ethic of nonviolence.

Or at least mostly nonviolence. Sherman's, which looked like a modest ranch house from the outside, was grittier on the inside. Claude's daughter Deborah Ricks recalls, "I remember my dad taking me there only once, during the day, for potato chips, but it just seemed that, well, it was not for kids."[102] The place saw its share of chaos. Sherman Morgan, in many ways as quietly charismatic and tough as Frank was, did not respond passively to intimidation. On April 28, 1968, his request for an ID from a surly patron was met with a spray of gunfire. The culprit was, according to Fayetteville's *Arkansas Times*, "a Fayetteville Negro" named Bobby Joe Carr. The soft-spoken owner's response was loud: Morgan grabbed his own gun, leaped over the bar, and fired repeatedly toward Carr as he chased him into the dusty parking lot. At the end of the affair, Carr (unharmed) was caught and convicted and spent three years in prison.[103] George's Majestic Lounge this was not.

"He was really at ease in that community," a close friend recalled of Frank and Sherman's. "He belonged there—he had fast, fast friends who were Black."[104] This community offered a new culture for Frank, who, from Sunday lunches at the Peabody Hotel to an elegant house on Lake

Norfork to an elite boarding school in the Ouachita Mountains to a frat house on the other side of town in Fayetteville, had lived a life of southern white privilege. He offers an exaggerated sense of the place's novelty in a line from an unpublished story: "Sherman has a little joint on the creek. In Tin Cup. The church with no preacher is on the other side.... A mule wandered up to the Tavern, walked in, leaned against the juke box, and dropped dead."[105]

Frank's experience with Fayetteville's Black citizens strongly evoked for him the most exceptional aspect of his past—namely, his time at the levee camps. Just when Frank and Jimbo were becoming close friends and when Frank was spending considerable time at Sherman's, he began to revisit the Black characters he'd known at the camps. Willett recalls how, after they moved into the Buchanan Street house, Frank kept talking about how he "was with those kids at an early age." For all the banter about Baby Gauge, O. Z., BoBo Washington, and Six Toes, Willett said that Frank talked about them earnestly and all the time.[106] Another friend remembers how Frank "started to recall his earlier life." He was "always exposed to Black people, and he had previously not given that a lot of thought."[107] In a letter to the poet Alan Dugan, Stanford, in a fit of overstatement, wrote, "You probably think I'm fucked up with my 'association' with Blacks. This is the way I've always been: most of my life was *not* spent with white people."[108] This was an obvious exaggeration but a telling one. It suggests that he was, with the help of a new historical narrative and social group, adjusting his persona to reject the son-of-the-South character.

Frank's integration into this new social group reflected an inclusion he had been unable to achieve at Subiaco, and it extended beyond Jimbo Reynolds, Sherman Morgan, Claude Ricks, and the "honky tonk on the creek."[109] When Willett moved from his previous section of the duplex at 221 Buchanan into the bottom section with Frank (at some point in late 1967), two of the university's most politically active Black students—James Seawood and Carl Moore—moved into the apartment above them. "Frank and I would talk with these guys quite a bit," Willett recalled. "They were very intellectual."[110] Dick House, who recalls his new neighbors as being "very, very good students with good minds," said that there was so much social interaction between the whites downstairs and the Blacks upstairs that they eventually agreed to "open the doors ... so we could all just mix."[111] Seawood and Moore would often invite over another Black student activist—R. D. Rucker—who led an effort to end the playing of

"Dixie" at university football games. Frank got to know Rucker too, as well as the issues that engaged him.[112]

Seawood (a sax player for the Arkansas marching band) and Moore (a business major with Frank during their first semester) had a local band they called Nits, Grits, and Soul. They would host frequent parties at their duplex, and as House said, "Bill, Frankie, and I were the only white faces you'd see." Word got around. So much so that when Dick House went back to Mountain Home in 1968, a local businessman—a "pretty influential guy in town"—chided him, saying, as House edited it: "I understand you and Frank have been associating with some goddamned N-word over there in Fayetteville."[113] There was even talk back home that Frank was dating a Black woman named Yvette, a claim that Willett verifies.[114] Carl Launius, an early Stanford scholar, writes that "Frank had a special fondness for Black women, and Sherman Morgan ... recalls that on many occasions Frank left the bar with one of his female patrons."[115]

James Seawood was as active in civil rights issues as any student at Arkansas. He served as first president of the university's Black Americans for Democracy (BAD), a group formed in 1968 to increase Black enrollment. When Martin Luther King Jr. was assassinated in 1968, Seawood was chosen to represent the university at his funeral in Atlanta. "He was," a mentor of Seawood's said, "a quiet conscience for social justice."[116] And he had stories to tell—stories that surely came up during the long conversations he had with Frank, House, and Willett at 221 Buchanan. Seawood had grown up in Sheridan, Arkansas, a town that had forced out most Blacks when integration was imposed on public schools. But the Seawood family had stayed behind. His mother was the principal, head teacher, and janitor of his high school, the only one in town for Blacks. Enrollment eventually shrank to one student—her son James. When Seawood finished school, as he later told National Public Radio, "a big bulldozer came and dug a deep hole and ... just pushed our beloved school in the hole and covered it up. And it was as though it was never there."[117] Stories like this one echoed those told at Sherman's. In a 1971 letter to Dugan, Frank referred to Seawood as "my friend and old roommate" and noted that when he had parties at a cabin where he later lived, "there were just as many or more blacks" as there were whites, a detail he felt was important to note.[118]

Frank's integration into the Black community took place at a time when racial tensions on campus were higher than usual. Fayetteville was relatively progressive compared to the rest of the state, but still, Black students were not allowed to live on campus until 1965.[119] White students would routinely drive cars through town honking horns and waving Confederate flags. A student who attended the university in the late 1960s recalled how students at an off-campus fraternity "were known to throw, shout things, shoot BB guns and pellet guns at black students."[120] Tom Whalen, who attended the university from 1966 to 1970, recalls that the place "was a nightmare for Black people."[121] Responding to this aggression, the roughly 150 Black students on campus intensified efforts to improve race relations and make progress toward equality on campus. Seawood and the Black Americans for Democracy were at the center of these initiatives. To honor Martin Luther King, Seawood announced to the crowd gathered around Old Main: "Let's gather our forces together and fight for freedom today—not tomorrow."[122] Many whites on campus, if not a majority, were not so thrilled with such a bold call to arms.

Several issues on campus converged to make the late sixties an unusually tense time for Blacks in Fayetteville, especially Black students at the university. A March 1969 visit to campus by Muhammad Ali, who was on a tour throughout the state promoting Black Power and proudly singing songs such as "It's All Over Mighty Whitey," did not help ease tensions on campus.[123] Black students had aggressively—and, to the consternation of many whites, successfully—lobbied to start a Black Studies program.[124] While there was support among a small cadre of the white faculty for this, even the advocates signed internal memos and notes with such closes as "yours darkly."[125] BAD, led by Rucker, fought not only to end the playing of "Dixie" at pep rallies but to eliminate the song at football games too, notably at the "Game of the Century" against the University of Texas on December 6, 1969. The week leading up to the big game saw members of BAD being harassed, and on the night before the game, a Black student named Darrell Brown was shot in the leg on Buchanan Street, while walking to Seawood's apartment after a basketball game.[126] That same year student Jack Kearney wrote in *Black Americans for Democracy News* that Arkansas "has fewer black players on their team than any other major university."[127]

Game day was a bad day for BAD. Members needed a police escort to get to the stadium, where they all sat together in a section of the arena reserved for them. According to Gordon D. Morgan, author of *The Edge of Campus: A Journal of the Black Experience at the University of Arkansas*, "During the game there was jeering and the hurling of racist epithets. A few objects, such as plastic seats and cups of ice, were hurled at the blacks. Telescoping flag poles, umbrellas, clubs, sticks, and other weapons were brandished by angry whites."¹²⁸ After the game the Black students on campus "vacated their dormitories and kept together at the Buchanan Street House," the house behind which Frank had lived.¹²⁹ A few years before his death, Frank, looking back on his time at the levee camps and in Fayetteville as a college student, said, "My only friends, usually, and certainly my closest, even my idols, were Black kids. Even after I got to college, my best friends were Blacks, some of them."¹³⁰ As a college student in Fayetteville, he saw firsthand the issues that defined their lives.

## An Orphan

Frank's integration into Fayetteville's Black community coincided with his decision to openly embrace the reality of his adoption. The timing of this move was not random. In the literature on Stanford, few issues have generated as much commentary as his supposed discovery that he was adopted. The consensus is that it crushed him. Stanford scholar A. P. Walton writes that its "emotional and psychic impact on him is considered to have been formidable, metaphoric."¹³¹ Another scholar has called it "a traumatic event."¹³² Bill Willett recalled how Frank's realization that he was adopted caused him "an emotional breakdown," leaving him with "a feeling of hollowness."¹³³ His late sister Ruth remembered near the end of her life how the adoption news turned him from a voluble, easygoing kid into a quiet, brooding adult. "The difference in him before and after he learned he was adopted was like day and night," she said.¹³⁴ Matt Henriksen, a poet who researched Stanford's life and art, wrote of the adoption discovery that "the script to Stanford's life as he had imagined it suffered a heavy rewrite just as he was coming into his own as a poet."¹³⁵

Henriksen's remark reveals an essential point about Frank's adoption narrative—he definitely was most vocal about it when he was realizing that he was a poet. But we cannot forget something critical: Frank wrote his own script. And by 1968 his script had changed in a way that an adoption narrative could accommodate especially well. He was not going into business. He was done with the Mississippi Confederate act. He'd quit the country-club style fraternity. The allure of old southern heritage now meant nothing to him. Instead, while integrating himself into a radically different culture in Fayetteville, he was becoming a poet who thrived on the appealing versatility of that culture's vernacular. His adoption by his mother was a fact he had likely long suspected but, while he was identifying at Subiaco as a proud Mississippi blue blood, had not been motivated to confront. Father Fuhrmann said that "I still wonder if Frank, sharp as he was, did not catch the meaning of the 'chosen child' line"—that is, if he was not in on the literal meaning that his mother really had chosen him.[136] As C. D. Wright later noted, this "was a strategy that he worked out with his family," one that he pursued "to protect himself."[137] But that protective strategy was, as he integrated into a new community in Fayetteville, becoming less necessary for Frank. As his productivity as a poet intensified, as his time at Sherman's grew, and as his loyalty to his mother's blueblood obsession faded, he needed the liberation that adoption offered. "I know I must set my own course in the stars," he would later write to Willett.[138] It was time for ties to be cut.

Frank aimed to fashion a new persona consistent with the powerful voice driving his poetry. He addressed the matter a few years later when he told Irv Broughton that "to be adopted, for better or worse, is like the second coming, man." He added, "I'm not a Great Dane, maybe a Heinz 57."[139] Essentially, as a Heinz 57, Frank decided he could make up his heritage.[140] In an untitled and undated poem he writes, "I thought up no[m]-de-plumes in the outhouse."[141] Ruth Rogers stated: "Frank realized that he wasn't who he thought he was. He realized that he didn't have the same Southern Mississippi blue blood as all our high society family. He just said, *What the hell. I'm going to do what I want to do and be who I want to be.*"[142] Being who he wanted to be is exactly what Francis, indulging in a bit of Audre Lorde–like biomythologizing, does early in *The Battlefield*:

> the principal that old crawdad asked me my name I told her I am
> the Marquis de Lafayette Marie Joseph Paul Yves Roch Gilbert du Motier
> I got it down pretty good don't I
> better known around these parts as Francois Gilbert the gambler and
>     duelist
> sometimes I am Jean Lafitte the pirate I am the Japanese bowman
> if I go into all my past lives it will take all day
>     (350–55)

Two hundred fifty pages later Francis says:

> I had changed my name so many times I couldn't
> recollect which one I was using ...
>     (10286–87)

In a poem called "The Lies," Stanford, who portrays his mother as "imperial night," writes:

night has put her coins over my eyes
I don't know my past.¹⁴³

In a random note where Frank doodled ideas, he reminds himself, "Create birth certificate."¹⁴⁴

Reiterating a sense of lost identity, *The Battlefield* frequently highlights orphans, the most notable of whom is, of course, Francis himself. When Francis is cruising with Charlie B. Lemon through downtown Memphis, he asks Charlie B., "hey boss we got time to go by the orphanage and spring somebody today" (1320) and adds:

> I think the best thing in life is to help an orphan escape from Saint
> Blaise Home of Destitute Children . . .
> (1323-24)

In another context Francis thinks, "call me the orphan of silence" (4319). He recalls "the bad food at the orphanage" (6621-22) and how he once "got caught in the girls' orphanage" after "suffering from somnambulation" (8999-9000). Because Francis caused so much trouble there, "the authorities at the orphanage made certain I could / never return disguised or not" (9047-48). In a more poetic vein, there is "the one who looks in the mirror and the one in the mirror / a fire as silent as an orphan" (10033-34). And tragic:

> in the field Van Gogh is fainting and yet another
> orphan hangs herself in the attic with the belt of her lover
> (12207-8)

Father Fuhrmann said of Frank that "he became irritated when he read or heard about orphan children—when he saw suffering children, he felt close to the suffering."¹⁴⁵

Frank's embrace of orphanhood eased his path into Sherman's. Willett observed how Frank's declaration of independence from his Earl of Sandwich lineage "made it so much easier for him to associate with the Black people that he knew."¹⁴⁶ Another friend said that the explicit acknowledgment of adoption motivated Frank "to go back to his childhood," where he'd experienced "a baptism of language" at the levee camps by "being around all these young and old rural Black country people." This friend explicitly drew a link between "the childhood experience of being around a lot of Black folks" and "his friends in the Black part of Fayetteville."¹⁴⁷ In *The Battlefield*, Stanford, as he so often did, leaves a crumb on the trail with this passage:

> I came home one evening my folks were
> dead and gone all I said was good now I can be alone...
> (12016–17)

What he does with that solitude becomes the premise for the poem: Just as Frank was doing at Sherman's, Frank's alter ego integrates himself into a Black world. In this way, Frank relished that "baptism of language" as a force merging the levee past and the tavern present.[148]

As usual, Frank's poetry offers the best insight into this psychological shift in identity. In the poetry we find evidence of his association between adoption and his cultural allegiance with the Black communities in Fayetteville and Snow Lake. In *The Battlefield*—which Stanford may have started to excerpt and revise from "St. Francis and the Wolf" around 1968, at a time when he was going to Sherman's—he does something he could not have done while identifying as southern aristocracy: He routinely suggests that the protagonist, Francis Gildart, is mixed race. Relatively early in the poem, Francis and his older Black friend Sylvester fall into yet another one of their verbally thrilling debates. The following dialogue ensues:

> you better not hit me I said
> you bettah shut your mouf then
> I can say whatever I please
> pot calling the kettle black he said
> well this here pot is white then
> I thought you was a slop jar he said got you didn't I ha ha
> fuck you I said
> well the way they got dis Mississippi law I could tell you a few things
> but you'll find them out later
> find out what I said
> bout this who's a nigger and who ain't bizness
> I'm white as the moon I said
> yea well the moon ain't all the time white
> (4183–95)

In this scene Sylvester begins to introduce young Francis to the reality of miscegenation in the South. Francis at this point somewhat fearfully clings to his whiteness, refusing to speak like Sylvester ("bettah," "mouf," "ain't"), as he'll later do. He observes that the "pot calling the kettle black" phrase won't fly with him, because "this here pot is white," and "I'm white as the moon." Sylvester, older and wiser, suggests otherwise when he compares Francis to a "slop jar" and reminds him that the "moon ain't all the time white." As if to make the point official, he cites "dis Mississippi law" that would confirm Francis to be part Black.

Later, Francis overcomes his fear and embraces this notion. When he is on the freedom bus to Mound Bayou to settle a biracial utopia, a character named Vico says to Francis how impressed he is with how he can "change your dialect like the gait of a / horse" (9495–96). Francis attributes that ability to the fact that he's "double exposed"—that is, both Black and white. He tells a story about asking a boy to stab his double with a fork but the boy stabbing him instead and being terrified because "I heard me a nigger boy yell ough when I stuck / him [Francis] with that fork I swear on a grave I did" (9506–7). After a long discussion over this matter, Francis turns to Vico and says:

> I don't want to
> talk about it cause I go crazy and so I have to be of a different mind when I talks to different people . . .
> (9507–9)

More crudely and in a dream phase, he highlights the diverse origins of his body:

> the negro gave me
> his lips and his butt where the white man gave me his skin and the pony gave me his dick . . .
> (4474–76)

In another dream/trance phase he mentions "my body that casts two shadows" (9748) and in another "I could see my brother on one night beside me his was black" (6686). In an early published poem, which appeared in the *West Coast Review*, Stanford states, "I am black I am white."[149]

In 1975, Stanford published a book called *Arkansas Bench Stone*, his fifth book of poems, dedicating the volume to "my mother, Dorothy, my grandmother, Carolyn, and to the memory of my father, Albert Franklin, legendary figures."[150] The poem "Will" in the collection provides an allegory that connects his adoption story to his Sherman's experience. It starts:

> My father left me his wool shirts
> And a promise that I would take whiskey

> And cured hams to the family
> Of the man he shot fifty something years ago
>
> All through high school and college
> I kept his word
> And wore his shirts
> Until I had to go away[151]

These stanzas highlight Frank's commitment to a past that his family implicitly asked him to honor. The line "I kept his word" suggests that there were challenges in doing so, that he knew his place in the family narrative was fictional but still had a duty to carry it out. His father provided well for his adopted son and protected his South, their immediate and ancestral home, from the rage of rivers. He deserved to have his son adhere to the fiction. In another poem, this one from *Field Talk*, called "Fire Left by Travellers," Stanford writes:

> I walked down these levees
> my father's long graves
> which he raised like a pharaoh[152]

In "Will," though, there's a disruption to this obligation:

> One day in the planetarium
> Word came I was a bastard so
> I rode out to the country
> With a kid in a logging truck[153]

The sense of dislocation to come once the reality of adoption sank in cut him off from his fictional past. More important, it did so in a way that muted his role in Dorothy's ongoing narrative, as in the poem's eighth quatrain:

> Old colleagues see me sometime
> They wave me down
> Wanting to talk
> But I no longer have anything to say[154]

The last stanza of "Will" confirms the transition to Sherman's, suggesting his identification with the Black patrons, not to mention his own "coat" of blackness, while also associating the banter of the tavern with the levee camp days:

I left the heavens for the taverns
And the shirts for the old men on pensions
My coat is black
Like the nights I have long forgotten[155]

The influence of Stanford's Black friends and Sherman's Tavern on his poetry can be further glimpsed in his use of a single word in a single poem. In 1968, Frank wrote a poem titled "The Kite," which was published in 1971 in the *Little Review*. The poem opens with a reference to "Mr. Charlie's sedan" getting stolen. But the line that stands out is this: "All his tunes have lost their hinkty licks."[156]

*Hinkty.* The word, sometimes spelled "hincty," comes directly from a deep Black vernacular tradition. It means "a snobbish or pompous person," a person putting on airs. Its earliest recorded usage is in a 1924 song called "The Basement Blues":

the man I love
got lowdown ways, for true
well, I'm hincty, and I'm lowdown too[157]

In his book *Laughing to Keep from Crying*, Langston Hughes writes about "a hinkty hussy." Chester Himes's 1969 Harlem-based novel, *Blind Man with a Pistol*, refers to "all those hincty bitches" who "fell on those whiteybabies like they was sugar candy." In *A Chosen Few* (1965), Hari Rhodes writes, "You got a lotta nerve bringin' your fancy-talkin', northern-raised hincty ass down here and criticizin' us for what we do."[158] The appearance of this hip and signifying word in a poem that Stanford wrote around 1968 suggests how his poetic efforts were building on the Arthurian, warrior mode of *Saint Francis* to ground themselves in a more local vernacular tradition that he was able to more easily embrace without the encumbrance of his white-privileged past.

The question of Frank's race preoccupied his peers when he began to visit Sherman's and hang out with Jimbo. "He probably wished he were Black," said Frank's first wife.[159] Her comment echoes a version of what many people who got to know Frank often said: It seemed he was part Black, or might have been part Black, or at least wanted people to see him as part Black.[160] All we know is that his biological mother was white because Emery Memorial Home, where he was born, admitted only white women. And while there are an endless number of possible reasons why a white woman might give up her child in the South in 1948, one could certainly be that the father was not also white. But such was and is no more than speculation. All Dorothy would offer—once she later admitted that "chosen ones" meant "adopted"—was that Frank's biological mother was a cheerleader and his biological father was a football player. Later Dorothy suggested that the father might have been Italian. Whatever the case, the scenario hardly negates the possibility that Frank Stanford was, as he often suggested, part Black.[161]

## "This Is a New Voice"

Frank and a fellow student named Bob Ward went to Sherman's Tavern one night. What Ward saw there left an impression that helps us better understand the impact of the place on Frank's mindset and poetry: "We went down there. We drove past all of these trees. We get down to this tavern, and there it was with all of this great music, and there were all these Black guys and a few white guys dancing together. It was like the rest of Fayetteville was segregated and this place was just the opposite. Basically, it was really poor white people and poor Black people; it was strange. There was no separation."[162]

Ward's observation of poor Blacks and whites is crucial. He continued: "I figured that if you were middle class and white, you were probably racist down there [Arkansas], not a nasty one or one that's going to shoot people; you just didn't want to be around Black people. But if you were poor like these people [whites who went to Sherman's] were—and a lot of them were dirt poor—you didn't have any of that. It was really interesting, and I'm not sure why all of them got together, but there were even interracial couples there."[163]

This interracial space shaped Frank's thinking starting in his second year of college. His exposure to Fayetteville's Black community informed the mysterious process whereby *The Battlefield Where the Moon Says I Love You* was excerpted from the ever-shifting compilation called "St. Francis and the Wolf" and then revised. The *Sir Gawain* and Arthurian themes, the bravado of Bushido and the Japanese warrior ethos, and the raw expressions of youthful lust—all these early preoccupations of Frank's poetry—are evident in *The Battlefield*. They just become less conspicuous, thinner threads in a broader and more intricate tapestry, one that—in delving into race, language, and geography—transitions heavily to the syntax, vernacular, dialect, and idioms of Black culture throughout the American South.

But not Black culture alone. It is easy to miss something critical in Ward's observations: By exploring the vernacular traditions of poor Blacks in Tennessee, Mississippi, and Arkansas, Stanford was capturing the traditions of the impoverished rural South *as a whole*. The southern speech habits that Stanford explores in *The Battlefield* did not differentiate between white and Black southerners. Instead, they became a blended form of expression that defined the landscape of language for all southerners living on the margins of industrial capitalism. Stanford's pathway into that vernacular happened to be conversations with (and memories of) mostly Black people. But, had circumstances been different, his immersion in rural southern speech could have come through the expressions of peckerwoods, sapsuckers, and hillbillies.[164]

Contemporary assumptions about the Old South make it seem as if society consisted of rich white masters and poor Black laborers whose paths rarely crossed. That the races, and their voices, were otherwise separated. What Stanford's poetry understands is that beneath this stereotype there was another world of social interaction that, whatever the power dynamics, shared language habits to create a common aural landscape of rare power, humor, and beauty. This is what *The Battlefield* began to explore as Frank fashioned it into a regional poem with a global perspective.

Sociolinguistic research confirms the way disenfranchised whites and Blacks in the American South forged common speech patterns as far back as the seventeenth century. By the nineteenth century, according to scholars, these patterns had evolved to a point where "VBE [Vernacular Black English] was . . . the same as, or only slightly different from, the dialects of disadvantaged southern whites." In this assessment, "VBE is an ordinary development from the dialects of the British colonists—the same as, or only slightly different from, the dialects of disadvantaged southern whites."[165] A late-nineteenth-century linguistic comparison of "illiterate whites" and "the negro dialects" listed hundreds of words that were pronounced similarly "by negroes and illiterate whites alike" while only being differentiated by the "cultivated whites."[166] To wit, the word "hinkty," as we have seen, was a commonly used Black term, but it was shared by Scots-Irish Appalachian hill folk as well.

Southerners around Frank did not need academic studies to appreciate this overlap. They knew that he was doing much more than mimicking a Black way of talking. The writer and translator John Biguenet, who knew Frank and studied with Miller Williams at Arkansas, said that

"Frank liked the way Southerners talked," adding that it was "not so much African American dialect [that defined *The Battlefield*] as it was *southern*."[167] Sam Gwynn agreed, noting the "syntax of southern speech" that both poor Blacks and poor whites shared. Biguenet believes that Frank "was translating standard English into the kind of English that had been suppressed in national publications," that he was, in essence, seeing the neglected poetic brilliance of an overlooked and largely rural habit of speech.[168] C. D. Wright, who praised *The Battlefield*'s "cross cultural vision" noted that its syntax reflected how "he was a true southerner." She insisted that "he made his bed on that rock: Delta speech, manner, blues, literature." Like Whitman, Frank knew that language sprung from the ground up, and the deeper it was in the ground, the more universal and accessible and *interesting* it was. "Naturally," Wright wrote, "he preferred the lower tones."[169] What caught his ear was the unrefined language of people on the fringe. It was precisely this element that led Biguenet to declare, as so many did when they read Frank's work for the first time, "This is a new voice."[170]

In *The Battlefield*, Francis Gildart gradually assumes that new voice, adopting the vernacular expressions of his Black friends. "[T]hat astronomer back in Memphis," Francis explains to his Black friend Rufus Abraham, "wants me to be well," which means "I has to stay inside and read books and talk right" (1708–9). As the phrasing "I has" suggests, Francis naturally resists the language of cultivated society, in this case doing so as he discusses his inherited obligation to it. In one telling scene, while he and Rufus are swapping stories as a constipated Rufus struggles to initiate his morning "grunt" in the outhouse, Francis thinks:

> they is folks back in Memphis that would laugh and make fun
> of me a hepping a old man take his grunt but that ain't right I don't
>   care
> bout myself but when folks get old they can't do things right anymore
>   they
> cant zactly shit right you know ...
>   (1638–41)

Over the course of the conversation Francis, feeling his orphan status, starts to talk more like Rufus. When Rufus, referring to the property he will bequeath to Francis (called Abraham's Knife), says, "boy by the time you is growed the Knife will be worth plenty," Francis responds, "sho it will" (1665–66). He mentions the transistor radio he bought Rufus "for his birfday," finds a program on the dial that "don't have / no advertisements excepting for the hog prices," notes that "I seen / a good pitchu show the other day," and, referring to Rufus's later death, says, "I knew his / heart was gone give the day he passed" (1653–55, 1687–88, 1752–53). Francis and Rufus share slang terms, such as "job" for "defecate." Francis says to Rufus, "I reckon you might job some this morning," and while making the jobbing effort, Rufus moans, "Lawd it's me or this crap take me now or let me job how about it" (1680, 1755). Observing this shift in Francis's speech habits is one of the more fascinating aspects of reading *The Battlefield Where the Moon Says I Love You*, especially when we consider how Frank's social life was immersed in Black Fayetteville in the late 1960s.

It might be tempting to see Francis shifting his speech patterns as mocking Black culture or as an example of Stanford employing cultural appropriation in his work. A more grounded interpretation—that is, one that reflects what was happening in his life while he wrote—is that he was accessing language spoken by an overlooked class of people who populated the most ignored corners of the American South, the people, in short, that Frank was getting to know at Sherman's starting in 1968 and the people he knew as a kid at the levee camps in the 1950s. In the early 1970s, Frank lent insight into this poetic ambition when he explained to Irv Broughton that, regarding the levee camp workers, "I really don't like to think about these people dying. I don't like to think about people that never, will never, go noticed dying because the position it puts me in—as an artist—is that if you don't recognize them immortal, nobody else will, nobody else will, and to tell you the truth, I don't think anybody else will."[171]

In other words, Frank's language reflects a sentiment that transcends race to emphasize the hidden appeal of the eccentrics who earn Stanford's attention throughout the text and, in the end, become its heroes. The fundamental obsession with justice—cast in the tone of Beowulf versus Unferth—finds validation in *The Battlefield*. Driving that expression is affection for those on the subservient side of power in the Deep South. The struggles of Sylvester the Black Angel, Jimmy Lee, Mr. Rufus Abraham, BoBo Washington, Count Hugo Pantagruel the world's smallest man, Charlie B. Lemon, Jesus Christ, Sonny Liston, the "infants of the wood" (4693), and many scores of other poor characters in *The Battlefield* reflect Francis's conviction, to reiterate an expression just a few pages into the poem, that "I take to / people that are all fucked up" (467). In an interview with Broughton, Stanford said, "I'm sad when I see really indigent people, people that are down in their hearts and soul. I want to help them."[172] Honoring them with words was Stanford's way of doing that.

During his first two years in college, Stanford was becoming consciously fascinated with how people who were different from him spoke, and that fascination derived from an interest in how words sounded and even how *sound* sounded. It was the same kind of interest he'd cultivated at Subiaco while reading Chaucer and *Beowulf* with Father Fuhrmann. Throughout *The Battlefield*, Stanford pays close attention to preverbal expressions and noises. "I asked her what her favorite sound was," Francis says, referring to a teacher who has been trying to seduce him on a field trip to a lake.

> she said she liked the hum of the arrow
> the whine of the bowstring the unsheathing of swords the piccolo and
>   dirt
> and a shovel and the flamenco guitar the heels of an eighteen year old
>   wild
> like an animal a black hat alone a gypsy humming while he ties a knot
> in the tails of his shirt a greek fisherman thumping the hull of his boat.
>   (805-9)

The overt interest in the basic tenor of things—another aspect of *The Battlefield* worth tracing while reading—informed the connection Stanford would make with the Black people he met in Fayetteville. In the most fundamental way, sound presaged the language that would inform his next decade of poetic output. It would be an output fueled by more and more of the world pouring more and more of its noise into an ear no longer listening to his mother and the history she peddled.

## "We Pissed off the Same Bridge"

What was happening with Stanford during his first two years of college—his distancing himself from his son-of-the-South past and connecting with Fayetteville's Black community—reflected nothing short of a conversion. Thomas Merton may have helped it along. The famous monk's influence guided Frank's shift from privileged white southerner to a person who identified with the voices of the oppressed. Merton's appeal to Frank over the years makes sense for many reasons. Merton shared Stanford's André Breton–inspired inclination to erase the line habitually drawn between reality and surreality, the conscious and the unconscious, and Black and white. He ushered Frank into liminal space, insisting that "what matters now is for the conscious to realize itself as identified with and illuminated by the Unconscious, in such a way that there is no longer any division or separation between the two."[173] This perspective dovetailed nicely with Frank's own quest to live and write in an altered mental state. Furthermore, Merton, like Stanford, valued the basic sensuality of daily life, vesting the mundane with visionary power, blending the high and low into a poetic amalgam. Merton's Zen mysticism was no airy affectation; it was rooted in the physicality of existence, be it asleep or awake or in between, the same physicality that pervades Stanford's work. Stanford affirmed his connection to Merton poetically when he wrote in the poem "The Moon and the Mime" in 1965:

> He and I drank too much wine
> Waiting on the eclipse
> We pissed off the same bridge
> Into two different creeks can you beat that[174]

Reinforcing Frank's affection for Merton's melding of high ideas with more common expressions is a line that soon follows: "And so he went on about Yeats and Blake and The Little Rascals."[175] With Frank's namesake Francis riding mules around Snow Lake levee camps, feeling the blues with Born in the Camp with Six Toes while carrying John Milton and *Moby-Dick* in his saddlebag, this Mertonian erasure of cultural hierarchy underscored Frank's conversion to a new way of seeing and writing about a fresh reality.

What also made sense was Merton's view of what a conversion entailed. It was an experience that hinged on, in Merton's words, "the explosive rediscovery of the hidden and lost reality within us." This was a reality that embraced instincts brought to the surface through current events (Frank's time at Sherman's) that connected one to the past (the levee camps).[176] For a man who had recently converted from an implicit and unexamined assumption of racial superiority to being an advocate for the oppressed, and for a man long moved by the spirit of Zen mysticism, Merton's voice anointed his conversion, his compassion for the disenfranchised, and his poetic love of registers sacred and profane. As late as 1974 Frank was still claiming that "Merton is with me."[177]

IN THE SUMMER OF 1968 Frank told Bill Willett that he was working on a long poem.[178] He said that it was "really, really long but that it'd be worth something someday."[179] He said he would give Willett a manuscript copy of it. This was almost certainly a revision of the longest poem to be taken from "St. Francis and the Wolf." It was a project informed by Frank's integration into Fayetteville's Black community, his declaring himself adopted, his commitment to writing in a trancelike state, his recovery of the levee camp days, and his emotional openness to a Merton-like conversion to a new persona. Mirroring these changes were changes in Frank's physical appearance. His hair, once straight and practically plastered to his head, became an unruly mass—"a big head of girly curls," as C. D. Wright would later refer to it.[180] His preppy clothes stayed preppy, but they relaxed a bit, hanging off him untucked rather than clinging tight, and his shoes became more casual, the kinds that did not require polish. His hazel-brown eyes deepened, the bones in his face became more defined, and his expression grew more intense. He was every bit the beautiful, wild poet, his quest to be a local legend enhanced by his looks.

There was another conversion in Frank's life accompanying the poetic one: from wealthy to poor. Frank's good looks did nothing to alleviate the fact that he was, for the first time in his life, flat broke. Dorothy, now a fixture at Subiaco's Coury House, was living in a small home off campus while supporting her mother, Carolyn Gilbert, with a modest salary. She was becoming increasingly dependent on the monks for meals and a car allowance. Moreover, her growing disappointment with her son's decision to leave the business school and the fraternity disinclined her to keep helping him out financially. Father Fuhrmann, who spent a lot of time with Dorothy after Frank graduated from Subiaco, said that Frank's decision to leave the business school "was Dorothy's first step up the ladder of discontent."[181] A Subiaco classmate of Frank's recalls that "she turned on him" when he left the business school.[182] Father Fuhrmann agreed, claiming that although Frank only wanted "a roof and money for liquor," Dorothy cut him off "in the hopes that Frank would change his lifestyle."[183] Whatever the reason, Frank could no longer rely on his mother for financial support.

So at the start of the summer of 1968, Frank, Bill Willett, and another friend of theirs from Mountain Home, "Big Time" Sonny Morris, headed to Chicago to find high-wage work, hoping to get something in a car factory or on a construction crew. Willett found a construction job, but Morris and Stanford struck out in Chicago. They ended up in Saint Louis, spraying tar under car carriages at the Fisher Body Company plant, which made General Motors cars and trucks. It was nasty work. To get to Saint

Louis, Frank had first gone back to Subiaco and then Mountain Home. It was from there that he got a ride from Dorothy, who took him across the river on the ferry and said good-bye on the bank of the Mississippi River. Ruth, who'd gone along for the ride, cried as she watched her brother, who planned to hitchhike the rest of the way to Saint Louis, walk along the levee into the black night.[184]

Frank in Fayetteville, ca. 1970. *Photo courtesy of Carrie Prysock.*

## SEVEN

# College, Part Two

## 1968–1971

TARRING THE UNDERBELLIES OF CHEVIES was rough work, but it paid. When Frank returned to Fayetteville from Saint Louis in August 1968, he did so with a burgundy '67 Camaro and some spending cash. Passing through Subiaco to see his mother and his grandmother for a few days, he heard from his sister, Ruth, whose '64 Corvair that Dorothy had just gotten her for graduation was sitting in the driveway at Dorothy's, that she preferred the Camaro.[1] Frank, happy to appease his sister and proud of her for her stellar grades, drove the Camaro to Fort Smith, gave her the car, and hitched a ride back to Subiaco, where he took the Corvair back to Fayetteville.[2]

Frank faced a busy semester in fall of 1968. He was enrolled in Greek Philosophy, American National Government, and surveys of American and English literature. He ended up doing little else all semester except reading and writing poetry, evidently ignoring his classes even more than during his first two years. His transcript, marked with mostly As and Bs in his first year (1966–67) and Bs, Cs, and Ds in his second year (1967–68), became less impressive still starting in the fall of 1968. He failed the government course and received WPs (passing withdrawals) in his three other classes. On December 18, 1968, with his cumulative GPA having plummeted to a 2.6, Frank officially withdrew from the university.[3] He sold the Corvair, bought a rusty "little green bug"—a Volkswagen—and lived for a while off the profit, using his time to write.[4]

The irony of his situation in the fall of 1968 is noteworthy. Frank was like an athlete with Olympian skills who, without being aware of it, lived next door to a world-class training facility. He was producing poetry that would soon captivate readers with its raw originality, but the only notable academic feedback he had received on it was an accusation of plagiarism by an English professor. Yet right there in Old Main was a freshly minted MFA program coming to life with incredible literary talent. In 1964, the writer Bill Harrison had been asked by the university to start a graduate program for writers and poets, the first of its kind in Arkansas. At the time, Harrison was a thirty-one-year-old novelist who'd studied at Vanderbilt before going to the Iowa Writers' Workshop. He aimed to replicate the Iowa template at Arkansas but with a more southern twist. To that end, he called up his Vanderbilt graduate student peer James Tillotson Whitehead, "Jim" to everyone who knew him, and lured him to Fayetteville from Millsaps College in Jackson, Mississippi, where he was then teaching.

Harrison's vision for the poetry program was clear enough. He wanted it led by "a big guy, a manly poet, not some wistful little suck up." At six foot five and 250 pounds, Whitehead, a former Vanderbilt football player, not only fit the bill but was, by Harrison's account, "a force field."[5] One of his students described him as "generously endowed with faults and virtues."[6] Whitehead was, according to John Wood, an MFA student and peer of Stanford's, "phenomenally well read" and had a tendency, as Wood put it, "to roar."[7] One student called him "a big, huge sweetheart of a man."[8] Sam Gwynn, who noted admiringly how Whitehead made himself vulnerable in front of his students, said he was "the world's slowest moving target."[9] Whitehead did indeed roar. But he did so as a poet deeply rooted in the American literary tradition. Students noticed and, overwhelmingly, approved. They loved him, and he loved back.[10]

Masculinity mattered to Jim Whitehead. One of his children recalled how "Dad always wanted to counter the image of the sissy poet."[11] One of his students agreed, saying how "he brought to the program the sense that you could be manly and a poet."[12] To that end, "he cussed, drank, and smoked."[13] Whitehead was not oblivious to these characterizations. In a 1966 letter to poet and translator Miller Williams, he wrote, "You want the big man to be big inside, too, I know, I know, and, sure man, that's what I want."[14] And a year later, again to Williams: "I will continue to react and overreact in the tested fashion."[15] In a confessionally poignant poem about his wife and seven children, titled "I Write in a Peculiar Mood Unworthy of the Trust," Whitehead hinted at what might have lain beneath the big man and his bluster:

Your father is a tulip
A withdrawn man who won't outgrow his fears
Of pleasant husbandry and ignorance
Learn to avoid his awkward mental dance.[16]

Jim Whitehead, in other words, blended vulnerability and strength to offer students mentorship that was impassioned and imperfect but always genuine. He started a poetry workshop that would earn him lifelong loyalty from scores of students, most of them male, while sending many of them on a path toward becoming professional poets and writers.

Frank Stanford could not have imagined a sweeter spot of talent. Between 1968 and 1970 Whitehead's workshop, which Whitehead described as "soul work with the students," included Leon Stokesbury, who came from Lamar University armed with a poem published in the October 21, 1967, issue of the *New Yorker*.[17] There was also John Wood, who moonlighted as an antiques dealer, had a pet tarantula and a published book to his name (with an introduction by Allen Ginsberg), and cooked meals from centuries-old cookbooks; Jack Butler, a former Baptist preacher from Alligator, Mississippi, who was into Zen meditation; and John Stoss, who came from a Kansas farm by way of Fort Hays State University and had an alter ego named Honey the Hobo.[18] Later came poets Ralph Adamo and R. S. "Sam" Gwynn, among others. This mostly southern lineup was, as one student recalled, "tight-knit."[19] Stanford scholar Murray Shugars notes "a wonderful atmosphere of sharing among the writers of this group."[20] Gwynn described the members of the workshop as "the Algonquin Round Table of Fayetteville."[21]

Frank Stanford was, as we'll see, incredibly fortunate to be part of this group, and his involvement in the program would spark his publishing career. By most accounts, as we'll also see, he was among the most talented of the lot. "They do have confidence in me," he wrote to friend and poet John McKernan during his final semester of academic studies in fall 1970—when he was taking the fiction workshop.[22] But in the end Frank downplayed, and even seemed to dismiss, the opportunity the workshop afforded him. He eventually downplayed this literary community and any clique of writers with even a whiff of academic pretension. "The academic scene is getting all fucked up," he wrote to Allen Ginsberg in November 1969. "I just want to leave this place and camp out sometimes."[23] Looking back on the workshop, he told Broughton, "I disliked scholars."[24] Frank took Whitehead's workshop for two semesters—spring and fall 1969. He was not inclined to thank another person for the opportunities he gained there. In fact, he ended up doing the opposite when it came to Whitehead, the workshop, and his peers: He scorned them.

But the upshot should not be questioned: The workshop, and Whitehead in particular, catapulted Frank Stanford. They catapulted him to a kind of qualified fame that, however brief it was, he knew he deserved but had never thought he'd get, the kind of fame that might, as it's woven into myth, make one a slave to its obligations.

NOBODY KNOWS HOW JIM WHITEHEAD "discovered" Frank Stanford, but people have theories. Frank's fellow student Sam Gwynn recalls that "somebody told Frank he needs to see Whitehead, and the word gets around."[25] According to another student, "Stanford was discovered in Bill Harrison's class," which he may have taken in the fall of 1968.[26] Another remembers that "Whitehead brought him in because he saw some poems."[27] However the introduction came about, Whitehead's offer to attend his workshop was seductive enough for Frank to reenroll at the university shortly after dropping out at the end of the fall semester of 1968, evidently determining that the chance to be in a graduate poetry workshop was worth the cost of tuition. Even before the workshop began, as Ralph Adamo remembered it, "Whitehead was blown away by what he'd seen."[28]

Frank arrived in the workshop in January 1969. The MFA students were immediately dubious. For one, Frank looked different from the other poets, men whose unifying feature was a frumpy lack of athleticism. "He did not look like a poet," said one workshop veteran. "He looked like a weight lifter or boxer."[29] Another agreed, noting that he was "no effete English major."[30] Frank was also the only undergraduate in the seminar, a fact that made him an especially appealing target among seasoned graduate students who came to class aiming to put blood in the water. Stanford's credibility was further compromised because his first-year status as a business major had followed him to the workshop, and what could a bunch of starving poets possibly learn from a guy who had even momentarily considered being a business major?

Neither did it bode well for Frank that Whitehead's workshop was, like Whitehead himself, openly combative. Well-read second-year poets such as Leon Stokesbury, John Wood, and Jack Butler wielded knowledge to intimidate as much as to enlighten. Gwynn, who arrived in the fall 1969, called the workshop "fast, furious, and rough" and remembered how "people tended to get in arguments and yell at Whitehead."[31] Bruce Taylor, who came to the workshop from Boston in the fall of 1969, deemed the atmosphere "harsh, macho, and deeply southern." Taylor remembers how, when the poets got going, he didn't know what anybody was talking about. He'd go home and cram literary facts and theories into his head in a desperate attempt to catch up or maybe just embarrass himself at a slightly slower rate. "You had to know the poems, the poets, and the history. You had to know the literature—you couldn't just sit down and write a good poem," he said.[32]

And woe to the guy who sat down and wrote a bad poem. When Taylor introduced his first attempt to the seminar, the southern phalanx ambushed him. "I got unloaded on," he said, still feeling the sting a half century later. "One person said that 'I think this poem would be a good goddamn poem if a cannon went off in the middle of it.'" Another followed with "I don't think I've ever seen a poem before where I did not like one word—or maybe 'the.' Yeah, that's an okay word."[33] Demoralized, Taylor planned to quit and drive north toward home, but Jack Butler, the ex-preacher from Alligator, Mississippi, got Taylor drunk for three days and talked him back down south.

Bill Lavender, who joined the workshop in the summer of 1970, similarly recalls the cutthroat environment that Whitehead cultivated. "I had a couple of poems that tanked," he said, "and when poems tanked in those days, it was really a horrible experience." Everyone, he added, "took pride in its failure, making it as humiliating as possible. They'd quote lines back at you and laugh about it." But Lavender identified an upside to this ritualistic torture: "You felt like, if you worked through a workshop without getting slammed, you really accomplished something. When the group liked something and you actually got some praise and laughter, it was amazing."[34]

The assumptions behind the workshop were ultimately well intentioned: (a) The critics were harsh but well informed, and (b) their aim was to generate great poetry, accepting the fact that a little humiliation was part of the process. In a poem, John Stoss recalls how the criticisms "were so true and devastating you swear it's some crazy / demonic force" taking you down.[35] Lavender knew that he was in a group that was obsessed with poetry—its history, reading it, judging it, breathing it, writing it, talking about it endlessly. "People took it *really* seriously," he said. "That workshop made me decide what I wanted to do with my life."[36] Even a demoralized Bruce Taylor had to concede that, when it came to the harsh critiques, "I deserved it."[37] Such honesty, in the end, led to close friendships as well as better poetry.

For all the eagerness to take people down a few notches, or leave them in the fetal position, the workshop found Frank to be comparatively untouchable. It helped that he had the good sense to keep his head down. "He was very quiet in the workshop," said Gwynn, a recollection others repeatedly corroborated.[38] When Frank spoke, he did so only with Whitehead's prompting and, according to Stoss—whose long poem "Always Looking for a Safe Place" recalls many details of the workshop—revealed "an accent / [that would] make a tree stop growing for a few seconds."[39] (Once when a woman commented on Frank's accent, he said, "Well, guess you heard the pig shit in my voice.")[40] Stoss also recalls him "looking down from his monster eyes like maybe he should return to the wild Arkansas swamp for all we knew he came from." Adding to the mystique was an undeniably seductive factor that Frank, especially as he outgrew adolescence, would capitalize on for the rest of his life: "He was handsome beyond belief."[41] "He rarely said anything at all," another student remembered. "He was really quiet." But everyone sensed from the start that they were in the presence of a "dark, deep, southern voodoo genius."[42] One student went so far as to say Frank was shy.[43] In any case, much as he had done at Subiaco in Father Fuhrmann's classes, Frank walked into the workshop, met the room with a hard stare, let his looks do some work for him, and absorbed everything.

Then came the day he first workshopped his poems. John Stoss—described by one peer as "intuitively a poet"—remembers the impact that Frank's work had on the workshop veterans in one of his poems. "[W]e second-generation [as in second-semester] poets were moving / in and taking over," he wrote, but "the best poet of us all / was Frank Stanford . . . it was beyond belief that he / could handle words and intellect on such / a high realm. . . . You could almost hear Whitehead / and Harrison cheering their discovery."[44] Another student said, "Frank's poems were not like the others. He had a different way with language."[45] "Almost from the beginning," recalls Stokesbury, who was considered the program's leading poet before Frank's arrival, "there was a unique voice in the poems Frank submitted."[46] Another veteran said that Stanford "was considered the best writer" and that the poets in the workshop "almost thought he was a god."[47]

These accolades accumulated into something mythical, an amalgam of associations that went beyond the poems. By the end of the semester, Frank Stanford was "a legend," one who was "beyond admired."[48] In an atmosphere where, as Stoss wrote, "most of us / [were] trying trying trying and having the class / pick us apart like our poems were worms / turned out of the Arkansas soil," Stanford's work earned so much praise that he became "a little / embarrassed about the nice things said about his poems."⁴⁹ He was just twenty, and if nothing else, the encouragement got him back into the classroom and kept him there for a year.⁵⁰

Part of Stanford's immediate appeal in the seminar was the sheer novelty of his poems. While no poet was expected to adhere to a genre, Frank's work countered the MFA program's purported aesthetic focus. To the extent that the workshop favored a style, it leaned more neo-formalist than experimental, more what Frank dismissed as "Southern Writers Inc."⁵¹—writing in a self-consciously southern literary tradition—than international surrealism, objectivism, or confessional poetry. Whitehead, according to Gwynn, embraced "a fugitive tradition of the South," coming as he did from Vanderbilt, the home of Allen Tate, Donald Davidson, John Crowe Ransom, and Robert Penn Warren—the self-styled Agrarians. "There was a lot of 'mind of the South' type of stuff going on in the seminar," said Gywnn, referring to W. J. Cash's classic study of the Old South.⁵² Gwynn and Stokesbury favored a more formalist approach to poetry and found the program a good fit.⁵³ Student Bob Ward, who was from Baltimore by way of San Francisco, thought the dominant perspective of the workshop strange, noting how everyone seemed to be "writing in sort of Faulknerian styles . . . and they were *all* southerners. . . . It was like walking into the past."⁵⁴ Bruce Taylor, whom the graduate program housed in foreign student housing because he was from New England, was similarly taken aback by "the deep southern guys like Leon and Sam" who seemed to best reflect the program's focus.⁵⁵

Into this traditional atmosphere stepped Frank Stanford. He later said that he was more influenced by Byron than Flannery O'Connor and Carson McCullers, more attuned to "Beauty and the Beast" than Robert Penn Warren.⁵⁶ He submitted to the workshop poems such as "Living," "The Pump," "The Singing Knives," "Wishing My Wife Had One Leg," "The Picture Show Next Door to the Stamp Store in Downtown Memphis," and "The Gospel Bird" to magazines for publication. These poems defied the prevailing notions of formalism and regionalism. As Gwynn put it, they fell into the category of "didn't fit into the category of anything anybody else was writing."⁵⁷ As Frank would learn when he started to submit his work to small literary magazines—magazines with acceptance rates lower than 5 percent—Gwynn was not talking about the workshop alone. He was referring to the world of poetry at large, which would find Frank's work equally out of time. Because the freshness of Frank's voice was so thoroughly unmistakable, Whitehead overlooked its resistance to categorization and seized on what Gwynn called a Stanford poem's "defining elements." Whitehead went on and on, for example, about "The Gospel Bird," if only because he was in on the southern secret that a gospel bird was the bird you cooked on Sunday when the preacher was invited over for supper (something Frank had certainly learned from his mom having the monks over on Mallard Point).[58]

Frank's success was hardly a case of beginner's luck. He had likely been writing poems for much longer and with greater intensity than any other student in the program. His poems that made the "worksheet" (submissions to be critiqued the next day in class) in 1969 reflected a relatively mature poetic vision. Many of the icons and themes that animate the complete body of his writing are already evident in microcosm: the blues, dreams, the innocence of childhood, rural violence, Memphis and Snow Lake as cultural focal points, Jimmy as a recurring and subversive character ("I just got a soft spot in my heart for trouble" [8665]), sexual tension, horses, the moon, grotesques, myth, fish, and hoodoo. Less evident at this point are what would eventually become an Emily Dickinson–like obsession with death and a commitment to racial justice, a commitment that would reach fruition in *The Battlefield Where the Moon Says I Love You*.

Dean Young, a young poet in the 1970s, recalls his impressions when Stanford's poems were first passed around from reader to reader at the time in the introduction he wrote to the first collected poems edition of Stanford's work. The poems seemed to Young "far outside any known curriculum," "profoundly intoxicating," "authentically raw, even brutal," "both very old and utterly new," and evoking "a mythology beneath us."[59] The worksheet poems from 1969 bear out these assessments. A signature dream sequence, the kind that would define *The Battlefield* and that serves as a kind of DNA marker in Stanford's poetry, offers the kind of César Vallejo–inspired surrealism that struck students as something new:

> I dreamed the blacksnake rode the guitar
> Down the river
> I dreamed the clouds went by
> The moon like a dead fish
> I dreamed I was dragging
> A cotton sack with a dead man in it
> I dreamed the fish bandits stole the hogs
> Off my lines
> And one of them was a hunchback[60]

Nobody in the seminar room had ever heard anything like this. *Hunchbacks stealing catfish? A blacksnake floating down river on a guitar?* This was fresh and exciting, strange and dreamy, real and raw. While students were quick to identify hints of poetic realism, magical surrealism, and deep imagery, these poems ultimately landed in the workshop as sui generis realism. "Imagine Vallejo growing up in a tent on the Mississippi" was as close as poet Dean Young could get to describing a Stanford poem.[61] Stanford was unquestionably *southern* in his idiom, and his frequent evocation of familiar characters and places echoed the interlocking towns and family trees of Faulkner's Yoknapatawpha. "I live in the South, and I write about the people here," Frank once said, and that is in part what he showed the students in Whitehead's seminar.[62]

But Stanford's South was different. It was something both more accessible and less predictable. It rejected the Agrarian reverence for traditional values and classical forms. It was a South devoid of nostalgia or romance for the Confederate dead. It did not "struggle" with race in an obvious political sense so much as allow characters of all racial and ethnic persuasions to exist through language that linked them to one another and their landscape—and to worlds beyond. It was free of ideology and abstraction and instead deeply imbued with the sensuality of objects, people, places, smells, sounds, sensations. Stanford's South was becoming rather than being; it looked more outward than inward. John Biguenet, the poet and translator who first met Stanford in 1970 at a writer's conference at Hollins College, said of Frank's South: "I don't think people had seen anything like it."[63] Which could also be taken to mean that people saw something like it every day of their lives. They had just never seen it reflected back at them in such terms as those of Stanford.

Frank's South was also a child's view of the South. A child's perspective opened Stanford to the thingness of things in a way that evokes the poetic objectivism that was, at the time, in the air. One recalls William Carlos Williams's notion of "no ideas but in things" or Jasper Johns's "things the mind already knows" or even the Mississippi painter Walter Anderson's notion that "all things exist in themselves."[64] Two poems Stanford presented in his first semester in the workshop reflect this objectivist quality nicely: "Living" and "The Pump." In the latter, a well pump becomes a character in a low-stakes drama set in rural life. Frogs and lizards congregate around it, Johnsongrass grows under it, and in the winter, when covered with frost, the old pump could "bite" you, as it once did Jimmy ("and wouldn't let go"). The speaker uses the tongue of a Buster Brown shoe as a makeshift sucker washer. A sense of rural ingenuity and innocence marks the first four stanzas. But the fifth and last switches abruptly to something more serious:

> Sometimes the pump seemed like Jesus.
> I liked bathing buck naked
> Under the pump,
> Not in a goddamn washtub.[65]

This was powerful and wonderfully unexpected, as if adulthood arrived with a lightning bolt. Whitehead loved it. The only critical mark he made was in the line "I got the worms under the soggy boards." He suggested "slick" instead of "soggy." Frank, uncharacteristically, accepted the change.[66] According to Stoss, "if we criticized / he never changed one word or phrase."[67] In "Living," Stanford takes the innocence of childhood and nearly elevates it into a state of grace. The opening stanza approaches the edge of parody but never crosses it:

> I had my quiet time early in the morning
> Eating Almond Joys with Mother.
> We'd sit on the back porch and talk to God.
> We really had a good time.[68]

In this prelapsarian realm of tranquil mornings, a sweetly attentive mother, and God, the speaker gets to the business of "living." This means pursuing a Huck Finn–ish life of sorting baseball cards, looking for bottles, and shooting popguns at blackbirds. Jimmy makes the truck backfire to please his little cousin, and it works every time. A hint of violence creeps into the fourth stanza, but it's quickly defused by a joke that Jimmy makes:

> In the evening the cottontails ran across the groves.
> I shot one and put him in the backseat.
> He went to the bathroom.
> Jimmy said I knocked the shit out of him.[69]

The poem ends with references to baseball, a famous Memphis DJ, and a blues song whose message is, basically, "If my good fortune ever comes to an end, I'm gonna die from the pain, so prepare yourself."

> At night we would listen to the ballgame.
> Then to Hoss Man.
> Jimmy liked "Take Out Some Insurance On Me Baby" by Jimmy Reed.[70]

People started talking about these poems outside of the workshop. By the end of the spring 1969 semester, according to a member of Whitehead's class, some of Frank's poems "were already considered classics." Frank had gone from total obscurity to local cultlike fame in a matter of months. When new students arrived in the fall of 1969, they heard about this charismatic young poet named Frank Stanford. Cheering the loudest was Jim Whitehead. "Whitehead was the one who talked about him the most," said student Bob Ward. "He knew Frank was going to be a major poet."[71] Sam Gwynn said that "Jim took on Frank as his protégé."[72] One of Whitehead's daughters, who was fourteen at the time, remembered how there was often talk about Frank around the house. "My dad just loved Frank," she said.[73]

It seemed everyone was rooting for the moody, curly-haired undergraduate from the hills, or the lowland swamps, or wherever they wanted him to come from. Students remember how Stokesbury, although quickly developing something of a Salieri complex, also took Frank under his wing. Frank's poems might have been sui generis, but Frank needed context. To that end, Stokesbury and the workshop introduced him to living poets he did not know, primarily those in that year's *The Contemporary American Poets*. Stanford was one of only a few poets to escape Stokesbury's signature seminar sneer, a reaction to workshop poems that ended with his leaning his head back and staring at the ceiling in dismay. Stokesbury would always vie "for the title best poet in the MFA program," as John Stoss observes in his poem "Always Looking for a Safe Place," but Stokesbury knew his chances slimmed with every poem Frank showed the class. Stoss left the workshop thinking that Frank "never wrote a wrong / word or sentence."[74] One student recounts how someone convinced the secretary in the English Department to secretly make copies of Frank's worksheet poems and circulate them before class.[75] "He became a kind of legend," Ralph Adamo recalls, because of these poems written for the workshop.[76]

To cap off his stellar first semester, Frank scored his first publication. "Living" was added to that year's issue of the university's annual literary magazine, *Preview*, edited in 1969 by Stokesbury. Excited by this acceptance, he sent a poem ("The Gospel Bird") to *Poetry*, but it was rejected ("I didn't feel as bad as I thought I would," wrote Frank).[77] But consolation came when Frank was chosen to edit a future issue of *Preview*—a top honor—in 1971. Through these kinds of accomplishments, Frank Stanford started to become a known quantity in the streets of Fayetteville.

## "Well, What Was *That* About?"

For the University of Arkansas MFA students (and perhaps MFA students everywhere), the line between poetry and social life was, to put it mildly, blurred—inappropriately, shamelessly, and sometimes dangerously blurred. Parties became an extension of the workshop but with alcohol, drugs, sex, and, on at least one occasion, gunfire thrown into the mix. Bill Harrison, with a wife and three kids, said *no* to parties at his house from the start. "I don't think Bill ever let us in," recalled one of his students. "He was smarter than that."[78] Whitehead, with a wife and seven kids at his sprawling home, opened wide the doors. The Whitehead house was made for it. The family lived in walking distance of campus, on East Lafayette Street, in a house with a sizable yard and huge basement. According to his wife, Gen, Jim Whitehead viewed his parties as a way to create solidarity among students.[79] A Whitehead party for the poets was a coveted invitation. "I just felt so cool and special," said one English major about getting to go to one.[80] Whitehead's only rule (never followed) was that his liquor cabinet be left alone.[81] On these evenings, Whitehead also invited students into his home office. Students were free to come and go and talk to their professor about poetry and life. Gen Whitehead and her kids remember heading to their rooms for bedtime only to be kept awake until three in the morning by loud, drunken, happy poets.[82]

In the fall of 1970, the poet and translator Miller Williams joined the Arkansas MFA program's faculty. He came to Fayetteville from Loyola University in New Orleans. Williams was accomplished and professional. He had translated to great acclaim the poems of the Chilean poet Nicanor Parra and had recently founded the *New Orleans Review*, which placed unique emphasis on poetry translations. He was also known by colleagues for his rigorous organizational acumen, a disposition perhaps reflecting his early training as a biologist. "Miller exuded discipline," said Sam Gwynn, "and he came with the idea of bringing it to the program."[83] Williams also brought with him from New Orleans several young poets, including Ralph Adamo and John Biguenet, not only adding to the program's impressive depth of talent but also deepening its self-consciously southern focus. Stoss remembered Miller as "a short man with not a very big head balding and with thick black glasses his eyes glowing in the dark of day."[84] Glowing or not, Miller's vision, not unlike Whitehead's, owed a debt to the southern Agrarians. If Whitehead was, as Taylor put it, "the southern man," Williams let it be known that two men could play that game.[85] "Miller masqueraded as a country southern manners type," Gwynn said.[86] Fellow student Paul Lubenkov agreed, noting Miller's "southern style."[87] Williams said that the best compliment he ever got from a critic said, "Miller Williams is the Hank Williams of American poetry. While

Miller Williams (*center*) at home with his poetry workshop, 1970.
*Photo courtesy of David Reich.*

his poetry is taught at Princeton and Harvard, it's read and understood by squirrel hunters and taxi drivers."[88]

Williams insisted on a hierarchical relationship between students and faculty.[89] Unlike Whitehead, with whom he became very close, he would not engage in shouting matches and open debates with kids half his age. That seemed undignified and out of order.[90] He held forth during classes from a recliner that eased his chronic back pain. Students fanned out around him on the floor or in chairs, gazing at the master, awaiting pearls of wisdom. "We gather around the great mentor," writes Stoss in a wryly humoristic vein, "on his / king's chair."[91] Adamo recalled, "He was a good teacher up to a certain point, and then it was the kind of influence you have to pull away from. I pulled away early."[92] After the workshop, before the partying began, Williams sometimes made the students listen to his daughter, the future Grammy Award winner Lucinda Williams, play guitar and sing. "We all had to be quiet, sit still, and listen," Gwynn recalled, noting how when she sang the song "Season of the Witch," he thought she was singing "season of the wench" because of her accent.[93]

Like Whitehead, Williams believed parties promoted cohesion among the graduate students. "My feeling is that one of Miller's gifts was creating that welcoming, communal feeling among writers," said one writer close to Lucinda Williams. "Some writers are competitive and hardly ever come out of their shells. Miller really loved hosting parties and I think that rubbed off on a lot of people."[94] Some remember how Miller was "something of a freewheeler" when it came to social interactions.[95] He was not shy, for example, about how he and his wife, Jordan, were swingers, and, as many did in the 1970s, he supported a "playboy atmosphere" in general.[96] But many students, sometimes female ones, did not feel comfortable in that atmosphere, even in the sexually fluid era of the early 1970s. The only two women in the poetry workshop during its first few years—Nancy Harris and Julia Alvarez—never finished the program. Harris, for her part, was clear about why. A male professor wanted to sleep with her, and she had no interest in such a prospect. In the wake of this rejection, he was soon explaining that the program might not be the right kind of place for her and suggesting that she might consider leaving.[97] Harris went back to New Orleans, where she got a job at the *Times-Picayune*.

These parties were by contrast terrific for male bonding. Bob Ward, who was in the fiction program, remembers how, despite a roomful of women at the parties, the male poets "all stuck together." He said, "These poets always ended up in the kitchen in what looked like a football huddle. I would be in the other room trying to hustle one of the girls, and I would think, *What are these fucking poets doing?*" On the rare occasion when Ward poked his head into their huddle, he heard nothing but poetry gossip. In one instance he overheard a throng of poets debating which famous poet had had the most consequential death, one of them recalling what Robert Frost supposedly had said when he learned that Yeats had died: "Good now I have no more competition." Ward took it all in and said, "You guys are the gloomiest people in the world," to which "they looked at me like, fuck off, Ward. You're just a fiction writer."[98] Frank, never one to go with the team, stayed out of the huddles. While he did not avoid the MFA parties, he stuck to their periphery, entering the fray in bombastic and attention-grabbing ways rather than through normal social interactions. Alcohol, which he continued to consume heavily, fueled his outbursts. During one party, on New Year's Eve at the close of 1969, according to a student named Larry Johnson, Frank had gotten very drunk and had "torn out of the house and was running down the street." It was icy cold out, and the poets feared their young star would pass out and freeze to death, so several people chased him down. "When we caught him," Johnson wrote, "he had fallen into a shallow ditch and was rolling around acting crazy." Johnson was able to haul him out and help him stagger back to the house. Frank thanked him by grabbing him in a "somewhat sexual way."[99]

Ward recalled a similar incident at another party. This gathering had gotten more out of control than usual; "There was all kinds of wild shit going on," he said. On occasion, including this one, Williams's wife-swapping ethic extended to the students. Larry Johnson fell for John Wood's wife, John Wood's wife fell for Larry Johnson, and John Wood, many suggest, fell for Frank Stanford, but Frank Stanford, at least on this evening, was hitting on a woman, so John Wood fell for Larry Johnson too. It was that kind of night. Threesomes were not uncommon among the poets. Wood was "a fucking crazy character," according to Ward. Stoss, usually excluded from sexual threesomes, attempted to line up a twosome by walking around and asking women point-blank if they wanted to have sex. Anyway, "everybody was drunk," said Ward, "I mean really drunk, and there was pot and speed as well."[100]

Amid this chaos Frank, again, burst out of the house and into the street, this time frantically chasing the woman he was hitting on. Ward recalled looking up and seeing Frank "running out there with his shirt hanging off, completely nuts." The woman was nowhere to be seen, but Frank was heading blindly into oncoming traffic. Ward thought, "This isn't going to end well" and ran out and tackled Frank (no mean feat), yelling, "You can't just run out in the middle of the street!" Frank looked at him and started laughing hysterically. Then he said, "Yeah, I guess you're right" and walked back into the house, leaving Ward thinking, "Well, what was *that* about?"[101]

Socially speaking, Frank often left many people asking the same question. Random acts left people miffed. Jim's wife Gen remembers Frank coming to their house and, still out of breath from running over, telling her that "I just had sex with the same woman nine times."[102] ("[I]t is as simple as that," Stanford writes in *The Battlefield*, "sexual and frank" [12690–91].) When John Stoss went to see Frank in his studio on Dickson Street above the old UARK Theatre, which he'd moved back to in the summer of 1969, Stoss joked that he could take Frank, the judo master, down in a fight. Stoss was obviously joking with Frank. But Frank, lacking any sense of irony, later tracked him down and said that, as Stoss later recalled, "he could have ripped / me and tore me up good" and "almost did."[103] When Jack Butler took a karate lesson with Frank, Frank, as Butler later recalled it, "shoved me in the chest and I fell over backwards," and then "he broke my toe with a downward block." The experience left Butler motivated "to develop my own martial art, which was never get in a fight."[104] Disparate as these events seem, they were all just off-kilter enough to leave people asking the same question Ward had asked: What the hell was *that* about?

Perhaps Frank's most famous theatrical and mythmaking performance in Fayetteville came in the late fall of 1970. By this point the MFA parties had become legendary throughout the English Department. So much so that it was not uncommon for PhD students to show up, as well as a few undergraduates, if only to say that they'd been to an MFA party. Most of the time, their presence was tolerated as they usually brought their own booze and pot and only stayed long enough to say they'd been there. But Frank had a different reaction when some outsiders showed up at the party he was hosting up on Mount Sequoyah, about a mile off campus. "There was a pretty good crowd," said Gwynn, "but when people from the regular English program started showing up, Frank decided he didn't want all these people around." Willett, who was at the party because Frank was hosting it (Willett did not normally hang out with the MFA group), remembered how "there were a lot of hangers-on that just didn't know how to party and would just get in everyone else's way. Even sorority girls."[105]

Frank decided he'd had enough. These imposters were not up to the standards of the wild poets. He went over to the record player, cranked up an album called *Blues Classics by the Jug, Jook and Washboard Bands*, grabbed a loaded rifle (Willett says it was a Parker rifle), and promptly pumped a round through the ceiling of the cabin, blasting out a hole the size of a basketball.[106] Adamo, who was outside when Frank took his shot, remembers hearing the blast.[107] Gwynn, who knew this was only a stunt, looked at the PhD students, who looked back at him for some clue as to how to react. With debris falling and gun smoke hanging in the air, Gwynn yelled as loudly as he could, into Frank's face: "Freak, man! Freak!" At this the interlopers poured out of the place in a panic. "After that," Willett remembered, "we had one hell of a good time."[108] Adamo speculates that "this was the beginning of a kind of mythologizing" of Frank.[109]

### "That's Frank"

Frank generally knew what he was up to with these stunts. The adulation he achieved in the workshop ensured that his outbursts were taken to be evidence of precocious genius fueled by poetic madness rather than alarming signs of disordered social behavior. The sheer theatricality of his antics enhanced the "angry wild beast" image that Father Fuhrmann remembered Frank cultivating once he got to Fayetteville.[110] It was precisely that image that the poet Alan Dugan, who may have been at the party when Frank fired away, had in mind when, responding to Frank's wayward proposition to move himself to Provincetown, Massachusetts, wrote, "I think you are better off in Fayetteville or in Mississippi where your violence of behavior is relatively acceptable. If you came to Provincetown for example you'd be in jail after a couple of nights."[111] This kind of response was exactly what Frank wanted to hear. This was exactly how he wanted to be perceived, and shooting out a roof was a quick way to ensure it.

While Frank had been prone to outbursts since at least middle school—biting the heads off fish in Mountain Home, threatening to chop off his penis at Subiaco—these recent ones were behaviors as strange as his poems, just as unpredictable and unsettling, and to some extent reflective of the same creative act of writing poetry. As such, they were, as Adamo noted, easily molded into myths, ones that glorified the handsome, dark, mysterious, wildly talented, and mercurial poet.

But Frank knew the theatrics meant nothing without the published poems to back them up. Here he delivered. In 1970, after his only two semesters in the workshop, he began a terrific five-year publication run, drawing not only on his growing corpus of work but also on what he had learned from Whitehead and Stokesbury about how and where to submit poems. In addition to "Living" coming out in *Preview: 1968–1969* in the spring of 1969, he published the poems "Elegy For My Father, 1883–1963," "The Picture Show Next Door to the Stamp Store in Downtown Memphis," "The Gospel Bird," and "The Albino," in the 1969–70 issue of *Preview* in early 1970; "Early Times in a Mississippi Liquor Store" and "The Hole" in *Tansy* in 1970; "The Professors," "The Solitude of Historical Analysis," "The Politicians," and "Holy Night" in *Mill Mountain Review* in 1970; and "Wishing My Wife Had One Leg" in the 1971 issue of *Preview* that he edited himself. This was an exceptional publishing debut.

There is much to admire in these early publications. The poet Rodney Jones notes that "most poets are too unformed at this age, but Frank skipped that stage."[112] This point was similarly expressed by the Pulitzer Prize–winning poet Richard Eberhart, who wrote that it was "hard to realize how he could be so good in so relatively short a time."[113] There's the perfect evocation of place (levee camps) and childhood in "Elegy for My Father, 1883–1963":

> I had one finger in my ear
> And one in my toes looking for jam,

Waiting for the Negro
To set off the dynamite[114]

In "Early Times in a Mississippi Liquor Store," there's the elevation of countrified diction into something between operatic elegance and gangster rap—for example, when a store owner named James Jefferson asks a group of Black men just off work how he can help them:

Wild Turkey, suh, most would say.
Mr. James Jefferson said he enjoyed
Waiting on the wonky gandy-dancers,
He liked to watch them rock
In their toe holed Johnny Walkers
And he liked their conversation
I'm low like a toad,
A taradiddle, dippy, and dumb,
But I ain't no thimblerigger, Mr. James.[115]

Or, in "The Picture Show Next Door to the Stamp Store in Downtown Memphis," there's the almost impossibly achieved elision between mechanized urbanity and rural violence. The setting is a movie house in Memphis where the narrator, right in front of a group of Catholic schoolgirls who are waiting to see a film, cups his hands to catch the ice and soda from the drink dispenser because the actual cup failed to drop:

I am holding my hands together
like a gloveless hunter
drinking water in the morning
or calling up owls in the forest;
I am holding my hands together
like a hunter in winter
with his hands in the water
washing away the blood.[116]

One would be hard-pressed to find in the traditional Agrarian canon an expression as effectively critical of mechanization, even if it's only through a Coke dispenser, as this is. Equally compelling is Stanford's evocation of country life, with the speaker's cupped hands mirroring the primitive and sacred hunting ritual of washing off animal blood after the kill, in addition to calling owls and drinking water. The juxtaposition of these gestures with the violence of hunting further merges mechanization and its discontents with the more honest values grounded in the natural world. It is as if Stanford is telling the poetic ancestors he disavowed that while he has no interest in their collective Agrarian vision, for the record, this is how you do it.

By the end of 1970 Frank knew full well that it was not only Whitehead and the workshop poets who wanted more of his poems. Soon editors at the nation's leading little magazines were showing a keen interest in his work, encouraging him to send more poems. There is no doubt some of this attention went to his head. It is perhaps not surprising that Sam Gwynn said, "I can't think of anybody he'd consider an equal."[117] As his star started to rise, Stanford made sure it rose in the way that best suited him. "He was always a self-promoter," said Larry Johnson.[118] But Frank's brand of promotion, one that would never change, did not necessarily translate into greater exposure in commercial venues. He began to manipulate his nascent image in ways that highlighted his status as a prodigy from the hills, a reclusive poet more comfortable with Fayetteville's eccentric outcasts than the overly schooled types in the "Algonquin Round Table," a loner and an orphan who was his own act more than a team player.

This disposition meant, among other things, alienating himself from the MFA poets, the poetry workshop, and even Jim Whitehead. This transition was a marked one. When Frank first joined the workshop, there was a sense that he had found a new home. After a few weeks of the workshop, "Frank started fitting in with all of us," one student recalled.[119] John Stoss remembered how, at one party in the spring of 1969, Frank and Leon Stokesbury "went around shoulder to shoulder like little boys . . . welcoming us all and dancing all night."[120] But when John Biguenet arrived in the fall of 1970, after Frank had left the poetry workshop, it was obvious to him that something was wrong. "There had been a breach from his relationship with the MFA program," he said. "Frank was keeping his distance. . . . Whatever happened, it was substantial enough that people were talking about it."[121] Gwynn agreed, noting how "Frank grew distant from the poetry workshop."[122] In 1972 a psychiatrist seeing Frank noted in his report that "there is the feeling that this patient had quit his studies at the University of Arkansas due to disagreements with other people with whom he was studying."[123] What is so strange is that nobody can recall what those disagreements were or whether they even happened.

Despite the admiration and support from Whitehead and the workshop poets, Frank orchestrated his exit from the workshop with a measure of hostility. It began with small gestures before escalating into explicit condemnations. In March 1971, he wrote in a "Dear Sir" letter to the editors at *Partisan Review* that the MFA students "laughed at me at first;

now they don't like me" and that "I can't show the writers here poems or say anything because they steal it."[124] To John McKernan, who was working as an editor at the *Little Review*, he wrote, "If you knew how many knives were in my back."[125] To another editor, Eleanor Bender, he claimed, "Everybody started analyzing me."[126] When Stokesbury asked him for a biographical note for the 1970 *Preview* issue he was editing, Stanford wrote, "An undergraduate, Frank thinks, 'most of the people in this book, and most of the people in this school, are tight-assed honkies.' "[127] Funny, sort of. But hostile too.

Then there were the shenanigans over the moon. When Frank edited *Preview: Eight Poets* in 1970–71 for the magazine's 1971 publication, he consulted all of nobody as he assembled what proved to be a tastefully minimalist issue. "He was doing it in a fairly secretive manner," Gwynn said. "He just told people he wasn't accepting editorial suggestions." And while "it seems like small pond stuff now, people thought it was big stakes." Frank assigned each poet in the volume a drawing of a phase of the moon. Stoss got what looked like a fat zero; Gwynn earned a half moon; Stokesbury got almost a full moon. Gwynn recalled looking at his moon and thinking, "Ahhh, okay, I get it."[128] Stokesbury later remembered how Frank "pissed us off" because the moon phase "was a comment by Frank on that poet's poetry."[129]

The eighth poet, representing the volume's denouement, was, of course, Frank himself. He gave himself a new moon followed by the powerful poem "Wishing My Wife Had One Leg." In the biographical notes he stresses that he is the only undergraduate in the issue—even though he had by then dropped out of school—but was nonetheless the issue's editor. Last, by changing his birth year to 1949 (instead of the actual year, 1948), he made it known that he was the youngest poet in the volume (both Gwynn and Adamo were also born in 1948).[130] The overall message was unmistakable: He was younger and better and had a brighter future than the other poets. "He was remarkable enough," Stokesbury wrote. "But he had to have more."[131]

Later Frank openly and somewhat uncharitably disparaged the program and those in it. Frank's poem "Flies on Shit" refers to "the dumb-ass students" and "gentlemen from the South" who swarmed around poems and ruined them with their "institutional poetry criticism."[132] To an editor, Frank wrote that "when I was in college, the local poets and teachers *conditioned* me against my own natural inclination in poetry."[133] To another, Frank explained about his cohort of students and professors, "They are all good and honorable writers, only better poets advised me not to tow their line of neo-fugitive, neo-redneck verse. It is difficult to break with ties, but none I had there were over two years old."[134] *The Battlefield* mentions poets who "slept in one another's jockstrap" (12518). Frank's psychiatrist wrote in his 1972 patient report that "apparently he had someone advising him to not listen to what those people were saying but get away."[135] In a note to himself, Frank wrote, without further context, "I feel guilty ... goin [*sic*] along with JM [Jim Whitehead] like that."[136]

Still, much of Frank's vitriol may well have been manufactured by Frank for Frank. In a June 1971 note to Alan Dugan, he sounds almost paranoid about the workshop poets. "Most of them hate my guts," he wrote about the poets in the program, poets who generally admired him.[137] To Eleanor Bender a week later he wrote, "They had me tied up by the feet and they were ready to slit my throat, but I got away and I ran a long time until I quit."[138] This was a melodramatic Frank. John Biguenet remembers that "there was just so much bitterness that people expressed about whatever happened."[139] Another fellow student said, "It was like he just dropped out."[140] And another: "He had basically dismissed his old friends."[141] And Frank: "All everyone wants to do here is kiss everyone's [illegible] ass and play poetry politics."[142]

Frank held on to some of these grievances well into the mid-1970s. In some notes that C. D. Wright took on an interview Frank did with Irv Broughton, Frank calls his colleagues a "fraternity" that "used the South as a compost in the gardens of their work."[143] His second wife, Ginny, wrote to the editor Michael Cuddihy after Frank's death, responding to a note that Frank had written to Cuddihy wherein Frank made some critical, possibly indelicate comments about the MFA program. She noted that "the faculty at U of A is aware of franks feelings of disdain for a few of them—i.e., he's said plenty of stuff about the profs there." And then she noted the faults that Frank routinely observed about the program: "Franks speculations ... might offend miller williams or jim whitehead—they're easily offended by 'political things'—my guess is that everyone would say 'that's Frank.'"[144] Ralph Adamo remembers how Frank mentioned having to suffer fools in the program. He also remembers how badly that remark stung Leon Stokesbury, who so warmly encouraged Frank and, later, eulogized him.[145] Frank did not reciprocate the support. "Frank always said Leon tried to steal his material," Frank's publisher Irv Broughton recalls.[146]

Frank, in short, felt indebted to everybody and nobody at once. A line from the poem "Transcendence of Janus," published in *The Singing Knives*, captures the defensiveness that he would assume toward any suggestion or implication that he was influenced by contemporary poets, much less the peers he knew. He mentions "the dusty sockets / of poets, who have lost their eyes."[147]

## "I've Forgotten the Name of the Poet but I Liked His Poetry"

Frank forged a narrative that claimed he, the lone genius, had had little to gain from the MFA workshop. But there is no doubt that he benefited tremendously from his affiliation with the program. He did so specifically by meeting and impressing visiting poets with established reputations. Whether retiring and reclusive, explosive, or manic, Frank could pull himself together and act like a perfectly normal human being when the situation demanded it. When Allen Ginsberg showed up in Fayetteville with Peter Orlovsky on May 1, 1969, largely because of John Wood's intense lobbying to get Ginsberg to visit, Frank was quick to don his well-adjusted persona and hobnob with the famed Beat poet.

Ginsberg took an immediate liking to Frank—"They got along well," one student remembered.[148] "Ginsberg was clearly turned on by him," Stokesbury wrote, adding that "Frank played that for what it was worth."[149] When John Wood picked up Ginsberg and Orlovsky at the airport in Little Rock, Ginsberg expressed an interest in the folk traditions of rural Arkansas. This was right up Frank's alley, and over the weekend Frank advised Ginsberg on the best places to find fried dill pickles, catfish, and real folk musicians. Frank met Ginsberg on the second day of his visit and, along with Jack Butler and John Wood (and their spouses), went to the Ozarks National Forest with him, stopping off to have huckleberry pie in Eureka Springs before going to Magnetic Mountain.[150] Frank badly wanted to make a detour to Subiaco to introduce Allen to the monks, but "one of those professors in charge wouldn't let us go."[151] The group had a photo taken in front of the soaring Christ of the Ozarks statue and then hiked to a fire tower and climbed up and down it, hiked some more, and then drank Coca-Colas at a local convenience store. As they posed for the picture in front of the statue, Ginsberg, Frank later told Dugan, had "held my hand."[152]

Ginsberg was a fun guest. He became intrigued by a local word that happens to appear throughout *The Battlefield*: "peckerwood." The term is slang for a poor white person, implying "white trash." When Ginsberg was interviewed in the local newspaper, he gamely tried to use this new word in his vocabulary, but confusing it with redneck, he said "peckernecks." Malaprop aside, Ginsberg read that night to a standing-room-only crowd for well over two hours.[153] Student Larry Johnson says it was the best reading he'd ever heard. Everyone was thrilled that Ginsberg read a poem he had not read aloud in a long time, a poem with a message that resonated well in the heady days of 1969: "Howl."[154]

After the event, Frank joined a group of workshop poets who took Ginsberg out for pizza and beer. "Pitchers and pitchers" of beer were consumed, and the only topic up for discussion was, as always, poetry. The students were enthralled with the master, and their attention might have slightly irked their professor. Whitehead, true to form, went on the offensive, and as Wood recalled, "Allen and Whitehead got into it about prosody." Whitehead, whose poetry could not have been more different from Ginsberg's, ended up calling Ginsberg a "pedant." The students kept trying to shush their animated professor, but as always, "Jim roared on." The resolution to this conflict was, alas, more beer. Later in the evening, after Whitehead had gone home, Ginsberg and the students stumbled over to Stokesbury's house and crammed onto a sofa, where a picture was taken with Ginsberg and Frank pressed into each other, grasping cans of Budweiser.[155]

On the last day of the guru's visit came the moment all students were waiting for—Ginsberg would read and comment on their poems. The poets gathered anxiously in Old Main. Wood, a wonderful poet, hoped for anointment from the hero he had invited to the Ozarks. Ginsberg was tactfully noncommittal. However, five months later he felt confident sharing his opinions of what he'd read that afternoon. He wrote to Wood asking about "the poet with dungarees." "I've forgotten the name of the poet," he wrote, "but I liked his poetry." Ginsberg, once he'd discovered who this poet was, said Frank should "try sending it out to *Poetry* or *Evergreen* or wherever it interests him if it interests him to publish some."[156]

The endorsement made a significant impression on Frank. In 1975, recalling his time in the program, he wrote to an editor that the workshop would have been an intolerable fate had not "A. Ginsberg and Donald Justice on visits . . . told me I had nothing to fear."[157] Ginsberg was surely attracted to Frank, but there is no doubt that he admired his poetry as well. "Frank's poems always seem slightly electric," he wrote.[158] Stoss summed it up aptly when he said Frank was "exalted by Allen Ginsberg."[159] Another fellow student has said that Frank, as his note to Cuddihy suggested, felt the confidence to exit the program because Ginsberg convinced him he was ready to move on.[160]

Frank's next big networking coup came a year later at the famous Hollins Conference on Creative Writing and Cinema at Hollins College, a nearly two-week event organized by the poets George Garrett and R. H. W. Dillard.

Larry Johnson described the Hollins gathering as "the greatest of all literary conferences ever held."[161] When Jim Whitehead returned from it, he wrote to Miller Williams, who had not been able attend, that it "was a wonder I'd wish we shared."[162] Over 250 prominent writers, filmmakers, and students attended.[163] John Biguenet, who would start graduate school at Arkansas that fall, remembers being starry-eyed while talking to writers such as Richard Yates and William Manchester. Sam Goldwyn Jr. was there, as were James Dickey, Larry McMurtry, Shelby Foote, Brian Moore, and Ralph Ellison. "George Garrett knew everybody," Biguenet recalls, and he drew on his connections to make this conference a memorable one.[164]

James McAuley, a young creative writing professor at Arkansas with a large station wagon, loaded students and professors—including Stanford, John Little, Bill Harrison, Jim Whitehead, Kathy Walton, and Jack Butler—into it, and they drove the nearly one thousand miles to Roanoke, Virginia, with an overnight stop in Knoxville.[165] During the day the conference was all literature; at night, all movies. Biguenet thinks he may have seen as many as fifty films in those two weeks. "If I was not at a reading, I was at a film," he said.[166] The same held true for Frank, who exhibited a social energy and poise he sometimes lacked back home. Not only did he attend the Hollins Conference, but he was also, as Johnson recalls, "in the middle of everything."[167] Frank left behind the wild-man-of-the-backwoods persona, the white-kid-who-prefers-to-hang-out-with-Black-people persona, and the better-than-everyone-else persona. As he did during the visits of famous poets, he poured on the charm and integrated himself seamlessly into the graces of those who had more influence than he did. When it came to outrageous behavior, context mattered. Hollins was a place for the southern gentleman, not the southern wild man.[168]

Frank, who was attending the conference with financial support provided by George Garrett, had a blast.[169] Highlights for him included Richard Wilbur responding with enthusiasm to his poem "The Picture Show Next to the Stamp Store in Downtown Memphis," which Frank wrote that Wilbur talked about for forty-five minutes.[170] Larry Johnson, although "high on Vietnamese grass," remembers being amused when Wilbur had to have what "booties" were explained to him ("Their booties dance / in the leotards").[171] When a writer named David Slavitt, who had an elite East Coast educational pedigree (Andover, Yale, Columbia) and a best-selling novel, *The Exhibitionist*, to his credit, spoke, Frank leaned over to Johnson and said, "That guy's a shithook."[172] When he was drinking beer one evening under some trees in the quad and a thunderstorm rolled in, Frank, as he told Johnson, got worried and went inside. The

Hollins Conference, with its professional writers and poets and filmmakers, was not the place to be taunting lightning with metal rods, as Frank had done a few years earlier at Subiaco. Plus, he had other reasons to come in from the rain. Johnson is certain that "Frank was one of the lucky guys who got some sex at that event."[173] Gwynn recalled how "Frank had a big head at the conference."[174]

To top it off, Frank landed a book contract. It "made us all jealous," Gwynn remembers.[175] This life-changing moment happened because it was at Hollins that Frank first met Irv Broughton, who was then a Hollins graduate student. The two men introduced themselves in a parking lot outside an academic building on campus before going in to see a film. "I'm Frank from the University of Arkansas. You a poet?" Irv recalls him asking by way of introduction.[176] A year before he met Frank, Broughton had started a handsome semiannual "little magazine," *Mill Mountain Review*, which he'd funded with a $1,000 loan and ran "by the skin of my teeth." He was just finishing his degree at Hollins College, where he was studying with George Garrett and putting the final touches on the second issue of *Mill Mountain Review*. The magazine was printed on high-quality paper using an old Varityper machine "that fought with me every time I touched it," Broughton said. Whereas many little magazines at the time skimped when it came to design, *Mill Mountain Review*, because of art editor John Brust, was beautifully illustrated. It had a subscription base that, while modest, included the New York Public Library.[177] Frank was impressed with the issue that Broughton gave him, as it included poems by Annie Dillard, William Matthews, and Garrett. Frank specifically remarked on the quality of the paper. In exchange for it, Frank handed Irv a manuscript he was calling "22 Poems."

Broughton read it that night and was captivated. "I loved his work almost immediately," he said, adding that he knew he'd encountered a genius. At breakfast the next morning, he told Frank he wanted to publish it. He also took five other poems for his issue in progress, one that included work by Philip Levine, Fred Chappell, and Wendell Berry,[178] and six more poems for the following year's first issue, which included work by Tillie Olsen, Richard Wilbur, and Frank's teachers Jim Whitehead and Bill Harrison.[179] Frank's contributor's note in the first *Mill Mountain Review* issue his work appeared in was humorously pared down: "Frank Stanford is from the University of Arkansas. He is forthcoming in *Evergreen Review* and *New American Review*. He likes elephants."[180] His next contributor's note, however, was triumphant: "Frank Stanford's THE SINGING KNIVES is new from Mill Mountain Press."[181]

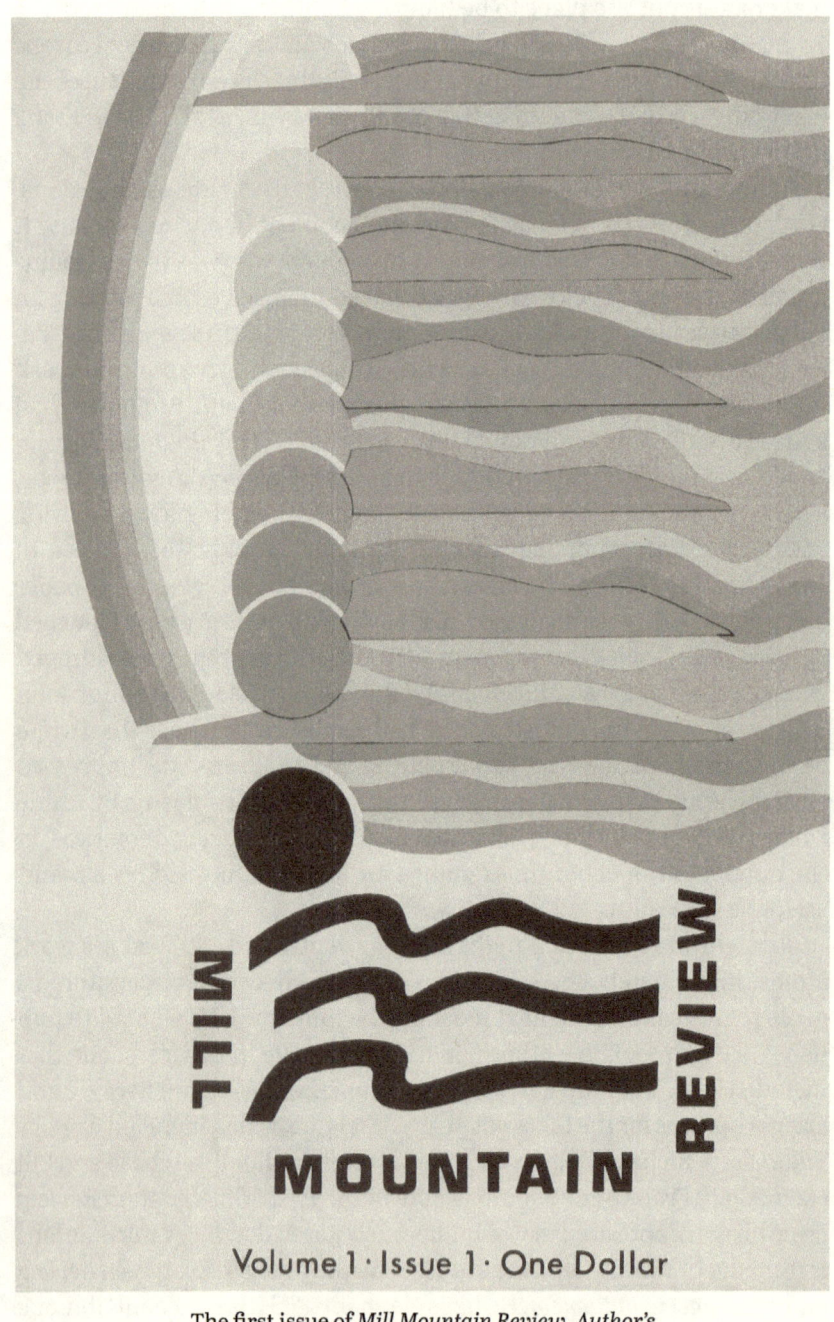

The first issue of *Mill Mountain Review*. Author's copy. Photo courtesy of the author.

For Irv, Frank's appeal went beyond the poetry. Whereas Irv could come off as nerdy, Frank was cool and handsome. Frank's rootedness in backcountry vernacular appealed deeply to Irv, whose suburban Florida upbringing lacked such exoticism. Frank was also more willing than most to share the inner process of his craft, something that Irv was intensely interested in documenting for all the artists he admired (and which, in fact, he would spend much of his career doing). In a March 1971 letter to Irv, Frank wrote, "What I like to do after getting the feel of each poem . . . is write the poems out and, or memorize some without writing them out. . . . The closer you get to *the* experience either by participating or feeling—reading or writing—the closer you can come to making it with somebody's poems."[182] This kind of creative introspection thrilled Broughton. He made it clear that Frank could expect complete loyalty from him, a promise he kept. Irv Broughton would spend the next five years putting Frank's interests ahead of his own. Without Irv Broughton we would not know Frank Stanford the way we do today.[183]

If Irv gave Frank a platform on which to build a legacy, the poet Alan Dugan gave Frank the confidence to start building it. Dugan, because of Stokesbury's lobbying, came to the Arkansas program in November 1970 to do a reading and meet with students. His visit was, by all accounts, another major victory for Frank Stanford. It was a meeting that would culminate with Frank finding his most influential advocate and active correspondent. Stokesbury wanted Dugan—a Yale Series of Younger Poets, Pulitzer Prize, and National Book Award winner—to visit Arkansas because he was certain that Dugan shared his own poetic vision. But Dugan, who despised the notion of anyone writing Dugan-like poems, did not agree. He made no friends on his legendary visit from coastal Truro, Massachusetts, to the hinterlands. With one exception. Frank, whom Dugan "named as the Anointed One," became close friends with him.[184] "Frank was," Gwynn noted, "the answer to Dugan's prayer." Ralph Adamo agrees, remembering how "Alan Dugan said 'Yeah you're the one.' "[185]

Dugan behaved badly in Fayetteville. He showed up armed with a suitcase packed with vodka, got thoroughly drunk, stayed thoroughly drunk, and became an increasingly ornery drunk. Gwynn remembers picking him up at the local airport: "Dugan steps off that frontier prop plane and looks around [at Northwest Arkansas], kind of like [à la Kurtz in Conrad's *Heart of Darkness*], The horror! The horror!" He also remembers a one-on-one visit with Dugan, an aggressively unhelpful meeting where the older poet kept pulling his bottle of booze from the trash can and swigging from it. "He was drunk the whole time," Gwynn recalls.[186] Bruce Taylor confirms that Dugan was, in his words, "drunk off his ass" for most of the visit. Taylor saw the evidence firsthand when he and his wife, fellow Yankees, were asked to "sort of watch [Dugan] the first night." When Dugan arrived at the Taylors' for dinner, he came with his suitcase and hit the vodka hard. When they sat down to eat, he was so smashed that he did a face-plant into a plate of fluffy mashed potatoes. "He just collapsed," said Taylor, "and then he lifted himself up—and he had potatoes all over his eyebrows and face—and he said, 'Uh, forgive me for my problems.'"[187]

Few students were able to forgive Dugan the next day when, in Old Main, he critiqued their work, and "critiqued" is putting it generously. Dugan would read a poem in a mocking monotone and mumbling voice, barely audibly—"Hum dum dum um," as one student described it.[188] He would then move to the next poem, where his comments would, again and again, be the same: "Hum dum dum um."[189] A few poets—Adamo was one, John S. Morris another—escaped this assessment, but most went home wounded.[190] Taylor remembers how "there were just bodies all over the floor after that workshop; we were just destroyed."[191] Dugan's own reading was met with indifference from the students, mostly undergraduates forced to attend, and by many accounts went on too long. Gwynn recalls how the audience "bailed in droves." He said that when the event seemed to be finally winding down, "some asshole named Fred McCuistion"— that would be Frank's friend "Bad Fred"—asked Dugan to read his longest poem, "The Branches of Water or Desire," thereby extending the torture for another twenty minutes.[192] Things were going poorly.

Leon Stokesbury was especially stung by the Dugan visit. Not only did Dugan fail to admire Stokesbury's poems, but he absolutely loved Frank's. And only Frank's. As Gwynn put it, Dugan "held in disdain everything in Arkansas with the sole exception of Frank."[193] Frank found a major poet who appreciated his work, bought into his backwoods mystique, and encouraged his status as an outsider able to write circles around the insiders. Within a matter of months, Dugan and Stanford were writing each other regular letters, sharing drunken deep feelings with each other about life, love, and poetry. In moments of sincerity, Dugan, who had left Arkansas with a pile of Stanford's poems to read, declared things such as this to Frank as early as June 1972: "Read this carefully: I think that you are a genius and a beautiful poet."[194] Stanford was thrilled. Shortly after Dugan's visit, he reported to a friend, "Alan Dugan was here for a week and he liked my poetry very much—better than anyone else here and said he thought I was the best young poet he'd seen."[195] He later wrote to Dugan in all sincerity, "You and your work mean a lot to me.... You helped me a lot while you were here."[196]

Other poets came to the University of Arkansas as well—W. D. Snodgrass and Donald Justice are examples—and Frank schmoozed with them easily (or at least with Justice). "I am getting to know people and know of them," he wrote to the poet Charles Plymell in July 1970, "people I have the deepest admiration for."[197] Frank gave Justice a copy of the 1972 *Open Places* volume where he had recently published several poems. He marked it up before handing it over. "Here are the poems you like," he wrote, saying that "Strappado" was "the most orchestrated poem I've written" and describing another poem as "like a dream of a chess game."[198] Justice directed Frank to the journal *Kayak*, where Frank soon published "Wishing My Wife Had One Leg," in *Kayak* 26, alongside James Tate, Gary Snyder, and Wendell Berry.[199] Justice also urged Frank to read Jean Follain, a French poet for whom Frank would develop an abiding affinity.

Frank, who despised the obsequious behavior of the workshop poets, twice wrote Justice notes of his own that, given that he did not know Justice very well, could be read as fairly obsequious. In his first note he declares, "Whether you know it or not, in your brief visit here ... you helped me very much. I don't know quite what to say except that I'll always remember you ... you + your poetry are in my thoughts often." He insists he is not "trying to be obeisant."[200] In the next note he gets on his workshop-complaint hobbyhorse and goes on about how: "The first thing they told me to do in the workshop was: 'quit being pretentious and punctuate'! I didn't have any idea I was being that way. Anyway, I took their advice." Then he enthuses, as if Justice is his savior, "Then you came here in 1969. You told me about Jean Follain. I will never forget.... I'll always be glad you told me he existed."[201]

## "You Need to and You Should Publish...."

Frank sent his new publisher, Irv Broughton, "twenty of the thirty poems I am giving you for the pamphlet" in January 1971. Frank knew that, as a publisher, Irv offered the one thing he could never relinquish: creative control over his poetry.[202] Irv's obvious deference to Frank's obvious talent suggested that he'd never meddle with his new friend's poems. Irv might be out of money or flying by the seat of his pants, but he would always cede to Frank's choices when it came to poetry.[203] Plus, he promised to get Frank's first book of poems out. In early September 1971 Irv arrived in Fayetteville, stayed a few days with Frank, and handed him "newly printed copies of *The Singing Knives*."[204] The rest of the copies would not be ready until the summer of 1972, but these mock-up copies were assurance enough for Frank that Irv was a man who followed through.[205]

A competing, if only potential, opportunity in the publishing world highlights Frank's interest in maintaining the exclusive creative oversight that Irv and his Mill Mountain Press offered. Shortly after meeting Irv and well before *The Singing Knives* was headed into production, Frank sent poems to the journal *Open Places*. Its editor, Eleanor Bender, accepted "Poem," "Strappado," "Bequeath," "Becoming the Unicorn," and "Narcissus." "I am really astonished by your poetry," she told him, wondering, "What are your publishing plans for a book?" Bender had good reason to ask. She had, through her own lobbying efforts, landed a big contract with Random House for a young poet she admired named Rosmarie Waldrop. Waldrop's book, *The Aggressive Ways of the Casual Stranger*, which would be published in 1972, had been acquired by Nan Talese. Bender saw this as a coup of sorts.[206]

"I would be interested in seeing your manuscript," Bender wrote Stanford, "and perhaps undertake to help you publish it."[207] Eager to capitalize on her success with Waldrop, Bender had already alerted Random House about Frank and said she "would be happy to submit a manuscript" for him. She thought that Frank could even submit his manuscript to the Yale Younger Poets contest and possibly win it. Her bottom line was simple and encouraging. Whether it was Random House or Yale, she wrote to him in August 1971, "You need to and you should publish a book of poems as soon as possible."[208] Bender's interest suggested a substantial opportunity for Frank to potentially achieve commercial success at a young age.

But Bender's enthusiasm for Frank's poetry was tempered by her belief that a poet's manuscript should be bulked up as much as possible. She encouraged Frank to send as full a manuscript as he could to her so editors could have more material to work with, allowing them to craft it into a marketable volume. "I say this," she said, "for practical reasons." Bender tried to explain why this move would help her sell a manuscript: "An editor likes to feel that he can edit your manuscript and you don't leave any room for him to feel that he can edit it." She correctly sensed that "you are very sensitive about what others say and do about your poetry." Still, she urged Frank to "put those feelings aside and get practical."[209]

Few phenomena are harder to imagine reconciling than "Frank Stanford" and "get practical." Frank certainly *could* be practical—his behavior at the Hollins Conference showed as much—but practicality would be on his own terms and serve his own principles. His correspondence with Bender over her interest in his work was consistent with the myth he cultivated of the radically independent outsider, the precocious-genius image that mattered so much to him, the image of the beautiful, wild poet who rejected commerce and answered only to the muse. On paper he offered Bender a mildly impetuous "If you want to show this to Random House you can."[210] But this was an opportunity from which he quietly distanced himself. Frank later wrote to Irv: "A woman says Random House will buy my book. She wants to be agent. I say no deal."[211]

Frank found Bender's interest in him "charming" but claimed he was not ready for the big leagues, noting that "I'm still a little bat shy." He then added that "I'm too young to be publishing anything besides a pamphlet." Elsewhere, and earlier, he'd explained, regarding the prospect of shooting for the stars, "I'm broke—but I'm not ready."[212] In the end what he was not ready for was losing creative control to a commercial outfit: "I would like people to read my poems first hand ... and not in other people's versions of them."[213] The poet Charles Plymell, for one, commended him, writing that "It's noble of you to realize you don't need a book out yet."[214]

Bender was nonplussed by Frank's seeming indifference to her offer to help him: "I am a little surprised that I have not heard from you. I can't believe that you would take any of my comments about your manuscript in such a wrong light." Her confusion was justified. Here she was, after all, offering Frank a chance to go for a major commercial press and help him submit his work for the nation's highest honor offered to young poets. And here Frank was saying he was not ready. In the end, all Bender could do was throw up her hands: "You poets are an unpredictable race of people!" she wrote.[215] Frank was contrite: "I hope you won't be down on me, Eleanor. . . . Please forgive."[216] Apology notwithstanding, Frank's opportunity—however distant it was—to introduce his work to a national audience came and went and never came back.

Frank picked up his poems and continued ahead with Mill Mountain Press. He did so even though, as Ralph Adamo later noted, "Mill Mountain was nothing but Irv publishing Frank."[217] But Irv was not asking for changes. Irv did not think the manuscript was too short. Irv did not want to make edits to poems or meddle with the title. Irv had an ace art director and professional printer. Irv visited Frank in Fayetteville in September 1971 to hand deliver some dummy copies. Irv had high-quality paper! And when it came to being practical, Irv summed up his approach to publishing *Mill Mountain Review* (at least in financial terms) by insisting that "it was a totally irrational act."[218] Irrational was okay for Frank, and he saw no need to bend over for Random House when you had Irv Broughton on your side.

ELEANOR BENDER HAD APPROACHED FRANK with her offer to help him submit to Random House right around his twenty-third birthday. After taking the Arkansas MFA program by storm in 1969 (through only two poetry workshops) and then publishing several impressive poems in respectable venues, he had distanced himself from the MFA poets and professors. And while he was or had been in contact with established poets across the country—Allen Ginsberg, Alan Dugan, Donald Justice—none of them were much inclined to act as professional mentors. Frank had abandoned the only men who at the time could have effectively and directly guided his career as a poet—Jim Whitehead, Miller Williams, and even Leon Stokesbury—and in so doing, he had effectively enhanced the image of himself as the loner genius. "I'm not in their *circle* anymore," he wrote to Donald Justice in 1971 about the poets in the MFA program.[219] To Irv he wrote that "I'm starving for good advice & help, but not for all this other shit—I'd rather do it alone."[220] Thus he removed himself from an otherwise nurturing network of professional expertise that might have advised him, for starters, to get over himself and work with Bender and go and enjoy a huge career as a professional poet.

But Frank was sticking to his script. Or perhaps to his principles. In 1971 he wrote to his friend John McKernan that "publishing, advertising, and theories are not at all connected to my poetry."[221] An antiestablishment ethic was percolating and starting to pervade not just Frank's work but his entire identity. Anything commercialized or hedged to hit a commercial market put him off. "I wonder," he wrote to Eleanor Bender in early 1972, "if Faulkner knew that the same people who took over the banks would one day have sons running writing programs + journals."[222] Hence his comment that David Slavitt, he of the novel with four million copies sold, was a "shithook" (slang for schemer). In an early 1972 letter to Dugan, Frank elaborated on this line of thinking. "Piss on St[i]rling Silliphant & Jesse Hill Ford," he wrote about two men known for achieving commercial success through connect-the-dots art (Silliphant was a screenwriter; Ford churned out trope-ridden southern-themed novels). As far as Frank was concerned, these men were "phony goddamn scalawags." While his own poems were "about what I know," he insisted "this other stuff is counterfeit." Still, he lamented that "they will always have the power." His opinion of this reality was succinct: "Fuck."[223]

His growing disdain for commercial success was not a pose. Frank was developing a deeply committed sense that the pursuit of marketable poetry automatically compromised art. "I really don't care for the way editors and teachers and writers *build* bleak auditoriums to house their future business of art," he wrote to a poet friend in April 1974.[224] Stanford resisted the tendency to, as Auden put it, "ruin a fine tenor voice / For effects that bring down the house."[225] In an unpublished essay-like fragment titled "In the Wet Fields," Frank, praising the poet R. S. Thomas (and again echoing the ideas of Flannery O'Connor) wrote, "Thomas, fairly unknown and definitely not *in*, confirms something I've ... suspected a long time in this country. There's a great fear of reality, a blind spot for the common process of mystery." Plus, added Stanford, "I like his quiet, brooding voice." By contrast, there was that wildly commercially successful poet, Robert Frost, whose "farmers were philosophers, not the beaten, bitter, tender men who have worked their minds as well as their bodies to death." Frost was a poet, Stanford wrote, who had "fixed eyes."[226] And too often they were staring at the almighty dollar.

The perceived vapidity of fancy publishing venues gets some attention in *The Battlefield*. "A man from New York"—a journalist—shows up in rural Arkansas looking "to get a slice of life for a magazine" and, in effect, bring down the house (8862, 8867). Francis continues:

> he wanted to know if I had
> a few ribald tales I said no I'm sorry he said that's too bad I said what's
> that you putting down he said how many times he'd been mosquito bit
> since he'd been in the state of Arkansas I said hell why don't you just go on
> ahead and get snake bit while you're at you'll have lot's to tell about then
> a marvelous idea he said ...
> (8870–75)

"When talking about art, he only said what matters," C.D. Wright noted.[227] The meddling of editors would only be to enhance Frank's work's curb appeal, which did not matter. It would, he was sure, diminish its integrity—and his legacy, which he clearly cared about. He once sent to an editor some poems that he noted had been "written a very long time ago ... unsubmitted and unseen." Of these he said, "Although I doubt they would ever meet contemporary publishing standards, I would be willing to be remembered by these, if I am remembered at all."[228] With pride, he wrote to Irv Broughton that "my poetry has nothing to do with the hist[ory] of literature, schools, magazines, etc." He believed (channeling Jean Cocteau) that the poet is "unskilled when he speaks," that "there isn't room for both the poet and his work," as if he wanted the ego out of the work. He went on, sounding almost Foucauldian in his analysis: "If they live in the means, they mean nothing. They are bureaucrats and the heads of associations. This is not poetry, this is power and organization." This is as close to a manifesto as he would get. For the moment at least, he wanted none of the taste of fame, sticking instead to his own beatitude: "Blessed are the composers nobody will listen to."[229]

But Irv Broughton listened. And then, even if it took longer than expected, he did exactly as he'd promised. As far as both men were concerned, the poems that made up *The Singing Knives* were ready to enter the world, in however small a way, without changes. The two men worked closely on the design and layout. Irv not only kept his hands off the poetry but even allowed Frank to make sketches for the cover design, sending him in return variations based on his suggestions. Frank responded with more ideas of his own: "Six possible designs for a cover enclosed.... I like the first three colors more than the rest.... Looked nice with your paper and print."[230] Irv chose a purple cover faintly illustrated with nine jellyfish-like balloon figures floating upward in three tiers. The same image appears on the title page, preceded by an illustration of Frank Stanford. This was the kind of control Frank craved and, with Irv, got.

But Irv could be slow. The copyright for *The Singing Knives* is 1971. However, in February 1972 Frank was writing to Irv about how he hoped the book was going to come out soon. Frank was anxious. At some point in the summer of 1972 it arrived, and it was adored in Fayetteville, where in no time copies were cleared from the shelves of the local bookstore. Critics would later effuse over the book: One novelist called it "one of the most savagely beautiful books I know."[231] But it got no contemporary reviews. By contrast, Rosmarie Waldrop's book of poems—*The Aggressive Ways of the Casual Stranger*, the book Eleanor Bender had ushered to Random House—came out at roughly the same time as *The Singing Knives*. It launched Waldrop's career, one that included induction into the Academy of Arts and Sciences and being named a Chevalier des Arts et des Lettres.

Frank's rise was of a more literal sort. By early 1971 he had left the workshop, left college, and abandoned most of his colleagues to live with a girlfriend way up on a hill on the outskirts of town. On Mount Sequoyah he made major progress on what would be his life's defining work, an epic poem, full of integrity, totally unconcerned with commercial viability, and a work that few people would see or read until nearly two decades after his death.

Frank and Linda Mencin, ca. 1970. *Photo courtesy of Blair and Jordy Bond.*

EIGHT

# "A Remarkable Chaos"

## 1970 to Early 1972

THE INTENSITY THAT FUELED FRANK'S creative accomplishments did not end with his creative accomplishments. Frank's creativity thrived alongside a destructive pursuit of sexual indulgence, alcoholic excess, and extreme emotional vacillations. At the very time that Frank was achieving success as a published and increasingly recognized poet, he was spiraling into obsessions that seemed manageable . . . until they weren't. Worse, Frank did not break down alone. He took others with him, almost always women, causing tremendous personal harm to people for whom he cared deeply. The harm engendered guilt, and the guilt made him sink into an even worse emotional state. A kind of charmed mania inspired his writing, which tended to blossom as everything else around him burned. This dark paradox left him feeling alone and self-centered in an adult world he could never quite accept or comprehend.

One of the first people to experience these qualities in Frank was a young woman named Linda Mencin. Frank met Mencin when he was finishing his second and last semester in Jim Whitehead's poetry workshop, in the fall of 1969. Almost exactly Frank's age, Mencin was beautiful, smart, ambitious, and politically engaged.[1] When she moved to Fayetteville, she began working as a bartender at the Library on West Dickson Street while taking summer classes at the University of Arkansas to complete her degree in sociology at Boston University, to which she transferred her course credits. Linda's parents lived in a stately waterfront home on Beaver Lake, about an hour north. Her father was a career military man who had served in World War II, the Korean War, and

Vietnam. He had acquired extensive property on the lake, designed his own home, and was overseeing the development of the entire subdivision, all to his considerable profit.[2] Aware of her privilege, Linda volunteered, and then worked full-time, for the War on Poverty through Fayetteville's Economic Opportunity Agency (EOA) branch, located in downtown Fayetteville. Much of her work involved helping underserved communities grow fruits and vegetables and then canning them at a facility that she helped establish.[3]

Frank and Linda met when Linda and her boyfriend, Keith Mills, walked past Frank's apartment—likely above the UARK Theatre on Dickson Street. Enamored as so many were with the emerging Stanford legend, Mills said, "This is where Frank Stanford lives. He is a poet, and you have to meet him." They went up the flight of stairs to say hello. "It was not long after that," Mencin recalled, that Keith was no longer her boyfriend. "Frankie and I hooked up," she said.[4] Less than two years later, despite Frank's romantic involvement with another woman, a talented musician, Father Fuhrmann married Frank and Linda in a small but elegant ceremony at her parents' house on Beaver Lake.

The period from 1970 to early 1972 was also a time when Frank continued to work on *The Battlefield Where the Moon Says I Love You*. Living with Linda was a boon to his writing. Despite Frank's troubling personal behavior, most of it involving sexual infidelity and alcohol, Linda supported him during this pivotal phase in his writing career. She shared her home with him (it was her name on the lease), cooked, kept house, paid rent, tolerated his bizarre working habits, and tried as best she could to stabilize the chaos that defined his life. Mencin was no pushover; she was a strong and independent partner who would eventually insist that Frank stop fooling around with other women and, when his behavior became intolerable, drop him without a regret. But until that breaking point came, the couple shared a fertile moment together. With Linda's support, Frank produced a manuscript that embraced the ideals of racial equality and justice from the bottom up—ideals the couple reinforced for each other.

These years were about more than just finishing *The Battlefield*. Frank began to garner considerable attention in the little magazines for his poetry. He was, with characteristic intensity, submitting relatively short poems to prestigious little magazines for much of 1971, and editors were accepting his work at an enviable rate. Frank was not shy about putting his work out there, and he drew on his new connection with Alan Dugan to send involved introductory letters, along with piles of poems, to leading journals and magazines such as the *Massachusetts Review*, *Partisan Review*, *Open Places*, *Kayak*, and the *Nation*, all of which embraced his work.

In these introductions, he made sure to play up both his outsider status and his charm. "You haven't ever heard of me," he opened a March 1971 letter to *Kayak*; "I don't know if you will like my poems or not," he wrote to *Partisan Review* (a phrase he also used in his introduction to *Kayak*); and, again, "I don't know if you will like my work or not," he wrote the *Massachusetts Review*.[5] He assumed this somewhat naïf stance knowing fairly well that his poems might certainly strike a mark with these journals. He was, in short, fully confident but acting otherwise. He also told these editors that his birth date was 1949 rather than 1948 and that he had been born in Greenville, Mississippi, rather than Richton. The fabrications were evolving into genuine beliefs. To Irv, a man to whom there was no reason to lie, he insisted that "I was not really born in 1948, but 1949."[6]

When it came to finances during these years, Frank's assessment was one that the once-rich kid from Memphis might never have predicted: "I'm broke."[7] Financial struggle gripped these years with an iron fist. Frank did eventually get a job, working on a surveying crew, that he always tolerated and often enjoyed. He had to report to work at 7:00 a.m., but when his coworkers were late or there was bad weather, he could, in his words, "sit in the truck and dream."[8] When he was working in the field, he did so while "dreaming about the lives and the poems I will participate in when I return home."[9] Whatever dreams he was having, it was all a bundle of tasks to manage: marriage, a job, and continued creative success. In this respect, young adulthood appeared to be a conventional affair for Frank Stanford.

But beneath the surface there were demons coming to life. Most notably, there was the love triangle that he established after falling for a woman named Cheryl Campbell in early 1971, only months after moving into Linda's Mount Sequoyah home. Frank lied and lived a dual life with Cheryl and Linda for about five months in 1971. While Frank was dating Linda, and living in her house, Cheryl, a 1969 Arkansas graduate with a degree in the French horn, moved into a "funky writing studio" that Frank rented on Lindell Avenue, a couple of blocks from the law school. Frank moved her in a few months after they met in early January 1971, and he spent most of the time between early March and late July of 1971 living with her in town.[10] Eerily foreshadowing future behavior, Frank maintained intense, conflicting relationships with both women and, simultaneously, casual sexual ones with others. He somehow kept Linda in the dark about Cheryl, and, as Cheryl recalled, "he told me that she [Linda] just would not except [sic] that they had broken up."[11] Cheryl recalls that she and Frank rarely left the studio, a fact that, in retrospect, led her to wonder whether Frank was afraid of running into Linda or her friends.[12] In any case, the two women somehow never met. Frank's new job on the surveying crew provided convenient excuses for him to be away—with "away" often being right across town. Within months of each other, both women became pregnant by Frank.

This reckless dishonesty warrants a look into the deeper influences on Frank's behavior. The intensity of his creativity resisted the reality of adult responsibility, and this resistance kept his poetry alive. He seemed unable to function as an adult burdened with the most basic and banal expectations of adulthood and, at the same time, expect to write the way he wanted to write. Responsibilities such as monogamy, commitment to a romantic partner, or even something as simple as housework clashed with his idea of being a poet. As he assumed the tasks of adulthood, he began to sense a diminishment of childhood innocence and freedom, qualities that had long supported his antibourgeois nonconformity. Expressed more in *The Battlefield* than anywhere else, such a childhood spirit fueled his creative productivity and sense of purpose as a poet. Losing that spirit, that sense of purpose, left him emotionally unmoored, depressed, drinking heavily, and—as the situation with Linda and Cheryl came to a head—frightened for his own sanity and even Linda's safety. The most alarming result of this darkening disposition was a fascination with the suicides of others and, if only hypothetically, of himself. By the spring of 1972, Frank was producing exceptional poetry at a breakneck pace. But as this output increased, his personal life threatened to implode. And then it did.

## "I Really Became One with That Place"

Linda's initial response after meeting Frank was to his body. "There was an instant attraction," she said. "Frank was gorgeous; he had luscious hair and muscles everywhere from the karate and judo lessons he taught." He was "exquisitely beautiful," much like, she noted, one of the smooth-skinned, fast-talking heroes Frank loved to praise: Muhammad Ali ("I have more respect for Muhammad Ali / Than any other living man"). But what made Frank most attractive to Linda was the genuine concern he showed for her values and ambitions. "He loved my interest in liberation and equality," she said. Linda had worked as a lifeguard at a Black beach in Maryland, so he admired her commitment to racial integration. Frank raved about Linda's blond hair and blue eyes and shapely figure. But he was more complimentary about her goals in life. "He loved my work," she remembered.[13] A later lover of Frank's said that "his enthusiasm for you was like a narcotic."[14] Linda would have been able to relate.

Soon after the couple met, they traveled with a friend of Frank's ("Big Time" Sonny Morris) to Washington, DC. They went in Morris's van to protest the Vietnam War.[15] The Moratorium March took place on November 15, 1969, a frigid day that drew hundreds of thousands of protesters from across the country. A week later Frank wrote to Allen Ginsberg and Peter Orlovsky, "I was in Washington last week and everything was beautiful. I got gassed but I didn't get hit."[16] Not only did this trip require Frank to do something he rarely did—leave Arkansas—but it also required him to leave his comfort zone. Throwing peace signs into the air on the East Coast with a crowd of hippies was not exactly Frank's style. But off he went, into the gas of a national protest.

Stanford was only strategically political. While he peppered his letters to Ginsberg the peace activist with obligatory objections to the Vietnam War, he had previously avoided the antiwar movements that gripped his campus in 1968. He avoided politics in general. Kathy Walton, an MFA student who met Frank that year and was fervently committed to protesting the war, remembered that Frank was indifferent to the opposition brewing on the home front.[17] All that he had done to resist Vietnam was write a letter to the draft council insisting that Bill Willett was totally unfit for combat. "Bill is a pacifist and has always been one as long as I've known him," Frank explained, conveniently avoiding the fact that his best friend had just actively beaten the shit out of three men in a bar fight before sustaining a stab wound to his chest that required thirty-six stitches. Frank elaborated on Willett's passivity for his commanding officer: "You see, sir, I know a lot about Bill and the unwillingness or willingness to fight and kill. I am a Karate Instructor and I hold a first degree black belt. I also have a brown belt in Judo. And, I am a nationally published writer. Bill cannot . . . kill."[18]

There it was. "I'm getting him out on a C[onscientious] O[bjector]," Frank bragged to Dugan. But in Washington, Frank was putting himself, and his opposition to the war, out in the crowd, marching with the masses, chanting with the herd, all for Linda. If this wasn't love, it had to be close.

Either way, the immediate payoffs of his relationship with Linda were worth it. One clear benefit of life with her was living with her in her excellent rented house. She rented a secluded cabin at 115 Skyline Drive on Mount Sequoyah. "I loved the place . . . top of the mountain," she later said.[19] It was a two-story structure set on a bluff overlooking the city. Adamo remembered "a cozy little cabin" that seemed "more isolated than it was."[20] Frank started living there with Linda around September 1970. There was no question about who was running the show financially on Skyline Drive: "I was supporting him," Linda said.[21] Frank, who told a friend that "I live on top of a mountain with my girl friend and I like that," had good reason to express as much. Very little was expected of him, and he could put his time and energy into writing.[22]

Frank was effectively useless when it came to domestic duties. He'd recently been kicked out of university housing, after a brief stint there in the fall of 1969, for repeatedly overturning common-room furniture and clearing it away to make space for judo and karate lessons.[23] Chores were anathema to the kid who grew up with servants; when messes were cleaned up by the help, one's time was one's own. "Frank was not very domesticated," C.D. Wright later remembered.[24] In Linda's cabin, he never repaired the hole he blew in the roof during that infamous party in November 1970, leaving her to complain about the draft chilling the house on winter mornings. "I was furious with him," she said. "Frankie didn't really clean or cook," she remembered. The laundry piled up so high it would stink up the kitchen. Linda did all the meal preparation, remembering that "Frank liked meat and potatoes" while watching his weight.[25] "She likes her boys on the thin side," Frank once said, patting his stomach, to a friend about Linda's preferences.[26]

Domestic life, if already unbalanced, soon went haywire. Between March and July 1971, life with his girlfriend Linda was marked by Frank's extended absences. In early 1971, Frank had met and immediately fallen for Cheryl Campbell. Born in Missouri in 1946, Cheryl, who'd grown up as Cheryl Crites in Batesville, Arkansas, was a musician recently separated from her first husband (whose last name was Campbell). She'd come back to Fayetteville, where she had gone to college, for a fresh start. She did temp work at an assessor's office, where she learned to type, and eventually got a job at the EOA, the same organization where Linda worked (although at a different branch).

Frank and Cheryl met at a party on Markham Hill, a forest on the edge of Fayetteville. The event was held on a one-hundred-plus-acre piece of property with hippie communes and cabins. A few weeks after the party, Frank and Cheryl spent four lost days together in Greenland, Arkansas, where Cheryl was doing some caretaking for a farm. Cheryl recalls, "We became hungry for each other not only physically but emotionally. The mind body meld was sweet." Cheryl moved into Frank's studio in or around

March 1971. According to Cheryl, he *moved her in*, carrying her "musical instruments, clothes, a few books" across the threshold into his big lie. Cheryl recalls how much interest Frank showed in her interests. He "always wanted to know how I constructed my theories of my worldview, my internal universe, what I saw as truth." She adored the attention he lavished on her ideas, noting how "Frank quizzed me a lot about my Eastern studies."[27] She remembers that "we had *incredible* conversations.... We talked about *everything*. He probed my mind."[28]

When Linda had Frank up on the hill, unaware of his double life with Cheryl, she was equally enthralled with his presence. Like Cheryl, Linda loved the chance to support Frank's work. She respected him unconditionally as a poet and later recalled how he read his work aloud to her. "You should have heard him read his poetry," she said.[29] The couple had a large round oak table where Frank did most of his writing. "The round table is old and pecan brown" is how he described it to Dugan, adding that "sometimes, cheese falls in the crack."[30] Irv Broughton remembered how when he visited the couple, Linda would always defer to Frank, making sure to stay out of the men's way when they talked shop or plotted out ideas for the films they would someday make.[31] Frank enjoyed everything about his living situation with Linda. "I have just stayed here alone with Linda," he wrote to Dugan. "I've done a lot of writing."[32] Later, Frank spoke to Broughton about the special connection between cabins and his writing routine. Describing a small cabin he later rented on the White River, he said: "This cabin had a lot of magical feeling to it. I could get up any time of the day, any time of the night, and I could write in it. I felt so at home in this place. It was so strange, when I think of it now, getting up in the winter, building a fire at three o'clock in the morning, making coffee, goin' down there and writin' or reading. It's a strange feeling. I really became one with that place. It wasn't a possession. It was just a place you could exist in."[33]

In another letter to Dugan, Frank elaborated on his work habits in Linda's cabin: "I get up every morning about 4:00 and everything is fine. I read over what I wrote the night before and whenever I use the T.W. [typewriter] the squirrels go nuts. I can call them with my mouth and they will come right up to the desk."[34] He never spoke with such affection about his studio in town.

Frank, literally looking down on the university he had abandoned, used the time on Mount Sequoyah to write his way out of the perceived damage caused to his poetry by the workshop. In early 1971 he recalled how, before the workshop, "I was writing good shitty poems." But when he "started in with the writing program, I started affecting bad shitty poems." He continued: "When I realized this, I was frightened. It haunted me like a nightmare. For a long time I eluded it . . . then I confronted it, and I was victorious. I was compelled to write so much. . . . Now, I write more than most I know, but the good poems have really increased, while the bad ones have almost gone away."[35]

Achieving this transition daunted Frank. "I've tried to meditate in stillness and inactivity . . . inert as an artist, and it is painful. . . . You just write—write—and finally a poem comes," he said. Contrasting this method to the freewheeling automatic writing of the surrealists, he identified his work habits and discipline as more akin to what Japanese sumi-e painters were seeking through carefully controlled strokes of ink, made in a state of Zen-like concentration—to reduce matters to their essential forms. He even began to attempt some of these paintings on his own, if only to foster this kind of focus.[36]

Both Linda and Cheryl watched Frank get sucked into his obsessive writing routine. "Frankie was writing day and night," Linda later recalled. "He wrote constantly, all the time—hours a day. . . . He was formidably prolific."[37] Cheryl, who did much of Frank's typing throughout the spring and early summer of 1971,[38] recalls how he would almost dictate current poems and write new ones at the same time. He was always at it—"a remarkable chaos," she called him. But she also loved it when "he was nearby, working on a letter to be typed . . . sometimes he would be writing, music was on, and I would be reading and holding quiet space for him."[39] Cheryl appreciated it when Frank read his work to her but ultimately valued "the importance of silence" she gave to Frank so he could write. "I accepted him for who he was," she said.[40] When Frank saw a psychiatrist in 1972, he was asked how he filled his days. "Writing (All the time!)," the psychiatrist wrote on the form.[41] Cheryl, like Linda, had no problem with this.

Isolated from the social life of the workshop, steering clear of the student-centered Fayetteville bar scene, removing himself from the local antiwar movement, moving between women who supported him in complementary ways, and no longer regularly attending classes or MFA parties, Frank could now revive the frantic writing habits that he had once pursued when living with Willett on Buchanan Street.[42] On the rare occasions when he did venture out socially—seeing movies, going to friends' houses for dinners—he got lost in his own head. "Wherever I am," he wrote to an editor, "I'm not really there."[43] Kathy Walton, who also had an on-again-off-again affair with Frank between 1969 and 1971 (yes, while he was with Linda and, very possibly, Cheryl as well), remembered that he was typically aloof, quiet, and in his own world, writing in his head, when he was ostensibly socializing.[44]

It would be easy to assume that Frank's obsessive, trance-induced work habits immediately resulted in polished gems of genius. This was hardly the case, though. He was always revising. When Irv Broughton asked him how many drafts of a poem he tended to write, he noted that sometimes one came out whole but also that "I might do a hundred." He said, "On shorter poems, I probably revise over and over and over, whereas the narrative poems under three hundred or four hundred lines, possibly forty or fifty revisions."[45]

Alcohol continued to fuel his creative fire and pose its share of problems. Interestingly, Cheryl recalls that Frank, who told her he was hypoglycemic, rarely drank when he was with her in the Lindell Avenue studio, maybe just a beer or a glass of wine.[46] But Linda reported the opposite. She said that while he avoided cigarettes and drugs, he drank, typically preferring hard alcohol.[47] She sometimes became upset enough about his drinking to leave the cabin and stay with her parents on Beaver Lake.[48] When Larry Johnson visited Frank on Mount Sequoyah, Larry found him listening to a Bessie Smith record while scribbling away on legal pads. It was late morning, and Frank opened a bottle of rosé, which he and Larry drained before Frank suddenly remembered he had to conduct a judo lesson in town.[49] Frank, in his own words, had no problem "working up a good sweat" while teaching a lesson and "then get[ting] drunk."[50] In the summer of 1971 Frank told Irv, "Excuse me for the delay in answering your phone call and letters, but I have been drunk all the times I have not been keeping up with the pen."[51] That same summer Frank wrote to another friend, "I am not as drunk as I was yesterday. Saying this is not an affectation, but a weakness, because I have turned into a sot part of the time."[52] When Frank saw the psychiatrist Dr. Ball, his answer to a form question about alcohol use was "lately—too much beer."[53] Whatever the poison, Frank, depending on where he was, took it in something between a slow and steady drip and a fire hose.

Frank also continued to write in a hyperfocused and trancelike state of mind. When Father Fuhrmann visited him at the cabin, probably in the fall of 1970, he walked in to find Frank writing. He vividly remembered the scene: There were books open all over the oak table, and Frank was ranging around it from text to text, "jumping from one to another," staring into space, and writing furiously on a yellow notepad. Fuhrmann said he stood in the room for nearly an hour before Frank acknowledged him, at which point Frank snapped out of it, marched into the kitchen, and brought them several bottles of cold beer. Switching his focus immediately, he demanded to know everything about what was happening down at Subiaco.[54] On another occasion Frank reported to an editor how watching the movie *Sundays and Cybèle*—about a psychologically traumatized war veteran—"put me in a trance."[55]

These altered states could make Frank unusually emotional. The smallest things might set him off. In June 1971, after going into town to eat dinner (likely from the Lindell Avenue studio) he came home and wrote to Irv: "I am back a little bit drunk. On the way I saw things that made me want to cry. I always do when I see something like it. An old fat woman girls are laughing at. People who are ashamed of the way they look. Cripples. I just don't know.... What is it about hate? Why do so many people seem only to thrive on it? ... Everyone hates one another so. I just don't know."[56]

Sleep deprivation certainly played a role in his fragile mood. Although Frank and Cheryl went to bed at a normal hour when Frank was staying in the studio, he rarely slept when he was living up on the mountain. Linda would often wake up in the middle of the night and hear him writing at the circular table.[57] This was common for Frank. When a former workshop classmate invited him to Memphis to hear a reading, Frank, who stayed in his friend's apartment, wrote until daybreak. This was after the two of them, as they had sometimes done in Fayetteville, drank four or five beers in one sitting at a bar.[58] In an untitled poem draft, Frank suggests that this manner of working suited him just fine:

I drink whiskey all day
Write poems in the night
I drink whisky all day
Write poems in the night

Life be so beautiful
I don't ever want to retire[59]

But more important than where he was writing, or what he was drinking while doing so, was what he was writing. Frank was no longer burdened with having to generate short and sweet verse for the MFA worksheet. He was freed from the weekly demands of the workshop, as well as other class requirements.[60] Frank was also coming to realize that he could get his stuff into print more or less whenever he wanted to ("A few editors + poets have written me letters asking to see my work," he proudly wrote Dugan).[61] So, with time to write, two ideal spaces to write in, no classes to attend, and at least two romantic partners on hand to offer moral support, domestic and financial help, meat and potatoes, and sex either up on the hill or down in town, Frank dove into the big poem he had been working on in one way or another since his Mountain Home days. When Leon Stokesbury visited Frank and Linda on Mount Sequoyah, he remembered that "Frank was cold grits" but "some pages of *The Battlefield* were on the desk."[62] "It was always *Battlefield*," Linda confirmed when asked the name of the epic he was writing on the oak table in the dining room in the middle of the night.[63]

## "I Run with Some Crazy People...."

It's impossible to say precisely at what point, and in what capacities, the longest poem in "St. Francis and the Wolf: Some Poems 1957–1964"—this manuscript being a compilation of forty or so long poems, mostly juvenilia—became *The Battlefield Where the Moon Says I Love You*. It would be like saying at what point one ocean becomes another. This manuscript was a huge and malleable text in a constant state of flux. What is certain, though, is that the birth of *The Battlefield* hinged on Stanford's systematic inclusion of at least two defining features not as evident in "St. Francis and the Wolf": The first was attention to the vernacular that characterizes both poor whites and Blacks in the rural South; the second was the theme of racial discrimination and justice. Both emphases are most evident in the bond that endures in *The Battlefield* between the white cousins Francis and Jimmy and the cohort of Black characters with whom they socialize. The adventures that Sylvester the Black Angel, Tang, BoBo Washington, Five Spoke O. Z., Ray Baby, Baby Gauge, and Charlie B. undergo, and the ways they articulate their experiences, make *The Battlefield* a work every bit as generous as Whitman's *Leaves of Grass* in its affection for human language, dignity, and transcendence.

*The Battlefield*'s emphasis on race and language reflects several developments in Frank's life in the early 1970s. His time at Sherman's Tavern—marked by his friendships with Black men such as Jimbo Reynolds, Sherman Morgan, and Claude Ricks—had diminished during his one year in the poetry workshop. Frank had become frustrated with the way his MFA social life conflicted with social life at his hangout. The two groups did not mix well. "Usually there are just as many or more blacks at Linda/my house (when I did have parties)," Frank wrote to Dugan, "but they won't come to one if Whitehead or any of the English dept. people are there."[64] In a letter to Eleanor Bender, he complained about how the MFA "sycophants... started telling my next door neighbors who are black what kind of music to sing in their next record."[65] Gwynn recalls how Frank never invited any of the MFA poets to Sherman's Tavern—"I never even knew where it was"—usually going alone or with "Bad Fred" McCuistion.[66] Frank purposely kept his white friends at bay, telling Dugan more than six months after his visit to Fayetteville that "I haven't seen anyone here [i.e., program poets or writers] since you left."[67] Frank was constantly explaining to Irv Broughton how much more interesting he found hanging out with Fayetteville Blacks than Fayetteville whites. This was exactly the time Linda was later referring to when she surmised that Frank "probably wished he were Black."[68]

After Frank severed his connection to the MFA program and its poets, he returned to Sherman's and rekindled his friendships at the bar.[69] He also reconnected with James Seawood, head of Black Americans for Democracy, from his Buchanan Street days while getting to know a Black country singer and his wife—Sarge and Shirley West—who lived in a cabin just down the hill from him and Linda.[70] "The blacks next door," he wrote, "are beginning to see other blacks and us too."[71] He mentioned another Black couple who were "our new best friends" and stressed that most of his socializing was with Black friends. "I don't associate with the writers here much," he wrote in March 1971.[72]

The lives of these Black folks were marked by different dramas than those characterizing the MFA crowd. And they were related in a fresh and vibrant language. "I run with some crazy people I wish you knew," Stanford wrote to Dugan, likely referring to Jimbo, Claude, and Morgan. "I told them about you at this tavern."[73] He told Dugan a story about Claude Ricks and his wife, Annie, going to Claude's sister's funeral in Mississippi and, in an echo of the plot details of Faulkner's *As I Lay Dying*, finding the corpse "sitting up, contorted on a piece of plywood" because she could not afford proper burial services."[74] Frank and Linda joined Claude and Annie for meals of pigs' feet and whiskey. Frank loved how Claude instructed his children, who were off to a party in the Black part of town, to never exit a room first in a gunfight. "You'll get shot first," he said, drawing on firsthand experience. Frank and Claude became especially close, drinking together, playing dominoes, and staying up all night talking. Frank called these evenings their "midnight talks" and said they were accompanied by music and discussions of death—"the feeling of the real taste of death."[75] His friendship with Jimbo Reynolds was tamer and more family oriented. Things reached the point where Jimbo was routinely bringing Frank to his mother's house for meals. Frank would regale Irv with stories of Jimbo-inspired culinary adventures, such as fried squirrel and raccoon.[76]

These friends were very much in Frank's life and on Frank's mind as he revised his work into *The Battlefield*. Accordingly, many of Stanford's unpublished prose fragments, which often appear to be outtakes from *The Battlefield*, include references to Frank's experiences and friendships at Sherman's. These scenes are frustratingly decontextualized—we do not know precisely where in the text (or even what version of the text) they were taken from. But they ring consistent with the tenor of the final poem, and tonally at least, one can easily imagine them having once been woven into a draft of it. For example: "Claude Ricks and I were frying a hand in a hubcap, cooking it like a frog leg"; "Sherman has a little joint on the creek.... Sherman sent word that his wife Minerva had killed a goat"; "I went to see Jimbo but he was in bed, drunk.... Jimbo is like Zorba."[77] Any of these outtakes, all of which are focused on his Sherman's Tavern friends, would have fit right into *The Battlefield Where the Moon Says I Love You*.

But Frank's tavern friends did not make it into the final version of the poem. Instead, it was the Black folks from the levee camp days—Baby Gauge, BoBo Washington, Born in the Camp with Six Toes, Emma, and Charlie B.—who became *The Battlefield*'s animating Black figures. More than a nitpicky observation, this is an important reminder that Frank was insistent about writing an autobiographical poem told from the perspective of a twelve-year-old named Francis Gildart rather than a twentysomething named Frank Stanford. It's an important reminder, also, that when he was writing, he was often, as he put it, "totally lost in the past," and it was a past that did not yet include Jimbo and the Sherman's group of friends but rather BoBo, Six Toes, and Baby Gauge.[78] It stands to reason that, in a testament to autobiographical accuracy, Frank—who knew that childhood was especially amenable to mythologization—would include the Black kids he knew when he was close to Francis's age, kids with whom he shared the magical levee experiences that defined his childhood summers.

But if the Black people in Frank's contemporary life in the early 1970s do not appear directly in the poem, their concerns and circumstances certainly do. *The Battlefield* abounds with hard cases of racial injustice, the types of cases he would have routinely heard about at Sherman's. Most of these scenes reflect lingering Jim Crow policies in the American South circa 1960—what C. D. Wright called "the dragons of the South."[79] When a Black kid whom Francis meets on the freedom ride goes to use the toilet in a general store, the boy reports:

> I just got off to pee
> but this hea man he wouldn't let me use his bafroom
> (10866–67)

When he goes to a gas station across the street, he discovers that "they bafroom said WHITE" (10982). When a white kid tricks him into sucking helium from the balloon he bought at the general store, the store owner catches the Black kid with his mouth on the balloon and says, "you little pickaninny get on out of heah," reprimanding him for putting "your fat filthy lips / on one of my balloons" (10979–80). When a white woman intervenes, the Black kid is eventually accused of asking "this white woman fah a piece of pussy" (10996). Echoes of Emmett Till—killed in 1955 only about fifteen miles from Mound Bayou, Mississippi—are unmistakable.

Francis often merges the experiences of Blacks in the South with the blues tradition forged in the very fields Dorothy's father had overseen as a Parchman prison officer. While his thoughts wander on the freedom bus, Francis Gildart thinks about how:

> some of them mens sing the blues with a high voice
> I heard them every night
> they were like the willows
> how does a man get sent up for forgery if he can't even write his name
> Tang wants to know somebody tell him I don't why
> memory won't go
> away it hangs on like a bloodsucking leech out of the bottoms
> (11498–504)

The forgery reference is to Furry Lewis, the iconic bluesman from Stanford's Memphis. In a 1960 recording of "Judge Boushay Blues," Lewis sings, "They . . . arrest me for forgery and I can't even sign my name."[80] This is just one example of how Stanford wove the blues tradition into his poetry, allowing the genre to help define *The Battlefield*'s "auricular Delta" (14266). The use of the name "Tangle Eye" is similarly apt. This was a nickname for the Delta harmonica bluesman Walter Horton, who also sometimes went by "Mumbles." Mumbling, not incidentally, is something that the character Tang is known to do.[81] Stanford himself was sometimes explicit about the connection between the Black musical traditions in the South and his poetry. In "With the Approach of the Oak the Axeman Quakes," he links the writing of his poem "Death on the Arkansas River" to work songs sung by field hands. He explains, "I had a year with this poem; . . . I never wrote a word down until I had it right in my mind. It became what they call a floater. That's a work song, a chant. . . . Men sing when they work, or at least they used to. I'm liable to talk to myself."[82]

If *The Battlefield* were sung, it might sound like a long and improvised blues number. Early in the poem, while Francis is in Memphis and hanging out with Charlie B., Stanford writes:

> Charlie B. said I need a beer let's take a
> ride we drove to the section they was frying catfish I asked the chef
> for an egg I walked out of the joint with the smells and the blues
> (980–82)

When Francis waits outside the outhouse for his friend Mr. Rufus to finish his morning "grunt," he reports how "I give him a transistor radio I got out of the mail / for his birfday three year ago the batteries was low or we'd a listened / to the blues" (1652–54). About his friend Sylvester, the man with whom Francis says that he is so close "we could finish one another's song" (3533), he recalls:

> when he got back from the doctor he always had bad news
> like he lost a payroll at the horse races
> he had the blues
> (3541–43)

In a dream sequence, when Francis is walking "down the road a piece" (4591), he says:

> for some reason I recollect some tune
> a tune like the chain gang sings in the winter a slow blues
> I mean real slow and cold like two rivers running into each other
> (4593–95)

The injustice that Francis witnesses is, in these ways, persistently integrated into the Delta's deepest musical heritage.

Responses to the blues often charge the text with heightened emotion. Referencing B. B. King's "Blues Before Sunrise," Francis observes how "a man coasted down the road on a bicycle with a mudflap / he was singing blues before sunrise and tears standing up in my eyes" (6359). In another dream sequence Francis describes how "I sit in the saddle with Dark the negro / and his crazy blues sinks down like a diver into the belly of my dreams" (7346). When he establishes his utopia at the poem's end, it's a "regular continent where the blues got to coming down / just like a little rain" (14949–50).

Frank's connection to the blues drew on his affection and admiration for people whose voices were more interesting to him than the ones in the lounge of the Peabody or the seminar room at Arkansas. This was the vernacular, the music, that sustained Frank's poetic voice. Frank knew the blues. The depth of his record collection confirms *The Battlefield*'s integration of blues and related musical genres. For popular music, Stanford tended to prefer the records of Black performers. His collection included Bobby Bland (three records), the Dixie Hummingbirds, John Lee Hooker, Son House, Skip James, Memphis Slim, Blind Lemon Jefferson, Jimmy Reed, Robert Johnson, Leadbelly, and Muddy Waters. Jazz-wise, he collected Charlie Parker, Pharoah Sanders, Miles Davis (eight records), John Coltrane (twelve records), Ella Fitzgerald, Thelonious Monk, Charles Mingus, Sonny Rollins, and McCoy Tyner. Most of the records were bought in Fayetteville's local drugstore, Collier Drug.[83]

Intuitively tuned in to the expressions shared between poor whites and Blacks, Stanford routinely used musical traditions to envision racial connections. In a letter to Alan Dugan, he writes, "Are you familiar with how the A. Saxon Ballad + Negro Blues spilled into the same body of water!?"[84] *The Battlefield* echoes a similar idea when Francis, after the racial utopia has been achieved, hears "the blues and ballads like two singers singing as one" (14548). This convergence reverberates across Stanford's South, reiterating an essential aspect of *The Battlefield*'s harmonious biracial pitch: While Stanford highlights the vernacular and experiences of poor Black southerners, he never does so exclusively. The experiences of poor whites and poor Blacks merge in shared expression throughout the poem. This should never suggest that the lives of southern Blacks and poor whites were the same but only that their differences came through interaction. Stanford honors this notion in his poem "The Mind Reader" when he writes, "I dream black hands and white hands like where two creeks meet."[85]

## "We Were Like Four Noblemen in the Loges at the Opera"

Many of *The Battlefield*'s most emotionally resonant scenes happen at this intersection of Black and white. Most notable is the one where Francis, Jimmy, Charlie B., and the character Tangle Eye (also called Tang or

Mr. Tang) plan to visit a drive-in theater located about twelve miles outside of the levee camp where they work. The theater has advertised "a all night picture show marathon" (7379). Francis is initially excluded from the venture because of his young age. But when he threatens to rat out Jimmy for his numerous infractions ("I'm gone tell I said I know plenty"), and when Charlie B. insists, "let the son-of-a-bitch go," Francis gets the green light to join the gang on their adventure (7379, 7399–400). Barely able to contain his excitement, he declares, "going to have a carload ain't we" (7402). Included in this carload are three cases of beer and six bottles of whiskey. And a loaded pistol. It is less a question of what could go wrong than when.

Francis offers a hint of the impending trouble when the men drive up to buy their tickets at the entrance booth of the drive-in theater, Clyde Miller's Sunset Drive Inn.

> but when we pulled up under the sign and waited in the car line
> all they had in bad spelling was science fiction and hillbilly music
> they weren't another colored person around
> let's get out of here Charlie B. said
> fuck Jimmy said
>    (7585–89)

Nothing screams "dumb redneck" more clearly than a misspelled sci-fi film title on a drive-in marquee. Sensing that they are victims of false and very white-focused advertising, they peel out and roam the back roads for a while. Stanford's poetry thrives in the interstices between events; like his characters, the poem rambles and plays. The men pull up to a general store so Francis can buy Tang some lunch meat. Francis daydreams about Jimmy's cool car, how much he hates school, how he resents the astronomer back in Memphis, and what Tang's Adam's apple looks like when he gulps his beer ("bob like a fishing cork" [7655]). They eventually return to the theater. As they approach it for the second time, Francis sees from a distance "a face in the moom pitchu" (7688)—up on the screen. It's James Dean. Tang immediately knows they've been had: "they just put that other shit up there," he says, referring to the title of the sci-fi film, "so they could turn those niggers away shit I know" (7698–990). This injustice—this refusal to welcome Black patrons—won't stand. Jimmy cuts a hard left, and they are right back at the ticket window, where a woman—the wife of the theater owner, Clyde Miller—"ducked her head and strained like a goose to look into the car" (7704).

Before the predictable moment comes when the Black men are denied entrance, it's important to recognize why this old movie marathon matters so much to Tang and Charlie B. It was common in the early days of film for producers to shoot movies in the Deep South. They did so because it was cheap and the locals worked as free extras. As a result, even decades later in the 1950s, people went to see these movies to get a glimpse of themselves, friends, or family on the screen. "Charlie B. hisself is in Baby Doll," Francis notes (7461), highlighting the presumed fact that the real Charlie B. Lemon was an extra in that movie, filmed in Benoit, Mississippi, in 1955. Francis also mentions that Tangle Eye played a "root picker" in the 1929 movie *Hallelujah* and that his late wife, a former singer with the Dixie Jubilee Singers, was in the film as well (7460, 8251, 8255).[86] Francis, who has been listening to the men talk, understands these connections, and he elaborates on their emotional significance. Interestingly, he observes that the white rednecks and poor Blacks who go to see themselves or their loved ones on-screen react in very different ways. Of the white reaction to the films, he says:

> these dumb rednecks the fucking idiots don't even know what
>     they're about
> they just go looking for their face on the screen
> the only ones that raises a ruckus is the ones that didn't get in it
> and they is liable to get drunk and kill somebody
>     (7438–41)

But as for the Black patrons:

> colored people like to go see themselves too
> why not they're just like everybody else
> they carry on to when they see themselves but it's different from
>     white people
> course there's always some jive cat yelling
> but the nodding and humming like they do like they was in church
> well it's different as if they was listening to what the pitchu is meaning
> as if they was looking for real at what the people was doing
> like they identify with the character . . .
> . . . . . . . . . . . . . . . . . . . .
> I want you to know they ain't paying no quarter just to see theirself
> I know that
>     (7443–50, 7452–53)

Note the affection here. Yes, there's always some character making too much noise among the Black folks, but mostly it's the beautiful and subdued hum of excitement that comes through, as if the deeper meaning of the art elicits reactions more appropriate for the church than the drive-in and just as spiritually resonant.

Back at the ticket window the woman leaning into the car "shined the light in Charlie B.'s eyes and then in Tang's"; the two men "squinted and turned their heads away" (7714, 7716). She summons her husband, Clyde Miller. Charlie B. and Tang, looking at Clyde, know better than anyone else how this script will play out:

> sorry you can't bring those niggers
> in here tonight we got a religious service at daylight
>   (7778–79)

The light irony is evident, as Francis has just noted that the Black viewers react to the film as if in church, whereas the white viewers act like "fucking idiots." In any case, Francis pulls his son-of-the-levee-boss card: "tell that mother fucker who I am" (7794). But Jimmy has a different, more rebellious idea. He picks up the loudspeaker that connects to all the cars and yells, "why don't you and Mrs. Miller go get fucked" (7811). Tang mumbles, "fucking shithooks" and then says to his white friends, "I told you ... y'all won't listen to an old man" (7830, 7841). Charlie B. says, "drive up to the levee I want to yell a little bit" (7856). Once again, Jimmy pulls out of the place, and as they drive the twelve miles back to the levee camp, Francis, set on revenge, thinks, "I'll dream something up" (7868).

But once they get to the levee, it's Charlie B. who plots the next move:

> hold your horses I got a fine idea
> he was so crazy drunk don't see how he had it
> with that wounded look in his eye he looked around the levee
> where bouts that engineer shack at he said
> to make a long story short what we did was stole
> four transits from the U.S. Corps of Army Engineers
> we stole some bottle cases too
> we sit on them
>   (7975–83)

Perched on the bottle cases atop the levee, the men peer into their borrowed transits—optical instruments used in surveying—and, from twelve miles away, watch a string of films at the drive-in. Francis, relishing the camaraderie, reflects:

> yea we sat up there on the levee like four generals looking at a battle
> Charlie B. said these here is what I call box seats hey Jimmy

> these is the white man's bench alright Tang said
> the two negroes and the white one Jimmy and myself sat in the balcony
> of the delta
> we were like four noblemen in the loges at the opera
> > (7995–8000)

Naturally, they can't see much. The outrage of their situation hits home when they discover that *Baby Doll* and *Hallelujah*—films that Charlie B., Tang, and Tang's deceased wife are extras in—will in fact be shown. Charlie B., of *Baby Doll* fame, is so excited when he hears this news that "he f[alls] off the bottle case" and runs over to Francis's transit to see himself on-screen (8735). But the image is blurred, and "both his eyes was fogged over" (8737). He gets angry:

> he was saying ain't this the
> shits can't even see your own ugly self in the moom pitchus
> > (8738–39)

As for Tang, he becomes sad to the point of tears when he cannot see his late wife in the film:

> then he broke down like a bulldozer his voice
> broke I mean he sobbed and couldn't talk . . .
> . . . . . . . . . . . . . . . . . . . . . .
> it was cause his wife of long ago was in it
> > (8248–49, 8251)

Their exclusion from the theater is commonplace discrimination. But Stanford again renders the commonplace profound. The men feel the personal slight of the injustice, and as their frustration mounts alongside their inebriation, they head back to the drive-in for a third attempt to enter, although this time they aim to wreak havoc. When they approach the ticket booth and see that *Hallelujah* is still playing, Tangle Eye, who desperately needs to see his wife on the screen, hands Francis the loaded gun and, gesturing to the racist owner, says, "if that peckerwood says a word shoot him" (8532). The men settle in to watch the film as Francis levels the piece at the racist owner. What follows is one of the more poignant scenes in all of Stanford's poetry:

> Tang got to see his young wife several times
> I could tell the way his bottom lip was just jumping and the way
> he crumpled his old dusty and oily hat in his hands
> and brought it to his breast when he sighed he sighed he sighed

> like chords on a guitar he let his quiet breaths out
> (8540–44)

With a hum that seems to come from deep within, Tang reacts to the movie—specifically his late wife's face in it—as if soft guitar chords were coming from his soul. At this moment, Francis—and, really, Frank—does something rare. He instructs the reader on *how* to interpret this poignant scene, what not to miss. It is as if Stanford himself was concerned that the otherwise madcap nature of the evening and the audacity of the impending revenge would prevent the reader from feeling the depth of his seriousness about Tang, racial injustice, and the legacy of its impact. It is as if he feared we might overlook the redemptive power of this emotionally intense moment.

> in the midst of all this commotion everything was silent
> like when you standing by yourself in a long grassy row of a morning
> how can that be you might say you might have it all wrong
> you might say all this was like a parade but to me it was a funeral march
> it was as quiet and listless as the mule I'm riding how can I tell you
> maybe I shouldn't tell you about drooping eyes and turned down lips
> if you think I'm trying to be funny you got me wrong
> (8545–51)

It is not until nearly one hundred pages later in the epic that Francis, circling back to this drive-in adventure, completes the scene with an act of revenge for the theater's discrimination. Morning breaks, the white preacher has arrived for the Easter service, and Tang, still drunk, once again commandeers the PA system.

> I'm calling the shots aint nobody going nowheahs till my wife's bless her
> soul face is off the screen . . .
> (11913–14)

Meanwhile, Jimmy and Charlie B. sneak off, leaving Francis to proclaim:

> uhoh Tang now Jimmy and Charlie B. done gone
> and done it
> (11907–8)

Jimmy and Charlie B. have gone and done it indeed. They have stolen a bulldozer and are now driving it full steam toward the movie screen:

> Jimmy and Charlie B. kept a backing up and running into the frame
> that held the screen up I couldn't hear what it was they was yelling

cause of the noise but Tang's show was still on but he didn't want to
look at it no more he was passing out and they was bringing it
down now the whole thing was flat as a piece of paper and they got the
bulldozer on it in the middle and spun around and around tearing it
to shreds
(11932–37)

They only stop when they pass out drunk. With the movie screen leveled, *Hallelujah* gets projected into the woods behind where the screen once stood, the past illuminating the present landscape of the Mississippi Delta.

This critical scene—the longest in the poem—epitomizes racially important aspects of *The Battlefield* and suggests what Frank was doing, and thinking, as he lived with Linda on Mount Sequoyah. The inclusion of racial discrimination, the confrontation of that discrimination, and the quest for an exaggerated fictional revenge reflects many aspects of Frank's life from 1970 to 1972: sharing Linda's commitment to social causes; socializing with his Black friends Jimbo, Sherman, and Claude; his active fascination with their struggles and the vernacular language they used to express them; his immersion in the blues and jazz traditions; and a growing habit of remembering the levee experiences of his youth while virtually erasing his status as a white and privileged son of the southern gentry. "I still have this fascination with the warrior and the coward," he wrote to Alan Dugan in February 1972.[87] But in *The Battlefield* the warriors are bulldozer-driving Black men rather than the abstract and fantasized swordsmen or knights-errant lopping off heads in the earlier poems he wrote as a kid. And the cowards are racist peckerwoods.

## "Frank Now Had to Choose"

Writing such outrageous scenes as the drive-in fiasco, Stanford was living vicariously through the adventures of a twelve-year-old kid. But when he looked up at the real world, he was an adult making some bad decisions. On August 21, 1971, he made a defining one that seemed, on the surface, like a sign of easing into adulthood: He and Linda got married in a ceremony officiated by Father Fuhrmann. "Frankie cried," Linda remembered, "sentimental tears, I think. He was happy."[88] But when he told Dugan about his impending marriage, Frank seemed less enthused. "I think things will be fine," he wrote, as if recovering from an injury.[89] Dugan hardly stoked

Frank's dubious enthusiasm for marriage when he wrote, "I suppose I should congratulate you and Linda (give her my love) getting married, but I don't know."[90] Fuhrmann's hunch about the marriage's prospects was less ambivalent: "If I had any nerve," he explained, "I would have stepped forth and said Frank and Linda have at least six more months to ponder what they plan to profess."[91]

Fuhrmann might have mustered that nerve had he known the recent history leading to this point. Frank had gotten Linda pregnant in the fall of 1970, just before he met Cheryl, and he had paid $1,000 for her abortion, likely in November. A few months later, he had told Dugan that he had dropped out of school to secure funds to pay for the abortion. Next, in or around June 1971, he got Cheryl pregnant (despite their being careful about birth control), but Cheryl had a miscarriage just before the planned abortion.[92] Despite impregnating both women within seven months of each other, Frank had somehow kept the two women apart between January 1971, when he had met Cheryl, and June 1971. It was then that Linda, fed up with Frank's absence, came down from Mount Sequoyah and banged on his studio's door when he was inside with Cheryl. Cheryl vividly recalls the incident, noting that the knocking was urgent and angry. "A screaming woman [Linda] was banging on the door, yelling, 'Frank! Frank! ... Frank Stanford! I know you're in there'—quite dramatic." Upon hearing his last name, Frank cowered. "He kind of froze," Cheryl remembers. "I'd never seen him that way."[93]

Eventually Linda gave up and left. But she soon delivered Frank an ultimatum: Pick a woman. "Frank now had to choose," according to Cheryl.[94] Frank, who was likely more in love with Cheryl than Linda, chose Linda, most likely because Linda had the resources to support him. Cheryl, who did not protest Frank's decision, moved on with her life. "I could not support him to write," she added, "and Linda could."[95] Cheryl briefly went to Eureka Springs in the first weeks of August 1971 to see a friend before moving to New York City. Astounding, even for Frank, is the fact that he sneaked away days before his wedding to see Cheryl in Eureka Springs, arriving unannounced and drunk. As if to memorialize their seven-month relationship, the couple spent several days making love in a room at the New Orleans Hotel. At one point, Frank whispered into Cheryl's ear that he wished they had not lost the baby that she had miscarried. She cried. Then Frank went back to Fayetteville and, within days of seeing Cheryl, got married to Linda, crying as she made her entrance descending the staircase.[96]

So Father Fuhrmann's skepticism was well placed as the ceremony got underway on August 21, 1971. Fuhrmann, who would have preferred a church to a lakeside mansion, said the event "seemed like a show but not a covenant." The scene was carefully choreographed, with style trumping the sacred. The bridesmaids wore designer gowns while Frank's two groomsmen, Bill Willett and "Big Time" Sonny Morris, sported rented tuxedos. The Mencins' home was grand, columned, and handsomely situated on Beaver Lake. As Linda came down the foyer's winding staircase, professional musicians played classical music instead of the religious hymns preferred by Fuhrmann.[97] As the bride descended, Frank whispered to his old teacher, "Isn't this poetic? . . . It's like a vision."[98] Fuhrmann dismissed the comment as "type talk" from Frank. "I should have brought the divorce papers along with the marriage license," he griped.[99]

It was not only Frank who brought fidelity issues to the marriage. When she was dating Frank, Linda had a fling with Leon Stokesbury, Frank's former classmate and arguable rival in Whitehead's poetry workshops. "Though I was connected to Frank," she said, "Leon and I had some kind of electric connection as well." On one occasion, before she married Frank, she was at Leon's house when she heard that Frank had come back to town early (likely from Subiaco or Mountain Home). "I didn't have time to have sex with [Leon] that night," she added, and she left his place in such a rush that she made an incriminating wardrobe error. "Why is your blouse on inside out?" Frank asked her. When he figured out the answer, according to Linda, "he decided to devirginize one of my [former] roommates—you know, his calling."[100] On another occasion, before Frank and Linda moved in together on Mount Sequoyah, Leon and Linda did find the time to have sex. "I was a bit stoned and it did not last very long," Leon recalled. Frank arrived thirty minutes later to find the couple still in bed. "I embarrassingly got out of bed and left," recalled Leon. The next day Frank called him and said, as Leon recalled in his own words, that "it was a pretty damned strange experience to get into a woman's bed and feel the wet sheets of the guy who had just left." Leon added that Frank "did not seem mad."[101]

Financial matters did not bode well for the marriage either. Aside from the negligible funds from teaching the occasional judo lesson, Frank was, in all likelihood, close to penniless when he moved in with Linda.[102] Plus there was her abortion to pay for.[103] Even if Frank's mother, Dorothy, had wanted to help him out financially, she could not have done so. She had a mortgage on her Subiaco home and was caring for her elderly mother. "He couldn't afford anything," Linda recalled about Frank. Even if her meager income might have been complemented by her well-off parents (although there is no evidence that it was), Frank's poverty meant that they had to try and live on an extremely tight budget. "He told me once that he and Linda could easily subsist on less than $2 a day," Sam Gwynn wrote. This meant, at least foodwise, eating "two Banquet frozen dinners and a can of ready made biscuits" for a typical meal. Although Frank could exaggerate, Gwynn wrote, "I suspect this was true."[104] Fuhrmann always noted that Frank cared little for money: "He had no money—it was not important to him."[105] Frank's time with Linda confirms as much.

## "Most Poets Work for the Highway Dept."

Still, two dollars a day would not hack it. Frank had to get a job. It was fortunately around this time, the summer of 1970, that Sam Gwynn approached Frank about joining the surveying crew that he ran for the firm Kemp, Christner, and Associates. Frank had zero experience surveying, but Gwynn reasoned that "it doesn't take a genius to hold a pole or stretch a tape" and welcomed Frank to his team. "I suspected," Gwynn reflected, "from the familiarity with nature in his poems that Frank could tell a brush hook from a handsaw."[106] Frank certainly could do that—and more. Although he would look back on his initial stint of surveying and say that "I really wasn't much count," he warmed to the task.[107] "The job *is* money and outside," he wrote to Dugan, adding how he liked being in nature, seeing bobcats, sidestepping snakes, and running into eccentric people in the hills.[108] He would only kill a snake, he once noted, if it was venomous and "it pushes me."[109]

He also found the work conducive to a poetic mindset. As Gwynn notes, "There may be something inherently poetic in land surveying, with its lines and measurements."[110] John Stoss said that "Frank convinced Kemp that it would be cool to have a poet hold a pole."[111] Stanford echoes this idea in a poem from a work called "Smoking Grapevine":

> Although I can't prove it,
> Most poets work for the highway dept.[112]

Gwynn recalls how, on one occasion, the men went back to the office after a day in the field, and Frank typed a poem on the company's IBM Selectric and handed it to Gwynn as a gesture of appreciation for the job.[113] Working with Frank was memorable. The daily labor, much of it clearing and platting land for a Fayetteville suburb and sewer line, was physically demanding, and Frank excelled at it. His primary task was to keep taut the back end of the chain, moving it forward as the surveying team progressed. But he really distinguished himself when it came to clearing brush with machetes and bush axes. "He could *work*," Gwynn recalled. "He could certainly brush."[114]

Frank got on well with his crew. "The guys I work with are good souls," he wrote to Dugan in June of 1971, "they could give a shit that I was a writer." Frank's behavior somehow convinced them that he was, as he put it, "an Indian or something because every time I called [for bad weather] the rain has come." He would playfully court inclement weather, in one case a tornado, by "fucking around—dancing out in the woods." Bad weather left him more time holed up in the truck writing poems.[115] All in all, Frank found peace with employment: "My land surveying job," he wrote Dugan in the spring of 1971, "is v. good."[116]

But in the field, there were some odd Stanfordian incidents. Once when Gwynn prepared to take a "long shot" with the transit—the culmination of hours of clearing brush—he turned the transit's cross hairs on Frank, and instead of finding his much-needed coworker holding the line rod like a good soldier, he encountered a man frozen, sitting on the ground in a rigid trance. He was "motionless far down in the woods, his red and white line rod leaning against a tree." Gwynn, who very badly needed Frank to steady the line *immediately*, went berserk. "I yelled my head off trying to rouse him, but naught availed." Gwynn still marvels at what happened next: "In a bit of a temper, I marched off downhill through the brush line, finding at its end Frank seemingly mesmerized by a swinging plumb bob he had tied to a sassafras branch. Even yelling from a close distance didn't work, so I had to shake him out of his reverie, put the rod in his hand, and stalk back off to the transit station. The ride back to the office that day was quiet."[117]

Stanford recalled this same event during a psychiatric evaluation. According to the doctor, "he stated that his friend [Gwynn] looked through the surveying transit and saw his face and said what is the matter with you and wanted to know what was wrong. The patient states that at this time he had a feeling of doom, no audible or visual hallucinations or delusions, but states that 'it was all conceptual.'"[118]

The second instance of "what was *that*?" behavior was a classic Frank outburst. In what almost seemed to be a staged performance for his fellow workers, Frank finished clearing brush up to the top of a hill and, as if to celebrate his remarkable prowess, began, in Gwynn's words, "to run amok with a machete, lopping the heads off of everything botanical in sight, all the while yelling 'I am superior, I am superior!'" The crew stood in collective witness of this act, bemused if not a little alarmed. The scene recalls his earlier rampage across the Subiaco campus, in the middle of a lightning storm, with metal rods, daring the heavens to strike him dead. In any case, it was, alas, "another quiet ride back to the office."[119]

But Frank's odd behavior was the least of the firm's or Frank's problems. "Working for Kemp and Herb Christner was like being part of a family," according to Gwynn, "a seriously dysfunctional one." The dysfunctional atmosphere tolerated a certain amount of delinquency. By no means chronically absent from work, Frank skipped his share of days. Gwynn recalls one of them well. Frank did not show up for a job that was long overdue and had to be finished. "I couldn't rouse him by telephone," Gwynn complained. But it was, in Frank's defense, the last day of Dugan's weeklong visit to Fayetteville, and Frank was not about to miss his final day with the poet who adored him by going to work on a sewage line survey.[120] Gwynn, bereft, called on Stokesbury to hold Frank's line. Leon agreed, if only to "get out of his head" after the disastrous Dugan visit. Substituting for Frank, Gwynn reasoned, "may have kept him from going crazy."[121] With this absence of Frank's, Gwynn stopped calling Frank to work surveying jobs. Frank reported the situation a little differently to Irv: "The company I work for has gone under," he wrote.[122] Whatever the case, by September 1971, Kemp and Christener had split up. Don Kemp took out an ad in the local paper insisting that "I will not be responsible for any debts other than those contracted by myself personally!" and then started his own firm.[123] Frank, meanwhile, worked on contract for three registered surveyors, possibly including Kemp, as an independent, albeit unlicensed, field chief. He would survey the landscapes of Arkansas until the end.

## "I Think You Are a True Poet"

If surveying was up and down, writing remained steady. "I've had some good luck," Stanford wrote to Dugan. He was referring to the ongoing interest that editors at literary magazines were taking in his poetry. Frank had an unusual ability to juggle, however imperfectly, full-time work and (after August 1971) marriage along with full-time promiscuity and drinking, all the while reading and writing prolifically. His reputation as a poet seemed to be spreading locally and nationally, by word of mouth and on a steady wind. He noted how he had poems coming out in *"Kayak, West Coast Review, Open Places,* and *Evergreen"* and was waiting to hear back from "the men at *Partisan R. + Chicago R.*"[124]

Frank's contemporaries would later often describe him as a self-mythologizing figure. But he rarely mythologized his publishing feats, if only because didn't need to. Except for the *Partisan Review*, which accepted his work but never published it, each of the journals he mentioned to Dugan, all highly regarded in poetry circles, ran Stanford's poetry in 1971 or 1972, as did other literary venues he did not mention, such as the *New American Review*, the *Nation*, *Tansy*, *Aldebaran Review*, and the *Little Review*. The publishing record he had initiated in *Preview: 1968–1969* in 1969 was growing and, by any standard, leading to a mature body of work for a remarkably young poet. If publishing well was the best revenge against the MFA program he came to disparage, Frank's was fierce.

This is not to say that there wasn't some mythologizing going on. As he had done when editing the student magazine *Preview*, Frank used contributors' notes to portray himself as a kid prodigy taking the poetry world by storm. In William L. Fox's *West Coast Poetry Review*, which published "The Mind Reader" in 1972, Frank's bio reads that he was "born in Mississippi, 1949," and lists the composition date of the poem 1959. Stanford was born in 1948, and "The Mind Reader" is a poem that may have been started in 1959 but was certainly revised for many years afterward. His contributor's note for the *New American Review*, where he published "The Gospel Bird," offer a different sort of spin. It declares that Frank Stanford is "an undergraduate at the U. of Arkansas"—which was true when the poem was accepted—and that "this is his first published poem," which would prove to be not true. Frank had poems published in *Tansy*, *Mill Mountain Review*, and *Preview* before "The Gospel Bird" came out. But the *New American Review* was a coup, and he wanted that point emphasized. It put Frank in the rarified company of Ginsberg, James Merrill, W. S. Merwin, William Matthews, Sylvia Plath, Robert Coover, and other stars. The name of the poetry editor of the *New American Review* was one of the biggest: Richard Howard. Frank wanted his star to rise here, amid established poetic greatness.[125]

Frank's main source of feedback during the early 1970s remained Alan Dugan. The lively letters Frank wrote to him in 1971 and early 1972 confirm not only a rare trust in Dugan's opinion but also the extensive volume of poetry Frank kept producing. In April 1971, Stanford, who was in the process of preparing the manuscript of *The Singing Knives* for Irv and Mill Mountain Press, sent Dugan the twenty poems slated to appear in it. He noted that for ten of them he "revised with your suggestions." He added that he harbored doubts about "Tapsticks" and "Bequeath" and that he had "changed up" "The Snake Doctors," a poem he had been working on for "a long time." Frank also mentioned "10 new poems I have been working on since you left," four of which were longer than "The Snake Doctors." As for a couple of books with about one hundred poems in them, Frank determined that "after what you said I don't think they are much good," but he thought that ten of the poems "are worthwhile—sometimes."[126]

Stanford continued to consume an ambitious and eclectic literary diet during this period. In June 1971 he noted in a letter that "my reading has really been wandering." It included: Yukio Mishima, Peter Quennell's *Byron in Italy*, G.K. Chesterton, Fyodor Dostoyevsky's *Memoirs from the House of the Dead*, Melville, the Bible, the Koran, *Don Quixote*, Miguel Serrano's *C.G. Jung and Hermann Hesse: A Record of Two Friendships*, Thomas Wolfe, the *Decameron*, Keats, Shelley, Michael Drayton, Christopher Marlowe, D.H. Lawrence, Conrad, Sophocles, Lowell Thomas's *With Lawrence in Arabia*, Whitman, Twain, Poe, Kafka, Hawthorne, texts on Japanese swords, northern and Celtic mythology, Faulkner, Dante Gabriel Rossetti, and some books on boxing.[127] This kind of eclectic reading seems to have been essential to his ability to churn out poetry.

He made this list for Eleanor Bender, editor of *Open Places* and a woman whom he knew responded well to erudition. Dugan could have cared less. What Frank wanted from Dugan was not admiration but validation. Dugan, who rightly sensed that Frank was a tender flower when it came to criticism, wrote to him in early May of 1971: "About your poems . . . they are so good that I am hesitant to write about them in a letter for fear that you might get the wrong impression of my criticisms." Dugan assured Frank that he was not only the best poet in Fayetteville but also on his way to developing a national reputation. Then, as if to evade the awkward task of criticism, he shifted gears to offer career advice: "<u>Don't let anyone stop you from getting wider attention</u>." The implication was that the Arkansas poets were holding Frank back or maybe forcing his ambitions into academic molds. "Notoriety," Dugan wrote, "is a means of liberation for a poet." A little bit of fame and money, Dugan went on, "can give the mad poets some freedom of action." And not to be second-guessed was the fact that both men surely qualified as mad poets. "You've seen how I behave in person," he wrote in reference to his disastrous Arkansas visit, "and I've seen how you behave," he wrote in reference to Frank's shooting a bullet through the roof of the cabin. Dugan concluded with a clarification: "I don't mean [you] being a self-publicist like J. Dickey." But he pleaded with Frank to "consider what I say."[128]

Frank did. Two weeks later, when Dugan sent Frank a letter with specific criticisms of the manuscript that would become *The Singing Knives*, Frank was eager to read his thoughts. "I find this letter one of the most difficult of its type that I have ever tried to write," he began. Most of the time, he noted, "I don't have much trouble writing what I think, probably because the mss are murderously convoluted, or mediocre, or both." But in this case, he wrote, "your poems are different." They were "strange, different, & extremely good." Before giving concrete suggestions, he offered a final padding of admiration: "I think you are a true poet." Then he launched into the task he was loath to undertake.

Dugan's touch was deft. He knew he was walking a tightrope, and he did so admirably. His primary concern was to not meddle too much with Frank's poems while, at the same time, ensuring that they avoided even a whiff of academic taint. He knew well the encyclopedic range and rare depth of Stanford's literary knowledge, and he understood the conformist pressures imposed by MFA workshops. He repeatedly warned Frank against any deviation from his "natural vein of passion." In that spirit, he advised omitting "The Solitude of Historical Analysis" because it was "academically learned." He called "Wishing My Wife Had One Leg" "a beauty" but suggested that "the formal structure of the poem" might be "too heavy." For "Bequeath" he recommended taking "some of the curse off the structure" by making an *A* lowercase. As for "Narcissus and Achilles," he wrote, "Learned—but shit, the poem is so beautiful I have to say keep it." The rest of the poems "are good poems—you're a poet, and more power to you."[129] It was excellent, measured criticism.

A month later Frank wrote back to Dugan. "I took your advice," he wrote. "You are right." He also included a copy of "The Singing Knives," the title poem, noting that it was "about myself I guess." This letter then took a bizarre turn into an eight-page rant. The Frank that comes through is in part the Frank he evidently wanted Dugan to know: a wild man, a man with Black friends and hillbilly friends, an autodidact who devoured books, an iconoclast who broke ties with the MFA crowd, a man with connections to Faulkner through his mother's friend, the writer Joan Williams. None of it was necessarily untrue. But the letter, with its occasional fawning tone, comes off as awkward. Frank presumptuously asks Dugan to send him the poems he's working on, calls him "one of the best living poets," and ends the letter by writing, "I hope I can be your student one of these years."[130] A week later, Frank explained this strange performance: "I guess you think I am crazy. I was drunk when I wrote that letter."[131]

Dugan, who would himself declare things like "DRUNK AS HELL!!" in his letters to Frank, could easily overlook an alcoholically unmoored letter. Later that summer, Frank sent Dugan a short and sober note along with the poem "Belladonna," to which he added a brief note regarding its inspiration: "Goethe was riding back from a girl's house and he saw himself passing on a horse. That mystified me."[132] Dugan, always quick to remind Frank that anything intellectualized cheapened his work, responded: "I had no idea you were using Goethe in making 'Belladonna', and it doesn't matter, to my mind. The poem stands as is, without the literary crutch."[133]

Dugan continued to avoid overly detailed commentary on Frank's work. Aware that his earlier comments had led Frank to kill some poems, he insisted that "if my criticisms influenced you in any way in this decision, I swear to Christ I'll never make a critical remark to you again." In case Frank missed the point, he added, "DON'T THROW WORK AWAY." Dugan was protecting his right to compliment without criticizing. He deemed "The Singing Knives" "magnificent" and, in possibly an even greater compliment, he wrote a poem titled "On a Professional Couple in a Side Show" (1974) that references "the knife thrower's lady," "the rage of knives," and "whistling knives"—signature images in Frank's poem.[134] But if Frank wanted line-by-line edits, he could, as far as Dugan was concerned, go elsewhere. Dugan simply wanted Frank to know that his biggest potential threat was his own ample store of literary knowledge. Other than that, he was eager to say it as often as he needed to: "You're a good poet."[135]

As a final act of support, Dugan handed a stack of Frank's poems to Stanley Kunitz, a prominent poet with an international reputation. Dugan clarified to Frank that he was not a fan of Kunitz's work—"he is not so good as a poet"—but trusted his ability to give fair feedback without "malice or personal vanity." Enclosed in a letter to Frank was Kunitz's response to his work. "This poet," Kunitz said of Stanford, "is obsessive, romantic, redundant—but he's for real, + a rare one." He asked, "What can we do for him?"[136]

## "The Slow Decline toward Adulthood"[137]

If Frank could have answered Kunitz's question, he might have said, "Stop time." Creatively speaking, he was living in a golden moment, he knew it, and he did not exactly relish the way adulthood threatened to interfere with it. From a distance he looked as if he were entering his early twenties with competence: He was married, held down a job (at times), was networking with prominent poets, and was pursuing a creative passion with tangible results. The problem was that his creative passion was an outlet from nothing at all—the creativity existed for its own sake. It was all that mattered to him. And it was consuming him. For Frank, being a poet required keeping the self-conscious habits of adulthood, habits that turned one into "a pile of shit," as Francis puts it (1710), as far away from his poetry as possible. For a man who wrote a 15,283-line poem from the perspective of a twelve-year-old boy, misrepresented his age in contributor's notes, and worked hard to highlight how he had written some poems at the age of ten or eleven, the connection between youth and language—the ability to hear and feel the voices that animated his poems—was as sacred as it was precarious. Adulthood was an imposition on everything that truly mattered to Frank Stanford.

Frank tried to explain how his ability to work from an undistracted inner sanctum was diminishing with the onset of adulthood. Quoting the French poet and filmmaker Jean Cocteau, he noted that he knew that "the poet is unskilled when he speaks, as he is awoken from sleep in which he composes his work." In terms of his creative disposition, "like a medium speaking out of a trance" was where Frank had long been and where he wanted to remain.[138] But adulthood made it harder to find that space and stay there. Referring to himself when he was a fifteen-year-old, he said, "I knew I was a poet"—perhaps because he didn't have to act like a poet. But now, at twenty-three, he thought, *It is all helpless*. When he had to *think* about being a poet—something he had never done before Whitehead's workshop—his ear wavered, and he wrote "bad shitty poems."[139] Adults must package themselves and think about how others see them as packaged selves, and the self-consciousness of this process challenged his natural, childlike approach to living and writing.

In areas where Frank might have really benefited from a little adult pragmatism, he failed especially hard. Frank's inability to mature into the profession—essentially to reconcile adult responsibility with his poetic ambitions—inhibited him from delving into the poetry business. Despite his publishing success, Frank remained mostly disconnected from poetry networks: "I feel like what I want to do in my poems has nothing to do with what I read in magazines and journals. Is there something I'm not facing up to?" he asked. As much as he valued it, he could become despondent over this self-imposed isolation: "I feel like a fool, an unoriginal thinker, and not a thinker at all." He was worried about how others might see him: "Some might think me apparently aimless, ostensibly gratuitous." A few years earlier he had been spending blissful days alone in his room, clad only in underwear, drinking whiskey and writing without care or distraction from the outside world. Before that he was writing most of his poetry at a boarding school or in secret. Now he was encountering a professional world marked by rules and responsibilities he found too tedious to endure. "I have a great contempt for the rules," he said. And as for the poetry world's attempt to categorize and assess work, he noted, "I despise the neurosis of aesthetic descriptions." The upshot: "So I'm crazy."[140]

Many scenes in *The Battlefield* reflect Stanford's veneration for the timeless spirit of childhood. But one especially stands out. After recalling "the bad food at the orphanage," Francis describes a chore the orphanage authorities required him to undertake (6621–22). The job "had not no hard labor to it or nothing / but it was the one I hated the most" (6631–32). Francis had to wind the orphanage's grandfather clock. This nine-foot-tall clock kept official time and, as such, "stood there like an evil and wicked king no a brutal general" (6639–40). To prepare himself for the literal task of furthering time, Francis anxiously pulls out his fingernails with his teeth, as if the clock's movement consumes him with every tick. His first strategy to endure this torment is a decision to "pretend the key was a knife and the slow levorotatory movements / I wound with was just a working that blade in his gut" (6644–45). But time's passage exacts its toll: "each time I left some of my blood in the clock and at night / I couldn't stop the tick tick tick like drops of water" (6647–48). His body diminishes while his childhood dies as the clock ticks.

Eventually Francis settles on a solution: "I unscrewed that which I was told never to touch"—whereupon he discovers the true source of the clock's power:

> I seen all it was too it just a goddam gimmick
> damn they hide I was thinking it weren't nothing but a fat tick tock
> it wasn't no general I seen it didn't have nothing inside but steel wheels
>     (6653–56)

And steel wheels can be manipulated, controlled, and even reversed, which is precisely what Francis does:

> the hands commence to going around and around
> backwards and so I didn't have to pluck my eye out
>     (6662)

To the contrary, he sees his way to an escape. With time moving backward, "I packed my bags that night and says to the ones that was up outside / kneeling in the snow on account of bad manners see y'all boys I'm getting / the hell out of here and I did" (6666–68). And with that the young runaway Francis is on the lam, thinking:

> I don't even know where I is but there is one
> thang for sure if I pull through ain't nobody gone have call to want me for
> no reason cause *I'll just be a kid*
>   (6673–75; emphasis added)

It's hard not to interpret this scene, and all of *The Battlefield*'s symbolic treatment of clocks and watches in general, as reflecting Lord Byron's theatrical destruction of his beloved watch near the end of his life. He "furiously dashed this watch upon the hearth," wrote Lady Byron, "and ground it to pieces among the ashes with the poker."[141] Regardless, for Frank to lose his ear in the flow of time, to miss the poetry in the face of the conventions imposed on him by adult responsibility, was a threat to his writing. It therefore makes sense when Francis, just before he murders the grandfather clock and escapes the onerous duty of keeping time ticking, recalls, "I dreamed of a thousand pocketwatches and I was pouring salt on them like slugs" (6350). When Frank, in a poem titled "Handling Paper with Cold Hands," describes a sensation with the lines "Like a watch with a black face / You dropped down the well of your childhood," the themes of childhood and time converge with unusual poignance.[142]

## "Poetry Takes Its Toll.…"

During these years Frank discussed suicide, that of others and his own. The global news in November 1970 of Yukio Mishima's suicide made an impression on Frank, not only because he read and loved Mishima, but also because he shared Mishima's fascination with the Japanese warrior ethic. The mark Mishima left on Frank was intensified by the dramatic nature of the Japanese novelist's final act: He seized control of a military general's office, delivered a martial speech from a balcony to a thousand servicemen, and then publicly disemboweled himself in a seppuku ritual. Writing to Dugan, Frank indicated he saw the suicide as a warning against his own tendencies: "After you left I thought about what you said, then Mishima killed himself. That did it for me. I think I quit 'indulging in romanticism' as you say." But he also thought highly enough of Mishima to dedicate an unpublished series of poems to him. Frank's fascination with seppuku extended to playacting performances of it on himself, as Lord Byron had also done.[143] "He really admired Mishima," said Sam Gwynn.[144] Irv Broughton suggested that Frank's unpublished book of poems called "Naegling," a reference to Beowulf's sword, was "in memory of Mishima."[145]

Another suicide victim Frank openly admired, even obsessed over, around this time was the early-twentieth-century Russian poet Sergei Yesenin. The two men had a lot in common: Yesenin wrote about Russia's downtrodden farmers and peasants; he did so in a vivid, Stanford-like voice; he found literary fame in his twenties; his fans were ordinary people rather than elites; and he was deeply admired for his charisma and good looks. Frank called him "a beautiful Russian poet."[146] In a poem dedicated to Yesenin, titled "Swimming Towards Women" (from "Automatic Co-Pilot"), he wrote:

> So long blood
> brother until then
> when we meet again
> why are you so black
> friend is it the moon
> that makes you sing your prayers to the dead
> it's a long swim back to our boat
> so we better be going[147]

Frank had discovered Yesenin in 1969 when he read a borrowed copy of *Poets on Street Corners: Portraits of Fifteen Russian Poets*.[148] The book's entry on Yesenin opens with a poem that begins:

> Already you've begun to fade
> to wither like a flower.[149]

When he acquired his own copy of this book in early 1972, Frank wrote a note about Yesenin in the back of it. "For some years now the spirit of Sergei Yesenin has been my comrade. . . . We are brothers." In a reference that seems to confirm Dugan's suspicion that Frank had destroyed some of his poetry, Frank writes in this same note to Yesenin, "I'm afraid I've burned your photograph, the one that's kept with my MSS over the years." Midway through the inscription, he addresses Yesenin directly, saying that the photo was one "where the vodka, the women, and the world was in your eyes." He continues, "You are like the passwords one hears in a dream."[150] Yesenin hanged himself in a Leningrad hotel room shortly after he turned thirty. He did so after writing a farewell poem in his own blood.[151]

These grandly performative suicides appealed to Frank. He was an intensity junkie who lacked the perspective to see through the histrionics to the underlying brutality of the act. The examples of Mishima and Yesenin almost certainly encouraged him to envision his own demise, which he was contemplating during these years. Bill Willett remembers how Frank said he was going to give him a manuscript, which he was calling "St. Francis and the Wolf," and that it would be worth something someday. "He was contemplating suicide obviously early.... One of the main points... was that he had to get it done and put it out because he wasn't going to be around much longer." Willett was stymied about how to respond: "I'm this guy's best friend, and he's my best friend, and he's telling me he's going to kill himself."[152] Frank's Subiaco classmate Martin Pendergrast recalled, "Some years after we left Subiaco, we sat down, drank, and had a full-on conversation in the middle of the night. He talked about killing himself."[153] Linda was certain about it: "The suicide was premeditated." In June 1972, immediately following her and Frank's separation, she told Dugan that "he didn't want to live anymore."[154] In a letter to Dugan, Frank could not have been more direct about the connection between poetry and suicide: "Sometimes it makes me want to shit, or kill myself. This bloodsucking poetry."[155]

FROM THE OUTSIDE, FRANK SEEMED to be doing well from 1970 to 1972. He was publishing up a storm in the little magazines, had a book under contract, was widely adored for his mystique and good looks, and was as mythological a figure as Fayetteville had ever known. But with Frank there was as always a darker story brewing. Between himself and the cabin walls on Mount Sequoyah, between himself and his studio walls on Lindell Avenue, Frank was becoming increasingly confused on the best of days, miserable on most others, and on the darkest days, suicidal. The moments of creative bliss he enjoyed on Mount Sequoyah were just that: fleeting moments. Mirroring the emotional swings he endured, that creativity was, after a heroic two-year outburst of poetic productivity, about to tumble down the mountain and, in a few months' time, land him in the state hospital in Little Rock.

The tipping point came when Linda, who sparked and supported so much of Frank's productivity during these years, left him in May 1972, after only nine months of marriage. "Poetry takes its toll," Frank wrote to Dugan. "It just took my wife." He then clarified, "Rather it took me and, while I wasn't looking, it took my wife."[156] Linda confirmed the assessment, noting that "Frankie was so entranced in his poetry" that she "fell in love with someone else to excuse [herself] from the opera."[157] She knew too well the aria she was going to miss. After months of writing and philandering and drinking, Frank faced what she saw as an inevitable crash, and he understood perfectly well why Linda had the foresight to get out of the way. As he wrote to Dugan, "She has grown up."[158]

Frank Stanford, Hanover, New Hampshire, August 1972.
*Photo courtesy of Irv Broughton.*

NINE

# "I Am Ready to Rise from My Ashes"

## 1972

HIS MARRIAGE MIGHT HAVE BEEN coming undone, but Frank began the year 1972 with an unprecedented creative outburst. "I am drinking too much and writing a lot," Frank wrote to Dugan, from the security of the Mount Sequoyah cabin, in January.[1] "I'm trying to lay off the booze," he said to Irv as a way of suggesting that he was not doing so well at it.[2] Drunk or sober, but frequently drunk, he was pleased with the written results: "The new poems I'm working on I like the best." He was confident in the independence of his artistic vision. "I have no stand when I write," he emphasized. "I write what I knew," he said, celebrating the power of his past. It was there, in his past experience, that he was most assured about "what is the truth."[3]

By early March the intensity of his behavior, fueled by insomnia and alcohol, supercharged his writing habits. "I'm writing more than ever," he wrote, sounding more desperate about it than proud. "I don't know where it's coming from." He captured the essence of the experience with a choice metaphor: "All the time I'm in a daze; like an 18 hr slow and easy orgasm." He understood the emotional consequences of such a release: "I put out like a ship," he wrote, "then, when it's over I'm depressed and want to get drunk." One outcome of this roller-coaster ride was his "big manuscript"—he once called it "the long son-of-a-bitch."[4] At any given moment between 1968 and 1972, trying to discern the difference between "St. Francis and the Wolf" and *The Battlefield*—or trying to figure out *The Battlefield*'s place in "St. Francis"—is like trying to nail jelly to the wall. But here is how Frank made sense of it to the editor of *West Coast Poetry Review* in 1972: "Maybe I can clean up some confusion by a few details. If you have the MS. 'St. Francis . . . ,' you should have over 50 poems, of all lengths, written anywhere from [19]57–64. You can distinguish these poems by the lack of caps. in title and the first line and first letter of every line. There is, extant, a long section from a very long poem 2/3s destroyed. It's called 'the battlefield where the moon says I love you,'—about 300 pages long. It is also from St. Francis."[5]

Whatever state of transition the poem was in, it reflected Frank's deepening confidence, creative autonomy, and increasingly global perspective. As *The Battlefield Where the Moon Says I Love You* took form as a one-of-a-kind creation, Frank began to openly detest the attitude he saw emerging among American artists who believed they should, as he put it to Irv, "Look at America," "forget Europe," and be "in favor of America." Regarding American poets, he wrote that they "are all paranoid and insecure now, and so they form these stupid little cliches of ways of writing poetry." Rather than follow trends, he wanted to broaden the range of what was possible. He opposed the notion of any school of writing as much as he did that of a single national voice, which could only reflect "America's neurosis." All he would hear was "just the animals and voices," the boundless sounds of a boundless world. "Artists of all persuasions and nationalities appeal to me," he noted.[6] Too many poets, in his view, were choosing what to hear rather than just listening.

Frank especially disliked what he once referred to as "Southern Writers Inc." poetry, the kind of mannered southern stuff he claimed tainted Whitehead's workshop.[7] Too many American poets were limited because "their suburban + urban backyards were . . . so small—so small." This opinion suggests that his recognition of his adoption offered him the freedom to think beyond his region to other vernaculars and styles. Frank's backyard would always be southern, but, as he qualified it, since "my backyard was infinite, anything and everything can and did happen."[8] It was an emerging perspective that complicated any effort to rope him into any genre, much less Southern Writers Inc.

## "Insane Reality"

Stanford's adoration of the French poet and filmmaker Jean Cocteau was critical to this broadening perspective. Frank described Cocteau as one of his "guardian angels." He knew intimately Cocteau's films and poems and had even read his biography.⁹ There are several noteworthy aspects to this attraction. Cocteau's international perspective defied the provinciality Frank condemned in many American poets. Whereas Americans were "trying to rediscover their own past + traditions," Cocteau's ideal artist was geographically located "in heaven, where everything is fine." As Frank noted, "I am in heaven with these artists. I may descend into hell occasionally, but no longer than DANTE!"¹⁰ The artistic sensibility that he was cultivating in the infinite backyard of Northwest Arkansas worked diligently to root itself in place and, at the same time, transcend it.

Cocteau's creativity also evoked the liberated spirit of Frank's childhood. Like Stanford, Cocteau was a child prodigy who, according to his most recent biographer, "loved his childhood," which was as free and "infinite" as Frank's.¹¹ Frank singled out *La belle et la bête* as a favorite Cocteau production. This film, according to one analysis of it, "dared to be naïve, asking its audience to revert to childhood, the better to accept its practical magic."¹² Frank keyed into this quality of Cocteau's work—the instinctual appeal of childlike wonderment in the face of bourgeois reality. It was a disposition reflected in *The Battlefield*'s protagonist, Francis. The idea of being naïve but adventurous not only spoke to Cocteau's trancelike visionary appeal but also supported Frank's disdain for conventional respectability. When poet Lorenzo Thomas famously described Stanford as "a swamprat Rimbaud," it was this subversive, unironic aspect of Stanford's aesthetic vision and its primitive sincerity that Thomas captured so well with that choice description.¹³

While Frank's European-surreal-ish focus might seem to run counter to his ear for local dialects, it in fact strongly complements it. Cocteau's nonconformist vision merged seamlessly with Frank's interest in the cultural patterns of Fayetteville's Black community. The anthropologist Hortense Powdermaker, who undertook an insightful ethnography of the Black Belt in the late 1930s, conducted studies that inform what might seem an unlikely connection between Frank's Cocteau obsession and his friendships with Jimbo, Claude, Sherman, Charlie B., and others. She wrote, "Jean Cocteau represents the Genius of his free creative spirit as a Negro." He reflected "the Negro as being undistorted by the cramping effects of our civilization."¹⁴ LeRoi Jones would later develop this idea, writing about how Black people in America, albeit through no choice of their own, were necessarily outsiders to "standard" American values. This outsider status was particularly pronounced when it came to music. "The young Negro musician," he wrote, "began to realize that merely by being a Negro in America, one *was* a nonconformist."¹⁵ The artist could do a lot with this nonconformity. Stanford's affinity for the country blues, the ultimate in outsider music, imbued his poetic process and informed his own fringe-dwelling persona.[16] One might even wonder if Frank's paranoia-infused story line of his workshop peers stealing his work mirrored in his mind the way white music producers capitalized on the talent of the Memphis bluesmen whose music Frank knew so well or the way that the goliath Atlantic Records scammed and sunk Stax, the little Memphis jewel, into oblivion. Whatever the case, Cocteau represented the stylish outlaws, the crafty subversives, who were so much like the men Frank admired at Sherman's.

But in the most fundamental terms, Cocteau appealed to Frank because his aesthetic vision blurred reality and fiction, the conscious and the subliminal, and the real and surreal. This blurring happened in ways that erased the significance of established boundaries, or what Pier Paolo Pasolini, another favorite filmmaker-poet of Frank's, called "the forms of the world."[17] Frank's poetry thrived in a formless realm that was inseparable from dreaming, but he still considered dreams to be grounded in reality. From this link one can deduce that reality for Frank was formless. Film reinforced this notion more than any other medium for him. In discussing Cocteau, Frank wrote, "Film (poetry) has nothing to do with dreams except that it borrows the vigorous illogicality of dreams, their way of giving during the night."[18]

To have visions or to be in a trance was therefore *not* to be out of one's mind or living in an alternate or unhinged reality. To the contrary, "I believe the visionary life has nothing to do with a necessarily transcendent existence," Frank wrote.[19] Visions appeared while one was sleeping and while one was awake, and the poet did not need to bother with the distinction between these arbitrary states. "My poems can't be classified as subliminal, dreams, un-conscious, automatic, etc.," he wrote. He wanted nothing to do with any conscious trend toward the unconscious, à la Robert Bly, or explicitly forced efforts to tap into the subconscious for poetic purposes. "I, deliberately, avoid these conscious + calculated + intentional manifestations of the unconscious," Frank explained. Instead, in a patchwriting of Cocteau, Frank wrote that he preferred "a kind of half sleep where I wander through insane reality." Insane reality was his infinite backyard; it was where poetry happened. In fact, it *was* poetry. As Irv put it, Frank "said he believed one dreams his own dream in the poem, that it isn't a matter of recounting; rather, it is a matter of actually having the experience in the poem itself."[20] Cocteau helped Frank appreciate this aspect of his creativity, one that's possibly only understandable if you as an artist experience it.

## "A Tragic, Labyrinthine Tale of Woe"

It would be easy to get entangled in these kinds of thoughts or attempts to convey these thoughts, and sometimes, while thinking about dreaming and reality and poetry, Frank did. In a way, it's satisfying to watch him elucidate and untangle his poetics through his growing interest in Cocteau and other European poets, philosophers, and filmmakers. But his insights into the creative process, especially when they became overly abstracted, sometimes drove Frank to frustration. Frank knew the dangers of this manner of thinking for him, primarily because he knew that "theories are not at all connected to my poetry."[21] One time, after an overwrought self-analysis of his poetry—one that touched on everyone from Parmenides to Rimbaud, Mallarmé to Apollinaire—he wrote how "these theories only delude and echo, driving you insane and impotent or at best sterile, as a poet."[22] When he waxed self-reflexive, he risked spiraling into turmoil. The result of the turmoil was poetry, and the result of the poetry was turmoil. And so the cycle spun, sometimes to the verge of disaster, as it did in the spring of 1972.

For about two months, most of March and all of April of 1972, the need to make a living temporarily slowed this spiral. With the weather improving, Frank's surveying work picked up, sometimes to eighty hours a week. "My time has become really valuable again," he wrote, noting that the work schedule "had certainly helped my insomnia + drinking."[23] The tight but more predictable schedule even inclined him to do something he enjoyed but rarely took time to do: bake. In late April the *Northwest Arkansas Times* published Frank's "Pumpkin Bread" recipe. Frank instructed, "Line bottoms of 2 bread pans or 1 10 inch tube pan with waxed paper. Pour [the prepared canned pumpkin mix] into prepared pans. Bake at 350 degrees 50–55 minutes for bread pan or 70–75 minutes for tube pan."[24] Enjoy.

During these relatively sober and hardworking couple of months, Frank focused on getting his ever-evolving big manuscripts into the hands of critical readers and editors. He pulled much of his "long son-of-a-bitch"—*The Battlefield Where the Moon Says I Love You*—together and sent three hundred pages of it to Dugan. To both Dugan and William L. Fox at *West Coast Poetry Review*, he sent the even larger "St. Francis and the Wolf: Some Poems 1957–1964." Fox said he was only browsing what Frank sent him because, well, it was hundreds of pages long and there were no page numbers in it. He was also waiting "for that other copy to come"—presumably *The Battlefield*—and this one hopefully with page numbers.[25] Frank reported to Eleanor Bender at *Open Places* that, even though he felt unstable, he was still "putting together the type script of a thousand page poem I wrote in 1964"—that is, *The Battlefield*. Then—offering a hint about how this poem was evolving—he noted that he was blending old material with new, a process critical to updating *The Battlefield*, which had begun life as an excerpt from "St. Francis and the Wolf." "While this past was being collated," he wrote, emphasizing his control of his own history, "the present was becoming new work."[26] Although this is hardly conclusive, few descriptions get us closer to the mysterious process behind the creation of *The Battlefield*.

However time-consuming Frank's surveying work and writing were, it was his philandering that would ultimately send him over the edge toward a breakdown. "Frank was screwing whoever he could find," Irv remembered.[27] He seemed to take this activity to a new level in the spring of 1972, with sex becoming a manifestation of his hyperactivity in general. His actions had serious emotional consequences for almost all involved. "I have done my share of ruining the lives of several women," he wrote in an agonized mood to Bender in July, no doubt recalling the pain he had caused Cheryl the previous summer and Linda that spring. But there were many others. *The Battlefield* may reflect something of Frank's actual situation in spring 1972 when Francis refers to "my eleven / girlfriends and twenty-two pen pals" (6133–34).

Francis the fictional kid was unfazed by this array of lovers. But Frank the actual adult was trapped in what he called "a tragic, labyrinthine tale of woe."[28] There was Kathy Walton, about whom Frank noted, "I hurt her. I can't talk about her now," but, he said, "She was in love with me. I did not love her." As for the uncountable flings, he wrote, "There were women, but nothing more than a man's pleasure."[29] He explained that there were "just too many lovely women to hurt and contend with," specifying "other women, married, divorced, single, and so on."[30] The promiscuity was out of hand and had to end. As he told Dugan, he had "more regards for the several women [in Fayetteville], I love, to ever see them again. Let them go their way. I'll go mine. Too many, too much to hurt."[31] At the root of this pain was guilt and fear that he seemed unable to control: "I don't want to hurt anyone. Really I don't."[32] But it was too late for that. As for Linda, "she has found out more than she should." Frank felt terribly for "her own sweet, hurt self."[33] The behavior was bad, the guilt was excruciating, and he kept doing it.

Additionally, he still longed for Cheryl. Her absence—recall that she left for New York when Frank decided to marry Linda in August 1971— allowed Frank to dramatize the emotional impact of his loss. He explained, "I betrayed a woman who was the Light to my Dark soul." Frank and Cheryl had been "bound as day and night." She "ruled the nights of my instinct."[34] Frank was certainly sorry about what he had done to Linda—"My wife had to endure so much"—but he was far more distraught over having rejected Cheryl. By any standard what he had done to her was cruel: He had shared an apartment with her for five months while also sleeping with Linda; he had pushed her to have an abortion (before she miscarried) and then lamented the loss of the child; he had agreed to marry Linda in August 1971 and then sent Cheryl packing; and he had visited Cheryl in Eureka Springs just days before his marriage ceremony to have days of drunken sex. But Frank still loved her. "As a poet, Cheryl is my wife," he wrote. "As just another citizen, Linda is my wife."[35] He told Willett, "Cheryl was my body soul and spirit mind all." He wrote, "I betrayed my mistress, and when you betray a lover as close to your soul as Cheryl was to mine, [you] must suffer the ultimate consequences, my friend." After Cheryl left for New York, Frank said, "I went mad."[36]

Indeed, the twenty-three-year-old poet was crushed. "Pages and pages would not describe C and my love for each other," he wrote to Willett.[37] He would lie in bed next to Linda and, fixated on Cheryl, "dream of the aborted children," remembering how "there is only one meeting of lovers like us."[38] He confessed that "at night, I dream of a fleet of coffins under sail, bearing the bodies of dead infants."[39] "Would I," he wrote, "ever return home on my horse with a dead child not in my lap."[40] As the next evening approached, as more nightmares awaited, he'd get drunk and go into town and, out of frustration or confusion, make another bad choice. "I'm getting horny," he wrote during one fit of emotional chaos, "so I'll probably fuck somebody tonight."[41] As far as he was concerned, the outcome of his betrayal of Cheryl, as well as his sexual experiences with countless other women, was foreordained and unavoidable: "madness and death."[42] For the moment, Frank, at least according to several angry women, became persona non grata. "It is guilt I feel, for doing what I've done.... I deserve nothing but death," he wrote.[43] For the time being, though, cosmic retribution came in the form of derangement bordering on madness.

As if matters on the infidelity front were not already bad enough, there was evidently an angry husband in the mix. It seems that this husband might have been closer to Frank than he would have liked. Frank alluded to an angry cuckold set on revenge: "I was a wanted man."[44] And, later, he wrote to a poet friend: "An irate husband was going to do me in."[45] He elaborated to his friend Willett: "There is one [woman] in Fayetteville who you know by acquaintance (but you don't know who I speak of), older than myself, a married woman with a family. No one knows about us. I will not tell you her name, as I promised never to do so: there is too much to lose, if others should find out. Anyway, it was brief and sweet." He noted that another abortion had resulted from their affair.[46] Frank paraphrased a letter that a furious husband had written him: "I thought you were a friend, I opened my doors to you, and all along you and my wife were..."[47] Whoever the angry husband was, the situation, as Frank characterized it, spelled trouble.

By May of 1972 all this drama culminated in a sense of acute desperation. Frank's letters went haywire, making statements throughout the early months of 1972 such as "The poet's work... devours him," "I'm crazy," "Everything is absurd" (a Cocteau quote), "I'm an outcast," and "Fuck words." He was despondent about the poetry world—"I have lost faith in poets"—bellowing out against "Dickey shit, Merwin shit, Bly shit, Ginsberg shit."[48] On May 10 he began a letter to Dugan by howling onto the page, "May Day May Day May Day."[49] He wrote Irv asking for $150 after he was fined for disorderly conduct for screaming Cheryl's name in the streets. "Otherwise, I'm going to jail.... Don't try to call me.... I'm ducking + dodging."[50] It was at this point that Linda, possibly worried for her safety, left him for good. "Frank's craziness drove her off," recalled Leon Stokesbury.[51] "I drove her crazy," Frank confirmed to Dugan, acknowledging that she feared being physically harmed by him. Something even went wrong with Frank's skin—"[I'm] shedding skin like a snake"—and his thoughts were a mess: "I don't have any control of my mind."[52] To an editor he apologized for an erratic letter he'd written, saying, "I'm just too goddam miserable."[53]

By the middle of May he was delirious and hopeless. "I don't know what to do anymore." Quitting booze, going back to school, getting "the fuck out of this place," and "mak[ing] up with my wife" were all floated as options but ignored. "I can't think," he complained. "When I get fucked up in the head I start shuffling and talking shit." He felt betrayed by himself: "I thought I had things by the horns," he lamented. And somehow during his outburst he posed a question that came from who knows where: "Is that Yale Univ. any good?"[54] It was during this time that he wrote what has to be one of the stranger biographical notes ever published (although it was made into a contributor's note by an editor who evidently mixed up Arkansas and Alabama). It was for four poems that were running in the summer 1972 *Iowa Review*, and it read: "Frank Stanford has got to be one the [sic] strangest poets around. Right now he is living in a monastery in Alabama where he likes to borrow a horse, ride into the mountains, and meet strange girls. He is 22 years old and the poems in this issue are from an early manuscript called *St. Francis and the Wolf: Some Poems 1957–1964*. This means, obviously, the poems in this issue were written when he was about 12 years old."[55]

This was, at best, cheeky and at least a little off-kilter. Frank was undergoing a genuine collapse fueled by shame, despair, mental instability, and an increasing desire to escape. He did not want to hurt the women with whom he was intimate. He was increasingly ashamed of himself as his infidelities multiplied and condensed into suffering that was mind altering. He was embarrassed when Linda's parents, who had always worshiped their Frank as a genius, came to get Linda's belongings and, as a parting shot, told Frank he had degenerated into a pathetic drunk. He knew he was going to have to leave the cabin and go home to his mother's house and work for the monks, and while he loved the monks, he didn't want to have to live at home with mother and grandmother. It was all deeply humiliating. Still, "it is for the agony of others that I howl," he told Willett, "not for myself."[56]

While his philandering partly precipitated this decline, Frank understood that at the root of this trouble was his obsession with poetry. It was therefore almost logical, considering this diagnosis, that in late May, he marked his decline by doing what qualified to him as addressing the ultimate source of his turmoil: He set fire to the vast archive of his writing. "I burned everything in the house," he wrote to Dugan on May 26, 1972. "There is nothing of mine existing in this house. Don't send me my poems, or I'll burn them."[57] He confirmed the act to Irv, writing, "Except for about 50 things I have out in the mail, all my manuscripts are burned. I burned them."[58] To clarify what mattered most to him, to stress what he saw as the greatest loss in this rueful act, he reiterated to Dugan: "There is no such thing as 'The Battlefield Where The Moon Says I Love You.' I burned it—the whole thousand pages."[59]

Fortunately, this was not quite the case. There was still such a thing as *The Battlefield*. It was just scattered. Stanford had recently sent three hundred pages of the manuscript to an editor at the *New American Review*, a few hundred pages to William L. Fox and Alan Dugan, and large excerpts to Bill Willett. In the letter in which he informed Dugan about the burning, he included some typed-up scraps from "The Moon Says I . . ."[60] The next day he revisited the extent of his destruction, assuring Dugan that he had burned over ten thousand pages of work.[61] Later he upped his estimation to fifteen thousand pages.[62] "There is no one here the least bit interested in what I write," he declared.[63] His recounting of the firestorm mentioned that he had also burned "stories, essays, novels (nascent), plays."[64] But he included a telling caveat. He confessed to Dugan that he had, in fact, saved "the rest of the Battlefield Where the Moon Says I."⁶⁵

A document Frank wrote a few months after the burning, appropriately titled "List of Ashes," helps clarify what may have been lost. He notes that "pages"—fifteen thousand, he reiterated—could refer to "any scrap of paper that was handy when the Muse wanted to make love." He also clarifies that there was no original manuscript lost that had been dated to before 1957. He mentions "several epic length prose poems" written when he was at Subiaco. Between 1966 and 1972 there were "novels, novellas, plays, stories, prose pieces." He notes that "in a sequence of dreams, Thomas Merton had given me instructions on a novel." Those instructions had evaporated. Out of the hundred stories that had burned, he remembered liking only twelve of them. One novel, called "ella," was about Keats, Bellerophon, Villon, Comte de Lautréamont, and others. There was "a recent little cycle of stories" called "Eleven Dark Women," "a long *good* poem called The Illustrated Boy," "a cotton sack full of unfinished poems," all written "since college." He had destroyed a novel titled "The Dream Children," a play called "The Black Patch," a cycle of poems titled "The Black Ship," a "ms of a hundred or so poems, each title being a girl's name." Most of "St. Francis and the Wolf" was "lost, burned, drowned, given away, confiscated long ago," but he still had "a pack of old and wild poems" he was calling by that name. "I feel as if an orphanage full of doomed orphans has burned," he writes.⁶⁶

Dramatic as this move was, Frank had made careful Stanfordian calculations. He wanted the satisfaction gained from the arch theatricality of burning his work while, at the same time, salvaging what would best enhance his literary reputation: *The Battlefield*. He would, even in the throes of his breakdown, protect what he wanted to outlive him while preserving the romance and agony of the grandiose gesture. In his last letter to Dugan before leaving the Mount Sequoyah cabin, Frank included a page torn from the preface of John Keats's epic poem *Endymion*. The preface begins: "Knowing within myself the manner in which this Poem has been produced, it is not without a feeling of regret that I make it public."⁶⁷ From there Keats, the precocious genius dead at twenty-five, charts his transformation from childhood to maturity, the duration of that journey being marked by feverish, trancelike, and familiar bursts of unfettered creativity. Frank needed to, and did, preserve the poetic starting point of that journey by making sure the big poem outlived his epic fire. "You caress me, Endymion," he wrote in July 1972, "as I sleep."⁶⁸

If *The Battlefield* would survive the inferno and live on in the world, the same could not be assured for Frank. Every indication was that he was on the brink of a fatal kind of crash. "Poetry has always been like breathing to me," he wrote to Irv. "Sometimes there is gasping, though."[69] "When I last saw him," Linda told Alan Dugan, "he did not want to live."[70] As always, Frank left behind a string of hints in his work. The manuscript he'd been writing in the cabin contained more than enough references to confirm his dark desire (including, in the third quoted line, a Keats quote): "I got drunk and wrote suicide notes" (11962), "I'll be dead before long so it don't matter" (8989), "I have fears that I may cease to be" (again echoing Keats) (12399), and perhaps most ominously "a person might have thought three shots were fired" (2527). Frank's assessment of his own condition aptly and clinically summed up his mental state at the end of May 1972: "I'm insane right now."[71]

## Patient LR105913

As she prepared to file for divorce, Linda called Dorothy to alert her that Frank had suffered a breakdown and was coming back to Subiaco.[72] Over the previous three weeks, according to Frank's subsequent Arkansas State Hospital report, he had been "experiencing despair [because] he was occupied only with himself." More so, "he was concerned about his marriage and felt sincerely that he would commit suicide since he already felt dead." Notably, given Frank's fascination with Mishima, he "considered the method of committing suicide with the knife as the Japanese commit hari-kari."[73] Father Fuhrmann remembered that Dorothy, who was still managing Subiaco's Coury House, was worried out of her mind when Frank got home. She had fretted about Frank's mental health ever since he was deemed a genius in the fourth grade by a Memphis testing agency. "He caused her some suffering," Linda said, adding Dorothy's name to the lengthening list of women Frank had recently hurt.[74] Frank showed up in Subiaco at the close of May 1972 with, as he later recounted, "nothing, only the clothes on my back."[75]

Dorothy could not afford to send Frank to a private clinic for treatment.[76] When Frank spoke with a general practitioner, his family doctor from Mountain Home, Frank told him, "I don't want to die."[77] Finally Dorothy urged Father Fuhrmann to get Frank, who was still going days without sleep, into treatment at the Arkansas State Hospital in Little Rock.[78] The pugilist priest's attitude was that real men handled these problems independently or through faith. But he agreed to do as Dorothy asked. On June 2 the two men left Subiaco for the hospital. Frank kept the conversation light as they made the two-hour drive, assuring Fuhrmann that he was not ashamed about checking into what he called "a nut house."[79] Linda wrote to Dugan that "Frank wanted me to tell you he committed himself to the state hospital."[80] Frank later wrote to Dugan, "I didn't exactly commit myself."[81] And then Frank wrote to the editor Eleanor Bender: "My wife had me committed."[82] Whoever was responsible for the hospital visit, and it does seem to have been his mother, Frank, who was exhausted, went without protest. "I don't recall any belligerence against the clinic or his mother," Father Fuhrmann noted.[83]

In the tempestuous months leading up to the hospital visit, Frank later told Willett, he was, with the Angel of Death hovering, "writing to live, creating to exist."[84] This need to write persisted in the hospital. He even worried that admitting himself would be, as his intake report noted, "a sacrifice to his writing."[85] The previous few months had certainly provided ample material to write about, and later in the year he told Willett about "my newest manuscript . . . recalling the last year in Arkansas."[86] Frank, whose work never veered too far from actual experience, mentioned a draft he had written in the hospital that was lost in the mail.[87] This could feasibly have been an early version of what would become *Ladies from Hell*, which Mill Mountain Press would publish in 1975 (copyright 1974). The events of the first half of 1972 have their imprints all over the book. The volume's opening quote is from Thomas Merton: "The sweet dark warmth of the whole world will have to be my wife." The poem titles alone arguably seem to connect the book to Frank's troubles with Linda at that time, promiscuity, angry husbands, and multiple affairs: "Where We Slept Together," "The Paramor," "Farewell," "Suspect," "Sudden Opera," "Women Singing When Their Husbands Are Gone," and "Linger."[88]

The content of these poems reflects Frank's recent experiences with despair, infidelity, and revenge. There's a young mother walking into the water "with her dress full of rocks," another woman who "took her own life on the levee / with a pistol," and a speaker who says:

> I am afraid a woman
> will burn my hair.

The poem "Suspect" opens with:

> He is the one
> They all know he done it

> He was
> Run out of the country
> For it

It goes on:

> In all my trials
> Saying to himself
> No one knows
> The trouble
> That comes looking
> For me

And, in a darkly mysterious vein, the poem "Dante Gabriel Rossetti with His Head on the Virginal" opens with:

> I give you the feeling
>
> That you are in danger
>   of a woman dressed in black
> Who walks down the hall with a candelabra
>   to burn the suicide notes she reads in braille[89]

References to escape—drifting, drinking, and dreaming—abound in these poems. The first in the collection opens with:

> We'd been dreaming
> Or at least I had

In the poem "Linger," Stanford writes:

> I dreamed someone's horse
> Had wandered out on the football field
> To graze
> And I was showing children through a museum

In "Chimera," Stanford opens with:

> I dream I am asleep in a boat
> with jars full of coins
> drifting through fine rushes.

The movement in these poems is slow and controlled—dreamy, as if Frank was containing the frantic turmoil of his life within the lugubrious beauty of words. The wind does not blast but rather "lifts a finger"; "A good memory moves me through the current"; "The wind blows through the trees / Like a woman on a raft"; "The moon wanders through my barn / Like a widow heading for the county seat"; "There are mountains that float like ashes"; and "*Frightened crayfish move in the mud / like lonesome women.*" Slowness prevails, the kind that makes you ease up on the gas and look more closely at the surrounding landscape.[90]

Drink provides perpetual solace in these poems, and "Blue Yodel of the Wayfaring Stranger" explains what comes next when the booze is gone:

> All my liquor is gone so is my land
> I got kicked out of school for sleeping
> And I spent what I had
> Going to the picture show
> Where I was arrested for putting my fist through a mirror
> When this song is finished
> I'm leaving this place . . .

For a man who had spent the spring of 1972 drinking heavily, fornicating widely, ruining his marriage and possibly another, cursing the MFA program, suffering self-loathing, and burning his work, the poem's images of consumed liquor, lost land, rejection from school, punching a mirror, and planning an escape track closely with his actual experiences during this time of crisis.

On June 6, four days after his admission into the hospital, Frank finally saw a psychiatrist. The doctor's initial report reveals a young man every bit as troubled as his "May Day" letters indicate. The doctor's primary reason for keeping Frank under close observation for ten days is listed as "depression." The symptoms specified are "Deeply depressed. Confused. Suffering greatly from fear—guilt." Additional notes add that Frank "cares only for books—his writing," that it is "difficult for him to take criticisms and rejection," and that he "resents advice." The report further observes that Frank had been drinking heavily, writing obsessively, loving "literature and philosophy" exclusively, and that his wife had recently left him after nine months of marriage because of his obsession with "the manuscript"—that is, *The Battlefield.* Still, on balance, the big poem was by his own calculation causing him "50% worry and 50% joy."[91]

Two days later the doctor wrote up a "psychiatric history and mental status" report. "No definite evidence of psychosis is demonstrated," he concluded. He determined that Frank was deeply upset about his broken marriage and that, again, according to Frank, the manuscript that consumed him was solely to blame. With respect to Linda, the doctor said of Frank that "his dealings with her within the past two or three months has not been that as he would think of as normal." The reason, the doctor determined, is that "he feels that he was too wrapped up in the manuscript in which he was writing and let it affect his ways with his wife to such an extent that she began to fear him actually physically although he stresses that he would not hit her." This fear may have come right after the mass burning of his work, when, Frank recalled, Linda told him to "shut up this rant; it was only paper." It was the kind of comment whereby, Frank admitted, "I might become violent from my grief," although he never did, at least not toward Linda.[92]

The report also makes it clear that Frank only felt in charge of his life when he was writing. When asked if there were thoughts he could not stop or words that kept entering his head, he said that "he had had melodies and phrases" that occasionally nagged him but that "he was always in control of phrases about his writing." He denied that he could read minds but clarified that "I can when I am writing; you know the people I am writing about I have to know what they are thinking." But Frank also knew that this authorial control, and the satisfaction it provided him (50 percent joy), was also at the core of his tribulations with Linda. The report continues: "He goes on to state that he had been working on a manuscript which he was rewriting from an old manuscript and he was probably relating his own life to that described in the manuscript and probably paying too much attention to the content of the manuscript and he states that he knows it had too much affect [sic] on his life with his wife and that he was unable to handle it and so this was the manuscript that he burned."[93] In this way, as Frank rightly noted to Dugan, poetry took his wife. And had Fuhrmann and Dorothy not intervened, it might have taken his life.

This fundamental conflict between poetry and life precipitated Frank's destructive feelings of insecurity and self-consciousness throughout the spring of 1972. When the doctor asked Frank to evaluate his own situation, Frank "smiled and stated well, I guess I'm just sensitive regarding people's thoughts about me because I am so self-conscious." After discussing a recurring nightmare of being decapitated, Frank noted his inability to deal with these visions. "He feels vulnerable now," the doctor wrote, "because he can't handle these [dreams] and since his wife is leaving has had a marked feeling of insecurity." This insecurity fueled his reckless sexual behavior ("I'm getting horny so I'll probably go fuck somebody tonight"), which in turn led to regret and feelings of being persecuted. When Frank was asked if people had a grudge against him, the doctor reported that Frank said, "Well, there is probably plenty of people who have a right to have a grudge against me." When asked why, he said, "Well, you know, girlfriends and things."[94] If this was a cycle he did not know how to escape, he was at least becoming aware of how "girlfriends and things" made it spin.

Dugan, living in Truro, Massachusetts, was nervous about Frank getting psychiatric help in what he saw as a backwater of psychiatric knowledge. Although Linda would later thank Dugan "for helping to keep him alive,"[95] Dugan had been stymied by the "May Day" missives Frank had sent the month before, and his response had been silence, an awkward silence as far as their letters go. He felt badly about not responding to Frank's "agonized and agonizing letters" but later absolved himself because "they tended to throw me, so answering them was a danger to my own precarious stability."[96] Now that Frank was hospitalized, Dugan's more immediate concern was that, being the type of mad poet Dugan understood all too well, Frank would be misunderstood by provincial medical professionals in Little Rock unable to appreciate the unique burden creative geniuses such as Dugan and Stanford had to bear. He explained:

> I have a worry about the Arkansas State Hospital because I know nothing about it: (Please show this letter to a psychiatrist and/or psychoanalyst you trust) I trust that there are sophisticated professionals on the staff, but even they could not know that you are an all-too-familiar phenomenon of our craft: an 1) excellent and 2) self-destructive poet. They could not know this because you are as yet unrecognized publicly and they might not believe my assessment of your genius either. If this is true ask your contact to look me up in *Who's Who* etc., or to call the English Department at the U of A at Fayetteville.[97]

A letter that Frank wrote to his editor at *West Coast Poetry Review*, William L. Fox, after he got out of the hospital suggests that Frank might have actually shown Dugan's letter to the doctor. Frank explained how he was "released from the hospital with these words: 'We can help you with the Dionysiac madness which flows from drink but we wouldn't dare tamper with that other, 'Divine Madness', as Plato says, which is particular to your orphic genius.'"[98] To Cheryl he wrote, "They say my only madness is from wine. The rest is divine, orphic, Bacchic."[99] Dugan tried to cheer Frank up by conveying a friend's comment on the recent rash of suicides: "I have a spiteful desire to stay alive."[100] A few weeks later the poet and editor David Walker, to whom Frank had described his descent into madness, also assured him that "things do get better after 30 . . . hang on, the best is yet to come."[101] Frank did not respond.

Frank's own assessment of his time in the mental hospital confirmed something about himself as an artist that he had long intuited but could now openly recognize: His identity was inseparable from his craft. Frank managed to describe this state almost clinically, without a hint of romance. "You have heard it said about others: a born writer," he wrote to Eleanor Bender just after his release. "Well, I tell you for the past year it has been antipodal to me. What I had already created made me live. I had to create to exist. I was hoping to be born again through this. Hopeless." He admitted that he existed in a "kingdom of melancholy" because of this antipodal relationship and that, because of his dependency on art, "love was not ever again to be found." Perhaps for these reasons—because he knew that the untenable mix of love and art spelled disaster—he was as committed as he had ever been to getting *The Battlefield* published. "If a book of mine could be published now it would mean much," he wrote to Bender. "This is what I'm asking: Would you be willing to read my manuscripts?"[102] He was now on his knees before the woman whose solicitations for a manuscript a year earlier he had rejected. But that ship had sailed; Eleanor's offer was no longer on the table.

Frank's one letter to Irv Broughton from the hospital is as honest and self-reflective as anything he'd ever before written, and it suggests that the visit did him good. "I'm in Little Rock," he explained, "where I've been committed to the state mental institution. I have very few rights here. I only wish I had one: the right to leave, but I am contained here until a team of doctors says I can go." Frank took solace in the only book he had with him—D. H. Lawrence's *Complete Poems* ("I see things, feel things, so much like him," Frank wrote). He felt sadness for "the poor, unfortunate, suffering creatures around me."[103] Suggesting that his sense of humor was intact, he later noted that his fellow patients were "murderers, rapists, multiple attempts at suicides, alcoholics, and just everything you see at town council."[104]

Frank also felt sorry for himself. "Irv," he wrote, "this is so humiliating for someone like myself. . . . I feel so ashamed to be in a place like this." He echoed this sentiment to Bill Willett a month later, telling him, "If you aren't mad when you get there, it takes all not to be when you leave."[105] Frank had no idea what he would do when he was released, but he knew "I need to be happy and carefree once again." Delving deeper into that ambition, one sparked by the pain he experienced in the hospital, he reflected on his behavior in a strikingly honest way. "I need to quit playing every role. I am a whole repertory company unto myself." As a child, Frank, by all accounts, had laughed a lot—he had a carefree spirit and a jovial attitude. He was a "motley boy on the loose." He wanted that side of himself back: "I want to laugh with no worries," he wrote to Irv. Moreover, "I want to be in love again," and not just any kind of love but love with a woman "deep as the night herself"—that is to say, with Cheryl. He ended the note with a poetic if ominous flourish: "This poet might as well do himself in if he can't let the bullcalf blood of his blindfold art bellow in the waters of the night running through his body like a silent fire."[106]

As a PS, he asked Irv a question: "Are there any film conferences this summer? Something like that would really help me."[107] Irv, ever attentive to his friend's interests, had a better idea: Frank should work on films. Irv insisted that Frank come on the trip he was taking at the end of the summer to the Midwest and New England to film famous writers. Frank declined. But, thankfully for him, only initially.

## "I Am in Love and Want to Live"

Frank was released from the hospital on June 12, 1972. Father Fuhrmann picked him up, and they arrived back at Subiaco later that day. Although he'd later call doctors "lousy poker players," Frank told Fuhrmann that he respected the staff at the hospital, noting how difficult their job was. He expressed skepticism that they could make accurate diagnoses in such brief periods but also added that it had been "worth the visit," if only because, as Fuhrmann recalled Stanford saying, "I picked up some images that were in the dark before."[108] A snapshot from June 18 of him standing in a swimming pool shows him looking at the camera with a relaxed, almost relieved, smile on his face. "Free at last," he wrote the next day in a postcard to a William L. Fox.[109] For the moment, he seemed scrubbed of anxiety.

The plan now that he was free at last was short term but focused. Frank would do chores for the monks for two weeks, and then, in early July, he would work for two more weeks as a guide at Camp Subiaco.[110] While Frank's recent stay in a mental hospital hardly enhanced his qualifications to be a camp counselor, his time as a guide on Lake Norfork and as a student at Subiaco outweighed that drawback. Plus, given that the camp, located on nearby Lake Dardanelle, focused on two passions of Frank's youth, fishing and water-skiing, Frank was further prepared for, and

Frank with his niece in Greenville, Mississippi, six days after leaving the state hospital. *Photo courtesy of Carrie Prysock.*

even excited about, these responsibilities. "I'm no monk," Frank wrote to Dugan, "but this monastery will do for awhile [sic]."[111]

"Working here with the good monks," Frank jovially reported right after camp started. He mentioned that they "have an unusual boys camp here" and that what he liked most about it was that the boys came from all backgrounds. They were rich and poor, both conditions personally familiar to Frank. They were also aged eight to fourteen, a not insignificant fact for a poet writing an epic poem from the perspective of a twelve-year-old boy. "I'm taking sanctuary here," he wrote. The kids' "innocence and joy," he added, "kept me alive."[112] Plus, it was always a boon to Frank to be with the monks. "I'll have to go now," he ended a short letter to Irv. "Tonight, a monk by the name of Wolfgang, really, and I are going to get drunk and listen to music. He's black—former dancer and opera singer."[113] Frank's affection for the monks endured.

But darkness soon descended on Frank's sanctuary. There was his health: "No sleep, and this ulcer hurts." There was alcohol: "Whenever I think about anything, I just want to get drunk, or worse." There was malaise: "Whatever solitary, miserable island where my soul has shipwrecked, been banished, is far more real than any work of art says it is."[114] And there was, more than anything else, Cheryl, who was still in New York.[115] "I knew not where Cheryl was," Frank wrote to Eleanor Bender.[116] Bereft, he "decided to wrestle the angel of death"—that is to say, try and kill himself. He'd already indicated as much to Dugan, warning, "On the tenth darkness will descend—The angel of Death." He'd added, "I will always be with you as poetry has always been with me." He reiterated the pain he'd caused, stressing how "Many close to me, in love with me, have suffered, become victims, on my behalf. To go on alone would mean more casualties." Dodging, he assured Dugan that "I'm not giving up the battle" and insisted he was wrestling with the Angel of Death "in your dreams." But at the same time Frank made his intention as clear as a bell: "I have no wish to further myself in this world."[117]

At the start of July, Frank went down to the lake and indeed tried to drown himself. He did so by attempting to swim until he gave out and sank. Leaving the camp's Lake Dardanelle cabin after listening to Mahler's *The Song of the Earth* (which is about the acceptance of mortality and overcoming the fear of death), Frank "wrote a poem, and swam off in the darkness into what I hoped would be oblivion." He described what happened next for Bender: "I swam into oblivion for eight hours, until dawn. I don't know what made my body keep on physically, but I knew where my strength came [from]. I thought of Cheryl."[118] The version of the story he told to Dugan was similar: "I went out to swim into oblivion. I swam from dark to dawn.... My body wasn't that powerful, it was Cheryl singing to my spirit."[119] He recounted the incident for Cheryl like this: "I took all of my clothes off, and set out to swim to my death.... I knew I was weak; knew I would drown. I set out from the solitary shore at darkness; I swam, and swam, saying 'Angel of Death, you have won,' but I kept on swimming. I don't know how many miles it was. What kept the muscles from giving out? You. You were all I thought of.... I swam from dark until dawn, saying your name.... I tried to swim into oblivion."[120] Oblivion, thanks to Cheryl's voice and spirit, did not conquer Frank on that good night. "Once again," he wrote to her, "you."[121]

Within a couple of days something remarkable happened. One of the monks walked into Frank's room and handed him a letter with a Staten Island return address.[122] It was from Cheryl, who was responding to a letter he had recently sent her. "She is in New York," he recounted to Bender. And even more important: "She loves me, forgives me, and we will get together as soon as possible."[123] Cheryl had decided to give Frank another chance. To Bill Willett he wrote that "on the day I was certain to lose [to the Angel of Death] I received a letter from Cheryl—forgiving me, saying she loved me, when could we meet, and live whatever is left."[124] He was, as he put it, "born again."[125] His response to Cheryl, written the same day he received her letter, was effusive: "I love you. I love you. . . . Because of you I live. I live for you. . . . Always, for all times, we have been, we will be lovers. . . . Your letter has saved me from death."[126]

Linda filed for divorce two days later, on July 7, 1972, and Frank returned full-time to courting Cheryl. The couple even discussed Cheryl's moving back to Fayetteville, but Frank, considering his recent troubles there, determined "Fayetteville would be hell." They batted around ideas about moving somewhere else together: "Where would [you] like to go?" Frank asked. "Do you have any ideas?"[127] It was at this point that Frank remembered Irv's invitation to travel east and do some filming. On July 20, with camp over, Frank wrote to him: "Believe it or not, I'm going to Staten Island to live with Cheryl. You said you'd be heading East the last of the month. I'd like to meet you wherever you make your lowest southern arc, and go north & work with you for awhile [sic]. . . . Let me know as soon as you get this."[128] To Cheryl, he wrote that he'd rather come to New York directly but that "this editor is looping down all the way from Seattle," and he had some film work for Frank to do.[129]

Frank's letter to Irv, reflecting his change of mind about the filming venture, if only because Irv was his free ticket to get to Cheryl, arrived just under the wire, as Irv and his filming partner were packing the car to leave the next morning. Irv, who was totally thrilled, told Frank to sit tight. They were on their way.[130] Frank was ecstatic. "I am in love and want to live," he declared.[131] And to Dugan, "I am in love and on my way to New York." The road trip was on. Cheryl was back in his life. And even the monks came through, giving him some "bread to hit the road."[132] It was late July 1972, and Frank was back on his feet. "I am so happy now I don't know what to say," he wrote a little more than two weeks after the drowning attempt. "To be in love again is like a ship embarking in my heart." He assured Irv that "I no longer walk with death."[133] He proclaimed: "Love calls."[134]

## "The Sensuous Elixir of Being Alive"

Irv Broughton arrived in Subiaco on a cross-country drive from the University of Washington to pick up Frank on July 30. He came with a communications student from the university named James Babij, a man Irv described as a "dark-haired string bean with chiseled features."[135] Everyone called him Jim. Their plan was to tour the abbey and school grounds for a couple of days and then head northeast to Kenyon College in Ohio to film an interview with the eighty-four-year-old Agrarian poet John Crowe Ransom. From there it would be on to other interviews in New Hampshire, Maine, Massachusetts, and Connecticut. This was Babij's first visit to the American South. He was charmed by "the mesmerizing nocturnal drone of its grasshoppers," "the richness of its settings," and the architectural grandeur of the boarding school. He wrote about "the first captivating views of Subiaco Abbey—a Renaissance-era transplant seemingly teleported across the seas from Lazio, Italy by divine intervention." He also noted Frank's "soft southern lilt," "the warmth of his smile," and his quiet charisma.[136]

Frank was not only proud to show off Subiaco; he was also proud to show off his book. At some point on the trip, he gave Babij a copy of *The Singing Knives*.[137] (As noted, the book's copyright is 1971, but it did not come out until 1972.) Back in September of 1971, Frank, under the impression that the book's layout preparations, printing, and binding were almost completed, had asked Irv for "15 copies of the pamphlet," adding how he would "be glad to see it."[138] But it was nowhere near ready then. An October 1971 postcard from Irv to Frank notes a kink in the book's production schedule.[139] By February 1972 Frank was as annoyed as he'd ever be with Irv: "I'm worrying that I won't ever see a copy of the pamphlet until spring."[140] Frank's subsequent reticence on the exact timing of his first book's arrival hasn't helped scholars trying to pin down when it materialized. But it seems safe to conclude that Frank, after the delay in publication, received official copies at some point between his bonfire in late May of 1972 and the arrival of Babij and Broughton in Subiaco in late July or, very possibly, upon their arrival. In any case, when Irv asked Frank to sign a copy for his brother, who was amazed at how young Frank was, Frank wrote, "To Bobby Broughton: Rimbaud quit when he was 19."[141]

Whenever it came into being, *The Singing Knives* revealed a twenty-three-year-old poet whose creative maturity was evident in his debut. While the title comes from a poem of the same name, the book could just as appropriately been named after another poem in the volume called "The Transcendence of Janus," a reference to the Roman god of gates, doors, and transitions. The frictionless moves Frank makes across multiple boundaries—from country vernacular to levee-camp jive to consciously juvenile reflections on family time to *Beowulf*-like imagery to Whitman- and Keats-inflected scenes—astound with their mix of poetic registers, local and global, high and low. The transitions are so rapid and subtle that the poems almost hum as if vibrating. While many poems are loosely rooted in the culture of the levee camp, the thematic range manages to encompass on-the-spot visual impressions, scenes of the natural world, stylized violence, weighty historical thoughts, and quickly sketched vignettes that seem both deeply rooted in place and transcendent of all context. Running through it all is a quality elusive and mysterious in the rawness of language—the quality that ultimately made Frank the poet he was.

Frank was not one to sit around and wait for formal reviews of *The Singing Knives* to pour in. Which was just as well, because they didn't, at least not during his lifetime. The slim volume achieved subcultural-icon status in Fayetteville, but there was no formal feedback. A couple of years after the book's publication, editor David Walker was lukewarm. Promising in a letter to "play it straight," he assured Frank that, of the twenty poems, "I liked several of them a lot." He noted that "you've got your style, your tone, [mostly?] assured + consistent." But "the ones I like the least are the shortest + longest," he wrote. "They aren't somehow inevitable enough," he explained (whatever that means). He thought that some of the poems felt like "too much a self-indulgence, a gesture."[142] Irv sent the book to Wesleyan University Press, which took over a year to write back, and when it did, it sent the kind of letter that makes a writer want to throw flames into someone's soul: "The Poetry Board has considered Frank Stanford's *The Singing Knives*—not so much as a submission but as an indication of his work so as to determine whether or not we should invite his next manuscript. I am sorry to tell you that they don't seem to want to. The book just did not seem to generate the kind of enthusiasm that we feel is the *sine qua* non of acceptance. I am quite aware that you feel very enthusiastic about Stanford's work, and I am sorry to be the harbinger of this news."[143]

The other "reviews" came from his mother and a couple of priests. "Dorothy," Fuhrmann said, "was disappointed" in the book. Irv remembered that she didn't understand it: "She was convinced poetry had to rhyme."[144] At least Jim Babij, who immediately saw the cinematic appeal of *The Singing Knives*, was thrilled with it, assuring himself that he was hitting the road with "a legendary talent."[145]

Before the team left Subiaco, Frank made sure that Irv and Jim met the monks. The monks, who were just as likely to be seen flowing around the grounds in their vestments as outfitted in work clothes, were for Frank the pride of Subiaco.[146] Late one evening Frank, Irv, and Jim were "covertly ushered up to a monk's room, each wall of which was festooned with glowing lights and religious objects d'arte [sic]."[147] Before taking off on his trip, Frank, to keep his work on the front burner while he was away, wrote a quick note to editor William L. Fox asking him to write Linda for a copy of "St. Francis and the Wolf: Some Poems 1957–1964." "I assume," Fox wrote back, "that you want me to browse thru it, take what we want in copy, and keep the thing until you call for it. Correct?"[148] The team hit the road around the close of July. Frank had $400 in his pocket and was happily unburdened by material possessions: "All that is left of my earthly goods are a few books, classical records. . . . No car . . . no house."[149] The time in the state hospital, only a month and a half earlier, seemed a relic of distant memory.

The drive northeast had its lighter moments, but the venture was ultimately about work. "The road trip was grueling," Babij recalled. For fifteen days, with Irv behind the wheel and Frank and Babij buying and pumping the gas, they drove with windows down, cramped in a sedan packed with books and camera equipment. Babij and Irv were on each other's nerves from the start. The old Buick Riviera, which kept on chugging, was usually, as Babij put it, "straining against its load." Frank, reserved and cool, generally stayed out of the fray. Babij recalled how readily Frank laughed about life's little absurdities, but Babij also noted that most of the time his traveling companion was lost in "a meditative state."[150] On one occasion, while in Ohio, Irv secretly filmed Frank pumping gas. Frank, annoyed, ducked and demanded that Irv not film him.[151]

Filming sessions were often marred by nagging technical challenges. "We were working with antiquated gear," said Babij. Even by the standards of the early 1970s, wielding a hand-cranked camera with a maximum capacity of one-hundred-foot reels of film that had to be changed in a black bag to prevent exposure required a lot of patience and technical acumen. Without a connection between camera and recorder, sound had to be synced to the film manually. If the camera operator's eye came off the viewfinder for a nanosecond, the film was exposed. The "technical newbieness" of the group, Babij recalled, often led Irv to lose his patience. "Frank," wrote Babij, "seemed frustrated by Irv's perceived attitude toward him as being nothing more than a tripod or camera holder."[152]

As they neared Gambier, Ohio—home to Kenyon College and John Crowe Ransom—some of the angst lifted. The cooler air coming through the car windows eased their road fatigue, as did the landscape growing rich with hickory and oak and corn and tomatoes, which they stopped to sample. In Kenyon's Waite House, as Ransom rhapsodized about prosody,

Frank ran the audio and Babij spent the session worrying about not giving Irv a heart attack by taking his eye off the viewfinder. Frank's assessment of the film work itself to Dugan was a terse "It's experience" and not much else.[153] Still, the team finished the Ransom interview in good order and got ready to get back on the road.

Frank wrote that while he enjoyed filming J. C. Ransom, he was sure "the old man will die pretty soon."[154] When Ransom died two years later, Frank was sorry to hear about him "kicking the bucket," as he put it.[155] He later recalled filming Ransom but pointed out, as he often did, that "the last thing in the world I care about is the Fugitives."[156] Frank found it alarming that Ransom dismissed the poet Galway Kinnell while praising the stuffy and long-dead Arkansas poet John Gould Fletcher. Frank decided that, with such a hoary endorsement, "Ransom had moved into a dark space."[157] Never one to miss making a potentially useful literary connection, Frank wrote an appreciative note to Ransom shortly after the interview, only to get, by way of response, a stamped and addressed but empty envelope. "He'd forgotten to put the note in," Frank bemusedly told Malcolm Cowley.[158]

After a night in Michigan with Babij's parents—"They didn't know what hit them"—the team made the twelve-hour drive to Dartmouth College in Hanover, New Hampshire. They arrived to find themselves at the Pulitzer Prize–winning poet Richard Eberhart's house around the time of his daughter's wedding reception.[159] The three wandering strangers were welcomed into the festivities by the one-time US Poet Laureate. Frank put on his white suit and panama hat and did some filming for Irv.[160] The team ate and drank and socialized throughout the night. Frank spent much of the evening talking to Eberhart's son, also named Richard, with whom he discussed the publishing industry. Babij hit it off romantically with a woman named Suzanne from New Mexico.[161] Irv socialized easily with everyone there.

The next day, Frank and Eberhart took a swim in a nearby pond. Eberhart recalled, "Frank could be the most silent of men. He was remarkably silent." But in time, "he loosened up and began to talk."[162] Frank commented that Eberhart "was a pleasant, wealthy kind of poet, who was very nice to me."[163] Frank told Eberhart he was a wanted man in Arkansas. He may have been alluding to the numerous women—and at least one of their husbands—who wanted him behind bars. Or he may have been furthering the myth of the wild-man backwoods poet that he peddled to Dugan. Either way, Frank was having fun—"This part of the world is like a dream for me," he wrote to Dugan.[164] Speculating

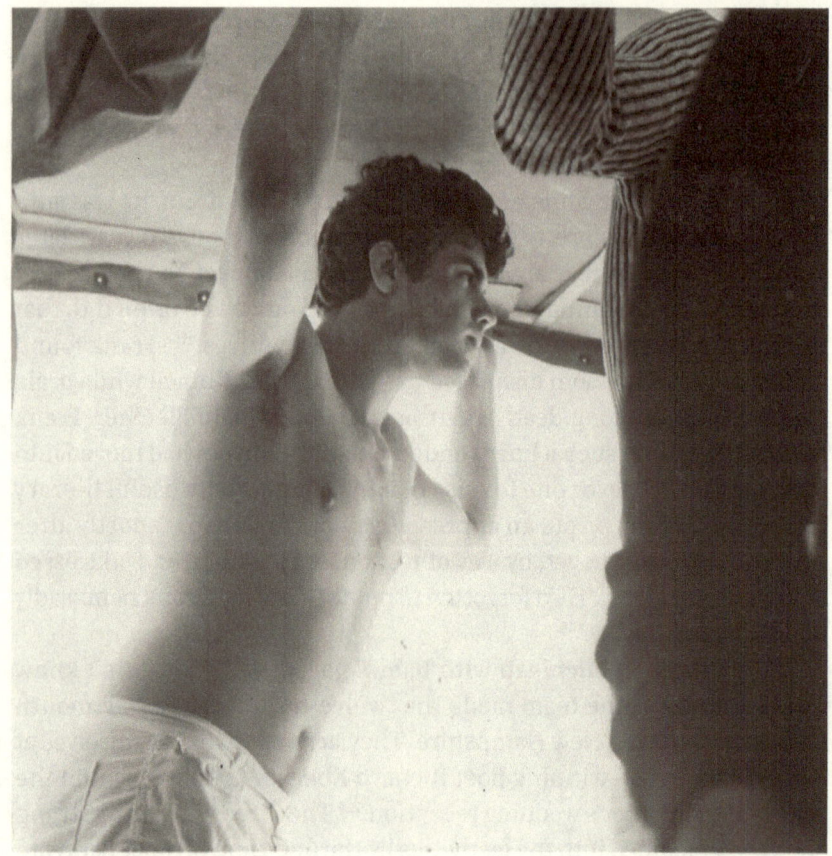

Frank on *Rêve*, enjoying his first time on an ocean, August 10, 1972.
Photo by Irv Broughton. Photo courtesy of Irv Broughton.

on Frank's thoughts during the trip, Babij said, "I'd like to think he was ardently imbibing the sensuous elixir of being alive."[165]

The team impressed the Eberhart family enough to get invited to their cottage in Cape Rosier, Maine, for a generous six-day visit starting on August 9.[166] Irv and Frank drove there in the Riviera while Babij went with his new summer girlfriend from Taos, "grateful to be free from the confines of the Riviera's back seat."[167] The crew converged for what proved to be a coastal idyll. Irv recalled how Frank was "obsessed with seeing the ocean."[168] Frank later told Eberhart that "I was still a virgin as far as the sea was concerned."[169] Frank also thought that "maybe the reason I never moved near to the ocean was because I always knew in my heart I'd run off to the sea."[170] Irv recalled, "You should have seen his eyes light up when we saw it."[171] In a conversation with Irv later on, Frank said of the experience: "You know one minute the poet stares at the ocean in the rain, the ocean he's just seen for the first time, but it is as if he is an orphan and the water his mother, a mother younger than he thought."[172]

Eberhart's cottage was nestled into a Maine hillside overlooking Penobscot Bay—"a beautiful old house on the shore," Frank called it.[173] Frank also recalled it being a hive of literary activity, buzzing with writers and literary talk. But he reminded Dugan that "I don't go in for any of the lit. business." He also noted that Irv and Babij "are nothing at all like me; they are mixers, conversationalists, etc."[174] Frank had told Irv, "I hate being with a lot of people unless I have known them a long time or have admired them," adding, "I don't think I'm much at all in company."[175] He found it exasperating to listen to the pompous drivel of East Coast elites, one of whom "said he wrote theological fiction" and "despised Kazantzakis and Merton." And when this blowhard declared himself "a New Critic of Cinema," Frank couldn't take anymore and went outside to watch shooting stars. Plus, Frank added, "I was too drunk to talk to him." He was relieved when, one evening, he and Eberhart and Irv skipped out of the salon and went to see a film.[176]

Eberhart's motor yacht (named *Rêve*) was, as Babij called it, "a hand-tooled and varnished wooden beauty." It was anchored below the house, next to the boathouse where Frank chose to sleep. On August 10, Eberhart took the team for an overnight excursion on the yacht. At one point they set anchor at an inlet where a wide stream entered the bay. Frank and Jim got off and rowed a punt up the stream to sun themselves on an outcropping of rocks. As the men were napping, they heard Irv hollering at them from the stern. The tide had turned, and unless Frank and Babij wanted to be swept out to sea while punting back to the yacht, they had to come back immediately. The two men powered forth with encouraging calls from Eberhart and Broughton, arriving, as Babij noted, "just in time."[177]

With that crisis averted, a more consequential one soon followed: Frank had a manuscript blow out of the boat into Penobscot Bay. In an undated two-page poem that appears to be an outtake from *The Battlefield*, Frank refers to a manuscript "hung in the bay by the wind." Elsewhere he writes, "I was smoking dope on Richard Eberharts' [sic] yacht keeping a divorcee warm . . . while my new brutal manuscripts were blowing out of the boat and I didn't care while I was drinking Cold Duck and lying naked on the prow with the finest of women."[178] Frank ended the evening curled in a sleeping bag back at the boathouse. He woke up to find Irv once again filming him as the sun rose. The noise of the camera stirred him awake, and Irv recalls, "This time he was really pissed."[179] (This moment before he woke up made it into the film *It Wasn't a Dream: It Was a Flood*.)[180]

In addition to comforting a naked divorcée on the prow of Eberhart's yacht, Frank met several notable people during his week in Maine. Most memorable was the back-to-land advocate Scott Nearing, whom Frank described to Willett as an "87 year old anarchist-farmer-philosopher." Frank was intrigued with Nearing's ideas about living closer to the earth and self-sufficiency. Later, while hanging out at "a shanty with fishermen," Frank met women from the Congo, Morocco, Greece, and Romania. He also met the poet Daniel Hoffman and was thrilled that Hoffman had seen his poems in the little magazines ("He had heard of me!"). His only major complaint about Maine was the typical southern lament about life up north: "Too cold. 38 degrees last night."[181] In a letter to Cheryl from Maine, he reiterated how strange the weather was and how excited he was to see her.[182]

In yet another reminder of how close Frank's life and thoughts were to his poetry, the people he met in Maine made it into an untitled poetry fragment. As an unnamed person waits "for Jean Cocteau to do his most blessed magic," Stanford mentions "making love to the darkest / woman from Morrorca [Morocco] with her little sister along atop Under / Cliff the mysterious hideout of the poets of New England." (Undercliff Road was the road running behind the Eberharts' Cape Rosier house.) Soon he was also "making love to a gypsy's daughter," a reference to the Romanian woman he told Willett about, and then "lying through my teeth with a woman from Greece." Circling back to the actual world from the poetic one, Frank wrote to an editor about "making love to some girl from Morocco who lives in Paris" while he was visiting Eberhart. Both Nearing and Hoffman get mentioned in this fragmented poem as well, the former praying for a revolution in buttermilk consumption and the latter having "caught the eyes of the mysterious young la dame aux the black ships." After citing "that old fool in Vermont," presumably Robert Frost, the poem adds this promise:

> We'll take off with everybody's wife for one night
> they can have them
> the rest of their natural lives.[183]

In the midst of his Maine revelry Frank said he was so sleep deprived that "I don't know how I can still see through the camera." Frank wrote to Cheryl, telling her about all the women he was meeting but assuring her, "I am enjoying their *company*—nothing else. . . . How I love you."[184]

*From left:* Irv Broughton, Daniel Hoffman, Richard Eberhart, and Frank Stanford, Cape Rosier, Maine, August 1972. *Photo courtesy of Irv Broughton.*

The team left Cape Rosier in mid-August. From Maine, they drove to Massachusetts and Connecticut to visit Alan Dugan and film interviews with the poet Richard Wilbur and critic Malcolm Cowley. Cowley suggested that Frank to apply for a fellowship at Yaddo, the prestigious writers' retreat. About Cowley, Frank said, "He thinks I'm a mixture of Crane and Faulkner, which would be a strange blend of tobacco no one, understandably, would want to put in their pipes."[185] Frank filmed Wilbur in an open field at his farm, leaning against a fence and discussing his poetic vision. But Frank ended up far more interested in the architecture of Wilbur's writing studio than in his poems; it was a converted silo that, as Irv described it, "rose into the sky like a huge crown.[186] A couple of weeks later Frank wrote to Willett, with Nearing's ethic fresh in his mind, suggesting they build something similar and live in it together. Later that year Wilbur sent to Frank an article detailing how to refurbish an old silo into a studio.

On Cape Cod, where Irv and Frank went to see some of Irv's family in Wellfleet, Frank made plans to reunite with Dugan in Truro. When Frank and Irv went to a graveyard to look at eighteenth-century gravestones, Frank traced some of the headstone inscriptions, and as he did so, Irv asked if he could go with him to see Dugan. But Frank, who, after exchanging thousands of words with his mentor, wanted Dugan to himself, held Irv at arm's length and went on his own.[187] "Frank could sometimes be catty," Irv later observed, recalling this soft rejection.[188] In Truro, Frank and Dugan got thoroughly drunk. Frank later noted how "our meeting was strange."[189]

But it really didn't matter much to Frank, because all he could think about by this point in the trip was Cheryl. "By the time you get this," he said in a letter to Dugan, "I'll be in New York making love to the woman I told you about."[190] Indeed, as the team's work came to an end, Frank decided to leave early and go to New York to find Cheryl, the supposed love of his life. He'd been calling her on pay phones throughout the journey, as well as writing her.[191] After the quick visit with Cowley in Connecticut, Frank went to New York and made his way to 56 Harvard Street, Staten Island. Cheryl was just as eager as Frank was. The letters he had written over the summer before coming to the East Coast, she said, "made me fall in love with him again."[192]

"Glad to be done with it," Frank told Willett about the filming venture shortly after arriving in New York.[193] "I don't have time to thank you for all you've done," he wrote to Irv, showing gratitude for what he had "given me the opportunity to do."[194] Irv recalled that it was on this trip that he finally broke through Frank's cool exterior. "We became friends," he said. "It was a good trip."[195] Babij was ambivalent about his own experience. His patience hit a limit with Irv, and forgoing the ride back to Seattle, he left of his own accord, abruptly and in something of a huff, claiming he had to get to UCLA to start graduate school. But Babij and Frank stayed on excellent terms. Frank—who now called him "Jim Baby"—wrote him a brief good-bye note, adding, "It's been good traveling + learning the camera from you" and hoping "we can resolve some of these visions on film."[196] What had begun as a grueling road trip ended as one where Babij and Frank were, as Babij put it, "on the road like Kerouac and Cassidy, a jug of wine in one hand and the world by the ass in the other."[197] Frank agreed, recalling the experience as "a maze of... enchantments."[198]

## "I Went Rollicking"

Frank arrived in New York on August 21, 1972.[199] For all his exuberance, he had some concerns. "I'm .. not as steady as I was when I left Arkansas," he wrote to Dugan just before getting to the city. "I'm still crazy as hell so I know I *must* be careful."[200] He had noted in a postcard in July that

"Lorca went mad in N.Y." but that it was no matter, as "I'm afraid but in love + willing to take chances."[201] Beyond his precarious mental state, there were the typical fears outsiders often have of New York City: "I'm liable to get killed in New York. Where I'll be staying, with all these Alvin Ailey dancers, they're liable to take me somewhere where I'll get cut." He told Irv about a friend of his who had been held up at gunpoint while going to confession at a Catholic church in the city.[202] He expected to stay a year.

Frank's fears of going mad or getting mugged were quickly alleviated. Shortly after arriving to Staten Island, he wrote to Bill Willett, "What can I say about Cheryl and New York: just in love." The accommodations were excellent. "C and I live on the third floor of a huge old house completely surrounded by trees. Like the cabin. Lots of room." They were going to museums and movies together—the Cloisters, the Museum of Modern Art, the Guggenheim, the Museum of Natural History, and even the Brooklyn Botanic Garden.[203] The house's company was exciting too. Cheryl lived in a large house owned by a Jamaican dancer named Clive Thompson, who had worked with Martha Graham, and his wife, Elizabeth Thompson.[204] Cheryl was also in a band whose members were always milling around the house, gossiping, drinking, and rehearsing. It was a kind of bohemian enclave, and Frank fit right in.[205]

New York's multiculturalism enthralled him as well: "It is, this city, like an infinite library of the world and its arts."[206] Cheryl worked weekdays at a data collection company in the Empire State Building from nine to five, with an hour commute each way. Frank, on his own, ferried into Manhattan daily and had the run of the city.[207] "I like writing poems on the Staten Island Ferry," he noted to Willett. As he roamed the city, Frank kept his ear to the ground. "You would really love walking around the various ethnic parts of the city, listening to their speech and music, eating and drinking in their hangouts," he told Willett.[208] Later, to Dugan, he wrote about how he "drank and ate at the ethnic bars, all the while listening to them talk."[209] The city—"a place to spend time in, studying others"[210]—washed over him like cacophonous music.

A few weeks later, reflecting on his New York experience, he wrote Dugan that he "had the time of my life. . . . I loved it." Central to his happiness was his knowledge that his time in the city was not permanent. He was a stranger in foreign territory, felt stranger the longer he was there, and he enjoyed how that strangeness made him feel—like a "transilient time tripper."[211] "I felt so free there, knowing I wasn't going to live there," he explained. "N.Y. and my blood mixed like swamp water and whiskey." While this mixture could be intoxicating, "after three days I knew I wouldn't stay." The city's pace and sensory onslaught overwhelmed him. "I don't see how any young artist could work here," he declared.[212] Still, he felt momentarily empowered. "Nothing intimidated me," he went on, again adding that "much of this was due to the fac[t] that I was not going to live there." Knowing all this, he decided to pursue his pleasure guiltlessly, fearlessly, without regret. "I went rollicking," he told Dugan. "I was so HAPPY."[213]

Rollicking for Frank, of course, meant women and, as his time in the city wound down, just one woman. And it was not Cheryl. In fact, the much-anticipated reunion with Cheryl wore off in a New York minute, in large part because she had to hold down a job. "You going to work, me being there was just too goddamn much," he later reflected.[214] Plus, he said in regard to Cheryl, "Once old loves meet, the spell is broken," as if issuing forth some sort of ancient wisdom.[215] The New York Frank soon fell into habits that looked a lot like Fayetteville Frank's. "I ran on to six or seven fine women," he explained to Dugan, "they were splendid."[216] As always, there was the hurt woman: Cheryl, he wrote, "was hurt that I went wild and free." He admitted that "I didn't spend much time with her at all,"[217] and to Willett he confirmed that "I'm never home with her."[218] Cheryl agreed, noting in a recent conversation how "he really got silent when he started getting into these other women—he wouldn't talk to me."[219] When home together, they got along fine. She enjoyed playing the flute naked in bed while Frank wrote poems. But the thrill was gone, or at least it was not thrilling enough to keep Frank from roaming around New York City looking for more and more women while the supposed love of his life brought home a paycheck and provided room and board.

In addition to the "six or seven fine women" he entertained in the city, Frank, clearly not having learned from his Fayetteville scare with an angry husband, also evidently had an affair with the wife of the dancer who owned the house. According to Frank, this woman was so taken with him and his exotic history that she wanted "to leave her family and run off to the South."[220] To Cheryl, Frank later admitted, "I could have stayed in N.Y. and helped complicate their already complicated marriage." As for her husband, Frank said, "I am most ashamed when I think of him."[221] Without apparent distress or angst, he explained his increasingly entangled situation with New York women to Willett as: "There is a white bird that keeps flying from one shoulder of a woman to another. Like Byron, I enjoy the chase: the joy + the misery." From this chase he began to discern something significant about himself and his relationship with women. To Willett he explained, "I seek out the mystery of all women. With some it takes seconds, others years. Like a priest, I transubstantiate the body + spirit one into the other. Once this is done, whenever I look into one woman's eyes, I see yet another woman, and so it is: I was able to capture my old, unfinished dreams, so that I could dream them once more."[222]

This vague idea got recycled a few weeks later for Dugan: "Whatever I say to one woman's beauty, I intend it for all."[223] When he was at the Arkansas State Hospital, Frank had said something along these same lines to his doctor, who wrote, "[Frank] said that when my wife and I were in love there was this other woman that I did get involved with, and then there was a third woman who looked like the second woman and therefore I thought that I likely would get involved with the third one because she looked like the second one and of course my wife would not like that."[224]

This blending of all women into an amalgam of sexual, emotional, and romantic feeling was, in a way, classic Stanford. It meshed smoothly with Frank's Cocteau-dream-infused poetic vision, one that refused to draw boundaries between surreality and reality, conscious and subconscious, love and art, past and present, and, it now seemed, lover and lover. There was something distinctly Keatsian in this view as well. As the poet Edward Hirsch has written about Keats: "He tended to displace and embody his quest for a highly sensual love, for superhuman beauty, in the form of various supernatural enchantresses and Muse figures."[225] It even echoed the philosopher and novelist Albert Camus, who wrote in his 1944 journal, "Those who love all women are those who are on their way toward abstraction."[226] And that, among other things, is how Frank's feelings were for women at this time—abstracted and distant but also inclined to a platonic notion of beauty.

The conception also revealed something essential about Stanford and his art. Everything about Frank was ultimately subordinated to the kinetic and boundless nature of his tangible and febrile poetry. Everything. It might seem pointless or indulgent to recount what seem like mundane details of Frank's life—his road trip, his time in Maine, and so on—but these events were the organic foundation of his work. The experiences were all raw material that got integrated into poetry. And no aspect of his life ever slowed or normalized enough to become something Frank could point to and say, *Mine, forever mine*, and hug to his chest with permanence. Love, beauty, place, passion, art, the joys and letdowns of everyday common experience—it all could become poetry only when everything and everyone else was fleeting and abstracted, thus making room for the single thread connecting Frank to his past and future: thousands of lines of poetry. This was a tragic disposition to cultivate when it came to forming stable human relationships and making plans for a stable future. But it was gold dust for the artist.

Frank's lofty assessment of Linda after their breakup illuminates this paradox. It reveals his aversion to commitment while, at the same time, preserving his passion for the abstractions of love and beauty. He explained to Willett, "It will always be possible to keep falling in love with Linda and others because we will never be together again. I can care for her and others, write poems to them."[227] Love and beauty could be experienced once they were abstracted from Linda, or any woman, but never when rooted in the realities of a relationship's daily and tedious obligations. He elaborated: "God bless the beauty in all women, in all things, wherever it hides like a wounded animal.... I am saying when Linda + I were together, it was difficult to love. Now, she is beautiful. Now I love her. For I know we will never again be together. I can be, only now, the poet, who she loved.... Apart forever, we can endure."[228]

In the same note Frank said of Linda: "She is all women, as everywoman is. What the poet sees, what the human being sees. I hope you understand. I am in love with beauty, for it is everywhere. Let her go her way, and I mine. Let us be happy always—and kind. For once I can be kind to her."[229]

In another piece of correspondence from this time period to Willett, this one written on a page ripped from the 1969 book *William Blake's Illustrations to the Grave*, Frank decreed that "death has always been my mistress."[230]

It could be tempting to dismiss these expressions as rambling idiocy, the warped ideations of a philandering man. But there was more going on than that. Frank was exploring, in his letters to Willett, something fundamental about what was required for him to be a poet. He was seeking a way of experiencing reality that was neither committed nor disengaged. He could love New York because he was going to leave New York. He could love Linda because she left him. He could love Cheryl once "the spell" broke after he moved in with her in New York. He could—he had to—experience all the beauty he encountered, but he could never own it or think of it as permanent. Beauty was more than Frank's "mistress"; it was the fleeting spirituality that never settled. But it had to be ephemerally experienced, remembered, and dreamed rather than anchored in the present and nurtured for the future through conventional behavior in a normalized reality. As with Keats, beauty had to bowl him over, transform him, and then move on. "You know what Keats and Shelley said," Frank told Irv, without specifying what Keats and Shelley said but nonetheless situating his sensibility alongside the radicalism of their romanticism.[231]

This perspective also highlights something fundamental about Frank's noncommittal character. When it came to art, it meant popping in and out of museums and theaters. When it came to the city of New York, it meant a monthlong visit rather than the anticipated year. When it came to women, it meant fleeting rather than stable relationships. When it came to his family, it meant being an orphan rather than a son of the South. Speaking of "the mystery of women"—but really speaking for himself as a poet in general—he wrote, "Once you have found it, the spell is broken. You seek another. The curse of the poet is: he can never see beauty and have it; it is one or another." The insane spell of beauty, like Pasolini's "stupendous monotony of the mystery," will indeed enchant, perhaps generously, but eventually "the mirror will crack and soak up all of anyone's beauty."[232] When that happened, the only option aside from death was to move on, to open the muse to something different, be it different women, sex, film, art, or poetry.

Frank would eventually abandon everything—including his poetry and his own life. But two notable exceptions persisted and sustained him before he did: dreams and language. These were the threads of continuity through Frank's fleeting and fragmented existence. Dreams and language were different from the rest of Stanford's reality; these were phenomena that washed over him, passed through him, cycled back to him with the warmth of eternal recurrence, flirted with him, and never settled or stabilized into the tedium of convention. As such, they fueled him, kept him alive. Dreams and language were vehicles of beauty and love that could be experienced without the burden of a commitment or sacrifice. This is what Frank discovered about himself in New York in the late summer of 1972; it was a realization that marked a critical shift in his approach to art and life. And it all hinged on one requirement: Life and love had to be subordinated to art. Balance was out of the question. Art was the only option, all there was, and it hinged on language and dreams.

Perhaps because of this burden—the commitment to frenetic imbalance—drinking remained a constant for Frank. Alcohol made dreams dreamier, language more interesting. "I was drunk all the time," he wrote to Dugan about his time in New York.[233] He spent most of his days in cinemas with a bottle of something alcoholic and cheap at his side, usually Cold Duck sparkling wine. In an unpublished poem titled "I foxed them alright," he writes:

> I only came to New York to go to the movies
> I bought a fifth of Gypsy Rose and a horse
> And left the country
> I got good and drunk.[234]

"Still drinking wine in picture shows," he wrote Willett. Repenning a letter he had placed in a manuscript that he had lost in a movie theater on Thirty-Fourth Street called the Murray Hill Theatre, Frank wrote, "I was in a trance, when I jotted the ideas down on the Staten Island Ferry rides I have to take every day to get into the city, and was fairly filled with that inner hush when I typed them. At the moment, I'm not in that state of the poet's grace; I'm just drunk, so what I say, how I say it now, won't be like I had intended it."[235]

This information about his drinking alone in movie theaters further elucidates how he lost yet another manuscript. Referring to some postcards that he intended to send Bill Willett, he wrote, "Alas, I left them inside the pages of my newest manuscript—the first draft of which I sketched out on the trip, recalling the last year in Arkansas, and had begun a second draft of—when I lost it at some theatre, including my long series of cards to you." Reflecting on these losses, he wrote, "Strange that all three manuscripts I've done since Fayetteville have been lost."[236] It's less strange when one considers how intoxicated he was for much of the trip. "I drank Cold Duck every night," he told Irv.[237]

Frank and Cheryl seemed to agree that whatever relationship they had anticipated together had yet again tanked. "I dreamed my old dream here," Frank wrote to Willett about New York and Cheryl. "It's done. I've stayed too long with the dream . . . it was time for my ship to journey."[238] On September 19, 1972, just after Frank left, Cheryl wrote to Willett, "I know Frank and I went too fast—We expected to [sic] much to be there. . . . with out [sic] knowing . . . taking for granted past feelings to be the same."[239] The hurt, in other words, that he meted out to women in Fayetteville continued in New York. Cheryl wrote, "Today I am calmer—But the pain in the pit of my stomach—still here!"[240] Frank knew it. "She was hurt," he admitted to Dugan, feeling somewhat ashamed.[241]

Frank's last hurrah with ephemeral beauty in the big city was with a Scottish woman named Deidre. Just when "the dancer's wife" started to get serious—"She wants to run away to Arkansas with me"—Byron's white bird left Frank's shoulder. "I've already become enchanted with yet another girl, Deidre, a well-off woman from England who works in the museum [the Museum of Modern Art]." She was, he told Dugan, "bright and lewd . . . wise and could drink in Plato's good form," which presumably meant drinking a lot.[242] Embracing his new commitment to not committing, Frank wrote to Willett, "I know from my instinct to survive and write, I must not become so involved with [her] realities." With Deidre, he recognized the warning signs. "The English girl," he wrote, "says she will support me and my writing, but I'll never do that again." Financial support from a romantic partner might be good for poetry, but, as Linda and Cheryl knew all too well, "It doesn't give love a running chance."[243]

Initially Frank and Deidre drew boundaries around their affair. They agreed that they "were just passing like the summer," as Frank put it. "We admitted our first intentions: sex and money." He was pleased that "there was no moon struck shit about it; it was all so sleek and mellow."[244] Later that fall Frank told Dugan that the reason he had been able to thrive as well as he did in New York was Deidre's generosity. "This was all made possible by a good-looking, rich, English girl . . . who took it upon herself to be my patron while I was there, and then some more."[245] He called what she offered him "patronized wanderlust."[246] Much of that wanderlust took place at the Museum of Modern Art, where she let him in for free every day.

The equanimity between Frank and Deidre did not last. Deidre was into Robert Burns, which pleased Frank, but she was also, "sorry to say, infatuated with the South, its violence, me." Frank detested "southerphiles," as he called them.[247] She wanted to quit her job, buy a car, and head south with him, but Frank had no patience with stereotypical outsider fetishizations of the American South. Frank wanted neither Deidre nor her exotic romanticization of southern snakebit violence following him back home. "She attributes things to me," he wrote to Willett, "I really don't consider having."[248]

Finally, after nearly a month in New York, matters came to a head for Frank. Again, the precipitating factor was his involvement with multiple women—all of them, he made clear to Irv, *quite* beautiful. Deidre was reneging on their pact to keep their fling a fling. Frank's realization that, as he told Dugan, "I'll never be able to be faithful to one person" perhaps reflected a modest boost in the self-awareness he had lacked back in Fayetteville.[249] Likewise, dissembling as it was, his recent pseudophilosophical transmutation of love for one woman into an abstract love for all women spared Frank the guilt that had reduced him to despair earlier that year. Now he could say to himself this is just how he was. Still, the noose of multiple infidelities was tightening to the point that it was time for another escape.

On September 15, Frank waited for Cheryl to leave for work, packed his bag, left a cryptic note in black marker on her bathroom mirror, and had

Deidre pick him up in the Mercedes-Benz she rented. "I had no idea he was leaving!" Cheryl recalled.[250] Frank and Deidre drove to Washington, DC, and then, when Deidre made a quick stop to visit a friend, Frank "skipped off from D.,"[251] found a bus station, and "caught a bus South."[252] On the ride from DC to Memphis, Frank sat next to an eighty-four-year-old Black man (or eighty-nine-year-old—Frank's stories vary). The man was, as Frank relayed it to Malcolm Cowley, "my drinking and tale spinning companion." The two got especially drunk together in Nashville.[253] The man had heard of Frank's father from the levee days, as well as his uncle, who was a "legal bootlegger" from the town of Three Way, Tennessee.[254] This old man said he was going back home to Cleveland, Mississippi, to die. Frank, who on the eve of leaving for the East Coast venture had told Irv that "I must create new life," had other plans.[255]

## "I'm Looking Forward to Living Things Out"

Shortly after his return to Subiaco, in late September or early October, an old acquaintance and roommate of Frank's named Neal Spearmon killed himself. He and Frank had lived together briefly in 1968 at 221 Buchanan Street in Fayetteville. A physics major, Spearmon put a noose on his neck, attached the other end of the rope to a cinder block, and tossed it over the footboard of the bed. An avid tennis player, a soft-spoken friend, and possibly a closeted gay man, Spearmon had recently broken up with a girlfriend but had had little to say about his feelings in the aftermath of the relationship.[256] He was a quiet and kind man who hid his suffering behind closed doors.

The news of Spearmon's suicide made a significant impression on Frank. His first reaction, notably, was to call Spearmon a poet, or "poet Manqué," so he could declare to Dugan, "Another poet, unknown, bites the dust."[257] Next, deeming his elegy to Spearmon "a gentle war song of the poet warrior battling to stay alive," Frank wrote two hundred pages "for my friend who hung himself" called "Blue Yodel of poets of times past."[258] Frank said that he "burned most of the poem at [Spearmon's] grave," but a page of it survives in Irv Boughton's private collection.[259] Its lines suggest a familiarity with Spearmon (with references in them to tennis) as well an interest in the impact of Spearmon's death on his reputation. He was now, as Frank put it:

> Something of a legend
> Cut into rock so we can only see three sides of you.[260]

The cloister walk at Subiaco Academy. *Photo courtesy of Ginny Crouch Stanford.*

Here was another suicide that Frank, after obsessing over it, added to his warehouse of dark examples of how a poet (or poet manqué) might die.

The Spearmon tragedy did not dampen Frank's mood. Frank Stanford was alive—as alive as he'd been in years. "I'm in the highest spirits I've been in for a long, long time—almost like after Hollins," he told an editor.[261] "My boat has made it through the shoals," he told another.[262] With Father Fuhrmann's help, Frank found lodging in a monk's cell on the fifth floor of the monastery.[263] Albeit temporarily, he was pleased to return to the monks, men who always welcomed home their prodigal son, the wandering poet with his mind aflame. "I walk around in a burnoose I bought in New York, over the roof, something of a vigilambulistic castelain. The stars, everyone asleep underneath my feet," he wrote. The setting was conducive to writing poetry, which Frank now tried to do regularly if less frantically. "I know I have to slow down if I'm going to survive," he wrote to Dugan, "and that is what I've done, except in my poems." Still, "I only write two times a day now. . . . I've put a little sheaf of things together. Not much, but a beginning."[264] Alcohol was under control: "Haven't had anything to drink," he told Cheryl, to whom he was still writing.[265] It also helped that there were not many women around to distract him. Although he did mention to Dugan that he was "having an affair with a high school girl," calling this one the "Greta Garbo of the Ozarks."[266]

He even had a temporary job that "keeps me sane."[267] Few would have argued with Richard Eberhart's remark that "Frank was not in a position to deal with the subtleties of the academy."[268] But the monks, at Fuhrmann's prompting, let Frank loose in the Subiaco classroom. Teaching literature classes was taxing; "Goddamn I have a headache," he said after a day in the trenches.[269] But he did well enough for Father Fuhrmann to write, two years later, "Anytime you find yourself in the position to come and talk to seniors will be appreciated."[270] In addition to part-time teaching, Frank coached boxing, took kids to a few Golden Gloves matches, and even did a little boxing himself: "Have you ever," he joked with Dugan, "written a poem with a boxing glove on?"[271] The problem, even at twenty-four, was "I don't seem to get in shape as I used to: I attribute this to my former self destruction." Another problem: "My face is getting beat in by these young brutes."[272]

The Ouachita Mountains around Subiaco kept Frank grounded for a while. The hills predisposed him to trancelike states of mind that supported his imagistic poetic imagination. The monks gave Frank occasional access to a cabin on Lake Dardanelle, from where he took long walks day and night, "abandoning myself," he wrote in high Keatsian mode, "to impossible, lyric plots."[273] To Dugan he wrote about "walking through the meadows and mountains," having Blake-like visions, and "not thinking at all in terms of the literary world" but instead staying attuned to "calls of inner worlds, almost audible in their movement." When he could not sleep, he took to the woods and, on occasion, had visions that fostered an altered state of mind, "the kind where you *write poetry*."[274] To Cheryl, he wrote in November that "here, alone, I've gone through some spiritual visitations." He added that "I hope you don't think I'm avoiding reality, if I say I have visions." He assured her that "I've talked to the brothers about them."[275]

One evening in mid-October he wrote, from his mother's house, a quietly charged note to Dugan: "I am sitting outside on a lifted porch; a quarter mile away on a hill, I can see the tip of the monastery bell tower, lit up, which strikes every quarter hour. There is heat lightening all around the dome of the hemisphere. There are 300 boys and 100 monks asleep, and dreaming the same things."[276]

Having set the scene, he then, as if going from waking to dreaming, seamlessly transitioned to a more poetic mode: "My mother's ducks are standing on one leg; her nine black cats are eating crawdads; the same old brother who walked in his sleep 8 years ago, is walking tonight. . . . The air smells like butchered hogs and soy beans at the feed mill. The homosexual barber who raises bloodhounds is out running his dogs, but the sound you hear is a pack of wolves. Yes, a pack of wolves are howling their crazy love."[277]

Frank was back in the infinite backyard of his native South. He was at Subiaco, nestled in the hills, among impassioned beer-brewing monks, his mother, and perhaps Greta Garbo of the Ozarks. If only for the moment, he wanted to be where he was. He felt recovered from the breakdown he had had in May and was free from the guilt and shame of the recent past in Fayetteville. Although he missed the gang at Sherman's, he was happy to be away from the snake pit of Fayetteville, the allure of too many women in one place, and the annoyance of the poets, the writing program, the pressure, and the endless and soulless talk of the poetry business. When he was in the state mental hospital in June, he had written to Irv, "I am ready to rise from my ashes. I am ready to spread my wings and have perpetual intercourse with the living."[278] His road trip east and monthlong stay in New York—ultimately made possible by his true guardian angel, Irv Broughton—had offered Frank a renewed glimpse into that perpetual intercourse with life. It had also given him the opportunity to look to the future rather than be tormented by the recent, terrible personal past. As the chill of fall settled over Subiaco, Frank, assessing the impact of his recent adventures for Dugan, concluded this roller coaster of a year with a message one can only wish he had, in the end, followed through on: "I'm looking forward to living things out."[279]

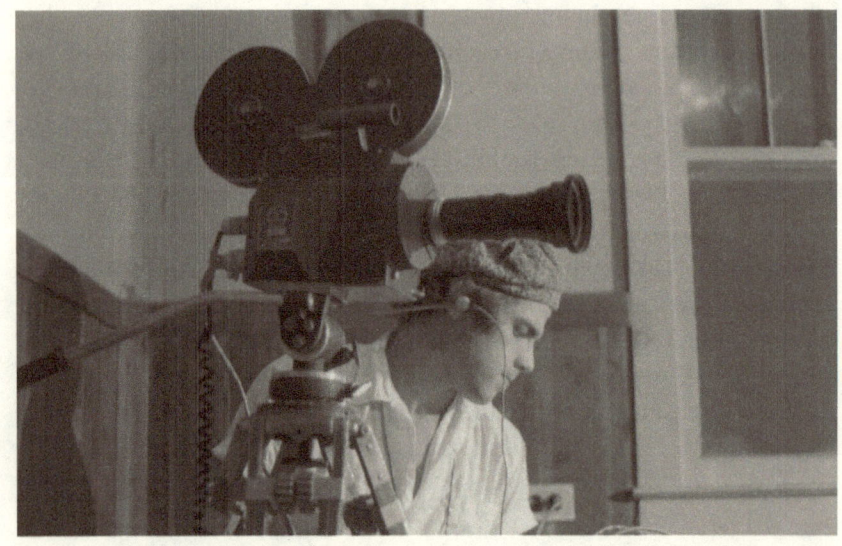

Frank filming for the documentary *It Wasn't a Dream: It Was a Flood*, summer 1974. *Photo courtesy of Ginny Crouch Stanford.*

TEN

# "A Syntax of Images"

## 1973

FRANK'S FEW WEEKS IN New York City, for all their drama, were ultimately about sitting in movie theaters and watching films. "When I was in NY," he wrote to Irv shortly after returning, "I saw over 100 films, mostly old classics from every country."[1] The pace at which he saw them was like "listening to all of Wagner's operas at once." But he knew he'd never get the chance again to see so many films, "so I must view them now," he wrote.[2] At these screenings, he encountered in person Tennessee Williams, Hal Holbrook, and Pauline Kael. Frank had been wanting to merge his interests in poetry and film since at least the spring of 1972, when Dugan expressed to him hope that "in the film you plan that you will have that kind of ample poetry on the soundtrack."[3] Frank would, again largely because of Irv Broughton's selfless commitment to his interests, get a chance to do just that—plan and make his own film.

Frank's passion for film was long-standing. Bill Willett remembers the two of them regularly seeing serious movies at the Starlight Drive-In and the Baxter Theater back in the Mountain Home days.[4] At Subiaco, Frank caught movies in Fort Smith whenever Father Fuhrmann arranged a field trip there. At the University of Arkansas, he nurtured his interest by seeing many movies shown at the UArk Theatre (above which he briefly lived) and helping manage the Student Union film series selections in 1969. When fellow student Bill Lavender took over that role in 1970, he scheduled films by Fellini, Godard, Bergman, and Pasolini. Frank never missed a screening.[5] Lavender remembers talking to Frank more about film than about any other topic.[6]

John Biguenet recalled how when he met Frank at Hollins back in June 1970, it was a big moment for foreign films, especially French and Italian, and that Frank knew them all. "I don't know where he got the education," Biguenet said. "My impression is that he had seen a lot of films and thought about them."[7] Biguenet saw almost fifty films in two weeks, and Frank was right there with him, attending screenings by, as Frank recalled for Irv, "Kurosawa, Bunuel, Mamoulian, Truffaut, Bergman, Rossellini, and all the old Russian films."[8] In February 1972, Frank urged Irv, "Remember to watch Cocteau's 'La Belle et la Bête' tonight.... Have you seen 'Les Parents terribles,' 'Orphée,' 'Le Testament d'Orphée,' and, of course, 'Le Sang d'un Poet'?"[9] Frank later remarked that he had seen *La belle et la bête* thirty times.[10] He told Irv that he wanted to make films about his poems, specifically of "Gospel Bird, Tapsticks, Snake Doctors."[11] When a friend at the University of Arkansas had to make a film for a class in late 1971, Frank told Willett that he was hoping to write and direct it.[12] In an unpublished essay that Jim Whitehead wrote after Frank's death he wrote, "If any poet ever loved the movies, Frank Stanford did."[13]

Combining literature and film seemed natural for Frank, whose poetic vision always had an intrinsically cinematic quality to it. In 1972, while revising *The Battlefield*, he noted to Irv that "much of this is poetry for the screen."[14] This convergence reflected Frank's interest the cine-poetic vision of his icons. In an unpublished interview he noted, "At the moment I'd say two of the most popular or well-known filmmakers, Pasolini and Bertolucci, are good poets; does anyone think they got into cinema first[?] Bertolucci... his family has a literary background. Pasolini is the one who's done all the research in dialect poetry and everything. He traveled around his country, listening, writing, and now goes around filming.... The beautiful poet Jacques Prévert did that.... And what about Jean Cocteau[?] Of course I could go on."[15]

Of course he could. Frank's friendship with Irv Broughton and their shared ambition to make films together allowed Frank to contemplate a future where film and literature merged, as they had done for his Italian heroes Pier Paolo Pasolini and Bernardo Bertolucci. On the last day of 1972, he wrote to Irv, "Remember the good summer! And all we spoke of doing [films on]: Missus Welty, Walker Percy, and on and on."[16] His commitment to film was both as a technical practice and an expansive form of poetic expression that could include in its realm artists ranging from Walker Percy to François Truffaut. It was a tangible way to challenge what Frank saw as so many "misconceptions of reality—due to the lack of perception of it"[17] while enabling him to build, furnish, and keep drawing on what his second wife, Ginny Stanford, would aptly call "his vast warehouses."[18]

## "So Long, Old Road Dirty with My Past"

After New York, the bus ride with the old Black man, and ditching Deidre, Frank had returned to Subiaco in or around late September 1972. The monks would do for a while. Subiaco was a reliable escape, good for temporary reprieves, but, especially after his acknowledgment of his adoption, it did not appeal to Frank as a permanent home. The main problem was his mother. Dorothy was hounding Frank again, much as she had in 1966 before he left for college. Her grievances were mounting and her inhibitions about expressing them lowering. She never approved of Frank's decision to be a poet and never understand why his poems did not rhyme as poems were supposed to rhyme (as the ones she once wrote did!).[19] She disapproved of his choice to not study business and, eventually, drop out of college. She was upset about his stint in the mental hospital, his and Linda's divorce, and his disappearance into the vice den of New York for a month. She did not like *The Singing Knives*.[20] Then there was the state of his soul. Since high school, his erratic behavior had worried her, and she often applied religious pressure to keep him in line (something the priests never did, ironically). Much of her attempt to control Frank's behavior conflicted with the loss of credibility she may have felt over his acknowledgment of what she still refused to discuss—his and Ruth's adoptions. Frank was no longer the southern gentleman he had been groomed to become, or at least he was no longer playing that role as dutifully as he was expected to play it. As far as Dorothy was concerned, this all constituted a betrayal.

A few months later, just after Frank left Subiaco, she fired away in a letter to him. We have only his response to it. Always sidestepping open conflict, Frank responded to his mother not directly but by writing to Father Herbert Vogelpohl, Dorothy's closest friend at Subiaco. Frank's letter confirmed his ongoing susceptibility to being guilt-tripped, as well as his refusal to engage his mother's evident ire. He wrote:

> Dear Father Herbert,
>
> Thank you for your note. I was getting a remarkable amount of work done, until I got this letter from mother, where she achieved her objective of making me hate myself, once again.... Those kind of letters were the reason I left in the first place. Hope everything is fine with you.[21]

In a late December 1972 note to Irv, Frank insisted that Irv not tell people, including relatives, where he was living or what he was doing when he left Subiaco.[22] He would never cut himself off from Dorothy, but he would create a healthy distance from her. That was hard to do at Subiaco, where, as the Coury House's matron for almost a decade at this point, she was a constant and beloved presence. "I'm not too comfortable around my mother and grandmother—they think I am disturbed, etc.," he wrote to Cheryl in November 1972.[23]

For all the stress with Dorothy, Frank's few months at the monastery in the fall of 1972 had benefits beyond part-time employment and a free place to stay. The priests continued to be rewarding company. After returning from New York, Frank wrote to Irv that his note would have to be short because "a brother is coming by to get me and do a little labor and go fishing."[24] Frank valued this kind of low-commitment camaraderie with men who read, recited verse, drank, and worked. Father Fuhrmann lent him an old army jeep owned by the abbey, and Frank drove it in the hills around campus. He stayed fit by climbing a steep cliff across Highway 22 called "St. Peter's Chair," which he often ran up, according to Father Fuhrmann, "faster than the bobcats that roam the region."[25]

Ensconced in the monastery, Frank could also return to his big poem without distractions. *The Battlefield Where the Moon Says I Love You* had not been his top priority during his road trip and New York adventure. But now, with some healthy distance from the manuscript and with a literal monk's cell to work in, he returned to it. He wrote to Irv soon after getting home, "Before I forget: unless you are planning to go to good press soon with that long ms., send it back to me right now . . . try not to mess up the page numbers. . . . Mail it first class."[26] Writing to Dugan, Frank requested that he also send the poem back. There would, Frank promised, be no more burnings.[27] In late January 1973 he sent a fresh version of the poem to the Antioch Press, where an editor named Eric Horsting wrote back to say, "Because it is long it will take me some time to get to it."[28] This was an early hint of how hard it would be for Frank to get someone, anyone, to read the poem the way it needed to be read—slowly and with an awareness of the poem's deep vernacular complexity. But it was also an indication that he used the fall of 1972 to keep working on this ever-evolving masterwork.

Stanford had paid relatively little attention to contemporary poetry up to this point in life but for one exception: his own. His "anxiety of influence" was, because of the attenuated nature of *The Battlefield*, about himself. He had been working on the same autobiographical poem, or at least a gestating version of it, for over a decade. During the previous few years, he had been forging something that was now officially becoming *The

*Battlefield Where the Moon Says I Love You.* Throughout the process the epic poem had expanded and contracted like an accordion, with some outtakes finding a home in some journals and in his books. But it remained at the center of Stanford's creative existence, and he was still eager to work recent and ongoing revelations and lessons into his project.

New York, and his immersion in the world of cinema had an enormous impact on *The Battlefield* and Frank's poetic thought in general. Not many months after leaving the city, he produced a manuscript titled "Automatic Co-Pilot." Not incidentally, it consisted of poems functioning as "my renditions of 20 foreign poets in someway [sic] connected to cinema."[29] In a post–New York interview that he did with Broughton, Frank explained that serious poets were culturally obligated to merge writing with cinema. "After all," he said, "we poets have to realize that . . . only a few of us have broken into the motion-picture industry. We have to do that. We just can't let these second rate novelists and playwrights keep jumping the gun on us."[30] Over the next two years, as he continued to work on *The Battlefield*, Frank integrated cinematic techniques, themes, and references into his big poem while looking at his world, literally, through a Bell & Howell movie camera.

Frank's emphasis on film allowed *The Battlefield* to become an even denser amalgam of people, places, themes, interests, and dreams that, without filmic thought and technique, might have seemed impossible to smooth into a workable narrative. Seasoned readers of *The Battlefield* know very well how Francis's dream sequences lend the poem a coherence that, without those cinematic shifts, would dissolve into chaos. The frequent repetition of intrusive dreams, which are departures from more narratively conventional stretches of text, allows the poem to absorb almost any possibility. Dreams, like films, don't follow normal rules about space and time. Frank, kind of quoting Jean Cocteau, wrote that "film . . . follows the vigorous illogicality of dreams."[31] In this sense, the poem reflects the vigorous illogicality of his life. He wrote, kind of quoting Byron, " 'I had a dream that was not at all a dream.' So far, that's how my life has been."[32] *The Battlefield* was no more or less coherent than Frank's own waking and dreaming mind, which the poem reflects. Put differently, the poem confirms Frank's belief that "the world . . . was written by an insane, bad poet, and all the main characters resemble a perverted, treacherous Marx brothers."[33] Film-like perspectives and techniques, with their image- and sound-driven segues, shifts, cuts, and diversions, inform the dream sequences that organize *The Battlefield*, imbuing the poem with a powerful cinematic spirit.

The beautiful heterogeneity of the foreign films that Frank saw in New York informed the beautiful heterogeneity of his evolving poem. The monks and their Mertonesque ways only enhanced that connection. Frank's ever-lengthening arcs of cultural associations—which created space for knights-errant, Japanese warriors, levee camp cooks, Memphis fat cats, carnies, con men, bad cops, freedom riders, bluesmen, gypsies, peddlers, rock and rollers, classical musicians, peckerwoods, levee workers, Renaissance painters, horny housewives, medieval philosophers, professional boxers, seasoned rednecks, Jesus and the apostles, Hollywood stars, you name it—appear to confirm the fact that a polymathic genius with a near photographic memory had been working on the poem since high school. One's interests change, evolve, shift, rise, fall, stabilize, and destabilize over ten years. Frank decided to preserve that helter-skelter process endemic to daily life and explore it through an image-obsessed consciousness that challenged conventional reality. Few places were as conducive to this effort as the monastery, and few media as conducive as film.

There seemed no limit to what *The Battlefield* could incorporate into its dense and dream-sequenced structure. Frank's cinematic immersion in New York, as well as his Cocteau-inspired blend of film and poetry, made this limitless integration of voice and dream possible. It is what John Biguenet had in mind when he said that "Frank was really serious about film and poetry."[34] It was what these media could do for each other, their symbiotic interaction, that most excited him. Of course, none of this should suggest that readers of Frank's manuscript, whatever version they read, would necessarily grasp that symbiosis. In December of 1973, William L. Fox wrote to Frank that "I spent some time going through that giant of yours, all the pages—I still can't find much to do with it." He complained that "it's all the same in a sense."[35] In fact the cinematic nature of the poem ensured just the opposite. The poem is a density of diversity. And the reason has everything to do with Frank's interest in film, his thinking through film, and his aggressive effort to integrate that interest and thought into a poem he started writing well before his immersion in film.

The few months he spent at Subiaco at the end of 1972 gave Frank both distance from Fayetteville and a much-needed ephemeral sense of being between places. Nobody, least of all Frank, was expecting him to stick around Subiaco for long. To merge film and poetry he needed isolation and, as he had learned in New York, the confidence that all things were, like a film, transitory. With the grim events of Fayetteville and the subsequent State Hospital visit still fresh in his mind, Frank craved the chance to start over, to steer clear of Fayetteville's MFA scene, and to nurture a sense of ongoing possibility. He needed to hear new voices and "work in peace," as he told an editor.[36] Subiaco gave him a respite to do that.

But after three months of some classroom teaching and boxing matches and fishing with monks and running up St. Peter's Chair, it was time for another move: "I'm lonely," he wrote Cheryl. "I'm thinking about hitchhiking over to Eureka Springs, hide in the bushes, walk the streets alone, the perpetual stranger."[37] He wanted to recover the odd equilibrium he had experienced in New York and maybe have the chance to reinvent himself in a place where he was far enough away from familiar faces that he could banish recent memory and emerge as a blank slate. "So long, old road dirty with my past," he wrote in a notebook around the time that he left Subiaco, in late 1972.[38]

But there was one memory he could not vanquish. Despite Frank's abrupt departure from New York, his infatuation with Cheryl remained as intense as ever. His loneliness only enhanced his longing. Whether she would go the way of that old road, though, remained an open question. "Cheryl wants to come here," Frank reported to Dugan when he was at Subiaco.[39] Although Frank had abandoned Cheryl in New York—after first ditching her for Linda in Fayetteville (in the summer of 1971)—the couple stayed in touch, and more important, they stayed in love, at least at a distance and on paper. On November 1, 1972, Cheryl wrote Frank an impassioned three-page letter reassuring him of her continued love for him: "I want to be with you—live with you—love you—have a home with you." She went on: "Frank—how much I love you. . . . I feel close to you & yet so far away. Are we a myth. Yes—and *know*—no!" She needed Frank to "lead me to the lake for a ride in your canoe." She reminded Frank, "With the moon we can sail—traversing—all worlds—only to race to the hearth—making love by the fire—and sharing our tales til the coals die—birth the morning."[40]

Frank returned the passion. "Your clitoris is a minnow I want to dip out and return to the water forever," he declared. "Oh let us go down the roads, love, smoking Coleridge's fantastic pipe together." Contemplating her possible move back to Arkansas, he hoped "to find a place by the end of the month," even if he had to "wade in that necessary branch of reality"— steady employment. He mentioned getting a job driving a truck, pursuing such a provincial ambition "so I can swim in your waters, so we can dream in peace, so we can live, and create."[41]

Frank was walking a tightrope with Cheryl as he prepared to leave the monastery. He wanted more intimacy with Cheryl. But for obvious reasons he was duly wary about pursuing a traditional romantic relationship with her, especially back in Arkansas, where the bridges he had burned were still smoldering. In December 1972, while living with the monks, Frank wrote Cheryl three long letters (one of them over six thousand words—the lengthiest of all known letters by Frank), delivering what amounted to a mixed message that confirmed both his desire and ambivalence. There was no question about the fire of his passion. Admitting that there had been other lovers, Frank told Cheryl that his feelings for her were different, unique. "There have been so many other women," he wrote on December 2, "but none of them like you." He said that "you are ... *so* different from all the other diversions," turning the liability of his promiscuity into a foundation for his compliment.[42] His urges were raw and unequivocal: "No one can screw like you," he wrote Cheryl. "I'm just longing for you." He told her to "pinch your nipples so you can come." He was thrilled by how "we still have a thousand ways to make love," predicting that "when we're free we'll die fucking" and observing that "coming with you is like a meteor shower in the middle of summer."[43] "I am very frustrated," he wrote, "SEXUALLY and everything."[44]

Raw desire for Cheryl notwithstanding, he had enough self-awareness to offer some ambiguous warnings, prefacing them with this advice: "Don't flinch." He said that his "doctor need[ed] to know" if she was "prolonging our relationship for my physical & mental well being, etc." He noted that "I'm animal like in my movements when I think you are having pity on me." He chided her for "writing me advice letters," something to which he did not cotton. "I know you mean well," he clarified, "but I think you are giving advice to yourself." Women and envious writers would always swarm around him, he warned, adding that "if we live our kind of life, there will be many jealous intruders." Because "I am a great poet," he wrote, Cheryl would have "to understand how volatile are the liquids and solids of my imagination." Last, out of nowhere, he explained that he suffered from memory loss: "Anyway, about this amnesia ... I guess now is the time to bring this up." He assured her that "I will cope with my amnesia myself; fuck the doctors." Then there was the point that "I could murder myself right now. ... You could call it madness ... but that is how LOST I am with the universe."[45]

Frank spent considerable time in this letter musing on the beauty and mystery of other women, including those with whom Cheryl lived and socialized in New York. He was fascinated by Elizabeth Thompson, the married woman he had had an affair with while in New York, because "being a dancer, she knows her body." He wrote to Cheryl that "the first time I saw her, her head was raised like a doe." He called her "rough and tumble like a barmaid" and noted that "the anxiety" between her and him "is sexual." He wrote to Cheryl that "since I was screwing somebody else while I was staying there, but no one you know, this guilt was like screwing everybody." Absconding with Deidre, he said, "was a way of keeping from the others." Still, he reassured her that when he was "making love with you everything was fine." He added, "You might as well know, I might be a father.... Whatever, I will never see her [the potential mother] again."[46] None of this was an eager endorsement of moving to Arkansas.

The takeaway from these long letters from the monastery, in the lonely days before his fateful move to Eureka Springs, Arkansas, is that Frank loved Cheryl, desired her, but knew these emotions might not mean he was ready to pursue a standard relationship with anyone. All complexity aside, one thing was clear: Cheryl would, for the time being, stay in New York.

## Eureka!

In mid-December 1972 Frank learned that a room was open at the New Orleans Hotel in Eureka Springs, located about forty-five miles northeast of Fayetteville.[47] The last time he was at the hotel it had been to have sex with Cheryl only days before he and Linda married in August 1971. Eureka Springs was (and still is) a unique place for any state, especially Arkansas. Located in the Ozarks, it welcomed with open arms hippies, lesbians, back-to-the-landers, commune dwellers, farmers, and tolerant locals who, as one resident at the time put it, enjoyed "the alternative world people" who populated their hills.[48] The hotel had recently been purchased by a feminist political activist from New Orleans who turned it from a haven for Baptist Evangelicals into a hive for feminism and gay rights. Eureka Springs became a seductive magnet for outsiders, many of them women who wanted to own land and live independently.[49] Frank paid around $130 a month in rent.[50] He ate sparingly, occasionally stole fish from a nearby hatchery and cooked it on park grills, wrote obsessively, picked up odd jobs, and did his very best to keep his location a secret.[51] "If any relatives or editors write you asking where I am," he told Irv, "don't say."[52]

Frank liked everything about the town. Eureka Springs, he told Irv, was "a testament to my clairvoyance."[53] It was perhaps the ideal location for Frank to continue exploring the relationship between poetry and film and work those discoveries into *The Battlefield*. "The place is," he wrote to his grandmother, "almost European." Situated in the Ozarks, it was home to fifteen natural springs, several annual folk festivals, a ring of communal/anarchist hippie farms, heaps of Victorian architecture wedged into steep hillsides, and enough backwoods hollows and hideouts for people to live and let live. Its European facade harbored hillbilly eccentrics, exactly the kind of people Frank enjoyed for their unvarnished ways of living. "Eureka was," said one resident who moved there in 1970 to start a writers' colony, "enchanted and out of time."[54] Frank was happy that "there are saloons to write in now."[55]

"This place is crazy," he told Dugan. On a postcard with a picture of a hulking man on horseback dressed as a gladiator, he wrote, "This is true: the fat Roman, leading the pack, is really a fishing guide, who also owns a grocery and a laboratory. He has his own 'Theory of Light,' but N.A.S.A 'refuses' to listen to him."[56] Frank assured his grandmother that "there are no negroes, only hill people"—the "billies," he called them—and reported a "date" he had had with a seventy-year-old woman: "She fed me supper, which was honey bread and shrimp and some dish I cannot spell ... and then we listened to Bruebeck [sic] and Mahler."[57] To Irv he noted, "Where else can you see a half-blooded Cherokee riding a camel and a former nuclear physicist blowing glass ships. Where else can one come see Judas hung nightly"—a reference to the town's legendary performance (still ongoing) of the Great Passion Play of Christ. "Jesus got too fat," he reported, "turned to liquor, so another was hired." These vignettes could easily have been *Battlefield* moments parading as reality, an art-life boundary where Frank was most alive. "Irv," he wrote after describing these eccentricities, "you aren't believing me." But he assured him: "All of this is so true it hurts."[58] New York paled in comparison.

The random characters milling around the town appealed to Stanford's Whitman-like craving for strangers and their stories. "The kind of people, the mixture, is so strange," he wrote to his grandmother. "On the one hand you have an elderly glassblower who was formerly a nuclear physicist"—likely a jeweler named Ira Whitney[59]—"and on the other hand you have someone murdered in a local saloon, hillbillies, easterners, Europeans, ex-bankers from New Orleans."[60] To Irv he marveled about how "all the hicks live in Victorian houses," a Stanfordian juxtaposition par excellence.[61] He added how "in the distance I can see the hut of Crescent Dragon, soi-disant appleative [sic] of a swan maiden from the Big Apple who writes famous herbal cookbooks, who is rich, and who has parents connected in some way with publishing the best line of children's book[s] in NYC."[62] This reference was to a woman named Ellen Zolotow, also known as Crescent Dragonwagon, who indeed wrote cookbooks and came from a publishing family in New York.⁶³ For a man whose autobiographical protagonist said, "I listen to the voices" (11577), Eureka Springs was the place to be.

For all Frank's efforts to disappear into the wonderful weirdness of the town, Deidre, the Scottish woman who was intent on experiencing Frank the southerner, found him there soon after he arrived. "The girl from Scotland," Frank wrote to his grandmother after he arrived in Eureka Springs, still wanted to "tour 'the South.' "⁶⁴ Frank obliged. To William L. Fox, Frank, on New Orleans Hotel stationery, reported how "I'm showing a lady from Scotland the South, touring with her, writing stories and screenplays, and blue yodels, and ballads." In an unpublished fragment he wrote, "I lay my head down in the lap of a woman with a Scottish brogue," noting the "chignon of her auburn hair."⁶⁵

They had quite the trip. For a week, probably in late January and early February 1973, the couple, as he wrote, "travelled in a wagon with a hobo." He recalled how "I met an old river rat I knew in my youth, and he offered me his floating shack for the rest of the winter."⁶⁶ He mentioned seeking refuge in "boxcars, mansions, dives, saloons, monasteries, and barges."⁶⁷ In a letter to Malcolm Cowley he noted that the venues on this trip included "a houseboat, a boxcar, a monastery, or a hotel."⁶⁸ To David Walker he recalled how he "met up with the girl again. SHOWED her the so-called south," a venture that included living in a "houseboat, whorehouse, and hotels."⁶⁹ Eventually Deidre "put out on a ship from New Orleans, headed toward Europe,"⁷⁰ floating out of Frank's life, possibly pregnant.

Frank, who had come to Eureka Springs eager to "walk the streets alone," soon found himself at the center of the town's social scene.⁷¹ This meant the usual pursuit of sexual adventure. Crescent Dragonwagon said that Eureka Springs was, at the time, a place where "everyone was having sex with everyone," which worked fine for Frank.⁷² Between January and March of 1973, he struck up at least two affairs. One was with a sixteen-year-old girl nicknamed Strawberry. She was, according to Frank, a six-foot-one-inch track star with ambitions to be a masseuse and was best known for beating up a high school boy—a son of a local bar owner—every day at school. "The other woman I'm seeing," Frank wrote, "is an artist, about thirty, seven years older than eye [sic], fourteen years Strawberry's senior, who is unmarried, but with a six month old child." He claimed to have had one of his prophetic visions of her before they met. She was, as he prophesized her, "in her black Napoleonic coat, and the papoose in an Aztec blanket." He said he wrote two short stories about their affair. "I made love to her while her child was nursing," he told Irv, to which he could only say, "Jesus Christ."⁷³

Frank felt liberated in this town, full as it was of characters who mirrored *The Battlefield*'s restless bullpen of castaways and outliers. This was a place where life chased art, where the theatrical and carnivalesque merged into genuine reality, and where weirdness, if not plain madness, was normal. "Borges, Brunel, and James Dickey could not contrive such a place and people as this, even if they were on DeQuincey's and Coleridges's pipe," he wrote.[74] And to his gran-gran he added: "This town is one of the strangest places I've visited."[75] A man could howl here with impunity, and Stanford often did just that. On another postcard, this one with a picture of an empty amphitheater, he wrote to Dugan, "I go [to] this place, and shout my grievances, and read my poems to the empty Elizabethan seats."[76] It was all a good fit for Frank.

## "How about That"

The only way to integrate all of this strangeness, all of these foreign expressions and personas, and give the Eureka Springs carnival some coherence, was through film. Bill Willett visited Frank that winter at the New Orleans Hotel and later recalled how "Frank continued his infatuation with film in Eureka Springs."[77] When a major ice storm shut down the town from January 6 to 12, 1973, Frank evaluated the scene in explicitly cinematic language, writing, "Many trucks, cars, buses have run off the roads in the mtns. and this Hotel **which is called the New Orleans because it looks like something in the French Quarter***is much like a movie*, due to all the stranded people who are staying here."[78] Describing the town in general, he wrote, "This place is like a movie by D.W. Griffith."[79] Frank was literally seeing reality in Eureka Springs as if it were a film. Of course, he also wanted to see actual films in reality. The problem was that, while he could make as many film analogies as he wanted, he could not see a hundred foreign films in Eureka Springs. In fact, he couldn't see one. "I haven't seen a film in god knows when," he complained to Cheryl in January 1973.[80] This was an old and ongoing frustration. His first wife, Linda, recalled how in Fayetteville "Frank did love movies, including foreign films, but there was only one theater in town."[81] A brief conversation between Jimmy and Francis in *The Battlefield* highlights this dilemma:

> You want to go to town I says
> What town you talking about there ain't a damn town for a hundred miles
> I thought we might go to a picture show
> I ain't driving a hundred miles to see no picture
> (6669–73)

Frank admitted that he would in fact drive twice as far. "I travel up to two hundred miles when I can to see films," he told Irv.[82] But still, outside of New York or other cultural metropolises, it was hard to see the foreign films he felt he needed to see.

To address this problem, Frank, emboldened by the artistic spirit of Eureka Springs, took charge. He rented space behind the hotel in late February, hit Irv up for "$$$$$$" (as he put his request in one note), sold an old spinning wheel he somehow owned, and opened what Bill Willett remembers as "a small, small theater."[83] To do this he drew on his past experience running the film series at the Arkansas Student Union in 1969.[84] As in his poems, he brought foreign, surreal, and abstract concepts into the heart of the Ozarks. Gwynn recalls that Frank was caught up in "a big Pasolini push at the time"—right around when Pasolini's poems were being published in the US—and that he showed *Teorema* (1968), *Medea* (1969), and *The Gospel According to St. Matthew* (1964).[85] To Dugan, Frank noted that "we watch, on the wall, Cocteau, Carné, and Renoir—also documentaries by [about] Rousseau, De Maupassant, Hugo, Proust, and so on."[86]

Frank called his little theater the Eureka Springs Theater. To acquire films, he would contact foreign embassies, request their catalogs, rent the films, show them for a couple of weeks, and send them back. "Somehow, through the French Embassy," he wrote, "I have some very fine films on loan."[87] He would also rent them from Janus, a foreign film distributor, a choice he made over Brandon Films, whose list he informed George Garrett "leaves much to be desired."[88] With Willett home from the army, Frank convinced him to come pick up the films after he showed them and screen them back in Mountain Home. "So I would travel back and forth to Eureka Springs," Willett later remembered, "and we tried to get something started over here [Mountain Home], but the nucleus for art wasn't here, so this part didn't work out." Still, Willett got to see films by Bergman and Fellini. These movies were, Willett stressed, "very important to Frank's poetry."[89]

Frank's approach to showing movies was like his approach to writing, sex, drinking, and reading: intensive and immersive. He screened movies either weekly or biweekly and usually as double features. The theater's debut weekend featured not one film but a string of them, shown back to back, relentlessly, for days. Frank wrote to Irv just before the doors opened: "The premier of my theatre this weekend: *Diary of Country Priest*, *Zero for Conduct*, *L'Atalante*, *St. Louis Blues* with Bessie Smith." Later in the spring, for four consecutive days, May 25-28, Frank scheduled eight screenings from 10:00 a.m. to 2:00 a.m., and over the course of those days he showed fifteen films, including Faulkner and Brown's *Intruder in the*

*Dust*, Fellini's *Nights of Cabiria*, Dreyer's *Vampyr*, Dalí and Buñuel's *Un chien andalou*, Godard's *Les carabiniers*, and *The Little Rascals*. Admission for the entire day was $1.50. Summing up these efforts, Frank, more than a little pleased with this marathon of film offerings, wrote to Irv with a little triumph in his tone, "How about that."[90]

Frank also opened his theater to the occasional variety show. David Zimmerman, an aspiring writer who came to Eureka Springs after studying literature with Andrew Nelson Lytle at the University of the South, recalls being "jealous of Frank's obvious brilliance, which radiated power." But this did not prevent him from performing an act in which he donned a long purple gown and vamped on stage while reading Emily Dickinson's "A rat surrendered here." The events at Frank's theater could occasionally draw a full house. Zimmerman recalls about thirty seats.[91] Steve Stern remembers going to a movie at Frank's theater before he ever met Frank and finding the room packed with maybe fifty people. He cannot remember the specific film being shown but does recollect seeing Frank in front of the theater before the show: "I remember a guy who was sitting on a log outside. I was a smart-ass. . . . I remember having words with him, and I was being my ironic Jewish self." But when Frank gave him a hard look in response, Stern toned it down. "I just hit an absence of irony and unwillingness to suffer fools," he remembers. "I thought, *This is trouble*, and I backed off."[92] Frank's theater, including the movies shown there, was no laughing matter.

High attendance was in fact rare. Willett recalled that "he made a good effort and showed very good films, but he didn't have the audience so it didn't last long."[93] Still, "Frank took it very seriously."[94] Frank later recalled to an editor how "I ran a small picture show of good films—you'd have to go to SF or NYC to see some of what we had." But in the end, he said, "we lost our ass," adding, "Only children, drunks, and hillbillys came, although there were enough tourists and so-called artists and intellectuals around. Boy did we lose our ass. We'd show movies, great films in 16mm, and nobody would come."[95] Some locals evidently thought the theater was "a good place to drink in the dark," but Frank decided such leisure was not worth subsidizing with the more than a thousand dollars a month he ultimately put into acquiring films and paying rent.[96] The theater ran out of steam by the summer of 1973.[97] "I'd like to know of a shenanigan better than that," Frank later said of this failed venture.[98]

When it came to money, Frank, confirming Father Fuhrmann's assessment that he never cared that much for it, was only as ambitious as he had to be. "Fuck money," he wrote to Cheryl in December 1972, summing up his general attitude toward material accumulation.[99] "I see money as dirt tracked into the home," he later wrote.[100] He only wanted enough cash to write, drink, and perhaps one day buy some land in a remote area and live off it.[101] In Eureka Springs he worked odd jobs, including feeding horses for a family that owned a stable in the hills, a task that required him to "take a very long walk... into the mountains." He preferred to do so, he wrote, while "mulling things over along the way." He mentioned how excited he was to try to purchase some land of his own. But for the moment he would "hire on to those around here."[102]

Appreciating the weirdness of Eureka Springs and channeling the autonomy and simplicity of the monks, Frank began to fantasize about living off the grid in a remote area. "As Robert Frost said," he wrote to his grandmother, "the only other thing a poet can do is farm."[103] To Cheryl he wrote in January 1973 that "a farm is the only thing."[104] The back-to-the-land communes in the area impressed him because they were full of young people who "grow and raise just about everything they eat, even down to the yogurt which they make, which comes from goats." He admired "a divorced lady with alot of children who paints and runs her own farm"—likely the woman he slept with while she was breastfeeding—and another woman with "1200 acres to herself on the Little Piney River."[105] Both women were beneficiaries of the female empowerment movement whose headquarters were at the New Orleans Hotel. His recent encounter with the self-sufficiency guru Scott Nearing in Maine and his fascination with Richard Wilbur's Massachusetts silo hideout only enhanced the potential appeal of this independent lifestyle.

Fayetteville was only forty-five miles away, but as far as Frank was concerned, it was another planet. He could not stress enough his desire to stay isolated from that part of his past. "I will keep your address secret," Irv promised.[106] It was not uncommon for correspondents to begin the letters they wrote to Frank with something like "We have no idea where you are & can only hope this finds you."[107] When John Wood, whom Frank knew from the workshop days, ran into Frank in Eureka Springs in the winter of 1973, Frank looked at him as if he did not know him, perhaps a response designed to complement his ambiguous claim to Cheryl that he was suffering from amnesia. No matter. Soon his acquaintances in Fayetteville were calling him "amnesia Frank."[108] Frank certainly might have been experiencing periodic memory loss.[109] He later recalled how, at this time, he was "recovering from amnesia" and had been told by doctors that some "term[inally] ill" condition he supposedly had was gone.[110]

Frank was not one to dwell on health issues, but he did allude to them frequently enough to raise questions about potentially deeper problems.

We do know that his stomach was in bad shape. His second wife recalls him saying that doctors told him to quit drinking or he'd soon be dead. In late February of 1972 Frank wrote to Irv that he "*MUST* stop drinking. Had to go to doctor about this."[111] In this case, though, he was referring to the ulcers with which he had been diagnosed at least twice and was suffering from that winter.[112] This was not new. Back in the summer of 1971 he had written to a friend that "my gut finally busted." He and Linda had been visiting her parents on Beaver Lake when "I started heaving blood. My ulcer came back."[113] Again, whatever the case, *something* seemed awry, however momentarily, with Frank's physical health. [114]

Frank's drinking during these first few months in Eureka Springs, despite medical concerns, seems to have been on par with the past: excessive and integral to his functioning as a writer. There were at least three bars he frequented: the Hi-Hat, which was for the hippies; the Wagon Wheel, which was for the "billies"; and Main Street Bar where all were welcome, including the town's only Black man.[115] Frank remarked how he bonded over drinks with the new people he met in Eureka Springs, saying of the "fat Roman" that "I drink with him." He continued to get drunk mainly on wine. Without noting his location, Frank mentioned how he almost "took off on a ship ... but got drunk and didn't make sailing time."[116] On one occasion he "passed out in a saloon here [in Eureka Springs] about noon one day."[117] At another time he drank so much he puked on his bed, a detail he shared with Dugan. "Happy and drunk and hope you are," he wrote.[118] It was an accurate assessment of his general condition, with respect to alcohol, in the winter of 1973 in Eureka Springs.[119]

Even his excess could be excessive. Bill Willett recalls an evening, right after Frank moved into the New Orleans Hotel, when the two of them went out drinking until eight thirty the next morning. It was a binge that began with them visiting the Roaring River Fish Hatchery to steal fish. This was a place, according to one local resident, where you could easily get away with such a thing.[120] But in this case they were deterred by two men playing cards in a shack who noticed them trespassing. Hungry, they drove to Linda's parents' enormous Beaver Lake house. Frank knew they were out of town and remembered where they hid the house key. Bill and Frank drank Adolph Mencin's bourbon while eating Ritz Crackers with cheese and jalapeños. To cap it off, Frank agreed to make a rare trip into Fayetteville as the sun came up. "Frank was feeling his booze a lot," Bill said.[121] But it did not bother Frank in the least. "I am living the good life," Frank assured Irv.[122] "I am living the life the poet dreams he lives," he wrote in another letter.[123]

Frank's confidence in his writing was on the rise during these few months in Eureka Springs, a euphoria that often overlapped with his heavy drinking. He told his grandmother how "MALCOLM COWLEY, Faulkner's editor, wants to sponsor me to 'Yaddo' in N.Y." He was also thrilled that "a few checks are starting to roll in from publications" and that he had "four, maybe five books coming out."[124] All of this was true. But there were times when he was writing letters to Irv when his confidence went haywire, flirting with delusions of grandeur. In the winter of 1973 he wrote, "Dugan said I was the greatest living poet, whether or not I wrote another line. . . . Ginsberg told me, in this very place, in the Spring of 69 . . . that I was the reincarnation of Robert Burns and Robert Johnson, and that I reminded him of neil cassidy [sic]."[125] In another letter to "Dear Lord Irv, Earl of Broughton," he effused about how "I feel the brotherhood of the spirits of poets of times past" as he prepared work he thought "will endure."[126] To George Garrett he explained, after mentioning how he was not in the least intimidated by "Dickey, Bly, and Ginsberg," that "since I don't belong to any of these schools, I am, so far, accepted by all of them."[127]

Frank received a special postcard in early January forwarded from his Subiaco address. It was a fan note and solicitation from the San Francisco poet Lawrence Ferlinghetti, founding publisher of the famed City Lights Books: "Dear Stanford—I do dig many of your poems and would like to hold on to the manuscript so that we might choose a poem or two to publish in a *City Lights Journal* next Fall."[128] To Irv, Frank flexed a bit over the letters he'd recently gotten from writers of luminary status: "Ferlinghetti, Malcolm [Cowley] (2), Dugan (12), letters from everyone, all kinds."[129] Frank reported to his editor at *West Coast Poetry Review*, William L. Fox, that both Ferlinghetti and Cowley were attending to his poems.[130] During one moment of self-confidence he diagrammed his poetic influences, attributing his genius to forces no less profound than "the holy spirit," "unconscious motive of poetry," "saints and anonymous great poets," and "Surrealists and Dadaists." Under this sketch he declared, "The holy spirit and the muse make love: my poetry." Then he added, "I said the above when I was 15. I don't feel pretentious in saying it either, but morally wrong by not! Now I have various poets and critics to believe *with* me, not just in me."[131] This was quite a shift and leap in mood and tone from his May 1972 "May Day" letters. Clearly, the pendulum had swung from a mood so dark he was burning his work because he felt confident that no one cared about it.

## "The Black Angel"

It was not only film and poetry that merged for Frank in Eureka Springs. Frank's concern and affection for those on the margins of society were reignited when he befriended Eureka Springs's only Black resident, a man named Richard Kenneth Banks. Frank's friendship with Banks would enable him to blend his cinematic and poetic ambitions by exploring Banks's status and history. Banks, whose grandfather had been enslaved in Missouri, had about four years of schooling and was considered by locals to be functionally illiterate. But the man loved telling stories and was at ease with and welcomed by the area's "alternative world people." "When Main Street Bar, a local bar, opened," according to local resident Clarke Freeman, "he was a regular—he talked to everyone."[132] He was also a fixture at the Hi-Hat, where he perpetually hung out by the cigarette machine and jukebox.[133] Basically he could be found wherever alcohol was served. Crescent Dragonwagon remembered him as a "benevolent drunk."[134] On several occasions, Freeman agreed to drive a drunk Richard home in Richard's crumbling Model A Ford. "He was simple and straightforward," Freeman said, and he liked to drink, qualities Frank could appreciate in a man.[135]

Frank never came to know Banks as well as he did Sherman Morgan, Claude Ricks, and Jimbo Reynolds, his Fayetteville friends. But he and Richard were close. For two years they shared a love of fishing, drinking, and storytelling.[136] Banks, born in 1915, had endured a legacy marked by the harshest racism. He was one of only a few Black people living in Carroll County and the only one in Eureka Springs, where locals jocularly called him "Nigger Richard," a name he eventually accepted and used to introduce himself.[137] Stanford called him "the only Black man in seven counties."[138] How Banks came to that status reflected the white supremacy and violent enforcement of it that Frank addresses in *The Battlefield*, which he was still writing. Richard's family—the Fanchers ("the Black Fanchers," as opposed to the white ones who had enslaved them)—was forced to leave Harrison, Arkansas, in two waves (1905 and 1909). They did so when the town, which had long peacefully harbored a Black population, became unnerved by the sudden influx of Black male railroad workers in the early 1900s and decided to make Harrison a "sunset town," a place where if Blacks were not out by sunset, they could expect to be lynched.

Richard Banks worked for the Freemans, a long-established white family in Eureka Springs, first as a grocery clerk and then, for decades, as a maintenance man at the Joy Motel, which the family owned and operated. There, among other tasks, he dug the foundation for a large pool,

Richard Kenneth Banks outside of Frank's theater in Eureka Springs, 1973. *Photo courtesy of Ginny Crouch Stanford.*

zoned as a public pool, that he was not allowed to swim in.[139] He lived for a time in a part of town long known as "Niggertown"—a name reflecting the Black people who came to Eureka Springs in 1913 after being chased out of Harrison—before moving to a house on the edge of town, where he lived alone. According to Frank's second wife, Ginny Stanford, Richard was "the object of persecution by many locals."[140] Some bars, according to a *Eureka Springs Independent* reporter, would only serve him outside.[141] Banks had to sit in the balcony when he went to the movies (Frank's theater being an exception—and not just because it lacked a balcony).[142]

Stanford and Banks became close enough in the two years they knew each other for Frank to base one of *The Battlefield*'s most intriguing and critical characters—Sylvester Martingale, also known as the Black Angel—on him. He also included Banks in the film he would start to focus on in the summer of 1973 with Irv Broughton called *It Wasn't a Dream: It Was a Flood*.[143] Stanford treats *The Battlefield*'s Sylvester with qualities and scenarios that both confirm and dramatize Banks's actual situation. While Banks was known in town as "Nigger Richard,"[144] Sylvester is, similarly, "the town nigger" in *The Battlefield* (2721). Stanford makes Sylvester the victim of *The Battlefield*'s most egregious case of Jim Crow–era violence. Although the event is never described, he's lynched after being falsely accused of raping a white woman. Sylvester's murderers are deemed by Francis to be "shiftless trash" (2723). Francis the crusader is enraged, recalling how "he was a friend we used to see how far / we could spit" (2729–30). Sylvester was "a dicty cat from way on back" (2783). His unjust death—"he was only a peanut farmer" (2735)—becomes the driving motivation behind Francis's dogged quest for racial redemption in Mississippi. It is important to note, if only to reiterate how close this poem hews to Frank's contemporary experiences, that *The Battlefield*'s driving premise—avenging the death of Sylvester—could not have made it into the poem until after Frank met Richard Banks in the late winter of 1973.

The relationship between Sylvester and Francis is fantastically entertaining, and their conversations constitute some of the poem's finer moments. They base their friendship on playful banter that relies on verbal digs and hijinks. Stanford skillfully pits Francis and his formal book learning against Sylvester and his homegrown wisdom, the sources for that being, as Sylvester proudly claims, "motherwit the bible and the Memphis newspaper I know it all he said" (3640). As far as Sylvester is concerned, book learning dulls the brain. He razzes Francis by calling him "a pen pusher and a book reader" (3867). The man and the boy compete good-naturedly over questions such as who has witnessed stranger events:

> I seen a man by hisself praying in a boat one time he said
> I seen a jew cut a hog's throat without hitting him in the head I said
> I seed a white horse break away from a funeral hearse he said
> I know a cowboy said he seen a ghost ship in the desert
> I seed a blind child dancing behind Mamma's house
>     (4205–9)

The surreal backcountry imagery in this scene seems effortless, showing how Frank's poems thrum with quiet power when the strange (a man alone praying in a boat, a kosher hog slaughter, a horse breaking from a hearse, a blind boy wandering in a backyard) comes to feel normal.

Sylvester and Francis routinely engage in verbal one-upmanship and demonstrate grudging respect for each other's descriptive skills:

> I feel like a spotlighted deer and the world is a pickup full of toothless hunters
> got a nice ring to it he said
> let's see he said this here world is a relief ditch of shit where you don't know
> whether to sink or swim
> that's a old one I said
> yeah but it still works
> just like that old time religion huh
> kind of like he said
>     (3991–98)

The excerpt suggests Frank's return to rural vernacular through his relationship with Richard, rooting that vernacular here in the spiritual rhythms of the church rather than the banter of the barroom.

But it's ultimately a tense but comical misunderstanding over the word "guerilla"—brought up in the context of an eponymous "Mexican border war"—that best exemplifies the talk between Francis and Sylvester, their friendship, and their differing educations. When Francis says the word, Sylvester hears "gorilla." This homophonic confusion—"them bombs ought to be killing them guerillas I said . . . ain't no goddam bumb gone kill no gorilla he said" (3572, 3593)—leads to a jesting insult fest between Francis and Sylvester. Eventually their debate boils down to that classic childhood tête-à-tête:

> I know a hell of a lot mo than you do
> no you don't
> yes I do
> prove it then I said
>     (3881–84)

Proof, Sylvester insists, is to be found on the big screen. He tells Francis that "I don't want no sass" and that, to prove his point, he is taking Francis "this Saturday night to the pitcha show" (3885–86).

> why I said
> so I can prove something prove it to you I mean something I been talking
>     about
> who going to be there
> never you mind you just wait and see
> what picture show I said
> the one over in the next county
> outside inside or in a tent I said
> tent he said
> what do you think you can prove I said
> don't think I can prove nothing I know I can
> what I said
> I'm gone prove about them gorillas and bumbs
> oh you are huh
> yea I is and I'm gone make sho you see it again
> see what again
> the pitchu pitchu boy you done seen it once already I know I's sitting
>     next to you see how short yo memory is
> what I'm gone see in the picture this time I didn't see the first time
> you gone see the truth and that I'm right
> when are you going to prove it
> when the lights go out
> what are we going to see anyway I said
> Kang Kong he said
>     (3887–909)

What's happening here is a subtle paean to the power of film. Francis insists that there is no such thing in real life as a guerilla that can survive an accurate bomb attack. Sylvester insists that—as he learned from the 1933 film *King Kong*—of course a gorilla can survive a bomb attack, and to prove it, he will take Francis to the movies. "[W]hen the lights go out"—putting them in the dark—"the truth" will be illuminated when King Kong wreaks havoc. Frank tips his hand in this scene, insisting that Sylvester is right because what happens in film is every bit as real as what happens in the newspaper, and accordingly, he gives Sylvester the last word on the matter: Film, in its projection of an alternate reality, can be more poetically true than the reality we experience. It was through his relationship with Richard, and Francis's relationship with Sylvester, that Frank was able to merge in his mind and work film, life, and literature.

## "The Dusty Book of Blake"

If Richard Banks as Sylvester represented Frank's blending of reality and fiction, turning to Cocteau and the Danish filmmaker Carl Theodor Dreyer allowed Frank to think about that relationship in more explicitly cinematic terms. These filmmakers helped Frank honor the deepest potential of filmic expression. Dreyer was an artist who, Frank explained, "says B+W is more realistic, where the abstractions lie in color." He went on to note how "Cocteau said, when dealing with mystery it's always best to use real cards, and, for me, reality has always been, and continues to be, the most mysterious of things."[145] Frank elaborated: "I believe that the metaphorical imagination can be authenticated by the cinema."[146] As his thoughts became more explicitly cinema based, he wrote to Dugan, "If Carl Dreyer were alive to listen to my ramblings! If Jean Cocteau could hear me now!"[147] It is with these filmmakers in mind that Stanford directed Sylvester to find the right answer to the dilemma he experiences at the movies through King Kong.

This form of authentication—through translation from one medium to another—began to powerfully command Stanford's attention in 1973. It did not require much of a leap for him to travel from life to poetry, poetry to film, film back to poetry, and then poetry back to life. His language began to center on metamorphoses of various media. "Cinema is my form," he wrote Irv, "it is my drawing."[148] In *The Battlefield*, Stanford explores his own past through Francis Gildart, an alter ego who exists in a fictionalized world every bit as real to Frank as his own personal history. Similarly, Sylvester, based on the real Richard Banks, draws out the truth about guerillas and war by taking Francis to a "pitcha show" shown in a tent at a levee camp, a world that is likewise displaced from conventional reality but also more "real" than the one where Sylvester and Francis, and perhaps Richard and Frank, argue their points. Frank hinted at this fluid form of translation and transposition in a letter to Dugan: "Sometimes I think all my songs [poems] are sketches that [need?] to be resolved in cinematic drawings. Shelley! Didn't Blake, in his *Poetical Sketches*, and later on, think in terms of his illustration, printing, with his *Songs of I. + E.*? ... Rossetti said his best poems were paintings, his best paintings, poems."[149]

William Blake, who merged poems and illustrations, was in Frank's immediate thoughts after his three-week-long film binge in New York. He wrote a letter to Richard Eberhart noting that "One day, I hope to make films side by side with my poems, as Blake drew and engraved. However, at the moment, paper is cheaper."[150] As Frank was riding the bus home from Washington, DC, in September 1972, he had scrawled a note to Bill Willett on a page torn out of *William Blake's Illustrations to the Grave*. It read, in part, "Death has always been my mistress." When Willett went to see Frank at the New Orleans Hotel a few months later, Frank gave Willett his copy of the book and told him to insert the torn page back into the book and keep it.[151] And then, as if to tie waking reality and poetry into a knot, he added a line to *The Battlefield*: "Billy opened the dusty book of Blake" (14327).

Blake's conflation of poetry and illustration modeled the way that Frank wanted to integrate film and poetry. In a letter to Irv, Frank wrote, "I confess in my youth, I was writing poetry, thinking of films, which isn't too unlike Blake—his illustrations and printing."[152] To George Garrett, Frank noted having composed failed "poetical sketches" that "need to be resolved in film."[153] If he were to do a Broughton-like interview with Dugan, Frank suggested he'd go about it in an entirely Stanfordian manner. "I would film you strange as you are in your poems," he explained to Dugan. Rather than having Dugan reflect and pontificate on his poems from an academic distance, as Irv often had writers do, Frank would "translate" Dugan's poems into a series of filmed images. He then listed the Cocteau-like scenes that he would choose for depicting Dugan's poetry: "Child with an amulet and a tattoo, eating shrimp. A mirror that comes to your waist. A country girl I fucked in the back of her daddy's truck. My saddle-sore ass. Phoenix with lips. The bottom of the glass. The hypnotist who can transmute words into acts." Imagining these scenes to match Dugan's poems led Frank to wonder: "Is there such a thing as a syntax of images . . . instead of a story accompanied by words?"[154]

Frank began to see that there was indeed a syntax of images and that he had as much warehouse space for them as he did a syntax of words. With a hundred films coursing through his mind, he started to think in terms of a "documentary of dreams." He appreciated film's translatability into other forms of expression, explaining to Broughton, "Dreyer says the poetry of the cinema is the concern with the human face. This carries on over to Bergman who says film has nothing to do with drama or literature and that it is most like music; others say it was most like sculpture."[155] Either way, he envisioned a cinematic reality that was more conducive to multiple poetic expressions coexisting in the same moment—words as visual image, cinematic projection as literal image, all of it enhanced by sound.

Frank sometimes struggled to articulate for others this desire to mix sound, words, and images. During an interview with Irv, he put on a record of African music, calling it "sort of a precursor to the blues," and explained how "I have written to that piece three different scenes." So far so good. But the challenge came when Frank, with the scenes written, declared that "but I would still like to use the music." That is, while the music inspired the writing, he did not want to lose its aural power once the words were set on the page. Pondering this dilemma, he said, "I don't know what you say to something like that." Pushing himself to say something about it, he went on, "I wish poets were as free in their form here as in some other places with the use of music." Other places such as film. Referencing Rachmaninoff's *Isle of the Dead*, he continued, "That was... a score which delineated all the beginning scenes of a screenplay I wrote ... even to the extent that all the camera shots and editing was prefigured in with the music." When Irv, the filmmaker, asked him, "Isn't that a lot to do at once?" Frank responded, "No, not for me it isn't."[156]

In his essay "With the Approach of the Oak the Axeman Quakes," Frank described the signature scene he wanted to film and score on Lake Dardanelle, outside of Subiaco, for the film he wanted to make with Irv. He envisioned a robed monk rowing a canoe with a draped black child-sized casket lodged in the bow. But this image alone was just the beginning of the fuller effect he wanted to achieve. Film permitted sounds and background dramas to coexist within the dominant mise-en-scène of the floating monk and coffin. "For the sake of rhythm I have the selection of Bach I will be using," he wrote, carefully orchestrating the experience in his head. He also added a signature Stanfordian high/low juxtaposition: Bach would soar in the midst of the sound of "fishermen beyond the point, cussing the moon, listening to country music."[157] This was one concrete way to achieve "the transubstantiation of imagination + reality."[158] A monk in a canoe carrying a child's coffin on a lake while men fished, cursed the moon, and blared country music, all with a background of a Bach concerto: This was pure Frank Stanford. This was the expansion beyond conventional poetry that Frank sought after his immersion in film. It was exactly the kind of lush poetic reality that he could not quite nail to the page with a typewriter alone. Film permitted greater immediacy, depth, and simultaneity. "Each day that goes by my senses is an intrigue," he wrote Dugan.[159] Film slowed the day's passage, leavened words into images, allowed him to experience the results in the flash and hush of a more sensorially rich moment.

Film enabled Frank to push the idea—one so important to him—that those who were quick to call something "surreal" lacked exposure to broader realities. Recall Frank's short story about a blind man who works at a factory making mirrors. Because the editor deemed the story's premise "too surreal," it was rejected, a decision that led Frank to protest that the actual blind person he knew who worked at an actual mirror factory might beg to differ. When asked about the deranged Georgia rednecks in James Dickey's *Deliverance* and whether they seemed to him exaggerated into surrealism, Frank said, "These people do exist" and "I don't think what happened in the story was strange to Dickey."[160] Francis's remark that "I don't know if what I see is what really is or what I don't see is so" evokes his living in several realms: the actual one in which Frank lived with the rest of the world, that of *The Battlefield*, the films within the poem, and the films outside of it, including one that Stanford himself would soon shoot. This blurring of realities was a habit that testified to Frank's self-assessment that "I'm bound to the natural strangeness of reality."[161] Film nurtured that bond.

## "I Can Send You My Bell and Howell..."

Frank's theoretical interest in film reached a point at which he had to make an actual film. He turned his attention to this ambition in a more concerted way after moving to Eureka Springs. Confidence was not the problem. "I can write any kind of dialogue," he told Dugan.[162] He just needed the opportunity. Knowing that "things would be a little easier if the big film companies . . . could patronize the beginner," he was skeptical of achieving anything high profile in the world of film.[163] But then Jim Babij, Frank's friend from the New England adventure, came knocking. "Jim Baby" was now in film school and reported that "UCLA turned out better than expected."[164] Right after their road trip, he had written to Frank about possibly working on a film together. In the letter, he wrote that he regretted that he "didn't get a chance to read your screenplay"—a story about "the young poet in the monastery" that Frank had given him in August during their trip. But he had enormous confidence in Frank, knew of his intimate knowledge of film, and observed that "there seems to be more than ample opportunity for TV & film projects to reach an eventual media outlet."[165] He desperately wanted Frank to come work with him in Los Angeles.

Despite feeling "like I'm bleeding when I don't have a chance at films," Frank seemed indifferent to Babij's proposed opportunities on the West Coast.[166] Babij wrote a follow-up note in December 1972, which he sent to Staten Island, still thinking that Frank was in New York with Cheryl. By February 1973 he had finally tracked down Frank, inquiring of him, "What the fuck are you doing in Eureka Springs[?]" He'd gotten an animated film made at UCLA on Super 8, and it had been well received. Things were moving in the right direction, and he wanted Frank involved. But then he brought up a sensitive topic for Frank Stanford: the necessity of making artistic compromises to reach larger audiences. "Puzzles the shit out of me what turns them on," Babij wrote. Still, he was playing the Hollywood game and going as far as he could "without compromising my creative thrust."[167]

The implication of this balancing act was not lost on Frank. As Babij put it, "The problem is that the audience reacts best, especially in shorter films—to two dimension images—simple-gripping-dynamic-movements & compositions." By contrast, they responded poorly to "the introduction of subtleties in terms of lighting, perspective, and depth of field." This appeal to what an audience wanted, as opposed to what the artist wanted, turned Frank off and explains why he was cool to Babij's offer. It was a logic he would never follow and would often mock. Nonetheless, Babij's solicitation of Frank continued—he wanted to lure him to film school, buttering him up as "a student of the cinema." Frank, who believed with Byron that "[i]f Commerce fills the purse, she clogs the brain," quietly resisted.[168]

But Babij kept at it, telling Frank that he wanted to make a "short ten-minute film in B&W based on your '*Singing Knives*' pamphlet," specifically adapting the book's title poem. He assured Frank that "it's not going to be a direct extraction, but an attempt at synthesizing the images you created, which are especially cinematic, in a short drama sequence." For a poet who had long fantasized about his poems becoming films, this was potentially very exciting. In Babij's screenplay, the plot was reduced to two boys, white and Black, who go on escapades, get in trouble, and find resolution. Babij planned to start making the film in March of 1973. "If you have any objections to my doing the film," he wrote, "I'll stop." Frank, obviously curious, never asked him to stop, and Babij, highly prolific in his own way, proceeded with the script. "I've been totally fucking involved with this project," he said of the *Singing Knives*–inspired film a few months later. "It will run about 7–10 minutes (all I can afford) & will be a drama in that there is a storyline—tying together images from your work. I'm just reluctant to use your title, mainly because I don't think the workmanship & impact is up to the quality of your work."[169]

Then the other shoe dropped. Babij wrote, a little defensively, "I had to create an environment where there was a tension, carried through to a catharsis, and the inevitable denouement & resolution." A three-act boilerplate structure, in other words. He conceded that "the situation that developed proved to be quite different from the one you related," admitting, "I confess that the realization that this difference existed threw me into *some* turmoil—but I eventually decided to shoot the film as I had written it."[170] This admission from Babij only confirmed Frank's sense that art could not thrive when the goal was to appeal to anything other than art.

Babij knew his film did not come close to honoring Frank's book. "This is a fuck of a lot to try and get across in only 10 minutes & I'm not sure I've accomplished it," he told Frank. In the end, he wrote, "I'm just disappointed in my work." Still, he continued to peptalk Frank, asking him to "send some story outlines and/or scripts." He had an upcoming meeting with a Hollywood producer who "might be interested and could possibly get your ideas sold."[171] Frank, whose notebooks during this time are full of dreamy Cocteau-like script outlines,[172] did not follow up with Babij for a year. And when he did, it was with a script for a film that was as aggressively unaccommodating of a Hollywood audience as it could be, if not an implicit message to Babij that his friend's values had been sadly compromised by the pressures of Hollywood.

If Babij and his commercialistic ambitions were a no go for Frank, there was always (and always would be) Irv Broughton. Irv was not only a committed and uncompromising Stanford loyalist, but he was a film professor, a filmmaker, a poet, and a writer. For three years they had known each other, and for three years Irv had been utterly selfless in his support of Frank's pursuits. Broughton was no Bill Willett—that friendship was Frank's deepest and longest running—but he was getting emotionally close to Frank in a way that was more personal than Frank typically allowed. For his part, Frank earned some of their friendship. When Irv came home from their 1972 filming venture flat broke and then slowly fell out with his colleagues before ultimately not being promoted, Frank rushed in with moral support. "Please get out of the dumps, boss," he wrote.[173] "Unlike your teaching associates," he wrote his friend, "I have not lost faith in you." He shared Irv's outrage at his not being appreciated: "Here you are spending your life's time and energy, not to mention your earnings, and they aren't even willing to help you." As ever, Frank could not help out with a loan, but he added, "I am with you in spirit, and will be with you in the small quaking bodies of singed poetry," so there was that. He assured Irv that "in the last hours of the year I'm thinking of you." As a postscript he suggested, "Read Whitman and forgive your enemies, friends, and self."[174] In another pep-talk note he reminded Irv to "keep that body fucking, whatever you do" and "listen to Mahler + read Byron, drool hopelessly over young girls."[175] The advice, if not altogether sound, was at least well intentioned.

Irv was grateful. "I think am coming out of the morass—thanks to you, and others. Your encouragement helped," he wrote to Frank. "You've done a lot for me believe me," he continued, adding that "one person who understands is equal to an army of unbelievers." He insisted that if Frank ever experienced another serious bout of depression, "I would definitely want you here [in Seattle] for what—if anything[—]I could do." As for the moment, he was excited about the Eberhart film but lamented as always that "I am still broke."[176] But he was finalizing some filming plans and wanted Frank involved. He wanted his help on a film he hoped to do on the writer Kay Boyle. He also had a tentative lead on "DH Lawrence's mistress," a woman in whom he saw "a filmic possibility."[177] He was planning to approach the poet Elizabeth Bishop, who was that semester's poet in residence at the University of Washington, about an on-camera interview. This was Irv at his best: a swirl of ideas.

All the while he was prepping for sixteen credit hours of teaching a week in the spring 1973 semester, including night school classes, "which I am too proud to work for, but too broke not to." Moreover, to keep his job at the university, Irv needed to publish something. To that end he asked Frank for "a ghost job." He did not bother equivocating: "If you come up with something I could sign my name for a quick publication."[178] Last, Irv was preparing a set of questions for Frank to answer. Stanford was slated to be included in a book of interviews that Irv, a man of many projects, was doing on American writers and poets. Last, and most notably, he wanted Frank's voice recorded for the film they were about to start making about Frank called *It Wasn't a Dream: It Was a Flood*.[179]

Frank was excited and ready to participate in all of it. "I'm rearing to go," he wrote. He thought the Boyle and Lawrence projects sounded terrific, stressing how he was "willing to do anything." He also suggested that Irv consider projects on "Percy, Welty, and Joan Williams" while he was at it. Frank massaged Irv's ego, assuring him that "all of your work is important and essential" and reiterating how appreciative he was of the support Irv lent him: "Who else would give of themselves as you've done?" As for ghostwriting the article, Frank said yes: "I've got an existing BRILLIANT piece ... !! It's yours. ... I've got enough 'begun' work that'd take most 10 years to finish."[180] He was in high-intensity mode, but it was an upbeat high-intensity mode, one he sustained throughout the winter in Eureka Springs and for much of the rest of 1973.

Wanting to strike while Frank's mood was hot, Irv began preparations for the film *It Wasn't a Dream: It Was a Flood*. He urged Frank to send some tapes back with his answers to Irv's interview questions, as well as more letters—"Between the sound of voice and ink I shall be kept consoled and good." He also reported having bought a Bell & Howell 70DR camera. "No business doing so," he conceded, "no money, but make the waiting fuckers wait even more." He added that "I might ask you to do some shooting" for a film based on the levee camp days, a topic of special interest to both Frank and Irv, who was fixated on Frank's mother's role in the levee camps.[181] Elizabeth Bishop gave Irv a firm no—she "won't be filmed"—but the Welty, Percy, Williams possibilities were still alive. Completing the swirl, Irv added, "How about a screenplay or two for *Mill Mountain Review* Cinema issue."[182] Why not? This exchange was the start of a constant and frenetic two-year working relationship between Frank and Irv, and this was typically how it went: Although short of cash, Irv would spitball a dozen expensive ambitions; Frank would say yes to them all; and every now and then, somehow or other, one or two ideas would stick. And Irv always paid.

Once, when weeks went by without a note from Frank, Irv got nervous, wondering, "Where are you? What are you doing? Do you have a phone?" He needed Frank to record answers to the interview questions he had sent. He also wanted Frank to do some filming in preparation for *It Wasn't a Dream: It Was a Flood*. There was a lot to discuss and plan, and Frank was dragging his feet. Finally, Irv got a response, and it no doubt came because of the offer he had made to Frank in an earlier note: "I can send you my Bell and Howell 70 DR, with some film and x-tra lenses, etc." Irv wanted Frank "to script and shoot" *Dream/Flood*. About the blank film he was going to send Irv added, "I would like to see this used capturing the weirdness you have described in Eureka Springs: the people, the images, etc."[183] This was all music to Frank's ears. Irv added, "You could go out and fire away."[184] With this request the process of making *Dream/Flood*, a film about Frank by Irv with Frank's ongoing input, was underway. Frank the poet was about to become a filmmaker.

A page in Frank's pile of handwritten notes suggests that he got right to the task. It contains Frank's description of many images that would eventually appear in the film: "Poet, blindfolded, pushing plow at night," "moth on window at night, reflection of poet," "montage of beautiful porches." Variations on these images are memorable moments in the final version of *It Wasn't a Dream: It Was a Flood*. Other images did not make it into the film but easily could have: "Richard leaning against Victrola in the woods," "breathing catfish under spring," "snake on alter," and "monks moving up and down stairs."[185] Irv ended his worried letter to Frank with a request: "Write me a letter in which you fixate the world." This was pure Irv. The film that Irv and Frank would make—*It Wasn't a Dream: It Was a Flood*— would indeed fixate on Frank's world, incorporating in *Battlefield*-like fashion Richard Banks, the visual language of Cocteau and Dreyer and Blake, the blues, classical music, the Ozarks, and the monks.

## "He Said He Was a Poet"

Frank's vision for this film was shaped by a woman—a painter—who would become his second wife. Frank and Virginia (Ginny) Crouch met on March 3, 1973, in Neosho, Missouri. Frank had driven up to see a friend from the University of Arkansas named Robert Carter. Ginny had just returned to her parents' weekend house in Neosho after eight months of studying painting in Brussels, where she had pursued her interest in Netherlandish art.[186] During the last week of February 1973 the cinematographer James Szalapski, whom she saw in New York on her way back from Brussels, had invited her to go to New Orleans with him to work on a film project. Because she did not want her parents to know about this trip, Ginny went to her friend Robert Carter's house to use his phone and let Szalapski know when her flight got in. She got there at about 8:00 a.m. While she was drinking a cup of black coffee in Robert's kitchen, Frank walked in.[187]

Ginny recalls their first encounter vividly. Frank came down the long staircase of Robert's farmhouse and "was wearing white painters overalls, a gray sweater and lace up boots with the laces untied."[188] "I remember," she wrote, "that he said Hello. He said it real slow and he nodded. His voice was so low he could have been humming." His eyes that day were "dark and deeply set," his hair "wild and uncombed, wavy, about to curl." His skin was "winter pale . . . like the underside of a barn owl's wing." He introduced himself: "He said his name was Frank. He said he was a poet."[189] Frank once told Irv that "I like to talk to women."[190] On this morning he proved it; he and Ginny talked for over two hours. She was so engaged with what he said that she associated their meeting with a vision of "super novas streaming out of his mouth."[191] And she forgot to call Szalapski. When she finally remembered to call him, she said she was not coming to New Orleans.[192] When she woke up the next morning, she woke up with Frank.[193]

A week later Ginny came to Eureka Springs, where Frank was still living. She later recalled that Frank "was in an upstairs room at the New Orleans Hotel that overlooked Spring Street" and that "his diet was mostly black coffee, Shasta Diet Soda, saltine crackers, and Campbell's soup which he warmed in the can on the radiator."[194] Frank had a fifth of vodka for his alcohol supply. His weight was down to 155 pounds, a low weight for him.[195] This would not do. Although Frank reported that " 'Nigger Richard' wants me to move in with him, take care of him," Frank took this option off the table with Ginny's arrival.[196]

Complicating matters was the fact that Cheryl, despite her decision in the fall of 1972 to stay in New York, was still in the picture. Cheryl enthralled Frank from a distance. In January 1973 he was still writing her sizzling lines such as: "If I could be between your legs," "Drunk, wanting you," and "When will we make love again?" But Frank's former thoughts about living on a farm with Cheryl seemed to diminish after he met Ginny. Once he had wondered to Cheryl what it would be like "if we had a shack and coffee in the morning."[197] He now knew that Ginny, fresh from self-funded study in Europe and the only child of a well-to-do family who owned houses and property throughout Kansas and Missouri, could offer more than a shack and a cup of mud. Ginny's father owned a Ford dealership that sold farm equipment—"big money in farm country," according to Bill Willett. She might have been cash poor when Frank met her, but she came from obvious resources.[198] Frank noticed these things.[199]

Eleven days after they met, Frank and Ginny decided to move in together. As they contemplated where to live, Frank drafted a letter to Sara Gragg, the woman from Mountain Home who may have lent him books when he was a kid, and asked, "Is anyone living in your cabin on the lake in Mtn. Home?"[200] His idea was to live there for free and "try to improve the place." When that plan did not pan out, he turned to Irv for financial help in renting a house. "I've found a cabin way away on the white river I can lease. . . . What I need to get this place is $150, to cover the first and last month's rent," he wrote. Frank noted that this location—just outside Eureka Springs in the town of Busch—would place him far away from the temptations of Eureka Springs bars (in fact they were only a couple of miles away), allow him to "catch and grow my food," and enable him to make money as a fishing guide. "This wouldn't be money down the drain," he assured his friend and publisher about his request, promising to pay it back at ten dollars a month by writing and publishing stories. Frank admitted that "I know you are broke," but he hoped Irv would help him get this cabin "to make an investment in my writing."[201] As always, Irv came through, no questions asked.

That spring, around the close of March of 1973, Frank and Ginny moved in together, but not into the cabin on Spider Creek that Irv subsidized. Instead, Frank kept that place for himself as a writing studio. He and Ginny moved into another cabin about a mile away, located on a compound called the White River Lodge. They rented this small cabin from a man named Eliot Brockman, a civil engineer for whom Frank had done some surveying work. Brockman owned the entire compound of cabins and a larger guesthouse where meals were served to fishing guests. By midsummer Frank and Ginny had upgraded to a two-bedroom house on the lodge's property, at the very end of Country Road 109, in Busch.[202] Frank built bookshelves for the house and, as Ginny recalled, "filled the shelves with books, plants, and ceramic bottles of German wine in bright colors."[203] Frank's time in the eccentric social network of Eureka Springs was drawing to a close. Still, he and Ginny would often go into town to watch movies in Frank's empty theater with a jug of wine and then visit Richard Banks on their way back to their house. Ginny remembers how they would barbeque with Banks and his friends.[204] "It seems as if you have an idyll," Dugan wrote to Frank that summer.[205]

Frank loved life in the cabin on the White River. Ginny picked up work painting the exteriors of houses while Frank, drawing on an old skill, got a job that summer as a part-time fishing guide—"more Keatsian than commercial," he noted—as well as working as the property manager, carpenter, and cook for the resort. Soon he was making more money than he ever had. "I've never made 3.50 an hour before, or $45 a day guiding, so this is the life," he wrote Dugan. "I know what it must feel like to be paid for writing poems, now."[206] The pace of work was relaxed, the lodge he tended generally empty; he loved being near the water, and surveying work was consistent. "You have been on my mind," he told Irv, "as I climb the mtns, search the fields for cornerstones." He was "working outside 10–12 hrs a day," he added, and "[e]arning all this living."[207] There were moments when he felt that Brockman, now his boss, was exploiting him, but there was at least one major novelty to report in the summer of 1973: "I pay the rent."[208]

Frank and Ginny thrived off each other's companionship, and to an extent, Frank found an unprecedented measure of peace in 1973. "I've managed to *finish* several stories, poems, short screenplays," Frank wrote to Irv in June 1973.[209] Ginny later recalled that he spent much of the summer working on poems, possibly *The Battlefield*. He would hand her portions to read and ask for her feedback. She remembered how "he wrote without hesitation" and how "the poem poured out of him in one continuous motion," like Mozart claimed to write "as the sows piss." She especially enjoyed the way "I could hear him mumbling to himself, saying the words as he wrote them."[210] Ginny began to make some drawings (in anticipation of paintings), and she and Frank bonded over their mutual commitment to their respective pursuits in a way that Frank had not been able to do with either Linda or Cheryl. Their situation, and Frank's steady work, was, he told Dugan, "as close as I'll come to a good and tenable situation."[211]

"Neither of us had the habit of sleeping in," Ginny explained. "We practiced our craft in the cabin. . . . Frank wrote mostly in the morning and late at night, but he did not have a strict schedule." Ginny, "at Frank's insistence," began to draw in ink, and Frank started to take an active interest in her work. "He gave me specific direction about what he wanted me to draw," Ginny said. A lot of these drawings were for Frank's chapbooks that were about to go into production with Irv, including *Ladies from Hell* and *Field Talk*. These volumes would come out in 1975. Eventually Frank pushed Ginny to return to painting, suggesting she do a portrait of Richard Banks "sitting next to his window with an oar, looking at the full moon," and one of "a woman asleep at a table with a snake on the table." Initially, Ginny could not get these projects going. "It was difficult to concentrate with Frank around," she said of their first summer together, "especially because I was in love with him."[212]

Frank soon began a habit that would never cease: He put her work ahead of his. He did this tirelessly, even aggressively. "The girl I am living with," he wrote to Irv that summer, "is a good photographer and a great artist. Her drawings are wonderful, and her paintings are coming along. You *must* see how she sees all my characters, images, and so on. Do enquire about her work, possibly of using some of it."[213] To Dugan, he wrote that, of all the things he loved about his move to the White River, "the best of all this" was "the artist I met in a field one day." He went on: "She is very good, and one day I hope both of you [Dugan and his wife] can see her work . . . especially the drawings + paintings she got from me." *Not meet her but see her work.* He explained their integrated working habits, noting how "she reads one of my poems, drinks a bottle of wine, sits by the river, listens to Mahler, and fill[s] up several sketch books before I return, at sundown, from work."[214] The romance of it all was, while it lasted, easy and unaffected.

But Frank was Frank, ever prone to "self-sabotage," as Cheryl put it.[215] While he was settling in with Ginny, he continued, however briefly, to court Cheryl. By the late spring or early summer of 1973, just as he was achieving that "good and tenable" situation with the woman he'd marry a year later, he convinced Cheryl to move to Eureka Springs from New York.

"I carry the sweet and beautiful remembrances of our pasts around like a sailor with an oar *looking* for the sea," he wrote her on May 15, 1973.[216] Cheryl, despite receiving thousands of words from Frank since he had left New York in September 1972, knew it was naïve at best to fully trust him. He had already ditched her twice, in the summer of 1971 and again in late summer 1972. But she took the risk anyway. She left New York City and returned to Arkansas, arriving in Eureka Springs in late May or early June of 1973, ready to see if the third time was a charm.

It wasn't. When she got to town, she found Frank in the Hi-Hat bar extremely drunk and with a woman hanging on his shoulder, an "an older woman known for being an alcoholic."[217] Cheryl dragged Frank, who was slurring and could hardly walk, out of the bar and took him to a restaurant to get some food and let him sober up. When they went back to the room he had booked at the New Orleans Hotel, Cheryl looked at his bed and noticed that it was covered with semen stains. He initiated sex with her, but, wising up to his ways, she turned him down. "He was shocked," she said. Less than two days later Cheryl left for Little Rock, where she got a job in a machine shop "making buckets for backhoes," never to see or speak to Frank Stanford again.[218]

Ginny, who may have been visiting her parents in Missouri during this episode, presumably knew nothing of the affair. She instead remembers an idyllic summer of art, music, friends, and food. The couple sometimes made the three-hour drive to Tulsa to visit bookstores and record shops. "Frank liked to shop," she recalled, especially for shirts.[219] On another road trip, this one to Missouri, the couple went looking for Langston Hughes's house in Joplin.[220] "We often listened to music," Ginny said, "mostly from Frank's extensive collection of classical, blues, and jazz." The soundtrack that summer included *The Best of Eddie Harris*, eighteenth-century Italian baroque music, Purcell's "Come Ye Sons of Art," Vivaldi's *The Four Seasons*, and a lot of John Lee Hooker.[221] Reflecting on the summer of 1973, Frank wrote, "We had some high times. . . . We'd stick the Cold Duck or cheap wine in the minnow cooler, and take off down the water, she with her sketch book and I with my marshmellows for bait. . . . No stink, just lick your finger after you bait your hook."[222]

Frank's diet progressed beyond saltines and canned soup, and for a brief period after he met Ginny, he quit drinking. The couple made occasional visits to Missouri to see Ginny's parents, who always sent them home stocked with homemade meals. Frank also began to cook. He made eggs and bacon for breakfast, barbecued chicken on the outdoor spits at the lodge, and baked cornbread and sourdough bread. When working

Ginny Crouch Stanford, ca. 1974. *Photo courtesy of Ginny Crouch Stanford.*

for Brockman at the lodge, he prepared meals for the White River Lodge patrons whom he took on fishing tours. Frank was quickly known for his signature hush puppies, which were, according to Ginny, "a hit with Brockman and the guests." Ginny remembers how he was always experimenting in the kitchen, once hitting the jackpot by adding tart cherries to the cornbread mix. The couple frequently had Richard Banks over for fried fish and, making an exception to Frank's momentary teetotaling, Jax Beer, Richard's favorite. Over time those exceptions became the norm. By summer Frank was regularly heading back into Eureka Springs, about twice a week, to drink at the Hi-Hat bar and, as Ginny recalls, "to hang out with old men and some of the real characters that frequented the bar."[223] But the drinking, unlike when he was with Linda, was moderate; it never sent Ginny running home to her parents. Describing his alcohol habits during these days to the poet David Walker, Frank wrote, "I quit whiskey, but I made friends with wine."[224] It seemed a reasonable compromise.

The Busch cabin, and much of life in the summer of 1973, was ideal until it got cold. The cabins that Brockman owned were unwinterized and lacked woodstoves. So, in October, Frank and Ginny moved about forty miles away to a modest farmhouse—at what is now 8475 Twin Coves Road—on the eastern edge of Rogers, Arkansas, with glimpses of Beaver Lake across the street. The location was rural, the property ample (four acres), the rent cheap (seventy-five to eighty dollars per month). The house was heated with either propane or a wood-burning furnace.[225] To Dugan, Frank called the place "a farmhouse in good condition a little closer to the lake than you are to the sea, but with not as good a view, but with plenty of wind, hawks, deer."[226] To David Walker, he called it "a farm with no animals on a big lake."[227] In a scrap of poetry left in his miscellaneous notes Frank wrote:

> The first thing a poet does is to make sure there is
> Always enough water around him
> and some dirt too.[228]

The Rogers house fit the bill.

Ginny and Frank had every reason to be excited about their new place, where they would live in a semblance of domestic stability for nearly three years. They wanted cats and a vegetable garden. The former happened right after they moved in. Ginny went to see her parents in Neosho, Missouri, one weekend and, "on the spur of the moment," adopted a tiger cat from the Joplin Humane Society. That same weekend, Frank went to the Rogers Humane Society, where he adopted a black cat. When Ginny got home, Frank ran out, and they said to each other, "Guess what I have?!" Frank named the cats Arletty and Deburau, the lead actress and lead character, respectively, in "one of Frank's favorite films," Marcel Carné's *Children of Paradise*.[229] Although the couple lived in a remote area with little traffic, Ginny worried endlessly about the cats getting run over.[230] But that was about the biggest of her concerns. "We had," Ginny wrote, recalling these times, "a good life for a while."[231]

## "It Was a Flood"

Although consumed with Ginny's art, Frank kept his promise to Irv about their film. Frank suggested that, rather than send the precious and un-paid-for Bell & Howell through the mail, Irv bring it to Arkansas in person. "You must come and visit," Frank wrote in June of 1973. He wanted Irv to meet Ginny, who would be directly involved in making the film. "I'll take you on the River at night in a canoe; drinking with hillbillies and negroes; fishing, and so on," Frank promised him.[232] Such talk thrilled Irv, who entertained a voyeuristic fascination with the more gothic aspects of the American South. Irv drove from Seattle to Arkansas, and he and Frank spent a lot of time on the White River during that trip, mostly writing poems. Irv warmly recalls a "feeling of camaraderie" between them and remembers how high Frank's spirits were that summer. "You want to think of him as dour, serious, but he could be raucously funny . . . sitting there drinking wine, reciting this and that."[233]

When it came to the South, Irv liked the stereotypical more than the typical. Frank could give him that. "Irv Broughton visited us around September," Ginny recalled, "and we went on the trip south to film footage for It Wasn't a Dream, It Was a Flood."[234] Irv later noted that his plan to do this film had begun the year before when he and Frank were traveling in Maine and Irv had filmed Frank sleeping in Eberhart's boathouse and on the road pumping gas. At the time, Frank had been furious about being filmed, but, as Irv recalled it, "A year later I showed him the footage, and he got excited. Somehow that sold him."[235] Frank liked how he looked on film.

The *Dream/Flood* film was a compromise. Frank and Irv had talked more seriously about doing a more standard documentary film on the levee camps and the Stanford family's role in building the Snow Lake levees in the 1950s. Irv's interest in Frank's levee camp experience, largely because of the interracial aspect of it, was especially intense, so much so that he would later publish a novel based on it called *The Levees that Break in My Heart*. But when Irv and Frank contemplated the logistics of this undertaking, they realized that the film would require scores of interviews, site visits, and extensive archival research. "We'd really be spinning our wheels," Frank later recalled in a letter to Irv, surely with finances in mind.[236] More important, not only would the project have been too resource intensive, but it also was not the sort of film that Irv and Frank could have made with Irv's camera, which did not have a sound recorder built into it.[237]

*Dream/Flood*, by contrast, not only was cheaper to make, but also could be made with "wild sound"—that is, with the soundtrack added separately. *Dream/Flood* could also be shot locally, near where Frank and Ginny lived, in Rogers and Eureka Springs; at Subiaco when they visited for camps; and regionally when he and Ginny traveled to Missouri. "It was a terribly ambitious film," Irv recalled about *Dream/Flood*, but it demanded nothing near what the levee camp film would have. "Whatever values and flaws

[*Dream/Flood*] had, it was certainly ambitious," Irv said, particularly in its "variety of directions."[238] Whether Irv knew it or not, it was also ambitious in a way that plumbed Frank's deepest aesthetic ambitions. His affection for Cocteau-like imagism interspersed with wild sound are evident throughout the final film.

When Irv returned to Washington to teach his fall classes, he left his camera, as promised, with Frank. By early 1974 Frank had shot scenes of Richard Banks in Eureka Springs, some monastery shots at Subiaco, some shots at Sherman's Tavern, and, although it is unclear where, shots of Joan Williams. Ginny remained constantly involved, doing all of the still photography for the film. Frank did not have much experience with any of this work, but Irv was thrilled with the initial results. He immediately began the back-and-forth process of sending Frank more tape and directing scenes via letters from Washington State. "The footage you shot is good—good beyond experience—and fine in any league," Irv wrote.[239]

After sending Frank more blank film, Irv urged him to double down on shooting and recording more of Richard Banks and a character named Sho-Nuff. Irv had his own vision of what he wanted from the film, and, somewhat aggressively, he continued to direct from a distance, sometimes pushing Frank into territory he resisted. Irv pleaded for raucous scenes of Black men telling stories of the kind that Frank sometimes captured in his poems or scenes of "old men, on benches, who hear stories coming to their stoic ears from elsewhere."[240] He wanted sound recordings of the "guys at Sherman's—talking about getting a loan," "about a whorehouse being there at one time," and of Richard Banks hosting a party, philosophizing, and serving a meal of raccoon. He wanted the poet's exotic underworld visualized. "Shoot some of Richard getting haircut," he added.

What he got from Frank may not have been exactly what he had requested, but it certainly scratched Irv's itch for backcountry exoticism. There was no raccoon skinning (but there was a hog slaughter), no Richard philosophizing, no Richard talking about Frank the poet, and no Richard in the woods with a Victrola. Instead, after passing beer after beer to Richard and two friends, Frank had handed the camera to a friend of Richard's, who had then filmed a slurring and wildly inebriated Richard Banks in a dark room with a flashing light, howling and laughing hysterically, hauntedly, and mumbling a blue streak that ends with "Hey, Frank."[241] It's unforgettable. This sound/image overlay, featured at the start and end of the film, was rough in a way that Irv could never have dreamed. As for further footage ideas, Irv suggested that Frank "shoot some lonely men on boxes and benches!—preferably

Richard Banks on set during the filming of *It Wasn't a Dream: It Was a Flood*, 1974. *Photo courtesy of Irv Broughton.*

singular men." In another note he added, "Need footage of lonesome old men near gen'l stores."[242] He wanted porch shots and music suggestions from Frank. "Record music for your film," he demanded. The directions, rapid fire as they came, exuded excitement for what was gradually coming together very well.[243]

Frank sent Irv eight more rolls of film by the spring of 1974. Again, Irv liked them. But this time his response was more critical and impatient in tone. "Please accept some suggestions," he wrote. When Frank filmed both Richard and the Sherman gang, they were all talking. Irv censured Frank about all these moving mouths without sound: "Try to separate functions of sound recording and filming," he wrote, as if teaching a film class. "Lip flap is a problem." Then he made some specific requests: "We need more close-ups. . . . The porch looks good and I maybe told you to shoot them at a distance (or it was dangerous to get closer?), but I think we need some intimate objects of porches. . . . How about tight shots of hammocks, swinging chairs, rockers, the bits and pieces of porches." In a postcard, he directed Frank, "Film the MILL for Mill Mountain," and in another note he requested, "Shoot the chandelier with toothbrushes."[244] Both of the resulting scenes are among the film's most visually arresting.

Irv wanted to exoticize Frank as the tortured southern writer. "I would also like you to shoot yourself writing a poem," Irv directed. "I would like an over the shoulder shot (you can be hunched over if necessary) and it should be close so we can jump cut from beginning to middle or completed poem." He urged Frank to "write several this way" as it was "perhaps suggestive of how rapidly, intuitively you are able to write." He added, "Write legibly if possible." And, as for filming, "Maybe Ginny can help you."[245] He also asked Frank to recite something along the lines of "I grew up in the levee camps in Mississippi" and then to "lead into a discussion of the people in the birthday picture," referring to the picture of Frank's fifth birthday at the levee camp. Irv was especially obsessed with capturing more scenes of Richard Banks. He suggested shots of "Richard going into a bar, visiting in town, or some of locals talking about him." It would be ideal, Irv said, if Frank could get footage of "Richard cleaning raccoons," noting that Frank should tell him not to talk (avoiding "lip flap") but "get him to smile, and clown" and then turn on the audio tape and "ask him to tell you about skinning coons." Irv wanted audio of "Richard predicting the weather," talking about what "dying unnoticed would be like," and "what it is like to be the only black man in the county." Frank, sensing the exploitative nature of these requests, did none of this.[246]

If Frank did not accommodate Irv's specific suggestions, Irv did not always agree with Frank's cinematographic choices. "I liked the plowing, but you might shoot the plow digging the earth, and you [sic] face straining in CU [close-up] as you push the plow," Irv wrote. He conceded that "maybe you have just the long shot in mind which is great but I worry if it is recognizable what you are doing." Frank blew Irv's suggestions off; there would be no shots of his straining face, and the only close-up of a porch was a posed photo in the finished film of Frank relaxing on one, taken by Ginny. He left the long plowing shot as it was, with him blurred and far in the distance; and while he had Ginny film him sitting at his desk in Rogers, it was not while he was writing but rather while he was staring out the window. The effect in every case is not only visually satisfying but also a Stanfordian tamping down of Irv's overdramatizing of the southern poet.

By the spring of 1974, the *Dream/Flood* footage, by no means complete, was ready enough for Irv to start editing. The rapidity with which Frank worked to get the bulk of the footage shot was remarkable and a reminder that when he was creatively inspired, he could produce with diligence and discipline. "The music is beautiful," Irv wrote to Frank, who had chosen Leadbelly's "Whoa, Back, Buck," James Brown's "Get on the Good Foot," W. D. "Bama" Stewart's vocally profound "Levee Camp Holler," and a Bach oratorio, *St. Matthew Passion*. Irv, for his part, was even more broke than before, getting cash advances on his gas card. "He was absolutely bleeding me," he later said of Frank and his film.[247] But at the time all he cared about was the art they were making together: "It will be a beautiful film," he wrote, "and I am excited about it."[248]

## "I Love Reading Your Poems, I Really Do"

Frank was a successful multitasker, a skill that peaked in 1973 and 1974. In addition to updating and revising *The Battlefield*, working several jobs, and making a movie, he continued to submit poems to journals throughout the year. This effort, too, was charmed in the way that these years were generally charmed. He scored repeatedly with the *Boston Phoenix*, publishing "BLUE YODEL a Prairie" in May of 1973, "The Moon" that August, and "Blue Yodel of poets of times past" that December. In the summer issue of the *New York Quarterly* he published the poem "Death in the Cool Evening." He also sent a bunch of poems to Eleanor Bender at *Open Places*, where he had last published in January 1972. She responded first to what she perceived to be his enviable life-work balance. "Your job as a caretaker and fishing guide sounds marvelous," she wrote, "especially for a writer." She warned him, Dugan-like, to "stay away from the academic institutions" because "they will drain your blood." She added, "I'd like a job as a professional landscape watcher myself." As for his poems, she was clear with Frank that "you are a very talented writer." But she wanted to know "Why are you so uneven?" She decided to hold on to the poems

"Dante Gabriel Rossetti with His Head on the Virginal," "Humming This Song . . . ," and "Blue Yodel of the Wayfaring Stranger" to consider for publication, though they never ran in *Open Places*.[249]

These deeply rural, cinematic, and Ozarkian poems—especially the ones submitted and published in 1973—evoke in various ways Frank's recent experiences of meeting Ginny, touring the river, making a film, working with the monks, absorbing the weirdness of Eureka Springs, and contemplating departure and isolation. "Blue Yodel of the Wayfaring Stranger," which is written "after Paolo Pasolini," opens:

> I lean my head up against the juke box in the mountains
> And think about the three Indian sisters tending bar
> The nighthawks come down to sleep
> On the knives in my shoulders
> As if I was St. Francis barefooted and all
> They come down to cut their own throats in the snow
> Which falls like the dandruff of Jean Cocteau[250]

This poem evokes Pasolini's "The Wealth of Knowing"—possibly the source poem Frank worked with—with the figure of Saint Francis serving as the connecting thread between the poems. "There was already in my soul, born to passion, / Saint Francis *in toto*," writes Pasolini, referring to the mystic Catholic poet who embraced the dignity of poverty. "Being poor was only an accident," Pasolini's speaker notes, but still "there belonged to me / libraires, galleries, tools of every discipline."[251] The lesson that poverty does not deny creative and intellectual wealth (quite the opposite in fact) is similarly evident in Stanford's "Blue Yodel of the Wayfaring Stranger." The poetic wealth in this poem, inspired by Jean Cocteau (and his dandruff!) and the eccentrics in Eureka Springs, is evident when descending nighthawks land "On the knives in my shoulders / As if I was Saint Francis barefooted and all." But there is in this act hidden danger, as one "tool of the discipline"—the poetic discipline—leads to the nighthawks being sliced up by the knives on their saint's shoulders. The avenue of transmission for this dark scene, the muse, is perhaps the jukebox in the Hi-Hat bar:

> I lean my head up against the juke box in the mountains
> And think about the three Indian sisters tending bar[252]

The poem reveals Stanford's new confidence in connecting what once seemed too distant to be connected—in this case the geography of the Ozarks to European, Indigenous American, and medieval traditions.

Another poem Frank published during this time, "Dante Gabriel Rossetti with His Head on the Virginal," is dedicated to Father Wolfgang (Mimms) from Subiaco. The opening reads like a description of one of the monastery scenes from *Dream/Flood*:

> I give you the feeling
>
> That you are in danger
>     of a woman dressed in black
>     Who walks down the hall with a candelabra
>     to burn the suicide notes she reads in braille[253]

The poem in its entirety has a floating quality to it, an atmospheric aura that marks many Cocteau films. "You might be drifting / on a raft with a sleepy Negro" and "There are mountains that float like ashes" are lines that make the woman moving down a dark hall not so much walk as levitate. One thinks of Father Mimms in his black robe moving down a long Subiaco courtyard walkway, echoing the motif of a woman in black, as if both are in mourning. All the pain Frank had caused women seems to flow with her as she proceeds down the hall, with his guilt flowing with the priest to whom the poem is dedicated. Cheryl gets referenced in the poem—written on Eberhart's yacht in August 1972—through her primary instrument: "You lay your head in the carousel / the lap of a friend's wild haired wife / And listen to the French horn." To further connect the suicide notes with Frank's scarred history with abortions, the poem ends with a child "coming from a coffin."[254] Lastly, there is here a Stanfordian play on language, as the woman reading the suicide notes in braille holds a candelabra (presumably lit?), as if to say that there is no escaping the all-consuming power of her knowledge, her ability to translate from the most obscure language and then destroy that translation. Frank's witnessing of that destruction might even be an attempt to reclaim that power.

Shifting and merging cinematic images are especially evident in "Blue Yodel of poets of times past":

> The montage of the spider's pony
> The sagegrass where the prisoners drink
> The canticles of fish that quiver in the schoolgirl's palm
> The book of moonlight and sudden danger[255]

The word "montage" nicely illuminates Frank's growing ability to think poetically and cinematically at once, which is happening vividly in this poem. One can visualize it as a series of shots in a Stanford movie, with minnows wriggling in the hands of a schoolgirl becoming a "canticle," thereby allowing the speaker to merge music and image as in a film. The choice to foreground the sagegrass ahead of the prisoners drinking is also a testament to the way that Frank's poems were choreographing images in space, highlighting as it does the power of a camera to direct attention away from the main act to the usually unnoticed periphery. The yodel to "poets of times past" seems to be Frank's way of noting that, without cinema, a poet could not get away with a phrase such as "book of moonlight," which comes off as literary and cinematic at once and is a phrase his idol Keats could never have summoned.

"Blue Yodel a Prairie" suggests Frank's domestic life with Ginny in Rogers:

> She has a pair of blue jeans and a brassiere on
> Holding the prairie
> With a clothespin in her lips
> Her husband is putting a new coat of lacquer
> On his canoe
> He still wants to kill
> Whoever it is that stole his birddog
> It's been a long time
> Since I smelled new laundry
> The days have gone into the ground
> Like rainwater strangers wipe from their eyes
> When they meet again
> In these drinking places[256]

As in many Stanford poems the tension in this one is just barely submerged. The scene at first seems innocuous in its domestic detail, with the husband working on his canoe and his wife hanging laundry. Their sense of isolation—and perhaps strength in that shared isolation—is reiterated by the beautiful lines "Holding the prairie / With a clothespin in her lips." But longing and loss simmer under the surface. The bird dog that the husband fumed over losing once went on thrilling hunts (one can't help but think of Frank hunting women in Eureka Springs bars). The speaker wants revenge for that loss, that theft, because the tedium of domestic life has driven the days, and his mood, "into the ground." Fresh laundry and rides on the lake are nice but, the speaker suggests, nothing close to the excitement of reconnecting with old lovers in "drinking places," where the thrill is so pure that the only thing that must be wiped from your eyes is rainwater.

Two final general notes about some of the poems that Frank was writing in 1973 and 1974: First, as should be obvious, they continued to hew closely to Frank's experiences in everyday life. Almost self-consciously so. One of the few Stanford poems from this period *not* touching on the contemporary events of 1973 was "Death in the Cool Evening." And, notably, at the bottom of that poem, as published in the *New York Quarterly*, Frank specified a composition year: "1964."[257] The themes of hunting, dreaming, and youthful lust in that poem—themes more relevant to his life in 1964 than 1972 (its acceptance year)—indicate that Frank was once again being meticulously accurate about when a given poem was born and that getting the date right mattered a great deal to him and the timeline of his posterity. It's a quality that reminds us how deeply Frank's biography is imprinted on his poetry and that, for all of his mythologizing, he never tried to throw anyone off that scent.

Second, these shorter poems center on women. This makes perfect sense given that Frank's primary emotional preoccupations (aside from his poetry) for the five years leading up to and including 1973 were with Linda Mencin, Cheryl Campbell, and Ginny Crouch. He treated these women poorly in many ways, and his mistreatment of them created considerable personal distress, an emotion often evident these poems. Bill Willett observed that, when it came to women, "Frank imagined himself the hunter when he may have been the prey."[258] This comment suggests not only that women went after Frank as much as Frank went after women but also that when he caught them, or they caught him, everybody ended up wounded. One might justifiably speculate that the shorter verse Frank was writing around 1973 not only reflected the drama of Frank's mercurial romantic life but also thrived on his immersion in it. As C. D. Wright wrote, "When he was breaking up with one woman to take room with another, his poems slowly moved out."[259] At the risk of overreach, I would say it seems as if Frank's philandering even sought to mirror the episodic and temporal qualities of a movie, removing the viewer from time with the assurance that the pleasures of the suspended moment, such as Frank and Ginny's moment, were not to last.

In the summer of 1973, Frank sent a cache of poems to an editor who would have understood these qualities in Frank's work better than anyone else Frank knew: Michael Cuddihy.[260] Cuddihy edited the journal *Ironwood*, which he had started with his wife, Mary Cuddihy, in 1972. He had founded the journal to create "a haven and support for those poets I most believed in." Frank could not have found a more sympathetic reader than Cuddihy to hit up with submissions. Cuddihy aimed to offer "increased attention to the neglected or forgotten poet, the one who shunned the limelight." The two men were as matched temperamentally as they were mismatched physically—Cuddihy was confined to a wheelchair by polio. But like Frank, he was a college dropout, an autodidact, a proud provincial who believed "you could find almost everything in your own backyard rather than travel to Europe or some recognized cultural center." He was a devotee of Thomas Merton, open to the allure of trances, a Catholic, a lover of "Kayak surrealism" (a reference to the little magazine *Kayak*), wary of "public relations," and a man who favored pure, gut-driven poetry unsullied by "cliques or fashionable disputes."[261] Michael Cuddihy was a level-headed and independent thinker who kowtowed to nobody. In a way, he may have been Frank's most trusted and honest mentor, one whom Frank loved because Cuddihy once told Frank that "I'm harder on you," and a man he wanted to please with his poems. "I only hope I'll be able to come up to your expectations," Frank wrote to him.[262]

Cuddihy well remembered receiving Frank's first shipment of poems in 1973. In a 1990 book on his time as editor of *Ironwood*, Cuddihy wrote, "Stanford sent us fat envelopes with brief notes written in brown ink with an old fashioned pen, possibly a quill. What impressed me was that his first submissions made no mention of publications, just the names and dates of manuscripts from which they were taken. Since some went back to the early sixties, I thought him a much older poet, possibly black, given the amount of rural southern dialect he used."[263]

These poems were, Cuddihy thought, "perhaps [among] the most significant work submitted during this period."[264] His first response to Frank was honest and unequivocal: "You're so good it's maddening." But he was not afraid to let Frank know that "I feel that you blow it many times." On balance, though, Cuddihy was hooked: "Please send more poems, as many and as often as you can."[265]

Michael Cuddihy was critically selective when it came to Frank's work. Whereas Frank had recoiled at criticism early in his publishing career, Cuddihy delivered it in a way Frank respected and accepted. Cuddihy asked questions about word choices, second-guessed specific lines in Frank's submitted work, and always delivered criticism that he had deeply considered. He pondered the poems, sat with them, and never rushed. He wrote to Frank in the fall of 1973, "I'm returning all of these, including 'Nautilus,' except 'Getting to Sleep' and 'Women Singing When Their Husbands are Gone.' I like those two, but want a little more time whether to accept either or both.... I love reading your poems, I really do. So please keep sending them."[266]

When Cuddihy asked about Frank's background in his first letter, Frank responded with a lie he had told before and maybe even believed at this point: that he had been born in 1949. He also wrote: "Thank you for your kind words. . . . I've been writing since 1957. *Esquire, Iowa Review*, and others have published poems I wrote when I was 12. I'm not a monk (although I went to a monastery for schooling after my father died) other than the kind Keats speaks of 'my imagination is a monastery and I am its monk.' . . . Will write as soon as the weather gets bad, get off work."[267] As promised, Frank did.

## "The Sound of a Line"

In many ways, the year 1973 was possibly the happiest and most stable year of Frank Stanford's adult life. "Good and tenable" it was. This was due to a steadier income, a partner with whom he could collaborate on shared artistic ambitions, the chance to pursue directly his passion for film (thanks to Irv), an introduction to a new cast of characters in Eureka Springs, the incorporation of Sylvester the Black Angel (via Richard Banks) into *The Battlefield*, ongoing success with the little magazines and literary journals, and getting to know a poetic soulmate and correspondent, *Ironwood*'s Michael Cuddihy.

Even a rare setback during this year came with a silver lining. Frank had done a substantial amount of carpentry work for the resort owner Eliot Brockman, about $1,500 worth, but Brockman had skipped town without paying him. The solution was to take on more land surveying, which he did "like Thoreau, so I can pull through it."[268] When Frank was in the field, visiting new places, he was always thinking about Ginny and her art. Frank was, Ginny remembers, always "scouting for places for me to show my paintings." One new surveying job took him to Springdale, where he met Bruce and Mary Vaughan. The Vaughans were leading local cultural figures who owned an art venue called Image One Studio and Gallery. Ginny recalls how "Frank made a connection . . . and they began collecting and exhibiting my work," a first for her and the start of her career as a professional painter.[269]

And this was how life was in 1973: a little charmed. Frank and Ginny were a couple. They had a home together that had views of a lake and cost them a modest seventy-five dollars a month. They had room to write and paint. They worked closely and symbiotically with each other. Ginny later recounted their creative life after moving into the propane-heated house in October: "[Frank] wrote in several hour stretches. The sound of his work is a strong memory—the clack of the typewriter alternating with his resonant voice sounding out the poem. He sometimes composed or edited as he walked back and forth by his desk, turning over the sound of a line." He had his tics when writing. "Every now and then," Ginny recalled, "he would abruptly scrub his head with his fingers." She remembers how, at Frank's urging to paint images from Eudora Welty's book of photographs *One Time, One Place*, she began to paint rather than sketch in ink. Successfully. They had their two cats. They drew diagrams of the garden they were about to plant. They ordered seed catalogs. They went outside and yelled into the black sky at night.[270]

Frank Stanford, ca. 1974, Rogers, Arkansas.
*Photo courtesy of Ginny Crouch Stanford.*

ELEVEN

# "The Untold Days of the Poet"

## 1974–1975

IN FEBRUARY 1974,[1] WHILE SETTLING into the Rogers house with Ginny, Frank did something most people don't do until they are much older: The twenty-five-year-old looked backward and summed up his life in a narrative. He did this for David Walker, a Maine poet with whom he had started corresponding in 1971. Walker wanted to know Frank's story, so Frank told it to him. He began with Linda on Mount Sequoyah: "I was living on top of a hill in a log cabin in Fayetteville, Arkansas, keeping strange company ... trying to plow through the bad soil of every genre known to man—and woman, while at the same time trying to make fourteen years of early, Huckleberry Rimbaud mss. readable."

The "strange company" likely included the regulars at Sherman's. The "Rimbaud mss." was "St. Francis and the Wolf." He then touched on his mental decline, which had bottomed out in June 1972 after his "May Day" letters to Dugan and Broughton: "You know, you go down to these strange and ungentle dives and gamble with the creatures and rebuses of your imagination and, by the time you wake up for air, you've lost everything and don't know it, and sometimes no longer know what hand or die or bone you're playing. Whiskey, women, and the bad nights of poetry will always fill your mouth with cold ground: I bit the dust."

Living "nine lives of mystery and real-life madness," he had no choice but to leave "Fayette Nam"—a local nickname for Fayetteville—with "only the clothes on my back." He was self-exiled. "The only safe place to go—after I set fire to my cabin, where nothing burned but all my manuscripts—boyuscripts, that's true, was this monastery, where the brothers were the finest consolation, their vision, wine, and song," he wrote.

He loved the monks and was happy to sojourn there. But there was just one problem with the monastery: "*No poontang.*" Still, the monks "let me share and work and dream with them." Then came the Irv Broughton–Jim Babij road trip: "Got a job with an editor doing films on older poets. Met, filmed, drank, etc. lived, with Eberhart, Ransom, Cowley, Wilbur, and so on. . . . Gained experience with camera and personages."

Realizing that his narrative had skipped the time he had spent at the state hospital, he added in parentheses that "I forgot the part where they put me in the horse pit et al, to dry me out, only Alan Dugan and Cowley and some others found out and called the nuts at the nut house and tole them let me go." He declared: "Here endeth the days of youth. . . ."[2] The transition to adulthood, according to the narrative, happened in New York: "Lived in NYC with some black dancers and some jamaicans. . . . I'd start to work on the cultural side of the city at daybreak and go until about that time the next day. Met alot of people by chance. Really. Everybody I met there, met by chance. Drank and sung in a lot of ethnic bars, hate that word. Saw everything in NYC. Helluvalot of experiences but can't go into them here."

He included his stealth departure from New York with Deidre: "Met rich woman from Scotland associated with museums etc. We rode all over in her M[ercedes] B[enz], leaving the city, until somewhere, I forget, I got on a bus with nobody but blacks, met an old man who had worked for my uncle in Miss., got drunk, rode busses, trains."

He mentioned that during fall 1972, in the monastery at Subiaco after leaving New York, he was "trying not to take advantage of anyone, trying not to rape experience, trying to think more than I feel." He explained, "If I was a pilgrim, I only had a raft and the river was low." In such a manner did he drift into the wonderful year of 1973: "I winded up in the Hotel New Orleans in Eureka Springs, Ark. Then from there to a cabin on spider creek on the river as a fishing guide. From there, a farm with no animals on a big lake, working as a field guide for land surveying, the mountains and hills and topography of my soul."

Which brought him to the present moment:

The poet finds another woman
She is an artist.

Time Passes.
There is rest for the wicked.
My wife love[s] living here . . . old house in timber in fields, with garden.
  Warm Morning wood stove, two cats, making bread for life and living,
  and the untold days of the poet.

It is a remarkable account. For one, it's accurate. For a man who has been incessantly described as a self-mythologizer and liar, Stanford shoots straight in this picaresque overview of his recent past. If anything, the account suggests that the mythical labels placed on him reflect the fact that he may have lived, more than most, something of a mythical life. Some people do. As if to stress this point, he wrote in this same note, "As Jean Cocteau said, I think, the old myths are constantly being reborn without their heroes . . . like lies who always tell the truth." The account is also noteworthy for the way Frank continues to see the people closest to him as abstract characters as much as actual people: Linda is (maybe) part of the "strange company" on Mount Sequoyah—and more likely left out; Irv is "an editor" who gave him a job holding a camera; Cheryl Campbell is omitted; Deidre is a "rich woman from Scotland"; Ginny is "another woman . . . an artist." This depersonalizing tendency at best highlights Frank's independence of spirit. Less flatteringly, it shows his periodic self-absorption and habit of reducing people to functionaries serving his interests.

At the same time, Frank expressed, if only vaguely, a new sense of redemption from the guilt that had plagued him after the spring of 1972. Trying to think more than feel, seeking not to exploit others, he revealed a growing moral and empathetic sensibility. Part of this awareness might have been due to his connection to the monks and his ongoing exposure to their bedrock principles. These values were evident not so much in their words as in their works, which included overt concern for the fate of Frank Stanford's soul. A man might not pray for his own soul, but when an abbey of monks pray for it, he's likely to notice. "I often think of some monk," Frank wrote, "down on his knees in the hogpen, a bucket of slop beside him like a censor for the hungry, praying for me—which they do, because they love me. And I love them." Much as Flannery O'Connor's work was assessed, as Frank told Irv, "by nuns and priests,"[3] so the monks nurtured Frank.

Walker's response to Frank's potent autobiographical sketch was intuitive and on the mark. He wrote, "Your fantastic (weak adj.) saga is matched by few among my friends: truly, Rimbaud-plus in sheer complexity of physical-cum-psychological plummetings, buffetings, rise + falls." But, as he rightly sensed, life seemed to be calming down for the wild poet, easing into a manageable pattern: "Hope you're in for a breathing spell to get self + poems etc. together. Sounds like you may be: sounds like a good interlude or resting-hole, to assemble—meditate over—put forth, your work."[4]

"Work" was the key word in Frank's life for 1974–75. In a way, Frank experienced the normal stress of competing tasks that adulthood brings for a man in his mid-twenties. He became more committed than ever before to his surveying responsibilities. He did so while continuing to write new poems and publish old ones at an impressive rate. "This job of land surveying takes from dawn until dark," he explained, "but it gives us a fair livelihood. And I still manage to write a lot." He was not exaggerating about writing a lot. During these years he juggled finishing *The Battlefield*, ushering four chapbooks (*Ladies from Hell*, *Shade*, *Field Talk*, and *Arkansas Bench Stone*) into publication, writing dozens of short stories, crafting a screenplay about the monks, and finishing the filming for *It Wasn't a Dream: It Was a Flood*. "I can do 18 hours a day," he told Irv.[5] To be sure, doing it all often left him frustrated, drained, and unsure of his future as a poet—again, all expected stresses that come with a creative life. But in terms of sheer output, 1974 especially was an unusually prolific year for Stanford.

In another sense, this life committed to many kinds of work was a breath of fresh air from his once singularly obsessed focus on writing poetry. The multitasking life brought novelties, ones that were stabilizing, sometimes pleasantly so, and maybe even conveniently distracting just when he needed them to be. These moderating influences included the simple pleasures of a domestic life with home and garden and wife (Frank and Ginny married in October 1974), the shared creative rapport he enjoyed with Ginny, a playful and somewhat lower-stakes commitment to writing poems based on translations of foreign poets he loved (French, Italian, Spanish), and a new ambition to overcome his past aversion to commercial exposure by aiming for larger publishing venues for his work.

In his letters, Frank captured during these years rare moments of ease and relaxation: "After walking miles through the mountains, hills, creeks, shores, draws, and fields I like to sit at my desk by the window, watch my dead peach trees trying to come back, smell my hickory curing, listen to the green horses, listen to Frederick Delius, eat tangerines, and sip straight bourbon whiskey."[6] In the end, the balance would not hold. But while it did, for a couple of years with Ginny in Rogers, a rare and soothing stability prevailed.

## "What Damn Good Poems..."

When it came to seeing his work published, the years 1974–75 were again banner ones for Frank. His first publication of 1974 was in, of all places, *Seventeen*. Back in October 1972, hard up for cash to help him move to Eureka Springs, he had sent a submission to the magazine under a pseudonym. It had earned a favorable response from Judy Culbreth, editor of the You the Reader section of the magazine. "I think your poetry is great," she wrote to this fifteen-year-old Francis, not knowing he was actually a twenty-four-year-old widely published poet. Culbreth bought two poems from "Francis Gildart" for the magazine's "unscheduled inventory." She offered the hefty sum of $40 ($275 in today's terms) and, in her acceptance letter, included rights agreement forms. "We'll also need to have your parents sign both copies," she explained, hoping that wouldn't "be a problem for you." Hard to see how it would have been. Frank surely forged those signatures, and one of the poems ran in the January 1974 issue. It contained perhaps the most innocuous lines of poetry Frank ever published. The poem was titled "He Was Talking to Himself about Butterflies," and it ran under the heading "Teen-Work":

> The farm boys have asked all their fathers
> if they can name their lands
> that will be theirs
> One night I was strolling through
> a clearing
> and heard a boy afoot
> coming through the acres of his dreams
> A tiger moth
> lit on the end
> of the straw he was chewing
> and he said "I call this place
> mine and yours"—*Poem by Francis Gildart, 15, Paris, Arkansas*[7]

It's hard not to imagine Frank laughing to himself about this little coup. Culbreth urged Francis to "keep in contact" and to send ideas for book reviews, articles, and In My Opinion columns. Given the high pay, it is likely that the only reason Francis did not keep submitting to *Seventeen* was a reporter at the Paris, Arkansas, newspaper. Benefiting from "the alert eye of a local reader," he reported the news that a local kid had cracked the pages of a national magazine with her poetry. After "a check at Paris High School, Subiaco Academy, and at St. Joseph's School found no Francis Gildart enrolled," the paper suspected they were dealing with a "nom de plume." With the hunt for the real poet on, Frank presumably thought it best to lie low rather than to cash in further on the talents of his teenaged pen name.[8]

But *Seventeen* was hardly alone in wanting to run Frank's work. Frank was putting his shorter poems into the world at a breakneck pace. He had a tendency in 1973 and 1974 to dump a lot of poems on overworked editors and was sometimes chastised for his overly voluminous submissions, even as poems were accepted. A. G. Sobin, after taking "The Unbelievable Nightgown" and "Soaking Wet" for the *Ark River Review*, wrote, "Well, it's taken a year to read through your poems." He apologized for the delay but added, "From now on send in 3-poem batches & we'll give you very quick decisions."[9] Eric Horsting at the *Antioch Review* wrote, "I've had a number of your poems for a number of months now as you are probably aware. You sent so many that it's taken some time more than usual for me to read them."[10]

But for every editor suggesting that he limit submissions, there were others asking for more. At the *American Poetry Review*, Arthur Vogelsang solicited submissions from Frank, noting that "I've seen your work in various magazines the past few years and always admired it." In another note Vogelsang added that "you're certainly an original and strange poet and if one reads the journals and magazines he has the impression that you've just burst on the scene in the last year or two."[11] He promised a "fairly quick decision" and meant it.[12] About a week later (the speed of light for literary magazines) Vogelsang had passed around Frank's poems in the office and was happy to report that "we all liked them quite a lot." He asked for even more poems so they could "have a large selection to choose from."[13] A month later they took "What about This" and "They Really Do" and ran both poems in the March/April 1975 issue of *APR*.[14] Frank's contributor's note read, in part, "Frank Stanford lives in Arkansas, by the banks of a stream. He has been a fishing guide, carpenter, and land surveyor."[15]

Another 1974 publishing accomplishment was with *FIELD: Contemporary Poetry and Poetics*, published out of Oberlin College. Early in the year the editor Stuart Friebert wrote to Frank that "we would love to print LINGER & BROTHERS ON SUNDAY NIGHT." Friebert was overjoyed with Frank's writing: "What damn good poems, original and haunting." Interestingly, he asked Frank to drop the last lines of both poems, and more interestingly, Frank did. Friebert thought the lines in question had "too much of the Homeric simile in them." *FIELD* was a big deal for any young poet. Stanford shared space with the likes of W. S. Merwin, Adrienne Rich, James Wright, Franz Wright, Ted Kooser, Thomas Lux, William Matthews, Bruce Weigl, Charles Simic, and William Stafford. The editors, who also included David Young and Alberta Turner, accepted more of Frank's poems for subsequent issues of *FIELD* as well. But Friebert, too, advised Frank to take it easy on the volume of his submissions: "Please, just 5–8 poems at most, OK?"[16]

The run of success continued throughout 1974. Frank landed older poems in the nation's best little magazines, including the Fall 1974 issue of *Prairie Schooner*, where he published "Sudden Opera," and the Spring 1974 issue of the *Iowa Review*, where he published "Rooms" and "Hidden Water." But in terms of continuity and building relationships with editors, it was *Ironwood* and Michael Cuddihy that continued to matter most to Frank. Cuddihy was the perfect poetic mentor for Frank, and Frank knew it, telling him, "You have a way with reading + helping my poems. I'm glad."[17] He asked Cuddihy in May 1974, "I wonder if we might exchange a few, long letters in the future?"[18] Frank opened up to Cuddihy in a way that was, for Frank, unusually intimate: "You know there are solar systems of ideas and poetry I'd like to wade off and wander in with you in letters and conversation."[19] Through the fulfillment of this desire, nurtured through extended phone calls and exchanged tape recordings, the two men, both outsiders in their own ways, would find solace in each other's lives, art, and voices. "Your voice has a raspy twang, nearly French," Frank wrote to Cuddihy after a phone call. And regarding Frank's voice, Cuddihy wrote, "So many layers in that voice of yours—like a good red burgundy."[20] Literally, these men heard each other.

Cuddihy understood Frank's poetic temperament and knew how and when to push him for better work. Commenting on "Lost Recipe," which ran with four of Frank's other poems in *Ironwood 4* (1974), Cuddihy told Frank, "It's so free, lots of interior space, you never know what is coming next in that poem. It's so full of wisdom, visionary in the best sense." About *The Singing Knives*, Cuddihy wrote, "I'd like to say one thing about your poems as a whole. I love the ones in the book."[21] Cuddihy never complained about Frank's massive submissions but instead responded by writing, "So many good things from you. Just when I'm about to respond, in comes another huge envelope. All that energy!" After Frank sent him a tape of himself reading in his Rogers farmhouse, Cuddihy responded, "I loved it. It was like being there in the room with you; soy sauce, chow mein, the cat walking up onto the recorder, you in your cups reading. It's nice, the way you stroke the words."[22] Nobody had ever written to Frank with this level of empathy for his identity as a poet.

Cuddihy's affirmations opened Frank to accepting critiques in a less defensive way. This was something that Alan Dugan, whom Frank had asked for feedback in 1971, could never quite achieve with Frank. "As good as it is, I'd like to see some changes in the poem," Cuddihy wrote about "Fire Left by Travellers."[23] His suggestions were consistently razor-edged and thoroughly explained. In the past, any meddling with Frank's lines would have sent him packing. But Cuddihy, with his deft touch, helped Frank overcome what his 1972 report from the Arkansas State Hospital identifies as one reason for his depression: "Difficult for him to take criticism—rejections."[24] With Cuddihy, he was buoyed by the sense that "you seem to go to the heart of things."[25] The eventual upshot of Frank's openness to Cuddihy's critiques was a remarkable chapbook that Ironwood Press published in 1978 titled *Crib Death*. It contains some of Frank's strongest poems—including "Death and the Arkansas River," "The Angel of Death," "Fire Left by Travellers," and "Amaranth." *Crib Death* is proof that, as C. D. Wright later said about Frank, "His work has tremendous continuity—from 1959 until 1978. It isn't by any means all great—but it grew as he grew."[26] Cuddihy was central to sustaining that continuity and growth, especially toward the end of Frank's life.

As always, Irv Broughton was still playing the role of Frank Stanford's most dedicated and loyal advocate. Most of the poems that Frank published in 1974 and 1975 came from the four manuscripts that Irv's Mill Mountain Press brought out as books during this period. *Ladies from Hell* came out in early 1975 with a copyright date of 1974.[27] It was the first book of poems Frank had published since *The Singing Knives*. This is the book that, as the name suggests, significantly echoes Frank's "May Day" experiences back in Fayetteville on Mount Sequoyah. It was also possibly one of the three book manuscripts that he lost—in the mail, on Eberhart's boat, in a movie theater in New York. The volume showcases early evidence of Frank and Ginny's creative collaboration. Ginny did the book's nine illustrations. Her ink drawings are of Black and white women, with the most notable one based on Eudora Welty's photo of a Black woman leaning languorously on a porch column, backside out, hands bent at the wrists, one foot pressing onto the other.[28] It was an image that Frank had, as he always did, instructed her to draw.

Feedback on *Ladies from Hell*, all informal, was mixed. David Walker replied that "there is no one poem in it which impresses me as much as a couple in *The Singing Knives*." But he did call it "a more consistent book."[29]

When Frank sent a copy to the poet William Stafford, alongside whom he had recently appeared in *FIELD* 10, Stafford wrote back with benign courtesy, "I am grateful to you and admiring of the book." The poem "Death in the Cool Evening," he claimed, was his favorite.[30] *Ladies from Hell* also includes early examples of Frank's poetic improvisations on the work of Continental writers and filmmakers. "Blue Yodel of the Wayfaring Stranger" was—as we've seen—written "after Pier Paolo Pasolini," while "Twilight" was written "after" César Vallejo, the Peruvian poet.[31] Frank had been interacting with and interpreting these foreign voices since at least 1970, but these two examples of Frank's "after" poems portended what he would pursue more concertedly in 1975.

It is also worth noting the way that Frank merged *Ladies from Hell* with both filmmaking and daily life at the Rogers house on Beaver Lake. In the film *It Wasn't a Dream: It Was a Flood*, Frank reads the poem "Linger" from *Ladies from Hell* in a voice-over in one scene. As he does, the camera scans the house's interior, with papers and books spread out on a table, then cuts to the exterior of the old barn that sits behind the Rogers property.[32] Later in the film, the visual reflects that aural element as Frank walks somewhat stiffly through the same barn, shirtless and drifting through a shaft of sunlight in his boxer shorts, moving not unlike, as the poem's last line reads, "a woman on a raft."[33] In a later letter to his friend Ralph Adamo, Frank, reiterating how film and poetry interacted for him, wrote, "I have finished another book. It is like a B&W movie made by a new director, except it is printed instead of filmed."[34]

Frank likely wrote the poems in *Ladies from Hell* while he was still finishing and revising *The Battlefield*. The most conspicuous crossover theme from the big poem to the chapbook is Stanford's ongoing preoccupation with dreams and dreaming. In January 1974 he described one of his dreams for Dugan, weaving into the description commentary on what the dream told him: "I also dream about Negro musicians and W.C. Fields and aureoles and Giotto. Is life a cryptic, tragic gag, a serio-comic vision. I can see myself by the sea in a white living quarters. I have on clean white pants—except for fish blood, piss stains, and grease—and a blue shirt. I look at boats undulating like bad girls and, when I pick my glass off the table, the pages of my manuscripts fly off like bent cards in beaks. Tough shit. Well, that's life."[35] A few months later, echoing the poet John Berryman, Stanford instructed Dugan to dream "especially about what I saw in the creek the other day: old doors in water, stained glass and all."[36]

Almost a third of the poems in the volume mention some variation of dreaming. The opening line in the book, from "Brothers on Sunday Night," is "We'd been dreaming,"[37] and the last poem in the volume is titled

"Pasture Dream." In between, Stanford reiterates his belief that dreaming is its own reality, its own kind of truth, driving home his notion that surrealism per se can be a creative cop-out, or a failure to look closely enough at reality. From "Linger":

> I dreamed someone's horse
> Had wandered out onto the football field
> To graze
> And I was showing children through a museum[38]

From "Twilight":

> I have dreamed of a mother
> some fresh greens in a newspaper
> and the stars of dawn's trousseau[39]

From "Death in the Cool Evening": "Dreams leave their hind tracks."[40] To Frank, these images were as real as any world he knew while awake. A final thing to observe in *Ladies from Hell* is the clear evidence of Frank's ability to establish potent poetic moments that feel transcendent. "Sudden Opera" opens with lines that can sneak up on a reader and steal some breath away:

> In Arkansas the liquor costs
> The wind lifts a finger
> And that is all[41]

In the poem "If She Lives in the Hills," the speaker, through Stanford's keen consonance of *z*'s, reports:

> I am told how to get there
> By the oozing blaze in the pine[42]

Frank's ability to sketch a Faulknerian novel in a twelve-line poem, like his ongoing attentiveness to women and their troubles, is on full display in "Do Tell":

> everyone says it's like a dream
> is it now
> it was a good year for soybeans and love
> Miss Lucy took her own life on the levee
> with a pistol
> she left everything she had
> to a gigolo from Memphis

in no time at all
he bought a sailboat
and a whorehouse
and no one
is ever heard of since[43]

"His poems talk so easily," poet Thomas Lux, who started corresponding with Frank in 1974, wrote about Stanford. He made this comment after quoting from *Ladies from Hell*.[44]

## "Lessons in Paradise"

Daily life in the Rogers house was anything but hell. It continued to follow a comfortable routine centered around making art, earning enough money to live, and taking occasional road trips. But what anchored Frank and Ginny's domestic life more than anything else was the garden that the couple planted in January of 1974. By early spring of that year—armed with a Henry Field seed catalog and a Shumway seed catalog (both of which Frank kept stashed behind the toilet)—Frank and Ginny had applied not very green thumbs to tending a sixteen-row plot they hoped would soon feed them.[45] This was an ambition Frank had started to entertain when he met Scott Nearing in 1972 and some back-to-the-landers in 1973 in Eureka Springs. His and Ginny's culinary ambitions hinged on "peas, beans, turnips, collards, corn, potatoes, radishes, lettuce, tomatoes, beans (soy), mushrooms, honey dew melons, strawberries, and 12 or fifteen kinds of herbs."[46] Another list includes sixteen separate sections and mentions beets, okra, and Chinese cabbage.[47] Random notes made on scraps and envelopes include reminders to buy fish fertilizer, cut zinnias, pick mint, and so on.[48] A list that Ginny included in a later account noted pattypan squash, Little Marvel peas, Yolo Wonder green peppers, Scarlet Globe radishes, Bloomsdale spinach, and Rutgers tomatoes.[49] They chose well to plant on a patch of ground where a previous tenant had penned hogs and mules.[50] The soil was musty and fertile; hopes were high.

A rough system soon fell into place. Ginny would garden for a couple of hours every morning after Frank left for his surveying job and then would turn to drawing and painting. When he came home, they worked in the garden until sundown.[51] "Maybe I shouldn't spend so much time in the garden," Frank wrote to Michael Cuddihy, "but it is time well spent."[52] Frank admired the flora already blooming on the property, especially the "plums, peaches, and sprouts in our *big* garden," which were "fine to see

Frank tending to the garden, ca. 1974–75.
*Photo courtesy of Ginny Crouch Stanford.*

and smell, their blossoms blowing sometimes like snow."[53] It gave him hope about the quality of the native, precomposted soil, and he looked forward to achieving some of the self-sufficiency he had long dreamed of pursuing.

Frank worried often about the plot they cultivated together: "Hope to hell our garden comes up," he wrote. Weather patterns, which he followed closely because of his surveying work, often concerned him more for the impact on the garden than for his job. "Had a big rain, chill. North and South of us there was considerable flooding." To avoid using chemical poisons, he wrote, "Ginny planted 12 different kinds of herbs to keep the bugs away."[54] Frank battled the possums with Mahler and gospel, which he blasted into the garden from hanging speakers. He had no idea how he was supposed to distract deer—killing them was out of the question for Frank; "I won't kill an animal," he said.[55] But Ginny recalls how he eventually devised a method whereby he "put out rose water for the deer to drink and maple sugar instead of salt licks."[56] Memories of their time together in the Rogers garden stayed with Ginny over the years. "I remember him smiling in the front yard," she wrote, "his teeth white and gleaming."[57]

By late spring of 1974 the botanical news was good. "I'm eating out of the garden every day," Frank eagerly reported to Dugan. "Everything is growing." He especially loved the turnips and strawberries.[58] By July severe heat had wilted and stressed everything standing, the well was low, and to "keep the garden going," Ginny and Frank started taking baths in Beaver Lake to conserve water.[59] Sometimes Frank skipped the ablutions altogether, once going nine days without a wash, a hygienic decision that left him smelling, by his own account, like "sod and olives."[60] No matter how he smelled, the garden was alive. "I just can't get over my strawberries doing so well," he exclaimed.[61]

August brought the dog days. The "critters" were attacking the sprouts, it was over one hundred degrees, and while "we eat everything we can," they were also "putting up for the 7 lean years" (a reference to Genesis 41:30). The "varmints and the sun" were stealing far too much of their food, as far as Frank was concerned. But the garden recovered, and by the spring of 1975 it was once again thriving. Looking back on his first year as a vegetable farmer, Frank was proud that "we raised enough to eat all year." He and Ginny were so upbeat about their improving gardening skills that they planned to double the size of their plot because, as Frank told Dugan, "there are a few people, older, in town who are a little down in the dumps; good food would help their health."[62]

Frank's chapbook *Field Talk*, another Mill Mountain Press production, also came out in 1975, and, not incidentally, the garden theme climbs through it like a vine. The opening poem, "Plowboy," starts with the lines "I came up on death and love / hung up like dogs in my garden" and ends with "I came up on death and love in my garden / lessons in paradise." In the middle of the poem Frank offers a stern directive: "stay out of my greens." The second poem (out of only twenty relatively short poems), titled "Lullaby to a Child Who They Say Will Not Make It through the Night," highlights the garden's vulnerability. The narrator wonders:

> have a one of you seen how long
> it takes to wave so long or lose a crop

In the same poem, the narrator continues:

> I plant my garden under the gradual pressure of the loveliest saddle
> forgetting the undergrowth of sorrow
> I make loops for the worms my darlings

Even his battle with the vermin gets mentioned: "I betroth myself to the tension of the raccoon's approach." In the poem "The River Is Some Time to Kill without Warning," Stanford writes, perhaps ominously, "in my garden there is no more plowing."[63]

The tension between gardener and garden is evident on a larger scale as well in these poems, where there is a continuum of natural imagery ranging from human helplessness under nature's power to absolute human control over the natural world. Occasionally, a fine balance prevails. The poem "Nautilus" opens with "a body comes apart in the bayou / like cardboard." In "Fire Left by Travellers," which also appears in *Crib Death*, the built and unbuilt merge in a murky underwater world:

> briars take over their boots
> which took journeys without walking
> half under water there's a chimney
> driftwood and broken oars and lost lures
> floating in the flue
> the current drawing them up the fireplace like smoke

A calming sense of equanimity comes in the one-line poem "Partner": "some owls leave midnight is close at hand." Dominance over nature comes like a punch at the end in "Fire Left by Travellers":

> before the river rose
> before I walked down these levees
> my father's long graves
> which he raised like a pharaoh[64]

The last line of the poem (and book) nicely sums up Frank's life as a writer: "I had things to say."[65]

## "I Work. I Like It."

The garden in Rogers was a tangible sign of Frank's effort to live a more stable and conventional life. Success in the garden was, unlike in a poem, unequivocally evident in the yields. Those yields helped the couple save considerably on food—they only spent about twenty-five dollars a month on groceries (not including alcohol). But other expenses, while relatively modest, constantly preoccupied Frank, who judiciously handled financial responsibility for the household. Rent was seventy-five dollars a month. Other expenses included a rowboat for twenty-five dollars, a new woodstove, and his own transit for work.[66] There were occasional "petty bourgeois" ambitions, "like getting a pick-up, etc."[67] His "little green bug"—which was worth only forty dollars—pooped out in late 1973, so he bought and made monthly car payments on a Volkswagen 412 station wagon. There were also doctor bills, likely related to Frank's ongoing ulcer troubles.[68]

Work, the kind that paid, was becoming more necessary and rewarding after the move to Rogers. Frank carried into his relationship with Ginny the guilt he had experienced with his first wife, Linda, over not making a living. He remembered how "for so long a time nothing ever weighed on my mind but writing and books, and experiences and people out there, and friends—that was it."[69] As his state hospital psychiatrist reported in 1972, "He then explained that his wife was regularly insisting that he get some type of regular employment and that this embarrassed him." When he was asked what he hoped to be doing in two years, he said, "Writing" but noted that he "would like to have a steady income from his job."[70]

He made excellent progress toward this goal in 1974 and 1975. When asked what weighed on his mind, it was no longer primarily *The Battlefield* but rather "providing for myself, or whoever I was with—that weighed on it a lot."[71] After surveying for three years as an independent contractor, Frank was newly reemployed, starting around late 1974, by Don Kemp's surveying company, where he took on greater responsibility than before. He now carried around business cards and liberally used a stamp with his name and job title. It all looked very official, and all things considered, it was a lot of responsibility. "Earning a living is taking up so much time," he complained.[72] Some of that time went toward learning trigonometry. "I got a *teach myself Trig.* [book] as I need it for my job," he reported to Dugan in the fall of 1974.[73] The growing popularity of the Ozarks among the "developers and out-of-state rich," Frank wrote, made it harder for landowners "to keep track of [their] stones"—cornerstones—thus leading to a surge in demand for surveyors to draw and clarify boundaries before land sales.[74] Frank taught himself how to survey horizontal and vertical curve chords, an advanced skill that meant he could now actively survey rather than do grunt work for a surveying crew or a contractor.[75] He made about $500 a month working for Kemp. He and Ginny managed their finances well enough for Frank to claim, in early 1975, that "things are finally looking up in our pocketbooks."[76]

Frank holding topographical maps, ca. 1975.
*Photo courtesy of Ginny Crouch Stanford.*

The surveying jobs got more interesting as his skills improved. "My only routine is not to become a victim of routine," Frank was now able to say about surveying. "I work. I like it."[77] Rather than dragging a straight line through flat suburban developments, he went into the hills to manage more difficult projects. These ventures often meant that he got to meet eccentric characters along the way. In early January 1974, Frank reported to Dugan that he was working from "dawn to dark" on land that had not been surveyed for over one hundred years. This plot was now being turned into "a new Holy Land. No shit"; there would be a Sea of Galilee and a Noah's ark, evidently as part of a religious theme park. "The rub," Frank explained, "is there is this old hillbilly and wife and company of coon dogs and ducks and rabbits who own a piece right where the trolley car (ski type) is to go over. They won't move." Characteristically, Frank got to know the hillbilly. "The old man really likes me and had promised to tell me where there's a patch of wild strawberries when the season is nigh," he wrote. "He also knows where some happy weed is."[78] The old man, as any *Battlefield* backwoodsman would be, was a Beckett reader. Frank the unlicensed surveyor, ever loyal to the eccentrics, rewarded his new friend for his literary taste and botanical knowledge by "chip[ping] off a few acres from the Holy City" and "giving the land, by rights," to the hillbilly.[79] Backwoods justice.

Occasional odd and entertaining encounters aside, surveying was sometimes dangerous, often physically demanding, and always time-consuming. In the late winter of 1974 Frank wrote, "I'm working in the fields 12 hours a day," adding that he and his team were "working in some rough timber now—a lot of it dead." Rough timber meant not only that Frank had to buy a new chainsaw ("a John Deere, naturally") but also that "when the wind blows, watch out." He and his crew once had to dodge a small forest fire. "There are many woods stories I can tell you," he wrote Dugan, "but I better save them."[80] On another occasion Frank lamented that he had to "take my crew two hundred miles from home, way in the hills, to find old cornerstones." His only solace was the whiskey he'd brought from home, which spared him from "the lightening available in these parts."[81] The job took a full week. The aftereffects of these extended trips were less than pleasant. "The underbrush and the ticks and the snakes can get to you," he wrote to Cuddihy. "Last year Ginny picked 48 [ticks] off me one evening. You can drink a special herb tea to keep them away, but nothing really works all the time. But what I can't stand are the goddamn chiggers."[82] In "Allegory of Death and Night," from the posthumously published volume *You*, Frank writes:

> She turns a flashlight on
> The man's body, looking for seed
> Ticks that have been there since dawn.[83]

As seriously as he took his job as a surveyor, Frank's biggest response to his work was to complain about it. This was the beginning of what would become a chronic frustration with that phenomenon he had spent a great deal of his short adult life fighting: time. Surveying cut into his writing. "I must write!" he practically screamed in a letter to Michael Cuddihy in the summer of 1974.[84] There was no question that his paid work "g[ave] us a fair livelihood" and that Frank could "still manage to write alot," but the hours on the job began to take a toll on his poetry.[85]

The complaints became a constant refrain in his letters: "I wish I had time to write," "This damn summer flew by before I had a chance to loaf a day of it off," "My job is keeping me busy," "I can't drink and stay up all night," "Today ... would be a good day to fish, but I have to do drafting of last week's work (not poetry, maps of the woods & terrain)," and so on.[86] "It is also my desire," he wrote to Cuddihy, "to find time to write over and above earning a living."[87] Cuddihy tried to reassure him: "I can see the problem you have finding time to write during your land surveying job and the hassle of sending out poems and keeping in touch with editors." He urged Frank to remember, "The writing is the important thing. The rest will catch up eventually."[88]

But Frank could not afford to think this way. To his credit, he took the task of earning a living, and living within his means, seriously. The reality was that his job as a surveyor almost always paid the bills for both him and Ginny. Frank was in the novel position of being a legitimate provider. A document typed out by Frank—titled "Essential Expenditures Down to the Bare Minimum We Have to Make Each Month"—shows how seriously he took this task and how close to the bone the couple lived in order for Ginny to paint full-time. The couple's complete monthly expenses included "car payment, lease, surveying transit & equipment, loan from credit union, Montgomery Ward bill, electric, insurance and car maintenance, gas for car, gas for house, phone; postage, painting, still photo supplies; food, booze, medical, cats, garden, emergency." It came to $690 a month. The car payment seemed high at $115 month—compared to $85 a month for the house (up from $75 when they first rented it). Gas for the car was high as well at $50 a month, but this may suggest that Frank paid for his own gas when surveying. Frank's total monthly income from surveying forty-four hours a week was now up to $600, and "income from poetry and painting" was $100. This left about $10 left over every month. So while money was always tight, Frank covered their expenses and avoided unreasonable debt. The couple was getting by, and Frank Stanford was momentarily giving the life of a family man a shot.[89]

Looking over the numbers, Frank said, "I know dough is toilet paper, and when I shit, I like to wipe." On only one occasion during these years did Ginny have to get a job—"hack work for a stupid kind of gallery, plus baby portraits, etc."—and an ashamed Frank hated that she had to do it.[90] It took her away from her painting, and Frank was committed to working enough that Ginny did not have to ignore her art. By March of 1975 he could brag that "I'm doing enough work steady and long to have us six months ahead in payments and bills, which is a miracle for us."[91]

## "I Have to Do More Than Write Poems"

Throughout Frank's adult life, the people who lived closest to him agreed on at least one thing about his writing: The man *cranked it out*. Nothing, including sleep, got in the way. "I'm getting a good 14 hours a day in on things," he wrote to Irv during some downtime from surveying, adding "which is as it should be with me."[92] Even as his surveying schedule got busier, Frank shifted his creative agenda—complicated it immensely, in fact—in a way that involved much more than writing and submitting poems. He did so in response to what felt like an impending repeat of 1972, when he had lost his wife and his mind to an invariable obsession with writing poetry. This time, rather than delving deeper and deeper into a narrowly focused writing routine, he backed up and, in a way, put up some important barriers between himself and the obsessive response that had sent him to the hospital a couple of years earlier. In this respect the complications and challenges of adulthood might be said to have served him well.

When Frank was having a breakdown when he was with Linda in the spring of 1972, he was doing nothing but writing poems, most of his attention centering on *The Battlefield*. Now, a few years later, five distinct creative concerns actively preoccupied Frank. These projects were hard to juggle, but the juggle itself was important; it was what prevented Frank from getting lost in a single task. These goals included: getting the newly revised *Battlefield* manuscript published, taking his work to larger venues, writing and submitting short stories, doing "translations" of Continental poet-filmmakers, and getting the *Dream/Flood* film finished. These were discrete undertakings that most artists might pursue serially over the course of a career. But Frank kept all the plates spinning at once. Some crashed; some spun; some wobbled. But Frank, who rarely slept more than four to six hours a night when living in Rogers, tended to them all and, with the help of gardening and Ginny's painting, balanced creativity with a semblance of sanity.

His shift in creative focus was precipitated by fatigue with the usual business of writing and submitting poems, mostly to the little magazines. One problem was obvious: "Don't have the time to send anything out now."[93] But more concerning about this fatigue was a nascent sense that his muse was growing drowsy, that the fire that fueled his poetry was fading. The selective callback to the levee days in *Field Talk*, quoted in the previous section, includes that haunting image of the speaker walking down a levee. The signal lines of that poem—"holding out my hands / trying to warm them on campfires long gone"—powerfully confirm Frank's traditional habit of mixing memories with current experience to enrich his poems. In the summer of 1974, he started to explore a larger concern with losing consciousness of the past. It was a time when he was so attuned to this loss that he had recurring dreams about "Baby Gauge sitting next to me eating ice cream."[94] This exploration began in earnest, appropriately enough, on his birthday, August 1, 1974, when he wrote to Dugan: "Today is my birthday; twenty years ago I was camped on a river in a tent with Baby Gauge and all his brothers and sisters and camp children, and I was blowing out the candles. You've seen the picture. And today they're giving me a little party at this black tavern where I will be ever content to be with my friends and colleagues, emeritus professors of the dark heart.... Yours after a ¼ century, Frank."[95]

There is a lot happening in this nostalgic little passage. Frank was acutely feeling childhood slip away, so much so that he (again) subtracted a year from his life (he was twenty-six on August 1, 1974, not twenty-five). And so much so that, as he told Irv, he had a dream where "suddenly I was very young again."[96] However old he thought he was, the weight of adulthood and its interference with the reveries of childhood bore heavily on him during this period. Now that he was in his mid-twenties, his mind returned to life before adulthood. Not only to childhood, but to childhood at its freest and finest—the levee camp days, those unstructured days captured so beautifully in *The Singing Knives* and *The Battlefield*, days that hummed with memories that sang into his ears and made poetry.

In his poignant birthday letter to Dugan, Frank reiterated his desire to revive that campfire at the bottom of the levee by making a documentary film "on the levee camp people." This would be his way to reconnect with those souls whose language had long piqued his interest and fueled his work. He had now put considerably more thought into this potential project, and the people he wanted to be in it, people who were "thriving in prison, and in little sheds out back, etc."[97] He and Irv visited Joan Williams in Clover Hill, Mississippi, to discuss her book *Old Powder Man* and her memories of her father's work on the levees.[98] Frank even applied (unsuccessfully) for a grant from the American Film Institute to make the film he and Irv did not have the resources to make. He also tracked down an old family friend who had worked for his father and claimed "to know where all the people I knew in my youth are," as well as information about "the levee legends."[99] He hoped to make this film soon, before these people were dead and gone. He elaborated: "Before someone throws a spade full of dirt over them who have hauled tons of dirt, I'd like to reveal them, in a New Realist Poet's way ... that nostalgic idealization of the country past.

I'm interested in the lives and times. I have the experience and the gift but I have to do more than write poems."[100]

The idea of someone throwing dirt over working men who spent their lives throwing dirt to build levees reignited Frank's passion for the voices too often unheard. Making a film about the levee camp days was one strategy for him to refresh the present with distant memories in a way that merged past and present through art that did more than sit on the page and hide in little magazines. Hanging out at Sherman's was another way. He was thrilled to spend his birthday back at the "black tavern," literally evoking the birthday he had spent two decades earlier with Baby Gauge, BoBo, and others at Snow Lake. But, overall, his engagement with Sherman's and his friends there had diminished significantly since he had left Fayetteville, and that absence affected Frank, who now lived about fifty minutes away from Sherman's. More than anything else, this loss altered his poetic consciousness. "I have forgotten Tangle Eye," Frank writes in "The Visitors of Night," the first poem in his chapbook *Arkansas Bench Stone* (1975), thus lamenting his distance from Tang in *The Battlefield*.

In April 1974 he planned a reunion at his house in Rogers "with three old friends"—Sherman Morgan, Claude Ricks, and Jimbo Reynolds. It had all the markings of a hootenanny. They were going to fish, "barbeque a goat," "throw a big drunk," and "put it on the PAST's tab."[101] Frank, who had otherwise been admirably sober, loaded up on whiskey and catfish in anticipation of this occasion.[102] But at the last minute the Sherman's gang had to cancel "because of death, or a death," Frank explained. A few months later another plan to get together was foiled by the fact that Sherman Morgan's son allegedly killed a man who tried to steal his watermelon that was possibly stuffed with pot.[103] Again, a *Battlefield* scene in real life if there ever was one. In a later letter to Malcolm Cowley, Frank noted that this murder took place with "a big pan."[104] Whatever the weapon used (and whatever happened), Frank was upset much in the way a child would be upset over missing the ice cream truck. He declared to Cuddihy, "SAD news," and then he tended his garden to calm down. Eventually he "put my boat in alone and, instead of taking a book, I took some paper, wrote about my friends not coming." He lovingly described these Black men for Cuddihy: "One man used to be a preacher [Claude], the other has shined shoes and cooked for thirty years [Jimbo], the other runs a honky tonk on the creek [Sherman]." The last line of his final paragraph fell like a tear: "But they did not come."[105]

Frank addressed this sense of loss by dreaming up another project that might throw a log on that diminishing fire at the bottom of the levee.

Frank revisiting friends at Sherman's, ca. 1974.
*Photo courtesy of Ginny Crouch Stanford.*

He explained to Dugan that he and Ginny had conceived of a project they were calling SHERMAN'S. Noting that a small publisher was already interested (probably Irv Broughton's Mill Mountain), he explained, "All we'll do is photograph a tavern, all the people who spend most of their lives there. Portraits, etc."[106] Ginny took scores of photos for this project, but they never followed up on publishing it. But Frank, by even mentioning it and going with Ginny to take so many photos, was clearly working to bridge the gap between the lost days at Sherman's and the wandering muse of his own writing.

Being away from the levee camps in his memory and Sherman's in daily reality were alienations that touched Frank deeply. Months later he explained to Cuddihy, "Regret: I wish I could write about the subject matter I once did." He began to wonder: "Perhaps I began my journey into the country of the lost rib a tad too early?"[107] Being isolated in the hills of Northwest Arkansas had its advantages. He could work outside naked. "I don't like clothes in the good weather," he said in an interview.[108] But he was far away from the language of the marginalized and eccentric people of Eureka Springs and Fayetteville, unable to regularly hear their voices and stories, thrill in their banter and insight, feel the weight of their lives. This dislocation sapped his poetic inspiration and made him feel detached from a major source of that poetic inspiration, a source that pulses through *The Battlefield*.

There were still odd and beautiful voices to hear, to be sure, and Frank did his best to find them. Surveying in rural Arkansas was a godsend for discovering weirdos and strange sounds. "You wouldn't believe what I've run into in the woods," he told Irv. He mentioned a classic Stanfordian mash-up: "professors," "a mafia man," "children from Japan," and "beautiful women."¹⁰⁹ His letters from this time period note how he bought his beer from "a negro bootlegger at 3.09 a case," encountered a "black preacher" whose sermons included remarks such as "men gone crazy as niggers," and hung out with a drunk hillbilly who called himself "the dream gypsy."¹¹⁰ There was a "coonhunter" who "raise[d] rabbits and fighting cocks."¹¹¹ Frank was especially excited about the time he and Ginny, driving to the state line for booze (Benton County was dry), "ran on to this guitar and harp playing boy named Snake Maynard." Maynard hopped in their car and, grounding the gothic in real life, "serenaded us all night, driving through the back roads."¹¹² He had eighteen siblings. But these experiences, wonderfully strange as they were, were too fleeting, too detached from a deeper familiarity with life stories and histories, for the language and characters to fully take hold of Frank's imagination.

Frank wrote to Cuddihy: "One is put at ease in his works and days by knowing there are a few people who can truly understand." For Stanford, those who truly understood were the folks at Sherman's, the kids from the levee camps, and those who were "fucked up" in ways that made their stories interesting to Frank. Pondering this loss of regular contact with these people, he added, "I suppose this is why I like to be around monks, the poor—white and black, and alone with myself." But now "the infernal business of this life" was interfering with those experiences and connections. As a person who was "involved in literature and film," he wrote that such "infernal business" kept him away from both the "emeritus professors of the dark heart" and "the quiet transactions of the poet and his soul."¹¹³ Not only were these two losses intimately connected, but he *needed* these things back. He ended a September 1974 letter to Cuddihy with a choice quote from the poet George Oppen: "Air, a child / Stands as a child . . ."¹¹⁴

A light malaise crept into Frank's voice when the topic turned to poetry. At the end of the summer of 1974, right around his twenty-sixth birthday, he admitted to Cuddihy that he was tired. "At times I do become quite weary of words," he wrote, "and leary of what others make of them."¹¹⁵ By the fall he wrote that "I wish I could say I was still tracking that lost dog in my writing, but for the time being Ginny, god bless her, is the only artist working." In an undated and unpublished (and unedited) poetry fragment he wrote:

> I am no longer the man I once was the one
> who was interes[t]ed in being a poet the one with the blood
> of his demon on his hands
> I am no longer interested in being a poet
> the man I once was the one with the blood
> of his demon on his hands so long fool.[116]

He felt out of step with contemporary American poetry. "I suppose I've led the life of a poet," he wrote to Cuddihy. The past tense is noteworthy. "But I really don't," he added, "see myself fitting in with poets these days."[117] To Dugan he made similar complaints: "Sometimes the eyes get tired and the ears get weary of listening to your own, so maybe I ought not to write so much."[118] He complained to Cuddihy that "words may not always hold you in orbit."[119] To Walker he conceded that he was writing more than he should be.[120] Rather than celebrating a slew of acceptances that he had recently received, he complained that journals "seem to publish whatever I send them, which doesn't mean it's any good."[121] "Perhaps now what we poets have to do," he hypothesized, "is un-learn."[122] Ralph Adamo said that "I think he had just lost interest, like, 'I've done that, and I've been successful.'"[123] Maybe he paid special attention to a line in a book he read at this time, Stephen Stepanchev's *American Poetry Since 1945*: "There is a point in the career of a poet when he is no longer excited by his own manner."[124]

Although many of Frank's letters from 1974 are voluminous and inspired, he sometimes got stuck while writing. "I was up at 3:00 am this morning," he wrote to Cuddihy, "working on a poem." He included a draft of it, noting that "it's coming along, but I can't seem to get the enclosed out of my mind." He was used to this manner of obsession, but now there was a glitch in an otherwise effortless process: "Like a turtle that keeps taking my bait, the poem moves under me, and everytime [sic] I think I have something—I know something is down there, I pull up my line—nothing."[125] This "nothing" was a departure, or at least a swerve, from the flow he was used to feeling while writing, a flow that made poetry come out as Mozart's "sows piss." By the end of 1974 he seemed frustrated with writing poetry and, in one case, could hardly focus enough to pen a letter. "For about four hours I haven't been able to finish what I was saying," he complained to Cuddihy. "I got waylayed [sic] by a thought."[126] Eventually he admitted to being obsessed with some idea—"Can't get off the subject"—and he signed off by saying, "Wish I could write a decent letter but this thought won't let me. I'll be keeping in touch as soon as I can concentrate."[127]

By March of 1975, Cuddihy advised him to shake up his usual way of writing. Of Frank's poems Cuddihy wrote, "I wonder if they are not some kind of incubus or vampire, draining off energy that might better be directed toward new work." In any case, he said of Frank's poetic style, "I feel like it's time to move on."[128] It would have been hard for Frank to hear this and not feel defeated.

## "Visionary Conjurings"

This writerly slump, if that what we can call it, had a whiff of déjà vu. But whereas Frank's response to his 1972 emotional crisis had been to burn his work, bolt from Fayetteville, leave his wife (or drive her to leave him), and check into the state hospital, this time he handled the episode in a more reasonable manner. Although his strategy was not necessarily conscious, Frank dove into several discrete activities that reminded him that he could viably pursue other creative ambitions aside from getting short poems published in the little magazines or perpetually perfecting *The Battlefield*. For a man who once declared "I want my words, and my images, and my music that I like to be heard," seeking other forms of expression was both natural and healthy.[129] Whereas poetry alone engulfed him mentally in 1972, this time he was able to avoid a similar fate by balancing poetry with a range of other pursuits. Early in 1974 David Walker wrote to Frank, "Seems to me that, as one goes along, other *poetry* is less an influence. I find films, situations, strange throwings-together, are more so."[130] Frank agreed.

The most obvious outlet for Frank was film. Frank once said to Irv that when he read Franz Wright's poetry, it was like "time passing in a film." Such an effect continued to excite and preoccupy Frank, and he wanted to try to achieve it on his own. To that end, Frank reconnected with Jim Babij in Los Angeles, sending him a screenplay in early 1974. Frank's Cocteau-inspired script, based on the Subiaco monks, included twenty-seven scenes. Frank described each one, noting, for example, "Egg in monk's hands," "Minnow swimming in chalice of wine," "Hoe working plowed field," "Monk on roof holding sword," "Monk putting butter on bread." Babij, perhaps a little miffed by all the monkish imagery, offered some perfunctory compliments, the most notable of which was backhanded: "But most of all it is cinematic!"[131]

And therein was the problem. Babij continued, "In terms of the marketability of scripts like these—I think it's questionable whether they'd be well received. This town [Los Angeles] is really into the entertainment end of cinema—visionary conjurings are placed on the back shelf of the vault." Babij added, "This is not to say that you're wasting time by writing scenarios like this one."[132] Of course, Frank knew that's exactly what Babij was saying. As he had written to Irv a year earlier, "The reason Cocteau, Carné ([and his collaborator] Prevert), Bresson, Tati, etc. never did have to worry about being commercial is because there was always someone to foot their bills. They never went out for an audience, betraying their art. . . . They created their own worlds."[133] Babij was a connection, not a patron and not necessarily a supporter of Frank's conjuring visions. Frank knew that, and so he returned to where he knew his noncommercial ideas were taken seriously, where he could create his own world in film.

He went back to Irv, Subiaco, and the monks. A June 1974 trip to Subiaco allowed Frank to continue shooting for *It Wasn't a Dream: It Was a Flood*. The official occasion for the three-week visit was to assist once again with the annual boys' camp. "The monks asked us to come help with a summer camp for orphans," he recalled, noting (correctly) how "it was nearly my birthday" and (incorrectly) how "I would be a quarter of a century old."[134] He described this year's camp to Cuddihy as one attended by "a band of poor kids" who "come from cities." "I like to take them out in the woods and water," Frank wrote. "They run you ragged, and there is no pay, but it is worth it." He would continue to shoot his film, he said, "while the monks are at office."[135] He was especially excited to bring Ginny, as she would get to sit around and paint, draw, take photos, and drink beer. But he claimed to be nervous about interacting with urban kids. "Don't know how to treat them. Don't know about the cities like you," he told Dugan.[136]

These few weeks at Subiaco and Lake Dardanelle were eventful ones for Frank. Being involved in Subiaco put him at ease. That spring, to help Father Fuhrmann prepare the school's literary journal, *Rock Quarry*, Frank used what clout he had to solicit poems from Allen Ginsberg, Malcolm Cowley, and Alan Dugan. He was pleased, as he told Father Fuhrmann, to "lend a little muscle to a fine project."[137] On May 20 Frank wrote to Dugan, "I need to tell you, ask you something. That bunch of monks and boys are publishing a magazine. . . . I'm supposed to ask you for a poem for it." Frank acknowledged "who in the hell would want to give a poem to a monastery, to a bunch of strange boys and monks." But he assured Dugan that it would never be seen beyond Subiaco and that the students would love it.[138] That same day Frank wrote Lawrence Ferlinghetti to get Ginsberg's address. He delivered his line to Dugan, writing, "Of course, no one is interested in a magazine from a monastery published by strange boys and monks, but they'd really be grateful if I could get a poem from Allen."[139] This was Frank at his most generous, helping his former teachers at his former school help their students love poetry. While Ginsberg

Frank filming a scene for *It Wasn't a Dream: It Was a Flood*, summer 1974. Photo courtesy of Ginny Crouch Stanford.

passed on the opportunity ("No typewriter no time to prepare"),[140] Dugan came through with an original poem. Father Fuhrmann was impressed: "I am astonished at your ability to line up the formidable giants to help us in our second *Quarry* attempt.... Thank you very much, Frank."[141]

When the city boys arrived, they were taken to Lake Dardanelle, a dammed portion of the Arkansas River about thirty minutes from campus. "Every night," Frank wrote, "the Brothers, the hundred boys, and I would swim in the Arkansas River" while Ginny sat on the dock and sketched. He mentioned how he enjoyed "being out on the river, scaring the hell out of a group of orphans who have only known the cities."[142] The lake became the focus of Frank's summer. Notably, it's where he shot one of the most visually arresting scenes in *Dream/Flood*, the one that makes the film essentially Frank's. In it, a robed monk with his cowl draped on his back, Brother Jude Schmitt, paddles a canoe holding a small, draped coffin across a serene lake. (Recall Frank's mention in a letter to Willett of how "I dream of a fleet of coffins under sail, bearing the bodies of dead infants.") Jude rows toward shore, where four other robed monks stand to welcome the wayfarer and his coffin home. Frank later described the canoe and coffin as being paddled "through the dark arms of the lake + river."[143] It's a beautiful, even breathtaking, flatly black-and-white moment. It is a moment that Babij, discussing Frank's cinematic vision in general, called a "cine-poem."[144]

Father Fuhrmann was on set that afternoon. He later recalled Frank's attention to detail as he choreographed the scene, a focus that evoked for Fuhrmann his experience watching an entranced Frank in his classroom as a student at Subiaco. To get the angle he wanted, Frank insisted that he needed to shoot from water level. He submerged himself to his chest; then, while following the canoe, he sank up to his nose; and finally, while holding Irv's camera a few inches above the lake, he went completely underwater. Father Fuhrmann prepared to jump in after him because he thought Frank was drowning. But then his head reappeared, and he walked out of the water onto the shore.[145] Frank recalled how, after he had shot the scene, Brother Tobias DeSalvo, who oversaw the monastery's vineyard, marked the occasion by uncorking several bottles of wine. Frank and the monks drank directly from the bottles and talked about Thomas Merton, Flannery O'Connor, Pasolini, and Bertolucci.[146] This, for Frank, was close to as heaven as he could get.

On July 18, 1974, shortly after Frank shot this scene, a tragic event with eerie echoes of Frank's film unfolded. A local Subiaco student—not a camper—named Mark Wiederkehr fell out of a motorboat and drowned on Lake Dardanelle. It happened at buoy 25, about a half mile from where Frank had earlier shot his sepulchral scene, a scene with a coffin and a scene during whose filming Fuhrmann had thought Frank himself was drowning.[147] This was also the same body of water where Frank had tried to swim until he drowned in the summer of 1972. As if the uncanny connection to water would not end, Frank and the monks were drinking wine and swimming in the Subiaco pool when news came to them of the accident. They immediately drove to the lake to help a search party find the body. The team waded to a sandbar while a priest stood on shore "praying and blessing the body."[148] It was "too dark to look," Frank recalled. "But the boy [was] found."[149]

This event had a powerful impact on Stanford. "I know Frank absorbed it all," recalled Father Fuhrmann, who was with Stanford in the pool when he heard the news. More than anything else, it was the accidental nature of the death that moved him, in addition to its odd juxtaposition with the scene he'd recently filmed, one that also involved death on the water, monks, and Lake Dardanelle. "He looked forlornly up the river," Fuhrmann said, and he kept saying, "What a tragedy" while lamenting the pain that Wiederkehr's family, prominent regional wine merchants, would feel.[150] The walk back to the car after looking for the body also stuck with Frank, inspiring some choice poetic reflections. "We traveled back [to Subiaco] in the fog," he recalled in an essay where he described the incident. "I looked up and saw a huge sphere of concrete. I found out it was a nuclear reactor. Near the water level hung the remains of a large flathead catfish. *Arkansas Nuclear One* said the sign." A fisherman opposed to nuclear power had vandalized it with the phrase "*The Devil's Machine.*" That same night, Frank recalled, the recent past and immediate present merged to give him "a title for a poem I will write a year later on the eve of my twenty-sixth [in fact, twenty-seventh] year."[151] It would be called "Death and the Arkansas River."

Frank recited the poem in his head as if it were an evolving prayer. "I had a year with this poem," he remembered. "Everyday [sic] in the woods at work I would say it. I never wrote a word down until I had it right in my mind.... Once I thought it sounded right, and undramatic, I wrote it down without changing a word."[152] The poem—which first appeared in *Constant Stranger* (1976) and then again, with light edits, in *Crib Death* (1978)—opens with an affirmation of the impact of the boy's death as Frank and the priests searched for it:

> Walking from the killing place,
> Walking in mud,
> The bootsoles leave little hexes in the kitchen.

The poem hints at the precipitating event through many details, with references to "one summer," how "everyone was in hipboots / Looking out for Death's forklift," and the way "Men cleaned their fingernails / In the moonlight,"[153] which is precisely how stoic men might have contained their emotions over Wiederkehr's death, heads down, picking at their nails.

This poem thoroughly drilled into the theme of death, perhaps with a new intensity for Frank. When Lorenzo Thomas called Stanford the "poet of death,"[154] he was referring to this poem and those that followed to culminate in the book *Crib Death*, published shortly after Frank's death. The poem marks, in this sense, an important thematic shift for Frank, who around this time began to center his poems on death and dying more than life and living. But this transition was not abrupt. The attentiveness to everyday language and speech habits persists in the face of death, and death even gets personified, sometimes humorously, in the commonplace expressions of daily life. Throughout the poem, for example, death is shown to have it made in the shade:

> In the winter Death runs snow tires on his truck,
> He makes long hauls at night.
> Death pays the best wage,

He can keep in touch on his two-way,
He's paid all the Laws off.

Death can afford whatever he wants.[155]

The poem goes on: "Death is one for fooling around"; "Death is fond of the double-entendre"; Death "wants cooking that will remind him of home." Linking death back to the lake where Wiederkehr was killed, the speaker toward the end of the poem says:

Death controls the journeys,
The fare and the gender,
And Death is around you
Like a lock and dam.[156]

The poem reveals Frank's remarkable ability to situate the most precise and seemingly timeless aspects of life—putting snow tires on a truck, collecting the best wage, talking on a two-way radio—on death's doorstep. That image of the lock and dam grounds the poem in the fettered certitude of death, which not only controls the journeys but also has you trapped in its power. The fact that Frank sat with this poem about death for a year and the connection between the cinematic death he choreographed for his movie and the actual death on the lake are just two factors that converge to make "Death and the Arkansas River" a truly pivotal poem in Frank's oeuvre.

So much of Frank's earlier work had come not just from immediate experience hewing closely to autobiographical reality but also from Frank's ability to turn that confluence into poetry with almost effortless immediacy. "I had the sense from the beginning," Ginny said, "that Frank's creativity was so intense and prodigious it was constantly outpacing the limits of his physical abilities to manifest what arose in his mind."[157] Cher Ross (formerly Cheryl Campbell) observed something similar, noting how "his mind was faster than his reflexes could bear."[158] This was a man, after all, who wondered aloud what it would be like to "send out a fleet of poems at the speed of light," a man who said, "Poetry has always been life breathing."[159]

But with "Death and the Arkansas River," Frank was able to rein in the rapid-fire force of his creativity, slow down, and let the process unfold more deliberately. Tempering his poetic impulses with other media—namely, film—also made this possible. What Frank was doing, in a way, was a form of translation, one that allowed him to focus less directly on channeling the mad rush of ideas into poetry and more on the tangible gap he was now trying to bridge between one medium and another. Ginny was critical to this process. She explained, "I translated his awareness into visual art by making photographs, drawings, and paintings, which he choreographed." This shift to another medium forced Frank to think differently, translationally. It enabled him to arrange—via film or poetry—as Ginny put it, "Subiaco the place, and the characters of Subiaco, just as he wrote about them and featured them in the film Irv produced."[160]

This mix of art and life, triumph and tragedy, film and poetry, was a microcosm of the larger transition that Ginny described Frank experiencing as an artist at this time. "I try to get at the taproot of poetry," Frank wrote in "With the Approach of the Oak the Axeman Quakes." He began with "that force drawing things upward," and that taproot, that upward force, started in this case on that summer day with Frank in the water filming a scene with a floating coffin. It graduated into a haunting middle-of-the-night search for the dead body of a high school boy and was then followed by a melancholic walk in the woods that was replete with choice visual imagery of a nuclear power plant. It finally culminated a year later with a poem that Frank wrote in his head and enhanced with the essay "With the Approach of the Oak," about the writing of that poem. Through these many translations—film, life, poetry, essay—Frank kept his creative forces from overwhelming him into another breakdown. Through them he kept his head, full of thoughts about death, just above water.

With the footage from Subiaco shot and Frank and Ginny back home in Rogers, Irv and an assistant came to see them in early September 1974 to wrap up the filming for *It Wasn't a Dream: It Was a Flood*. The overall working relationship between Frank and Irv remained a healthy one. Still, both men had their frustrations with each other. Frank was appreciative that Irv had allowed him to "film my poems," but he regretted that he agreed to let Irv film him "talking about my poems, which can only turn out badly I think." (It was true, and this is probably the one false note in the film.) Frank refused "to act" in the film, which Irv kept asking him to do as well. Most critically, Irv continued to push Frank for shots of "local color," as Frank had put it back in 1971. Frank complained to Cuddihy that "they wanted to film some things which I wouldn't agree to"—Richard Banks eating raccoon and so on. Finally, Frank got so annoyed that he "told them if they wanted to know all what they were after, why not just drive into the hills and places and ask others." To prove his point, Frank "took the camera one night and drove fifty miles and asked an old woman to talk about whatever came into her mind. She said that the possums were digging into the bodies in the graveyard.... I got back and gave them the 400 feet and said 'there.' "[161]

Irv in turn had perfectly good reasons to be annoyed with Frank. More than anything else, funding films (and publishing books) that did not sell was driving Irv even deeper into debt. "I am literally risking bankruptcy," he complained, a lament to which Frank's ears were always deaf.[162] Even in the depths of Irv's financial woes, even when he knew that Irv was "sinking everything but his teeth into his magazines and films," Frank would still insist that if Irv scored another grant, he should "hold out 300 bucks so I can pay my rent, car, and transit bills."[163] Frank was generally skilled with the camera, but he tended to treat supplies cavalierly, as if Irv had endless access to film. He "shot a lot of bad stuff," Irv recalled, noting that "a lot of it was out of focus and not usable."[164] In one instance Frank ended up with a thousand feet of bad footage, but he blamed it on "interval fuck up in camera."[165] Some of his inexperience is evident in the final film—for example, in the scene with the pig slaughter when there is a quick, bright flash. While it has a kind of interesting cinematic effect, it was due to Frank having improperly loaded the film.[166] At some point Frank, despite his confidence that "I can handle a camera,"[167] thoroughly broke Irv's camera. "A Bell and Howell Camera! It was indestructible," Irv said. "They used them during the Chicago riots [1968]. I don't know what he did, but you'd have to do something really dramatic to break it." Still, though, Irv nonetheless agreed that "Frank had a good eye—he was an artist."[168]

Once Irv finished editing the sixteen-millimeter, twenty-six-minute film, he screened it on September 20, 1975, at the Empty Space Theater on East Pike Street in Seattle, billing it as "a dreamlike documentary about poet Frank Stanford, filmed in Arkansas and Mississippi."[169] It went on to win one of the Judge's Awards at the 1975 Northwest Film & Video Festival. It was a film full of visual conjurings and cine-poetic moments Frank had been wanting to achieve ever since falling for Cocteau. Plus, for the first time since the fourth grade he got some formal recognition for his artistic vision.

## "Horseshit"

While Frank was increasingly bored and frustrated with writing and submitting new poetry, he still had piles of preexisting work he hoped to get into print. Another way that Frank confronted his creative anxieties in 1974 was trying to find a home for *The Battlefield* while attempting to usher his other writing into more prominent—that is, commercial—publishing venues. To say that he considered *The Battlefield* "a deed accomplished," to use John Keats's language about his long poem *Endymion*, might be an overstatement, but it was well beyond "a feverish attempt."[170] He was ready to find a permanent home for the big poem and, along the way, try to score with a commercial operation, despite his principled objections to that act's inherently compromising nature. It would be a sort of last-ditch attempt to get recognized by a venue that could pay him real money. The effort would go poorly, but in that failure, there was a sense of resolution, as well as confirmation that his instinctual disdain for commercial outlets had been right all along.

As for *The Battlefield*, Frank knew that to even get a manuscript of its size considered would be a challenge. In mid-1972, he complained to Irv that "two of the so-called best magazines in the country refused, when I submitted a letter beforehand, to even consider a poem this length."[171] Even Dugan, who was as big a cheerleader for the long manuscript as anyone ("He thinks this is a *blockbuster* manuscript"[172]), suggested that Frank pursue a "small book edition" and publish it in parts—or "books," as he put it. Frank was not interested in breaking up his poem.[173] He noted to Irv that "it is my blessing and my curse, as far as my 'furthering' myself in the literary world, that I refuse to limit what and how I make my art to any one man's vision."[174] A monster manuscript and an uncompromising attitude about how it should be published were factors that boded poorly for the prospects of *The Battlefield*'s publication.

But Frank persisted. In April of 1974 he pitched the manuscript to poet and pen pal David Walker, sending him "375 pages of a 500 page" manuscript. He had had these pages typed up by Cheryl about a year and a half earlier. Walker was an active correspondent with Frank and an experienced editor well connected in the poetry business. "The original was over a 1000 pages but I got rid of half of it," Frank assured him. Frank said the other 125 pages—which he called "a lot different" from the rest of the poem—were somewhere out in the mail. "The poem, at one time 40,000 lines, is called 'the battlefield where the moon says I love you' and it comes from a ms. St. Francis and the Wolf: Some poems 1957–64, which is also a partial MS," he wrote. He warned Walker that "this long poem will obliterate your eyes."[175] Again, not advice to ensure a quick turnaround.

Frank primed the pump for Walker by quoting, "in toto or in part," what other poets had allegedly already said about the poem. John Berryman: "Most poets would have given their left eye to have written this, and their other eye to have done what you've done." Alan Dugan: "This is better than good, it is great. Publish it with a small press, now, as is, no revision." Richard Howard: "Have some mercy and respect for your audience. Weed out most of it, type it up MLA style, and send it back to me as a book." Malcolm Cowley and Anthony Hecht, Frank said, "only saw parts of it but liked it," while William Fox "said he didn't like it as much as my other poems, too many run on sentences for him." The whole poem is a run-on sentence! Mixed reviews aside, Frank was nonetheless pleased. "I thanked all of the fine gentlemen," he wrote, "but flat-out rejected Howard's suggestion."[176]

Looking back on the manuscript after Frank's death, C. D. Wright reflected that "a 542 page poem without line integrity, punctuation or even space to facilitate breathing and eye movement, much less narrative clarity . . . is bound to be trouble."[177] David Walker wrote that while he was excited to read the draft, he approached it with something "bordering on trepidation. . . . I'll do my best but don't expect instant results." He pled being overworked, complaining that other writers were asking him to read drafts of their manuscripts and quipping that "maybe I should charge, since everybody is so fuckin grateful."[178] When Frank sent excerpts of *The Battlefield* to the *New York Quarterly*, the editors, according to Frank, told him how "extraordinary" it was. Frank subsequently sent the whole manuscript but, after two years, reported that "I haven't heard heads or tells [sic] from them."[179] This kind of silence in the face of a manuscript that weighed nearly five pounds was understandable but frustrating.

Stanford shared those 375 pages with Cuddihy and insisted that "I never meant, or intended, you publishing a book of it." He only thought that Cuddihy "might want a 'bit' of wild reading."[180] In fact Frank was assuredly hoping Cuddihy would have some idea of what he might do with it. Cuddihy recalled being enthralled with what he read—"It was endless, shot through with brilliant passages echoing *Beowulf*, Dante, the Troubadours, and others, yet rooted in Frank's own history"—but he offered no new ideas on how to get the beast published.[181] Thomas Lux, whose Barn Dream Press had long been wanting to publish a book of Frank's poems, thought the manuscript was "fantastic" but could only suggest that Barn Dream publish "parts of the long piece."[182] William Packard at the *New York Quarterly* confessed that "we're not clear as to how to excerpt from it."[183] Irv, whose Mill Mountain Press at this point only published the chapbooks of one poet—Frank Stanford—said he would happily publish it. "The man who is editor of Mill Mountain is bringing out a 20,000 line poem I wrote," Frank told Cuddihy.[184] But this was a bit premature, as Irv could only pull off a publication of such magnitude if he did it over a three-year period, doing six small books a year. Frank did not like this plan. "I'd rather have it all in one thick book," he said.[185]

By the fall he'd decided the best thing to do with *The Battlefield* was to send it to "that Walt Whitman Award by the American Academy of Poets." That year's contest was being judged by William Meredith. The winner would be published by Harper & Row.[186] Dugan cheered him on. But Frank, who had virtually no experience in this realm, immediately undermined himself. Blatantly ignoring the submission length guidelines (fifty to one hundred pages), Frank sent in the longest version of his manuscript, somewhere between eight hundred and one thousand pages.[187] This was possibly an exaggeration by Frank. Nonetheless, the rejection came in a flash: "We just cannot accept a manuscript . . . that is significantly longer than 100 pages."[188] He was indignant and immediately wrote to Dugan, "The Am. Academy of Poets wouldn't accept for consideration my ms. for the W. Whitman award; said it was too long to read. Horseshit."[189] Dugan shared the outrage. He sent a note to Jeffrey Mitchell, head of the academy, insisting, "I think you have made a mistake. Stanford is a brilliant poet and just because he is ample in his work, like Whitman, is no reason to not to consider his manuscript . . . he should be encouraged in his amplitude rather than rejected for it."[190] Thus the outsiders railed at the establishment. Frank was both appreciative of Dugan's effort and resigned. He wrote to Dugan, "Thanks for writing the jerks at the Am. Acad. of Poets. I figured they'd at least look at the thing, considering the name 'Whitman' was on their award. It cost me $200 to have the thing typed."[191] Frank had taken on extra surveying work to help cover the $200 fee.[192] More important, he had taken a risk on something bigger and more official than usual, and—granted, because of his own intransigence—he had gotten burned.

Rejection would become an all-too-familiar feeling in 1974 and 1975. Even as older material was being published as books and in journals, other writing was getting knocked down. Frank knew he was wading into new territory; he was going from the little magazines, where he was a star, to larger venues, where he was generally unknown. Indeed, aiming for the Walt Whitman Award was part of Frank's larger effort to break into more high-profile publishing venues. The fact that he had virtually no success in entering these more conspicuous pages (*Seventeen* notwithstanding!) should not obscure the effort he put into doing so, the rejections he stoically endured, and the lemonade he eventually made—by founding his own press, Lost Roads—from an amplitude of lemons.

Some hope came from Marjorie Finnell, office manager at the *New York Quarterly*, where Frank had published "Death in the Cool Evening" in 1973. It seems Frank sent the editor William Packard the 375 pages of *The Battlefield*. Packard's enthusiasm matched Dugan's. Finnell loved the work.[193] But then came the predictable problem of what to do with a poem of such length. Not only was the journal not clear about "how to excerpt from it," but it wanted Frank to resubmit in small parcels. Frank still refused to take this approach. Later, Finnell came back to Frank and said that she, not the journal, still wanted "to publish your long poem as a book." She said he could "run it off on a mimeograph machine for next to nothing" but that doing it right—and this one was "worth doing right"—was cost prohibitive, "and that's the hangup—money."[194]

After the Whitman rejection, Frank decided to submit a manuscript to the Yale Series of Younger Poets Award, which was being judged in 1975 by Stanley Kunitz. This boded well as Kunitz had, only a few years earlier, called Frank's poetry "obsessive, romantic, redundant" but nonetheless "for real."[195] In September, prior to the Whitman rejection, Frank had declared to Dugan, who still cheered him on, "I'm going to send a short manuscript to S.K. at that Yale Series."[196] Without clarifying which manuscript he sent, Frank assured Dugan that "I got my ms. off to Yale around the 1st of March."[197] Kunitz got back to Frank ahead of the form-letter rejection, assuring him that "yours was one of the outstanding manuscripts submitted in this year's competition."[198] But the 1975 award went to Carolyn Forché. Frank, who may have looked up the winner at some point before hearing the official results, mistakenly told Dugan just three weeks after he had sent in his manuscript that "a woman name[d] Stanton won." But Maura Stanton had won the year before—for the 1974 competition, with her book being published in 1975. Frank, in his eagerness, had seen an advertisement for her book and missed the fact that she was the winner from 1974.[199] If nothing else, the anecdote reminds us how eager Frank was to get a big break without compromising his art.

As he began to think about seeking greater commercial exposure, Frank also began to think about taking his books beyond Mill Mountain Press. Referring to Irv in a letter to Cuddihy, Frank wrote, "I think he is nuts for spending so much money accepting my little manuscripts, turning down others [from other poets]."[200] He wanted to pursue a *career* as a professional poet. He'd seen men who had done it—Eberhart, Wilbur, Dugan, Hecht, Ginsberg—and he began to think he'd rather be like them than a surveyor-poet covered in ticks. In that vein, he approached Michael Cuddihy in the summer of 1974 and asked him, "Could I impose on you for a little advice." Frank prefaced his request with the caveat that "there are a few people around who'd be upset, knowing I'm writing you instead of them... but you seem to go to the heart of things." He was likely thinking of Irv—a man who was clearly supportive of Frank but, for various reasons, may not have been the best source to help him pursue a professional ambition, which was, as he clarified it for Cuddihy, this: "The publication of a book of poetry by one of the well-known presses—which pay."[201]

Given how long Frank had been writing poetry, his questions were basic: "Do you, at this time, think such a move on my part is advisable?" He listed ten presses, half of them academic (Yale, Wesleyan, University of Massachusetts, Pittsburgh, and Louisiana State University) and half of them commercial, asking which ones Cuddihy would choose. Frank wanted to know how to arrange his manuscript and how many poems to include in it. "What kind of order?" he asked. He noted how he was "leary of putting early dates on poems... because I think people are offended." After asking these rudimentary questions, he admitted, as if exhausted by his own confusion, "In fact, I'm leary of taking the time to publish a book."[202]

Cuddihy certainly took Frank's concerns seriously, but a written response from him does not survive (although the men talked on the phone often). Arthur Vogelsang, at the *American Poetry Review*, to whom Frank wrote a similar note, responded with apt advice: "Sending a book out isn't all that much work—just pick out your 50 or 60 best poems and organize them in some kind of thematic or chronological order and send them off." Vogelsang added, "What kind of work do you do? Perhaps if you got a book published you could use it as leverage to do some other kind of work?"[203] Regardless, the needle did not move toward publication, as Frank was still writing to Dugan in March of 1975, "I figure it is about time for me to start looking for a publisher."[204]

## "You Seem to Have Lost the Best of It"

Yet another way that Frank worked to expand and diversify his creative interests and ambitions during these two years was writing more short fiction. True to form, he churned out an enormous amount of it, experiencing in the process "a poetry-prose crisis," one he was happy to note that Wolf [sic], Lawrence, and Faulkner had gone through as well.[205] It seems Frank began writing short fiction in earnest in the winter of 1973, right after moving to Eureka Springs, when he informed Irv that he had "drafts of 12 more stories."[206] Looking back on his summer in 1974, he wrote to Dugan, "I've written some poems... but mostly what I've got to show is a 300 page fiction manuscript of stories. The next time I look it will probably be 500 pages."²⁰⁷ The freedom to make this transition, according to C. D. Wright, came when Frank considered *The Battlefield* to be complete. "He did not go back and edit the *Battlefield* again after he lopped off another 800 pages of it," she wrote to a poet-correspondent, "he went on to the next project—his fiction."²⁰⁸

His first effort to publish a short story met with success. The *Iowa Review* published "A Past: Wintered Like a Circus" in its summer 1974 issue.²⁰⁹ Centered on a married woman's interest in a beautiful boy who passes her house with a French-speaking crow on his shoulder, the story reads like an intensely image-driven and rural prose poem, with stretches of vernacular dialogue woven through the tale. The continuity with Frank's poetic style is clear; there is no question that this is the same writer who wrote *The Battlefield*. Frank explained to Cuddihy: "I believe there ought to be more than one voice, sometimes, in a prose poem. . . . So, in my prose poems, rather than a paragraph of a monologue, there are lines of conversation."²¹⁰ It was a pretty good description of most of Frank's short fiction and so much of *The Battlefield*. Still, Frank noted to Dugan, "What I write isn't nearly as good as what I hear and see."²¹¹ The format might have changed from poetry to prose, but Frank's guiding star, as this comment indicates, remained the rawness of daily life and language, which he aimed to capture as much in his stories as his poems.

Frank aimed high with these new stories. He compiled some of them into a book-length manuscript titled "The Blackberry Tales" and, in early 1975, sent the manuscript to major commercial venues: the *Atlantic Monthly*, Simon & Schuster, Houghton Mifflin, the *Iowa Review*, and *Esquire* (and perhaps others). The *Atlantic* sent a form rejection letter.²¹² Nan A. Talese personally apologized for her long delay in responding but was "afraid the *Tales* are not for the Simon & Schuster list," calling them "too special for us."²¹³ In his submission to Houghton Mifflin,²¹⁴ Frank sent a quickly cobbled together résumé listing Dugan, Wilbur, Eberhart, Justice, Lux, and Cowley as references. He added in a strange accompanying note: "Although the late John Crowe Ransom told me I ought to plan my fiction manuscript more closely to Chaucer's work, I took a different approach."²¹⁵ Ruth B. Saunders from Houghton Mifflin wrote a personal note to say of "The Blackberry Tales" that it was "not suitable for our general list."²¹⁶ Hoping to score twice with the *Iowa Review*, Frank sent them "Delainey's Tale," but fiction editor David Hayman rejected it. However, a young writer and editor there—T. Coraghessan Boyle—read it and wrote to Frank that "I like the story, alot [sic]." He asked to hold on to it until Hayman's replacement, Robert Coover, arrived the following year.[217] But the story never ran.

The big bite on Frank's stories came from Gordon Lish at *Esquire*. At some point over the summer of 1974 Frank sent a bunch of stories—possibly "The Blackberry Tales"—to the glossy magazine with the legendary fiction editor. Sensing that submitting to *Esquire* might be perceived as a kind of creative sellout, or kowtowing to a hypermasculine lifestyle magazine, Frank almost apologized to Dugan for sending his submission to Lish, writing, "I'm waiting to hear from ESQUIRE about a story I hope they'll buy. It is a sad day in hell when that's all that's left to publish fiction in."[218] To Cuddihy he stressed how he "was hoping to hit the big money," which was a departure for Frank, who had spent much of his earlier writing career seeking prestige rather than payment when it came to publishing his work. But he added that he wanted the money to buy time to write poems.[219]

Lish had seen Frank's *Iowa Review* story and been impressed. When he learned that his assistant Julie Schwartz was holding some of Frank's submissions, Lish had her reach out to Frank on his behalf. Her immediate aim was not to accept a story but to keep Frank sending in more material.[220] She wrote to him in August 1974, "I hope your promise to send us one every month doesn't come unstuck," adding the encouraging words "You have all the earmarks."[221] After *Esquire*'s initial interest, Frank wrote to Cuddihy that "ESQUIRE has accepted my style of fiction they say, and now, they also say, it's up to me to send them a story to accept."[222] The fact remained that "I have certain reservations about their taste"—again, he wondered if this was a sellout—"but I would like to relieve them of some of their money."[223]

In November, Lish sent Frank a form letter explaining Lish's arrangement with McGraw Hill to effectively share the work of *Esquire* writers with the publisher, with the intention of soliciting and producing books from writers Lish commissioned for the magazine. The note remarked, "I am filled with an immense enthusiasm for the prospects this relationship will yield, and anticipate the publication of works of fiction and non-fiction that will in every wise matter to me and to readers whose attentions are most worthfully earned, and which will bring distinction and notice to the writers who are represented in this enterprise."[224] It would be hard to imagine a young writer with little commercial publishing experience receiving this form letter and not thinking he was about to break into *Esquire*. And even if Frank had stayed cool about the note, Lish would have fired him up with the handwritten note he sent two weeks later: "You have massively interesting ideas and a remarkable hand at housing them. Yet everything I've seen thus far...juuussst misses." Still, he went on, "I think you are very close to being an exceptional writer of short fiction. It will not take much for you to get all the elements precisely in place."[225]

Driven by Lish's encouragement, Frank persisted, sending stories monthly as promised. Telling Dugan that *Esquire* was asking him to "fix" a story, he said, "Man am I going to get drunk if they take it."[226] He often underwent intense bouts of shedding to churn out stories. "I haven't been to sleep in 4 days," he wrote to Cuddihy at one point, "working and trying to revise a story for *Esquire*. . . . Too much coffee and wine, maybe a little drunk."[227] Frank's efforts were met with an excruciating game of editorial dodgeball. It began in October 1974 with Lish telling Frank, "Have gone through these. They confirm my interest in your work—but only TANCREDI'S LIGHT comes close to really getting me. Yet it needs works [sic], mainly, in my view, sharpening, focussing." Lish admitted that this advice was not very practical and that he was "right now very rushed," but he insisted that Frank may "want to give the piece another once-over and show it to me again. I'd like that."[228]

Frank complied, sharpening and focusing as directed, but to no avail. Lish wrote, "This is scarcely an improvement—tho it is now plenty clear."[229] Frank wrote a few new stories. "These are notable, Frank," Lish wrote in December, "but too long for my uses. Sorry."[230] Another submission in early January of 1975—most likely another reworking of "Tancredi's Light"—led Lish to write that "you seem to have lost the best of it."[231] Yet another revision—"I cut 11 pages," Frank told him[232]—and Lish was back on the hook: "Frank— Better. I'm thinking. Soon, Gordon." Lish then handed the piece over to his new assistant, Anne Conover Heller, who was totally confounded by "Tancredi's Light." "Hey Gordon, I don't *understand* this story," she wrote. After a few technical suggestions, she concluded that "this story could be absolutely magnif, but works incompletely or not at all as it stands." Lish sent the comments to Frank and told him to "be guided by them."[233]

In the meantime, while Heller was working over "Tancredi's Light," Lish had become interested in another submission of Frank's called "In the Midst."[234] The familiar rigamarole ensued. Lish called the story "very anecdotal and very told." He said that he'd "be tickled to see them [the two stories Frank had submitted] dramatized rather than narrated." Tickled. But he also added something that must have kept Frank from giving up on

*Esquire*: "And hey, you're really good, you know . . . just in case you were wondering." He signed off, "Keep em flying."[235] Frank did keep them flying. I'm "not giving up the ship,"[236] he wrote to Lish before rewriting "In the Midst," only to be told in April 1975, "I'm sorry, Frank, but it more and more boils down to the anecdotal." Lish, refusing to end what was now six months of torture, asked, "What's next?"[237] This time the answer, at least in terms of sending new work, was silence. The experience with Lish beat Frank down and turned him off commercial options for good. He was done dealing with submissions—and not just to *Esquire*. The only further mention *Esquire* got from Frank was a line in a poem called "The Truth" from an unpublished manuscript called "Smoking Grapevine." He wrote:

> Of course I've tried *Esquire*,
> But my shoes aren't platforms[238]

And as for Lish, Frank advised Steve Stern a year later to "stay away from that guy; he's a snake."[239]

The *Esquire* mess coincided with other disappointments. The *Antioch Review*, which had been holding Frank's poems for years, finally decided in February 1975 that while "there are some lovely moments in all these poems . . . no single poem sustained itself throughout."[240] This, coming from a little magazine, was unusual. Rejections also came from *Choice*, the *American Review*, the *Ark River Review*, and *Poetry Now*—all coinciding with the *Esquire* letdown. Even the effort Frank had made to get stories into the *American Review*, surely an attempt to salvage nine months of wasted effort to hit the elusive *Esquire* bull's-eye, floundered. "I've looked at these stories," wrote an editor there, "but didn't find one that grabbed me sufficiently to compel me to publish it."[241]

These rejections seemed to tamp down Frank's previous fire-hose approach to submitting work. With few exceptions—including *FIELD* and *Ironwood*—Frank stopped sending out poems and stories for publication in early 1975. He was still writing them at breakneck speed—in fact he had finished two more book manuscripts, "Flour the Dead Man Brings to the Wedding" and "The Last Panther in the Ozarks,"[242] and he would finish three others between 1976 and his death in 1978. He remained, as he always would, entirely committed to writing intensely and all the time, even when he was, as C.D. Wright claimed he later was, "tired of writing poems."[243] "He went the distance with it," she recalled, stressing how he was "the most disciplined writer I have ever known or heard of."[244] Frank reiterated his ongoing commitment to writing, telling a friend, "Hell, it's late, and I have to draw a map and two mountains and a winding creek. . . .

Then, in the 4 hours of dark left before sunrise, maybe a poem."[245] Later on: "Although it seemed like I didn't have time to take a comfortable crap," Frank wrote about the years 1975–76, "I was writing all along. (Don't ask me how or when or where.)"[246]

He knew he still had "the gift," as he noted to Dugan, but was just done knocking on doors with it.[247] More notably, he was just fine with this decision. By late 1977, he wrote to friend and editor John McKernan, "Don't send out poems anymore at all," adding, "Would say 'don't know why' but that would sound too much like jazz."[248] Part of this jazz may have been declining confidence in his work. "Poetry busts guts," Frank wrote in "With the Approach of the Oak," and it's not impossible that he could have felt that his poems no longer did that. For example, when he read John Logan's poem "Poem for My Brother," Frank wrote to Cuddihy that "I am, in all frankness, reminded of the way in which *I used to* write." In the same note, referring to poetry written the year before, Frank added, "I wish I could return to that state of soiled grace."[249] In late 1974 he wrote, "I'm afraid I'm not in the same ballpark of what I see in *Poetry Now* and *WCPR*."[250] Soon afterward even Cuddihy declined to publish some of Frank's poems, causing Frank to lament, "The fact that you didn't like my new poems that much was a let down, but that is the risk we all have to take."[251]

Another part of the problem was an inevitable one that seemed to mount with quiet intensity: the ongoing fatigue of adulthood and its multiple and seemingly endless responsibilities. "One of these days," Frank wrote in the late spring of 1974, "I want to go back to dreaming for a living."[252] Whatever the ultimate reason that Frank stopped trying to publish in the little magazines, the outcome was clear: His remarkable stint of publishing his poems in little magazines was mostly over. From 1970 to 1974, he had taken the world of poetry by storm. Then, rare exceptions aside, he vanished from the world of poetry's pages.

ON JANUARY 23, 1975, Richard Banks, Frank's Black friend from Eureka Springs, died. "For the last few years he'd been telling me he had sawdust in his eye, and he always wanted Ginny to get it out," Frank explained to Dugan a month after Richard's death. "We found out it was cancer. They took his eye out. Cancer had set in on him and took hold like kudzu." Richard's pain had been so acute that his neighbors could hear him yelling at night. He had gotten so weak he could not lift a log of firewood. Frank finally took Banks to the hospital but noted, "I suppose he'd a rather died in his house with his dogs and cats, but he couldn't take the pain anymore—even whiskey wasn't doing any good. I knew he was done for when he said he didn't want a drink. He's gone, now."[253]

Richard's death only enhanced Frank's sense of dislocation from the Sherman's gang and his growing alienation from the levee days and characters chronicled in *The Battlefield*. Whereas Frank had previously sensed his distance from his past, he now felt cut loose from the most obvious sources of his poetic-historical consciousness: his childhood and the language that had animated the levee camps. Back in 1971, when Frank was in the thick of writing for the little magazines, he had written a letter to Donald Justice that confirmed his conscious awareness of channeling childhood into his poetry. He quoted Cocteau's line from a talk he had given about *Le sang d'un poète*: "When he plays the game of cards, he cheats by taking from his childhood that which he should draw from within himself." While Frank managed that concern by merging memories of childhood with present-day experiences and feelings, he was nonetheless concerned that by channeling so much youth into *The Singing Knives* and *The Battlefield*, he was "stealing the aces from a dead child." But steal them he did because, as he wrote to Justice in reference to "St. Francis and the Wolf," "I know if I wrote about other things it would be artificial."[254]

Was he out of cards? Not quite. Yes, the unrefined and vibrant language that he had long heard and remembered and loved, the rural and Black vernacular that infiltrated his dreams and made his poems dance on the page, the visceral resonance of the blues—all of it was now yielding to the demands of making a living, the demands of domestic life and a garden, and the demands of a wider range of activities he was pursuing after moving in with Ginny. The essence of his poetic life, in other words, was yielding to change, and Frank was going with it as best he could. He could no longer claim that "my life is all dreams now" or that "sometimes I'm totally lost in the past."[255] He was now sleepwalking down his father's levee, leaving those memories, only to seek warmth in embers that barely glowed. He had little sustainable connection to the past, a connection that had lit fire to every line in *The Battlefield*, and he was okay. But no more than okay. Frank Stanford was a poet to the core, and some poets to the core do not grow up so well and do not deal with okay so well.

But still, he was not yet ready to succumb to despair. He had to keep writing, and he did keep writing. Only now he had to refocus. Just as the character in the opening of one of Frank's favorite movies—Cocteau's *La belle et la bête*—erases the chalkboard and channels the impulse of "childlike simplicity," so Frank had to leave behind the past that was leaving him behind, confront the blank slate, and seek new ways to hear and write about his world. One way he did this was by writing about the loss of childhood. In other words, tracing in his poetry exactly what was shaping his life and thought on a deeply personal level during this transitional moment in his career.

Consider a few examples from *You*, published a year after Frank died. In "Source," the past and the experiences it nurtured are washed away when the speaker sees "dirt washing down the river / Into the gulf" and says of that dirt "I think I walked over that ground."[256] In "Everybody Who Is Dead," the speaker observes that when a grown man is being hunted down:

> He shuts his eyes
> Remembers himself as a boy
> Lying naked on a rock by the water.[257]

In "Search Party" the idea of "passion" is "Like the eyes of a child in the last hours."[258] In "You" we hear about "summer visitors / In the three story house of our childhood." In other poems a watch is "dropped down the well of your childhood," a doctor in a shack is "Beating a child's heart with his knuckles," and a character thinks, "what it would be like / Being children together."[259] These lines need not be over interpreted; Frank was looking back on childhood. As for death, well, as we'll see, he dives into that deeply in his posthumously published *Crib Death*.

In a way, it's almost as if these poems about the loss of childhood in *You*, with the hovering presence of death around it, were being written in retirement. The analogy makes sense if we observe that between 1970 and 1975 Frank had, in effect, gone through a career as a poet. He had published scores of poems in dozens of elite journals. Each acceptance was a mini coup, delivering a jolt of adrenaline that pushed him to keep sending out his work, which he did aggressively and successfully. In 1973 he practically woke up every day and did a jig, he so was thrilled with the chase. These poems led to him developing a national reputation as a relentlessly brilliant young poet. During these years, because of Irv and Mill Mountain Press, he published five short books of poetry that, while poorly distributed and never reviewed while he was alive, enhanced and solidified his reputation in Fayetteville, where graduate students came to worship him as a legend. But by 1974, the thrill of the early years began to fade. Frank continued to write, but this writing had to be balanced, as we'll see, with a multitude of competing responsibilities—adult responsibilities—that led his meteoric rise as a poet with a growing reputation to plateau.

Thinking about Frank's writing as a sort of truncated lifetime of poetic output, as if he were a kind of poet emeritus at twenty-seven, helps us understand his last professional act, which happened to be a very adult one: the founding of a publishing company. By March 1975, just as the *Esquire* saga was coming to an end, Frank was thinking about starting his own press. He wrote Cuddihy, "If I were to make any money, I would like to start a chapbook series in the form of a magazine."[260] At least two motives underscored this desire. Frank now knew that if *The Battlefield* was ever going to be published, he would be the one to publish it, so Frank was clearly thinking about building a foundation to nurture the publication of his magnum opus. But just as significantly, he came to appreciate how fortunate he was to have had the run he had had. With a renewed sense that the underdog poets rarely got their due, he wanted to establish a press that helped give them the same shot that Irv and the little magazines had given him.

To get there, to cross that bridge, Frank had to learn to do something that did not often do: put the interests of others ahead of his own. "While consistent," C.D. Wright said of Frank, he "seemed . . . committed to changing."[261] He had to now adapt his creative impulses to the mysterious intricacies of other artists' minds. Fortunately, by working closely with Ginny—that is, by supporting her career as a painter in every way—Frank had not only revealed a deeply generous and loving side to himself but also established the foundation for helping other poets find the lost dog he could no longer track in his own writing.

Ginny Crouch Stanford, ca. 1975. *Photo courtesy of Ginny Crouch Stanford.*

TWELVE

# "My Wife Is Painting Alot"

## 1974–1975

G INNY AND FRANK LIVED WELL together. "All in all," he assured Cuddihy, "we live a good life."¹ They did not argue. They shared time in the garden, gave each other space to pursue their artistic ambitions, took road trips to see gallery exhibitions and visit their parents, played records, collaborated artistically, and easily enjoyed each other's company. When the surveying work was quiet, because of bad weather or lack of business, Frank was able to live as balanced a life as he ever would. In the summer of 1974 he described for Cuddihy how "every morning I work in the garden, write, and take a swim. In the day I write. And in the evening, more garden and another swim."² He was even paying attention to his diet. "I don't eat meat much—not that I'm a veg," he wrote. Frank preferred to not eat animals but admitted to Irv that it "depends how hungry I am."³ He preferred his dinner rolls made with soya flour, buckwheat flour, and wheat germ, which indicates that while he never fell for poetic trends, he was not immune to dietary ones.⁴

Frank also had his drinking under control. Back during his 1972 psychiatric evaluation, his doctor had asked him to confront his destructive relationship with booze. The doctor summarized Frank's self-assessment this way: "If he is experiencing a 'low' he is a bad alcoholic and drinks to forget and this makes him unhappy and then he goes on to state that sometimes he would drink because he was too happy and doesn't seem to know how to express it to other people."[5] While living in Rogers with Ginny, he avoided these emotional extremes and therefore, it seems, the need to drink excessively. So removed was he from the heavy-boozing days that he could refer to a time long past "back when I stayed raving mad and drunk all the time."[6] In Rogers, he would sometimes mix a little whiskey with ice water and slowly sip it, and there were the occasional trips to the Hi-Hat in Eureka Springs for a couple of beers, but Ginny recalls that, more than anything else, he drank cases and cases of Shasta soda.[7] This choice, at least for a while, kept Frank unusually domesticated. "We took walks," Ginny recalled of their years living in Rogers, "and picked blackberries and made pies."[8]

Being relatively isolated on the edge of Rogers helped Frank as well. The house and landscape deeply appealed to him. He wrote to Cuddihy how "from our bedroom window we can see our wilted garden, the moon at some point above it, way in the distance the lake and the hills, and nearby, horseshoes and chains and bits of broken plows picked up out of the old field and secured to a tree." He went on to describe a flat-bottomed boat on sawhorses, a concrete watering trough, and a wooden ladder against the barn. To this description he appended the remark that "I think we poets can easily lose contact with that which we say we understand if we don't keep the connection with 'things.'"[9]

Ginny remembers how Frank would leave the house in the middle of the night, not to carouse, but to hum at owls by the toolshed and walk on a nearby bridge "like the tightrope artists we saw in town last year at the County Fair."[10] Of one of these outings, Frank wrote, "More in the night: a cold, moonless, clear night. Got out of bed to throw another log on the fire. Outside, wild geese flying over. Can't see them in the dark sky, but they're there."[11] A friend of Frank's from Fayetteville rightly observed how Frank "was a magnet for outcasts and misfits."[12] But in Rogers there were no immediately available outcasts and misfits to attract, and so Frank took in more things, objects and landscapes, with special intensity and at all hours. "I'm in awe of things," he told Irv around the time he was living in Rogers.[13] To Dugan he noted how he would often "stay up all night in a daze."[14] "Frank often stayed up late," Ginny confirmed.[15] Only now he woke up not mired in guilt due to terrible behavior but rather facing another busy day with what approximated workmanlike, bourgeois dignity.

Frank and Ginny continued to take trips to Liberal, Missouri, where Ginny's parents, who came to like Frank very much, had a farmhouse, and to Subiaco to see Dorothy and "Gran-Gran." Frank wrote about how the couple spent the 1974 Christmas holiday in Subiaco, noting how Ginny and his mother and grandmother were busy in the kitchen swapping recipes. He recounted how he and his grandmother spent time looking at a book about the handwriting of old poets. It was a rare and expensive two-volume set called *Autograph Poetry in the English Language: Facsimiles of Original Manuscripts from the Fourteenth to the Twentieth Centuries* and had been given to Frank by Ginny's parents. Frank remembered how he and Ginny drank beer and played poker with his uncle and his family, how Dorothy "*made* us all attend" midnight mass. Despite his vehemently not wanting to go, "the Gregorian chants were worth the late hour, as was the special and rare invitation to dine with the monks after the service." Elaborating on this meal, Frank wrote, "Monk bread, monk wine, and monk sausage and honey, etc."[16]

Ginny stressed that these trips to Subiaco were "all about connecting with family."[17] Disagreements over church attendance notwithstanding, Frank, now that he felt mentally stable and was remarried and domestic enough to have a garden, was able to interact with his mother and grandmother without excessive tension. To Cuddihy, in a rare mention of concern for his family members, Frank wrote, "I do worry about my old mother and grandmother, in their 60's and 90's living together, but the monks take care of them. My mother will be the only woman to have ever have been [sic] buried in the monastery cemetary [sic]. How about that. She wants me to help her write a cookbook so she can die rich. At least, that is what she says." Ginny noted that while there were occasional "complications with family," they diminished significantly with her in the picture.[18]

Back in Rogers, keeping the house warm was a constant task during winter months. Frank and Ginny had a propane heater but saved money by burning wood—or anything else that was flammable—in a salvaged woodstove. Frank's task, which he took seriously—"We've got to keep the stoves burning"—was to ensure that the supply of fuel stayed constant.[19] "Chainsaw went out," he wrote in January 1974, "so keeping warm with an ax."[20] In the fall: "Hauled in the wood stove the other day, pulled the guts loose out of my back, and now I can't sit or sleep."[21] Old papers went into the fire, sometimes too quickly. "Somehow," he wrote to Cuddihy, "the copy of Kayaks [the literary magazine *Kayak*] I found got burned up for kindling. I don't know how."[22] Frank and Ginny often brought back old furniture from Liberal to the house in Rogers; some of that furniture became fuel. Other pieces did not. Ginny recalled, "Frank wrote in the living room of the Rogers house in front of a large window that faced east toward Beaver Lake. The Lake was visible in the winter when the trees had lost their leaves. His desk was an antique oak library table that belonged to my maternal grandmother."[23]

We have seen how Frank was involved in many projects during this time period. We have also seen how many of these projects were reaching a culmination by the end of 1974: *The Battlefield Where the Moon Says I Love You*, although still without a publisher, was effectively done; *It Wasn't a Dream: It Was a Flood* was done; Frank had tried and, with the *Esquire* experience behind him, was done trying to reach a more commercial venue with his work; and while he continued to write shorter verse, he was done sending his poems out for publication in the little magazines. He was more geographically distanced from his friends at Sherman's Tavern than he had been since 1968, when he first began going there. That relationship was hardly over, but it was attenuated, relegated to Ginny painting Jimbo rather than Frank spending a lot of quality time with Jimbo and Jimbo's mother, as he once had.

These conditions predisposed Frank to think about art other than his own. This was a change in disposition that would lead to Frank becoming not only selflessly supportive of his wife's painting and the work of other lesser-known artists but also the founder of a press and a publisher of others' poetry. It was an endeavor rooted in a new sensibility that required him to place the artistic interests and idiosyncrasies of others ahead of his own, something he had never before done. For a poet who once aimed to "reclaim the landscape of American poetry," this was no minor transition.[24] Beginning this process of thinking about art through the eyes of others might have seemed a daunting task for Frank, but he knew exactly where to start. In fact, he did not even have to think much about it. He was married to Ginny. Ginny was a painter. And Frank *loved* the idea of being married to a painter. She became his first project.

## "Nothing Has Ever Drawn Me Away from Poetry... Except Her"

"Frank was very clear that he wanted me to focus all my energy on painting," Ginny remembered about their nearly three years in the Rogers house. "Usually he would say 'you should paint'... and then describe the image or point to a photograph." She recalled how he was especially fond of photos by Eudora Welty and the New Orleans photographer Clarence John Laughlin and would push her to do paintings based on their images. While Frank worked at his oak desk with a distant view of the lake ("he wrote in several hour stretches"), Ginny, by her own account, "painted in the room off the kitchen with a view south to the garden."[25] This collaborative arrangement—in proximity to each other but facing different directions—suited both artists well. It was an arrangement that had not been possible with Linda the social worker or Cheryl the French horn player. Like his mentor Alan Dugan, who was married to the professional painter Judith Shahn—daughter of the social realist / modernist painter Ben Shahn—Frank the poet lived with Ginny the painter, and they worked in symbiotic union.

But Frank was quick to assume the role of mentor, effectively dominating their relationship in these terms. As busy as he was during these years, Frank relentlessly dedicated himself to Ginny's progress as an artist. In its attention to detail, his aesthetic oversight was reminiscent of the kind of attention he had offered the freshmen judoists at Subiaco in 1965–66, who, it is worth recalling, ended up thriving out of nowhere. For Ginny this attention often meant receiving precise instructions. She recalled, "He gave me specific directions about what he wanted me to draw ... I had an easel set up, started a couple of paintings that never came to completion. Both were suggested and choreographed by Frank: a woman asleep at a table with a snake on the table, and a painting of our friend Richard Banks sitting next to his window with an oar, looking at the full moon. ... Another image that Frank really wanted me to paint during that time ... was a woman asleep on a boat."[26]

In an essay, she explained:

> He was wildly enthusiastic about my painting—there's nothing like being understood. In the weeks that followed I read from his manuscripts and made drawings based on the poems. He bought me notebooks and different kinds of pens to try out. He said, Paint an old man sitting by a coffin waving at the moon; a fat lady shelling peas and a centaur behind her; a blind Gypsy holding a conch shell. Paint a white horse breaking away from a funeral hearse; a scarecrow wearing a kimono. Paint smoke rings.
> 
> I'd never heard anything like it.[27]

In one of her sketchbooks, Ginny allowed Frank to scribble his poetic thoughts and images among her drawings. Later in the sketchbook they dedicated a page to scrawling their signatures together (there were many more of Frank's).[28] In a journal, Ginny made notes on the imagery in Frank's short stories, listing items to paint ("the bell tower at Subiaco at night," "black/blue of the sky"; "negroes giving the finger to a police car on the levee").²⁹ Frank once rhapsodized in a note to Irv about listening to Mahler under a full moon with "Ginny painting one of my mad visions."³⁰ Ginny sometimes struggled with the technical complexity of the assignments Frank gave her. To cope, she reverted to drawing, and Frank supported her here as well, all the while nudging her back to painting.

Ginny persisted and in time eagerly and deftly painted the images that Frank continued to suggest she paint. Frank would ask her to work faster, but this only led to her working slower.³¹ In her journal, after listing images she wanted to paint—"portrait of Frank," "girl at window," "old man on front porch," "levy [sic] builders," "nick," "St. Benedict," "old woman sleeping"—she wrote that she would be drawing "for the next three weeks."³² Frank told Dugan, "For awhile [sic] she was illustrating my mind; now . . . she's painting."³³ With the monastery always at the forefront of his thoughts, Frank, in another example of love-based artistic collaboration, had Ginny paint the monks. To Cuddihy, Frank wrote:

> She's doing one of old brother Jerry playing a flute in his fantastic museum [this painting is owned by Subiaco Abbey]. If she can get a subsidy on the series, I think it will really amount to something one day. She is a hard working artist. Up at dawn and to bed early. She never talks about what she intends to do, she does it, And she is tech[nically] very competent, so she doesn't react the other way. She approaches drawing like Blake. And her art starts from scratch. There is none of this prepared food, none of these 15 cents biscuits in a box.³⁴

Frank's friend Ralph Adamo, who watched Ginny mature as a painter under Frank's guidance, attributed to Frank "a lot of the creative force behind her paintings."³⁵ By early 1974, Ginny, although working at her own pace, never questioned Frank's judgment. She recalls that she was soon winning cash prizes in art contests for the paintings that Frank had urged her to do and submit. Whenever she sold a painting, Frank was ecstatic. "Ginny found out she sold a painting," he wrote, "so we'll get drunk, go fishing, buy a new pair of boots, get the cat spayed, etc."³⁶

By the fall of 1974, after a year of mentoring Ginny, Frank was more involved in her art than his own. "Ginny is the only artist working," he updated Michael Cuddihy. "[She] is doing a painting of me and the old black guy I've been drinking with for ten years [Jimbo Reynolds]. It ought to be good. I seem to be more interested in her 'future' than mine."³⁷ Using a more graphic description, he explained, "Since I was first astonished with blood going stiff in my prick, two-thirds of a lifetime ago, nothing has ever drawn me away from poetry, from actually writing it, except her."³⁸ He was absolutely convinced of Ginny's talent: "I think she has her voice."³⁹

And he knew he was sacrificing his own work to foster it. After telling Irv that Ginny was preparing to send him slides of her work to use in *Mill Mountain Review*, Frank added, "Christ, I wish I could send you something besides a river of love and determination." At a time when Frank told Irv that "I'm sure you'll understand that it is essential for me to create" and that "I have to see to my own, my own legions," he was doing the opposite by turning his focus to Ginny's work.[40]

As involved as Frank was in inspiring Ginny's development, he was even more committed to publicizing and praising it. His initial target in his PR campaign was Alan Dugan and, more so, Dugan's wife Judith, a professional painter. Believing their support could enhance Ginny's exposure, he could hardly write a letter to Dugan in 1974 without including at least one shout-out to Ginny's progress. At times it seemed as if Frank's mood hinged on her success. In January 1974 he wrote, "I am in good spirits. My wife is painting alot."[41] A few months later he wrote that "my wife is painting alot and I am getting jealous of her good work."[42] But even when Frank was writing to a person who had no ability to help Ginny promote her work, he was still thrilled to brag: "She really has a vision."[43]

Frank was especially eager to share news of her commercial success, however modest, and exaggerate it to drum up interest. "Just back from the monastery," he wrote in the summer of 1974 after his stint at the boy's camp. "There's a chance my wife might sell a painting for enough for us to live on in the month of August, so I'm really hoping."[44] And the next month: "My wife is painting an old photograph in three, large panels on a commission which, if accepted, will enable me to write the month of September." Another commission had come in as well, but as Frank reported, "the idea was so trite she really couldn't go through with it and I couldn't blame her."[45] They needed the money, but as Frank assured Dugan the purist, she would never sell out and make those "15 cents biscuits in a box." For all of Frank's singing of Ginny's praises, Dugan never seemed to be in the least bit interested in her work. One even imagines Dugan might have felt a little put upon, perhaps sensing that Frank was angling to get at his wife and her connections in the art world. At one point Frank was essentially asking both Dugan and Judith to teach them an art appreciation course. "Since neither of us know what we should about contemp. painting," he explained, "we both feel a little guilty and foolish trying to discuss it." He asked for "your ideas and opinions on the following: *Gustav Klimt*, Fernand Knöpff, Hippolyte Daye, W. Kuhn, Adrian Van Ostad [sic], Vermeer." Always speaking on behalf of his wife, Frank explained how these painters "fascinate Ginny, and the latter has influenced her the most, along with Matisse + Cézanne."[46]

Then he turned to his own assessments and questions. He wrote, "I think T. H. Benton looks too much like El Greco and Tintoretto. Ask Judith. I'm probably an idiot. And I think Grant Wood looks like early Flemish? Probably, I don't know shit." But he was trying to learn so that he could better assess Ginny's work. He was especially curious about Andrew Wyeth, whose style Ginny's work most obviously reflected. Frank wanted to know what Judy's father, Ben Shahn, thought of Wyeth. Frank noted how he had heard Wyeth's painting compared to William Carlos Williams, Sherwood Anderson, "and, oh my God, Faulkner."[47] When Dugan expressed his disdain for Wyeth, Frank wrote, "Good to know you think Andrew W. is a shit. I hate him." Frank assured Dugan that "Ginny intends to get a couple of these art magazines, track what is going on." But in the meantime, he asked, "For my benefit, what do you think of Chagall, Modigliani, Pearlstein, Will Barnett, Leonard Baskin, Perlin, Tooker, Castéllon[?]" Perhaps sensing the imposition in all of this, Frank ended, "I better quit, that's a big job."[48]

The denouement of Frank's campaign to get Dugan and his wife to take Ginny's painting seriously came when Frank finally got slides made of some of her work and sent them to the couple for an evaluation. Frank talked up how hard it had been to get these slides done because Ginny's best work was suddenly flying out of her studio and, as a result, terribly hard to keep up with and photograph. "Goddam, all the paintings I *want* you to see . . . I can't get at," he complained. "They're all sold or given away." He explained, "There's one rich buyer who is buying her best, freest, most original stuff. . . . A lot of these paintings aren't even finished." He lamented, "I can't get at them long enough to take slides."[49]

Frank sent the slides of Ginny's work to Dugan in August of 1974. "If you think her work is shit tell me why," Frank insisted.[50] In the meantime, mildly encouraging words came from Michael Cuddihy, to whom Frank had also sent some of Ginny's slides. Cuddihy was, for example, "struck" by one painting of a woman, adding that it viscerally evoked "a certain kind of pain beautiful women leave you with." Cuddihy was clear on where Ginny's work stood vis-à-vis Frank's—"I wish I could say that I like those photographs and slides as much as I do your poems and stories"[51]—but the overall positive assessment boded well enough for the opinion that really mattered, the one they awaited on pins and needles: Judith Shahn's.

Dugan's letter in response to the slides finally arrived, after more than a four-month wait, in December. Frank had primed the pump, writing in November (and likely using this update as a nudge for an overdue response), "Ginny has painted her best since I last wrote you. Will send you a few slides as soon as I have time, unless they get bought before I shoot them."⁵² In his note, Dugan said nothing about Ginny's work. But he did note, "Enclosed find a letter to you from Judy writing about Ginny's work." This was what Frank (and possibly Ginny) had been waiting for.

Judith Shahn's response was written on a separate sheet of paper in cleaner, more legible handwriting than Alan's scrawl. "I've never tried before to give anyone my opinions or relations to their work on the basis of slides, and I'm not sure how this will work," she began. Addressing only Frank, she explained how she could not determine the scale of the paintings. She asked whether "most of her work actually does have a brownish cast or whether this is due to poor processing of the slides (or even the projector we used to look at them)." Without a sense of scale and color, she told him, "I for one almost have to imagine what the paintings look like." She said that "the drawing, the draughtsmanship, seems fine: well practiced, well observed." But in her final analysis, "I think my strongest reaction is that she has not yet found her own voice." She explained, "The kinds of things she paints and the way in which she handles them don't always seem related. There seems to be in some of the examples you sent to be an easy prettification, a sort of surface sentimentalization. ... Perhaps an even over-refinement of what are basically pretty direct statements. ... I kept having the feeling that she was looking at things with various other people['s] eyes, as well as her own. ... This is often the case with young painters."⁵³

This stung. "Ginny appreciates the note from Judith," Frank wrote to Dugan. He agreed that "all the work does have a brownish [color]," but he reminded Dugan that it was "coming from that part of the Ozarks where the fields ... meet the plains." While never overtly disagreeing with Judith's assessment, Frank wrote in defense of Ginny that "one of these days she is going to amount to something."⁵⁴ Soon after Shahn's review arrived, Ginny won a significant art award. Frank immediately wrote to Cuddihy, "Ginny won first place in a fairly old & well known Art show. ... The juror was an old, well-known artist, here in this country and abroad."⁵⁵ The winning piece was a painting in honor of Richard Banks, an image of an older woman surrounded by seven younger women. As Frank reported, the portrait won first prize out of two hundred entries in the twenty-fifth annual Fort Smith Art Center Competition. The judge was, as Frank pointed out, fairly well known. He was Alexandre Hogue, a noted painter of the American Southwest and a member of a group of artists called the Dallas Nine.⁵⁶ In the privacy of Ginny's sketchbook, Frank sweetly wrote, by way of congratulations, "Once in a great while an artist is fortunate enough to acquire public acclaim and critical recognition. At 24, Ginny Crouch Stanford."⁵⁷

In keeping with his aversion to conflict, instead of using this relatively prestigious accolade to show that Ginny, contrary to Shahn's assessment, had found her voice, Frank suggested to Dugan that Ginny owed her success to Judy's sage guidance. "It always works when a well-known artist tells another not so known to use their 'own' voice," he wrote. "She's been doing that recently and what do you know? She won first place in a fairly old & well-known Art show in these parts."[58] This was a stretch, as Ginny had completed and submitted the painting well before she had received Judy's tepid opinion of her work. But for Frank being obsequious was better than confrontation or overt expression of frustration with Shahn's opinion. Frank might have adhered to his own assessment of publishing poetry: "I believe anybody trying to get himself established will do anything to do it," and "I want no part of this."[59] But such rules of principled engagement seemed not to apply when it came to promoting Ginny and her work.

No matter what Shahn thought of Ginny Stanford, Frank's immersion in Ginny's painting—and Ginny's reciprocal connection with his writing and filmmaking—sustained their relationship. Recall that when Frank first described Ginny for David Walker (in the letter that opens chapter 11), he wrote:

> The poet finds another woman
> She is an artist

Much in the way that Frank couched his identity in "Frank the poet," he saw his wife as "Ginny the painter." Not Ginny the person, not Ginny my wife, but Ginny the artist. It was as if he were admiring her from afar. Still, their working relationship was a relationship. His favorite paintings were the ones "where my imagination and her skilled imagination merge."[60] Frank refused to make the mistake with Ginny that he had made with Linda, who thoroughly lost Frank to his obsession with "the manuscript" of *The Battlefield Where the Moon Says I Love You*. He avoided this mistake by seeing the world, at least artistically, through her eyes and her photos, drawings, and paintings. But while his empathetic commitment to her work might have removed Frank from his own, that removal was never complete. Her paintings were the strongest, in his view, when "resolving my poetic sketches," when linked to his advice and his work. On one occasion, he explained, "She's doing a great one of this black monk I know [Father Wolfgang Mimms]. And she's trying to do one from an unfinished poem I wrote." The fact that this poem was "[a]bout a helmet diver being hauled up and a man with a torch cutting the steel off his head" might seem odd. But that mattered less than the fact that the poetic image was Frank's and that Ginny's painting followed it to its own fruition.[61]

It helped that Ginny honestly adored Frank's poetry. "Frank's poems," she wrote, "could sweet talk you into driving through a snow storm for a six pack of 3.2 beer"; they could "talk a cat down out of a tree."[62] Frank's poems "lived with the fishermen and kept their lines tended ... kept the grass cut at the cemetery ... told me what I wanted to hear and let me guess the rest." Frank's poems, Ginny wrote, "promised me everything."[63] And the poems kept their promises. Ginny's paintings reciprocated. Frank and Ginny loved each other in this way—through their shared creation of poetry and paintings. Frank's attention to Ginny's work had the significant impact of encouraging him to listen more closely to other voices and artists, something he would do until he died.

## "Ougi, Ougi Tell Me What This Dead Poet Said"

During his years with Ginny in Rogers, Frank also expanded his outward-looking interest in the creative processes of others by "translating" the poems of Continental poet-filmmakers who reflected the cultural heterogeneity he valued. His work with Ginny did not necessarily initiate this interest in doing these translation-like exercises, as he'd been dabbling in them for years. But it certainly coexisted with and intensified Frank's desire to connect with poetic worlds and creative endeavors outside of his own. Ginny had, to a degree, pulled Frank away from his own work, and the pleasures of their collaboration were pleasures Frank came to realize could be found in other venues as well.

Frank Stanford was no linguist. Although he had studied French, he was not fluent in a foreign language. This fact might surprise readers familiar with his work. *The Battlefield*, narrated by a boy who seems to know every language on earth—even the secret ones, even sign language, even *secret* sign languages—contains long stretches of German and French and a smattering of Latin, Italian, and Spanish. Frank's published books of poetry include scores of poems dedicated to international language artists he deeply admired, artists including Pier Paolo Pasolini, Jean Follain, Nicanor Parra, Federico García Lorca, Bernardo Bertolucci, Yukio Mishima, Jacques Prévert, Luis Buñuel, André Breton, Jean Cocteau, and many, many more. Frank's interest in film fed almost exclusively on his obsessive attraction to a gritty kind of European avant-garde that he turned into a kind of backwoods hyperrealism. Determining precisely what he was up to when it came to working with foreign poems—because it certainly was not standard translation—requires some explanation.

If he wasn't doing translations, then what was he doing when he tuned his ear to so many international poets? John Biguenet, who had witnessed Frank's insatiable interest in foreign films and poets at the Hollins Conference back in 1970, suggested that Frank's "after" poems were initially akin to what Robert Lowell was doing with his period imitations. Seeking something between a translation and a tribute, the poet takes a preexisting translation of a foreign-language poem or maybe even uses a dictionary to eke out a rough translation of his own and then basically riffs on it. Consider Frank's early example of this exercise in *The Singing Knives*. In a poem called "The Intruder," which is "after Jean Follain," Frank tinkers with a translation of Follain's poem "Exil":

### "The Intruder" by Frank Stanford

In the evenings they listen to the same
tunes nobody could call happy
somebody turns up at the edge of town
the roses bloom
and an old dinner bell rings once more
under the thunder clouds
In front of the porch posts of the store
a man seated on a soda water case
turns around and spits and says
to everybody
in his new set of clothes
holding up his hands
as long as I live nobody
touches my dogs my friends

### "Exile" by Jean Follain (translated by W. S. Merwin)

In the evening they listen to the same
music no one could call gay
a face appears at a corner
of the inhabited world
the roses open
a bell has rung under the clouds

in front of the pillared doorway.
A seated man says to all comers
in his gray velvet
showing his furrowed hands
as long as I live no one
touches my dogs my friends

Some of what Frank does here, in one of his least modified "after" poems, is just elementary word swapping—"tunes" for "music," "happy" for "gay," and "blooms" for "opens." But on another level Frank, as he did with Cocteau, ushers Follain into his home territory, weaves him into his native landscape and vernacular, and releases him to see where he'll wander. Follain's "a face appears at a corner / of the inhabited world" becomes Frank's more pared-down "somebody turns up at the edge of town." Follain's "a bell has rung under the clouds / in front of the pillared doorway" is countrified by Frank into "and an old dinner bell rings once more / under the thunder clouds / In front of the porch posts of the store." Stanford describes a man about to speak as "seated on a soda water case," and before he says his peace, he "turns around and spits." Follain's more formal character is not seated atop on a soda water case (he's just "seated"), does not turn around, and most certainly does not spit.

This exercise with Follain and so many other poets writing in foreign languages mirrored what Frank was doing with Ginny and her painting. By setting the scene for her work, by asking her to translate images that he described for her, he was having her improvise within a preexisting imposed form. Frank, with some of his "after" poems, was subjecting himself to the same exercise, only in his case the strictures were coming from European, South American, and even Russian artists and poets. Again, this process coaxed the foreign poets out of their shells and into Stanford's infinite backyard in a quest to discover something unexpected. Frank was less the lone artist working in the wilderness than the collaborative artist uniting with another to synthesize something new.

If Bertolucci and Pasolini and Cocteau served as effective and inspiring models for Frank, then Frank could just as well serve as an effective and inspiring model for Ginny. To that end, perhaps emboldened by being filmed so often in the making of *It Wasn't a Dream: It Was a Flood*, he began to model for her, literally and often. Frank would dress up—in a kimono, in a Wild West outfit, in a pair of linen pajama shorts, in a T-shirt and suspenders—and he would pose while Ginny took scores of photos. Ginny recalls that Frank frequently asked her to draw and paint his likeness from those photos.[64]

Painting of Frank by Ginny based on a photo she took of him in 1973. *Courtesy of Ginny Crouch Stanford.*

While this request surely involved a measure of vanity—and the photos do bear this out—the modeling takes on deeper significance in the context of Ginny and Frank's working relationship. Frank not only listened to and watched the work of avant-garde artists on whose work he improvised; he also delved into their lives, their images, their personal histories, and explored the physical ways that they postured themselves as personae for the world to consume. Idols of his such as Muhammad Ali, Marlon Brando, the Marx Brothers, and Mishima are notable cases. They exemplified performative brilliance and, in so doing, warranted his full attention to the way they posed and crafted their physical presence to complement their artistic ambitions. Likewise, it was no coincidence that Pasolini, Bertolucci, Cocteau, and so many other models of Frank's were filmmaker-poets who had started writing at a very young age. These were men to whom Frank had an enhanced attraction, often physical, and whom he'd eagerly take direction from. Why shouldn't Ginny do the same with Frank?

There was a definite intimacy to this relationship. Recall Frank's attraction to Mishima. "You know there is a writer you should read if you haven't already. His name is Yukio Mishima," Frank wrote to Irv in 1971.⁶⁵ Mishima's appeal to Frank was as much physical as literary, as Mishima was routinely draping his lithe, muscular physique in cotton *yukatas* like the one that Frank, always attentive to his looks, started to wear with Ginny and have her paint him in. In this way Frank tried to inject eroticism into her art, and many of their surviving photos show that he succeeded. A photographer who was in graduate school at Arkansas in the mid-1970s briefly rented a darkroom with Ginny in Fayetteville. He recalls that almost all of her prints were shots of Frank, many times nude and sometimes in a state of sexual arousal.⁶⁶ There was no body of work without a body, and Frank seemed intent on Ginny paying close attention to his not only as a lover but as an artist as well.

Whatever the inspiration Frank sought through collaborating with other people, his relationship with them ultimately went beyond the body to embrace sound, rhythm, and place. In January 1974 he wondered in a letter to Dugan: "What is happening to sound in American poetry?"⁶⁷ To explore this question, Frank was not trying to improve on Follain and other foreign poets with his "translations." Instead, Frank hoped to transport them into his familiar geography, if only to defamiliarize that geography and force himself to readjust. Frank captured this idea with a Borges quote: "What is truly native can and often does dispense with local color."⁶⁸ The goal was to hear something simultaneously recognizable and foreign and to plant that contradiction in local soil. Recall Francis of *The Battlefield*'s wish:

> I want people of twenty seven languages walking back and forth saying
>    to one
> another hello brother how's the fishing
>    (4493–94)

So it was with Frank, who would have been thrilled to listen to any idea, much less one about fishing, expressed twenty-seven different ways in the confined locality of some southern bayou. As John Biguenet explained (regarding Follain), "Frank was moving back and forth between what French he had and the English translation. Then he was creating a synthesis of that into his own poetry."⁶⁹ Whatever came of that back-and-forth process, it allowed Frank, as he wrote in one unpublished fragment, "to drift off into a thicket of berries, briars, and voices."⁷⁰

This playful tinkering and synthesizing, this drift into multilingual thickets, preoccupied many poets in the 1970s. They were building on the pioneering translations of W. S. Merwin, Robert Bly, Lawrence

Ferlinghetti, and James Wright.[71] Closer to Frank's home, Miller Williams's more formal translation of Nicanor Parra had generated some buzz in the poetry world as well, and while Frank had little to do with Williams, he certainly lived in the orbit of that work. In this respect, Frank, for once, was part of a loose trend. Consciously or not, he was stepping into what Biguenet called "a literary community that was opening itself up to the world." Biguenet elaborated: "Poetry in that period had a working man's relationship to translation. It's not that people were thinking, *I'm a translator, and I'm going to turn out translations*. It was more that this is what a poet did. A poet read widely, read internationally, ignored boundaries for the most part. Translation just seemed a natural progression."[72] For a man whose literary interests skipped freely from *Beowulf* to Chaucer to Mishima to Yesenin, Frank was at home in this freewheeling, unbounded, translational flirtation with foreign expression on native soil.

It was in this spirit that Frank finished a manuscript he never published titled "Automatic Co-Pilot." It was composed of twenty-seven short poems that he described as "versions & improvisations." Each poem is dedicated to an international artist, most of whom were writer-filmmakers of an avant-garde/surrealist persuasion and many of whom were preoccupied with dreams. With perhaps one exception (the poem "White Rose" after César Vallejo), these poems are generally far less hidebound to the literal structure of a foreign poem than was Frank's interpretation of Follain's "Exil." The translational ambition was now elevated, however, as it involved writing poems that funneled the amorphous spirit of an artist's work and life into a poem. In some cases the connection to the artist was obvious, as in a Mishima-dedicated poem that evokes the Japanese writer and filmmaker's self-disembowelment with the image "long strings of guts / Fantailing out like caladium roots, wet and strange."[73] In other cases, Frank offers a more direct affirmation of a kindred spirit, as is evident in his Yesenin-inspired poem "Swimming Towards Women": "So long blood / brother until then / when we meet again,"[74] an apt line for a poet Frank adored and who wrote his last words in blood. But most often these poems read like image-driven expressions—ones that eschew familiar autobiographical themes and instead signal, however elliptically, foreign voices external to Frank's experience. These were voices, moreover, that he needed to hear at a point in life when the old voices he had so long relied on were becoming distant echoes.

In May 1974 Frank sent his "Automatic Co-Pilot" manuscript to an editor named Thomas Johnson. Johnson edited a two-year-old little magazine called *Stinktree* that focused on translation. He had already accepted a Bertolucci- and a Pasolini-inspired poem from Stanford but had now requested "to see a good sized mss from you."[75] This was exciting news. But despite his enthusiasm, Johnson never got around to publishing "Automatic Co-Pilot." The journal and its press folded in late 1975. But he did dedicate more than a third (twenty-one pages) of the spring 1975 issue of *Stinktree* to Frank's work. Calling what Frank was doing translation, Johnson attributed the poems to Bertolucci, Pasolini, Cocteau, and Jacques Prévert, following each poet's name with the note "Translated by: FRANK STANFORD."[76] This was a little misleading at best. Frank was not especially proficient in Italian or French, so these were assuredly not translations, at least as the term was traditionally understood. The process was so vague that Frank wondered to Cuddihy if he needed to get permission from whoever owned the copyright. Johnson, for his part, seemed aware of the problem but told Frank after he sent the issue to the printer that "I've decided it best to print the Pasolini with the name affixed, as you gave me the option." He hoped "the decision is one you can abide."[77]

Mischaracterization aside, the *Stinktree* poems reflect a more involved process than the one informing the poems in "Automatic Co-Pilot." For the latter poems, Frank admitted to Dugan, "I didn't really translate much of anything, other than holding my hands over an old board with a bottle on it, and saying, 'Ougi, Ougi [sic] tell me what this dead poet said.'"[78] But to prepare for the Bertolucci and Pasolini poems that he "translated" for Thomas Johnson, Frank had to find someone with the language skills to do a legitimate translation, however rough. This initial translation—likely not done by him—allowed Frank to improvise on that result to create what he called a "version."

To this end, Frank wrote to Father Jerome at Subiaco. Back in the summer of 1974, when camp was rained out and outdoor activities were canceled, Frank and Father Jerome had "returned to the translations we were doing." They had experimented with translating Hebrew, Greek, and Italian short poems.[79] Now, a year later, Frank was knocking on his door again, only this time there was a precise goal at stake. "How is your Italian?," Frank's typed letter began. "What I'm doing is taking the originals, finding a literal-non-poetic translation of them into English, then adapting them to poems," he explained. This was no longer "Ougi, Ougi" work. Frank stressed to Father Jerome, "I don't even need the translations to be in poetry margins.... They don't even have to be that accurate." They only needed to offer Frank a viable point of departure. Acknowledging how busy both men were—"You're probably the most snowed under monk in America"—Frank assured Jerome that "it should only take up about

15 minutes of your time per poem." Unless, Frank added, "you have forgotten your Italian."[80] (He assuredly had not.)

With a Bertolucci focus and Father Jerome as a potential collaborator, Frank was working up to a much more interesting project. In March 1975 he wrote a letter to Cuddihy at *Ironwood* summarizing plans that he requested be kept under wraps "until I have it all worked out." Stressing how Rossetti and Blake had blended poetry and visual art, he reiterated that he had long been interested "in those poets who are also filmmakers," if only to better understand and enrich his own interests. Bertolucci—a child prodigy who had started writing poetry at six years old and later found himself torn between poetry and filmmaking—was an obvious figure of interest for Frank. Bertolucci's first book of poems, called *In cerca del mistero* (In search of mystery), was published in 1962, when Bertolucci was twenty-one years old. Some of the poems had been written when he was fifteen. The book had never been translated,[81] and it was so rare that it took Frank two years to acquire a copy of it. "You don't have any idea how hard it was for me to get the book!" he noted.[82]

Frank's ambition, a really fascinating one, was to take the "first book of young B. Bertolucci" and then "translate" it—he added, "if that is the word"—with Father Jerome's help. Frank hoped that by the time he finished tinkering with the translations, "they will be versions. [B]ut still good poems, I hope." He noted that he would not "stick with the end rhymes." Frank did serious research for this project. He rightly observed to Cuddihy how "no one had published anything by Bertolucci" in English before Frank brought his poetry to light for English-language readers in *Stinktree*. He was so excited about this idea (as Bertolucci's poems were indeed obscure) that he convinced himself that if "a big publisher" got wind of it, "they would only get a well-known poet to do the book, making a lot of money for all concerned."[83]

This big plan, like so many others he had, never materialized.[84] The reason, as usual, was feasibly due to a lack of time. By the spring of 1975, not only was Frank immersed in Ginny's work, but also his experience twisting at the end of Lish's rope was coming to an end, the garden needed to be planted, and he had a lot of drafting to do for a new surveying project. He reiterated his refrain for Jerome: "Infernal business gets in the way."[85] Thomas Lux, who read the *Stinktree* issue with Frank's translations in it, for one was pleased that Frank was going no further in this vein. He wrote, "Here's a question that's also a semi-chastisement: why the hell aren't you putting together [a] manuscript of your best poems to submit to a big publisher? Why fuck around with Bertolucci when you're probably five times the poet he is?"[86]

But Frank's passionate interest in this collaborative venture was real—real enough to shift his attention away from the autobiographical origins of his work. Making "versions" of another poet's poems was a genuine, and genuinely felt, form of communication with poets he admired, voices from other times and other lands. To take direction from Bertolucci and Pasolini was to connect Frank to a new world that he could explore and mingle with his own. It was to mix the sounds and images of his own poems with the sounds and images of Bertolucci's and Pasolini's poems and then to improvise, version, synthesize the momentary chaos into a new expression. "There are so many kinds of poetry spoken," Frank longingly wrote to Cuddihy.[87] Like *The Battlefield*'s Francis Gildart, Frank Stanford wanted to hear and feel every one of them, even if it meant leaving his own kingdom behind and visiting, via lost roads, new villages with new voices.

## "The Small Fish That Rumble in the Night"

Frank had always expressed opinions about contemporary poetry, often strong ones, but he was generally hesitant to express them openly. Fellow students from the Whitehead workshop days recall Frank's silence during class. Fellow student Tom Whalen remembers that Frank chatted easily before and after class but held his fire once the seminar was underway.[88] The reason for this reticence surely had to do with Frank's belief that the workshop was an artificial space where poets postured and peacocked, something he was loath to do. When it came to workshopping poems, "He found it tedious," Irv recalls.[89] Frank, always nurturing his outsider status, preferred what he called "informal organizations" or "informal groups of artists" who shared their work spontaneously and organically. He noted that this was what made the 1970 Hollins Conference so appealing to him. But he despised the way the workshop—which he saw as a "dues paying association of writers"—fostered literary pissing contests. If only people could have kept an "unselfish and potent spirit" alive in the workshop, he lamented to Irv, rather than "being arrogant and obsequious," then he might have been more involved. As he saw it, most poets "were patting some shithook on the back" to get noticed.[90] None of it was for him.

When corresponding with other poets, such as Dugan, Cuddihy, and David Walker, Frank also tended to continue erring on the side of silence, perhaps afraid that his opinion would contradict theirs. To the extent that he even addressed the topic of other living poets, Frank continued to complain about how unfamiliar he was with contemporary poetry, all the while downplaying his standing as a critic. "I am out of touch," he flatly stated to Cuddihy in 1975.[91] False modesty or not, this posture began to shift during the time that Frank was mentoring Ginny in her painting and "translating" a range of foreign poets. After confessing to Michael Cuddihy that he was not in the same league with the writers he read in the leading journals, he turned around to declare, "That doesn't mean I don't like to shoot off my mouth about poetry!"[92]

And he started to speak more openly than he once had. He was not interested, as Whitehead and the workshop students had been, in debating the merits or demerits of famous poets past and present. Innately suspicious of commercially successful artists and having recently failed in his own attempt to break into popular venues, Frank fostered a critical bias toward the voices that the commercial presses overlooked. The underdogs. As always, his sympathies were with those whose talent went unrecognized by those in power. His critical tone, as he gradually became more vocal in his opinions during these years, was emphatic, fair, and generous. He always tried to discover a poem's deepest wellspring. But if it was poisoned with anything disingenuous, he would call it.

Frank's assessment, in a letter to Cuddihy, of a poet named Michael Checchio offers a case in point. After reading his work in an early *Ironwood* issue, Frank wrote that "Michael Checchio impresses me very much." Drawing on wisdom borne of his own experience, he wrote, "The destiny and doom of the poet who writes short verse is this: Either you can write thousands of the 'short poems', as I have in the past, or you can now and then whittle the little poem." Either way, he continued, "the *short* poem is the hardest of all forms, past or present. . . . They seldom work." That said, "Checchio is *good* though. I have wasted many nice nights (when I should have been fishing, sleeping, or dreaming) trying to *do* what he has *done*." Frank ended his review with a metaphor expressing a wish that quieter voices such as Checchio's might more often prevail. "His poems," he wrote, "are like the small fish that rumble in the night. The big ones are what we usually hear."[93]

Frank's critical edge was further honed by his largely self-directed immersion in the history of literature, a remarkable self-driven education that went back to middle school. This impressive contextual awareness, as well as his unassuming ability to access it, was on sharp display as early as 1969, when Frank was taking Jim Whitehead's workshop and had to write reviews of several popular poets. It was a task Frank loathed, complaining to Allen Ginsberg that he had to "writ[e] all these goddamn papers" for Whitehead.[94] But those goddam papers were pretty revealing. In a paper on James Dickey's *Buckdancer's Choice*, the twenty-year-old critic writes that "Dickey is capable of some of the most complex verse I have ever read." To appreciate that complexity, though, the reader has to understand that Dickey's "use of the swift anapest insinuates the comic and recalls the doggerel of fifteenth century English poetry." Only from that perspective can Frank's claim that "Dickey's rough shifts of gears break up the easy grace found in a lot of new verse" make sense. Whereas "the successions of unstressed syllables found in much of contemporary poetry emit a sensation of speed and buoyancy," Dickey interrupts that predictable rhythm "with images that claw."[95]

This is a keen analysis for anyone, especially a college undergraduate. While Frank's classroom prose was brilliantly imitative of what academic prose should look like (hence that good ear of his), the sweep of his knowledge was formidable and generally expressed without pretension. Reviewing Edward Simmons's *Driving to Biloxi*, he writes, "The resonant intonations he achieves in his longer lines and the eccentric interpretations of regional images recall the poetry of R.S. [Thomas] and Dylan Thomas." Still, Simmons, in Frank's assessment, too often does not measure up: "Many of his shorter lines rely only upon a cohesiveness, which often fails, of a multitude of gaunt and abstruse images, refracted to the point of weightlessness." Frank's critical voice stayed even keeled in these college essays, refusing to ever bully or pile on or engage in snark (unless it was absolutely warranted). So while, with Simmons, "all the meditative homages, except two, are paltry redundancies," these redundancies did not negate the fact that (the possibility of mockery here notwithstanding) "the polyphonic buoyancy lifts the lines to opalescent stratums of softness."[96]

Frank's greatest asset as an evolving critic was an intuitive sense of when a poem reflected an honest process and when it rang hollow as an imitation. There is no overstating how his criticism never wavered from this lodestone. He explained, "It seems to me that whatever the poet writes down first is automatic, there is a basic design of wheels turning in which is his experience, his imagination, his reading, his spirited intellect." With another driving metaphor, he continued, "But then, when he goes over what he has written, he is in standard, he shifts things around according to the load and grade of his driving."[97] Frank was quick to call foul when this necessary and personal process, one that the real poet intuitively appreciated, was violated. When James Dickey and the painter Hubert Shuptrine published a coffee-table homage to *Let Us Now Praise Famous Men* called *Jericho: The South Beheld* in 1974, Frank, for all his earlier admiration of James Dickey, pounced. "What a pile of shit," he wrote to Dugan, adding how "Willie Morris, who raved about it, is a complete fool."[98] This was exactly this kind of phoniness, a toadying to commercially driven art, that Frank despised.

Again, Frank's uncanny attunement to poetic honesty was deeply rooted in the wide range of his reading. He had a rare ability to access his encyclopedic but precise knowledge of the history of poetry and how it was written. In an undated letter to Irv, Frank wrote, "Try and recall the way in which Blake conceived his poetry: he inaugurated . . . a new aura around poetry (to this day, all the technical engineers still kissing the ass of the new critics believe that T.S. and Wallace were the first to adapt musical forms to poetry.) Shit. In the eighteenth century De Quincey was using the fucking fugue, not quartets." As evidence of this point he suggested that Irv "Read Blake's letter of 1803, April 25, to Thomas Butts."[99] Then he turned to a paraphrase of Coleridge that went right to the essence of poetic genius: "It is the prerogative of poetic genius to distinguish by parental instinct its proper offspring from the changelings with the gnomes of vanity or the fairies of fashion may have laid in its cradle or called by its names."[100] Frank, in other words, could smell a fairy of fashion a million miles away.

Frank's nascent critical philosophy also had an agenda. It ultimately addressed the disparity he perceived between undeserving writers who got commercial and critical attention and deserving ones who did not. Dominant categories and personalities—Walt Whitman's "schools and creeds"—too easily obscured talent that did not conform to what Pasolini dismissed as the preexisting "forms of the world."[101] "What I worry about," Frank wrote, "are these infernal descriptions: 'light verse,' social-realist, magical realism, surrealism, etc."[102] Pigeonholing poets into genres allowed for a savvy but mediocre poet to achieve undue fame only by imitating really well the forms in a particular realm. With established categories, a slavish adherence to a style rather than the inner brilliance of the work could too easily prevail, turning a mediocre poet into a magnet for awards and accolades.

"[W]e have set up all these dichotomies," Frank complained to Cuddihy, and poets were too easily locked into them.[103] Frank singled out Robert Bly and the Deep Image school. "When I read the shit that Robert Bly writes about poetry," Frank wrote, "I'd like to see all these little magazine editors quit trying to write about poetry like him." This kind of herd mentality with regard to poetic categorization annoyed Frank, who had at this point been following the poetry business long enough to voice more aggressively his opinions on the matter. "I wish somebody would write about poetry like Grocho [sic] Marx or Harpo Marx." In other words, with "silence."[104] In case there was any doubt about where he stood among the various typologies within the poetry world, he assured David Walker, no doubt with a little flex behind the statement, that "no theory accommodates me."[105] He clarified this position for Irv by noting, "I like those poets who are writing from a flowing intensity and not from a stance."[106] Frank had recently spent over a decade with that flowing intensity, and he knew the results of it when he saw them.

"The poet contains tragedy in his epic self," Frank wrote to Cuddihy. Tragedy in the epic self was where real poetry originated; it refused to conform to external categories of poetics. When poets were fashioned (or fashioned themselves) into something they were not—something that preexisting categories and trends tended to require—the result was a diminishment of the individual's inherent epic nature. The poems they produced inevitably confirmed that diminishment. "The man acting outwardly," he wrote, "is not so different than the man acting inwardly—unless he really is acting."[107] Frank—despite his self-deprecating claim that "I am inept in all gestures of criticism"[108]—was in fact becoming a powerfully astute critic, increasingly confident in his ability to tell the difference between an act and the real deal.

Michael Cuddihy, with his piercing poetic insight and generous disposition, was the ideal sounding board for Frank's critiques. George Oppen, Frank wrote to Cuddihy, commenting on the poets in *Ironwood 4*, was doing more than "writing good lines." Oppen was allowing them "ever so gently, but with a marked force, [to] become a poem."[109] Frank suspected the poet John Logan of having "learned" from James Wright. Or, Frank wondered, "are they both gliding over the same territory?" Jane Lippe—"hers really gets to me" (in a good way)—and William Stafford, along with Nils Nelson, struck Frank as being "very natural." He also knew all too well what poetic honesty such as Nelson's, completely yielding oneself to that "flowing intensity," could do to the poet emotionally. "I hope Nelson," Frank wrote, "can live with himself long enough to write more of his kind of poems."[110]

As Frank worked with Ginny and the "translations," he honed a critical voice attuned to the inner experience an artist went through to craft original art. He believed there was, despite the radical individuality of writing a poem, something universal about such an experience, and that every true poet eventually touched Pasolini's "inexpressible at the source of what I am" when that process was honored. "I do love to read good poems," Frank wrote to Cuddihy. "Just as I love to work and sleep and have pleasure."[111] What deeply frustrated Frank was how so many good poems written by honest poets never saw the light of day. In November 1974, he asked Cuddihy if they could turn the tables for a moment. He wanted to read some of Cuddihy's work—not the poems of others he edited but the ones he wrote. Cuddihy's work had been rejected by some magazines, but Frank wanted to read them and understand why they were not being accepted.[112] In the end, he loved them, and all he could say about them was "I wish other people could read them."[113]

This was not a rhetorical wish. Just as justice ignored the characters in *The Battlefield*, so the tastemakers ignored the artists who mattered. Frank felt the same way about so many disparate and hidden voices and not just voices in the American South. Consider the Japanese poet and translator Shozaburo Nakayama. According to Frank, he was "virtually unknown in this country and has only recently been 'discovered' in Japan." Frank's interest in him certainly involved the fact that Nakayama had attended a monastery at the age of twelve, been taken captive in World War II, survived a kamikaze attack that took out an American ship, and starved himself to death as a POW. In other words, he was an eccentric and brilliant hero who lived off the radar of public recognition, did not get the attention he deserved, and died heroically. But more important than anything else, Nakayama's voice also seemed to come from an honest and primitive place. "The poems which survive are of two natures: violence and peace," Frank wrote. "He signed poems with other poems." So, Frank concluded: "I would like to see his poems published in America."[114]

Likewise, Frank wanted to see Ginny's paintings hanging next to Vermeer's and thought he would in a just world. He wanted American schoolchildren to read and recite Bertolucci and Pasolini—and, why not, Frank Stanford—rather than old Robert Frost. Frank wanted poets to be real rather than suck-ups to fame. For all the angst generated by the MFA workshop back in 1969–70, there were a handful of poets from those days whose work Frank genuinely admired: Ralph Adamo, John Stoss, John McKernan, John S. Morris, and Justin Caldwell. Frank wanted these poets to get their due and win awards and have yachts like Eberhart. Frank wanted his own stories to fill the pages of *Esquire*. He wanted artists not concerned with fame, fortune, and the trappings of the literary business but only concerned with the honesty of their art to have time in the spotlight of literary recognition. "I've read quite a few books and poems by any given poet, usually the older ones, and it is mostly dull, but it is published and it is published not because it is good poetry but because it is supposed to be, given who wrote it," he told Irv.[115] Too many poets rode on their laurels rather than talent. It outraged Frank.

But by 1975 Frank knew better than to stew in that juice. He had learned enough about art and its market, art in the American South, art and the general public, and art and the underdog to know that cream rarely rose to the top. And he knew that when it did, it was quickly skimmed off to make room for the thin stuff. "His ideas," C.D. Wright wrote of Frank after his death, "seemed committed to changing."[116] This claim applied to more than Frank's art. It was true in his daily life, too, and in the flow of his ideas and ambitions. Remember how his ideas changed when he got to Subiaco and there was no judo team, when he met Ginny and realized she lacked a market for her incredible talent, and when he moved to Eureka Springs and could not see films by Bertolucci or Cocteau or Bergman. Frank changed the situation to get what he wanted: a judo team, a connection with a gallery, a movie theater. And so now, with his eyes full of shooting stars that only he could see—that is, writers he admired who had no home for their work—he realized that he would have to once again embrace the flux and, somehow or another, find a way to put these writers on the road to readership.

## "The Fucking Press Broke Down"

This kernel of a desire, fueled by a sense of injustice, would eventually lead to a publishing company called Lost Roads. To begin the process of creating that company, Frank turned, yet again, to Irv. Not only was Irv Broughton always there for Frank, but he was always there at the right moments. When Frank wanted to publish *The Singing Knives*, Irv brought him to Mill Mountain Press. When Frank wanted to try his hand at film, Irv literally put a camera in it. When Frank wanted to write screenplays, Irv sent him books on how to do it. And now, with Frank wanting to start a press to publish books of poetry by lesser-known writers, Irv was, yet again, there to help his friend. More than anything else, Irv had already set an example. As a scrappy publisher who thrived best when determination exceeded resources, he had demonstrated that, with patience and a suspension of disbelief, gorgeous little books came to life. Brilliant books. Underdog books. "Trying to do publishing without money is tough," Irv explained to Frank.[117] But, as Frank understood, a lack of consistent funding did not prevent Irv from eking out four of Frank's chapbooks in 1975. Notably, Frank did not sit back and watch that happen. He was by this time thoroughly familiar with how the books were made, and he knew that the birth of these lean volumes obscured the messy slow-motion chaos and uncertainty behind their production. Finding high-quality talent to publish was the easy part. Putting a book together was another story. But Frank was well aware of what had to be done.

Much of the work that went into publishing Frank's books, as Frank well knew, was done in a necessarily ad hoc fashion. Rather than adhere to any sort of marketing schedule, these books emerged only when Frank or Irv or both were somehow able to access paper, typesetters, and printers and then have Irv pay the bills. Typesetters were not to be taken for granted—"Not enough type and typesetters on your part?," Frank once impatiently inquired of Irv.[118] "PLEASE LET ME KNOW IF YOU ARE GOOD FOR SETTING THE TYPE," Frank wrote on another occasion.[119] Something as basic as getting decent paper could also be a challenge. In late spring 1974, Frank excitedly wrote that "I now have the paper and the covers, very high quality, for two books, 250 copies of a 36 page pamphlet."[120] But he lacked the time to properly package and send the material. Later that year, he effused to Irv how "I've got a real good 'hot' source for a bulk of paper."[121] And Frank could report, "I've got everything you need for yourself + magazines, but not time to type + revise it. No time with this fucking job."[122] Nothing, in short, was assumed to be on hand and accessible when needed. Time—as in having enough of it—could never be taken for granted either. And if time was available, he and Irv might be out of paper, or the gas card might have been maxed out.

Finding affordable printers was probably the biggest hurdle Frank and Irv faced in the effort to publish Frank's chapbooks and for Irv to run the *Mill Mountain Review*. Drawing on his Ozarkian connections forged in Eureka Springs, Frank eventually found an unlikely solution: a Eureka Springs turkey hunter who ran a print shop on Highway 187 called Elk Ranch Printing. His name was Burt Camp. Frank, who never referred to Camp by name in his letters, instead described him to Irv as "the fat hillbilly, bowhunter, treasurehunter, turkeyhunter, small engines mechanic." All correct—Camp was that rare local figure who still hunted with a bow and arrow, a treasure hunter, a tinkerer, and a big man. Ginny recalls seeing his operation and noting "a collection of brass bedsteads in the yard" and "a heavy set man in overalls and a woman missing a few teeth."[123] Frank said that, among Camp and his clan, "only one woman can read"—which was not quite the case. Camp was certainly literate, and his mother had even published a book that Elk Ranch had printed called *9 Flags: Cherokee Trail of Tears, Battle of Pea Ridge*. Camp propositioned Frank to write a book for them on, of all things, turkey hunting. Instead, Frank, who did not hunt and did not even own a gun, brought them Mill Mountain's business, including his books.

The turkey hunter was affordable because evidently neither he nor anyone in his family felt qualified to do adequate proofreading.[124] Camp, who relied on family alone, was always short of labor, so Frank and Ginny helped arrange the volumes after they were printed. The company offered various kinds of binding: "Perfect glued and staples, perfect glued and stitched, or a regular book binding."[125] Determining which Mill Mountain books and magazines were printed when and by whom is nearly impossible, but it seems quite likely that Burt Camp printed Frank's four books after *The Singing Knives*. Why Frank insisted on perpetuating the myth of his printer's illiteracy is unclear, but Frank, in an uncharacteristic instance of obvious impatience as he oversaw the printing of *Mill Mountain Review* 5, erupted: "The MMR V is driving me crazy. How would you like to work with printers who couldn't even read? They're so fucking slow and stupid."[126]

For his part, Irv had a printer in Bellevue, Washington, who had agreed to print *Mill Mountain Review* issues in exchange for Irv doing proofreading for the press, which he often did at night after a long day of teaching film classes as an adjunct.[127] In a rare moment of prosperity, Frank wrote, "As see[ing] that I have money for the printer, I'll send you the poems, about twenty or thirty short ones"—although it is unclear which book this was for or which printer they used.[128] Further complicating the printing picture is the presence of two other printers in and around Rogers, both of which Frank mentioned on occasion and possessed stationery from: Ro-Ark, which was established by a local fisherman named Dean Garman in 1974, and the more established Overstreet Printing Company in Bentonville and Fayetteville. Whatever printer was drafted into service, this was how the production schedule went for all of Frank's Mill Mountain books: catch as catch can. And when things were on track, they could just as easily go off the rails, as they did with this news, delivered by Frank to Irv in late March 1975, presumably regarding the turkey hunter: "The fucking press broke down."[129] At times the production of a book could even be delayed because neither Irv nor Frank had enough money for stamps. Making a book was, in short, chaos barely controlled, and Frank was well schooled in it.

But at the end of the day the chaos and uncertainty were all worth it. Because on the other end of it all, as Frank also knew very well, there it was: the book. The thin physical volume you got to hold in your hand, sign for friends, send to local bookstores, display on shelves, and maybe even sell. It justified all the frustration. *Shade* and *Arkansas Bench Stone*, which both came out in 1975, were especially important ones in Frank's career. They marked a sharp turning point in his work; namely, these books were the last stop for his childhood-inspired poetry. The poetry that was rooted in the youthful antics at Snow Lake among Francis, Jimmy, and their Black friends yielded after *Shade* and *Arkansas Bench Stone* to more conventionally adult themes reflecting Frank's contemporary immersion in adulthood and its many concerns (like death). Ralph Adamo brought this distinction to light when he said that, in *The Battlefield* and *The Singing Knives*, Frank was "calling on an incredibly rich sense of his own experience, especially on his childhood." But the later books, such as *Constant Stranger* and *You*, as Adamo observed, were different. They revealed "a very worldly and sophisticated sense of adult circumstances."[130] *Shade* and *Arkansas Bench Stone* offered the final expressive burst of childhood in Frank's published work.

Shade echoed familiar *Battlefield* themes. Passages such as "And the barefoot gypsy slicing her melon / Will kiss the ground you walk on / The rest of your life" recall a memorable scene in *The Battlefield* where Francis gets an erection while buying a melon from a topless gypsy hawking fruit near the levee camp:

> but on the floor on a patch quilt was a girl dirty as sin
> she was waking up and she didn't have a blouse on
> I said excuse me mam
> she said whata you want
> I said a honey dew melon mam
> (3705-9)

There are also many familiar characters from *The Battlefield* who appear in *Shade*: "I licked all of my mashed fingers / and read the books that smelled of Will Percy's stables," "Why be so damned faithful / to the way it is Rufus asked me," "The book is full of my father's eyelashes," "Of my sister I can only say / She was like a long feather / Who could breathe under the water," "Dark and I we shared quicksongs hollered at the top / of a loft," "Miss Emma has passed away," "I just had the pleasure of speaking / with Mr. Hank Williams." There are also the familiar territories: "Midnight Mississippi," "Panther Burn," "Snow Lake," "Moon Lake," "Trueblood's Drive Inn." And there are the frequent references to dreaming: "If you could do anything / You would dream," "Tomorrow night I dream," "I am going to dream," "the smiling / Chiropractor said dreams are funny like that," "This is an adventure / And I am a rider / Riding two plumed horses at once / The one is a dream and the other is real."[131]

In "St. Francis and the Wolf" and *The Battlefield* lines run long, often to the standard margin. But in the outtakes and reworkings from the big poem, Stanford truncated the lines. A majority of the poems in *Shade* do not exceed a page in length. Many are less than a half page. A lot of white space remains on the page. However, Frank notably left two poems— "Field Hands on Plantation Night" and "Slow Rag of the Yearbook"—in their original long-lined, untruncated form. These poems go on for several unpunctuated pages, exactly as in "St. Francis" and *The Battlefield*. "Field Hands" sounds, in a way, like an outtake that ended up not fitting into the levee-camp sections of *The Battlefield*. It features the levee-camp relationship between Dark (a Black man who is something of a hero to Francis) and Francis, which gets replaced in *The Battlefield* with Francis's relationship with Charlie B., BoBo Washington, Tang, Ray Baby, Born in the Camp with Six Toes, O. Z.—a more closely networked Black community bent on antics, mayhem, and backwoods justice. In *The Battlefield*, while Dark remains in the story, he plays a different role than in "Field Hands"—a more serious and mentoring one in the realm of social revolution, especially when Francis takes his freedom ride toward Mound Bayou at the end of the poem.

The limited second edition of *Shade* notes that "these poems were written during the time: 1964–1968." This detail is a bit of gold when it comes to understanding how Frank managed his constantly growing and shifting cache of poetry. The dates encourage us to speculate even further about the elusive timing of when Frank excerpted *The Battlefield* from "St. Francis and the Wolf." The year 1968, a time when the original draftings of the *Shade* poems were completed, was when Frank had just begun to frequent Sherman's Tavern and spend time with Sherman Morgan, Claude Ricks, and Jimbo Reynolds—all Black men that Frank came to socialize with regularly. Therefore, what we might be seeing in the outtake poem "Field Hands on Plantation Night" is a nascent version of the Snow Lake levee camp, one in which the character Dark begins to school Francis in the ways of subverting white power:

> who's trying to swamp your dory with the bilge of your own blue
> blood Me and a man named Dark did it We did it all most of it.[132]

But in *The Battlefield*, which Frank worked on diligently between 1968 and 1974, there may have been an effort, inspired by Frank's evolving friendship with the men at Sherman's, to rework the levee camp into a place marked not by subversion and revolution but by storytelling, banter, and adventure. Dark, who is at the levee camps in the *Shade* poems from the 1964–68 period, gets moved by Frank after 1968 to the end of *The Battlefield*, where his strategies of subversion are in service of utopia.

"Slow Rag of the Yearbook" is the other *Shade* poem that looks and sounds a lot like a *Battlefield* outtake, and the form suggests that Frank was, between 1964 and 1968, less interested in the role of race in his poem than he would be after 1968. The outtake is peppered with Mountain Home school references, which is appropriate given the 1964–68 time of its writing. The speaker remembers how "I'd stroll around the Library checking out books," much as Frank did at Subiaco; he mentions girls who "came past you in the halls with someone older"; he talks about walking "across the gymfloor in your cleats in the middle of the night"; he notes that "in bad weather the principal lets the girls wear boots and jeans"; and he recalls how "the English teacher got me back / on the team He's got pull." And then: "The season ended We didn't do any good." This poem is littered with such flash vignettes, ones that seem nostalgic for Frank's early high school years.[133]

*Shade* is thematically loose. Aside from being time stamped by Frank's childhood, the book has a haphazard and catchall feel. Whereas the twenty poems in *The Singing Knives* centered on life in the levee camps, with many poems and characters cross-referencing one another, the thirty poems in *Shade* lack a clear unifying thread. This is not necessarily a bad quality, as the staunch independence and decontextualized nature of the poems give them an innate and atomistic uniqueness. Take this excerpt from the poem "Leer," one that highlights Frank's ability to blend nature, violence, and beauty in a thumbnail sketch:

> The weeds give you something
> you want to fall into
> like a trap set with whittled cane
> With holes in your body
> something could blow
> clean through you
> and play a tune[134]

There are Tom Sawyer–like evocations of Mountain Home life, such as this stanza from "Night Time":

> When I was twelve I had to
> wash my mouth out with soap
> for taking the deaf girl to the woods
> and holding a lantern
> under her dress[135]

A poem titled "Tryst," written "after Jean Cocteau," shapes Cocteau's opium-driven hallucinations into thin daggers of text down three largely white-space filled pages:

your deadly fingers going
over my letters
like starfish making love
wherever you are
I want the last drink
of brandy which seeps
from your lips on the pillow
in your sleep I know you
fortune teller
of sinister signs[136]

Then there's the attention to the reality of lynching in "The Silence the Thicket the Sniffing":

Just like that
is what she meant
when she shook her head
and snapped her thick fingers
at the same time
They call it murder in some places[137]

And there's the subsequent Jim Crow deafness to the injustice, as shown in this excerpt from "Fair Trial":

And all his friends
Showed up
Not that they carried any weight
In the town
But they came
To give him soul support
Because they knew
He'd didn't have a whore's chance
In heaven
You can't touch
The wife of the Law
And expect to getaway
With it hell
The paper's bound to be against you[138]

Coming out around the same time as *Field Talk* and *Shade* was *Arkansas Bench Stone*. "ARKANSAS BENCH STONE looks great," Frank wrote to Irv in the summer of 1975.[139] This thin volume of just sixteen poems is a loyal addendum to *Shade*, one that also highlights precise memories of the levee camp days. In the poem "Inventory," Frank recalls one of his mother's many roles in the camps while using the quick-sketch storytelling technique he excels at in so many of his shorter poems:

> A man came into the store
> Told Mother he was looking for a good knife
> She took him behind the counter
> And let him look a spell under the glass[140]

Toward the end of this poem Frank gives a glimpse of O. Z. "hoeing weeds around the monuments." In "Island," he appears again: "Me and O.Z. walked everywhere. We had a seine a compass." Ending the poem is a Leadbelly lyric from a song used in *Dream/Flood*: "Whoa back boys oh goddamn." In a poem called "Lap" Frank pays homage to his family's cook in the levee camps, Emma:

> She pours sweetmilk over me before the sun comes up
> Her dress is like a tent in the desert
> Her whippings don't count
>
> . . . . . . . . . . . . . . . . .
> She cuts her snuff with happy dust
>
> . . . . . . . . . . .
> Emma is humming[141]

There's still a strong whiff of *The Singing Knives* in *Arkansas Bench Stone*. Take the opening to "Mouths Full of Spit," which involves several motifs from *The Singing Knives*, including the gar, the moon, the mother, and a kid running down the road:

> The gar weaved around the moon
> Like a child running down the road
> Towards the next lighted house
> Asking help for his mother[142]

Several poems in *Arkansas Bench Stone* address the one man who made the levee camps, and thus Frank's poetry, possible: Frank's father. Most notable is "Lament of the Land Surveyor," a poem Stanford scholar Murray Shugars calls "a son's longing for his dead father."[143] It ends:

> And the smell of those flowers
> Floating to the foot of the mountain

Reminds me of my hair
Falling on my own father's boots
And the smell of his jacket
And his straight razor like a lamp
Glowing in the window before me[144]

With *Shade* and *Arkansas Bench Stone*, that lamp glowing on Frank's memories begins to dim, reiterating for Frank a new adult reality, one where, as he writes in "Monk's Dog" from *Arkansas Bench Stone*, "you don't have a past."[145]

## Lost Roads

Frank's helping Irv wrestle these books into print offered its own kind of education. It's likely that, as early as the summer of 1973, Frank had written most of the poems for *Ladies from Hell, Shade,* and *Arkansas Bench Stone*. In August of that year he mentioned "small manuscripts" that needed to be "set up," but he did not have the time, or maybe the inclination, to send them to Irv.[146] Nearly a year later, he mentioned giving Irv "enough material for two books"—possibly *Shade* and *Ladies from Hell*—instructing him "to set what you wish" and assuring him that "the paper has already been cut," almost certainly by Burt Camp the turkey hunter.[147] Frank may have dragged his feet a bit because he wanted to sell as many poems as he could before putting them out in book form. Noting in August 1974 that the turkey hunter was ready to print *Ladies from Hell*, Frank wrote, "I've got those three other smaller books [*Shade, Arkansas Bench Stone,* and *Field Talk*] but want to wait on the magazines to publish the work."[148] As late as December 1, 1974, Frank, who had just completed a long stint of surveying, wrote to a friend, "The galley proofs of four of my pamphlets are sitting on the desk but I'm not interested in looking at them. I'm reading maps and listening to music and cutting wood."[149]

When it came time to publish, the haphazard nature of that process reminded Frank of how fine the line was between poems that sat in a drawer and poems that built a legacy. Stone by stone, Frank had been able to construct a legacy. Two hundred copies of *Shade*, which contained four drawings by Ginny, were bound by Overstreet Printing Company in June 1975;[150] two hundred copies of *Arkansas Bench Stone* were bound by Overstreet on Frank's birthday (August 1) in 1975.[151] These books joined *Field Talk, Ladies from Hell,* and *The Singing Knives* to comprise the first phase of Frank's career as a poet. Granted, it was only a four-year phase;

granted, only a few hundred books were made; and, granted, the next and last phase—which would include *Constant Stranger* (1976) and the posthumous *Crib Death* (1978) and *You* (1979) —was even shorter. But that's how it went for a poet who published a career's worth of work in less than a decade.

As his books came together, Frank, despite his admirable efforts on the ground, knew the only reason they were possible was because of Irv Broughton: "If I write poetry the way I want to," Frank wrote, "I doubt that anyone would publish it—except you."[152] While he was not one for excessive gratitude, even for the man who was going bankrupt on his behalf, Frank had the decency to thank Irv after the publication of *The Singing Knives* with what he called "my only cherished object": an old butcher knife taken from a shed on William Faulkner's property in Oxford, Mississippi. Frank also thought about giving Irv a horseshoe from one of Faulkner's horses, also purloined from Rowan Oak, but in the end, he decided it was "too heavy to mail."[153]

More importantly, though, Frank Stanford, who was quietly burying his past, was preparing to pay forward his gratitude. "You are one of the only people in existence who spends himself and his money on other artists, whether they be great, forgotten, unknown, or lurking—such as myself," he told Irv.[154] Frank, who had spent years getting a bowhunter with a small press in a tiny village in the woods to print some of the most exciting poems being written in America, was at this point fully committed to the notion that true talent was ignored because of lack of resources and opportunities. In early 1974 he wrote that he had a practice "of sending bad poems to large magazines, and good poems to small publications" to "prove the sincerity of small editors" and "the foolhardiness of big ones."[155] Frank now wanted to join Irv and the league of small presses to offer poets who were working in relative obscurity a chance to get noticed. Frank railed about "the bullshit most of the second rate people thrive and get wealthy on."[156] While there were "legions" of bad poets, "there are so many good poets, now, all young."[157] It was one's duty, as he explained to Irv, "if you see something beautiful and see something truthful and no one else sees it," to ask oneself, "How can you exist without putting some dark or light on it to bring it out?"[158] Knowingly or not, since meeting and working with Ginny, Frank had been preparing himself in various ways to pursue this ambition.

Since spring 1973, Frank had dedicated almost two years supporting Ginny's work as a painter, very much at the expense of his own writing. It had been a simple but profound reorientation, especially for a man in his mid-twenties. "You can well imagine the toll it has taken on my poetry," he told Irv about working so much with Ginny. To the extent that he did focus on his own poetry, Frank began to collaborate with foreign poets by writing versions of their roughly translated poems, a sort of homage-driven approach that took him away from his past, his childhood, the levee days, and his family history—only to send him on an empathetic journey into other poetic minds and contexts. Both endeavors coincided with—and surely fostered—Frank's evolution as a savvy critic who was especially attuned to a poem's deeply personal, emotional, and psychological origins. All of these developments, which intensified between 1973 and 1975, positioned Frank for his next and last move: publishing books of poetry for talented poets that he would select and then nurture.

Frank first raised the idea of starting his own publishing company in the late summer of 1974, when Irv was visiting Rogers to finish shooting *Dream/Flood*. By December the idea had evolved into a more concrete ambition. Frank wrote, "If I had 500.00 I'd start a little publishing company in the form of a magazine/pamphlet."[159] By March 1975, the idea was still alive. He wrote to Cuddihy, "I would like to start a chapbook series in the form of a magazine. . . . If I could print 8 or 10 books by people I think deserve books, then I would feel more like I was doing my part."[160] By August, Frank had reconnected with Leon Stokesbury, who was teaching classes at Arkansas, and solicited his participation in the project, to which Leon responded, "Your idea about the book periodical still sounds fine to me. . . . I think it can be done."[161]

Frank also wanted to do it as an homage to the little magazines that nurtured his career. "I believe 100% in the small magazine," he told Irv.[162] "I'm not one of those who condescend to the little magazine," he wrote to Cuddihy, whose little magazine, *Ironwood*, Frank adored. "Any poet who does is something of a lickspit. There is only one train running for poets and the good magazines are the boxcars, hauling our goods."[163] He described his desire to publish books as an "unrequited need."[164] Although he did not specify whom he had in mind, he noted to Irv that "I know four real good unpublished bookwise poets, and I know four fine published poets." As for the four fine published poets, he was referring to John S. Morris, John Stoss, Ralph Adamo, and John McKernan. Frank said to Irv, "I could do one of yours and one of your choices, or one of mine, too." Frank's idea was to do about ten books at one hundred copies apiece and publish them anonymously out of Neosho, Missouri, where Ginny's parents lived. "I'd call the magazine," he concluded, "XXXXXX    LOST ROADS    XXXXXXX."[165]

Frank most likely took the name from his own poem "Circle of Lorca," the lead poem in *You*, which includes the lines:

> When you take the lost road
> You come to the snow
> . . . . . . . . . . . .
>
> When you take the lost road
> You find woman
> Who has no fear of light
> . . . . . . . . . . . .
>
> When you take the lost road
> You find the bright feathers of morning
> Laid out in proportion to snow and light[166]

Irv knew exactly what Frank had to do to get Lost Roads going: get funded by someone besides him. To that end, he advised that anyone hoping to start a small press or a little magazine would need mock-ups, some sample copies to show off, to use to apply for a National Endowment for the Arts (NEA) small press grant. Irv, who wrote some poetry, happily made himself available to serve as Frank's first experiment. After receiving a batch of Irv's work, Frank shape-shifted quite convincingly into a seasoned editor. He wrote that "for me to give you any help—if I can at all—I will have to keep them [the poems] several months." His reason was that he needed to try to get as close to the poems as possible. "Some poets don't like you to get well acquainted with their work," he went on, because "you end up knowing more about it than they do." That was just step one. Frank then explained how only once he got to know the poems would he then turn to the task of making a book out of them. Foreshadowing the depth of attention he would offer his future poets at Lost Roads, Frank wrote to Irv back in March 1971:

> What I like to do after getting the feel of each poem, then the feel of the book, is write the poems out and, or, memorize some without writing them out. That is what I'm doing with yours now. Some days I might spend a lot of time with your poems and on others little or no time, then if I get up early . . . I will read say about a dozen or so at random. The closer you get to *the* experience, either by participating or feeling—reading or writing—the closer you can come to making it with somebody's poems.[167]

It would be a stretch to say that Frank ever "made it" with Irv's work. Frank had been reading Irv's poetry since at least 1971 and was not afraid to speak his mind about an Irv Broughton poem, as he had back in February 1972 when he wrote, "I don't think it is much account." He had long urged Irv to "make your poems come from a different terrane [sic], a place other, in motive, than the impulse which makes you a good editor."[168] After reading some of his poems "over and over," Frank concluded, "There are so many things you can do"—which is an ambiguous comment at best. As with his earlier criticism, he tended to register his opinions through carefully calculated metaphors. He wrote to Irv that "there are about seven poems where you stand on the ground with your feet and say 'I'm standing here.'" These poems were "like 7 rivers a crazy dog follows and when he dies an old man and a boy with one-eye come along and whittle his ribs into knives." In case Irv somehow mistook this extended metaphor for a compliment, Frank drew at the bottom of the page the outlines of a tent with connect-the-dot numbers and wrote, "Give up *this* property. Forget these boundaries—go out there. Infinite." In another assessment, he wrote, "For me, to read you is like having a rock thrown at you. Many times I have missed your poems for fear of getting hit by them. I did a lot of ducking." Eventually, though, Frank recovered his balance and decided, "I feel easy with them."[169]

For the moment, an easy feeling was all that was needed. The goal for the mock-up was not publishing poetic genius; it was the creation of a pretty little thing to show off for a grant application to get Lost Roads some funding. Frank suggested to Ginny, whom he assigned to design Irv's book, a solid white cover, and she approved. Frank wrote to Irv in the early summer of 1975, "Your book will have a gloss white cover with green ink. ... Really look professional."[170] Frank followed through, contracting with Burt Camp, the turkey hunter, to do the printing and Overstreet Printing Company in Bentonville to cut and bind two hundred books.[171] The title was printed in deep evergreen: *SURVEYING: Poems by Irv Broughton*. There is an endorsement by Richard Eberhart, who noted, "Irving Broughton can write a poem about anything and does. ... His work is refreshing to read. ... He gives lively pleasures."[172]

An unexpected stroke of financial luck made printing Irv's books possible. Frank had done two surveys for the turkey hunter and had yet to be paid. Frank initially said he had put about $800 of work into the plot (later he estimated it to be $1,000). But in the meantime the land Frank had surveyed—"I ran the lines honest, so I don't have to worry"—got tangled up in a lawsuit because "there was a fist fight among the turkey hunters [sic] women and a no count preacher and real estate agent."[173] Because the Camps could not pay Frank for the survey, Frank explained, "they'll do small books of mine for cost." In other words, "rather than have an uncollectable bill," Frank had a $1,000 credit.[174] It was because of this credit, the result of a backwoods brawl between the turkey hunter's mother and a preacher, that the first Lost Roads volume was born in the summer of 1975 (although the copyright date is listed as 1974). The bill from the printer came to $245. Frank sent it to Irv.[175]

Frank did one more mock-up—a 1975 edition of a book that Lost Roads would issue a longer version of in 1977. This was John S. Morris's *Bean Street*. Frank knew Morris from the workshop days and had published him in the *Preview: Eight Poets* issue (the one with the moons) he had edited in 1971. He admired Morris's poetry as much as the work of any contemporary poet he ever mentioned, calling it "real and good and down to earth in my book."[176] "I know a poet who I've lost contact with," he wrote to Cuddihy, "named John S. Morris." He was "pushing 40, but I hate to think of him at that age and still unknown."[177] Frank, who remembered Morris as "one of the nicest people I've ever known in my life" and a man of mixed heritage ("His Cherokee-Welsh-Arkansas self is beautiful"),[178] contacted him in early 1975 in West Virginia, where he was working as a campus representative for the Veterans Administration.[179] Frank requested a manuscript, and Steve (as Morris was called) sent it, assuring him that the poems had not been published anywhere and complaining how nobody was publishing his work anymore. "Hope you can do something with it—so far I haven't had any luck," Morris added.[180] His wife, Phyllis, assured Frank that her husband "is excited about his book."[181] Frank had the book out by October of 1975.[182] There are two illustrations in it, one by Morris's daughter. The inside cover reads: "Rogers, Ark.: Published for Frank Stanford, by Lost Roads Pub. Co., © 1975."[183]

On October 1, 1975, Irv alerted Frank to the November 1 NEA deadline and urged him to order the "Assistance for Small Presses Guidelines." He reminded Frank that, when he applied, he could "show a book or 2 from Lost Roads."[184] Frank, despite having gotten the mock-up books together for exactly that purpose, never followed through on that recommendation. He was not ready to apply for the grant. This was partially due to the fact that many of the Morris volumes fell apart when opened. Phyllis wrote to Frank after receiving the books, noting how "the printer seems to have done a good job, except for the binding is poor—the pages literally fall out as you turn them. But nothing is perfect."[185] And while an editor at the Catholic magazine *America* called *Bean Street* "a triumph of its kind," he chose not to review it, because it was so slim and "no price is mentioned."[186] Irv, for his part, applied for that NEA grant, got it, and used most of it to help Frank.[187]

Meanwhile, Frank accepted an invitation that would fundamentally alter his life one last time. At some point in the fall of 1975, perhaps deciding to bask in a little fame generated by a local screening of *It Wasn't a Dream: It Was a Flood* in Fayetteville, Frank went to a party at Jim Whitehead's house. This was likely just after late September 1975, a time when Bill Harrison wrote to Frank, "I take it you will be drifting into town for all the Fellini films. Good."[188] Whatever his exact reason for going back to Fayetteville, Frank went to Whitehead's party and met a young female poet in the MFA program, a woman who had had no intention of going to the party until she heard that Frank Stanford, the legend, might be there.

"I spent the evening talking to him in Whitehead's workroom," she recalled, after asking for an introduction to Frank by Miller Williams's wife.[189] The air-conditioning was blasting in the room as Frank and the young poet talked—"Whitehead kept it on high because he was always sweating."[190] "We had a long talk," she recalled.[191] As with Linda, Cheryl, and Ginny, the attraction between Frank and this poet was immediate. "It got serious rather quickly," she said. "It was all romantic, and I was a romantic young woman."[192] In a matter of weeks, both of their lives centered on each other. It was an all-consuming relationship—poet to poet— and it would result in what she would later call "three painful, exhilarating, life-changing years."[193]

Frank and C. D. Wright with the printing press Frank purchased in 1977. *Photo courtesy of Shiloh Museum of Ozark History.*

THIRTEEN

# Lost Roads

## 1976-1977

CAROLYN DORIS WRIGHT ("C.D.") WAS born in 1949 in Mountain Home, Arkansas, the town where Frank lived from 1961 to 1964. In 1956 her family moved to Harrison, where her father, Ernest Wright, worked as a judge, and her mother, Aline, as a court reporter.[1] After graduating from Memphis State University in 1971 with a degree in French, C.D. attended law school at the University of Arkansas. Law school had at least one unexpected benefit: Wright became friends with a law school professor, a woman with "coke bottle sunglasses and messy hair,"[2] named Hillary Rodham and as a result would go on to lunch now and then at the Governor's Mansion, once Rodham became Clinton.[3] After only a semester of law school, according to Forrest Gander, whom C.D. married in 1983, "she was pretty unsatisfied and wanted to write."[4] Her friend Ralph Adamo said that C.D. only went to law school "because her father was a lawyer."[5] With the endorsement of Ben Kimple, a professor in the English Department with whom she'd taken a class on the classical modernists (Pound and Eliot especially), C.D. entered the MFA program and began to write poetry.[6] This shift from law to literature meant, along with other perks, getting invited to Whitehead's parties.

Frank recalled that fateful evening in the fall of 1975 when he and C.D. met in Whitehead's office. "I met C. at a gathering of writers," he later remarked.[7] They discussed the city of Memphis, where they had both once lived,[8] and of course they discussed poetry. She was putting the final touches on her thesis, a selection of poems called "Alla Breve Loving." "I loved her poetry," Frank wrote, "not so much for what it was then, but for what it was to become."⁹ Soon after they met, Frank gave her "an onion-skin carbon of the manuscript in two bulging brown folders." It was around five hundred pages.¹⁰ This was, of course, *The Battlefield Where the Moon Says I Love You*. Frank had, by the fall of 1974, finished writing it but had yet to find a publisher.

His finishing it meant, among other things, that Francis the character had completed his freedom ride to Mound Bayou, Mississippi. From there he had established a biracial utopia on an island in the Mississippi Delta that he had inherited from his Black friend Rufus Abraham. He called the land "Abraham's Knife." In an easy-to-miss plot twist earlier in the poem, Francis *accidentally* boards the freedom bus, much in the way that Frank accidentally discovered Sherman's by meeting Jimbo. Francis's first thought is that the bus is going to get bombed. But instead he experiences nothing but love as he is welcomed by the Black activists on the bus and, after going to the back, eases into the freedom ride. A man says, "glad to have you along" and Francis responds, "well it took me a long time getting here" (9360–61). Soon enough "everybody goes Amen we going to ride ride ride Amen" (9367), and Francis, warming to the atmosphere, reports, "I clapped yassuh brother" (9378). Before you know it, the metal firecracker is barreling hard down a rural Mississippi blacktop.

At the end of the poem Francis, as if tying a contemplative past-present-future knot, sits on the bank of the river and reflects while a preacher prepares for a mass baptism:

> there was twelve race of people living on the bend
> Abraham's knife was a big island with good land
> Mr. Rufus was kind to leave it all to us like he did
> lots of folks come back from Chicago and Harlem and out west
> when they got their share of the deed
> Tang said it better not be no communism or no notci living
> he said it better be like the Indians
> it was like a tribe on the farm just like the tents on the levee camps
> were I used to dream when I was little
> 	(14793–801)

Remarking on this utopian community, populated in part by a reverse of the Great Migration of Black people out of the South early in the twentieth century, Frank, using a surveying analogy, said to Irv, "I learned that there can be a perfect society even if all the corners on it aren't ninety degrees. That there is such a thing. I learned what Blake knew and tried to teach and not didactically but tried to teach in poetry."¹¹ This strategy definitely worked for C.D. Her ultimate takeaway from the poem was that "Blackness empowers *The Battlefield*."[12]

## "Well, Yeah"

C.D. took the two brown bags of onionskin paper to her brother's house in Harrison and, as snow fell, read Frank's long poem. Frank, as she recalled it, "stopped by sometime in the night, on his way to or from somewhere, and we walked up and down my brother's street in the snow." Her brother's cat rode on Frank's shoulder as they walked. When he left, C.D. read the rest of the poem through the night. Her first reaction upon finishing it was to feel "a personal blow." She explained, "Here was someone barely five months older than me whose geography I knew, whose lexicon I could grasp." As C.D. put it, "I felt absolutely helpless to so much wildness of heart, so much fury and hilarity, such language."[13] C.D.'s close friend, the photographer Deborah Luster, remembers that C.D. "was blown out of the water by it."[14] As she fell in love with the poem, she fell for the poet as well, a man whose "unruly, lost tongue" she kept close for the rest of her life.[15] After a few weeks of spending more time together, C.D. and Frank "rented a house across [from] the co-op on Watson St."[16] It was around this time—by late November at the latest[17]—that Frank wrote a poem called "Directions from a Madman." It would appear the following year in his sixth chapbook, *Constant Stranger*. Coincidentally or not, the first stanza speaks to the moment in which he wrote it:

> Tonight you better listen because I'm going to tell you
> What you always wanted to hear.
> All you bad hombres better take a deep breath.
> I shit you not,
> This is the night of nights.
> Take a chance on love.[18]

For Frank, a man who believed all women blended into one, taking that chance seemed the natural thing to do. Yes, he had settled into a stable and predictable situation with Ginny in Rogers. But C.D. was in the magical process of becoming a poet, and recalling what that felt like, Frank was hooked, ready to take a chance. The progression from Linda the social worker, to Cheryl the musician, to Ginny the painter had been as fluid as it was painful, and however perversely, the arc of his love followed a logic of its own. With each romantic partner he was moving closer to the ideal way for him to be with a romantic partner: merging his art with theirs.

One Fayetteville woman who met Frank in 1975, and had a brief affair with him, wrote, "I don't know that I've ever met another ultra creative man who celebrated the talents of female partner(s!) with such unabashed enthusiasm."[19] Nurturing another's art was essentially how he expressed his love, and what art did he know better or more intimately than poetry?

As he had schooled Ginny with her painting, he would become involved—but to an even greater degree—in C. D.'s poetry. Like Ginny, C.D. was eager to learn from Frank, a poet whom she called "profound."[20] "He educated her," Forrest Gander remarked, "and she loved the aid." Gander noted how "he talked to her about metaphor and analogy, and she got really good at it." Frank gave her tacit permission to bring, as Gander put it, "a rural voice" to her work. "Before the poems [became] really very good," Gander added, "[Frank] was finding the best things about them to talk to her about."[21] David Reich, who was in the program when Frank and C.D. met, noticed that her writing "took a big leap under Frank's influence."[22] Whereas Frank and Ginny were separated by the gap between poetry and painting, any gap, under Frank's guidance, closed for him and C.D., and their connection to poetry soon kept them connected to each other in a remarkably tight, affectionate, and passionate way.

C. D.'s biggest concern was how to learn from Frank Stanford without imitating Frank Stanford. She initially struggled with this challenge. John McKernan, editor of the *Little Review*, who published fifteen of Frank's poems across three issues, wrote to C.D. after reading her poetry: "Boy was I tricked. You and Frank sound so much alike you might be the Wordsworth and Coleridge of our day."[23] This certainly rankled. Michael Cuddihy, who rejected some of C. D.'s submissions to *Ironwood*, wrote to her about her poetry that "my chief problem with it was that I often found it too close to Frank's."[24] Deborah Luster read some of C. D.'s work after she met Frank and remembered thinking that it was "*so* Frank."[25]

C. D. did not necessarily disagree with these assessments. After Frank's death she wrote to Cuddihy, "A woman left a batch of poems in my door the other day. Heavy under the influence. Of F[rank] S[tanford]. Mirrors, roses, moons, knives, horses—the whole bit. I guess it can't be helped. I think I'm outgrowing it myself, which is not as good as making a clean break, but it's better than staying in the same pot."[26] Gander said that "she was depending upon the things she'd learned from Frank too entirely."[27] Wright would assuredly become her own poet, and a MacArthur genius along the way, but Frank's unruly tongue could be hard to escape.

Throughout the fall of 1975 and into 1976, Ginny had concerns about her relationship with Frank. She quickly sensed that he was drifting from the idyllic life they had made together in Rogers. "The night he met her [C. D.] he pulled up anchor," she later wrote. "I didn't notice right away, but over the months she drew him further out into her ocean."[28] Ginny remembered that it was during "the third week of October" (1975), an evening when the woodstove needed a fire, that "he didn't come home" when he was supposed to.[29] There were more no-shows to come in November.[30] ("I who must cut your firewood," goes a line from *The Battlefield*, "so the suicidal lovers may fuck one another's eyes out" [13248–49].) She recalled how she would wait up for him: "I sat out on the front porch after supper, first in one sweater and then two, watching the leaves from the blackjack oaks fall in long slow spirals ... I thought I would hear his car when it turned the corner.... About nine o'clock, I gave up and went inside." Frank's absence from the Rogers house became even more common by the spring of 1976. "I remember the next spring," Ginny wrote, "after the woman." As if keeping vigil, she "slept on the floor of the living room beside his desk with all the curtains drawn. Day and night."[31] By the summer of 1976 the garden was dead.

While Ginny was waiting for Frank to round the corner, Frank was enjoying the electrified attention generated by his return to Fayetteville. For the Fayetteville writers, his reappearance was like a second coming. Poets had been passing around precious copies of *The Singing Knives* for years, the years he was away and being mythologized in this town shot through with artists. More recently, *Shade*, *Arkansas Bench Stone*, and *Ladies from Hell* were all on display and for sale at the House of Books.[32] David Reich, who was finishing his MFA when Frank returned, recalled how Frank was "extremely charismatic," was known as "the wild man who dropped out," and, as he walked around Fayetteville, "almost seemed to glow."[33] The writer Steve Stern wrote, "He pressed his poems on us like snapshots of an unnamed country." Frank was hardly flamboyant about his accomplishments. "[He] never seemed to have anything particular to prove," Stern said.[34]

"He was really isolated when he was up around Eureka," Deborah Luster recalled. But his work was known and worshiped: "He had a kind of celebrity."[35] Stern, reflecting on the legend's return, recalled "a character who was quite larger than life and I think it's very seldom that you experience that with someone." He added, "This is a guy who has a sense of his own destiny and the sense of his own mythical stature, and good God he's getting away with it." To have a Stanford sighting, according to Stern, was to have a story worth telling. "To see Frank in the streets of Fayetteville ... was like meeting Marco Polo back from Cathay."[36] Francis from *The Battlefield* took the comparison to another level: "I intend to come back out of exile / one these days like Odysseus done with a magic bow" (9334–35).

It took the combined skills of Odysseus and Marco Polo to sustain the love triangle with Ginny and C.D. for nearly two and a half years. Willett, very concerned about Frank's strategy, confronted his friend about it:

> Frank and I were talking one day, and I said, "Frank, this situation you got with [C. D.] and Ginny," I said this is going to come to a head at some point in time, I said, "What are you telling these ladies?" And he says, "Well, I tell Ginny that I do see C.D. but I don't go to bed with her, and I see C.D., and I say, 'Yes, I do go home to my wife, but we don't sleep together anymore' ..." and I said, "Do you really think they believe that?" and he says, "Well, yeah."[37]

Steve Stern described the situation this way: "He had convinced Ginny that the relationship was purely business and that their connection revolved around beginning this press ... and it was taking up a lot of his time in town. And I think he had pretty much convinced Carolyn that his relationship with Ginny was essentially just a marriage of convenience."[38]

Everyone around them at the time had something to say about what was really an open secret. Sam Gwynn recalls that "I didn't know exactly what their relationship was, but I know Frank told Ginny that Carolyn was a lesbian," while Luster said, "He told Carolyn that Ginny was just a platonic relationship between them."[39] Frank mentioned to Adamo that C.D. was gay.[40] The photographer Richard Leo Johnson, who knew C.D., Frank, and Ginny well, said that he was "never clear about the relationship" between them but that "I really think he was in love with both women." He also added that, because of a general "lack of boundaries sexually" at the time, nobody morally condemned anyone for whom they slept with or under what circumstances.[41] A love triangle was a love triangle—not huge news. Steve Stern agreed, noting how at one point he and Johnson had shared the same girlfriend.[42] "Our biggest fear," Johnson said, "was that we were going to get crabs."[43]

Frank would not directly confront the fullest consequences of his big lie (at least not in writing) until a couple of weeks before his death, when its precarious foundation cracked and crumbled. He would then admit that he told the women "C. was gay and a bitch and that G. was spiritual and celibate."⁴⁴ In the meantime he only dropped poetic hints, such as this fragment:

> So I could become two different people I devised
> a kite which would fly by itself when I tied it
> to the pommel on the Shetland pony Blue yodel of the formal feeling that
> came to the drifter
> with one foot still in this world.⁴⁵

The poem (which could have possibly been written in 1971 about Linda and Cheryl) is striking in the speaker's admission of leading two lives, being compelled by forces beyond his power, and the drifting sense that, with one foot in the muck, it would not last, that the other foot would leave too. And then there was this, from the posthumously published *You*:

> I keep two kingdoms of firewood
> Two loaves of cornbread and two key
> Holes...⁴⁶

Logistically, Frank's systemic deception fundamentally depended on maintaining geographical distance between life with C. D. and life with Ginny, to keep them, as Stern put it, "from comparing notes."⁴⁷ (He had done this with surprising "success" in 1971 when he lived in the studio on Lindell Avenue with Cheryl Campbell while dating Linda on Mount Sequoyah.) Frank and Ginny continued renting the Rogers house into the fall of 1976, when their lease expired. In early November, Frank completely shut down his surveying office in Rogers and disconnected the phone. It was around then that Ginny (and technically Frank) moved to a large farmhouse that her parents had recently inherited from her maternal grandparents in Liberal, Missouri. Frank, who called it "the farm," described it as "just out of the Ozarks and at the edge of the plains, so near Kansas, not too far from Oklahoma."⁴⁸ To Irv, Frank noted that it "was in the middle of nowhere" and with "a big old house."⁴⁹ Ginny recalled "our rambling old house with the front porch that wrapped around two sides, the elaborate garden we had, all the land."⁵⁰

With Frank no longer having to pay rent in Rogers, he and C. D., on October 1, 1976, signed a yearlong lease on a one-bedroom house at 705 Jackson Drive (now East Jackson Drive), about a mile and a half from the university. The house was owned by the writer Douglas C. Jones. C. D. and Frank paid $190 a month for it.⁵¹ This is also where Lost Roads—the office and its equipment—would find a home, with a press that "chewed up," as C. D. would recall, "every room in my house except the john."[52]

For the last nineteen months of his life Frank shuffled between the farmhouse and the house on Jackson Drive, with many amorous diversions along the way. "Frank would travel back and forth for years," Ralph Adamo recalled.[53] Surveying demands and the responsibilities of Lost Roads were viable, and sometimes legitimate, excuses for not being "home." Ginny recalled how "every week he had a new story to explain where he had been and why," adding how she "bought them all like they were the best crop of peaches at the farmer's market."[54] C. D. remarked how Frank "put thousands of miles on his new white truck, but he really didn't go far." As for explaining these regional meanderings, she said, "he always said just the right thing . . . he lied brilliantly." She elaborated: "I experienced him as a man living more than one life—one with Ginny, one with me, and never the twain were to meet. We, Ginny and I, were kept apart by an elaborate hive of lies. . . . There is the added factor that he had two pathetically willing subjects. He moved her from the rent house on Beaver Lake to her family farm in Missouri. He moved her further from Fayetteville because he had moved in with me. He never moved into the farm. He visited her there twice a month. Never more."[55]

"His relationship with the two of them," said Forrest Gander, "was so distinct: With Ginny, he was out in a rural area; they'd listen only to opera. And with C. D., they'd listen only to jazz. He was like a different person in both places."[56] C. D. and Ginny, while both gifted artists, also had distinct personalities. Ginny was, according to Richard Leo Johnson, "dreamy and flighty,"[57] while Irv Broughton called her "cautious and fearful."[58] Steve Stern said she "had an aura of mystery around her," while Ralph Adamo called her "warm, open, curious . . . with a sweet nature."[59] C.D. was, again according to Johnson, "more bang bang bang."[60] Gander said that she "was really direct, really honest, and really ethically based,"[61] while Kathy Thompson, a local potter, called her friend "real strong willed . . . a woman who spoke her mind."[62] Stern said C.D. had "a sharp tongue" and a "strong sense of right and wrong."[63] The kid who mowed the yard at 705 Jackson was afraid to go pick up his payment when C. D. was home because she'd criticize his yard work as lazy. Frank, when he answered the door, wouldn't even check the kid's work and would give him a big tip.[64]

Bill Willett was not the only one of Frank's friends who was dubious about this arrangement with Ginny and C.D. Others recall being bemused at best, not the least because Frank, while keeping these women apart, seemed to worry very little about getting caught. "I was aware of the love triangle, at least heard about it," recalls one woman who was in the MFA mix in 1976. "Kinda mystified about it all."[65] A painter in the MFA program at the time recalls how "people were well aware that Frank was married but living with C. D."[66] At times he could be shameless about the situation he had so strategically engineered. "Frank would often have a wry attitude," said Stern, recalling how Ginny once drove into Fayetteville from the farm to look for Frank and, not finding him, called Steve for help in locating her husband. Not wanting to land Frank in hot water, Stern gently encouraged Ginny to go back to Missouri and promised that he would let Frank know she was looking for him. Later that evening Stern saw a carefree Frank and C. D. having a nice dinner in downtown Fayetteville. "He had that very entitled way about him," Stern observed. During a 2020 group discussion about Frank, C.D., and Ginny, Stern marveled at the stress that going "back and forth between Missouri and Fayetteville" must have caused Frank, but Ralph Adamo was quick to note, "I don't think it's quite as important as you think it is. Stuff just didn't matter to him as much."[67]

This insouciance led at least one woman who knew Frank during these years to determine that he "was not even a real person but a kind of made-up person in a way."[68] Richard Leo Johnson, who cared about Frank but saw that he was a deeply wounded man, likewise remarked on how careless Frank could be about juggling attachments to Ginny and C. D. Johnson explained that, while Frank was living with C.D. in Fayetteville and Ginny was in Rogers (before the move to Missouri), Ginny regularly came to Fayetteville to work in the darkroom she shared with Johnson.[69] Another artist who kept a studio in the same warehouse also recalls Ginny frequently being in the heart of Fayetteville while Frank was carrying on his affair with C. D. When Stern eventually told Frank about the time Ginny contacted him to find Frank in Fayetteville, Frank just rolled his eyes and muttered, "Women."[70]

Frank's behavior reflected the attitude toward women that he had described to Willett back in 1972, when he was seeing about a half dozen girlfriends in New York while reuniting with Cheryl. He had then written, "I seek out the mystery of all women. With some it takes seconds, others years. Like a priest, I transubstantiate the body + spirit one into the other. Once this is done, whenever I look into one woman's eyes, I see yet another woman."[71] A typist for Lost Roads, working in the 705 Jackson Drive house, recalls how "Frank was hardly there"—as in rarely physically present. She guessed that he was "always off" because "he had girlfriends all over the place, you know, New Orleans and Eureka Springs and everywhere."[72] Steve Stern agreed, saying that when it came to lovers during this time period, "Frank cast a wide net." The yields were prolific. Stern said, "There was always a whole circle of women who were happy to sleep with the poet.... He was a very busy man."[73]

Stern always wondered if these affairs reflected "some deep insecurity inside Frank."[74] The behavior was notably chronic. Deborah Luster said that she and Frank entered C. D.'s "orbit" at about the same time and that "Frank would end up having an affair with most of the women in that orbit."[75] One of those women was Merideth Boswell, a member of Calabash Pottery Collective and a future film set designer. "He really loved women," she explained. While recalling that "sex with Frank was the least memorable part of Frank," she remembered his "extreme interest! in so MANY things I found seductive."[76] Frank later admitted, "Merideth wanted a friend and a lover. I was her lover but I was not a good friend."[77] Now that he was back in Fayetteville, Frank asked after his old flame Kathy Walton, a woman with whom he had had an affair while he was with Linda and Cheryl in or about 1970 and 1971 and a woman who also remembers little about sex with Frank aside from his deep attentiveness to her.[78] Ginny remembers how he "stole my jar of cold cream off the dresser and gave it to a sixteen-year-old who worked at the drive-in."[79] There were waitresses. There was (possibly) Strawberry, who was nineteen years old at this point and still up there in Eureka Springs. There was a random note left by one "Megan" claiming that Frank was the father of her child. When Frank and C. D. attempted a threesome with a friend of C. D.'s, C. D. ended it the second Frank turned his attention to the other woman. "She was fiercely protective of him," Jessica Slote, who worked briefly at Lost Roads, recalled.[80] Overseeing Frank's fidelity must have been a full-time job, one that even C. D., for all her heroic efforts to overlook or compartmentalize his philandering, had to admit was nearly impossible. "He collected women," she later said.[81]

## "The Surveyor and His Catspaw"

None of the intrigue with women kept Frank from working regularly as a surveyor, work that became significantly more critical as the costs of running a press mounted. Frank continued to operate under the arrangement that he had established with Don Kemp in 1974. As Frank proposed it in a letter to Kemp: "I get the job, do the job paying all labor in the field and vehicle and expenses, and what office work I can, and you approve it. I collect the bill, and we split, after wages & wage taxes, 50–50."[82] Frank was still an unlicensed surveyor; Kemp was fully licensed. The arrangement kept Frank in the field often, making around $500–$600 a month when business was good and driving hundreds of miles a week around the state. Plus, Frank's relocation to Fayetteville and the fact that it placed him amid a thriving social life, a community that warmed to his mere presence, intersected with his business in an interesting way.

"He made himself socially available in Fayetteville," C. D. wrote. "I think he needed that," she added, alluding to the fact that he had been living in relative isolation with Ginny since 1973.[83] Frank combined friendship and business to his advantage by convincing the artists he knew and sometimes the writers he was publishing to do some basic surveying tasks for him when he was engaged with getting the business of Lost Roads off the ground. Luster was called to duty, along with their mutual friend Fred McCuistion. "We were enlisted to do this one survey," Luster remembered, "and I think we completely screwed it up. I'm terrified of snakes, so I remember just tromping through it." Luster summed up her knowledge of surveying this way: "Well, I knew nothing."[84] John Stoss, another poet from the MFA program, frequently trudged into the woods on Frank's behalf, despite having no inkling what he was doing.[85] Bruun Whitehead, one of Jim Whitehead's sons, sometimes got the call. When asked if he knew how to survey, he said, "Oh, I had no idea."[86]

On other occasions, C. D. would join Frank in the field. In an essay written after Frank's death, she reminisced about "the surveyor and his catspaw. The poet and his follower. Poking around in the woods with a transit. He shot the lines. She held the plumb bob. Squatted in a stand of cedar to pee. Watch yourself: copperhead country."[87] Once when they were in the woods together, Frank buried some change and told her to come get it in an emergency and use it to see a movie. It says something about Stanford that he convinced poets and writers and photographers with zero experience to work as land surveyors. It says something else about the accuracy of the boundary lines marking Northwest Arkansas in the late 1970s.

Kemp of course was thrilled with the arrangement that Frank had proposed, especially now that Frank was in Missouri part-time. Kemp was, because of his contract with Frank, able to assure his clients that "we now have a crew working full time ... in the Fayetteville, Springdale, Rogers, Bentonville, Neosho, and Eureka Springs areas." "This," Kemp went on in a letter mailed to all his clients, "will enable you to have 48 hour service on small jobs, providing all essential information can be relayed over the phone or picked up at your office."[88] This expansion happened right around the time that Frank moved Ginny to Liberal, only an hour by car from Neosho. When he listed their address for Cuddihy, he explained that it was "for Ginny all the time and for me some of the time."[89] This was another way that Frank was molding his surveying work to his personal life, as business in Neosho meant that he could stop by "the farm" and check in on Ginny while telling C.D. he was off to do some surveying in southern Missouri and proceed to actually do both things.

As with almost everything Frank did during his last couple of years, he took his surveying business to another level of complexity. One critical decision was at the heart of it. In 1975 the company Precision International put on the market an electronic distance measurer known as the Beetle 500S. This state-of-the-art surveying machine, about the size of a brick, went for nearly $3,000.[90] Don Kemp gave Frank access to bigger jobs, and on large boundary surveys (forty-plus acres), especially around the lakes, this kind of instrument was invaluable. Using a chain and transit would require a party of about four and a lot of brush cutting; everything had to be chained one hundred feet at a time. The Beetle, with its infrared distance measuring, only required "line-of-sight" to give an accurate readout. If one could see the "prism" five hundred feet away, the distance could be automatically computed.[91] Frank, whose fetish for advanced technology occasionally had him writing camera companies about theodolite technologies still in the research stage, decided that he needed a Beetle 500S.

In the summer of 1977, he got one. A quote from the Trion Company, the Dallas-based firm that sold Frank the equipment, revealed that the Beetle 500S was just the start of his investments. The infrared distance measurer required a mount, a power pack, a prism, a prism rod, prism bag, a tripod, and other accouterments. Frank found himself on the hook for $4,765. This amount was more than double what he had invested in surveying equipment in 1974, and it put him in debt. He paid $762.40 down and financed the rest with a thirty-six-month installment plan at $190 a month—the same amount he and C.D. were paying in rent for their house.[92] This investment was intended to improve efficiency and save labor costs, and on paper, it was not a terrible idea. "I can," he had written to Kemp a few years earlier, "make more money with my equipment than without it."[93] But it would take many years for such benefits to fully materialize, and in the meantime, Frank compounded the problem, as we'll see, by assuming debt in other endeavors, most notably in investments in Lost Roads Publishers. With these decisions, Frank's financial life, which he had always managed judiciously, began to spiral into deep trouble.

## "He Never Hogged the Road"

Frank and C. D.'s relationship intensified in Fayetteville. They became known around town as "a glamour couple."[94] C. D. recalled in her notebooks that, right after Frank moved in with her, "we were a match made in heaven. We clicked and we clicked. Tremendous big hits we had."[95] When they argued, often because of Frank's suspected dalliances, Frank always talked her down with the perfect words.[96] "He always said just the right thing," she later wrote.[97] After Frank's death, C. D. wrote with a "whole black heart," "If you are not going to be on top of my body this Friday would you glide past my window. I want to dig you up my friend. Carry you home."[98] She missed "the residual scent of our constant screwing."[99] In the two and a half years before his death, Ginny, by contrast, sank further into desperate isolation, first in Rogers and, after the move to the farm in September 1976, then in southern Missouri. "He left me to the wind and the dust and the darkness," she wrote. When the annual seed catalogs arrived, she "read them like some read Scripture. For solace and hope, the promise of better days to come." She missed "the music of his voice." Frank's poems "dropped me off where I'd never be found.... I should have seen it coming."[100]

Frank's attachment to C. D. was inseparable from his attachment to her poetry. As he had done with Ginny, he put her work ahead of his own. Commenting on the state of her poetry when she met Frank, C. D. said, "I was just learning. I did not know what I was doing. I was just writing *stuff*. Nothing but stuff."[101] The fact that she included her thesis, "Alla Breve Loving," in the category of such "stuff" did not keep Frank from getting it published for her in 1976. For this to happen, of course, he went directly to Irv and Mill Mountain Press. Frank never applied for the National Endowment for the Arts grant for Lost Roads in November of 1975. But Irv had succeeded on that front, receiving funding for Mill Mountain. In typical fashion, Irv, who thought Frank's romantic arrangement with C. D. was "all fucked up," nonetheless agreed to use $500 from his grant to fund the publication of her first book. Frank oversaw this project from beginning to end. Irv picked up the tab.

Five hundred copies of *Alla Breve Loving* were printed by Overstreet Printing Company in March 1976.[102] The chapbook is a modest thirty-pages long and, unprecedentedly for a Mill Mountain book, devoid of artwork. Relatively speaking, this thin and spare volume was not an expensive publication to produce. But still, it was a publication. Frank was elated for C. D. "Carolyn's book is out," he alerted Irv in June, "and I'm sending you a good many copies."[103] By July it was on sale at House of Books in downtown Fayetteville (now Dickson St. Bookshop). By March 1977 C.D. had sold three hundred books and netted $42.50 from the sales.[104]

It is critical to remember that, during the time when Frank was using Mill Mountain and his influence with Irv to get *Alla Breve Loving* published, much of his own work was, as he put it, "sitting in the closet."[105] This was a choice. Frank simply, miraculously, never stopped writing, but when it came to supporting C.D.'s work, he placed the publication of her first book ahead of his books. He did so without complaint or ever drawing much attention to this fact. He also drew on his contacts at the little magazines to encourage editors to read and hopefully publish C.D.'s work, even though he himself had stopped submitting poems. Again, this was how he loved.

Shortly after Frank died, C.D. commended Frank's commitment to her early career. She wrote to Father Fuhrmann that "he was my friend, teacher, editor, and publisher" and said, "He never hogged the road when it was time for me to get my due."[106] He was, as she knew quite well, "the full blown poet," while she had "roots that had yet to outgrow a coffee can."[107] She was more than ready to follow his lead. The more she did, the more effusively Frank championed her work. "She has moved beyond what she was doing," Frank wrote to Irv after *Alla Breve Loving* was published, "and is writing some of the best things I've read."[108] To Cuddihy, he wrote, "I can't wait to lay ten of C.D. Wright's poems on you. I think she is the most powerful poet I've read since Ai—but oh so very different." He added, in a rare challenge to Cuddihy's editorial opinion: "I hope you will have time to read & consider them. Of course, if you don't like the poetry, I want to know why."[109] Whatever Cuddihy's sense of C.D.'s poetry, Frank's faith in her was such that he determined that her next book must be the first of the six Lost Roads books he had planned for publication in 1977.

Frank may never have hogged the road with C.D., but he surely stayed in a lane. Before he turned to Lost Roads and the production of chapbooks by lesser-known poets in whom he deeply believed, Frank planned to move his own manuscripts for *Constant Stranger* and *The Battlefield* toward eventual publication. The former, at only twelve poems, was easier and cheaper to do. *Constant Stranger* was the last book that Mill Mountain Press published (on its own)[110] for Frank. It was his sixth book. The manuscript was completed as early as June 1976, and the book's copyright is 1976, but it likely was not printed and bound until the spring of 1977. A May 3, 1977, letter from Overstreet Printing Company to Frank shows that

*Constant Stranger* had indeed been printed and bound, and an August 1977 receipt shows Mill Mountain paid roughly $1,100 to have it done. The book was a mere forty-eight pages with five blank pages at the end. The cover had an image of a Gauguin painting called *Spirit of the Dead Watching*.[111]

This was an apt choice of artwork. Death pervades this chapbook. In addition to the opening poem, "Death and the Arkansas River," which we have seen is an ode to death, there is the poem "No Sign of Life: A Tragic Gag of Raymond Radiguet," which is "after Jean Cocteau." Radiguet died at the age of twenty from typhoid fever after writing a virtuosic novel as a child prodigy (aged seventeen). In this poem Stanford writes:

> I have seen doors
> through which Death comes and goes
> picked clean[112]

In "A Black Cat Crossed the Road I Was Born On," death is a constant and even amusing character: "But Death knows my ass / from a hole in the ground," "Death is no chauffeur," "When Death beats his child / Nobody listens," "Death is two-timing me," "Some people I knew hired death by the hour," "There is no doubt in my mind, / Death is a bad hog."[113] Finally, in the last poem, Stanford opens it with, "I am going to die."[114]

Stanford's preoccupation with death in these poems is inseparable from, and in fact directly responsive to, his own late experiences with love, lust, and fading memories. Heavy as this foray into the not-too-distant past and the emotions it inspired could be, he keeps the poems balanced on the edge of whimsy. As he did in his personal life, these poems deflect the inner gravity of death, reminding readers that Stanford might not be taking matters as seriously as we are. It's as if he's inviting us into the depths of an emotionally charged and deeply personal memory (in a way that Elizabeth Bishop or Robert Lowell would never have dared to do) and reminding us how utterly weighty it is before cracking a joke or rolling his eyes and telling us to lighten up because, after all, death knows our ass from a hole in the ground. The insouciance he brought to his love triangle is echoed in these poems. He's laughing a bit at an inevitable fatalism.

In "Directions from a Madman" Frank writes that "You run off into the ditch of your past / And love spins like a wheel." In the same poem he moves from the generalized to the autobiographical:

> Years now I've been walking these goddamn hills,
> No telling how many lies.

Nearing closer to the bone of recent events, he writes:

> What you go and have in the night
> Is strictly your business.
> Keep it on the road.

And, more prophetically:

> For soon it will be time to go
> From the one love to another,
> Time to buy a home on wheels
> And honeymoon until death.[115]

The poem "Blue Yodel of the Desperado" repeatedly evokes his New York experience. No doubt referring to his first wife, Linda, he writes:

> I went to New York to leave you
> Flowers of blood and light
> In the Picture Shows I dreamed
> Of your birthmark in the shape of a pistol

In another section, he writes:

> I only went to New York to go to the movies
> I got good and drunk in the dark

He even revives his double escape from Cheryl and his rich British lover, Deidre:

> When luck and money ran out
> I deserted you somewhere in South America
> It was on a Sunday I remember
>
> I met up with this English woman with plenty
> That very night
> While she was in the powder room
> I went back to the hotel
> Stole her rubies
> And stowed away on the first rig I saw
> A ship full of wild horses
> Bound for America[116]

A few lines later, recalling the beauty of the women he met in New York, he adds:

> your legs are still
> To be reckoned with

The last stanza declares "And when I got to where I was going / The place I come from / I needed a knife to clean my fingernail,"[117] as if to say, I got away with it all up there in New York. It's clear from these lines that these escapades and observations thrilled Frank with their mayhem, absurdism, and trickery, and it comes through in most of these poems. He ends *Constant Stranger* with a resort to the second person:

> And if you have no enemies, inquire of me,
> Your troubles are just beginning.[118]

*Constant Stranger*, at 48 pages, was affordable to produce. But the other book Frank wanted to get into print, *The Battlefield*, at 542 pages, was not. However, having worked on it for well over a decade, having had the manuscript (or variations of it) ignored or rejected by outside publishers, having the new and enthusiastic insistence from C.D. that it be published, and now having his own press about to start churning out a slew of books, Frank was as well placed as he would ever be to get his magnum opus into the world. He was determined to make that happen before death two-timed him.

## "The Longest Poem Ever Told"

The copy of *The Battlefield* that Frank gave C.D. to read in late 1975 was, with the exception of the last fifty pages, most likely the only copy he then had.[119] After reading it and becoming enthralled by it, C.D. retyped it on her Olympia typewriter so the typescript could eventually be used by a typesetter.[120] Forrest Gander, who edited the original manuscript for the book's republication in 2000, recalls that those early pages were "thin and yellowing, marked now and then by hand (at least two hands), with occasional words over-typed or misspelled, rendered ambiguous sometimes, but rarely incomprehensible."[121] C.D. remembered how, in 1976, as she retyped it, she "stripped in hundreds of corrections and missed hundreds more." Frank told Irv that "I took it upon myself to make minor revisions,"[122] but C.D. recalled that "Frank took little interest in the process." Either way, the result was a corrected (sort of) and complete (sort of) manuscript to haul off to the printer, a printer who, C.D. remembered, "said it read as if the author was hopped up on something." C.D. added how Frank "did not cotton to this unsolicited remark."[123]

Money, as always, would dictate the book's haphazard journey toward publication. In September of 1976 Overstreet Printing Company let Frank and Lost Roads know what to expect: It would cost $3,549.34 to produce fifteen hundred copies of the big book. The cost of binding alone—$700 for a book that would weigh in at nearly four pounds—was almost equal to the total price of producing *Constant Stranger*. Typesetting came to $276.[124] This was, in short, a prohibitively expensive venture, and the quote was yet another reminder that the greatest inhibiting factor preventing this poem from entering the world was its massive size. The extraordinary cost of producing *The Battlefield* forced Frank to make two key decisions. The first was to reduce expenditures by having Overstreet provide the paper, print the book, cut and fold the pages, and do the cover. Lost Roads would take care of the typesetting and, when it could eventually afford to, the binding. This lowered the bill to $1,987.[125] The second decision, because this price remained far too much for Lost Roads to cover (it did not get the NEA grant it applied for in early 1977), was for Frank to publish *The Battlefield* jointly under both the Mill Mountain and Lost Roads labels.[126] While hardly flush with cash, Mill Mountain still had NEA money in its account, and Irv, to the very end, would support his friend in getting his life's defining work published.

For nearly a year after it was printed by Overstreet—between May 1977 and July 1978—unbound and folded pages of *The Battlefield* were, as Frank ruefully noted, "sitting in boxes getting wet."[127] But when it finally came together—and this it did slowly—the book itself became more of an instant literary artifact than an enduring classic. There are perhaps around 850 copies of the original *Battlefield* in existence today (certainly no more than 1,000). The volumes are hard to miss when encountered. Type was set on C. D.'s Olympia typewriter and reduced 40 percent in the camera copy.[128] Frank noted to John McKernan that "the reduced type was my idea," and he did it knowing full well that "some won't like" it.[129] The print is indeed small and faint, and Frank predicted that, in terms of production value, it "won't have much quality printing to it."[130]

Binding of most volumes did not take place until shortly after Frank's death, when C. D.—using an NEA grant Lost Roads finally received in the summer of 1978—took the printed pages to a Tulsa-based binder named Robert T. Motter.[131] The cover photo of a pile of dead children with crying mothers behind them, in what appears to be Southeast Asia, was reportedly "lifted," with Frank's approval, from the Louisville *Courier-Journal* on the last day of the Vietnam War (April 30, 1975). The decorative ring circle preceding the half-title page, following page 542, and on the back cover recalls what Frank had done in *Preview: Eight Poets* (and his experimental foray into Japanese painting). The white cover with lipstick-red lettering was a signature Lost Roads aesthetic for the press's first seventeen volumes.

The Battlefield's copyright is 1977. "The release date," Frank wrote to Michael and Mary Cuddihy, "is Dec 31 77."[132] But the book's release on that date did not happen. It is common for Stanford scholars to highlight the fact that The Battlefield was bound posthumously. The claim, while true, should not suggest that Frank never held his book in his hands. He almost certainly did. Overstreet printed and cut The Battlefield's pages in May 1977. While they did not bind it—recall that Lost Roads and Mill Mountain determined they would find another source for that task—they did make, at Frank's request, some mock-ups. Frank wrote to Fred Overstreet that "we will have to make at least three dummies up" to use for promotional purposes. He reiterated that "you would have to make at least one dummy anyway to know where and how to locate spine, cover, back material on cover."[133] In June 1977 Frank wrote to Michael and Mary Cuddihy that "some make-up dummy copies of THE BATTLEFIELD WHERE THE MOON SAYS I LOVE YOU, all 550 pages, should be done by the 20th of this month."[134] Ralph Adamo remembers visiting Lost Roads while Frank was alive and how C. D. "gave me a completed bound copy."[135] Leon Stokesbury saw copies of the book in the late fall of 1977 or early 1978. "Frank," he said, "brought it into a bar/restaurant called The Restaurant on the Corner. . . . it was out."[136] Or at least some bound copies of it were. In any case, it seems certain that Frank held his book.

In terms of Frank's expectations about The Battlefield being *out* out—that is, its volumes bound and displayed in bookstores, reviews in the little magazines, a literary event that the poetry world would discuss—he kept them appropriately modest. On the first day of 1978 Lost Roads informed its readers that "another book of poetry co-published with Lost Roads and Mill Mountain, at 552 pages long, will appear . . . sometime in 1979."[137] While this estimate indicates that Frank continued to resign himself to the book's unbound pages sitting in boxes at 705 Jackson Drive for a while, that did not prevent him from drafting promotional copy for The Battlefield. Poignantly, he begins by listing the book's title and author and then dramatically adds, "THE LONGEST POEM EVER TOLD."[138] Noting the price for a softbound ($8) and hardbound ($16) copy,[139] he then offered a few typo-ridden attempts at self-generated blurbs:

> Stanford who is 26, has received high praise from many of America's greatest poets as well as his poet-editor contemporaries, and leading younger poet-editors.
>
> Stanford, who is 27 and the author of ten other books of poetry, has received high praise from many of America's greatest poets. He is considered

by the younger poet-editors as ibe if tge most powerful and original voices in contemporary poetry. The Battlefieddl Where The Moon Says I Love You is destened to reclaim the landscape of American poetry.

Stanford, the 27 year old Land Surveyor from Arkansas, the author of ten other books of poetry, and the subject of an award winning documentary film, has received high praise from many of America's greatest poets, and is considered by the younger poet-editors as one of the most powerful and original voices in contemporary poetry.

The Battlefield Where The Moon Says I Love You is a brilliant achievement, destined to reclaim the landscape of American poetry.

Available XXXXXXX[140]

Yet while preparing the chapbooks that Lost Roads would publish, he told Ralph Adamo that he'd never include a blurb on his books, calling blurbs "sparrow shit."[141]

## "Each Poet Is Beautiful"

As Frank was finalizing plans to publish *The Battlefield*, he and C. D. worked to publish no fewer than six Lost Roads books of poetry by 1977. Five of these books would be from lesser-known poets in whom Frank deeply believed—C. D., John Stoss, Ralph Adamo, John S. Morris, and John McKernan. The sixth would be Irv's book. It was a lot to stay on top of, and Frank would spend the last two years of his life struggling to do so. He could occasionally lose his patience. "My life is all work and no play," he wrote to Irv in the summer of 1976 while he was sifting through hundreds of manuscripts for Lost Roads to consider. "Fuck it," he added.[142]

Lost Roads began to solicit manuscripts in the spring of 1976. Frank knew from the start that Lost Roads would publish the work of McKernan, Morris, Stoss, and C. D. Wright. He had known and admired McKernan's poetry since at least 1970, when he said of McKernan's poems, "Listen— and someone will tell you these poems will make a racket. They do, the racket of a powerful river, or of a goatsucker singing in a spruce tree in Alabama."[143] John S. Morris's poetry had already appeared as the Lost Roads mock-up that Frank had technically published as *Bean Street* in 1975. All that needed to be done in his case was to cut forty-one poems down to twenty, and that manuscript was good to go. As for John Stoss, Frank had published him back in 1971, when he edited *Preview: Eight Poets*, and viewed him as "a rare poet," a natural, and a poet on the level of C. D.[144] He was also fond of Stoss personally, describing him to Dugan as "big, fat, crazy, but a kind an[d] genuine soul."[145] Frank's poem "The History of John Stoss," from his collection *You*, portrays a man more generous than Jesus, a poet "Coming across the prairie in his wagon / Playing his tuba." Frank added:

> John Stoss gave away his lunchmeat and buttermilk
> And drove on
> Getting heavy on his love.[146]

C.D. Wright's poetry was as exciting as any young poetic voice out there. Her book, *Room Rented by a Single Woman*, was slated to be Lost Roads' first official title. Number one in a series that, as of early 2025, is still going.

Frank's decision to publish Irv's poetry was more fraught. Surely it was influenced by a sense of obligation to his most supportive friend. "I've spent lots of time with your ms. as of late and I have these things to say," Frank wrote to him in October 1976. He regretted that "I never got to know your poetry very well" and admitted "I feel bad about that." He urged Irv not to treat his poetry "as a past time [sic]," which was one way to say that the poems did not reflect the obsession Frank recognized in the best poems. "Much like an actor gets into his role" is how he described the way Irv got into his poems. Frank assured his friend that he would have been interested in the poems "regardless of our relationship, based on the merits," and that of the several hundred manuscripts he'd read "yours is one of the better ones." Better, not best. Frank would, in the end, publish Irv's book. It was called *The Blessing of the Fleet* and contained fourteen poems from the early mock-up, *Surveying*, and six new poems. At the end of the letter expressing his ambivalence about this decision, Frank asked Irv for $963.66. He needed it to get *The Battlefield* printed.[147] "Hurry," he wrote.[148]

Beyond these six poets was an anxious horde of poets seeking to break into Lost Roads. When the call for Lost Roads submissions went out—word of mouth was the primary means of dissemination—Frank and C.D. found themselves swamped with over six hundred manuscripts to evaluate. Frank read and vetted, by his own assessment, over twenty-four thousand poems in the late spring and early summer of 1976. This context is significant when it comes to appreciating his decision to publish Ralph Adamo's *Sadness at the Private University*. Ralph, whom Frank had also published in *Preview* in 1971, was back in his hometown of New Orleans. He sent Frank his manuscript in March 1976 after C.D. urged him to do so.[149] Frank, with uncharacteristic curtness, told him, "I have a surveying business to run" but said that he'd have a decision by June.[150] He was late in getting back to Ralph but responded in mid-July with good news. "You are a poet and you write poetry—rare," Frank wrote. "Your ms is very good as is," he went on, "but knowing you I think you can come up with something incredible." And then, "I really like you."[151]

Lost Roads also approached a few established poets and editors to publish their books. Frank asked Alberta Turner, who had cofounded *Field* and edited his work there, to submit a manuscript. Turner was grateful but said she only had about thirty-five unpublished poems on hand and was hoping to submit her "ripening book manuscript" to the University of Pittsburgh Press.[152] That book came out as *Lid & Spoon* in 1977. Frank also solicited manuscripts from Dugan and Cuddihy. Dugan, with whom Frank had lost touch over the past two years, passed, but Cuddihy sent poems in 1977. Frank worked on Cuddihy's manuscript—tentatively called "Bark"—but after Frank's death, Cuddihy withdrew it when C. D. took over Lost Roads, a decision she resisted.[153] A month after Frank's death, she wrote to Cuddihy: "I am disappointed in your decision to recall it for two reasons: I think it's a good book and because it's good I think it strengthens the series." She was also concerned because the NEA grant Lost Roads had (finally) received listed it as one of their prospective titles. She hoped he would reconsider but, in the end, conceded that "I completely accept your reasons."[154]

Frank also tapped Leon Stokesbury to publish a book with Lost Roads. But Frank was scooped by the University of Texas Press. Stokesbury's *Often in Different Landscapes* came out in 1976. There were no hard feelings— Frank said they were "nice poems, funny"—and Leon gave Frank a copy with the inscription "For Frank, an old friend."[155] Perhaps the most unconventional effort at recruitment came from John Stoss. He wrote to the New Orleans poets Everette Maddox and Rodney Jones, at 2900 Prytania Street, in pencil, on the front of a file folder: "Frank is looking for good books to publish. Mine is the 3rd. He is going to publish ten books. Frank is honest & _____. Rodney and you should send a manuscript."[156] Stoss routinely sent mail by putting a stamp and an address on anything that would pass through a mail sorter, be it a folder, a scrap of paper, a paper bag, but this particular file folder lacked a stamp, and in 2023, Rodney Jones was as surprised as anyone to hear that he'd been solicited by Frank, via Stoss, nearly fifty years earlier.[157]

Despite Lost Roads' unconventional recruiting techniques, a nation of budding poets bombarded Frank and C. D. with manuscripts. The poets of Fayetteville were especially insistent. Rejecting the manuscripts of local friends and acquaintances became an inevitable and awkward task. Steve Stern, who submitted a book of short stories, notes that when Frank declined to publish it, he did so with considerable tact and empathy for Stern's feelings. "Frank came over and we had a lengthy conversation about why he didn't think it was good enough," Stern recalls. "It was a good conversation, and I didn't resent it in the least. I mean, I was disappointed but at the same time I thought that his reservations were valid and he was a good reader."[158] He remembers that Frank "was a decisive critic, and the language of his criticism was always original."[159] Stanford still included the proposed title of Stern's book, *Goldfinch & Son*, a book he chose not to publish, in his 1978 grant application to the NEA.[160] Another local writer, a man named Reed Durbin, reacted less magnanimously to his Lost Roads rejection. A rumor spread that he was going to shoot Frank. He was eventually committed to an institution (much to the relief of Miller Williams, whom Durbin definitely wanted to shoot).[161]

By the late fall of 1976, with editorial decisions finalized about Lost Roads' first six volumes, Frank sounded burned out and short tempered. When Adamo disagreed with Frank's title for his book and offered alternatives, Frank snapped: "I can't accept any of those titles, or even come close.... Do you know anyone who has read your poems more than a hundred times—except you? I have."[162] John S. Morris, Irv Broughton, and John McKernan were all nagging Lost Roads to hurry things up, a request that rankled an overworked Frank. Frank told Cuddihy in November of 1976 that these poets "have been a little difficult to deal with" because they were "pushing me to get their books out" without appreciating his struggles with "time and money." Frank, who was as cranky as he had ever been in his letters, even went so far as to express boredom with the work of Broughton, McKernan, and Stoss, stressing his recent "lack of enthusiasm" for their poems. Stoss, about whom Frank had once been full of praise, was demoted to a guy he hated having to "run into... all the time." Still, as annoyed as he was, Frank had to admit that, for all the stress these poets were causing him, "each poet is beautiful."[163]

With the editorial work behind them by the end of 1976, Frank and C. D. turned to the always daunting technical logistics of getting the manuscripts made into books. This micromanaged work, which Frank hoped would be smoother than what he experienced with Mill Mountain and the turkey hunters, would eat up much of his time in 1977. In pencil and on Lost Roads stationery, Frank sketched out and estimated the "Cost per Book @ 40 pages per book" to be $1,275.80. As of fall 1976 the plan was to use Overstreet Printing Company and a local bindery to print, as Frank wrote to the binder, "250–500 books (80 % paperback & 20 % hardback), glued or S[myth] sewn."[164] The problem, as 1976 became 1977, was that Lost Roads once again could not afford to finish what it started. It could not pay for any of its promises, and Frank was deeply frustrated. Then he and C. D. got a break, and her name was Ellen Gilchrist.

## "I Did Not Fuck Frank Stanford"

At this point it is worth stepping back and recalling a few critical moments in the life of Frank Stanford, particularly those moments that demanded advanced organization and communication skills. As a twelve-year-old in Mountain Home he led grown men on guided fishing tours of Lake Norfork, managing a fleet of two motorboats to do so. At Subiaco as a high school junior, he single-handedly founded a judo club, recruiting students, training them, getting approval from the school administration, and arranging refereed matches with regional high schools. When he moved to Eureka Springs and wanted to see foreign films, he scouted out the adequate space, acquired a projector, rented dozens of obscure films, and opened a small theater. Since 1971 he had been working as an independent surveyor who could boast that he had botched only two jobs in all his years of surveying, a profession that required high technical ability to operate complex machinery and even do trigonometry. In short, when Frank wanted to accomplish something of an organizationally complex nature, he had not only the drive but also the skills to do so.

Frank knew how to get a book published as well as anyone. The ad hoc landscape of little magazine work was, after all his work with Irv and Burt Camp's Elk Ranch Printing, no mystery to Frank. After *The Singing Knives*, he worked closely with Irv to get his five other Mill Mountain titles published while also publishing two early Lost Roads mock-ups for John S. Morris and Irv Broughton. When he looked at the task he faced in early 1977, a contractual promise that required publishing six books in the upcoming year, and when he looked at the six authors who were on tenterhooks about their books coming out beautifully and on time with Lost Roads, Frank knew the only challenge he faced was paying for it all. To that end, on February 15, 1977, he applied for a $9,870 grant from the NEA.[165] He explained to the director of the literature program at the NEA that without this grant, "the only way I have to fund this is with the money I make in my business."[166]

But Frank was in debt for the sophisticated surveying equipment he had purchased. His boss, according to their contractual arrangement, got half of what he made. He had a rent payment ($190) and a truck payment to make every month. There was nothing left from his surveying business to sink into Lost Roads. It is in this context that the arrival in Fayetteville of a forty-year-old MFA student named Ellen Gilchrist was a godsend. Gilchrist, who would go on to become an award-winning fiction writer (*Victory over Japan* won the National Book Award in 1984), came to the Arkansas MFA program in the fall of 1976. She had done her BA in philosophy at Millsaps College in Jackson, Mississippi, where she took classes with Eudora Welty, and now she wanted to study with the novelist William Harrison and the poet Miller Williams. Soon after her arrival in Fayetteville she met, probably through Jim Whitehead, Frank Stanford, and she fell for him.[167]

"I can remember the temperature of certain rooms when he would hand me poems," Gilchrist recalled. "He was a beautiful man."[168] She was, like so many others, mesmerized by the "simple dazzling images he could create."[169] Frank was not quite as smitten or dazzled in return, at least not with her writing—few of the Fayetteville writers were. "Nobody took her seriously as a writer," one student said.[170] Ralph Adamo, putting it more delicately, said, "She was just beginning to start her writing."[171] Whatever people perceived about her talent, though, Frank could not help but notice the one thing everyone agreed on about Ellen Gilchrist: She was rich—"filthy rich" as one student put it.[172] More to the point, as Steve Stern noted, "she could be very generous."[173]

Not only did Gilchrist come from a wealthy family, but she was also married to a successful New Orleans attorney named Frederick Kullman. With three kids from a previous marriage and a grand house in uptown New Orleans at 1563 Webster Street, Gilchrist was an unconventional Arkansas MFA student. "She had been divorced, married, and had children. She had life experience," Jessica Slote, who came to the program from Vermont in 1974, recalls about Ellen when she arrived.[174] But Ellen was languishing in the role of the good wife in New Orleans, and after a year writing for the *Vieux Carré Courier*, she needed a radical change and a literary one at that. She wrote to Miller Williams about her husband, "I am abandoning as quietly and as neatly as possible this ridiculous marriage—it is very destructive to me to live with this nice, decent capitalist jerk."[175] Bored at home, Ellen wasted little time blending into the bohemian honeypot that was Fayetteville, albeit not always as successfully as she hoped. "Why are so many poets impotent?" she asked Miller. "All the ones you introduce me to are. Is it pain or terror? This is a *serious question*."[176] Despite her interest in virile male poets, Gilchrist was unequivocal about her relationship with Frank: "I did not," she insisted in an interview, "fuck Frank Stanford."[177]

But she did something far more productive: She funded him. Ellen, who was commuting weekly between New Orleans and Fayetteville, quit the program after a semester. She explained to Miller Williams, "I went to Arkansas without missing more than two classes for two months—flying back and forth from New Orleans wasting a lot of money and studying on airplanes and learning a lot of invaluable things but finally I started seeing spiders in the corners of the woodpile and never knew where I was when I woke up in the morning so I gave it up."[178] Despite "feeling like a deserter," she left Fayetteville having made new friends and discovered a new purpose. Essentially, she bought her way into the literary epicenters of Fayetteville and New Orleans, keeping herself in the mix despite leaving the program. She earmarked three loosely interrelated projects worthy of her investment and involvement: Frank and Lost Roads, a New Orleans–based journal called *Barataria*, and the painting career of a woman she came to adore and correspond with for decades: Frank's wife Ginny Stanford.

On January 15, 1977, a month before Frank applied for the NEA grant, Ellen gave Lost Roads $5,000. She did so in exchange for 50 percent of the sales from the books that Lost Roads would publish for C. D. Wright, John Stoss, and Ralph Adamo, as well as *The Singing Knives*, which Lost Roads planned to republish in the near future. The timing of this gift could not have been better or the terms more generous. "There is no way I can thank you," Frank wrote to Ellen, "except with the publication of great poetry.... What you are doing for these authors, including myself, is very fine." He closed this note with a hopeful flourish: "I believe we all may be stepping into that big cow chip called literary history?"[179] Ellen was more than happy to be included, no doubt with the implicit agreement that this cow chip of literary history would eventually include her own book of poetry, which it did in 1979 when Lost Roads published her first of twenty-six books, *The Land Surveyor's Daughter*. In any case, Ellen was pleased to help Lost Roads, predicting that "this will be a good year for everyone, I feel it coming—it's our turn."[180]

Ellen's funding, coming at the start of 1977, was the fuel Frank and C. D. needed to dive into the business of turning Lost Roads' six manuscripts into six books. In March Frank wrote to McKernan, one of the writers pestering him about a publication date, to assure him that galley proofs and a contract for one thousand books (all paperback) would be coming soon. "Sorry this has taken so long," Frank added.[181] On April 1 he sent all six authors the typescripts being used to set their books. Once corrections came back, he promised to send galley proofs and new contracts. The contract, as he described it, bent over backwards to treat the poets well. The writers would receive $100 in advance of publication ($200 if the NEA grant came through), $300 worth of free books ("Please don't give your books away to people who will buy them"), and 30 percent of royalties ("six times what a University Press gives"). He assured the authors that they were all treated the same—"No poet has over 20 poems in his book," he said, because "I have never read a book with over 20 or so good & powerful poems in it." He reminded them how "this all started out on a small scale in a small way" but said that "the more I read your poetry the more I knew I had to make it reach the most people."[182] Even as Frank soured on the obligations of running a press, his belief in publishing the underdog poets never wavered, nor did his willingness to keep the press alive.

Frank followed up with his stable of poets on May 1, 1977, elaborating on his requests and requirements for publication and on postpublication plans. He urged his writers to contact their local bookstores about carrying their books and to think about where they wanted review copies sent and where to advertise. He chided the group for only one of them having sent him the requested author photo. "I guess you are all ugly," he concluded.[183] On June 1 (he had clearly reserved the first of the month as the day to contact his "Dear Six Authors"), he wrote, "I hope the Galleys look O.K.," adding that it was high time for everyone to "shit or get off the pot."[184]

At some point in the spring of 1977, while Frank and C. D. were ironing out the details of advertising, sales, and distribution, as well as the galley proofs for the first six volumes, Lost Roads lost its printing company, Overstreet Printing. With Ellen's $5,000 loan Frank had paid 50 percent in advance for printing the six Lost Roads volumes. But Overstreet—which had already printed and bound *Constant Stranger* and was about to print *The Battlefield*—hit a roadblock that would delay the six books. Fred Overstreet explained to Frank in a handwritten note that his company had recently changed ownership. This had led to disruptive equipment and personnel issues as well as "countless problems," including "a bad roof."[185] While Frank was relieved that "things are clear on the big book"—that is, *The Battlefield*—he decided that he "could not prevail on the other six books." He asked Fred Overstreet for a refund of $815.84. "Please work with me on this," Frank wrote.[186]

Overstreet did, and Frank and C. D. quickly turned this setback into a potential opportunity: They decided to start their own printing press. In mid-May of 1977 Frank noted how "I have recently found[ed?] a printing company to do the work on a lower cost basis."[187] The company Frank and C. D. started was named White River Printers (WRP). Through a "long term low interest note," Frank purchased "a complete print shop: about 16,000 worth of new and used and new equipment and supplies."[188] This exaggerated figure may have referred to the printing press that came from Burt Camp, the turkey hunter who had run Elk Ranch Printing. Camp had been grumbling about having to sell the operation back in 1975, when Frank was using him to print *Surveying* and the early version of *Bean Street*.[189] Wherever the press came from, Frank and C. D. drew on a $5,000 grant/loan from her father, Ernie Wright, to pay around $4,000 for the equipment.[190] They then hired an ex-convict named Jess Henderson to run the press at White River Printers. He "hasn't been out of prison long—manslaughter or murder?," Frank wrote to the Cuddihys.[191] Henderson had indeed been imprisoned for the "unlawful delivery of heroin" to a young woman who overdosed.[192] While incarcerated he had learned the trade of operating a printing press. Lost Roads was happy to have him on board.

The acquisition of this equipment changed the scene at 705 Jackson Drive dramatically. "It just seemed normal that they had a press and they were using it," recalled Kathy Walton, who briefly worked at Lost Roads.[193] "It was a really old printing press they used," Ralph Adamo recalled.[194] "The books were hand pressed. Even then it was old fashioned. They had a press they used to roll out the pages and hung the pages. They had to take the pages to Rogers [probably referring to Elk Ranch here] for the binding. It was very labor intensive."[195] Even so, Lost Roads could, in conjunction with White River Printers, better control the production of its own books.

Establishing White River Printers also created a potential source of income to fund Lost Roads. Lost Roads certainly saved money with WRP printing the press's first six books. At least Wright's *Room Rented by a Single Woman*, Stoss's *Finding the Broom*, and Adamo's *Sadness at the Private University* were all printed (although still unbound) by June 1977. Frank also planned to use WRP to print *Mill Mountain Review* issues and books for Irv, so long as *MMR*'s grants kept coming through. Frank told the Cuddihys that he "declined to do printing jobs for crummy books" but felt like "this was an error," one that was "elitist and undemocratic." He estimated that WRP would "need the accounts of about nine other fairly regular small press/little magazines" to recoup their investment. He further noted that WRP could do work at about "⅔ cost in Northwest and Deep South." If nothing came through soon, though, Frank said he and C. D. would have to swallow their pride and print "menus and letterheads and advertisements," trying not to care what the press pressed.[196]

Fortunately, a couple of things did come through. Further acts of generosity from Ellen Gilchrist and C. D. Wright's father, Ernie Wright, kept WRP and Lost Roads afloat through 1977 and into 1978. After two editors at the New Orleans–based magazine *Barataria* hired Ralph Adamo as poetry editor for its third issue in late 1976, Ralph, on hearing about Ellen's support for Lost Roads, called on her for financial help with the magazine. Ellen, who was thrilled to be even informally part of Lost Roads, was happy to expand her literary involvement. She delivered in more ways than one. In addition to making an unspecified financial contribution (in exchange for becoming an associate editor), Ellen sent *Barataria* to White River Printers. "Next," Frank wrote with enthusiasm to the Cuddihys, "we do issues of the BARATARIA out of New Orleans."[197] A week later—in late June—he wrote to *Barataria* editor Louis Gallo about how to save money by buying paper in bulk. "This is the only way to fly," Frank assured him.[198] Although the issues would not be ready until November—"I apologize for being behind schedule," Frank wrote—*Barataria* 3 and 4, beautiful volumes, would be printed by C. D. and Frank's company.[199]

All that was left to do by the fall of 1977 was make covers for all six of the Lost Roads books and bind them. Frank was proud of several of the covers, noting to John McKernan how his would be designed by the photographer Richard Albertine, "a man ... who was with Minor White at APERTURE," Morris's by Albertine's student Richard Leo Johnson, and Broughton's and Adamo's by Ginny.[200] By late 1977 all six books would be published. On October 31, 1977, Frank wrote to Ralph perhaps the shortest letter he ever wrote: "Ralph—Your book came out today! Frank." He later told Ralph to celebrate—"Have a weenie roast."[201] For whatever reason, the six writers would not have their books delivered to them until February 1978, the total number of copies of each book printed and bound was likely closer to five hundred than one thousand, and, as Ralph Adamo noted, "there was just no plan for distribution beyond listing it with a small press distributor." He added that he was "not sure any review copies were ever sent."[202] But the books were published. With their signature white covers and red lettering, they were, as Frank had intended, circulating in the world. They still are. And while the writers might have experienced that all-too-common feeling that writers have when their book finally drops—the calm before the calm—the momentum for Lost Roads and WRP leaned forward as 1977 moved into 1978.

But at the end of 1977, Frank and C.D., at least in terms of their business, were in the same boat as they had been at the end of 1976. Goals far exceeded resources. The NEA grant Frank had applied for in February 1977 was denied. Frank claimed he was never notified, a claim duly backed by the repeated letters he sent to the NEA asking what was up. Nonetheless, he and C.D. had a list of new plans that they wanted to achieve with Lost Roads. These included publishing Ellen Gilchrist's first book, *The Land Surveyor's Daughter*, and C.D.'s third book, *Terrorism*; getting *The Battlefield Where the Moon Says I Love You* bound and distributed (as Lost Roads no. 7–12); publishing three photography books, especially one by Frank and Ellen's favorite photographer, the ever-irascible Clarence John Laughlin; and trying to get the first six Lost Roads titles reviewed.

After having achieved their goals for 1977, they were once again broke. But that changed in November of 1977 when Ernie Wright gave his daughter $5,000–$2,500 as a gift and $2,500 to assume Frank's loan on the printing equipment (he was to pay Ernie back at $100 a month).[203] Freshly bailed out, Frank and C.D. signed another year's lease on the 705 Jackson Drive house, reached out to a new stable of artists, and dove back into their lives as live-in poets-publishers-printers.

## "I Mean He Was Wore Out"

Running a press kept Frank close to C.D., it enabled him to support her poetry, and it made the Fayetteville side of his double life possible. Otherwise, it was *work*. It was tedious and time-consuming and largely unrewarding work. And with C.D. doing much of the behind-the-scenes heavy lifting, it was still work Frank was not especially good at doing, at least in terms of meeting deadlines and managing finances. After his death, C.D., addressing Frank directly, wrote in her notebook, "The publishing company my friend is going to make it.... You didn't make it easy for us, but you made it possible."[204] Money was always scarce. They were subsidized by friends and family and not even breaking even. Everything took longer than anyone expected.

Plus, the publication of a book did not mean that anyone noticed the publication of a book. People nagged. Poets Frank had liked when he started working with them he liked less when he was done working with them. Of Morris, Broughton, and McKernan, Frank wrote to Cuddihy, "I will confide this to you only, I am not too thrilled anymore with their poetry."[205] He had to balance book publishing with surveying. He had to balance book publishing and surveying with two romantic relationships in two different states. He somehow continued to write poems—he had three new manuscripts finished by 1977 and was working on *Crib Death* for Ironwood—but he still chose not to submit to journals. His once active and deeply satisfying correspondence with other poets was effectively dead. In late 1977 he wrote a one-off note to Dugan: "Never hear from you anymore? How is everything going? Here is what I've been doing with most of my money and time the last three years. I still have the surveying company, which made a publishing company, which made a printing company. I am still poet company, but never in company with poets."[206]

Frank ended by recalling a letter that Dugan had written to him in 1973, one with a swatted fly taped to the page: "I would appreciate a line or two, maybe another dead fly; I still have the one you sent me."[207] Nothing came. After Frank's death, when Michael Cuddihy was working to get poets to write a tribute to Frank's career, Dugan "just couldn't make the deadline with a short piece on Frank."[208] Frank had even lost touch with Jimbo Reynolds. An office note in the Lost Roads archives reads, "Jimbo called and wants to keep in touch."[209]

Additionally, the birth of *The Battlefield* was not a satisfying book drop but a laborious release that took place throughout the year 1977 and into 1978. Frank seems to have experienced the publication of his life's great work as a slow and unsatisfying drip-drip-drip of a release. While the printing and binding of a few copies of the book allowed Frank to turn his attention to Lost Roads' first six books, the final completion of his most important work removed him from a heady experience that had occupied nearly half his life. Nothing better improves a writer's work than being able to finish it, put it away for a while, and take it back out to read with the fresh eyes of an objective editor. Frank had been putting his poem away and taking it out for over a decade, and it had indeed gotten better and better. It had improved because his assessments of it—because of his maturing critical voice—had also improved. This ongoing experience—having the "anxiety of influence" be about your own work—kept Frank connected to his past, allowed him to mold his contemporary persona to it, shaped the range of his contemporary social relations (Sherman's, Richard Banks), and continually refreshed the deepest source of his need to write. To see this massive book printed and bound, even if only in a few volumes as mock-ups, must have been equally gratifying and terrifying.

Then there was the impact of daily correspondence. Stanford letters are a form of expression every bit as unique as his poems. They have a literary style all their own and often have the power to stun. When he was writing regularly to Dugan, David Walker, Michael Cuddihy, and Irv Broughton, as well as many other editors, Frank wrote with gusto and without inhibition. His epistolary style, often enhanced by alcohol consumption, howled over poetry, artistic ambitions, critical opinions, and even a little po-biz. "His letters were full of warmth, wild tales, and an intense love of poetry," wrote his pen pal Thomas Lux.[210] But in mid-1975, 1976, and 1977, this freestyle approach came to an end. Frank's letters stopped going for broke. They became all business. They were more frequently typed. They had to be. The conformity required to run a press and a publishing company numbed him. For a man whose persona was created through writing letters, the new imperative to communicate precise information rather than unleash uncontained ideas and opinions deflated the chaotic spirit of this once-liberating activity. While engaged in the business of poetry more than the writing of poetry and focused more on the accomplishments of others than those of himself, Frank, along with his letter writing, became purposeful and prescribed rather than full of play and possibility. The letters became adult. Pure adult.

For all these reasons, there's no surprise that, after two years of running a publishing company and a year of running a publishing and a printing company—all the while running a surveying company—Frank Stanford was worn out. After his death, C.D. Wright wrote that "he finally got tired—he got tired of writing poems because he said it came too easy, he got tired of surveying because he hated business, he got tired of his love life because it was a mess, he got tired of paying his bills but he still owed them, I mean he was wore out."[211] Forrest Gander noted that "he stopped writing a lot, he felt like he'd sort of run out . . . that he'd done what he had to do."[212] Ellen, who also witnessed Frank's growing fatigue, urged him to drop everything and go to film school: "My friend . . . teaches at the University of Maryland at Baltimore and wants to meet you . . . he is *one of us*."[213] Frank, who put it as clearly as anyone could about these last few years when he wrote that "sometimes just the everyday things became so difficult that it was very tempting to stop it all,"[214] never followed up on Ellen's offer.

In the past, there had always been something exciting just about to materialize, something he hoped *might* happen, and he only had to steady his ship on turbulent seas and lean in that direction for life to take on new meaning. For a while this excitement had centered on himself and his publishing, sexual adventures, and movie ambitions: The progress of his books and poems and film ideas and encounters with women were like drug hits. And then, when the drug hits got old, or too costly, or too easy, he turned to the task of helping others get their hits. Since 1973 he had transferred that sense of artistic emergence to Ginny and her painting and, since late 1975, to C.D. and her poems as well. Frank was an excellent and heartfelt mentor. The work of mentoring gave him—and his wife and lover—real pleasure. But he never stopped to wonder how long this mentorship could sustain him or them or if mentoring people he was not also sleeping with, such as the other five of the Lost Roads six, possibly might not be as fully gratifying as mentoring his lovers.

This was a problem, if only because by about 1977 neither C.D. nor Ginny really required the guidance they once had from Frank. Their training wheels were wobbling and about to fall off, and they were riding strong. The coping strategy that Ginny mentioned after Frank died—"I anchored myself to painting"—was clearly in use while Frank was slowly abandoning her in Liberal, Missouri, and her efforts were paying off. She continued to paint what Frank suggested she paint, most notably portraits of Frank in a blue and white kimono, and her confidence and connections had improved considerably. She won several awards at the Arkansas State Festival of the Arts in Little Rock in 1975, and that same year, she won the Ozarks Merit Award at Point Lookout, Missouri.[215] Ellen Gilchrist became Ginny's most important fan and patron; Frank had routinely bragged about her paintings to Ellen. In late 1976, she drew on some New Orleans connections to arrange a show of Ginny's paintings. As Ellen took over Ginny's mentorship from Frank, he faded a bit from Ginny's professional life. Frank worried about this distance, admitting that "as time went on I wondered if the only reason either one of you had any thing [sic] to do with me was because of my eternal and constant belief in your work."[216] He was onto something there.

Ellen had constant belief in Ginny's work too. But she also had more resources. She began playing the role of Ginny's de facto agent. "Ginny Stanford coming Friday for her show opening January 16. I'll send you the rave reviews," Ellen wrote to Miller Williams.[217] This show was at A.L. Lowe in the Carrollton section of New Orleans, and it was Ginny's second solo exhibition, the first having been a year earlier in Fayetteville at the Union Gallery.[218] Ellen, enlisting her rich friends, had masterfully arranged the whole thing. Lowe was not really a gallery but a frame shop, but no matter so long as Ellen's friends were on hand with their checkbooks. Ellen soon reported how "Ginny has sold 3 or 4 paintings for $1600—the reviews were raves. Compared her to Emily Dickinson."[219] On May 12, 1977, at Ginny's second show there, Ellen wrote: "ginny stanford has been here many days—she is besieged by offers of portrait commissions at 15 hundred bucks a throw—there are so many it is frightening to her—also she sold 11 paintings here and has entered an incredible canvas in the n[ew] o[rleans] biennial—I am certain she will be one of the six winners—she is reacting to the terrible onslaught of attention as we all do—fearfully and has been drinking wine for the first time in two years which frightened me."[220]

She concluded, "perhaps my whole reentry into this world has been designed to help her."[221] Ginny, in short, no longer needed Frank to manage her career or advise her on her art, much less bring home firewood to keep her warm.

C.D. was also breaking free. Thanks to Frank's help, she was working on her third book of poems in 1977, a manuscript that Lost Roads would publish in 1979 as a collection titled *Terrorism*. Only four years earlier she had been in law school, but now she was a prolific experimental poet. She was beginning to emerge from Frank's shadow and become noticed by the little magazines on her own terms. David Young at *FIELD* wrote to Frank in May of 1977 that "we didn't finally find anything we wanted in the Stoss book, but we were more and more interested, as we worked along, in C.D. Wright's work: there's a real world there, and it's unique."[222]

While grateful for Ellen's generosity, Frank must have been frustrated with the way she used Lost Roads and *Barataria* to leverage her transition from bourgeois housewife to bohemian literatus. *Barataria* was named after the bayou just south of New Orleans where Jean Lafitte and his pirates bivouacked. The magazine was committed to "the eccentric and peripheral concerns amidst a local culture devoted to extravaganza and metropolitan progress, a central drive that destroys all vestiges of present originality and past accomplishments as it advances itself."[223] After her donation to join this club, Ellen made the *Barataria* masthead as associate editor and a member of the editorial board, listed alongside local legends such as Everette Maddox, Ralph Adamo, and Louis Gallo. Ellen, despite her constant railing against corporate elitism, seemed unabashed about this method of entry, gloating to Miller Williams, "Ralph is doing the *Barataria* all by his lonely self—; I have nothing to do with it but money."[224]

Ellen applied a similarly imperious attitude to Lost Roads, an attitude that especially irked C. D. In her letters to Miller, Ellen made it sound as if she and Frank were the ones running the press together, an attitude assumed solely based on her financial support of it. "I am excited about the books Frank and I are publishing—they will be absolutely beautiful physically—we are going to reissue *the singing knives*," she wrote.²²⁵ In another note, she bragged, "Frank and I are publishing 3 books." By January 1977, she was thrilled that she was going to "help publish the incredible books by stoss, wright, and adamo which frank and I are so excited about we forget our own work." She added that "whenever beauty and art happen—I want to serve it for all my days—fuck oil and gold and terror and death and war."²²⁶

As Frank's artistic influence on Ginny and C. D. diminished during these years, his relationships with them became increasingly conflicted and indifferent as well. Deborah Luster recalled how Frank and C. D. started to argue, one time so viciously that C. D. "came banging on my door" and asked her to leave town with her. The two flew to Dallas to see their musician friend Steve Allen play the saxophone at the Playboy Club.²²⁷ Luster and others noted that C. D. began to demonstrate an unhealthy possessiveness over Frank, and Frank later recalled how she would often insist on having sex with him before he left for the farm. "I think she was afraid I would make love to G. . . . C. was always afraid I'd leave her," he wrote.²²⁸

Possessiveness and fear could work in both directions. Louis Gallo remembered a small blowup between the couple once when Frank and C. D. were at Gallo's New Orleans house on North Miro Street, working on *Barataria* 3: "Frank seemed sort of—I'm not gonna say deranged but very upset. I remember his face: He was pale and the main feature was this curly shock of black hair. He seemed beside himself, upset, and he was following [C. D.]. It was obviously something wrong, some kind of psychic badness." He was, Gallo explained, "hounding her."²²⁹ Ellen recalled that when Frank and Ginny were visiting her in early 1977, C. D. "was calling all the time for Frank" and Frank was "increasingly harried by it."²³⁰

In the notebooks she kept after Frank's death, C. D. included stream-of-consciousness entries that noted a decline in passion after their first year together. In one entry she wrote, "I was so disappointed in your love as it grew older but I was so mad about its youth."²³¹ In another, she wrote, "Miss the whole shebang touch kiss sweat tongue fucking the first year we never slept through the night we never quit morning night afternoon but that beautiful stuff in the first year what happened what terrible wind blew your love so far away."[232] Ginny also wondered about that same terrible wind and where it had taken the man with whom she had lived in relative isolation and domestic comfort back in Rogers. "He left me to his lies and failures," she recalled, "no firewood, no grocery money, the pipes frozen solid, no gas for the car." She fumed that "he had forgotten his home"—and her— by the end of 1977. "A week between [visits] stretched into two, then three," she wrote.[233]

For Ginny, her reaction to this diminishing closeness and decline in artistic mentorship manifested itself in growing anger at her husband's absence. She recalled him as having "no shadow, no footprints."[234] Frank himself did not disagree, saying that "I knew I was a ghost." When the lid finally came off the big lie, Frank was surprised to learn how long Ginny had resented him for what he was doing to their marriage. "I came to see how much you despised me," he wrote.[235] When he told her he loved her, she said, "Don't give me that crap."[236] With C.D., Frank's reaction to the decline in passion, the increase in possessiveness, and the sense that they were inching into bland unhappiness manifested itself, oddly enough, in his increasingly bourgeois habits. Frank and C.D. began to run on the track together because Frank wanted to stay slim.[237] Frank was eating a mostly vegetarian diet and was rarely if ever drinking—"Been off liquor and meat for a good while now," he said in the latter half of 1977.[238] A scrap of paper from his Lost Roads records has the phone number for Alcoholics Anonymous listed.

It was a good thing that Frank was taking care of himself physically. Lord knows the man had been hard on his body, with ongoing bleeding ulcers to show for it. But these behaviors coincided with a workaday life of writing business letters and paying bills. It was adulthood layered over adulthood. There is no law dictating that a poet's quest to find the primal origins of language through the voices of hillbilly geniuses must necessarily be fueled by alcoholic binges, sleepless nights, and trancelike states of mind. But, for better or worse, that's how it had always worked for Frank. And now he was writing contracts, watching his waistline, and apologizing for being late and, really, for not being terribly good at what he was doing.

But what tormented Frank during the years he ran the press more than any other factor was the fact that the big lie, the love triangle, was proving to be, as C.D. put it, "more than he could hold." Frank began to sense the impact that his secrecy was having on the artistic autonomy of these two brilliant women whom, in his own way, he loved. It is important to remember that love for Frank was inseparable from art. He loved Ginny and C.D. as women *artists*. "The more I dreamed my way into your art, the more I needed you both," he wrote.²³⁹ He knew that his lie was forcing them to accept false realities. He feared that living a life that required them to hide, however subconsciously, their suspicion that they were fostering his double life would compromise their art. "I fell in love with Carolyn and what her work would become in the same way I fell in love with Ginny," he wrote. "Like a charge of lightning I suddenly saw I was in love, very deeply, with two women, and their work."²⁴⁰

This was honest, but it was a tragic way to be in love. His support for these women as artists was negated by the fact that he became "the person you have not trusted for so long." His love triangle and his "eternal and constant belief" in their art were, he came to realize, incompatible. In the last note Frank wrote to Ginny and C.D., he pleaded with them not to allow the understandable hate they felt and the pain they were going to feel "drive you off course."²⁴¹ Frank betrayed Ginny and C.D. as human beings. But never as artists.

## "What I Wanted to Do Was Run"

In early fall 1976 Michael Cuddihy received "an envelope from Frank Stanford, thick with poems."²⁴² These were the first poems Frank had sent to him in more than a year.²⁴³ Cuddihy read them and immediately concluded that something terrible had happened to Frank or Ginny or both. The poems were that grim. He picked up the phone and called Frank's laundry list of phone numbers (getting messages at each of them saying find me at the next number) before getting a hold of Frank's mother at Subiaco and getting Frank's number at the farm in Liberal, Missouri, from her. Cuddihy told Frank "how moved [he] had been by the poems, and how worried." He then proposed that *Ironwood* do a book with these poems at its core.²⁴⁴ Frank agreed and apologized for the worry he had caused his friend, adding that "for the past year (at least that long) each day was a tick that sucked on the hours I would have liked to have been free."²⁴⁵ The book, which would not come out until shortly after Frank's death, was appropriately called *Crib Death*.

While a third of the book's thirty poems were verifiably written (and several published) prior to Frank's having met C.D., the majority of the book's poems sound as if they were written during the time when he was shuffling between Ginny and C.D.²⁴⁶ They explore themes such as the loss of voice, the death of youth, fatigue with existence, the end of dreams, declining health, and the desire to escape. Summarizing the book, Michael Cuddihy wrote, "Of the poems in Stanford's *Crib Death* many had achieved a new intensity. Here love and death circled each other, with death the ultimate victor. In some of the most wrenching, the real world of the poem would literally shove aside the metaphors in the last stanza and declare itself. No wonder I was afraid that someone had died when I first read the poems that became the foundation of this book!"[247] Cuddihy had advised Frank a couple of years earlier to try something new. This was it—a profoundly dark book with a single underlying message that declared it would have been better never to have survived childhood.

As always with Frank's poetry, the "real world of the poem" mirrored the real world of Frank Stanford. Loss pervades these poems. In "Taking Your Life," the speaker talks about being silenced:

> One night the man woke and had no voice.
> He felt his mouth, saw that his tongue was gone.

This man, who thought "his tongue was his wife," went looking for it in bars and in dreams.

> He dreamed he was a musician,
> That his tongue heard him one night,
> Fell in love with him,
> Came back to live in his mouth.

But in reality, the last line suggests, he was abandoned by his tongue, his wife. He was "The man with no voice, no lovers."[248] In ways like this, Ginny and C. D. are all over the poems. In "A Woman Driving a Stake into the Ground at Midnight," the narrator declares:

> I wanted my love to be an orchard,
> Rows of thornless berries.
> I wanted my love
> To be death for the suffering.[249]

But as it turns out, the speaker's love, for all his desire for it to heal suffering, "Is a dark and rotten fruit on the ground."[250] It is a poem, in its expression of love and death, that echoes the suicide notes Frank would later be writing and may have already been composing in his head.

The poem "Strange Roads before Light" concerns the loss of access to Frank's iconic poetic touchstone: the moon. "At midnight I am alone / And my love is with someone else," it begins. A one-legged kid looking for his dog looks at the moon, but "It was like a plate with no supper." A salesman looks at the moon and sees "a clock with twelve numbers," but "he had no arms to hold her." A child who dreams about sleeping next to a woman when he should be practicing the piano "thought the moon split the key to her room." The poem ends by circling back to the first person and linking the moon's diminishment to the speaker's promiscuity:

> The woman blowing smoke in the dark,
> Her fingers looking for the ashtray,
> She thought the moon
> Was a piece of stationery
> In a drawer she would not open
> She would have written there was no moon,
> That I am screwing somebody else,
> Trying to remember your telephone number.[251]

These lines eerily foreshadow Ginny's discovery of Frank's infidelity with C. D. by finding the evidence "in a drawer she would not open" but where, when she did, she found that he was "screwing somebody else."

But the poems exceed the suffering of the moment to encompass the suffering of all his failed relationships and the many abortions that defined them. Aborted children and the longing for a youth that has passed into distant memory are constant themes in *Crib Death*. "A Woman Driving a Stake into the Ground at Midnight" opens with "God, I have not forgotten you / For sending all my children into your old iceboxes." Later, it proceeds:

> Like you, I knew a woman once.
> She was carrying a child.
> One night she cut it
> Out like a vine
> With her husband's razor.[252]

In "Amaranth," Frank writes, after an early line that declares, "I would like to look under the bed of your childhood":

> When you come down to the heart
> Bring your posthole diggers and crowbar.
> Do not set a corner, a fence won't last.
> Do not bury our first child there[253]

In other poems are lines that declare "I'm sorry to break this to you / But a child of yours was killed today" and "Who calls you his wife now, / And your breasts will never be / Heavy with milk."[254]

In "Would You Like to Lie Down with the Light On and Cry," the narrator says:

> Nine months from tonight
> A woman will be holding
> Her belly in pain.[255]

In "Lost Recipe," he notes:

> I buried the afterbirth in the sawdust
> On the floor of the barn.[256]

The theme of fatigue is also prevalent. In the poem "The Angel of Death," an orphaned narrator declares:

> My shoes are wore out
> Like a thousand years in the desert.

The exhaustions of adulthood make one miss the time, as noted in "Women Driving a Stake into the Ground at Midnight," "When they were young and unfucked / And old friends with the moon." The only solution, as "the Angel of Death" explains, is to flee:

> I am getting out of here, I told the man.
> . . . . . . . . . . . . . . . . .
> What I wanted to do was run.[257]

WHILE OVERSEEING A PUBLISHING COMPANY and a press, even while loving two women, Frank was doing what he thought he wanted to do—publish the work of underdog artists. But it was not going as planned. He was rotting from within. Throughout this time, he claimed, he all the while knew what was coming. Two weeks before he died, just after the love triangle had imploded, he wrote, "I could foretell everything that was going to happen."[258] He explained how "I saw my destiny become wonderfully but dangerously encircled in this idea of 3 people willing to change things." He said that "I have known about this journey for a long time, I even know how it would come about."[259]

It was for these reasons, or even just an echo of these reasons, that back in November 1975, weeks after he met C. D. at Whitehead's house and soon after they shared their poetry with each other, that Frank (knowing what was coming, knowing how this would end) went home to his and Ginny's quiet house in Rogers—the house with a garden and a lake view and two artists doing their work in peace. He walked in, and, as Ginny remembered it, "he put his head in my lap and cried."[260]

Frank posing for Ginny in Liberal, Missouri, ca. 1977.
*Photo courtesy of Ginny Crouch Stanford.*

## FOURTEEN
# "I Wandered I Sang"
## 1978

"WE MUST SEARCH FOR STANFORD through his writings. There he left us field guides, maps, and compasses." These words by Murray Shugars, an early pioneer of the study of Frank Stanford's life and work, have the deep ring of truth. Frank's guides and maps and compasses bring us to the end. An immersion in Stanford's work is not required to see his itinerary toward death come into focus. Not only had Frank long been fascinated with the dramatic suicides of others, not only had he discussed killing himself with at least four people over the previous ten years, and not only had he tried to do so at least once, but Frank also left far too many hints on his path toward death for anyone to be surprised by the way this story ends:

> "A rifle in my hands a bullet in my heart"[1]
> "I can go get my pistol anytime"[2]
> "I have come to know the timing of my death."[3]
> "no one takes my life from me / I lay it down myself"[4]
> "Alive I announce my own death to the world of the living"[5]
> "a person might of thought three shots were fired" (2507)
> "I who will be dead before one word is read a suicide note which is sung too late" (13282)

Frank even left behind a poem titled "The Cape," an inverse of Whitman's "Song of Myself," written from the other side:

> in my heart I knew I was mad
> I wandered I sang

I made promises to death and I kept them
so having done
with my work in this world
I dove into that pool.[6]

For a man who so often boasted of having the powers of prophecy—"I warn the harbinger," he wrote in *The Battlefield* (12414)—these passages portend an almost inevitable conclusion. The immediate circumstances surrounding the fatal moment, Frank's fight with Ginny and C. D. at 705 Jackson Drive, only intensify the tragedy. It seems certain that the path toward death for Frank was also a path toward self-mythologization, the kind meant to turn attention to him and his art. Thomas Lux thought the claim that Frank would live on through his art was "bullshit." But Frank certainly didn't. When he killed himself, he did so with at least two things in mind: his poetry and the two women he loved. A few months after the suicide, C. D. wrote in her notebook: "I can only get better. You have only to get famous."[7]

None of this is to suggest that the last six months of Frank's life were a linear march toward a premeditated demise. Instead, it was a time marked by the routine tedium of work, a welter of surveying headaches, the downward spiral of personal debt, and during his last two weeks in New Orleans a convoluted attempt to merge work, love, and art into something quixotic, enduring, and possibly life affirming. It ended, of course, with the "three lead thuds," in Lux's words, that Frank had long predicted.[8] To say that Frank died because he got caught in a trap of his own design seems fair. But that does not mean he did not make an eleventh-hour effort to imagine a way out of it.

## "He'd Heard Some Great Jazz..."

What is ironic about the last five months of Frank's life is how much fun he had. In 1978, Lost Roads turned to its next round of projects. More than for the first round, the work this time blended social relationships and professional duties in Fayetteville and New Orleans. Equally ironic is that Frank, as down as he was, was as ambitious with Lost Roads' plans as he'd ever been. Anticipated projects included books by poets and photographers including Justin Caldwell, Michael Cuddihy, Clarence John Laughlin, Richard Leo Johnson, Richard Albertine, C. D. Wright, and Ellen Gilchrist. Fewer than half of these projects would materialize, but Frank made various levels of progress on most of them. The ones that would become Lost Roads books—volumes by Gilchrist, C. D., and Justin Caldwell—would be finished shortly after Frank died. He essentially saw them to completion.

This second round of writers was an easier crew to manage than the original six. C. D. had brought Caldwell to Frank's attention, and much to Caldwell's own surprise, Frank loved his poems. Frank noted that Cuddihy had read Caldwell's manuscript and been "knocked over" by it.[9] Caldwell never liked what he called Frank's "backwoods surrealism," but he "instantly" liked him as a person when they met in 1976 and was touched by how both Frank and C. D. "were very encouraging of me." He was especially impressed with the way Frank, the man's man, did not care that Caldwell rejected "the macho element of writing" that the MFA program continued to promote under big Jim Whitehead's guidance. When Caldwell's book *The Sleeping Porch* came out after Frank's death, Caldwell had only one complaint: Frank, in an initial printing, made Caldwell five years older than he was. "Frank did that," C.D. later explained to Caldwell, "because he [Frank] thought he was growing old." Frank, as had been the case his whole young adult life, did not want anyone to be younger than he, the lone prodigy, was.[10]

Ellen Gilchrist, whose book of poems was in the works, was a more complicated case. By February 1978 Frank reported to Ellen his progress with her book, conspicuously saying nothing about the poetry itself. Before describing his daily life as "flood control," Frank went into one of his convoluted explanations for why he wanted the title of her book to include some variation of either the word "anchorite" or the word "anchor." He wrote, "Pursuant to a dream lecture in my sleep by CJL [Clarence John Laughlin] . . . I looked up the word anchorite, thence anchoress, thus to find anchor light, and so on to your available light, then again back to CJL feelings about light, then into metaphorical adventures of tombs as anchors of light then to the light anchors of the light anchor." He ended this digression by saying, "Tell me what you think."[11]

Ellen was not sure what to think, but she quoted Frank's letter at length to Laughlin three weeks later, explaining, "I thought it might amuse you to imagine [Frank] dreaming of you teaching him—as I once did." This was a flattering prologue to thanking Laughlin for allowing her to use his beautiful photo on the cover of her book, which she never did call "The Light Anchor" despite telling Laughlin that "it is an exact description of the function my work has in my life."[12] (Frank, in his third application for an NEA grant in early 1978, still listed her book as *The Light Anchor*.) Where the final title of her book, *The Land Surveyor's Daughter*, came from is unclear, but we know based on her financial support of the press that it was certainly Ellen's choice. As C. D. complained to the Cuddihys shortly after Frank's death, Frank was always doing Ellen's bidding. Ellen, for example, wanted a glossy cover on her book. Nobody else asked for a glossy cover. But Ellen did. And Frank promised her one. (C. D. reneged on that after Frank died).

Michael Cuddihy, as a potential Lost Roads author, was a dream. His poems for a book tentatively called "Bark," as well as Cuddihy himself, were the easiest to manage, so Frank turned to them late, in March of 1978. He genuinely admired his friend's writing. "I can see my way into 18 poems at the moment," Frank wrote to the man who had so lovingly mentored him, "but I am more interested in coming up with either 24 or 30 for a book." Frank especially liked the poem "Loyalties," writing that "you take a different turn with this poem." He had critiques to make, but he was "trying to beat the Spring leaves on many jobs so I won't have to work my ass off come full bloom," highlighting once again the growing challenges of surveying while running a publishing company.[13]

Frank was especially excited about taking Lost Roads in the direction of publishing photography books. Clarence John Laughlin, whom Ellen rightly said "was mad for poetry," made perfect sense in terms of a shared aesthetic view with Frank.[14] He was a self-taught New Orleans photographer with minimal formal education who blended words and photographs to capture what he called the "hyper-real" rather than "surreal" (a word that he also had mixed feelings about) in the images he shot. His earliest work was as a photographer with the Army Corps of Engineers, where he documented levee construction in the late 1920s and 1930s.[15] Add in the fact that he was obsessive in his work habits and favored marginal subjects, and Frank's attraction to Laughlin as a kindred spirit came naturally.

Frank began to discuss doing books with two other photographers besides Laughlin: Richard Leo Johnson and Richard Albertine. All three photographic projects were closely related. Frank and Ginny had admired Laughlin's brand of southern hyperrealism for years, and when Laughlin, with Ellen's encouragement, founded a photography lab in Fayetteville in the mid-1970s, that lab became the epicenter of the Fayetteville photography scene. This is the lab where Johnson and Ginny, who was taking some photos in the Laughlin style, shared a darkroom. Frank met Laughlin on a trip to see Ellen Gilchrist in New Orleans and liked him immensely. "I hope to be seeing him again this spring," he wrote to Johnson. Frank suggested to Laughlin that he do a book with Lost Roads, and according to Frank, Laughlin was open to the idea.

For whatever reason, this plan fizzled, but Frank got much closer to publishing a book of photography with Richard Leo Johnson. "My company is in favor of the artist totally," Frank assured Johnson as they worked to settle the details of the book contract. Sobered by the reality that the first six Lost Roads volumes had made nobody rich, Frank advised Johnson, "Please don't anticipate your book as a money making project for either of us." Frank was not posing in the least bit when he added, "Money is not my interest."[16] It rarely was.

Frank convinced Johnson's mentor Richard Albertine to do a Lost Roads book as well. Albertine had studied under the poet-photographer Minor White at MIT. But Albertine was slow. Frank chided him for not getting his portfolio to him in a timely manner. "I would like to get beyond the tentative stage," he told Albertine in February 1978. He noted that "I have three jobs, and help out 12 artists, so I don't like to be tentative very long." He also wanted to get the ball rolling on photography exhibits to accompany these proposed books. He gave Albertine a deadline of April 1. "I know your life is rocky now," he wrote, "but please count on this as easy going, at least until camera, plate, and proof time."[17] Albertine apparently never met the deadline, but he would move on, getting a job with Baton Rouge's alternative weekly *Gris Gris* and taking photos of Louisiana fauna such as Edwin Edwards before turning to the flora of Avery Island.

Frank kept in touch with the original Lost Roads six. John Stoss was becoming a thorn in his side. When Frank and C. D. told him that C. D. was working to get his manuscript of a novel titled *Machines Always Existed* "into shape," Stoss, according to Frank "got furious," presumably thinking it was already in shape. John McKernan, on the other hand, was Frank's golden boy, at least so far as marketing was concerned. Frank reported that he "sold 100 books in a month" and "got 25 bookstore orders." Frank was annoyed with Ellen because she had promised to get the original six Lost Roads volumes reviewed but had nothing to show for her promise. Judiciously, given Ellen's financial support, Frank vented his frustration with her to Ralph. "She promised," he complained. Adamo, for his part, came into Frank's best graces as a poet and budding critic. Frank approached him to write reviews of some poetry books that had recently come out. "I am interested," Frank explained, "in that free space as yet untraveled between prose poem and essay." Channeling his antiestablishment angst, he argued that "for a long time only shit hooks and political powers were doing essays and reviews," but "now young poets are." He concluded, "You could do it Ralph." As far as C. D. and her work went, Frank was unwavering in his take on her: "TERRORISM [her third book] is very good, the best so far." He even had a rare assessment to make about himself, saying of *Crib Death*, "It is my best."[18]

Despite the complexity of a relationship mediated by her financial donations to Lost Roads, Ellen and Frank became friends, not lovers, but friends bound by Frank's mentorship of Ellen. Frank went to New Orleans several times to work with Ellen on her manuscript and check in with *Barataria*, whose issues White River Printers was printing. Frank was also going to New Orleans because of New Orleans itself, a city he was growing to love. The streetcar, the city's bookstores and artists—most notably Maple Street Book Shop and Clarence John Laughlin—appealed to Frank, as did the music venues, including Tyler's, located uptown on Magazine Street; Rosy's at Valence and Tchoupitoulas; and the Maple Leaf Bar on Oak Street, where Everette Maddox had started his legendary poetry readings. Frank enjoyed being out of the fishbowl of Fayetteville and in the jazz clubs of New Orleans, and Ellen and *Barataria* offered enough justification for him to make several trips there in the last year of his life.

On one occasion, Ellen recounted how—likely in mid-January 1978[19]—"carolyn, frank and friend, Peggy Kon[e]rt have been here for eight wonderful days of museum ballet music music music." She wrote to Miller Williams, "guess who we kidnapped one night at the mapel [sic] leaf—your youngest chicken—I love her and got drunk and told her to move in with me—maybe she will." That youngest chicken was Miller's daughter Karyn Williams, younger sister of Lucinda. Also along for the ride on that drunken evening were Ralph Adamo, Everette Maddox, and the writer Tom Whalen. "We had all the poets in town together for days doing quiet things and sitting on the floor and just loving each other—it was nice."[20] Ellen's salon was for all involved a kind of well-funded euphoria that contained multitudes.

Frank and that young chicken's sister, Lucinda, became close as well. Lucinda spoke in clear terms about her attraction to Frank—he was, with his brooding manliness and poetic sensibility, exactly her type. Frank wrote to C. D. and Ginny in the last couple of weeks of his life, "Lucinda was wonderful to be with when C. was gone. I felt free from danger."[21] Deborah Luster recalls how, in the spring of 1978, she frequently saw Frank and Lucinda together at George's Majestic, the pub and music venue on Dickson Street in Fayetteville. As was so often the case with Frank and the women he fell for, people were left scratching their heads over the nature of the relationship. Luster supposed that Lucinda "was quite smitten with him and they had a little affair."[22] But Ellen, who was closer to Lucinda than Deborah was, insisted that they were only close friends, in love in a platonic way, and that Frank was more interested in an artistic than in a sexual liaison with her. Ellen remembered the two of them discussing the phrase "make me a pallet on your floor," recalling Frank's ability to trace the lineage of that lyric deep into the blues tradition.[23] These discussions played a pivotal role in Lucinda's songwriting. She was, when they had that conversation in 1978, working on her first album, *Ramblin' on My Mind*. When it came out a year later, it contained the cover "Make Me Down a Pallet on Your Floor."

Frank seemed to always be balancing one lover with another, so of course Lucinda was not alone in vying for Frank's attention. Frank may have been seeing during his New Orleans visits—and certainly did see on his last visit—an equally charismatic artist, a photographer named Kay DuVernet.[24] Frank and DuVernet had likely met when he moved into the New Orleans Hotel in Eureka Springs in December 1972, fresh from his New York adventure with Cheryl Campbell and subsequent escape and escapade with Deidre. In early 1973, DuVernet left New Orleans for Eureka Springs to explore the lesbian art community for which the town was becoming well known. When she arrived, she booked a room in the New Orleans Hotel, where she met the owner, Barbara Scott. It was an unconventional meeting (although not for Eureka Springs). Scott and DuVernet had gotten in the elevator together, and DuVernet had immediately grabbed Scott by the shoulders and kissed her. They dated for several years, and DuVernet became manager of the hotel for a while. It seems nearly impossible that, while managing the place, DuVernet did not meet the poet staying in room 308.[25]

In any case, DuVernet and Frank became quite close in New Orleans, again as much emotionally as physically. According to Leslie Parr, a friend of DuVernet's in New Orleans, DuVernet saw "things other people would not see." She was "dreamy and ethereal." She was the kind of person who might spend an entire day on the porch or balcony just looking out at the world. She loved Japanese scroll painting and photography and was drawn to odd abstract images. She "did not see the world as most people did."[26] Barbara Scott said that Kay "knew how to hold a mystery," and Scott could easily see how this quality might have appealed to a poet like Frank.[27] Ellen recalled that Kay adored Frank, while Ralph noted that Kay taught Frank a certain intimate maneuver requiring the use of a fist.[28]

Whoever was there and whatever they were doing with or to each other, these evenings in New Orleans with poets and painters and photographers were everything Ellen could have dreamed of. She was finally hanging out with people who loved literature and the arts, and she was the resourceful

Kay DuVernet, ca. mid-1980s. *Photo courtesy of Leslie Parr.*

executrix of her own salon. Frank was just as excited about the city. He spoke to Ralph about how fun it would be to rent a place there.[29] Although this is entirely speculative, it's hard to think that Frank wasn't in the early stages of coordinating his third attempt to live in two different places with access to two different but remarkable women—Kay DuVernet in New Orleans and Lucinda Williams in Fayetteville. Frank even advised Kay, who was considering moving to Fayetteville to go to the MFA program, not to do so, even though, as Kay later wrote to C. D. and Forrest Gander, "Ellen advised it."[30]

In any case, the only person who suffered from all this bohemian activity was Ellen's husband, Fred Kullman, the attorney rubbed the wrong way by the scruffy scene Ellen ushered into her refined Uptown home. Ralph Adamo remembered, "By spring '78 things were really bad between them; I remember Freddie being pretty hostile to all of us who were sitting around in his house. On one occasion, Frank was playing jazz records but Freddie wanted to hear the album from 'Nashville,' (which is a terrific album), and Frank said something disdainful about music with words or songs with words. He'd heard some great jazz at Tyler[']s and wanted to hear that."³¹ In the will that Frank wrote two weeks before he died, he lists under "JAZZ TO GET" the great New Orleans drummer Johnny Vidacovich and Astral Project, both acts that he saw while visiting New Orleans during his last two weeks on earth. Ellen continued to generously fund all the musical outings for the starving artists she adored, taking care of cover charges and drinks.³² Frank, who had been relatively isolated from any sort of lively social scene since the spring of 1973, was having a good time in New Orleans.

## "I Would Like for Frank to Start Making Payments"

But everything else in his life was a mess that just got messier. Surveying work proceeded but it was hampered by Frank's indebtedness for his sophisticated surveying equipment. Worse, even with the more accurate equipment, he was making errors in the field. A big job that Frank did for Greer Real Estate in January of 1978 was botched, or at least his client believed it had been. It insisted that the surveying pins were misplaced and thus refused to pay the $700 balance it owed on a $5,800 job. Frank, who was baffled by the accusation, had to hire C. D.'s father, Judge Ernie Wright, to represent him and his boss, Don Kemp. "This I don't understand," Frank explained. "Any error like this would have turned up in our computer." And if it had turned up, "we could have adjusted easily," he wrote.³³ Frank could not understand how the pins had been improperly set. "I hope no one has tampered with any of our stakes or pins" was all he could offer by way of an explanation. When he relayed the matter to his boss, Kemp also insisted that there was no error "unless it is some kind of clerical error we can't find."³⁴ The fact that Frank had been using notably inexperienced labor—namely, poets and photographers—to do some of the fieldwork went unmentioned in these exchanges.

Kemp and Frank were eventually persuaded to let another surveyor confirm the accuracy of their work. If an error turned up, Frank agreed to fix it at no charge.³⁵ From there the paper trail runs dry. But something Frank did a couple of weeks later suggests that he may have been at fault: He purchased even more advanced surveying equipment. In early April, Frank signed a thirty-six-month lease with a Dallas-based operation called Surveyor's Leasing Company for $7,339 worth of new surveying tools. He put down a security deposit of $1,174.24 and took on payments of $293.56 per month. The equipment included an updated Beetle, a Nikon NT-2 camera, a Trion mount and power pack, a triple prism. and a prism holder.³⁶ Later that month, in a long overdue letter to his mother and gran-gran, he explained how he hoped to "average out my time better" by purchasing "expensive distance measuring equipment (Electronic Infra-Red), which I have already done last month." To assuage any concerns about his being overcommitted financially, he wrote that "it is very expensive on the lease-purchase plan, but we [he and Kemp] share the cost."[37] Only Frank's name, however, is on the lease.

Frank made this investment to better balance the work triangle—surveying, publishing, printing—that mirrored his love triangle. But it came amid several other financial pressures that, while individually manageable, were collectively becoming untenable. Ernie Wright had originally demanded that Frank begin paying back his March 29, 1977, loan for the printing press on September 1, 1977, but then had given him a two-month extension. Judge Wright wrote to C. D. in November: "I would like for Frank to start making payments. Of course, as soon as he is in a position to pay off his half of the notes in full, so much the better."[38] Frank made the minimal $100 payments to Wright on December 27, January 27, February 27, March 27, and, last, on May 15. With the annual interest on the loan, at a rate of 8 percent, coming to $144, Frank had barely made a dent in the principle. Plus, he was making these $100 payments not from his personal accounts but with Lost Roads checks.

All in all, Frank's finances were becoming an unprecedented and irreparable wreck. This was new for him. When he was with Ginny in Rogers and working solely as an independent surveyor, the couple had practiced great discipline to live within a tight budget—right down to the last dollar every month. They appear to have never gone over. But now that Frank was running a business—or three—he lost all financial control. In addition to the roughly $1,800 still due Judge Wright, Frank owed (with C. D.) $190 per month in rent on 705 Jackson Drive, $128.80 per month for his white Datsun King Cab pickup truck, $293 per month for the new surveying equipment, and $190 per month for the surveying equipment he had leased back in August 1977. Then, as if the debt load was not bad enough already, Frank's student loans came due. As of late 1977 he carried a past-due balance of $362.21 and was getting notices for that payment. There were also unspecified monthly payments on an unspecified piece of surveying equipment he had bought in November 1977 and still owed $515 on. In February 1978 he took out an auto insurance policy from Montgomery Ward and had monthly payments for that of $73. Frank had John Stoss, with whom he was reconciled and who somehow had decent credit, take out a $400 loan from a credit union to help Lost Roads pay some bills, but that note was coming due in May. Frank owed Ellen 50 percent of sales on three of the Lost Roads titles, per her January 1977 $5,000 grant, and by May 1978 that figure came to $150. The financial burdens just seemed endless, directionless, relentless, as the spring of 1978 slogged on.[39]

More: Frank and C.D. failed to file taxes for White River Printers, and Frank was being hounded by the IRS for that. Lost Roads was raiding its inventory by sending complimentary Lost Roads books (including some *Battlefield* dummies) to reviewers who requested them—Stephen Harrigan at *Lucille*, Scott Davidson at *Book News*, Douglas Blazek of the Mimeo Revolution, Karl Elder at *Seems*, Bruce Weigl at *Quarterly West*, and Frank Graziano at the South Carolina Arts Commission—but they never published reviews. Lost Roads just needed some good ink to generate some sales, and maybe they could get out of the hole. "Frank Stanford is very busy," the acting Lost Roads secretary, Deborah Luster—then Deborah Nolan—wrote, "but he is hoping you might find something to say, a couple pages or so, about Lost Roads."[40] Nothing. Nolan reached out to Alan Dugan for some help: "We would like to hear what you have to say about the books."[41] Nothing. "A review of these books would help if you can get into it," Frank wrote to Elder.[42] Nothing.

Social consequences followed the financial ones. As the economic noose tightened, as Frank worked harder and harder only to go deeper and deeper into debt, he was increasingly stuck in Fayetteville. He rarely made it to "the farm" to see Ginny, or to Subiaco to see his mother and grandmother. And he was getting an earful about it. "I've had to stay away from the Farm a lot because of everything I do," he wrote to his mother and grandmother, "and that hasn't set too well with Ginny." He added that "I certainly don't blame her." Since Christmas of 1977, he explained, "I haven't really been living there." Frank hated the idea of his mother and grandmother worrying about him and his marriage. "I hope you don't think there is anything very wrong with us, because there isn't," he told them. "We aren't getting a divorce or anything like that." He also apologized for not making it down to Subiaco, as he had promised to, for his grandmother's birthday in mid-March. "I've just been snowed under," he wrote.[43]

"Everything had you down," C.D. wrote in her journal three months after Frank's death.[44] She knew where he was emotionally. But a lot of that emotion reflected the financial burdens that had begun to weigh on him starting in early 1977. "The present is a little dark here and there," Frank told his mother and grandmother one month before he left for New Orleans in May of 1978. This was understatement by the son who did not want to cause people he cared about undue concern.

## "All 3 of Us Loving"

On September 3, 1976, Ginny Stanford, who worked in isolation in the southern Missouri farmhouse, finished an unusually large painting—about three by five feet. It's notable for more than being large: The painting is three renditions of her husband's lover C. D. Wright. There she is in a mustard-yellow dress, standing near a window revealing a crescent moon in an equally yellow sky, surrounded by purple plants growing from a smooth hardwood floor. In one of the three images, C. D. has lowered the top of her dress to expose her breasts. She looks down in a gesture of possible shame. The painting is titled *Carolyn Wright readies herself for another evening*.[45] As we have seen, Ginny almost always painted from photographs that Frank gave her or that she took of him. In May 1978, Frank recalled "how G. cried when she saw pictures I took of Carolyn."[46] Frank had likely taken photos of his girlfriend, some of them topless; shared them with his wife; and instructed her to paint these images. And Ginny did.

This *what were you thinking?* moment starts to explain what Frank was thinking when it came to the other big disaster brewing in his life: the love triangle. The painting helps us to see how he negotiated the more or less secret romantic arrangement that, maybe even to his surprise, he had successfully maintained for over two years. In his final notes addressed to both women (there were three suicide letters), Frank was clear that he fully understood "how you hate me for my manipulations and not telling you the truth." He never tried to excuse or downplay the lies. But, until the occasion of his May 21, 1978, letter, there was a deeper truth he had yet to tell them, one that he could not bring himself to reveal and one that they would not read about until it was too late: He was in love with both women. Deeply and genuinely in love only as he knew how to be in love. He felt no need to have exclusive control over either of them. He wanted to find a way for all of them to live together, "all 3 of us loving," as he put it.[47] A way to somehow be as one in a shared network of love and art was something he desperately needed to discover.

How to do so was the problem. Open discussion, and thus very likely verbal warfare, was something he could neither initiate nor abide. But getting from the lie to the truth preoccupied his thoughts nonetheless, much more than his poetry, for the last few months of his life. "God how I wanted us all to be together," he wrote a couple of weeks before he died. Again he addressed both women in a letter they would not see until after his death: "I missed you so much, Ginny.... And Carolyn, it was so lonely to be at the farm or at Subiaco without you." He explained, employing the plural you, how "wherever I was, whoever I was with, you were in my thoughts."[48]

After his big lie was revealed, he confessed that he was sure that they must have known about each other, that they had to have been implicitly aware of the game that the three of them were playing. He reasoned that, much as he and his mother never openly discussed his adoption, he and Ginny and C. D. never openly discussed their arrangement. "I thought in your hearts," he wrote, "you knew I was in love with you both and loving you both." He supposed that, much as he as a kid had had his reasons for not calling out his adoption to his mother, neither Ginny nor C. D. ever exposed or confronted the obvious truth, because they needed him to support their art. Frank knew that C. D., who had once tried to overdose when a boyfriend broke up with her, obsessed over losing him.[49] For Frank, it was less an inability to sustain this fiction that led to the love triangle's collapse—a collapse that, as we'll see, he likely orchestrated—than what was happening to him beneath the scrim of their shared fiction. He wrote to them, "As time went by I saw how impossible it would be for me to live without you both." In this respect, the inseparability of art and love went all the way to the end. He wrote, "The more I dreamed my way into your art, the more I needed you both."[50]

It is tempting, and perhaps narratively satisfying, to portray the legendary showdown among the wife, the lover, and the poet as a case where the lying man gets duly busted by the innocent women for his manipulations and infidelities. The wife and lover crush him with revenge ("We sliced and diced him," Ginny recalled[51]); and the guilt-ridden bad man punishes himself with a self-inflicted death ("one might have thought three shots were fired" [2507]). It's a reductively clean story line, almost Shakespearean in its power. But the actual situation was more convoluted, and Ginny's painting *Carolyn Wright readies herself for another evening* shines an unlikely light on that complexity, placing Frank's May 18 departure for New Orleans and Ginny's discovery of his big lie in a fuller and more complicated context.

When Frank showed Ginny seminude pictures of C. D., a woman Ginny knew he was living with in Fayetteville, he was ostensibly doing so to foster, as he had long done, Ginny's art. *You should paint this.* But given the fact that this was a woman he was spending more than half his time with, a woman whom Ginny presumably sensed he had sexual feelings for, this could also be seen as a tactic to nudge C. D. and Ginny into each other's lives. "I wondered how I could ever bring you two together," he lamented in one of the last letters.[52] Well, here was one way: Have Ginny paint C. D., warm up to her image—her eroticized image no less—think about her as a real person through contemplation of her sexualized self (something Frank had Ginny do with him by taking hundreds of photos of him); evoke Ginny's curiosity about C. D. as a poet and person. It's hard to imagine any portrait painter not doing this, not experiencing some emotional or even carnal connection to the subject whose image they were sitting with for hours. This was one way Frank could help Ginny get beyond his claim that C. D. was, as he had once described her, a lesbian and a bitch and come to see her as a woman and an artist worthy of their love.

Of course this tactic didn't work. The move did not quite backfire—Ginny clearly got over the pain of seeing those photos—but it did not initiate the deeper curiosity Frank was seeking. The situation remained the same as it had been before: "G. knew nothing," Frank recalled, even though "C. thought G. knew about our love."[53] Ginny just would not bite at the suggestion that Frank was intimate with both women. When Ginny's first show at the A. L. Lowe frame shop in New Orleans was over, Frank, not wanting Ginny to take the painting of C. D. back to the farm, walked *Carolyn Wright readies herself for another evening* down Prytania Street and gave it to Ralph Adamo, who was living near the Prytania Theatre. Ralph thinks Frank may have given Ginny the impression that Ralph bought the painting, which he did not. Today, the evidence of Frank's failed effort to bring these women together still sits in Ralph's living room.[54]

Not incidentally, this wasn't the only time Frank attempted the paint-the-lover strategy. He also did it with Merideth Boswell, whom he was occasionally sleeping with while he was with Ginny and C. D. Recollecting the story, Boswell recounted what led her to finally break it off with him:

> I had let Frank use my car (an old Triumph convertible he loved to drive) while I was out of the country. He picked me up at the airport and drove us straight to McIlroy Bank which at the time was having a show of Ginny's paintings. All I knew was he had a "big surprise" for me. We rode the escalator up to the lobby exhibit where I was met with an almost life-sized painting of myself, oddly, in the same dress I was wearing. I didn't pause but immediately descended on the elevator and left. I was furious that he had taken a photo of me (on the porch of the farmhouse where I lived) and had Ginny paint my portrait.[55]

Looking back on her affair with Frank, she noted, in a reminder of the promiscuity that was prevalent and condoned at the time, "It WAS the 70's.... I only knew about Carolyn and Ginny."[56]

It is also worth pointing out that what Frank wrote to Willett back in 1972 was still very much his guiding approach to women and relationships in 1978. Again: "I seek out the mystery of all women. With some it takes seconds, others years. Like a priest, I transubstantiate the body + spirit one into the other. Once this is done, whenever I look into one woman's eyes, I see yet another woman."[57]

But now "all women," according to Frank's letters, had become two women, and when it came to them and his emotions for them, the stakes were as high as they had ever been in his life. He had become, in essence, deeply dependent on them. "I did not know how to live if we were apart," Frank wrote them. He spent his time "worried about keeping you [Ginny and C. D.] apart until the right moment." But when was the right moment? How could he tell? For now, he was so viscerally drawn to both women that "one time, after C. and I had come back from a movie, I put the covers in my mouth and said your [Ginny's] name." And then, "Once, at the farm, while Ginny was asleep, I was writing; all I could type was your [C. D.'s] name over and over."[58] This is yet another example—an especially raw one—of the way that Frank translated the emotions of his experiences into the written word, albeit this time in a suicide note.

On one especially odd occasion, C. D. and Ginny were literally steps away from meeting each other and maybe even steps away from finally liberating the secret. Looking back on the evening with regret, Frank wished he had decided to make this the "right moment." C. D. and Frank, for an unknown reason, were driving to Kansas from Fayetteville. On their way they had to drop something at the farm in Liberal. When Frank and C. D. arrived, Frank went into the house, and Ginny said to him, "Tell her [C. D.] she can come in and I can leave." Likewise, C. D. had said to Frank, "Tell her it's OK I won't come in." Putting aside the fact that these reactions suggest that these women had knowledge or suspicions about each other, Frank recalled this close encounter as a missed opportunity. This could have been the much-longed-for reckoning. He wondered, what if "C. had stepped in the door," and what if "G. had gotten out of bed and told C to come in"? This near meeting was "the closest things ever came to fulfillment"—a fulfillment that Frank was, awkwardly and haltingly (perhaps stupidly), trying to achieve. Frank wrote about how "I meant everything I said to C. that night—my feelings about all of us, all 3 of us," suggesting that he did in fact open up to C, at least to some extent, about the truth.[59]

Another bizarre way that Frank attempted to escape being locked into his own lie and in turn seek an honest, aboveboard ménage à trois alternative was tacitly encouraging Ginny to see another man. Perhaps this kind of sexual openness, he thought, would ease the transition toward what he wanted to achieve: "all 3 of us loving." For all of Frank's possessiveness of his poetry and for all his dependence on Ginny and C. D., he was never conventionally possessive of his girlfriends or sexually jealous of other men. He particularly felt no threat whatsoever from his friend Ralph. Moreover, Frank did not miss the fact that when Ginny first visited New Orleans in January 1977 for her first show there, she and Ralph hit it off. "Ginny and I started seeing each other," Ralph explained. "I understood at some point," he said, "that Frank wanted us to do that so that Ginny would feel less lonely." One evening in Fayetteville, at a party, someone made a joking remark to Frank about him having two wives. Frank immediately turned to Ralph and said, "Yeah, but I'm sharing one with him."[60]

Frank took a slightly different, and in some ways, more direct approach with C. D. on the prospect of seeking sexual openness. Basically, he encouraged her to share sexual fantasies for Ginny with him, and then together they would imagine being with her. "Sometimes C. and I would fantasize in our love about G.," he wrote. But C. D. eventually put an end to this experiment. "This went on," he recounted, "until one day C. pulled away when we were making love." In time, he wrote, "C. would never let me express anything sexual about G. without hurting her feelings or disturbing her." Similarly, "G. would flinch when I spoke of love or loving with another woman."[61] Again, none of these tactics qualify as especially logical or even remotely achievable ways to reconcile the situation. But they belonged to a strategy nonetheless. General outlandishness notwithstanding—Frank himself said that "I'm sure this is all bullshit to you"—the effort spoke to his desire to destroy the lie and do what he did so well in his poetry: manipulate fantasy into reality.

Resolving this love triangle would involve not simply a mental adjustment but rather something in the deepest core of his emotional life. He was, in his words, "waking up with one woman in Fayetteville, or with one woman on the farm, and knowing wherever or whenever you wake another part of you is missing." He could no longer carry the weight of this ongoing feeling of loss. As a result, "my only desire was to achieve a new kind of experience." He insisted, referring to the three of them, that "I would do anything to [e]nsure the existence of our love, its future." Being nurtured and openly loved by C. D. and Ginny had become "my secret, my reason for existence."[62]

Just as *The Battlefield*'s Francis creates his utopia, Frank was making a last-ditch effort to make his own, and it looked something like this: "An ideal life of us together as friends, lovers, workers, and artists, working to change things." Because of his relationship with them, he explained—again, all in notes C.D. and Ginny did not read until after his death—"I peered into a new world, much more desirable than the old world, where everyone was equal." He let both women know that "I saw my destiny become wonderfully but dangerously encircled in this idea of 3 people willing to change things." This destiny became so all-consuming that, he told them, "Each of you became more and more essential to my work and my life. I felt myself undergo great changes. My love for the ideal and my desire were so great I knew my existence was founded on its conception." He became "obsessed in any way whatsoever in bringing my idea to fruition."[63] On the wall of Ralph Adamo's bathroom on the day of his death Frank wrote, "What is Frank looking for?"[64] Well, this was part of what he was looking for, and the fact that, after his death, C.D. and Ginny lived together for several months suggests he was not totally out of bounds to seek it.

## "Ain't Life Sweet"

Frank eventually realized that finding a solution required delivering a more extreme and direct message. Insinuations and hints were not working. The lie, he decided, would have to be exposed with less artifice. He'd have to risk what he had long tried to avoid—the verbal showdown, the open conflict. He would have to face reality and see if he could handle it. But first, in case he couldn't, there were other people to put at ease, primarily his mother and Father Fuhrmann. On May 12 Frank wrote to Dorothy promising that he and Ginny would be in Subiaco for "the 14th on Sunday, or the day after on Monday?" He despaired that his mother and Ruth were still fighting. "This just goes on and on," he lamented. But he took pride in the fact that "you and I haven't had a real argument in over five years going on six." He added, poignantly, "I think this is pretty good don't you?" As for Mother's Day, Frank insisted that his mother not "go to any trouble fixing anything big" but noted that "if you want to make a dessert, I sure won't stop you." Then, in this note, written three weeks before his death, he wrote: "Speaking of eating, I've been running for several months now. Always run two miles every day, and three and four when I'm feeling good. I like to run early in the morning before work. The other day I got up real early and drank some coffee, then ran. What a mistake! Give everybody my love and we'll see you shortly. I love you, Frank."[65]

During his visit he told her, "I have made so many mistakes," to which she replied, "You can't look back and say that." This was also the Mother's

Frank and Father Fuhrmann, undated. *Photo courtesy of Ginny Crouch Stanford.*

Day visit where Frank sat on the steps outside the Subiaco Abbey with Father Fuhrmann and said that he wished he had the faith that the monks had. Fuhrmann convinced him to watch a short promotional film about becoming a monk. Frank did. When he left Subiaco, he told his mother, "Don't ever let anything happen to think I don't love you."[66]

The day after their Mother's Day visit to Subiaco—either May 15 or 16—Frank dropped Ginny in Liberal and went back to Fayetteville. About two days later—May 18—he flew from Fayetteville to New Orleans, with a layover in Dallas. The official reason for the trip was to continue working with Ellen on her book *The Land Surveyor's Daughter*, as well as the next issue of *Barataria*. He flew out of Northwest Arkansas on a $130 round-trip ticket with a scheduled return date of May 28. As he had done for everything that month—including records, food, prescription drugs, and liquor—he purchased the ticket with Lost Roads checks. On his way to the airport, he realized that he had left his Saint Francis necklace at the Jackson Drive house and insisted that C.D. drive him back to get it. He came within seconds of missing his flight, but he and Saint Francis made it to New Orleans, which was soupy hot.[67]

Frank had his arrangements for New Orleans carefully in order. He gave Ginny an assignment to copy a Gauguin painting "and paint me standing in front of it. Call it *Spirit of the Dead Watching*." This painting (Gauguin's) had also been the cover of *Constant Stranger*.[68] Once in New Orleans, Frank went to Ellen's on Webster Street, where he stayed in one of her many extra bedrooms. On his boarding pass he had written down in black ink the address of the woman he would spend most of his time with over the next two weeks, the poet and photographer Kay DuVernet. There were shows at Tyler's and Rosy's to see. Last, and most significantly, back in Liberal, Missouri, he had left more than a hint: He had evidently left visible some incriminating love letters from C. D. to be easily found by Ginny.[69] The evidence on this point is less concrete than one might hope, but Frank knew how to hide things—secrets, feelings, and surely love letters. He did it scrupulously back when he was with Linda and Cheryl, depositing Cheryl's letters with Irv so Linda would never see them. That Ginny discovered C. D.'s letters, which she did on May 18, the day Frank left for New Orleans, is almost evidence enough that he wanted them discovered. Ginny was not one to snoop. Frank was not one to be careless with his secrets. Whatever the strategy, she found them.

When the call came, Frank was at Ellen's house on Webster Street. The big lie finally collapsed, and it collapsed all over Frank Stanford. Reality immediately got real. Upon discovering the letters, Ginny, who later wrote simply that "he had betrayed me," went straight to Fayetteville to confer with C. D.[70] The two women spent most of the next two weeks together, driving back and forth between Fayetteville and Liberal, fuming as they attempted to iron out the intricate details of their betrayal, comparing notes and merging their individual fury into something profound. They lambasted Frank during several angry phone calls to New Orleans. These women understandably spent hours and hours mining the depths of the deception they had endured—trying "to figure this labyrinth out," as Frank explained, and then throwing it all back at him like rocks.[71]

Frank was a man who wilted under the softest criticism. But C. D. and Ginny laid into him, deeming Frank weak, insecure about not getting enough attention for his poetry, a sexual monster who made "'conquests' of women." They called him ruthless, manipulative, mad, evil, a "Rasputin." They said that his behavior, as Frank put it, suggested that he "had no respect for either of you." Frank did not deny these charges. But he sounded defensive, wondering why they were "in a frenzy." He suggested their vituperation was the wrong reaction, one "arising from another part of your brain." He wrote how he thought they "were making a terrible mistake." And then this: "I don't think you know what you are doing, what you've done, what you will do." He wished they would stop obsessing over "the bad plumbing of the moment," stop trying to "explain or figure out or fathom everything about me."[72] He did everything but call them hysterical. Frank was scared; he wanted forgiveness without punishment.

One thing was now certain for Frank Stanford, and it was a certainty that came to him immediately after the first phone call on May 19: There would be no utopia. There would be no living together in love and through art, no grand experiment in alternative living, no foreseeable forgiveness, no "all 3 loving." And thus, for Frank, there would be no future. After his death C. D. wrote in her notebook: "I would have been your friend again. I think you could tell that."[73] But Frank could not tell that. On May 21 he wrote his first and longest suicide note to C.D. and Ginny. On May 22, he wrote his will, dividing everything he had—namely, his work— between Ginny and C.D. He dedicated his future books. *Crib Death* was for Pharoah Sanders and Muhammad Ali. *You* was for "for Carolyn & Ginny." "One Finger Zen," a manuscript of poems, was for Kay DuVernet and Ellen Gilchrist. Some short stories went to Ginny and the "new poems" to C. D. He insisted on a "Non religious burial, no family, no friends, cheapest place + cheapest way. Fayetteville." (None of this would happen; he had a burial in Subiaco officiated by Father Fuhrmann in the cemetery across the road from the school.) He gave Ginny his half of the Lost Roads company and joked, "If the NEA should give me a grant, make sure L.R. gets it even though I'm dead. The pentagon will just buy a TANK TRACK with it."[74] The grant—the first for Lost Roads—came through a few days after Frank died.

Frank extended his New Orleans trip twice, choosing not to go home on May 28 as originally planned. In his mind and while in New Orleans, he retreated into the only world where he ever felt right, felt in control, felt he could say the things he needed to say: his poetry. "The person who is writing this," he explained, sounding a lot like Kafka, "is Frank Stanford, poet," and "the man writing this is the creature of the poems."[75] In the end, it was in his poetry that Frank the poet lived, and in the end, its where he returned when everything else in his life crumbled. It was only in poetry that Frank Stanford was fully Frank Stanford. It was there that Frank the poet could dream into reality his elaborately vernacular utopias, his ingenious solutions to unfathomable rebuses. What was before him now was, of course, a different reality—an artless mess of immutable reality—one where Frank had no place, where he had never been able to properly function, where he had always escaped into realms more alive with beauty and sounds and sensations that intoxicated him.

Frank did what he had long wanted to do: He stepped aside from the horrible actuality of his adult life. "The poet is writing to you now under the full powers of love, freedom, and joy," he wrote to C. D. and Ginny hours before his death.[76] Ralph, who saw him frequently during these two weeks, confirmed Frank's thoroughly upbeat mood. Ralph wrote on June 2 to John Stoss, "Frank's doing fine. Says he is feeling good. That is, very good, unusually good. Has something to do with Ginny and Carolyn bonding together and 'finding him out.' Apparently they called and told him off a few times."[77] They had. And they had made something clear to him that he could not, despite his delays, forget: He would have to come home and face the consequences, and he could be sure that it was not going to be pleasant. But Frank, riding the streetcar at night in New Orleans, alone, determined that he would, at least in his heart, not face those consequences, not in the way they wanted him to. While "preparing for something which will soon take place," he decided to free himself of all angst, get lost in New Orleans with his friends and, on his last night, with a lover every bit as soulful as he was.[78]

These last few days were eventful and light. While he was drinking with Ralph at a bar on Saint Charles Avenue, they were approached by a bedraggled and despairing Everette Maddox, the brilliant but forlorn and alcoholic poet, who kept taking desperate swigs from his flask. "I wouldn't want to live if I were that guy," Frank said as Maddox walked back to the streetcar. Frank and Ralph went to Tyler's to hear jazz, and Ellen joined them. She paid for them to get into Rosy's Jazz Club to see a violin player "who was all the rage." After the show, according to Ralph, "We were smoking out by the car, and I turn around to shotgun Frank. As I'm blowing smoke into his mouth, Frank says, 'Look, Ellen, me and Ralph are kissing.'" Nobody was aware, and certainly nobody could tell from his jovial behavior, that Frank had made his plan. Ralph recalled, "Everything seemed okay. We knew—I guess from Frank—we knew that Ginny and Carolyn had gotten together. I guess we just didn't realize how heavy a prospect it was."[79] Frank himself seemed to have forgotten.

Then there was Kay DuVernet. "She has been my companion and friend most of my stay in N[ew] O[rleans]," Frank told Ginny and C. D. Within hours after Kay dropped him off at the airport on June 3, Frank wrote that "she revived something in me . . . she completed something in me." Had it not been for Kay, he said, "All my feelings would be dark and terrible." But instead, "I feel light and I feel pain going away."[80] Ralph's June 2 letter to Stoss noted that Frank "has linked up with . . . Kay, who is a poet, and he and she have been working together on her stuff." While it seems logical that Frank would have twice delayed his trip back to Fayetteville to avoid the inevitable confrontation, it's just as feasible that he wanted to extend his time with Kay, a woman with whom he had likely been close since before he knew either C. D. or Ginny. Frank and Kay left for Pass Christian for a few days on May 28 and stayed at the home of a friend of Kay's, and they got back to New Orleans on May 31. On that day Frank wrote his last note to his mother, the woman who had adopted him nearly thirty years earlier: "I'm fine and having a very good time. This is a wonderful city full of wonderful people.... Been in Pass Christian and other parts of the coast last few days. Don't worry. I'm well, fine, feeling good.... See you this weekend or before. Love, Frank (Hello, Gran-Gran if you are there)."[81]

He asked her to deposit a check in his account, promising to pay her back when he returned. This could have been to cover the $150 that Frank had paid Ellen for her investment in Lost Roads. He then wrote to Ralph on the same day:

> Got back from 2 days on coast. Sorry to miss you brother. Will be going back early in the morning. Take care of everything, keep your eye on the moon, your poetry.
>
> Love, Frank[82]

But Frank, making one last change of plans, did not go back on the morning of June 1, a Thursday. Instead, he went to Ralph's house with Kay. On the night of Friday, June 2, the night before Frank finally did fly home and end his life, Kay and Frank retired to Ralph's bedroom and loved each other in the night, and when Frank got up early, he walked into the bathroom and stared at the image of Michelangelo's *The Last Judgment* tacked to the wall, and then he left us with the question that not even the man himself could answer.

"What is Frank looking for?"

# *Coda*

LOOKING BACK ON FRANK'S LIFE, *we might shift the tense and ask a variation of his question: What was Frank looking for? Well, he wanted to live in poetry, in art. It sounds clichéd and childish even. But that's what he wanted—and he did it. The man—the boy who was the man—published seven books of poetry while he lived. He saw with his own eyes. He saw with his own eyes one of the longest poems ever written, the result of his life's work, bound into dummy copies. He wrote it and brought it into being, and he loved it. He called it* The Battlefield Where the Moon Says I Love You. *He read and listened to and watched everything, and his ear and eye heard and saw so much of what others missed. The published work scratched the surface of an archive, a wealth, a hidden treasure of a manic and furious lifetime of writing. All of it, aboveground or below, in print or not, was personal and autobiographical and southern and foreign and historical, and it became inseparable from life to the point of becoming and being life. And it just bulldozed anyone who got in the way. "I go to the extreme," he wrote (12319). But my God, the costs of doing so. The immense, immeasurable, terrible, tragic costs. Were they worth it? What did Frank want? Lust, the chase, nineteenth-century-style romance, romance more Bryonesque and Keatsian than akin to any other tradition his mythologizers wanted to drape on him. He wanted the company of lovers, a constant rotation of lovers. And he had them, and they had him back, craving and consuming his lavish attention, his medusoid thatch of hair, his white teeth, his karate body, his earthy odor of olives and dirt. What did Frank* want? He wanted others to have the publishing joys that he had. He wanted other poets to hold their own words in their own hands, to their chests, and have others hold them, too, and maybe love them for it. He wanted good, high-quality paper and access to the best films and cats and beer and bourbon. Twenty-nine years of life, and he wrote and fucked and mentored and read and drank and nurtured more than the most productive and amorous and ambitious and mentoring of us could do in multiple such shots at existence. Yes, those costs. Those horrible, horrible costs. But what if, to him, it was all worth it? What if every fuckup was worth the words it generated? What if longevity and stability and predictability and financial responsibility weren't all there was for Frank Stanford? What if life wasn't everything to him? "He may see something the rest of us don't," George Garrett said.[1] What light did Frank see in this world of darkness? C.D. said that Frank's favorite line from the fifteen thousand or so in The Battlefield was "Ain't life sweet" (6357).[2] It seems right and proper to at least wonder if Frank Stanford, right up to the very end, even moments before he did it, perhaps even at the instant he fired those shots, believed exactly that. And, I mean, wouldn't that be sweet?

# Bibliographical Note

WHEN I BEGAN THIS PROJECT, I did so incredibly grateful that Yale's Beinecke Rare Book & Manuscript Library held the papers of Frank Stanford, Ginny Crouch Stanford, Lost Roads Publishers, and C. D. Wright. When I finished this project, I did so even more incredibly grateful that the Beinecke held these collections. The research librarians and archivists there were, particularly during COVID-19, beyond incredible. I am especially grateful to John Singleton, Moira Fitzgerald, Matt Nelson, and June Can.

But what future Stanford scholars must appreciate—if not come to terms with—is that the Beinecke holdings are the tip of the iceberg when it comes to researching Frank Stanford. When I visited Frank's publisher Irv Broughton at his house in Spokane, Washington (twice), I was stunned by the extent of Irv's archive of Stanford materials. Deep and eclectic, it includes scores of letters, documents relating to filmmaking, photographs, pamphlets, and seemingly endless surprises such as a small painting by Frank, the records of the levee camps that Frank's mother kept, transcripts of interviews Irv did with Frank, and so on. There is, in short, no writing about the life and work of Frank Stanford without accessing the private archive of Irv Broughton, who is now in his eighties. One can only hope that this collection will find a more public and accessible home for the next generation of Stanford researchers to access.

If Irv's collection takes us down from the tip of the iceberg, another private archive—this one belonging to Frank's niece Carrie Prysock—brings us even further into the thick of Stanford research. Carrie's holdings, which I organized in the summer of 2020, center on Frank's earliest years, in addition to records and documents relating to Frank's parents and his sister, Ruth Rogers. Carrie also has Frank's mother's collection of Frank's published books, articles about Frank in which she left marginalia, yearbooks from Mountain Home with Frank's classmates' notes to him, and a trove of photos circa 1948–70. These documents, in addition to Subiaco yearbooks that Frank signed (which have been gathered by Leo Lensing), constitute another cache of material highlighting the alarmingly centrifugal forces that have scattered Frank's archive to the winds.

Everything Frank loved doing he did with intensity. This was especially true for letter writing. While the archives noted above contain scores of Frank's letters, the decade-long (and tireless) effort on the part of A. P. Walton to collect the letters of Frank Stanford has turned up hundreds of Stanford letters. Walton has archived and annotated these into an unpublished collection called "The Letters of Frank Stanford," a manuscript continually in progress. He generously shared this collection with me even as he was (and still is) doing the work of compiling it. A select number of these letters, more than 150 of them, will soon be published by the University of Arkansas Press as *Letters of a Poet Dying*. I had access to this critical manuscript as well. The implication for future researchers is this: While *Letters of a Poet Dying* will be absolutely essential to your research, there are many more Stanford letters to consult, and you will not find a more knowledgeable expert on that front than A. P. Walton. Regarding my notation methods, given the lay of the land regarding Frank's letters, it is currently possible to find the same letter in the Beinecke, in *Letters of a Poet Dying*, and in "The Letters of Frank Stanford." When I encountered a letter in multiple sources, my approach was to cite the most accessible one.

Letters we know were written have been lost but not necessarily destroyed. Frank actively corresponded with the poet Thomas Lux, who died in 2017. Both Claudia Lux and Jennifer Lux—Tom's daughter and wife—recall him noting on many occasions how he regretted losing his file of letters from Frank. Lux claimed to have lost them in one of his many moves in the 1990s, and while Jennifer was kind enough to let me rummage through her late husband's papers in the attic of her Atlanta home, nothing turned up other than a handwritten draft of an elegy that Tom wrote for Frank. Judging from Lux's letters to Frank, this file of Frank's letters was assuredly pure gold, and I for one literally dream that it will turn up one day. Much more likely to be found is a lost file of letters that Frank wrote to the poet David Walker. David's ex-wife Frances assures

A.P. Walton and me she has that folder but, like Lux, misplaced it in a move, to a house in Maine. Walton went to look for it and could not find it. It's a blue folder. This story is still in progress.

A major figure in Frank's life was Father Nicholas Fuhrmann, teacher at Subiaco and friend of Frank's into adulthood. Fuhrmann, who died in August 2019, corresponded extensively with a New York poet and Stanford researcher named Ata Moharreri. Over many years of email exchanges, Father Nick sent to Ata several unpublished essays on Frank and his memories of Frank at Subiaco and beyond. Ata kindly shared these essays and his correspondence with me, and these documents allowed me to develop aspects of Frank's character in high school and college that would have been impossible to develop otherwise. A similar kind of email correspondence about Frank between A.P. Walton and Leon Stokesbury, who died in December 2018, proved equally helpful. Also included in this category of "work others did long ago that I benefited from" are Murray Shugars's transcribed interview with Frank's mother Dorothy Stanford from 1997, which he shared with me in 2018; A.P. Walton's transcribed 2014 interview with Frank's first wife, Linda Mencin Bond (who is now in poor health); and filmmaker John Erwin's transcriptions of several interviews done for his documentary film in progress, *You*. There is no way I can thank these researchers enough for sharing these invaluable documents. And, again, I cannot overstate how fragmented the Stanford archive really is.

I spoke to hundreds of people for this book. Many of these conversations were brief, done by text, email, or a quick phone call. But others were full and more formal interviews, and for most of these longer interviews I have excellent transcriptions. This trove constitutes hundreds of pages of people discussing Frank and their memories of him. On one occasion in the winter of 2020, driven by the hunch that we tend to be more open and speculative when talking in a group, I arranged a group discussion with many of Frank's friends, including Steve Stern, Ralph Adamo, Deborah Luster, John Biguenet, and R.S. (Sam) Gwynn. This conversation took the better part of a full day and may have been the smartest research move I made over the course of writing this book. Anyway, I hope to make these transcripts available to the public in the near future, although I have yet to determine in what manner or format this will be done.

Last, instead of citing *Battlefield* references in the footnotes, I decided to cite the line numbers in the text. All references to *The Battlefield* are from the 2000 Lost Roads edition.

I once joked that I could write a book about writing this book. But it's no longer a joke. These brief bibliographical notes only touch on the wonderful chaos involved in researching the life and poetry of Frank Stanford. While it was thrilling to play the part of a private investigator, psychologist, archivist, road tripper, cheap motel enthusiast, and professional nag—in addition to being a professional historian and amateur literary critic—my hope is that future Stanford scholars might benefit from a more streamlined and conventional research experience. My hope, in other words, is that there is more to come.

—JM

# *Acknowledgments*

I AM SITTING AT FRANK STANFORD'S desk as I begin to write these acknowledgments. The fact that I am sitting here speaks to the support and generosity of Frank's niece, Carrie Prysock, and her husband, the musician Michael Prysock. I open my acknowledgments by thanking them not only because they—along with their sons, Scout and Samuel—are wonderful people who opened their home and family to me very early in my research but also because they intuitively understood why I needed to take a bus to Dallas and sit where I am sitting to thank the people that made this book possible.

As I look at Frank's desk, I see layers of colors. The surface is brown, but chips and dings reveal evidence of other, older paint jobs. There's a pretty good metaphor in this. Just as Frank's life was layered, so was the experience of discovering those layers. To do this, I relied on the most generous people I have ever met. I never knew Frank Stanford personally, but I'll tell you one thing about him for certain: The man's friends and family are angels who walk the earth. Over my many years of writing this book they have repeatedly reminded me that grace is no joke.

As I assembled chapters, I shared my progress, in many cases chapter by chapter, with several critical readers. Feedback from Leo Lensing, Molly Gaines, Dwight Watson, Michael Parker (the nice one), Ward Keeler, and Ralph Adamo was invaluable and validating and critically precise in ways that made me scrutinize every sentence I wrote. Cecily Parks took the task of giving feedback to another level, writing a reader's report that should be the platonic ideal of a reader's report. Knowing that I was going to send drafts to these incisive scholars inspired me to work more diligently, to be clearer and more judicious with my interpretations, to *impress* them. Any sentence that happens to shine in this book owes something to these brilliant minds.

I have dedicated my book to Ralph Adamo. I have done this not only because Ralph read my work so closely and critically but also because he read *me* so closely and critically. When I needed an emotional boost, when I needed to be talked down from insecurity and despair, he not only sensed my drama but also did something out of fashion these days: He asked me about it. It's truly amazing what an unsolicited "Are you doing okay?" can do to reset your confidence. When I tell people that writing this book has led to me making so many close friends, Ralph comes to mind real quick.

So does Leo Lensing. Lensing's extensive Stanford knowledge—compiled as research that he shared with me while writing his own book on Frank's high school years (Leo shared two of those years with Frank)—made chapter 5 possible. The reason I was able to track down and speak with so many of Frank's Subiaco classmates has everything to do with Leo. But more than that and just as critically, there was an implicit paternal quality to Leo's guidance that made me feel cared for—nurtured, even—as a person undertaking a scholarly endeavor I kind of had no business doing. I could never have dreamed of finding such a wise and supportive and deeply kind mentor as Leo.

Irv Broughton opened his home and his archive to me with the same generosity that he showed Frank fifty years ago. On my last research visit to Spokane, Irv and I spent the day watching college baseball, talking about Frank, digitizing photos, and going through Irv's incredible collection of rare and signed first editions—of Frank's books and so many others. Irv remains every bit the optimistic dreamer, full of ambitions and projects, that he was when he and Frank were at it in the 1970s. We should all be so lucky.

I hope my book obscures this fact, but even though writing a biography demands preternatural organizational talent, I do not have preternatural organizational talent. Not even close to it. To address this concern, I benefited from yet another act of immense generosity. Carolle Morini, a research librarian at the Boston Athenaeum who appreciated my disposition toward chaos, put into digital form nearly every word ever written about Frank, affording me the secondary material in one place. She also compiled what must be the most complete bibliography of Frank's work, annotating it with the biographical statements published in journals. And if that wasn't enough, she digitized every page of *The Battlefield*, allowing me to search it as a private digital file rather than flipping through my battered copy looking for that obscure reference to whatever. Oh, and if *that* wasn't enough, she found through endless Interlibrary Loan requests copies of all the journals where Frank published. I am in awe of this work. And undeserving.

Writing a book can be a lonely business, but I was much less lonely with the company of the most knowledgeable Frank Stanford scholar on the planet: A. P. (Adam) Walton. Adam, who is compiling and editing Frank Stanford's letters, ushered me into Frank's world in a way I am certain I'd never have been able to do on my own. He's a dogged and meticulous researcher and writer, and I learned from him every day I worked on this project. There were long phases of research, usually when we were both free of teaching duties, when Adam and I were communicating daily, even multiple times daily, trying to iron out the complexities of the thorniest details of an elusive life. Adam's company in this respect was invaluable, but his scholarly standards are so high that it made me work harder to get things as right as I could. They say to surround yourself with people better than you are and you'll rise to the mean. Thank you for that, Adam.

I spoke to, emailed, texted, and visited hundreds of people for this book. But a handful of them I connected with so often, and with what I'm sure seemed like ridiculously obscure questions and sometimes deeply personal ones, that they would have been justified in blocking my number and getting a restraining order against me. Bill Willett elucidated Frank's Mountain Home years and early Fayetteville experience with incredible insight and passion. R. S. (Sam) Gwynn, Steve Stern, Deborah Luster, Forrest Gander, Merideth Boswell, Irv Broughton, Kurt Lipschutz (pen name klipschutz), Kathy Walton, Gen Whitehead, Kat Paulsen, John Biguenet, Father Jerome Kodell, John Erwin, Anna Journey, Ata Moharreri, Jennifer Lux, Cher Ross, Jennifer Steinorth, and Ginny Stanford endured my repeated calls, texts, emails, and visits, enabling me to write with growing confidence about Frank's adulthood and work. I am deeply grateful for my loyal *Battlefield* readers. It's a poem best read aloud and in company—"let no one read me alone" (12746)— and I thank Peter Young, Chad Holley, and Michael Parker for reading it aloud with me a couple of times a month. Other people in my life just listened, asked questions, and listened some more. In the category of "Sorry you got roped into this," I thank Yetik Serbest, Kevin Rowe, Dan Hannon, Sam LaBrie, Doug Dempster, Elsbeth Fast, Brian Rogers, and Greg Harkins. Friends: My gratitude for your patience is immense.

# ACKNOWLEDGMENTS

When I started this book, my two kids—Owen and Cecile—were in high school and middle school, and when I finished it, Owen graduated from college, and Cecile was more than halfway through college. Along with my wife, Leila Kempner, they did exactly what I needed them to do as I wrote this book: They stayed safely on the periphery of my obsession and dove into their own fascinating interests. I hate the idea of a family dropping everything so one person can do what he needs to do; I love the idea of everyone exploring their own passions in their own ways. I would like to think that, together, we as a family minimized the former and maximized the latter. Either way, as I wrote, I benefited daily from being around the smartest, most compassionate, funniest, and unconditionally loving people I know. Squad: I love you.

Several people who were alive when I was researching this book no longer are. I feel grateful to have personally met and gotten to know Father Nicholas Fuhrmann, Ellen Gilchrist, Frank Coleman, John Stoss, and Ruth Rogers. And while I never met the poet Matt Henriksen in person, my correspondence with him offered invaluable insights into Frank's poetry. I will miss all these people and regret that I cannot hand them a copy of this book.

When I first got the idea to undertake this project—a lightbulb moment for me—I asked a friend who had published with the University of Arkansas Press what her experience had been like working with them. She immediately said, "You and David Scott will really hit it off!!" Hi howdy was she right. Working with my editor David Scott Cunningham and the University of Arkansas Press has been a gift. David Scott is an almost impossible combination of patience and brilliance, forthrightness and understatement, style and substance. He intuitively understood this project from the very start and knew when to trust me and when to gently intervene, and he always made me feel better about my repeated technological failures. Somehow, he never rushed me. Be it tennis, bourbon, oysters, or books, I look forward to more with him.

—JM

# Notes

## Abbreviations for frequently consulted archives and volumes

ADP   Alan Dugan Papers. Stuart A. Rose Manuscript, Archives, and Rare Book Library. Emory University.

BSPM  Black Studies Program Materials. Special Collections. University of Arkansas Libraries.

CDWP  C. D. Wright Papers. Yale Collection of American Literature. Beinecke Rare Book & Manuscript Library.

FSP   Frank Stanford Papers. Yale Collection of American Literature. Beinecke Rare Book & Manuscript Library.

GCSC  Ginny Crouch Stanford Collection of Frank Stanford. Yale Collection of American Literature. Beinecke Rare Book & Manuscript Library.

LFS   "The Letters of Frank Stanford." Edited by A. P. Walton. Unpublished manuscript, shared with the author on August 23, 2023.

LPD   *Letters of a Poet Dying*. Edited by A. P. Walton. Fayetteville: University of Arkansas Press, forthcoming.

LRPR  Lost Roads Publishers Records. Yale Collection of American Literature. Beinecke Rare Book & Manuscript Library.

| | |
|---|---|
| MCIP | Michael Cuddihy and Ironwood Press Records. Special Collections of the University of Arizona Libraries. |
| MWP | Miller Williams Papers. Harry Ransom Center. University of Texas at Austin. |
| SAA | Subiaco Academy Archives, Subiaco, Arkansas. |
| WCPRR | West Coast Poetry Review Records. John Hay Library, Brown University. |

## PRELUDE

1. Ralph Adamo, in discussion with the author, September 19, 2019, New Orleans, LA. C. D. Wright also mentions this detail in her September 16, 1978, notebook entry, C. D. Wright Papers, Yale Collection of American Literature, Beinecke Rare Book and Manuscript Library (hereafter cited as CDWP).
2. Ellen Gilchrist, in discussion with the author, November 21, 2019, Ocean Springs, MS.
3. Ralph Adamo, in discussion with the author, February 10, 2023, New Orleans, LA.
4. Adamo, discussion, February 10, 2023.
5. Trayce Wear, in discussion with the author, April 25, 2024.
6. Quoted in Robert Trussell, "Frank Stanford: A Poet's Dreams, Death and Legacy," *Stage & Scream in Kansas City* (blog), January 16, 2012, https://kansascitytheater.wordpress.com/2012/01/16/frank-stanford-a-poets-dreams-death-and-legacy/.
7. C. D. Wright to Brent Long, May 22, 1997, CDWP.
8. Wear, discussion.
9. Trussell, "Frank Stanford."
10. Frank Stanford to Dorothy Stanford, May 31, 1978, Ginny Crouch Stanford Collection of Frank Stanford, Yale Collection of American Literature, Beinecke Rare Book and Manuscript Library (hereafter cited as GCSC).
11. Bill Willett, in discussion with the author, September 18, 2019, Mountain Home, AR. The "holy water" comment came from C. D. Wright in a letter to Ellen Gilchrist, n.d., ca. fall 1978, Gilchrist MSS, CDWP.
12. Lucinda Williams, "Don't Tell Anybody the Secrets," unpublished manuscript, shared with the author in November 2020. A revised version has been published as *Don't Tell Anybody the Secrets I Told You* (New York: Crown, 2023), where the quote can be found on page 99. Of Williams, Stanford wrote, "Lucinda was wonderful to be with." Frank Stanford to C. D. Wright and Ginny Stanford, May 21, 1978, Frank Stanford Papers, Yale Collection of American Literature, Beinecke Rare Book and Manuscript Library (hereafter cited as FSP).
13. Frank Stanford to Wright and Ginny Stanford, May 21, 1978.
14. Trussell, "Frank Stanford"; author's visits to the house at 705 Jackson Drive, September 18, 2019, and August 12, 2023.

15. Margaret Salassi, in discussion with the author, October 19, 2019.
16. Adamo, discussion, September 19, 2019.
17. Ruth Rogers, in discussion with the author, July 9, 2019, Dallas, TX; Willett, discussion. Rogers mentioned only the underwear. Willett added the cut-up Stetson and the album cover.
18. Ginny Stanford, "Requiem: A Fragment," *New Orleans Review* 20, no. 3/4 (Fall/Winter 1994): 150.
19. Ginny Stanford, account of Frank's final day, unpublished manuscript, [early 1990s], shared with the author by Ralph Adamo, April 19, 2024.
20. Wright to Long, May 22, 1997, CDWP.
21. Ginny Stanford, "Death in the Cool Evening," in *Saltwater, Sweetwater: Women Write from California's North Coast*, ed. Barbara L. Baer and Maureen Anne Jennings (Forestville, CA: Floreant, 1998), 5.
22. Quoted in Trussell, "Frank Stanford."
23. Wright to Long, May 22, 1997, CDWP.
24. C. D. Wright, interview by Murray Shugars, n.d., transcript, CDWP.
25. Gen Whitehead, Ted Whitehead, and Katherine Paulsen, discussion with the author, April 2021, Fayetteville, AR.
26. Whitehead, Whitehead, and Paulsen, discussion.
27. Irv Broughton, notes taken when Ginny Stanford called him to tell him about the suicide, private collection of Irv Broughton. The detail about the CPR attempt and Ginny going across the street comes from an unpublished account of the incident written in the early 1990s by Ginny Stanford and shared with Ralph Adamo, who shared it with the author in May 2023.
28. Ginny Stanford, "Death in the Cool Evening," 3.
29. Ginny Stanford, draft of a novel/memoir, unpublished manuscript, n.d., sent to Ralph Adamo in the early 1990s, shared with the author in May 2024. In her cover letter she writes, "About what I have sent: . . . I go from Frank's, to a first person Ginny character, to a third person describing Ginny's experience."

**INTRODUCTION**

1. John Biguenet, "Frank Stanford: After the Fact," unpublished manuscript, n.d., FSP. This sentiment was echoed by Forrest Gander, in discussion with the author, August 4, 2023, San Francisco, CA.
2. Bill Willett, "Dream of the Alluvial Field: An Interview with Bill Willett," interview by Peter J. Moore, *Rain Taxi* 13, no. 3 (Fall 2008): 37.
3. Thomas Lux, "Elegy for Frank Stanford," in *Sunday* (Boston: Houghton Mifflin, 1979), 17. The poem ends, "Frank, you dumb fucker,—who loves you / loves you regardless."
4. John Wood, "With Allen in Arkansas: An Ozark Diary," *American Poetry Review* 41, no. 5 (September/October 2012): 47–49.
5. Alan Dugan to Frank Stanford, March 23, 1972, FSP.
6. Thomas Lux to Frank Stanford, July 20, [1972?], GCSC.
7. Quoted in A. P. Walton, "Toward Innumerable Futures: Frank Stanford & Origins" (master's thesis, Lund University, 2015), 79.

8. Quoted in Walton, "Toward Innumerable Futures," 79.
9. Lawrence Ferlinghetti to Frank Stanford, January 3, 1973, FSP.
10. David Alexander, in discussion with the author, August 10, 2021.
11. C. D. Wright, "Frank Stanford of the Mulberry Family: An Arkansas Epilogue," *Conjunctions* 29 (Fall 1997): 303.
12. Ellen Gilchrist, in discussion with the author, November 21, 2021, Ocean Springs, MS.
13. Frank Stanford, "Miscellaneous" file, FSP.
14. Frank Stanford to John McKernan, summer or early fall 1970, in "The Letters of Frank Stanford," ed. A. P. Walton, unpublished manuscript, shared with the author on August 23, 2023 (hereafter cited as LFS).
15. Frank Stanford to Irv Broughton, February 18, 1972, private collection of Irv Broughton.
16. Frank Stanford to Irv Broughton, August 2, 1974, private collection of Irv Broughton.
17. James Whitehead to Thomas Lask, June 8, 1978, unprocessed letter, James Whitehead papers, University of Arkansas, shared with the author by A. P. Walton, June 19, 2023.
18. LFS.
19. Ralph Adamo, "Frank Stanford's Lost Roads: The Heart as a Broken Landscape," in "10 Great Neglected Poets of the 20th Century," special millennial issue, *Asheville Poetry Review* 7, no. 1 (Spring/Summer 2000): 228.
20. Michael Cuddihy to Ginny Stanford, n.d., after June 3, 1978, Lost Roads Publishers Records, Yale Collection of American Literature, Beinecke Rare Book and Manuscript Library (hereafter cited as LRPR). This comment was supported by C. D. Wright, who wrote to Father Nicholas Fuhrmann in February 1979 that Frank "bequeathed to Ginny and myself the more than fifty complete, unpublished, manuscripts he wrote, including books of poetry, short fiction, screenplays, and essays." C. D. Wright to Nicholas Fuhrmann, February 13, 1979, CDWP.
21. Frank Stanford, *What about This: Collected Poems of Frank Stanford*, ed. Michael Wiegers (Port Townsend, WA: Copper Canyon, 2015).
22. Recognizing this common thread, the poet Lorna Saunders wrote in 1979 that Stanford "certainly grew tremendously from the poems in *The Singing Knives* to those in *You* and *Crib Death* but all the gold was there even at the beginning." Lorna Saunders to C. D. Wright, October 2, 1979, CDWP.
23. John Stuart Mill, "Thoughts on Poetry and Its Varieties," *Crayon* 7, no. 5 (1860): 123–28, https://doi.org/10.2307/25528049, quoted in Lisa Lai-ming Wong, "A Promise (Over)Heard in Lyric," *New Literary History* 37, no. 2 (2006): 271–84. Thank you to Cecily Parks for pointing me to this term.
24. Willett, "Dream of the Alluvial Field," interview, 38.
25. Cher Ross [Cheryl Campbell], in discussion with A. P. Walton, September 18, 2023, transcript, shared with the author on September 27, 2023.
26. LFS.
27. Frank Stanford, interview by Irv Broughton, 1973–74, FSP.

NOTES 519

28. The phrase "redneck surrealist" comes from a scrap of typed paper in "Miscellaneous" folder, FSP. It attributes the phrase to "Thomas, S+M." Thomas is likely Lorenzo Thomas. I have not been able to determine what "S+M" means.
29. Frank Stanford to Eleanor Bender, February 1, 1972, in *Letters of a Poet Dying*, ed. A. P. Walton (Fayetteville: University of Arkansas Press, forthcoming) (hereafter cited as *LPD*).
30. Wright, "Frank Stanford of the Mulberry Family," 299.
31. Quoted in Walton, "Toward Innumerable Futures," 2.
32. As A. P. Walton notes in "Toward Innumerable Futures," p. 15, it can be a difficult to accurately rank poems by length, but there is no question *The Battlefield* is one of the longest.
33. Quoted in Paul Wilner, "The Swamp-Rat Rimbaud: *What about This: Collected Poems of Frank Stanford*," review of *What about This: Collected Poems of Frank Stanford*, by Frank Stanford, ed. Michael Wiegers, ZYZZYVA, November 30, 2015, https://www.zyzzyva.org/2015/11/30/the-swamp-rat-rimbaud-what-about-this-collected-poems-of-frank-stanford/.
34. Leon Stokesbury, "A Few Words for Frank Stanford, 1948–1978," in *The Royal Nonesuch* (Tallahassee: Anhinga, 1984), n.p.
35. Lee Upton, email message to author, November 12, 2020.
36. Lucinda Williams, "Don't Tell Anybody the Secrets," unpublished manuscript, shared with the author in November 2020. A revised version has been published as *Don't Tell Anybody the Secrets I Told You* (New York: Crown, 2023), where the quote appears on page 98.
37. C. D. Wright, "Frank Stanford," in *The Before Columbus Foundation Poetry Anthology: Selections from the American Book Awards, 1980–1990*, ed. J. J. Phillips et al. (New York: W. W. Norton, 1992), 340.
38. Frank Stanford to David Walker, April 1, 1974, *LPD*. The manuscript of *The Battlefield*, housed at the Beinecke Rare Book & Manuscript Library at Yale, confirms that Stanford did indeed count the lines that he wrote. There are break marks in the margins every forty lines.
39. C. D. Wright to Pamela Stewart, n.d. [after June 1978], CDWP.
40. Wright, "Frank Stanford," in Phillips et al., *Before Columbus Foundation*, 340.
41. Frank Stanford, *The Battlefield Where the Moon Says I Love You* (Barrington, RI: Lost Roads Publishers, 2000), line 2625. Text references are to line number.
42. Wright to Stewart, n.d. [after June 1978], CDWP.
43. Bill Carpenter, "Frank Stanford's *The Battlefield Where the Moon Says I Love You*: Introduction," Eratosphere, forum of *Able Muse Review*, August 27, 2012, https://www.ablemuse.com/erato/showthread.php?p=257356.
44. Stanford, interview, 1973–74.
45. Murray Shugars makes this point in his essay "Searching for Frank Stanford: Finding a Critique of Literary Biographies," in *Constant Stranger: After Frank Stanford*, ed. Max Crinnin and Aidan Ryan, 2nd ed. (Buffalo: Foundlings, 2019), 190.

46. Adamo, "Frank Stanford's Lost Roads," 229.
47. Chet Weise, email message to author, April 28, 2020.
48. C. D. Wright, preface to Stanford, *Battlefield*, second page of the preface (unnumbered).
49. Dugan to Frank Stanford, March 23, 1972, FSP.
50. Walt Whitman, *Leaves of Grass* (New York: Bantam Dell, 1983), 29.
51. "Can't Get There from Here," by R.E.M., written by Bill Berry, Peter Buck, Mike Mills, and Michael Stipe, produced by Joe Boyd, I.R.S. Records, released as a single in June 1985. Thank you to Michael Parker for recommending the phrase "muddy two-track."
52. C. D. Wright to Carl Launius, April 2, 1986, CDWP.
53. Wright, "Frank Stanford," in Phillips et al., *Before Columbus Foundation*, 340.
54. Frank Stanford, *Hidden Water: From the Frank Stanford Archives*, ed. Michael Wiegers and Chet Weise (Nashville: Third Man Books, 2015), 70.
55. Wright to Stewart, n.d., after June 1978, CDWP.
56. Frank Stanford to Walker, April 1, 1974, *LPD*. This description was Frank's account of what Dugan said.
57. Walton, "Toward Innumerable Futures," 2.
58. Leon Stokesbury, introduction to *The Light the Dead See: Selected Poems of Frank Stanford*, by Frank Stanford, ed. Leon Stokesbury (Fayetteville: University of Arkansas Press, 1991), ix.
59. C. D. Wright, "A Note on *The Battlefield Where the Moon Says I Love You*," *Ironwood 17* 9, no. 1 (Spring 1981): 105.
60. Adamo, "Frank Stanford's Lost Roads," 229.
61. Michael Cuddihy, editor's note, *Ironwood 17* 9, no. 1 (Spring 1981): first page (unnumbered).
62. Frank Stanford to Alan Dugan, February 14, 1972, Alan Dugan Papers, Stuart A. Rose Manuscript, Archives, and Rare Book Library, Emory University (hereafter cited as ADP).
63. Stanford, interview, 1973–74.
64. Frank Stanford to Richard Eberhart, December 27–31, 1972, LFS.
65. Frank Stanford to Alan Dugan, October 10, 1972, FSP.
66. Frank Stanford to Dugan, February 14, 1972, ADP.
67. Frank Stanford to Alan Dugan, May 16, 1972, ADP.
68. Stanford, *Hidden Water*, 167.
69. Frank Stanford, "Sunday Services," n.d., Prose Fragments, FSP; Flannery O'Connor, *Mystery and Manners: Occasional Prose* (New York: Farrar, Straus and Giroux), 199.
70. C. D. Wright, interview by Murray Shugars, n.d., transcript, CDWP.
71. Frank Stanford to Ralph Adamo, July 15, 1976, LFS.
72. Wright, interview.
73. C. D. Wright to Jim Hartz, November 24, 1978, LRPR.
74. R. S. Gwynn, in discussion with the author, January 4, 2022, New Orleans, LA. He added to this quote, "Not even Miller [Williams]."
75. Malcolm Cowley, *The Portable Faulkner* (New York: Viking, 1966), 3. I am grateful to Michael Parker, the nice one, for this reference.

76. Frank Stanford to Alan Dugan, May 21–22 1972, ADP.
77. Frank Stanford, "Snatches from a Wandering Interview on Film and Poetry," interview by Irving Broughton, *Ironwood 17* 9, no. 1 (Spring 1981): 153.
78. Wright, "Frank Stanford," in Phillips et al., *Before Columbus Foundation*, 339.
79. The year 1971 is usually given as the official publication date of *The Singing Knives*, but while 1971 is the copyright date, the printing was delayed, and the book was not actually bound and distributed until at least May 1972.
80. Irv Broughton, in discussion with the author, December 21, 2019.
81. Frank Stanford to Alan Dugan, May 1972, ADP.
82. Two exceptions to the anthology claim are Miller Williams, ed., *Ozark, Ozark: A Hillside Reader* (Columbia: University of Missouri Press, 1981), and Leon Stokesbury, ed., *The Made Thing: An Anthology of Contemporary Southern Poetry* (Fayetteville: University of Arkansas Press, 1987). Both Stokesbury and Williams knew Stanford from the University of Arkansas.
83. klipschutz, "Where There's a Will: The Moon Retake the Stage," in *Best of the Sucks: High-Octane Poetix from the Legendary "Toad Suck Review*," ed. Mark Spitzer (Cheshire, MA: Mad Hat, 2022), 167.
84. Matthew Henriksen, "Another Part of the Flood," *Fulcrum: An Annual of Poetry and Aesthetics*, no. 7 (2011): 368.
85. Wright, "Frank Stanford," in Phillips et al., *Before Columbus Foundation*, 340.
86. Wright, "A Note on *The Battlefield*," 157.
87. Frank Stanford to Michael Cuddihy, August 6, 1974, Michael Cuddihy and Ironwood Press Records, Special Collections of the University of Arizona Libraries (hereafter cited as MCIP).
88. Stokesbury, introduction to Stanford, *Light the Dead See*, xi.
89. Wright, "Frank Stanford," in Phillips et al., *Before Columbus Foundation*, 340.
90. Walt Whitman, preface to *Leaves of Grass* (Brooklyn, 1855), vi.
91. Stanford, *Hidden Water*, 5, 7.
92. Clyde Woods, *Development Arrested: The Blues and Plantation Power in the Mississippi Delta* (New York: Verso, 1998), 6.
93. Wright, preface to Stanford, *Battlefield*, fifth page of the preface (unnumbered).
94. Jody Stewart, "Toward Innumerable Futures: The Offering of Frank Stanford's Poetry," in Crinnin and Ryan, *Constant Stranger*, 151.
95. klipschutz, "Where There's a Will," 203.
96. Eileen Myles, "A Man's World," review of *The Light the Dead See: Selected Poems of Frank Stanford*, ed. Leon Stokesbury, *Village Voice*, October 6, 1992, 93.
97. Anna Journey, "The Nijinsky of Dreams: The Legacy of Frank Stanford," *American Poetry Review* 44, no. 4 (July/August 2015): 21.
98. Stanford, interview, 1973–74.
99. A copy of the award is in "Awards," FSP.
100. Frank Stanford to Alan and Judith Dugan, August 1, 1974, ADP.
101. In a masterpiece of understatement, the poet Richard Eberhart, whom Frank met in August 1972, explained that "Frank was not in a position to deal with the subtleties of the academy." See "Frank Stanford," *Ironwood 17* 9, no. 1 (Spring 1981): 137.
102. Adamo, "Frank Stanford's Lost Roads," 228.

103. C. Vann Woodward, "The Search for Southern Identity," *Virginia Quarterly Review* 34, no. 3 (Summer 1958): 321–38.
104. C. Vann Woodward, *The Burden of Southern History*, 3rd ed. (Baton Rouge: Louisiana State University Press, 1993), 6. The material cited here comes from an updated version of "The Search for Southern Identity," which appears as the first chapter of this book.
105. Woodward, *Burden of Southern History*, 7.
106. Woodward, *Burden of Southern History*, 16.
107. Woodward, *Burden of Southern History*, 24.
108. John Crowe Ransome, "Reconstructed but Unregeneate," in *I'll Take My Stand: The South and the Agrarian Tradition*, by Twelve Southerners (Baton Rouge: Louisiana State University Press, 1977), 1.
109. Frank Stanford to Dugan, February 14, 1972, ADP; Frank Stanford to Michael Cuddihy, late September 1974, MCIP; and Frank Stanford, scrap of paper, n.d., "Miscellaneous" folder, FSP.
110. Woodward, *Burden of Southern History*, 25.
111. Woodward, *Burden of Southern History*, 25.
112. Frank Stanford to Michael Cuddihy, n.d., ca. late September 1974, MCIP.
113. Woods, *Development Arrested*, 23.
114. Wright to Long, May 22, 1997, CDWP. This book was never written or at least never published.
115. Wright to Long, May 22, 1997, CDWP.
116. Wright to Long, May 22, 1997, CDWP.

## ONE

1. Dorothy Stanford, interview by Murray Shugars, June 1997, shared with the author in 2019; C. D. Wright, introduction to "Frank Stanford: Blue Yodel of a Wayfaring Stranger, Nine Previously Unpublished Poems by the Virtuoso Dreamer of the Ozarks," by Frank Stanford, *Oxford American*, Winter 2006; A. P. Walton, "Toward Innumerable Futures: Frank Stanford & Origins" (master's thesis, Lund University, 2015), 82; copy of adoption decree, State of Mississippi, Washington County, private collection of Carrie Prysock, Dallas, TX, accessed April 26, 2020; and Frank Stanford's baby book, private collection of Carrie Prysock, Dallas, TX, accessed April 26, 2020. Carrie Prysock is the daughter of Ruth Rogers, Frank Stanford's sister.
2. Copy of Emery Memorial Home stationery, private collection of Carrie Prysock, Dallas, TX, accessed May 3, 2020; see also "Rites to Today at Richton for Rev. Mabel Cooper," *Hattiesburg American*, August 21, 1961.
3. "History of the Emery [Memorial] Home," last accessed July 11, 2023, http://www.emeryhome.com/; Murray Shugars, "What the Moon Says: Frank Stanford's Quest for Poetic Identity" (PhD diss., Purdue University, May 2000), 59. Mabel Cooper, a minister in the Missionary Bands of the World, ran Emery. Walton, "Toward Innumerable Futures," 82.

4. Clipping from Rosie Smollen Wilson, *Richton... Remembered and Retold* (n.p., 1977), box 6, MSS 295, FSP.
5. Ruth Rogers, in discussion with the author, July 9, 2019, Dallas, TX.
6. Dorothy Stanford, interview.
7. Dorothy Stanford, interview.
8. Clipping from "Women on the Home Front," July 16, 1944, private collection of Carrie Prysock, Dallas, TX, accessed April 26, 2020. This clipping unfortunately clipped off the name of the newspaper.
9. Neil R. McMillen, *Dark Journey: Black Mississippians in the Age of Jim Crow* (Urbana: University of Illinois Press, 1990), 161.
10. Dorothy Stanford, interview.
11. "Women on the Home Front," July 16, 1944, private collection of Carrie Prysock.
12. James C. Cobb, *The Most Southern Place on Earth: The Mississippi Delta and the Roots of Regional Identity* (Oxford: Oxford University Press, 1994), 198–99.
13. Dorothy Stanford, interview.
14. Dorothy Stanford, interview.
15. "Mrs. Dorothy Alter to Run Poultry Farm," *Delta Democrat-Times* (Greenville, MS), May 15, 1945.
16. Dorothy Stanford, interview; see also Admission and Discharge Records, Social Service Report, Arkansas State Hospital, case history 105913, private collection of Carrie Prysock, Dallas, TX, accessed May 3, 2020.
17. "An Honor Well Deserved," editorial, *Delta Democrat-Times* (Greenville, MS), May 17, 1953.
18. Dorothy Stanford, interview.
19. Ex Parte Petition of Dorothy Gilbert Alter, August 20, 1948, State of Mississippi, Washington County, Mississippi Bureau of Vital Statistics.
20. Dorothy Stanford to Michael Cuddihy, April 8, 1981, MCIP.
21. Frank Stanford's baby book, private collection of Carrie Prysock.
22. Carrie Prysock, text message to author, April 1, 2020; Walton, "Toward Innumerable Futures," 6.
23. Dorothy Stanford, interview.
24. Frank Stanford's baby book, private collection of Carrie Prysock.
25. Cobb, *Most Southern Place*; see also "History and Culture of the Mississippi Delta Region," National Park Service, accessed July 7, 2023, https://www.nps.gov/locations/lowermsdeltaregion/history-and-culture-of-the-mississippi-delta-region.htm.
26. Robert McElvaine, ed., *Mississippi: The WPA Guide to the Magnolia State* (Jackson: University of Mississippi Press, 1938), 47.
27. "I knew William Percy, and Hodding Carter, and many other writers and artists." Dorothy Stanford, interview.
28. Frank Stanford, *What about This: Collected Poems of Frank Stanford*, ed. Michael Wiegers (Port Townsend, WA: Copper Canyon, 2015), 104.
29. Dorothy Stanford, interview.

30. McMillen, *Dark Journey*, 238.
31. Dorothy Stanford, interview.
32. Rogers, discussion.
33. Shelby Foote, "Shelby Foote, the Art of Fiction No. 158," interview by Carter Coleman, Donald Faulkner, and William Kennedy, *Paris Review*, no. 151 (Summer 1999), https://www.theparisreview.org/interviews/931/the-art-of-fiction-no-158-shelby-foote.
34. William Alexander Percy, *Lanterns on the Levee: Recollections of a Planter's Son* (Baton Rouge: Louisiana State University Press, 1941), 280.
35. Hodding Carter to William Alexander Percy, March 23, 1941, Correspondence, 1941, Hodding II and Betty Werlein Carter Papers, Mitchell Memorial Library, Mississippi State University.
36. Clipping from the private collection of Carrie Prysock, Dallas, TX, accessed April 26, 2020.
37. "Green Acres Is Scene of Informal Graduates Party," *Delta Democrat-Times* (Greenville, MS), May 24, 1946.
38. Clipping from society column in the *Delta Democrat-Times* (Greenville, MS), private collection of Carrie Prysock, Dallas, TX, accessed April 26, 2020.
39. Hortense Powdermaker, *Stranger and Friend: The Way of an Anthropologist* (New York: W. W. Norton, 1966).
40. Quoted in Shugars, "What the Moon Says," 65.
41. Dorothy Stanford, interview.
42. "Descendants of Joseph Stanford of Somerset County Maryland," Herbert W. Stanford, III (website), p. 573, http://herbstanford.net/joseph%20stanford%20family.pdf.
43. Rogers, discussion.
44. Dorothy Stanford, interview.
45. Dorothy Stanford, interview.
46. Dorothy Stanford, interview.
47. While it is true that Judd Gilbert worked at Parchman, Stanford has his dates off, as Vardaman was governor from 1904 to 1908, two decades before Judd Gilbert worked there.
48. John A. Lomax, *Adventures of a Ballad Hunter* (1947; Austin: University of Texas Press, 2017), 108. Citations refer to the 2017 edition.
49. Dorothy Stanford, interview.
50. Frank Stanford, interview by Irv Broughton, 1973–74, FSP.
51. Dorothy Stanford, interview. Dorothy's son would go on to think differently, writing in his poem "The Mind Reader," "blessed is Abe Lincoln he was a good man I believe." In Frank Stanford, *Hidden Water: From the Frank Stanford Archives*, ed. Michael Wiegers and Chet Weise (Nashville: Third Man Books, 2015), 7.
52. Dorothy Stanford, interview.
53. "Prisoners at Parchman Go Back to Work," *Daily Herald* (Chicago), May 6, 1936.
54. "Shooting of State Engineer Mystery at Parchman Camp," *Biloxi Daily Herald*, June 5, 1930.

55. Bob Gilbert, in discussion with the author, May 5, 2020.
56. "Convict Slayer Finally Taken," *Lincoln Star*, December 31, 1928.
57. Frank Stanford, interview.
58. Quoted in Cobb, *Most Southern Place*, 126.
59. John A. Lomax, *Adventures of a Ballad Hunter*, 108.
60. Alan Lomax, *The Land Where the Blues Began* (New York: New Press, 1993), 258.
61. Alan Lomax, *Where the Blues Began*, 257.
62. Quoted in Lawrence Levine, *Black Culture and Black Consciousness: Afro-American Folk Thought from Slavery to Freedom* (Oxford: Oxford University Press, 1977), 237.
63. Richard McKinley Mizelle Jr., "Backwater Blues: The 1927 Flood Disaster, Race, and the Remaking of Regional Identity, 1900–1930" (PhD diss., Rutgers University, 2006), 5.
64. John A. Lomax, *Adventures of a Ballad Hunter*, 117, 119.
65. Quoted in Marybeth Hamilton, *In Search of the Blues* (New York: Basic Books, 2008), 125.
66. Quoted in Levine, *Black Culture*, 243–44.
67. Levine, *Black Culture*, 226.
68. Dorothy Stanford, interview; notebook, private collection of Carrie Prysock, Dallas, TX, accessed April 26, 2020.
69. Clyde Woods, *Development Arrested: The Blues and Plantation Power in the Mississippi Delta* (New York: Verso, 1998), 20.
70. Dorothy Stanford, interview.
71. "Descendants of Joseph Stanford," p. 604. In Greenville she worked at a grocery and fruit store her parents established in 1930.
72. Dorothy Stanford, interview.
73. Rector St. James to Dorothy Gilbert, September 17, 1935, private collection of Carrie Prysock, Dallas, TX, accessed April 26, 2020.
74. "Descendants of Joseph Stanford," p. 573.
75. Dorothy Stanford, interview.
76. Carl Alter, newspaper clipping, private collection of Carrie Prysock, Dallas, TX, accessed April 26, 2020.
77. Excerpt from the journal of Dorothy Gilbert Alter, private collection of Carrie Prysock, Dallas, TX, accessed April 26, 2020.
78. Dorothy Stanford, interview.
79. Journal excerpts, private collection of Carrie Prysock, Dallas, TX, accessed April 26, 2020.
80. Dorothy Stanford, interview.
81. Newspaper clippings in scrapbooks, private collection of Carrie Prysock, Dallas, TX, accessed April 26, 2020.
82. Journal entry, 1944, journal of Dorothy Gilbert Alter, private collection of Carrie Prysock, Dallas, TX, accessed April 26, 2020.
83. Advertisement, *Delta Democrat-Times* (Greenville, MS), October 3, 1950, 3; ellipsis in original.
84. Classified advertisement, *Delta Democrat-Times* (Greenville, MS), August 19, 1949.

85. "First Baptist Women Meet Monday," *Delta Democrat-Times* (Greenville, MS), March 23, 1950.
86. "Miss Nell Tate Has Luncheon for Her Bridesmaids," *Delta Democrat-Times* (Greenville, MS), August 17, 1950; "DAR Will Meet at the Hide-Away," *Delta Democrat-Times* (Greenville, MS), April 19, 1951.
87. Advertisement, *Delta Democrat-Times* (Greenville, MS), March 29, 1951, 2.
88. Advertisement, *Delta-Democrat-Times* (Greenville, MS), March 27, 1950, 3.
89. Announcement, *Delta Democrat-Times* (Greenville, MS), December 19, 1950, 7.
90. "Old Stuff," *Delta Democrat-Times* (Greenville, MS), September 15, 1965.
91. Dorothy Stanford, interview.
92. Joan Williams, "Remembering," *Ironwood 17* 9, no. 1 (Spring 1981): 108.
93. Frank Coleman and Carole Hess, in discussion with the author, November 19, 2019.
94. "Descendants of Joseph Stanford," p. 572; Nicholas Fuhrmann, in discussion with the author, August 9, 2019, Subiaco, AR.
95. Fuhrmann, discussion.
96. Williams, "Remembering," 109.

## TWO

1. David L. Cohn, *Where I Was Born and Raised* (Boston: Houghton Mifflin, 1948), 1.
2. "Learn More About One of the Most Iconic Historic Hotels in Downtown Memphis," the Peabody Memphis, accessed October 28, 2024, https://www.peabodymemphis.com/history; Ruth Rogers, in discussion with the author, July 9, 2019, Dallas, TX.
3. Frank Stanford, *Hidden Water: From the Frank Stanford Archives*, ed. Michael Wiegers and Chet Weise (Nashville: Third Man Books, 2015), 16.
4. Clyde Woods, *Development Arrested: Race, Power, and the Blues in the Mississippi Delta* (New York: Verso, 1998), 40.
5. Frank Stanford, interview by Irv Broughton, 1973–74, FSP.
6. Neil R. McMillen, *Dark Journey: Black Mississippians in the Age of Jim Crow* (Urbana: University of Illinois Press, 1990), 131.
7. Ben Ehrenreich, "The Long Goodbye," Poetry Foundation, January 18, 2008, https://www.poetryfoundation.org/articles/69003/the-long-goodbye.
8. Leon Stokesbury, introduction to *The Light the Dead See: Selected Poems of Frank Stanford*, by Frank Stanford, ed. Leon Stokesbury (Fayetteville: University of Arkansas Press, 1990), xi.
9. Carole Hess, email message to author, July 17, 2020. Carole Hess is the granddaughter of Albert Franklin Stanford.
10. Dorothy Stanford, interview by Murray Shugars, June 1997, shared with the author in 2019; "Descendants of Joseph Stanford of Somerset County Maryland," Herbert W. Stanford, III (website), p. 577, http://herbstanford.net/joseph%20stanford%20family.pdf.
11. Hess, email message to author, July 17, 2020.
12. Frank Stanford, interview.

13. Dorothy Stanford, interview, quoted in Murray Shugars, "What the Moon Says: Frank Stanford's Quest for Poetic Identity" (PhD diss., Purdue University, May 2000), 119.
14. See "Descendants of Joseph Stanford," pp. 572–77. I am also drawing information from a clipping of an obituary sent by Albert Franklin Stanford's great-grandson Robert Gilbert, email message to author, July 19, 2020.
15. Dorothy Stanford, interview.
16. Clipping, journal entry, 1944, private collection of Carrie Prysock, Dallas, TX, accessed April 26, 2020.
17. Alan Lomax, *The Land Where the Blues Began* (New York: New Press, 1993), 230.
18. Lomax, *Where the Blues Began*, 9; John Barry, *Rising Tide: The Great Mississippi Flood of 1927 and How It Changed America* (New York: Simon and Schuster, 1997), 173–200.
19. William Alexander Percy, *Lanterns on the Levee: Recollections of a Planter's Son* (Baton Rouge: Louisiana State University Press, 1941), 258.
20. "Work or Die of Hunger is Dixie Order," *Chicago Defender*, June 4, 1927; "'Work or Die Edict' Perils Race," *Chicago Defender*, June 16, 1927. See also Richard McKinley Mizelle Jr., *Backwater Blues: The Mississippi Flood of 1927 in the African American Imagination* (Minneapolis: University of Minnesota Press, 2014), 38.
21. Mizelle, *Backwater Blues*, 125. See also Roy Wilkins, *Standing Fast: The Autobiography of Roy Wilkins* (New York: Penguin, 1982), 119–30.
22. Mizelle, *Backwater Blues*, 3.
23. Quoted in Woods, *Development Arrested*, 9.
24. Kevin Young, *Brown* (New York: Knopf, 2018), 153.
25. Dorothy Stanford, interview.
26. It is possible that the phrase "Mr. Cholley," or "Mr. Charlie," was a generic reference to the boss that might have had roots in the antebellum era. But, as Alan Dundes writes, "Mr. Charley was used in hollers and work songs up and down the Mississippi, it is likely to have been sung with Charley Lowrence in mind." Alan Dundes, ed., *Mother Wit from the Laughing Barrel: Readings in the Interpretation of Afro-American Folklore* (New York: Prentice Hall, 1973), 482n.
27. Frank Stanford, interview.
28. Quoted in Woods, *Development Arrested*, 130.
29. Lomax, *Where the Blues Began*, 249. The stories that dogged him did so for decades. "I saw Charley Lowrance strip a bad nigger and carry him in his tent buck-naked and whip him," recalled a worker interviewed by Lomax, specifying how he "whipped him with a buggy strap." Another said, "He had a voice that would scare you to death." Quoted in Lomax, *Where the Blues Began*, 508.
30. John Cowley, "Shack Bullies and Levee Contractors: Bluesmen as Ethnographers," in "Labor Song: A Reappraisal," special double issue, *Journal of Folklore Research* 28, no. 2/3 (May–December 1991): 153.
31. Son House, Fiddlin' Joe Martin, and Willie Brown, "Camp Hollers," recorded 1941–42, track 5 on *Son House Library of Congress Recordings*

1941–1942, Document Records, DOCD-5689, YouTube video, 2:24, https://weeniecampbell.com/yabbse/index.php?topic=8952.0.
32. Cowley, "Shack Bullies," 139.
33. N. H. Olds, *Report of the Preliminary Sanitary Surveys of Labor Camps... 1920–1929*, p. 929, Box 43, RG 90, United States Public Health Service Files for 1924–35, Box 43, folder 161, National Archives.
34. Dorothy Stanford, interview.
35. Rainer Maria Rilke, *Letters to a Young Poet*, trans. Stephen Mitchell (New York: Vintage Books, 1986), 7.
36. Entry for Hilda Jordan, US Census Bureau, Sixteenth Census of the United States: 1940, Ancestry.com.
37. City directories, birth certificate, and draft registration documents found on "Charlie B. Lemon," Ancestry.com.
38. Frank Stanford to Michael Cuddihy, ca. late September 1974, MCIP.
39. Dorothy Stanford, interview.
40. Frank Stanford, *What about This: Collected Poems of Frank Stanford*, ed. Michael Wiegers (Port Townsend, WA: Copper Canyon, 2015), 177.
41. Frank Coleman and Carole Hess, in discussion with the author, November 19, 2019. "He always had a chauffeur," Frank Coleman recalled.
42. Dorothy Stanford, interview.
43. Ruth Rogers, interview by John Erwin (director and producer of *You*, a documentary film on the life and work of Frank Stanford), n.d., transcript, shared with the author on July 12, 2023.
44. Dorothy Stanford, interview.
45. Coleman and Hess, discussion.
46. Frank Stanford, interview.
47. Coleman and Hess, discussion.
48. Camp payroll records, private collection of Irv Broughton, accessed August 7, 2023.
49. Dorothy Stanford, interview.
50. Rogers, interview.
51. Coleman and Hess, discussion.
52. Coleman and Hess, discussion.
53. Frank Stanford, interview.
54. Rilke, *Letters to a Young Poet*, 8.
55. Dorothy Stanford, interview.
56. Frank Stanford, interview.
57. Dorothy Stanford, interview.
58. Quoted in Cowley, "Shack Bullies," 144. The bluesman Son House, in a 1941 camp holler, sang of the camps that "ain't nothin for us nohow but livin' and killin'." See House, Martin, and Brown, "Camp Hollers."
59. Dorothy Stanford, interview.
60. Stanford, *What about This*, 177.
61. Dorothy Stanford, interview.
62. Coleman and Hess, discussion.
63. Dorothy Stanford, interview.

64. Coleman and Hess, discussion.
65. Bill Carpenter to C. D. Wright, June 19, 1989, CDWP.
66. Quoted in Murray Shugars, "Searching for Frank Stanford: Finding a Critique of Literary Biographies," in *Constant Stranger: After Frank Stanford*, ed. Max Crinnin and Aidan Ryan, 2nd ed. (Buffalo: Foundlings, 2019), 184. This quotation is from an interview of John F. Stanford conducted by Murray Shugars in 1999.
67. Frank Stanford, interview.
68. John Krupa, "Town Where the Highway Ends," *Arkansas Democrat-Gazette*, August 17, 2008, https://www.arkansasonline.com/news/2008/aug/17/town-where-highway-ends-20080817/.
69. Coleman and Hess, discussion.
70. Rogers, discussion.
71. Frank Stanford, poem draft, n.d., Prose Fragments, FSP.
72. Dorothy Stanford, interview.
73. Stanford, *What about This*, 179.
74. Coleman and Hess, discussion.
75. Frank Stanford, interview.
76. Snow Lake Levee Camp account records, item number R-689, private collection of Irv Broughton, Spokane, WA, accessed August 7, 2023.
77. Coleman and Hess, discussion.
78. Durrett's age was confirmed through Ancestry.com, and the detail about his mother is from A. P. Walton, "Compendium of Characters in Frank Stanford's Poetry," in Crinnin and Ryan, *Constant Stranger*, 127.
79. Frank Stanford, "Those Fools Who Try to Write Books but Not That Russian," unpublished prose fragment, n.d., FSP.
80. Stanford, *What about This*, 179.
81. Walton, "Compendium of Characters," 126.
82. Dorothy Stanford, interview.
83. Frank Stanford, *What about This: Collected Poems of Frank Stanford*, ed. Michael Wiegers (Port Townsend, WA: Copper Canyon, 2015), 4–5.
84. Stanford, *What about This*, 10.
85. Stanford, *What about This*, 22.
86. Stanford, *What about This*, 59.
87. Dorothy Stanford, interview.
88. Frank Stanford, interview.
89. Dorothy Stanford, interview.
90. Stanford, *Hidden Water*, 16.
91. Frank Stanford, interview.
92. Frank Stanford, interview.
93. Rogers, discussion.
94. Editor's note, *Blytheville (AR) Courier News*, November 29, 1957.
95. Frank Stanford, unpublished poem, n.d., Poetry Fragments, FSP.
96. Dorothy Stanford, interview.
97. Dorothy Stanford, interview.
98. Frank Stanford, interview.

99. Quoted in Shugars, "Searching for Frank Stanford," 187–92.
100. Frank Stanford to Michael Cuddihy, May 30, 1974, MCIP.
101. Cohn, *Where I Was Born*, 276.
102. Stanford, *Hidden Water*, 9.
103. McMillen, *Dark Journey*, 79, 87.
104. James C. Cobb, *The Most Southern Place on Earth: The Mississippi Delta and the Roots of Regional Identity* (Oxford: Oxford University Press, 1994), 112–16.
105. Quoted in Bertram Wyatt Brown, *Southern Honor: Ethics and Behavior in the Old South*, 25th anniversary ed. (New York: Oxford University Press, 2007), 439.
106. Frank Stanford, interview.
107. Dorothy Stanford, interview.
108. Quoted in A. P. Walton, "Toward Innumerable Futures: Frank Stanford & Origins" (master's thesis, Lund University, 2015), 64.
109. Stanford, *What about This*, 157.
110. Frank Stanford, unpublished typescript, n.d., Poetry Fragments, FSP.
111. Frank Stanford, interview.
112. Rilke, *Letters to a Young Poet*, 8.
113. Charles Baudelaire, *The Painter of Modern Life and Other Essays*, 2nd ed. (London: Phaidon Press, 1995), 6.
114. William Stafford, *Writing the Australian Crawl* (Ann Arbor: University of Michigan Press, 1978), 86.
115. Peter Szondi, "Hope in the Past: On Walter Benjamin," trans. Harvey Mendelsohn, in *Berlin Childhood around 1900* by Walter Benjamin, trans. Howard Eiland (Cambridge, MA: Belknap Press of Harvard University Press, 2006), 10.
116. Frank Stanford to Michael Cuddihy, July 18, 1974, MCIP.
117. Stanford, *What about This*, 612.
118. Stanford, *What about This*, 65.
119. Stanford, *What about This*, 83.
120. Stanford, *What about This*, 172.
121. Stanford, *What about This*, 206.

**THREE**

1. Frank Stanford to Alan Dugan, June 21, 1971, ADP.
2. A. P. Walton, "Toward Innumerable Futures: Frank Stanford & Origins" (master's thesis, Lund University, 2015), 8.
3. Frank Coleman and Carole Hess, in discussion with the author, November 19, 2019.
4. Coleman and Hess, discussion.
5. Ruth Rogers, in discussion with the author, July 9, 2019, Dallas, TX.
6. Coleman and Hess, discussion, November 19, 2019.
7. Frank Stanford, interview by Irv Broughton, 1973–74, FSP.
8. Walton, "Toward Innumerable Futures," 4. Stanford was in a way the opposite of Flaubert, who argued "one must not write down oneself," or

even Henry James, who valued "the impersonality . . . of the artist." Not so for Stanford. See Joshua Landy, "The Point of the Pyramid: Michael Fried's Flaubert's Gueuloir," *Los Angeles Review of Books*, July 20, 2013, https://lareviewofbooks.org/article/the-point-of-the-pyramid-michael-frieds-flauberts-gueuloir/; Miranda Miller, "The Madness of Art: Henry James' Notebooks," Royal Literary Fund, November 22, 2021, https://www.rlf.org.uk/posts/the-madness-of-art/#:~:text=Because%20he%20disliked%20writing%20in,about%20the%20artist%20Angelica%20Kauffmann.

9. C. D. Wright, introduction to *The Battlefield Where the Moon Says I Love You*, by Frank Stanford (Barrington, RI: Lost Roads Publishers, 2000), last page of preface (unnumbered).
10. Frank Stanford, interview.
11. Frank Stanford's baby book, private collection of Carrie Prysock, Dallas, TX, accessed April 26, 2020.
12. Frank Stanford's baby book, private collection of Carrie Prysock.
13. Rogers, discussion.
14. Frank Stanford's baby book, private collection of Carrie Prysock.
15. Frank Stanford to Eleanor Bender, November 10, 1971, LFS.
16. Olivia Bethany Moore, " 'Black and White Together, We Shall Win': Southern White Activists in the Mississippi Civil Rights Movement" (master's thesis, South Mississippi University, 2016), ii, https://aquila.usm.edu/cgi/viewcontent.cgi?article=1215&context=masters_theses.
17. Laura Helper, "Whole Lot of Shaking Going On: An Ethnography of Race Relations and Crossover Audiences for Rhythm & Blues and Rock & Roll in 1950s Memphis" (PhD diss., Rice University, 1997), 1.
18. Murray Shugars, "Searching for Frank Stanford: Finding a Critique of Literary Biographies," in *Constant Stranger: After Frank Stanford*, ed. Max Crinnin and Aidan Ryan, 2nd ed. (Buffalo: Foundlings, 2019), 181.
19. *The Cambridge History of American Literature*, ed. Sacvan Bercovich, vol. 8, *Poetry and Criticism: 1940–1955* (New York: Cambridge University Press, 1996), 21.
20. Murray Shugars, "What the Moon Says: Frank Stanford's Quest for Poetic Identity" (PhD diss., Purdue University, May 2000), 128.
21. Frank Stanford, "In the Wet Fields," n.d., Prose Fragments, FSP.
22. William Faulkner, *Requiem for a Nun* (1951; repr., New York: Vintage, 2012), 73.
23. Edward Hirsch, introduction to *Complete Poems and Selected Letters of John Keats*, by John Keats (New York: Modern Library, 2001); the quote is from Dorothy Benden Van Ghent and Jeffrey Cane Robinson, *Keats: The Myth of the Hero* (Princeton, NJ: Princeton University Press, 1983), 7.
24. Frank Coleman and Carole Hess, in discussion with the author, December 5, 2020.
25. Rogers, discussion.
26. Coleman and Hess, discussion, December 5, 2020.
27. Coleman and Hess, discussion, December 5, 2020.
28. Rogers, discussion.
29. Coleman and Hess, discussion, December 5, 2020.

30. Dorothy Stanford, interview by Murray Shugars, June 1997, shared with the author in 2019.
31. Coleman and Hess, discussion, December 5, 2020.
32. Carrie Prysock, in discussion with the author, December 30, 2020, Dallas, TX.
33. Frank Stanford to Dorothy Stanford, May 5, 1978, GCSC.
34. Rogers, discussion, Texas; Prysock, discussion.
35. Coleman and Hess, discussion, December 5, 2020. "Let's just face it," Hess said, "she wasn't a very cute little girl."
36. Coleman and Hess, discussion, November 19, 2019.
37. Irv Broughton, in discussion with the author, July 19, 2019.
38. Coleman and Hess, discussion, December 5, 2020.
39. Rogers, discussion. About Dorothy, she said, "She used horrible, racist language, and she never encouraged me" and "When friends would come over, they would show us off and put us back on the shelf."
40. Dorothy Stanford, interview.
41. Rogers, discussion.
42. Coleman and Hess, discussion, December 5, 2020.
43. This document was kept by Ruth in her small collection of scrapbooks and memorabilia, which her daughter Carrie Prysock made available to me in April 2020, a few months after Ruth died.
44. Frank Stanford's baby book, private collection of Carrie Prysock.
45. Frank Stanford to Irv Broughton, April 16, 1971, LFS.
46. Dorothy Stanford, interview.
47. Rogers, discussion; Walton, "Toward Innumerable Futures," 7–8.
48. Frank Stanford, *Hidden Water: From the Frank Stanford Archives*, ed. Michael Wiegers and Chet Weise (Nashville: Third Man Books, 2015), 7.
49. Brown v. Board of Education, 347 U.S. 483 (1953).
50. Daniel Kiel, "Exploded Dream: Desegregation in the Memphis City Schools," *Law & Equality: A Journal of Theory and Practice* 26, no. 2 (2008).
51. Frank Stanford's baby book, private collection of Carrie Prysock.
52. "Poetry Contest Winners are Announced," clipping, private collection of Carrie Prysock, Dallas, TX, accessed April 26, 2020; see also a copy of the certificate in Frank Stanford, *What about This: Collected Poems of Frank Stanford*, ed. Michael Wiegers (Port Townsend, WA: Copper Canyon, 2015), x (page unnumbered but located between ix and xi).
53. Dorothy Stanford, interview.
54. Dorothy Stanford, interview.
55. Frank Coleman and Carole Hess, in discussion with the author, December 3, 2020.
56. Frank Stanford's baby book, private collection of Carrie Prysock.
57. Coleman and Hess, discussion, November 19, 2019.
58. Rogers, discussion.
59. Ruth Rogers, interview by John Erwin (director and producer of *You*, a documentary film on the life and work of Frank Stanford), n.d., transcript, shared with the author on July 12, 2023.

60. Coleman and Hess, discussion, November 19, 2019.
61. Rogers, discussion; Broughton, discussion.
62. Shugars, "What the Moon Says," 68. The detail of Dorothy's insisting that she be called "Mother" was revealed in the interview Shugars conducted with her on June 12, 1997.
63. Stanford, *What about This*, 186
64. Coleman and Hess, discussion, December 3, 2020.
65. Rogers, discussion; Rogers, interview.
66. Coleman and Hess, discussion, November 19, 2019. This fact is confirmed by Rogers, interview.
67. Frank Stanford to Alan Dugan, 1972, ADP.
68. Frank Stanford, interview.
69. Coleman and Hess, discussion, December 3, 2020.
70. Rogers, interview.
71. A. P. Walton, "Compendium of Characters in Frank Stanford's Poetry," in Crinnin and Ryan, *Constant Stranger*, 118.
72. Stanford, *Hidden Water*, 6.
73. Bill Willett, in discussion with the author, October 26, 2019, Mountain Home, AR.
74. Coleman and Hess, discussion, December 3, 2020.
75. Rogers, interview.
76. Dorothy Stanford, interview.
77. "Mr. and Mrs. Stanford Invite Friends to Game," clipping from unidentified newspaper, October 23, 1953, private collection of Carrie Prysock.
78. Frank Stanford, interview.
79. "Mr. and Mrs. Stanford," October 23, 1953, private collection of Carrie Prysock.
80. Dorothy Stanford, interview.
81. Lisa C. Hickman, "Tiger Lady: On Joan Williams," *Los Angeles Review of Books*, December 11, 2011, https://lareviewofbooks.org/article/tiger-lady-on-joan-williams/.
82. Joan Williams, "Remembering," *Ironwood 17* 9, no. 1 (Spring 1981): 108.
83. Joan Fargason (née Williams) to Ginny Stanford, June 27, 1978, GCSC.
84. Dorothy Stanford, interview.
85. Stanford, *Hidden Water*, 38–39.
86. Frank Stanford, interview.
87. Walton, "Compendium of Characters," 114.
88. Isaiah Berlin, *Liberty: Incorporating Four Essays on Liberty*, ed. by Henry Hardy, 2nd ed. (New York: Oxford University Press, 2002), 202.
89. Frank Stanford to Alan Dugan, April 27, 1971, ADP.
90. Dorothy Stanford, interview.
91. Dorothy Stanford, interview; "Surprise Visit by Louise Fazenda," n.d., clipping, private collection of Carrie Prysock, Dallas, TX, accessed April 26, 2020.
92. Coleman and Hess, discussion, November 19, 2019.
93. Rogers, discussion.
94. Frank Stanford, unpublished poem, n.d., Prose Fragments, FSP.

95. Michael Waters, "In the Wake of Huck Finn," *Ironwood 17* 9, no. 1 (Spring 1981): 117.
96. It is helpful in this context to recall the idea of the psychoanalyst Adam Phillips that "constructions in autobiography can be inaccurate but sufficient." *On Flirtation: Psychoanalytic Essays on the Uncommitted Life* (1994; repr. Cambridge, MA: Harvard University Press, 1996), 73.
97. Peter Guralnick, *Last Train to Memphis: The Rise of Elvis Presley* (Boston: Back Bay Books, 1994), 96; Robert Gordon, *It Came from Memphis* (New York: Faber and Faber, 1995), 45.
98. Gordon, *It Came from Memphis*, 45.
99. Stanley Booth, *Rhythm Oil: A Journey through the Music of the American South* (New York: Da Capo, 1991), 97–99.
100. Gordon, *It Came from Memphis*, 12.
101. Stanford, *Hidden Water*, 16.
102. Guralnick, *Last Train to Memphis*, 370.
103. Guralnick, *Last Train to Memphis*, 39.
104. Gordon, *It Came from Memphis*, 11.
105. Charles L. Hughes, "'You Pay One Hell of a Price to Be Black': Rufus Thomas and the Racial Politics of Memphis Music," in *An Unseen Light: Black Struggles for Freedom in Memphis, Tennessee*, ed. Aram Goudsouzian and Charles W. McKinney Jr. (Lexington,: University Press of Kentucky, 2018), 235.
106. Hughes, "'You Pay One Hell of a Price,'" 236.
107. Frank Stanford to Irv Broughton, November 20, 1973, *LPD*. The spelling "alot" is a stylistic quirk of Frank's that he used consistently throughout his writing.
108. Frank Stanford's baby book, private collection of Carrie Prysock.
109. Williams, "Remembering," 109.
110. Montgomery Kurt McBee, "They Also Played the Game: A Historical Examination of the Memphis Red Sox Baseball Organization, 1922–1959" (PhD diss., University of Memphis, 2001).
111. McBee, "They Also Played," 253. Bankhead also accomplished another first by hitting a home run on his first major league at bat.
112. Quoted in McBee, "They Also Played," 253.
113. McBee, "They Also Played," 143. To drive home the message that a team without a ball is a team that's ignored or neglected, Stanford describes the tiny town that the freedom bus passes through as "like a ball nobody will ever catch" (10372); for more information on "shadow ball," see Evin Demirel, *African-American Athletes in Arkansas* (n.p.: ED Productions, 2017).
114. Wikipedia, s.v. "George H. Tichenor," last modified December 9, 2023, 4:23, https://en.wikipedia.org/wiki/George_H._Tichenor.
115. McBee, "They Also Played," vii, 277.
116. Stanford, *What about This*, 94.
117. C. D. Wright to Pamela Stewart, n.d., CDWP.
118. The name Pantagruel is ironic. In Rabelais's *Gargantua and Pantagruel* novels, these characters are giants.

119. Cynthia Sadler and Beverly Greene Bond, " 'On Parade' Race, Gender, and Imagery in the Memphis Mardi Gras, Cotton Carnival, and Cotton Makers' Jubilee," in *Tennessee Women: Their Lives and Times*, ed. Beverly Greene Bond and Sarah Wilkerson Freeman (Athens: University of Georgia Press, 2015), 127.
120. "Memphis Cottons to Cotton Again during Cotton Week," *Kingsport (TN) News*, May 4, 1948.
121. Coleman and Hess, discussion, December 3, 2020.
122. Quoted in Sadler and Bond, " 'On Parade,' " 140.
123. Beverly Greene Bond, "Taylor Made: Envisioning Black Memphis at Midcentury," in Goudsouzian and McKinney, *Unseen Light*, 108.
124. Hughes, " 'You Pay One Hell of a Price,' " 233.
125. Sadler and Bond, " 'On Parade,' " 127.
126. Donna Elizabeth Reeves, "Battle for an Image: Black Memphians Define Their Place in Southern History" (PhD diss., University of Memphis, August 2008), 129.
127. "Cotton Makers Jubilee Opens," *High Point (NC) Enterprise*, May 13, 1937. This was a rare case of the white press covering the event. Most white newspapers steered clear, as a rule, of publishing photos of Black people.
128. Reeves, "Battle for an Image," 130.
129. Thomas J. Hirsch, "Insults for Sale: The 1957 Memphis Newspaper Boycott," *Tennessee Historical Quarterly* 72, no. 1 (Spring 2013): 31.
130. Gordon, *It Came from Memphis*, 37.
131. Frank Stanford, unpublished prose fragment, n.d., FSP.
132. Gordon, *It Came from Memphis*, 36.
133. Paul Conkin, *The Southern Agrarians* (Knoxville: University of Tennessee Press, 1988), 150.
134. Conkin, *Southern Agrarians*, 150–51.
135. Frank Stanford to Alan Dugan, n.d., in Stanford, *Hidden Water*, 167.
136. R. S. Gwynn, in discussion with the author, September 9, 2019, Beaumont, TX.

## FOUR

1. Frank Stanford to Michael and Mary Cuddihy, November 9, 1976, *LPD*.
2. Frank Stanford's baby book, private collection of Carrie Prysock, Dallas, TX, accessed April 26, 2020.
3. Dorothy Stanford, interview by Murray Shugars, June 1997, shared with the author in 2019.
4. Dorothy Stanford, interview.
5. Joan Williams, "Remembering," *Ironwood 17* 9, no. 1 (Spring 1981): 109.
6. Dorothy Stanford, interview.
7. Frank Stanford, interview by Irv Broughton, 1973–74, FSP.
8. Frank Coleman and Carole Hess, in discussion with the author, December 5, 2020.
9. Dorothy Stanford, interview.

10. "Lake Norfork," advertisement for A. C. Haskin Real Estate Co., *Blytheville (AR) Courier News*, July 2, 1964, 11.
11. Dorothy Stanford, interview.
12. Frank Coleman and Carole Hess, in discussion with the author, November 19, 2019.
13. Coleman and Hess, discussion, December 5, 2020.
14. Nicholas Fuhrmann, in discussion with the author, August 9, 2019, Subiaco, AR.
15. Donald Lovelady, in discussion with the author, July 15, 2021.
16. Dick House, in discussion with the author, October 26, 2019, Mountain Home, AR.
17. Flannery O'Connor, *Mystery and Manners* (New York: Farrar, Straus and Giroux, 1969), 84.
18. Adam Phillips, *On Flirtation: Psychoanalytic Essays on the Uncommitted Life* (1994; repr. Cambridge, MA: Harvard University Press, 1996), 53.
19. Ruth Rogers, in discussion with the author, July 9, 2019, Dallas, TX.
20. Bill Willett, in discussion with the author, October 26, 2019, Mountain Home, AR.
21. House, discussion.
22. Dorothy Stanford, interview.
23. Rogers, discussion.
24. Dorothy Stanford, interview.
25. Willett, discussion.
26. House, discussion.
27. Frank Stanford, interview, 1973–74.
28. Wick Temple, "Economic Boom in Northwest Arkansas," *Blytheville (AR) Courier News*, February 11, 1963; "Drug Product for Sale," *Blytheville (AR) Courier News*, August 2, 1962; and "Bond Issue Okayed," *Northwest Arkansas Times* (Fayetteville, AR), March 6, 1963.
29. Dorothy Stanford, interview.
30. Temple, "Economic Boom."
31. Carl Judson Launius, "It Was a Flood: The Life and Poetry of Frank Stanford" (PhD diss., University of California, Davis), 82.
32. Bill Willett, "Dream of the Alluvial Field: An Interview with Bill Willett," interview by Peter J. Moore, *Rain Taxi* 13, no. 3 (Fall 2008): 38.
33. Ruth Rogers, interview by John Erwin (director and producer of *You*, a documentary film on the life and work of Frank Stanford), n.d., transcript, shared with the author on July 12, 2023.
34. Williams, "Remembering," 109.
35. Frank Stanford, *Hidden Water: From the Frank Stanford Archives*, ed. Michael Wiegers and Chet Weise (Nashville: Third Man Books, 2015), 5.
36. Williams, "Remembering," 108.
37. Willett, discussion.
38. Willett, discussion.
39. Willett, "Dream of the Alluvial Field," interview, 39.
40. Rogers, interview.

41. CALS Encyclopedia of Arkansas, s.v., "Norfork Dam and Lake," by Scott Branyan, last modified June 21, 2023, https://encyclopediaofarkansas.net/entries/norfork-dam-and-lake-3529/.
42. Don Miller, "Afloat and Afield," *Chronicle Telegram* (Elyria, OH), April 19, 1963.
43. Harold Ensley, "Along the Ozark Trails," *Lawrence (KS) Daily Journal-World*, January 11, 196. On the Silver Maple Resort, see *Blytheville (AR) Courier News*, June 14, 1960, 8.
44. Rogers, interview.
45. Willett, discussion.
46. Rogers, discussion.
47. Rogers, interview; Frank Stanford, interview, 1973–74.
48. Frank Stanford, interview.
49. Dorothy Stanford, interview.
50. These feats are recorded in copies of the "Lake Norfork Fishing Letter," private collection of Carrie Prysock, Dallas, TX, accessed October 8, 2021.
51. Frank Stanford, *What about This: Collected Poems of Frank Stanford*, ed. Michael Wiegers (Port Townsend, WA: Copper Canyon, 2015), 109.
52. Stanford, *What about This*, 108.
53. Rogers, discussion.
54. Dorothy Stanford, interview.
55. Rogers, interview.
56. Dorothy Stanford, interview.
57. Rogers, interview.
58. As previously noted, while 1971 is the copyright date of *The Singing Knives*, and the book was not actually bound and distributed until at least May 1972.
59. Stanford, *What about This*, 4, 7, 23, 25.
60. Frank Stanford, "The Albino," *Chicago Review* 23, no. 1 (Summer 1971): 9–11.
61. Frank Stanford, "The Smoking Mirrors," *West Coast Review* 6, no. 2 (October 1971): 29.
62. Williams, "Remembering," 109.
63. Rogers, interview.
64. Williams, "Remembering," 109.
65. This line also appears in Frank Stanford, "St. Francis and the Wolf," n.d., Fragment 309, FSP.
66. Rogers, interview.
67. Elise Lee, in discussion with the author, March 3, 2020.
68. Coleman and Hess, discussion, November 19, 2019.
69. Dorothy Stanford, interview.
70. Frank Stanford, interview.
71. Dorothy Stanford refers to this critical meeting in a letter she wrote to the Reverend Benno Schluterman, a priest at Subiaco Academy, in 1964. This letter is housed in Stanford's Subiaco file in the Subiaco Academy Archives, Subiaco, AR (hereafter cited as SAA), and was kindly shared with me by Prof. Leo A. Lensing, who was a classmate of Frank's at Subiaco.
72. Ata Moharreri, "Frank Stanford: In Leenus Orth's Words," in *Constant Stranger: After Frank Stanford*, ed. Max Crinnin an Aidan Ryan, 2nd ed.

(Buffalo: Foundlings, 2019), 42; Nicholas Fuhrmann to Ata Moharreri, email, n.d., shared with the author by Ata Moharreri on September 9, 2021.
73. This account draws on three sources: my own interview with Nicholas Fuhrmann, August 9, 2019, Subiaco, AR; Moharreri, "Frank Stanford," 42; and Fuhrmann to Moharreri, n.d., shared with the author on September 9, 2021.
74. Nicholas Fuhrmann, in discussion with the author, August 9, 2019, Subiaco, AR.
75. Coleman and Hess, discussion, November 19, 2019.
76. "Hither'n and Yon," *Delta Democrat-Times* (Greenville, MS), June 23, 1964.
77. Rogers, discussion.
78. A. P. Walton, "Compendium of Characters in Frank Stanford's Poetry," in Crinnin and Ryan, *Constant Stranger*, 123–24.
79. C. D. Wright to Bill Carpenter, July 2, 1989, CDWP.
80. Stanford, *What about This*, 4.
81. Stanford, *What about This*, 6–10.
82. Stanford, *Hidden Water*, 9.
83. Williams, "Remembering," 107.
84. Willett, discussion.
85. Stanford, *Hidden Water*, 10.
86. Frank's complete Mountain Home grades can be found in Transcript of Record, Mountain Home High School, June 3, 1964, Subiaco Academy file, SAA. On the form his birth date is wrong, listed as July 1 instead of August 1, and his place of birth is listed as Greenfield, an obvious error for Greenville, Mississippi, a place of birth that is itself a deliberate fabrication by Dorothy, as he was born in Richton, Mississippi.
87. Clipping, January 1, 1963, private collection of Carrie Prysock, Dallas, TX, accessed April 26, 2020.
88. These are inscriptions in Frank Stanford's 1963 Mountain Home High School yearbook, private collection of Carrie Prysock, Dallas, TX, accessed May 3, 2020.
89. Beverly Franklin, in discussion with the author, March 19, 2020.
90. C. D. Wright to Carl Launius, April 25, 1986, CDWP.
91. Matt Horan, in discussion with the author, April 28, 2021.
92. Wright to Launius, April 25, 1986, CDWP.
93. Franklin, discussion.
94. Launius, "It Was a Flood," 81.
95. Frank Stanford's 1963 Mountain Home High School yearbook, private collection of Carrie Prysock.
96. Franklin, discussion.
97. Frank Stanford's 1963 Mountain Home High School yearbook, private collection of Carrie Prysock.
98. Frank Stanford to Irv Broughton, ca. February 1973, FSP. Her name is spelled Davalee.
99. Irv Broughton and Frank Stanford, *It Wasn't a Dream: It Was a Flood* (1974), 16 mm film, posted August 22, 2019, YouTube video, 26:19, https://www.youtube.com/watch?v=aPS1tXOvoC8, at 2:02–5.

100. Frank Stanford, interview, 1973–74.
101. Dorothy Stanford, interview.
102. Bill Willett, quoted in Launius, "It Was a Flood," 81.
103. Frank Stanford, unpublished poem draft, "Notebook 2," GCSC.
104. Frank Stanford, interview, 1973–74.
105. Danny Keeter, in discussion with the author, August 12, 2021.
106. Stanford, *Hidden Water*, 39.
107. Stanford, unpublished poem draft, "Notebook 2," GCSC.
108. Willett, discussion.
109. Willett, discussion.
110. I have drawn on three separate accounts to reconstruct this event. In addition to my own interview with Bill Willett in Mountain Home, AR, on October 26, 2019, there is Carl Launius's interview with Willett, quoted in Launius, "It Was a Flood," 81, and J. Peter Moore's interview with Willett, "Dream of the Alluvial Field," 38.
111. Bill Willett, "Dream of the Alluvial Field," interview, 38.
112. Vernie Harris, in discussion with the author, June 26, 2021.
113. Frank Stanford's 1963 Mountain Home High School yearbook, private collection of Carrie Prysock.
114. Franklin, discussion.
115. Rogers, interview.
116. Frank Stanford and Bill Willett, "Correspondence from Frank Stanford to Bill Willett, with Commentary by Bill Willett," ed. Matthew Henriksen, *Fulcrum: An Annual of Poetry and Aesthetics*, no. 7 (2011): 414.
117. Harris, discussion.
118. Franklin, discussion.
119. Willett, discussion.
120. Frank Stanford's 1964 Mountain Home High School yearbook, private collection of Carrie Prysock, Dallas, TX, accessed May 3, 2020.
121. Frank Stanford, interview, 1973–74.
122. Williams, "Remembering," 108.
123. Williams, "Remembering," 109.
124. Keeter, discussion.
125. Frank Stanford, interview, 1973–74.
126. Lovelady, discussion.
127. Nicholas Fuhrmann to Ata Moharreri, email, n.d., shared with the author on November 12, 2020.
128. Bob Gilbert, in discussion with the author, May 2019.
129. Bill Lux, in discussion with the author, December 19, 2019.
130. Fuhrmann, discussion.
131. Willett, "Dream of the Alluvial Field," interview, 39. The researcher mentioned here is J. Peter Moore, who conducted this interview.
132. Keeter, discussion.
133. Launius, "It Was a Flood," 82.
134. Stanford, *Hidden Water*, 151.
135. Frank Stanford, unpublished poetry fragment, n.d., FSP.

136. Willett, "Dream of the Alluvial Field," interview, 39.
137. Williams, "Remembering," 108.
138. Dorothy Stanford's copy of *Ironwood 17* 9, no. 1 (Spring 1981), with marginalia, private collection of Carrie Prysock, Dallas, TX, accessed May 3, 2020.
139. Dorothy Stanford to Michael Cuddihy, April 21, 1987, MCIP.
140. Willett, discussion.
141. Keeter, discussion.
142. Frank Stanford to Michael Cuddihy, September 1974, MCIP.
143. Stanford, *Hidden Water*, 49.
144. Frank Stanford, unpublished poem fragment, n.d., Poetry Fragments, FSP.
145. Frank Stanford, unpublished prose fragment, n.d., Prose Fragments, FSP.
146. Frank Stanford to Dugan, June 21, 1971, ADP.
147. Frank Stanford to Eleanor Bender, June 28, 1971, LFS.
148. Irv Broughton, in discussion with the author, August 3, 2021.
149. Nicholas Fuhrmann to Ata Moharreri, email, n.d., shared with the author in May 2021.
150. Frank Stanford to Alan Dugan, April 27, 1971, ADP.
151. Steve Stern, in discussion with the author, September 5, 2019.
152. R. S. Gwynn, Deborah Luster, Ralph Adamo, John Biguenet, and Steve Stern, in discussion with the author, January 18, 2020, New Orleans, LA.
153. C. D. Wright, "Frank Stanford of the Mulberry Family: An Arkansas Epilogue," *Conjunctions* 29 (1997): 298.
154. R. S. Gwynn, "Lies," in Crinnin and Ryan, *Constant Stranger*, 28.
155. Frank Stanford, interview, 1973–74.
156. Rogers, discussion; quotation is from Rogers, interview.
157. Dorothy Stanford, interview.
158. Rogers, discussion; Bill Willett, interview by John Erwin (director and producer of *You*, a documentary film on the life and work of Frank Stanford), n.d., transcript, shared with the author on July 12, 2023.
159. C. D. Wright to Joan Williams, August 9, 1978/79, CDWP.
160. Quoted in A. P. Walton, "Lives & Works: From Myth to Mythology," in Crinnin and Ryan, *Constant Stranger*, 93n4.
161. Frank Stanford to Carolyn Gilbert, 1973, LFS. This letter was typed in all capitals to make it easier to read. I have changed it to standard capitalization.
162. Frank Stanford to David Walker, February 1974, GCSC.
163. Frank Stanford, *What about This*, 730.
164. Frank Stanford to Alan Dugan, May 10, 1972, ADP.
165. Frank Stanford, "With the Approach of the Oak the Axeman Quakes," in *Fifty Contemporary Poets: The Creative Process*, ed. Alberta Turner (New York: David McKay, 1977), 301; Frank Stanford to Alan Dugan, June 21, 1971, in Stanford, *Hidden Water*, 156. Murray Shugars concludes in his dissertation on Stanford that "by the time he entered Subiaco Academy, Stanford was writing poems in the vernacular rhythms of the Delta." "What the Moon Says: Frank Stanford's Quest for Poetic Identity" (PhD diss., Purdue University, May 2000), 126.
166. Walton, "Lives & Works," 123.

167. Frank Stanford to Alan Dugan, May 10, 1972, ADP.
168. Frank Stanford to Carolyn Gilbert, ca. January 7–12, 1973, LFS.
169. These lines also appear in Frank Stanford, "St. Francis and the Wolf," n.d., Fragments 292 and 301, FSP.
170. Frank Stanford to George Hitchcock, November 30, 1971, LFS.
171. Frank Stanford to Irv Broughton, February 27, 1973, LFS.
172. Frank Stanford to Irv Broughton, January 22, 1971, LFS.
173. Frank Stanford to Eleanor Bender, November 10, 1971, LFS.
174. Frank Stanford, notebook, 1973, Notebooks, GCSC.
175. Stanford to Dugan, May 10, 1972, ADP.
176. Stanford, *Hidden Water*, 4–11.
177. Elise Lee to Carrie Prysock, Facebook message, shared with the author by Carrie Prysock, August 1, 2021.
178. These lines first appear in Frank Stanford, Fragment 293, in Wiegers and Weise, *Hidden Water*, 11.
179. Frank Stanford, unpublished poem, n.d., Poetry Fragments, FSP.
180. Willett, discussion.
181. Stanford, *Hidden Water*, 21.
182. Rogers, interview.
183. Franklin, discussion.
184. Stanford, *Hidden Water*, 6.
185. Frank Stanford's baby book, private collection of Carrie Prysock.
186. Frank Stanford, interview, 1973–74.
187. Willett, "Dream of the Alluvial Field," interview, 39.
188. Broughton and Stanford, *It Wasn't a Dream*, at 24:10–25.
189. On an undated scrap of typed and handwritten paper in his Prose Fragments, Frank lists "Blue Yodel The Many Evenings" as a "series of poems beginning in 1957–1964, along with 'Nocturnal Ships of the Past' and 'Crest Part III Some Past Twelve.'" FSP.
190. Frank Stanford, handwritten note, n.d., "Miscellaneous" folder, FSP.
191. Stanford, *Hidden Water*, 27–29. Various drafts exist of this poem. I have chosen to use the one published in this volume. It's possible that Frank considered a version he published in the *Little Review* in 1974 to be the final version, but it is hard to say. See Frank Stanford, "Blue Yodel of Those Who Were Always Telling Me," *Little Review* 5, no. 1 (1974): 13.
192. Stanford, "Approach of the Oak," 303.
193. Stanford, *Hidden Water*, 38–39.
194. Stanford, *Hidden Water*, 39.
195. Stanford to Dugan, May 10, 1972, ADP.
196. Stanford, *Hidden Water*, 8.
197. Rainer Maria Rilke, *Letters to a Young Poet* (New York: Vintage Books, 1984), 26.
198. Frank Stanford, "Frank Stanford," interview by Irv Broughton, *The Writer's Mind: Interviews with American Authors*, ed. Irv Broughton (Fayetteville: University of Arkansas Press, 1990), 3:302.
199. Quoted in Shugars, "What the Moon Says," 142.
200. Rogers, interview.

201. Stanford, "Approach of the Oak," 301.
202. Stanford, *What about This*, 641.
203. Stanford, "Frank Stanford," interview, 303.
204. Stanford, *Hidden Water*, 6.
205. Rogers, discussion.
206. Quoted in Shugars, "What the Moon Says," 142.
207. Harris, discussion.
208. Launius, "It Was a Flood," 83.
209. Quoted in Shugars, "What the Moon Says," 142.
210. Stanford, "Frank Stanford," interview, 304.
211. Admission and Discharge Records, Social Service Report, Arkansas State Hospital, case history 105913, private collection of Carrie Prysock, Dallas, TX, accessed May 3, 2020.
212. Shugars, "What the Moon Says," 147.
213. A. P. Walton, "Toward Innumerable Futures: Frank Stanford & Origins" (master's thesis, Lund University, 2015), 8.
214. Coleman and Hess, discussion, December 5, 2020.
215. Sister Louis Joseph to Dorothy Stanford, August 30, 1963, private collection of Carrie Prysock, Dallas, TX, accessed May 3, 2020.
216. Frank Stanford, interview, 1973–74.
217. Admission and Discharge Records, Arkansas State Hospital, case history 105913, private collection of Carrie Prysock.

**FIVE**

1. Dorothy Stanford, interview by Murray Shugars, June 1997, shared with the author in 2019.
2. Transcript of Record, Mountain Home High School, Mountain Home, AR, June 3, 1964.
3. Confirmation Program, May 14, 1961, All Saints' Church, Memphis, TN, private collection of Carrie Prysock, Dallas, TX, accessed October 8–9, 2021.
4. Fr. Jerome Kodell, email message to author, June 11, 2020.
5. "To Clifford and Literary Monks," included in an email from Nicholas Fuhrmann to Ata Moharreri, n.d., shared with the author in October 2021.
6. Bill Willett, in discussion with the author, October 26, 2019, Mountain Home, AR.
7. Nicholas Fuhrmann, "Feast of St. Joseph the Worker, May 1, 2018," unfinished entry in an unpublished autobiographical manuscript, private collection of Ata Moharreri, shared with the author on November 18, 2022.
8. A photo of Dorothy's inscription in this Bible was provided to the author by A. P. Walton.
9. "Ruth: Essential Docs," file, private collection of Carrie Prysock, Dallas, TX, organized and accessed by the author October 8–9, 2021.
10. Dorothy Stanford to Father Herbert Vogelpohl, n.d., "Correspondence from Dorothy Stanford," SAA.

11. Bill Willett, interview by John Erwin (director and producer of *You*, a documentary film on the life and work of Frank Stanford), n.d., transcript, shared with the author on July 12, 2023.
12. Dorothy Stanford to Vogelpohl, n.d., SAA.
13. Sister Louise Joseph to Dorothy Stanford, August 31, 1963, private collection of Carrie Prysock, Dallas, TX, accessed October 8–9, 2020.
14. Application for Admission to Subiaco Academy of Francis Gildart Stanford, SAA.
15. Dorothy Stanford to Rev. Benno Schluterman, OSB, July 1, 1964, copy provided to the author by Leo A. Lensing in September 2021.
16. Joseph to Dorothy Stanford, August 31, 1963, private collection of Carrie Prysock.
17. R. S. Gwynn, in discussion with the author, January 4, 2021, New Orleans, LA.
18. Fuhrmann to Moharreri, n.d., shared with the author in October 2021.
19. Leo A. Lensing, in discussion with the author, August 8, 2023, Old Saybrook, CT.
20. Dorothy Stanford to Rev. Benno Schluterman, O.S.B., July 1, 1964, copy provided to the author by Leo A. Lensing in September 2021. This job offer is also discussed in Dorothy Stanford, interview.
21. Dorothy Stanford to Schluterman, July 1, 1964, SAA.
22. Leo A. Lensing, *"Subiaco's Unofficial Poet Laureate": A Memoir of Frank Stanford in High School* (Buffalo: Foundlings Press, 2022), 39.
23. Bill Lux, "My Classmate, Frank Stanford," interview by Nicholas Fuhrmann, n.d., shared with the author by Ata Moharreri, October 2021.
24. Nicholas Fuhrmann, "Frank Stanford: Like Rain Falling and Night Falling," unpublished manuscript, n.d., shared with the author by Ata Moharreri, May 2023.
25. "Subiaco Academy Begins 86th Year," *Periscope* (Subiaco Academy, Subiaco, AR), September 1964.
26. Fuhrmann to Moharreri, n.d., shared with the author in October 2021.
27. Fuhrmann, "Feast of St. Joseph the Worker," private collection of Ata Moharreri; "'B' Team, Sophomores, Freshmen Ready for Competition," *Periscope* (Subiaco Academy, Subiaco, AR), September 1964.
28. Fuhrmann to Moharreri, n.d., shared with the author in October 2021.
29. Nicholas Fuhrmann, in discussion with the author, August 10, 2019, Subiaco, AR.
30. Nicholas Fuhrmann, in discussion with the author, August 9, 2019, Subiaco, AR.
31. Fuhrmann to Moharreri, n.d., shared with the author in October 2021. "I did suspect something different about Frank," Fuhrmann says in this email. The comment highlights a red flag in this kind of attention from Fuhrmann. In the 1980s and '90s Nicholas Fuhrmann was accused by as many as eight students of sexually abusing them. As for the mid-1960s, not a single Subiaco classmate interviewed about Frank claimed to have witnessed such behavior by Fuhrmann, which is why you are reading this as a footnote. While

Fuhrmann was defrocked in the 2000s (although allowed to keep living in the Abbey), no evidence suggests sexually inappropriate behavior when Stanford attended. For more information see Lensing, *"Subiaco's Unofficial Poet Laureate,"* 25–26, and James McWilliams, "What about *That*: Reframing Frank Stanford's Muses," *Smart Set*, June 3, 2019, https://www.thesmartset.com/what-about-that/.

32. Murray Shugars, "What the Moon Says: Frank Stanford's Quest for Poetic Identity" (PhD diss., Purdue University, May 2000), 181.
33. "Faces in the Crowd Features Fr. Nicholas," *Periscope*, May 1966.
34. Leo A. Lensing, in discussion with the author, December 30, 2021.
35. Fuhrmann, discussion.
36. Lensing, *"Subiaco's Unofficial Poet Laureate,"* 15. Another version of this event can be found in Shugars, "What the Moon Says," 181.
37. Quoted in Lensing, *"Subiaco's Unofficial Poet Laureate,"* 13.
38. Kodell, email message to author, June 11, 2020.
39. Emmett Hawkins, in discussion with the author, March 18, 2020.
40. Martin Pendergrast, in discussion with the author, March 5, 2020.
41. Omar Greene, email message to author, March 5, 2020.
42. Lensing, discussion, December 30, 2021.
43. Greene, email message to author, March 5, 2020.
44. Pendergrast, discussion.
45. Pendergrast, discussion.
46. "Subiaco and Its Students," *Periscope* (Subiaco Academy, Subiaco, AR), April 1965.
47. "Judo Team Stages Demonstration; Stanford Starts Subi Judo Club," *Periscope* (Subiaco Academy, Subiaco, AR), January–February 1965.
48. Greene, email message to author, March 5, 2020.
49. Fuhrmann to Moharreri, n.d., shared with the author in October 2021.
50. "Judo Team Stages Demonstration."
51. Pendergrast, discussion.
52. "Subiaco Judoists Hurl Northside in First Competition on April 23," *Periscope* (Subiaco Academy, Subiaco, AR), April 1965.
53. Frank Stanford, *Hidden Water: From the Frank Stanford Archives*, ed. Michael Wiegers and Chet Weise (Nashville: Third Man Books, 2015), 6.
54. C. D. Wright to Pamela Stewart, n.d., CDWP.
55. Pendergrast, discussion.
56. Lensing, *"Subiaco's Unofficial Poet Laureate,"* 13.
57. Shugars, "What the Moon Says," 173.
58. Pendergrast, discussion.
59. Stanford, *Hidden Water*, 9.
60. Shugars, "What the Moon Says," 174.
61. Inazo Nitobe, *Bushido: The Soul of Japan; An Exposition of Japanese Thought* (1905; republished Santa Cruz, CA: Evinity Publishing, 2009), chap. 12, https://sacred-texts.com/shi/bsd/bsd17.htm.
62. Bill Lavender, in discussion with the author, December 14, 2021, New Orleans, LA.

63. Daisetz Suzuki, *Zen Buddhism and Its Influence on Japanese Culture* (London: Routledge and Kegan Paul, 1959), 70, https://archive.org/details/in.gov.ignca.16794/page/n69/mode/2up.
64. Suzuki, *Zen Buddhism*, 70, quoted in Shugars, "What the Moon Says," 176.
65. Suzuki, *Zen Buddhism*, 70, quoted in Shugars, "What the Moon Says," 176.
66. Frank Stanford, "Frank Stanford," interview by Irv Broughton, *The Writer's Mind: Interviews with American Authors*, ed. Irv Broughton (Fayetteville: University of Arkansas Press, 1990), 3:303, 309.
67. Frank Stanford, "With the Approach of the Oak the Axeman Quakes," in *Fifty Contemporary Poets: The Creative Process*, ed. Alberta Turner (New York: David McKay, 1977), 302.
68. Suzuki, *Zen Buddhism*, 71.
69. Stanford, "Approach of the Oak," 302.
70. Stanford, "Approach of the Oak," 302.
71. Quoted in Shugars, "What the Moon Says," 70.
72. Bill Lux, in discussion with the author, December 19, 2019.
73. Lensing, discussion.
74. Frank Stanford, interview by Irv Broughton, 1973–74, FSP.
75. Quoted in Shugars, "What the Moon Says," 75.
76. Quoted in Shugars, "What the Moon Says," 75.
77. Lensing, "*Subiaco's Unofficial Poet Laureate*," 4. I saw the yearbooks that this information came from at Lensing's home in Old Saybrook, Connecticut, on September 8, 2023.
78. Fuhrmann, discussion, August 10, 2019.
79. Lensing, "*Subiaco's Unofficial Poet Laureate*," 9.
80. Hawkins, discussion.
81. Kodell, email message to author, June 11, 2020. Lensing writes that they decided to do so as early as 1955, a year after *Brown v. Board*. Lensing, "*Subiaco's Unofficial Poet Laureate*," 8.
82. Fuhrmann, "Feast of St. Joseph the Worker," private collection of Ata Moharreri.
83. Al Adams, "Educational Home Visits Complete Seniors' Study of Civil Rights," *Periscope* (Subiaco Academy, Subiaco, AR), January–February 1966. The *Periscope* praised "the opportunity to meet the Negro and discover his attitude towards the race question."
84. Lux, interview.
85. Lux, discussion.
86. Lensing, "*Subiaco's Unofficial Poet Laureate*," 8; Kevin Griesemer, in discussion with the author, September 19, 2021.
87. Quoted in Shugars, "What the Moon Says," 75.
88. Fuhrmann, "Feast of St. Joseph the Worker," private collection of Ata Moharreri. Bill Willett, Frank's closest friend, always found these stories about Frank's racism at Subiaco to be baffling. He never recalls any racist behavior coming from Frank. But, as noted, there were no Black people where they lived, in Mountain Home. Willett, discussion.
89. Lux, discussion.

90. Lensing, "Subiaco's Unofficial Poet Laureate," 8–9.
91. Lux, discussion.
92. Lensing, "Subiaco's Unofficial Poet Laureate," 9.
93. Hawkins, discussion. Lensing notes that the school eventually convinced some places to allow Hawkins in, under threat of a boycott.
94. Lensing, "Subiaco's Unofficial Poet Laureate," 10.
95. Hawkins, discussion.
96. Lux, interview.
97. Fuhrmann, discussion, August 10, 2019.
98. Fuhrmann, "Frank Stanford."
99. Nicholas Fuhrmann to Ata Moharreri, email, n.d., shared with the author in September 2021.
100. Fuhrmann, discussion, August 9, 2019.
101. Dorothy Stanford to Father [Hubert?], July 1, 1966, Correspondence from Dorothy Stanford, SAA.
102. Fuhrmann, discussion.
103. Fuhrmann, "Feast of St. Joseph the Worker," private collection of Ata Moharreri.
104. Fuhrmann to Moharreri, n.d., shared with the author in October 2021.
105. Frank Stanford, interview, 1973–74.
106. Frank Stanford, *What about This: Collected Poems of Frank Stanford*, ed. Michael Wiegers (Port Townsend, WA: Copper Canyon, 2015), 322.
107. Ginny Stanford, email message to author, November 16, 2019.
108. Subiaco Academy, *This Is Subiaco....*, brochure (Subiaco, AR: Subiaco Academy, early 1960s), private collection of Carrie Prysock, Dallas, TX, accessed in April 2020 and October 2021.
109. Irv Broughton and Frank Stanford, *It Wasn't a Dream: It Was a Flood* (1974), 16 mm film, posted August 22, 2019, YouTube video, 26:19, https://www.youtube.com/watch?v=aPS1tXOvoC8, at 7:30–8:05.
110. Frank Stanford, prose fragment, n.d., Prose Fragments, FSP.
111. Fuhrmann, "Frank Stanford."
112. Fuhrmann, discussion.
113. Broughton and Stanford, *It Wasn't A Dream*, at 8:25.
114. Fuhrmann, "Frank Stanford."
115. Broughton and Stanford, *It Wasn't A Dream*, at 8:49–51.
116. "Subiaco and Its Students."
117. Lux, "My Classmate, Frank Stanford," interview.
118. Frank Stanford, Subiaco Academy: Permanent Record, completed May 27, 1966, SAA.
119. Fuhrmann, "Feast of St. Joseph the Worker," private collection of Ata Moharreri.
120. Frank Stanford to Eleanor Bender, June 28, 1971, *LPD*.
121. Lensing, discussion, May 28, 2024.
122. Greene, email message to author, March 5, 2020.
123. Fuhrmann to Moharreri, n.d., shared with the author in September 2021. Fuhrmann always downplayed his influence, saying in this email, "I had no

real direct influence on Frank's creations, although I do think I had some indirect influence."
124. Pendergrast, discussion.
125. Frank Stanford, interview, 1973–74.
126. Fuhrmann, discussion, August 9, 2019.
127. Frank Stanford, "List of Ashes," July 25, 1972, private collection of Irv Broughton, accessed August 7, 2023.
128. Griesemer, discussion.
129. Lux, discussion.
130. Shugars, "What the Moon Says," 160.
131. Lensing, *"Subiaco's Unofficial Poet Laureate,"* 38–39.
132. Pendergrast, discussion.
133. Quoted in Lensing, *"Subiaco's Unofficial Poet Laureate,"* 12.
134. Lensing, *"Subiaco's Unofficial Poet Laureate,"* 10.
135. Lensing, *"Subiaco's Unofficial Poet Laureate,"* 40.
136. Pendergrast, discussion.
137. "Competent Staff Runs Improved Library," *Periscope* (Subiaco Academy, Subiaco, AR), October 1964. To stress the impressiveness of the library, classmate Martin Pendergrast recalled developing an obscure interest in Greek footraces and, to his surprise, finding a row of books on the esoteric topic. Pendergrast, discussion.
138. Pendergrast, discussion.
139. Frank Stanford to Alan Dugan, May 27, 1972, ADP.
140. Lux, interview.
141. Lux, discussion.
142. Fuhrmann, discussion, August 10, 2019.
143. Fuhrmann to Moharreri, n.d., shared with the author in September 2021.
144. Frank Stanford, interview, 1973–74.
145. Fuhrmann, discussion, August 9, 2019.
146. Fuhrmann, discussion, August 9, 2019.
147. Frank Stanford to Michael Cuddihy, May 22, 1974, MCIP.
148. Frank Stanford to Richard Eberhart, December 27–31, 1972, LFS.
149. Frank Stanford, interview, 1973–74.
150. Fuhrmann, "Feast of St. Joseph the Worker," private collection of Ata Moharreri.
151. Fuhrmann, "Frank Stanford."
152. C. D. Wright to Michael and Mary Cuddihy, November 9, 1978, LRPR.
153. Lux, discussion.
154. Fuhrmann, "Feast of St. Joseph the Worker," private collection of Ata Moharreri.
155. Lensing, *"Subiaco's Unofficial Poet Laureate,"* 40.
156. Greene, email message to author, March 5, 2020.
157. Fuhrmann to Moharreri, n.d., shared with the author in October 2021.
158. Fr. Gregory Pilcher, in discussion with the author, September 23, 2023, Subiaco, AR.
159. Lux, discussion.

160. Fuhrmann, "Feast of St. Joseph the Worker," private collection of Ata Moharreri.
161. Lensing, discussion, December 30, 2021.
162. Lensing, discussion, December 30, 2021.
163. Quoted in Lensing, *"Subiaco's Unofficial Poet Laureate,"* 39.
164. Dan McGrath, "Shoe Shines," *Periscope* (Subiaco Academy, Subiaco, AR), November 1964.
165. Lensing, *"Subiaco's Unofficial Poet Laureate,"* 39.
166. Lux, discussion.
167. Pendergrast, discussion.
168. A version of this story is published in B. C. Hall, "Death of a Major Voice in Arkansas," *Arkansas Times* (Little Rock, AR), December 1978.
169. Stanford, interview, 1973–74. "We all had good cologne," Frank added.
170. Lensing, *"Subiaco's Unofficial Poet Laureate,"* 17.
171. Lensing, *"Subiaco's Unofficial Poet Laureate,"* 40.
172. Pendergrast, discussion.
173. Nicholas Fuhrmann to Ata Moharreri, email, n.d., shared with the author on May 5, 2021.
174. "Junior Class Planning Jaunt to Lake Norfork," *Periscope* (Subiaco Academy, Subiaco, AR), April 1965.
175. "Various Excursions and Outings Mark Windup to Another Year," *Periscope* (Subiaco Academy, Subiaco, AR), May 1965.
176. This story was told to Leo A. Lensing by John Weinsinger, who was on the trip, and shared with the author by Lensing in a discussion on June 7, 2024.
177. Kevin Griesemer, email message to author, March 16, 2020.
178. Leo A. Lensing, in discussion with the author, September 8, 2023, Old Saybrook, CT.
179. Lux, discussion.
180. Pendergrast, discussion.
181. Fuhrmann, "To Clifford."
182. Dorothy Stanford to Father [Hubert?], n.d., Correspondence from Dorothy Stanford, SAA.
183. Dorothy Stanford to Father [Hubert?], June 21, 1966, Correspondence from Dorothy Stanford, SAA.
184. Dorothy Stanford to Father [Hubert?], n.d.
185. Dorothy Stanford to Father [Hubert?], June 21, 1966.
186. Stanford, "Frank Stanford," interview, 308.
187. Fuhrmann, "To Clifford."
188. Stanford, *What about This*, 64, 118.
189. Frank Stanford, "Snatches from a Wandering Interview on Film and Poetry," interview by Irving Broughton, *Ironwood* 17 9, no. 1 (Spring 1981): 154.
190. Frank Stanford, "Strappado," *Open Places* 11 (January 1972): 21. The comment in written in black marker on a copy of the journal that Frank gave to Donald Justice, with a note on the outside asking, "Mr. Justice, would you mind turning to my poems inside. F.S." This copy of *Open Places* is in FSP. See also Frank Stanford to Irv Broughton, February 10, 1971, LFS.

191. Irv Broughton and Frank Stanford, questions for *It Wasn't a Dream: It Was a Flood*, FSP.
192. C. D. Wright, "Frank Stanford of the Mulberry Family: An Arkansas Epilogue," *Conjunctions* 29 (1997): 298.
193. C. D. Wright, interview by Murray Shugars, n.d., transcript, CDWP.
194. Stanford, *What about This*, 4–5.
195. A. P. Walton, "Compendium of Characters in Frank Stanford's Poetry," in *Constant Stranger: After Frank Stanford*, ed. Max Crinnin and Aidan Ryan, 2nd ed. (Buffalo: Foundlings, 2019), 118.
196. Stanford, *What about This*, 4–5.
197. Stanford, *What about This*, 4–5.
198. Frank Stanford, handwritten notes, ca. early 1970s, FSP.
199. Frank Stanford, draft of *The Singing Knives*, FSP.
200. Stanford, *What about This*, 626.
201. Stanford, *What about This*, 626.
202. Dorothy Stanford to Father Herbert Vogelpohl, July 1, 1966, Correspondence from Dorothy Stanford, SAA.

## SIX

1. Frank Stanford, "Frank Stanford," interview by Irv Broughton, *The Writer's Mind: Interviews with American Authors*, ed. Irv Broughton (Fayetteville: University of Arkansas Press, 1990), 3:302.
2. Murray Shugars, "Searching for Frank Stanford," in *Constant Stranger: After Frank Stanford*, ed. Max Crinnin and Aidan Ryan, 2nd ed. (Buffalo: Foundlings, 2019), 182.
3. Nicholas Fuhrmann to Ata Moharreri, email, n.d., shared with the author in September 2021.
4. William Stafford, *Writing the Australian Crawl* (Ann Arbor: University of Michigan Press, 1978), 139.
5. Ruth Rogers, in discussion with the author, July 9, 2019, Dallas, TX.
6. Bill Willett, interview by John Erwin (director and producer of *You*, a documentary film on the life and work of Frank Stanford), n.d., transcript, shared with the author on July 12, 2023.
7. Bill Willett, in discussion with the author, October 26, 2019, Mountain Home, AR.
8. Nicholas Fuhrmann, in discussion with the author, August 10, 2019, Subiaco, AR.
9. Willett, discussion, October 26, 2019.
10. Willett, discussion, October 26, 2019. Frank's official transcript lists two English courses in fall 1966, but the professors' names are not listed on the transcript.
11. Willett, discussion, October 26, 2019; Bill Willett, "Dream of the Alluvial Field: An Interview with Bill Willett," interview by Peter J. Moore, *Rain Taxi* 13, no. 3 (Fall 2008): 38.
12. Willett, discussion, October 26, 2019.

13. Willett, discussion, October 26, 2019.
14. Willett, discussion, October 26, 2019; Fred McCuistion, in discussion with the author, April 12, 2022, Little Rock, AR.
15. Willett, interview by Erwin.
16. Rogers, discussion.
17. Vernie Harris, in discussion with the author, June 26, 2021.
18. Dick House, in discussion with the author, October 26, 2019, Mountain Home, AR.
19. "Nine Business Students Make All A's at UA," *Northwest Arkansas Times* (Fayetteville, AR), June 20, 1967.
20. This is from the bio in Frank's first book, Frank Stanford, *The Singing Knives* (Seattle: Mill Mountain, 1971), 57.
21. Frank Stanford, interview by Irv Broughton, 1973–74, FSP.
22. Official Transcript, Frank Gildart Stanford, University of Arkansas, Academic Record 39298.
23. Willett, discussion, October 26, 2019.
24. Frank Stanford, unpublished poem fragment, n.d., Prose Fragments, FSP.
25. John Biguenet, Ralph Adamo, Steve Stern, Deborah Luster, and R. S. Gwynn, in discussion with the author, January 20, 2020, New Orleans, LA.
26. Irv Broughton, draft of an autobiography, n.d., shared with the author on June 17, 2024.
27. Frank Stanford to Irv Broughton, February 10, 1971, *LPD*.
28. Willett, discussion, October 26, 2019.
29. Leon Stokesbury, "A Few Words for Frank Stanford," in Crinnin and Ryan, *Constant Stranger*, 24. The poem continues:
    He could write
    about swine. He could
    write about starfish,
    lunchmeat, Memphis,
    minnows and bay rum,
    Robert Desnos. He had
    the blue flow. He had
    the red hand. My God
    he had the touch, my friends.
30. Willett, discussion, October 26, 2019.
31. Stanford, "Frank Stanford," interview, 304. When he tried to distract himself from being unable to distract himself, Stanford did some painting. But he chose to do sumi-e painting, which required staring at a black piece of paper for hours on end before finally executing a quick slashing move with the brush. So hardly a way to reduce his obsessive focus.
32. Quoted in Edward Hirsch, introduction to *Complete Poems and Selected Letters of John Keats*, by John Keats (New York: Modern Library, 2001), xxvi.
33. Quoted in Murray Shugars, "What the Moon Says: Frank Stanford's Quest for Poetic Identity" (PhD diss., Purdue University, May 2000), 142.

34. Paul Valéry, "The Course in Poetics, First Lesson," quoted in Christopher Bollas, *Being a Character: Psychoanalysis and Self Experience* (London: Routledge, 1993), 86.
35. Frank Stanford to Bill Willett, 1972, *LPD*.
36. Willett, discussion, October 26, 2019.
37. Quoted in Shugars, "What the Moon Says," 142.
38. Stanford, "Frank Stanford," interview, 304.
39. Irving Broughton, "Playing the Child: Frank Stanford's *The Pump*," *Ironwood 17* 9, no. 1 (Spring 1981): 116.
40. Lee Upton, in discussion with the author, November 16, 2020.
41. Frank Stanford to Allen Ginsberg and Peter Orlovsky, n.d., LFS.
42. This despite telling Allen Ginsberg and Peter Orlovsky that he had been "writing a lot of surreal stuff lately." Frank Stanford to Ginsberg and Orlovsky, n.d., LFS.
43. Frank Stanford to David Walker, April 1, 1974, *LPD*.
44. Frank Stanford, unpublished prose fragment, n.d., Prose Fragments, FSP.
45. O'Connor, *Mystery and Manners*, 113. She added, "A thing is fantastic because it is so real, so real that it is fantastic."
46. Frank Stanford, "Snatches from a Wandering Interview on Film and Poetry," interview by Irving Broughton, *Ironwood 17* 9, no. 1 (Spring 1981): 155.
47. James Dickey and Robert Lowell, "James Dickey and Robert Lowell Discuss Dreams, c. 1969," ca. 1969, YouTube video, 1:51, https://www.youtube.com/watch?v=_C_oPjBr4Tg, at 1:20–25.
48. C. D. Wright, preface to *The Battlefield Where the Moon Says I Love You*, by Frank Stanford (Barrington, RI: Lost Roads Publishers, 2000), third page of the preface (unnumbered).
49. Biguenet, Adamo, Stern, Luster, and Gwynn, discussion.
50. Frank Stanford to Bill Willett, September 15, 1972, *LPD*.
51. House, discussion.
52. Stanford, interview, 1973–74.
53. Willett, discussion, October 26, 2019.
54. Leo A. Lensing, *"Subiaco's Unofficial Poet Laureate": A Memoir of Frank Stanford in High School* (Buffalo: Foundlings Press, 2022), 16. The exclamation points are in the written response by student Jim McDaniel.
55. Willett, discussion, October 26, 2019.
56. Frank Stanford, Handwritten Notes, FSP. The note continues, "He could be on a hill, overlooking water. He could be throwing them no one [sic] to somebody, or into the water."
57. Bill Lux, in discussion with the author, December 19, 2019.
58. Nicholas Fuhrmann, "Feast of St. Joseph the Worker, May 1, 2018," unfinished entry in an unpublished autobiographical manuscript, private collection of Ata Moharreri, shared with the author on November 18, 2022.
59. Dorothy Stanford to Father Herbert Vogelpohl, July 1, 1966, Correspondence from Dorothy Stanford, SAA.

60. Admission and Discharge Records, Social Service Report, Arkansas State Hospital, case history 105913, private collection of Carrie Prysock, Dallas, TX, accessed May 3, 2020.
61. Linda Mencin Bond, interview by A. P. Walton, n.d., shared with the author on December 7, 2023.
62. Tom Whalen, email message to author, July 13, 2023.
63. Willett, discussion, October 26, 2019.
64. Official Transcript, Stanford, University of Arkansas.
65. "Shoe Shines," *Periscope* (Subiaco Academy, Subiaco, AR), November 1964.
66. "He met Jimbo Reynolds when he attended the U of Arkansas. Jimbo was the shoeshine man in the student union." Ginny Stanford, email message to author, May 8, 2020.
67. Bob Ward, in discussion with the author, November 5, 2020.
68. Frank Stanford, unpublished prose piece, n.d., Prose Fragments, FSP.
69. A. P. Walton, "Compendium of Characters in Frank Stanford's Poetry," in Crinnin and Ryan, *Constant Stranger*, 123.
70. "Philosopher Finds Things are Better," *Northwest Arkansas Times* (Fayetteville, AR), March 28, 1976.
71. Willett, discussion, October 26, 2019.
72. Semon Thompson, in discussion with the author, June 13, 2020; Gordon D. Morgan and Izola Preston, *The Edge of Campus: A Journal of the Black Experience at the University of Arkansas* (Fayetteville: University of Arkansas Press, 1990), 43.
73. R. S. Gwynn, in discussion with the author, September 5, 2019, Beaumont, TX.
74. Deborah Luster, in discussion with the author, September 19, 2019. A few months before passing away in 2022, "Bad Fred" McCuistion, bedridden and fogged with dementia, finally opened his eyes and smiled when asked about "Frank and Jimbo in Fayetteville."
75. Thompson, discussion. See also Olivia Bethany Moore, " 'Black and White Together, We Shall Win': Southern White Activists in the Mississippi Civil Rights Movement" (master's thesis, 2016, University of Southern Mississippi), https://aquila.usm.edu/cgi/viewcontent.cgi?article=1215&context=masters_theses; Evin Demirel, *African-American Athletes in Arkansas* (n.p.: ED Productions, 2017), 20.
76. Ward, discussion.
77. Biguenet, Adamo, Stern, Luster, and Gwynn, discussion.
78. Thompson, discussion.
79. Ward, discussion.
80. Thompson, discussion.
81. Frank Stanford to Alan Dugan, December 1972, ADP.
82. Thompson, discussion.
83. Ralph Adamo, in discussion with the author, December 20, 2020, New Orleans, LA.
84. Rogers, discussion.
85. C. D. Wright, "Frank Stanford of the Mulberry Family: An Arkansas Epilogue," *Conjunctions* 29 (1997): 302.

86. "Philosopher Finds Things are Better," *Northwest Arkansas Times*, March 28, 1976.
87. R. S. Gwynn, in discussion with the author, August 20, 2019, Beaumont, TX; Thompson, discussion.
88. Deborah Ricks, in discussion with the author, July 5, 2020.
89. "Kiwanis Kids Football has 1 Win, 1 Tie," *Northwest Arkansas Times* (Fayetteville, AR), August 20, 1966. On bricks thrown at the house, see Ricks, discussion.
90. Demirel, *African-American Athletes in Arkansas*, 63; "Youth Leadership Training Program Planned," *Northwest Arkansas Times* (Fayetteville, AR), July 25, 1972.
91. Frank Stanford, unpublished story, n.d., Prose Fragments, FSP.
92. Pat Donat, "School Board Seeks to Better Slipping Racial Relations," *Northwest Arkansas Times* (Fayetteville, AR), February 9, 1972; "Youth Leadership Training Program Planned."
93. Willett, discussion, October 26, 2019.
94. Frank Stanford to Willett, 1972, *LPD*.
95. Frank Stanford to Willett, 1972, *LPD*.
96. Frank Stanford to Michael Cuddihy, April 1974, MCIP.
97. Stanford, interview, 1973–74.
98. Frank Stanford, unpublished story, n.d., Prose Fragments, FSP.
99. Frank Stanford to Alan Dugan, February 14, 1972, ADP.
100. Lux, discussion.
101. "Recommendation from the Ad Hoc Committee on Black Studies," Black Studies Program Materials, Special Collections, University of Arkansas Libraries (hereafter cited as BSPM).
102. Deborah Ricks in conversation with the author, June 10, 2020.
103. Crime News, *Northwest Arkansas Times* (Fayetteville, AR), April 29, 1968; Crime News, *Northwest Arkansas Times* (Fayetteville, AR), April 26, 1968.
104. Luster, discussion.
105. Frank Stanford, unpublished story, n.d., Prose Fragments, FSP.
106. Willett, discussion, October 26, 2019.
107. Lux, discussion.
108. Frank Stanford to Alan Dugan, February 14, 1972, ADP.
109. Frank Stanford to Michael Cuddihy, April 1974, MCIP.
110. Bill Willett, in discussion with the author, September 9, 2023.
111. House, discussion.
112. Willett, discussion, September 9, 2023.
113. House, discussion.
114. Willett, discussion, October 26, 2019.
115. Carl Judson Launius, "It Was a Flood: The Life and Poetry of Frank Stanford" (PhD diss., University of California, Davis), 147.
116. "Rev. James Seawood, 66," *Staten Island Advance*, January 22, 2014; see also Morgan and Preston, *The Edge of Campus*, 26.
117. Rev. James Seawood, "A Minister Recalls the Pain of Segregation," interview by Ari Shapiro, *Morning Edition*, NPR, February 20, 2009, transcript,

https://www.npr.org/transcripts/100885469. After graduating from Arkansas, Seawood went to Princeton Theological Seminary, where he trained to be a minister.
118. Frank Stanford to Alan Dugan, April 27, 1971, ADP.
119. Demirel, *African-American Athletes in Arkansas*, 36.
120. Demirel, *African-American Athletes in Arkansas*, 155.
121. Tom Whalen, in discussion with the author, July 18, 2023.
122. "U of A Campus Reacts," *Arkansas Traveler* (University of Arkansas, Fayetteville, AR), April 8, 1968.
123. Demirel, *African-American Athletes in Arkansas*, 142.
124. Unmarked folder, BSPM.
125. Tom Scott to Elaine McNeil, January 8, 1971, BSPM.
126. Demirel, *African-American Athletes in Arkansas*, 177. Brown had played for the Razorback football team as a freshman walk-on, in 1965, and was the first player to integrate the team, a factor that may have made him a target.
127. Jack Kearney, "Razorbacks Need More Blacks," *Black Americans for Democracy News* (University of Arkansas, Fayetteville, AR), November 1972.
128. Morgan and Preston, *The Edge of Campus*, 29–32; Joshua Youngblood, "Campus in 1969, Part II: Dixie, Nixon, and the 'Game of the Century,'" *365 McIlroy: Research, News, and Events from the University of Arkansas Libraries* (blog), December 5, 2019, https://librariesblog.uark.edu/campus-in-1969-part-ii-dixie-nixon-and-the-game-of-the-century/.
129. Morgan and Preston, *The Edge of Campus*, 32.
130. Stanford, interview, 1973–74.
131. A.P. Walton, "Toward Innumerable Futures: Frank Stanford & Origins" (master's thesis, Lund University, 2015), 3.
132. Launius, "It Was a Flood."
133. Bill Willett, in discussion with the author, October 18, 2019, Mountain Home, AR; Willett, "Dream of the Alluvial Field," interview, 37.
134. Rogers, discussion.
135. Matthew Henriksen, "Another Part of the Flood," *Fulcrum: An Annual of Poetry and Aesthetics: An Annual of Poetry and Aesthetics*, no. 7 (2011): 413.
136. Fuhrmann, "Feast of St. Joseph the Worker," private collection of Ata Moharreri.
137. C.D. Wright to Carl Launius, April 25, 1986.
138. Frank Stanford to Willett, September 15, 1972, *LPD*.
139. Frank Stanford to Irv Broughton, July 25, 1972, LFS.
140. Steve Stern, in discussion with the author, September 5, 2019.
141. Frank Stanford, *Hidden Water: From the Frank Stanford Archives*, ed. Michael Wiegers and Chet Weise (Nashville: Third Man Books, 2015), 38.
142. Quoted in Shugars, "What the Moon Says," 65.
143. Frank Stanford, *The Light the Dead See: Selected Poems of Frank Stanford*, ed. Leon Stokesbury (Fayetteville: University of Arkansas Press, 1991), 86.
144. Frank Stanford, "Notes," misc. scrap, 1975, GCSC.
145. Fuhrmann to Moharreri, n.d., shared with the author in September 2021.
146. Willett, discussion, October 18, 2019.

147. Biguenet, Adamo, Stern, Luster, and Gwynn, discussion.
148. Ralph Adamo, in discussion with the author, September 6, 2019, New Orleans, LA.
149. Frank Stanford, "The Smoking Mirrors," *West Coast Review* 6, no. 2 (October 1971): 29.
150. Frank Stanford, *What about This: Collected Poems of Frank Stanford*, ed. Michael Wiegers (Port Townsend, WA: Copper Canyon, 2015), 172.
151. Stanford, *What about This*, 186–87.
152. Stanford, *What about This*, 167.
153. Stanford, *What about This*, 186.
154. Stanford, *What about This*, 186.
155. Stanford, *What about This*, 186.
156. Frank Stanford, "The Kite," *Little Review* 2, no. 4 (1971): 20. Also published in Stanford, *Light the Dead See*, 79.
157. Clarence Major, *Dictionary of Afro-American Slang* (New York: International Publishers, 1970), 66.
158. Langston Hughes, *Laughing to Keep from Crying* (New York: Henry Holt, 1952); Chester Himes, *Blind Man with a Pistol* (New York: Knopf Doubleday, 1989); and Hari Rhodes, *A Chosen Few* (New York: Bantam, 1965).
159. Bond, interview.
160. Forrest Gander noted, "I think Frank played up the Black connection." Email message to author, April 18, 2022.
161. Ruth Rogers, in an undated interview with John Erwin (director and producer of *You*, a documentary film on the life and work of Frank Stanford), said, "Mother told me . . . his mother was a cheerleader, his father was a football player, they messed around, and she got pregnant . . . so they gave the baby up." Then she said of Dorothy, "She made stuff up all the time." Interview transcript shared with the author on July 12, 2023.

    The question of Frank's race preoccupied his peers. Deborah Luster said, "You know, I always suspected Frank had a little Black blood in him." Ruth said that "he might have been the son of a Black parent." In a group conversation about Frank having won the first annual Zora Neale Hurston Award (because the judge, Ishmael Reed, thought Stanford was Black), Steve Stern (only partially in jest) said, "I think he's one of the great Black poets of the twentieth century." In response, Sam Gwynn said, "Except he's not Black," to which Ralph Adamo said (and nobody disputed it), "But he sure looked like it." Another one of Frank's contemporaries put it this way: "He had features that were I guess slightly negro. Even the physique, he had a really high butt and all." Biguenet, Adamo, Stern, Luster, and Gwynn, discussion; Rogers, interview.
162. Ward, discussion.
163. Ward, discussion.
164. There is no escaping Mark Twain on this point. As William Ferris has written, "Twain blends both black and white voices within Huck's consciousness and awareness—in Huck's speech with Jim." "Southern Literature: A Blending of Oral, Visual & Musical Voices," *Daedalus* 141, no. 1 (2012): 139–53.

165. Ralph Fasold et al., "Are Black and White Vernaculars Diverging?," *American Speech* 62, no. 1 (1987): 3–80.
166. Hubert Anthony Shands, *Some Peculiarities of Speech in Mississippi* (Boston: Norwood, 1893; n.p.: Kessinger Publishing, 2010).
167. John Biguenet, in discussion with the author, October 22, 2019.
168. Biguenet, Adamo, Stern, Luster, and Gwynn, discussion.
169. C. D. Wright to Carl Launius, April 25, 1986, CDWP.
170. Biguenet, Adamo, Stern, Luster, and Gwynn, discussion.
171. Stanford, interview, 1973–74.
172. Stanford, "Frank Stanford," interview, 312.
173. Thomas Merton, "The Zen Revival," *Continuum* 1 (Winter 1964): 533.
174. Stanford, *Hidden Water*, 93.
175. Stanford, *Hidden Water*, 93.
176. Thomas Merton, *Mystics and Zen Masters* (New York: Farrar, Straus and Giroux, 1961), 24.
177. Frank Stanford to Alan Dugan, July 1, 1974, ADP.
178. Walton, "Toward Innumerable Futures," 10.
179. Willett, discussion, October 18, 2019.
180. Wright, "Frank Stanford of the Mulberry Family," 301.
181. Fuhrmann, "Feast of St. Joseph the Worker," private collection of Ata Moharreri.
182. Martin Pendergrast, in discussion with the author, March 5, 2020.
183. Fuhrmann to Moharreri, n.d., shared with the author in September 2021.
184. Rogers, interview.

## SEVEN

1. Ruth Rogers, interview by John Erwin (director and producer of *You*, a documentary film on the life and work of Frank Stanford), n.d., transcript, shared with the author on July 12, 2023.
2. Ruth Rogers, in discussion with the author, July 9, 2019, Dallas, TX.
3. Official Transcript, Frank Gildart Stanford, University of Arkansas, Academic Record 39298.
4. Paul Lubenkov, in discussion with the author, June 19, 2022. The "little green bug" reference is from Frank Stanford to Irv Broughton, November 20, 1973, *LPD*.
5. Bill Harrison, "Jim Whitehead at Vanderbilt," in *For, From, About James T. Whitehead*, ed. Michael Burns (Springfield, MO: Moon City Press, 2009), 22.
6. C. D. Wright to Michael Cuddihy, n.d., CDWP.
7. John Wood, "With Allen in Arkansas: An Ozark Diary," *American Poetry Review* 41, no. 5 (September/October 2012): 47–49.
8. Bruce Taylor, in discussion with the author, February 24, 2022.
9. R. S. Gwynn, in discussion with the author, January 4, 2022, New Orleans, LA.
10. Wright to Cuddihy, n.d., CDWP. Wright noted that his "moralizing makes me batfuck."

11. The Whitehead family, in discussion with the author, June 9, 2021, Fayetteville, AR.
12. Taylor, discussion.
13. Anonymous, in discussion with the author, May 2020, Fayetteville, AR. By mutual agreement, this discussion was conducted in confidentiality, and the name of the interviewee, who was close to Whitehead, is being withheld.
14. Jim Whitehead to Miller Williams, May 27, 1966, Miller Williams Papers, Harry Ransom Center, University of Texas at Austin (hereafter cited as MWP).
15. Jim Whitehead to Miller Williams, November 2, 1967, MWP.
16. James Whitehead, *Local Men* (Urbana: University of Illinois Press, 1979), 30.
17. Jim Whitehead to Miller Williams, October 9, 1970, MWP; Leon Stokesbury, "The Lamar Tech Football Team Has Won Its Game," *New Yorker*, October 21, 1967, 60, https://www.newyorker.com/magazine/1967/10/21/the-lamar-tech-football-team-has-won-its-game.
18. Ralph Adamo, introduction to John Stoss, *Nobody Loves Me: Collected Poems of John Stoss*, ed. Justin Chimka (New Orleans: Lavender Ink, 2021), vii.
19. Gwynn, discussion, January 4, 2022.
20. Murray Shugars to C. D. Wright, 14 November 1992, CDWP.
21. Gwynn, discussion, January 4, 2022.
22. Frank Stanford to John McKernan, November 18, 1970, LFS.
23. Frank Stanford to Allen Ginsberg, November 10, 1969, *LPD*.
24. Frank Stanford to Irv Broughton, 1970, letter fragment, p. 10, private collection of Irv Broughton, accessed August 7, 2023.
25. Gwynn, discussion, January 4, 2022.
26. John Stoss, in discussion with the author, December 13, 2019, Salinas, CA. Stanford's Arkansas transcript lists courses but not professors.
27. Ralph Adamo, in discussion with the author, September 6, 2019, New Orleans, LA.
28. Adamo, discussion, September 6, 2019.
29. Bob Ward, in discussion with the author, November 5, 2020.
30. Matt Horan, in discussion with the author, April 28, 2021.
31. R. S. Gwynn, in discussion with the author, December 14, 2022, New Orleans, LA
32. Taylor, discussion.
33. Taylor, discussion.
34. Bill Lavender, in discussion with the author, December 14, 2021, New Orleans, LA.
35. Stoss, *Nobody Loves Me*, 389.
36. Lavender, discussion.
37. Taylor, discussion.
38. Gwynn, discussion, December 14, 2022.
39. Stoss, *Nobody Loves Me*, 392.
40. Ralph Adamo, in discussion with the author, June 3, 2023, New Orleans, LA.
41. Stoss, *Nobody Loves Me*, 393.
42. Taylor, discussion.

43. John McKernan, in discussion with the author, June 28, 2022.
44. Stoss, *Nobody Loves Me*, 392–93.
45. Horan, discussion.
46. Leon Stokesbury, introduction to *The Light the Dead See: Selected Poems of Frank Stanford*, by Frank Stanford, ed. Leon Stokesbury (Fayetteville: University of Arkansas Press, 1991), x.
47. Ward, discussion.
48. Taylor, discussion.
49. Stoss, *Nobody Loves Me*, 392.
50. In a letter that appears to be from the fall of 1969, Stanford tells Allen Ginsberg and Peter Orlovsky that "I've been so busy it's been terrible, writing all these goddamn papers" and then signs off, "I've got to go to class, so I'll say goodbye." Frank Stanford to Allen Ginsberg and Peter Orlovsky, November 23, [1969], in *Hidden Water: From the Frank Stanford Archives*, ed. Michael Wiegers and Chet Weise (Nashville: Third Man Books, 2015), 185.
51. Frank Stanford, interview by Irv Broughton, 1973–74, FSP.
52. R. S. Gwynn, in discussion with the author, September 9, 2019, Beaumont, TX; W. J. Cash, *Mind of the South* (New York: Knopf, 1950).
53. Gwynn, discussion, January 4, 2022.
54. Ward, discussion.
55. Taylor, discussion. Even if Ralph Adamo, born and raised in New Orleans, dismissed it all as "rigid formalist bullshit," the emphasis centered on, as he put it, "formal issues when talking about poetry." Adamo, discussion, September 6, 2019; John Biguenet, email message to author, June 17, 2022.
56. Stanford, interview.
57. Gwynn, discussion, September 9, 2019.
58. R. S. Gwynn, Deborah Luster, Ralph Adamo, John Biguenet, and Steve Stern, in discussion with the author, January 18, 2020, New Orleans, LA.
59. Dean Young, introduction to *What about This: Collected Poems of Frank Stanford*, by Frank Stanford, ed. Michael Wiegers (Port Townsend, WA: Copper Canyon, 2015), xi.
60. Stanford, *What about This*, 7.
61. Young, introduction to Stanford, *What about This*, xii.
62. Stanford, interview.
63. John Biguenet, in discussion with the author, October 22, 2019.
64. Craig Morgan Teicher, "William Carolos Williams: 'The Red Wheelbarrow,'" Poetry Foundation, November 15, 2006, https://www.poetryfoundation.org/articles/68731/william-carlos-williams-the-red-wheelbarrow#:~:text=He%20had%20a%20famous%20maxim,is%20devoted%20to%20one%20image; "Jasper Johns," Guggenheim New York, Solomon R. Guggenheim Foundation, accessed November 6, 2024, https://www.guggenheim.org/artwork/artist/jasper-johns; and Anthony Thaxton and Robert St. John, *Walter Anderson: Extraordinary Life and Art of the Islander*, aired November 4, 2021, on PBS, video, 56:46, https://www.pbs.org/video/walter-anderson-extraordinary-life-and-art-of-the-islander-gyc1yb/.
65. Stanford, *What about This*, 12.

66. Workshop draft of Frank Stanford, "The Pump," in the possession of George Paulson. A copy of this draft was generously provided to me by Matthew Henriksen. The final version of the poem I consulted was from Stanford, *What about This*, 12.
67. Stoss, *Nobody Loves Me*, 393.
68. Stanford, *What about This*, 12.
69. Stanford, *What about This*, 12.
70. Stanford, *What about This*, 12.
71. Ward, discussion.
72. Gwynn, discussion, September 9, 2019.
73. Gen Whitehead, Ted Whitehead, and Katherine Paulsen, in discussion with the author, April 2021, Fayetteville, AR.
74. Stoss, *Nobody Loves Me*, 393.
75. Larry Johnson, email message to author, May 24, 2021.
76. Ralph Adamo, interview by John Erwin (director and producer of *You*, a documentary film on the life and work of Frank Stanford), n.d., transcript, shared with the author in July 2023.
77. Frank Stanford to Ginsberg and Orlovsky, November 23, [1969], 185.
78. Taylor, discussion.
79. Gen Whitehead, in discussion with the author, June 6, 2021, Fayetteville, AR.
80. Annette Gorden Tippen, in discussion with the author, December 15, 2023.
81. Taylor, discussion.
82. Whitehead, Whitehead, and Paulsen, discussion.
83. Gwynn, discussion, January 4, 2022.
84. Stoss, *Nobody Loves Me*, 397.
85. Taylor, discussion.
86. Gwynn, discussion, January 4, 2022.
87. Lubenkov, discussion.
88. "Miller Williams," Poetry Foundation, accessed November 6, 2024, https://www.poetryfoundation.org/poets/miller-williams.
89. As with Whitehead, many students could expect unstinting support from Miller Williams. One of his students says that, when Williams arrived, "he needed some boys. . . . He did not have any boys." Taylor, discussion. Williams took pride, according to Stoss, "in whipping us into not only good poets but his followers." *Nobody Loves Me*, 292. For students such as Bruce Taylor, the northern transplant who was kept at arm's length from the "Algonquin Round Table," Williams was a godsend. "He saved my life," Taylor said, explaining that Williams got him an assistantship and "bullied other people out of my way" when necessary. He called him "a mentor and friend and a teacher." Taylor, discussion. Others, in turn, spitefully deemed Taylor to be Williams's "puppet." Adamo, discussion, September 6, 2019. Williams was hardworking and generous. He invited all students to leave poems for him to look at and would have comments back to them by the end of the day. One student called him a "very encouraging teacher and mentor." Taylor, discussion.
90. Gwynn, discussion, September 9, 2019.
91. Stoss, *Nobody Loves Me*, 397.

92. Adamo, discussion, September 6, 2019.
93. Gwynn, discussion, January 4, 2022.
94. Sam Stephenson, email message to author, December 2, 2020.
95. Whitehead, Whitehead, and Paulsen, discussion.
96. The Whitehead family, in discussion with the author, July 12, 2023, Fayetteville, AR.
97. Nancy Harris, in discussion with the author, December 12, 2021, New Orleans, LA.
98. Ward, discussion.
99. Larry Johnson, email message to author, May 23, 2021. Johnson realized that he had to "lure Frank back to the house with my body."
100. Ward, discussion.
101. Ward, discussion.
102. Whitehead, Whitehead, and Paulsen, discussion.
103. Stoss, discussion. The quotation is from Stoss, *Nobody Loves Me*, 393.
104. Jack Butler, "Southern Baptist Zen," *Author Jack Butler* (blog), April 13, 2013, https://authorjackbutler.wordpress.com/2013/04/13/southern-baptist-zen/.
105. Gwynn, discussion, September 9, 2019; Bill Willett, in discussion with the author, October 26, 2019, Mountain Home, AR.
106. Gwynn, discussion, September 9, 2019; Willett, discussion.
107. Adamo, interview.
108. Gwynn, discussion, September 9, 2019; Willett, discussion.
109. Adamo, interview.
110. Nicholas Fuhrmann, "Feast of St. Joseph the Worker, May 1, 2018," unfinished entry in an unpublished autobiographical manuscript, private collection of Ata Moharreri, shared with the author on November 18, 2022.
111. Alan Dugan to Frank Stanford, January 6, 1972, ADP.
112. Rodney Jones, in discussion with the author, June 9, 2022, New Orleans, LA.
113. Richard Eberhart, "Frank Stanford," *Ironwood 17* 9, no. 1 (Spring 1981): 138.
114. Stanford, *What about This*, 19.
115. Frank Stanford, "Early Times in a Mississippi Liquor Store" and "The Hole," *Tansy* 1 (1970): 38–40.
116. Stanford, *What about This*, 26.
117. Gwynn, discussion, January 4, 2022.
118. Johnson, email message to the author, May 24, 2021.
119. Johnson, email message to the author, May 24, 2021.
120. Stoss, *Nobody Loves Me*, 394.
121. Biguenet, discussion, October 22, 2019.
122. R. S. Gwynn, "A Brief Survey of Frank Stanford," in *Constant Stranger: After Frank Stanford*, ed. Max Crinnin and Aidan Ryan, 2nd ed. (Buffalo: Foundlings, 2019), 56.
123. Admission and Discharge Records, Social Service Report, Arkansas State Hospital, case history 105913, private collection of Carrie Prysock, accessed May 3, 2020.
124. Frank Stanford to *Partisan Review*, March 8, 1971, LFS.
125. Frank Stanford to John McKernan, ca. Spring 1971, LFS.

126. Frank Stanford to Eleanor Bender, June 28, 1971, LFS.
127. "Staff," *Preview: The Literature* (University of Arkansas) (1970): 5.
128. Gwynn, Luster, Adamo, Biguenet, and Stern, discussion, January 18, 2020.
129. Leon Stokesbury to A. P. Walton, email, February 28, 2015, shared with the author by A. P. Walton.
130. *Preview: Eight Poets* (University of Arkansas) (1971).
131. Leon Stokesbury to A. P. Walton, email, March 3, 2015, shared with the author by A. P. Walton.
132. Quoted in Murray Shugars, "What the Moon Says: Frank Stanford's Quest for Poetic Identity" (PhD diss., Purdue University, May 2000), 22.
133. Frank Stanford to Michael Cuddihy, ca. January 1975, MCIP.
134. Quoted in Shugars, "What the Moon Says," 32.
135. Admission and Discharge Records, Arkansas State Hospital, case history 105913, private collection of Carrie Prysock.
136. Frank Stanford, note, n.d., Miscellaneous, FSP.
137. Frank Stanford to Alan Dugan, June 21, 1971, ADP.
138. Frank Stanford to Eleanor Bender, June 28, 1971, *LPD*.
139. Gwynn, Luster, Adamo, Biguenet, and Stern, discussion, January 18, 2020.
140. Lubenkov, discussion.
141. Gwynn, Luster, Adamo, Biguenet, and Stern, discussion, January 18, 2020.
142. Frank Stanford to McKernan, November 18, 1970, LFS.
143. C. D. Wright, notes on an interview of Frank Stanford by Irv Broughton, n.d., Miscellaneous, FSP.
144. Ginny Stanford to Michael Cuddihy, December 1980, MCIP.
145. Adamo, discussion, September 6, 2019. "Leon," according to Adamo, "had really watched out for Frank."
146. Irv Broughton, in discussion with the author, August 7, 2023, Spokane, WA.
147. Stanford, *What about This*, 31.
148. Adamo, interview.
149. Leon Stokesbury to A. P. Walton, email, March 6, 2015, shared with the author by A. P. Walton.
150. Frank Stanford to George Garrett, ca. January 7–12, 1973, *LPD*.
151. Frank Stanford to Lawrence Ferlinghetti, May 20, 1974, *LPD*.
152. Frank Stanford to Alan Dugan, January 12, 1973, ADP.
153. John Wood, "With Allen in Arkansas: An Ozark Diary," *American Poetry Review* 41, no. 5 (September/October 2012): 47–49.
154. Johnson, email message to author, May 24, 2021.
155. Wood, "With Allen in Arkansas," 47–49.
156. Allen Ginsberg to John Wood, October 9, 1969, LFS, n11.
157. Frank Stanford to Michael Cuddihy, ca. January 1975, LFS.
158. Wood, "With Allen in Arkansas," 47–49.
159. Stoss, *Nobody Loves Me*, 394.
160. Lubenkov, discussion.
161. Johnson, email message to the author, May 24, 2021. Irv Broughton said, "I don't think there's ever been a literary festival to equal it." Broughton, discussion, August 7, 2023.

162. Jim Whitehead to Miller Williams, June 30, 1970, MWP.
163. LFS, 47n.
164. Gwynn, Luster, Adamo, Biguenet, and Stern, discussion, January 18, 2020.
165. Irv Broughton, in discussion with the author, June 23, 2022; Kathy Walton, in discussion with the author, April 28, 2022, Fort Worth, TX.
166. John Biguenet, in discussion with the author, January 20, 2020, New Orleans, LA.
167. Johnson, email message to author, May 24, 2021.
168. John Biguenet, Ralph Adamo, Steve Stern, Deborah Luster, and R. S. Gwynn, in discussion with the author, January 20, 2020, New Orleans, LA. "He could not have been any kinder," Biguenet recalls. "I remember sitting on one of the many verandas with him just talking about books, and we really hit it off." He continued: "Frank was knowledgeable and serious. He cared mostly about international literature—one of the reasons that I think we connected and talked so much was because in those days there weren't many people who were reading internationally. He had educated himself. He was very kind. I really enjoyed being with him." Irv Broughton remembered Frank being humble and self-effacing, noting all the doubts he harbored about his work. Broughton, discussion, August 7, 2023. It is hard to find people back in Fayetteville, where Frank raged and retreated and raged some more, who observed these things about Frank.
169. Frank Stanford to Irv Broughton, August 2, 1974, LFS.
170. Frank Stanford to *Massachusetts Review*, March 1, 1971, *LPD*.
171. Johnson, email message to author, May 24, 2021; Stanford, *What about This*, 27.
172. Larry Johnson, email message to author, June 4, 2021.
173. Johnson, email message to author, May 24, 2021. Irv Broughton also remembers that "Frank screwed a gal up there at Hollins." Broughton, discussion, August 7, 2023.
174. Gwynn, discussion, January 4, 2022.
175. Gwynn, discussion, January 4, 2022.
176. Irv Broughton, interview by John Erwin (director and producer of *You*, a documentary film on the life and work of Frank Stanford), n.d., transcript, shared with the author in July 2023.
177. Broughton, discussion, August 7, 2023.
178. *Mill Mountain Review*, no. 1–2 (1970).
179. *Mill Mountain Review*, no. 1–4 (1971).
180. *Mill Mountain Review*, no. 1–2 (1970): 91.
181. *Mill Mountain Review*, no. 1–4 (1971).
182. Frank Stanford to Irv Broughton, March 1971, LFS.
183. Irv was tirelessly seeking opportunities for Frank. Irv, who had a brief fling with a children's book editor named Fran Manushkin, encouraged her to write Frank about him doing a children's book. Fran Manushkin, email message to author, June 9, 2023.
184. Gwynn, "Survey of Frank Stanford," 56.

185. Gwynn, Luster, Adamo, Biguenet, and Stern, discussion, January 18, 2020; Adamo, interview.
186. Gwynn, discussion, January 4, 2022. "God, he was an awful man," added Gwynn.
187. Taylor, discussion.
188. Gwynn, Luster, Adamo, Biguenet, and Stern, discussion, January 18, 2020; R. S. Gwynn, email message to author, July 13, 2020.
189. Ralph Adamo, in discussion with the author, September 19, 2019, New Orleans, LA.
190. John S. Morris to Frank Stanford, February 10, 1976, FSP; Ralph Adamo, email message to author, July 9, 2023.
191. Taylor, discussion.
192. Gwynn, email message to author, July 13, 2020.
193. Gwynn, "Survey of Frank Stanford," 56.
194. Alan Dugan to Frank Stanford, June 1, 1971, FSP; Frank Stanford to *Massachusetts Review*, March 1, 1971, LFS.
195. Frank Stanford to McKernan, November 18, 1970, LFS.
196. Frank Stanford to Alan Dugan, April 27, 1971, ADP.
197. Frank Stanford to Charles Plymell, July 13, 1970, *LPD*.
198. Copy of *Open Places* 11 (January 1972), with marginalia, FSP.
199. Frank Stanford to Michael Cuddihy, September 10, 1974, MCIP.
200. Frank Stanford to Donald Justice, 1971, *LPD*.
201. Frank Stanford to Donald Justice, October 1, 1971, LFS.
202. Frank Stanford to Irv Broughton, February 10, 1971, *LPD*; Frank Stanford to Irv Broughton, January 22, 1971, LFS.
203. In October 1971, Irv Broughton sent Frank Stanford a postcard claiming, "I called Len, my printer, and gave a plea. He said he'll get on the ball. Here's hoping."
204. Irv Broughton to Frank Stanford, September 21, 1971. This authentication letter was in the private collection of Irv Broughton. In late 2019, he consigned it (and other documents) to a bookdealer in California who, in an attempt to sell them, posted the documents on his website, from which I obtained screenshots of them.
205. Eleanor Bender to Frank Stanford, August 5, 1971, LFS.
206. Eleanor Bender to Frank Stanford, June 10, 1971, FSP.
207. Bender to Frank Stanford, August 5, 1971, LFS.
208. Bender to Frank Stanford, August 5, 1971, LFS.
209. Bender to Frank Stanford, June 10, 1971, LFS.
210. Frank Stanford to Eleanor Bender, July 27, 1971, *LPD*.
211. Frank Stanford to Irv Broughton, February 8, 1972, FSP.
212. Frank Stanford to *Massachusetts Review*, March 1, 1971, *LPD*.
213. Frank Stanford to Eleanor Bender, July 28, 1971, LFS. To George Hitchcock he wrote that "I've had another offer for a book, but I'm still too young." June 23, 1971, *LPD*.
214. Charles Plymell to Frank Stanford, December 10, 1970 (postmark), GCSC.

215. Eleanor Bender to Frank Stanford, November 8, 1971, FSP.
216. Frank Stanford to Eleanor Bender, November 10, 1971, LFS.
217. Ralph Adamo, discussion, September 19, 2019.
218. Broughton, discussion, June 23, 2022.
219. Frank Stanford to Justice, July 27, 1971, *LPD*.
220. Frank Stanford to Broughton, 1970, letter fragment, p. 10, private collection of Irv Broughton.
221. Frank Stanford to John McKernan, June 14, 1971, LFS.
222. Frank Stanford to Eleanor Bender, February 1, 1972, *LPD*.
223. Frank Stanford, *Hidden Water: From the Frank Stanford Archives*, ed. Michael Wiegers and Chet Weise (Nashville: Third Man Books, 2015), 167.
224. Frank Stanford to David Walker, April 1, 1974, *LPD*.
225. W. H. Auden, "In Praise of Limestone," All Poetry, accessed November 8, 2024, https://allpoetry.com/In-Praise-Of-Limestone.
226. Frank Stanford, "In the Wet Fields," n.d., FSP.
227. C. D. Wright to Carl Launius, April 25, 1986, CDWP.
228. Frank Stanford to Michael Cuddihy, March 15, 1975, MCIP.
229. Stanford, *Hidden Water*, 167.
230. Irv Broughton to Frank Stanford, n.d., private collection of Irv Broughton. In late 2019, he consigned it (and others) to a bookdealer in California who, in an attempt to sell them, posted the documents on his website, from which I obtained screenshots of them.
231. Steve Stern, "Frank Stanford (1948–1978): An Appreciation," in Crinnin and Ryan, *Constant Stranger*, 57.

## EIGHT

1. "Social issues were always her biggest platform," her daughter Blair recalls. Blair Bond and Jordy Bond, in discussion with the author, December 11, 2023.
2. Bond and Bond, discussion, December 11, 2023.
3. Linda Mencin Bond, interview by A. P. Walton, January–July 2014, shared with the author on November 23, 2020.
4. Bond, interview.
5. Frank Stanford to *Partisan Review*, March 8, 1971, LFS; Frank Stanford to *Massachusetts Review*, March 1, 1971, *LPD*; and Frank Stanford to *Kayak*, March 15, 1971, *LPD*.
6. Frank Stanford to Irv Broughton, 1970, letter fragment, p. 10, private collection of Irv Broughton, accessed August 7, 2023.
7. Frank Stanford to Irv Broughton, May 24, 1971, LFS.
8. Frank Stanford to Eleanor Bender, June 28, 1971, *LPD*.
9. Frank Stanford to Eleanor Bender, January 25, 1974, LFS.
10. Cher Ross (formerly Cheryl Campbell) remembers that Frank was at the Lindell Avenue studio "all the time," recalling only one or two nights when he was away. Cher Ross [Cheryl Campbell], in discussion with the author, December 20, 2023.

11. Cher Ross [Cheryl Campbell], text message to A. P. Walton, December 17, 2023; Ross, discussion, December 20, 2023.
12. Ross, discussion, December 20, 2023.
13. Bond, interview. The quotation about Muhammad Ali is from Frank Stanford, unpublished poetry fragment, n.d., Poetry Fragments, FSP.
14. Merideth Boswell, email message to author, April 11, 2021.
15. Bill Willett, interview by John Erwin (director and producer of *You*, a documentary film on the life and work of Frank Stanford), n.d., transcript, shared with the author on July 12, 2023.
16. Frank Stanford to Allen Ginsberg and Peter Orlovsky, November 23, [1969], in *Hidden Water: From the Frank Stanford Archives*, ed. Michael Wiegers and Chet Weise (Nashville: Third Man Books, 2015), 185.
17. Kathy Walton, in discussion with the author, July 28, 2022, Fort Worth, TX.
18. Frank Stanford to commanding officer of Bill Willett, May 5, 1971, LFS; Bill Willett, interview by the author, Mountain Home, AR, October 16, 2019. In a letter to Alan Dugan, Stanford, referring to this incident, wrote of Willett, "He got stabbed. It didn't kill him. It made him so mad, he beat the shit out of the other guy." Frank Stanford to Dugan, June 21, 1971, ADP.
19. Bond, interview.
20. Ralph Adamo, in discussion with the author, September 19, 2019, New Orleans, LA.
21. Bond, interview.
22. Frank Stanford to John McKernan, November 18, 1970, LFS.
23. A. P. Walton, email message to author, May 7, 2021; Dick House, in discussion with the author, October 19, 2019, Mountain Home, AR.
24. Notebooks of C. D. Wright, CDWP.
25. Dorothy Stanford, interview.
26. Ralph Adamo, in discussion with the author, March 21, 2021, New Orleans, LA.
27. Cher Ross [Cheryl Campbell], text message to A. P. Walton, October 7, 2023; Ross, discussion, December 20, 2023.
28. Cher Ross [(Cheryl Campbell)], in discussion with A. P. Walton, September 18, 2023, shared with the author by A. P. Walton on September 27, 2023; Cher Ross (Cheryl Campbell) in conversation with the author, discussion, December 20, 2023.
29. Bond, interview. To the best of my knowledge there are only two recordings of Frank Stanford reading his work, and one is in the film *It Wasn't a Dream: It Was a Flood*; the other is a file called "The Boathouse," cataloged by the United States Copyright Office at https://cocatalog.loc.gov/cgi-bin/Pwebrecon.cgi?v1=1&ti=1,1&SEQ=20240603160433&Search%5Farg=stanford%20frank&Search%5Fcode=NALL&CNT=25&PID=z_2GwTf17gr3j-Oo5SuanZlrREbleof&SID=2, which I have not been able to access.
30. Frank Stanford to Alan Dugan, January 13, 1972, ADP.
31. Irv Broughton, in discussion with the author, August 7, 2023, Spokane, WA.
32. Frank Stanford to Alan Dugan, April 27, 1971, ADP.

33. Frank Stanford, "Frank Stanford," interview by Irv Broughton, *The Writer's Mind: Interviews with American Authors*, ed. Irv Broughton (Fayetteville: University of Arkansas Press, 1990), 3:309.
34. Stanford to Dugan, June 21, 1971, ADP.
35. Frank Stanford to Irv Broughton, February 10, 1971, *LPD*.
36. Stanford to Broughton, February 10, 1971, *LPD*. Irv Broughton owns an example of Frank's sumi-e painting.
37. Bond, interview.
38. Once, when Irv needed some poems typed, Frank told him that he could have "my girlfriend type them." Stanford to Broughton, 1970, letter fragment, p. 10, private collection of Irv Broughton.
39. Cher Ross [Cheryl Campbell] to A. P. Walton, September 20, 2023, shared with the author by A. P. Walton; Ross, discussion, December 20, 2023.
40. Ross, discussion, December 20, 2023.
41. Admission and Discharge Records, Social Service Report, Arkansas State Hospital, case history 105913, private collection of Carrie Prysock, accessed May 3, 2020.
42. Stanford to Broughton, February 10, 1971, *LPD*.
43. Frank Stanford to William L. Fox, ca. December 24, 1972, LFS.
44. Kathy Walton, discussion.
45. Frank Stanford, *What about This: Collected Poems of Frank Stanford*, ed. Michael Wiegers (Port Townsend, WA: Copper Canyon, 2015), 726.
46. Ross, discussion, December 20, 2023.
47. Bond, interview.
48. Nicholas Fuhrmann, in discussion with the author, August 9, 2019, Subiaco, AR.
49. Larry Johnson, email message to author, May 24, 2021. When Ralph Adamo made his first trip to the cabin to see Frank, he found him sitting outside with a typewriter on a milk crate and a bottle of bourbon at the ready; he recalled that Frank was "friendly but not very talkative." Adamo, discussion, March 21, 2021.
50. Frank Stanford to Bill Willett, October 7, 1971, LFS.
51. Frank Stanford to Irv Broughton, June 18, 1971, LFS.
52. Frank Stanford to John McKernan, June 14, 1971, LFS.
53. Admission and Discharge Records, Arkansas State Hospital, case history 105913, June 6, 1972, private collection of Carrie Prysock.
54. Fuhrmann, discussion.
55. Frank Stanford to Eleanor Bender, November 10, 1971, LFS.
56. Stanford to Broughton, June 18, 1971, LFS.
57. Bond, interview.
58. Paul Lubenkov, in discussion with the author, June 19, 2022.
59. Frank Stanford, untitled poem draft, n.d., Poetry Fragments, FSP.
60. Frank Stanford to Alan Dugan, June 6, 1971, ADP.
61. Stanford to Dugan, April 27, 1971, ADP.
62. Leon Stokesbury to A. P. Walton, email, March 9, 2015.

63. Bond, interview.
64. Stanford to Dugan, April 27, 1971, ADP.
65. Frank Stanford to Eleanor Bender, July 28, 1971, LFS.
66. Fred McCuistion, in discussion with the author, April 11, 2022, Little Rock, AR; R. S. Gwynn, Deborah Luster, Ralph Adamo, John Biguenet, and Steve Stern, in discussion with the author, January 18, 2020, New Orleans, LA.
67. Stanford to Dugan, June 21, 1971, ADP.
68. Bond, interview.
69. Stanford to Dugan, June 21, 1971, ADP.
70. Kathy Walton, discussion.
71. Stanford to Dugan, January 13, 1972, ADP.
72. Stanford to *Massachusetts Review*, March 1, 1971, *LPD*.
73. Frank Stanford to Alan Dugan, February 1, 1972, ADP.
74. Frank Stanford to Alan Dugan, February 14, 1972, ADP.
75. Stanford to Dugan, January 13, 1972, ADP.
76. R. S. Gwynn, in discussion with the author, January 4, 2022, New Orleans, LA.
77. Frank Stanford, Prose Fragments, FSP.
78. Stanford to Bender, November 10, 1971, LFS.
79. C. D. Wright, preface to *The Battlefield Where the Moon Says I Love You*, by Frank Stanford (Barrington, RI: Lost Roads Publishers, 2000), third page (unnumbered).
80. "Judge Boushay Blues," Genius, ML Genius Holdings, accessed November 28, 2024, https://genius.com/Furry-lewis-judge-boushay-blues-lyrics.
81. A. P. Walton, "Compendium of Characters in Frank Stanford's Poetry," in *Constant Stranger: After Frank Stanford*, ed. Max Crinnin and Aidan Ryan, 2nd ed. (Buffalo: Foundlings, 2019), 129–30.
82. Frank Stanford, "With the Approach of the Oak the Axeman Quakes," in *Fifty Contemporary Poets: The Creative Process*, ed. Alberta Turner (New York: David McKay, 1977), 300.
83. Frank Stanford, *Hidden Water: From the Frank Stanford Archives*, ed. Michael Wiegers and Chet Weise (Nashville: Third Man Books, 2015), 135–37; Richard Leo Johnson, in discussion with the author, August 5, 2022, Savannah, GA.
84. Frank Stanford to Alan Dugan, late October 1972, LFS.
85. Stanford, *Hidden Water*, 7.
86. Walton, "Compendium of Characters," 129–30.
87. Stanford to Dugan, February 14, 1972, ADP.
88. Bond, interview.
89. Frank Stanford to Alan Dugan, July 26, 1971, ADP.
90. Alan Dugan to Frank Stanford, July 30, 1971, FSP.
91. Nicholas Fuhrmann, "Feast of St. Joseph the Worker, May 1, 2018," unfinished entry in an unpublished autobiographical manuscript, private collection of Ata Moharreri, shared with the author on November 18, 2022.
92. Frank Stanford to Álan Dugan, April 27, 1971, ADP; Ross, discussion, December 20, 2023.
93. Ross, discussion, December 20, 2023; Ross to Walton, September 20, 2023.

94. Ross to Walton, September 20, 2023. She added: "I declared my feelings but if he did not choose us I was leaving. I did not demand." By contrast "she [Linda] demanded," and Frank "acquiesced."
95. Cher Ross [Cheryl Campbell], in discussion with the author, September 20, 2023.
96. Fuhrmann, discussion.
97. Fuhrmann, "Feast of St. Joseph the Worker," private collection of Ata Moharreri.
98. Fuhrmann, discussion.
99. Fuhrmann, "Feast of St. Joseph the Worker, " private collection of Ata Moharreri.
100. Bond, interview.
101. Leon Stokesbury to A. P. Walton, email, February 23, 2015, shared with the author by A. P. Walton.
102. Stanford to Willett, October 7, 1971, LFS.
103. Stanford to Dugan, April 27, 1971, ADP. Frank wanted Linda to have the child—he had already named the baby Avalon—but Linda insisted on the abortion. "Who would have taken care of the child?" she said. "Can you imagine [Frank] taking care of an infant while writing *The Battlefield*?" Bond, interview.
104. R. S. Gwynn, "A Brief Survey of Frank Stanford," in Crinnin and Ryan, *Constant Stranger*, 64.
105. Fuhrmann, discussion.
106. Gwynn, "Survey of Frank Stanford," 57.
107. Frank Stanford to Don Kemp, October 6, 1974, *LPD*.
108. Stanford to Dugan, June 21, 1971, ADP.
109. Frank Stanford, interview by Irv Broughton, 1973–1974, FSP.
110. Gwynn, "Survey of Frank Stanford," 57.
111. John Stoss, in discussion with the author, December 11, 2019, Salinas, CA.
112. Stanford, *What about This*, 432.
113. Gwynn, "Survey of Frank Stanford," 57.
114. R. S. Gwynn, in discussion with the author, September 9, 2019, Beaumont, TX. Bill Willett, who sometimes joined Frank in the field, agreed: "He was good at his work, and he didn't screw around. He went and got it done." In discussion with the author, October 26, 2019, Mountain Home, AR.
115. Stanford to Dugan, June 21, 1971, ADP.
116. Stanford to Dugan, April 27, 1971, ADP.
117. Gwynn, "Survey of Frank Stanford," 64.
118. Admission and Discharge Records, Arkansas State Hospital, case history 105913, private collection of Carrie Prysock.
119. Gwynn, "Survey of Frank Stanford," 64.
120. Gwynn, "Survey of Frank Stanford," 64; Gwynn, discussion, January 4, 2022.
121. Gwynn, discussion, January 4, 2022.
122. Stanford to Broughton, June 18, 1971, LFS.

123. "Public Announcement," *Northwest Arkansas Times* (Fayetteville, AR), September 1, 1971, 17.
124. Stanford to Dugan, April 27, 1971, ADP.
125. Frank Stanford to Alan Dugan, June 28, 1971, ADP.
126. Stanford to Dugan, April 27, 1971, ADP. Dugan likely made the suggestions Stanford refers to in November 1970, when visiting Fayetteville.
127. Frank Stanford to Eleanor Bender, June 28, 1971, *LPD*.
128. Alan Dugan to Frank Stanford, May 5, 1971, FSP.
129. Alan Dugan to Frank Stanford, May 19, 1971, FSP.
130. Stanford to Dugan, June 21, 1971, ADP.
131. Frank Stanford to Alan Dugan, June 29, 1971, ADP.
132. Stanford to Dugan, July 26, 1971, ADP.
133. Dugan to Stanford, July 30, 1971, FSP. Frank noted in a July 29, 1972, letter to Cheryl Campbell—now Cher Ross—that "Belladonna" was written about her. Frank called her Belle. LFS.
134. Dugan to Stanford, July 30, 1971, FSP; Alan Dugan, *Poems Seven: New and Complete Poetry* (New York: Seven Stories, 2001), 222.
135. Dugan to Stanford, July 30, 1971, FSP.
136. Alan Dugan to Frank Stanford, August 11, 1971, FSP.
137. Michael Waters, interview by John Erwin (director and producer of *You*, a documentary film on the life and work of Frank Stanford), n.d., transcript, shared with the author in July 2023.
138. Stanford to Dugan, February 14, 1972, ADP.
139. Stanford to Broughton, February 10, 1971, LFS.
140. Dugan to Stanford, February 14, 1972, ADP.
141. Quoted in Thomas Moore, *The Works of Lord Byron: With His Letters and Journals, and His Life*, vol. 14 (n.p.: Palata Press, 2015), 464.
142. Stanford, *What about This*, 334.
143. Ralph Adamo, in discussion with the author, March 3, 2022, New Orleans, LA. On Bryon, see Kay Redfield Jamison, *Touched with Fire: Manic-Depressive Illness and the Artistic Temperament* (New York: Free Press, 1993), 176.
144. Gwynn, discussion, September 9, 2019.
145. Stanford, interview, FSP.
146. Stanford to *Massachusetts Review*, March 1, 1971, LFS.
147. Frank Stanford to John McKernan, July 13, 1971, LFS; Stanford, *What about This*, 465.
148. Frank Stanford, Handwritten Notes, FSP.
149. Olga Carlisle, *Poets on Street Corners: Portraits of Fifteen Russian Poets* (New York: Vintage Books, 1968), 223.
150. Frank Stanford's copy of Carlisle, *Poets on Street Corners*, with marginalia, Handwritten Notes, FSP.
151. "Sergei Yesenin (1895–1925)," *Cradle: Language, Literature, Arts and Roots*, accessed November 30, 2024, https://thecradlemagazine.com/sergei-yesenin-1895-1925/.

152. Willett, discussion.
153. Martin Pendergrast, in discussion with the author, March 5, 2020.
154. Bond, interview. A photocopy of the note from Linda to Alan Dugan, dated June 4, 1972, is included in this unpublished interview, conducted by email by A. P. Walton, called "Frank Stanford's Linda Years."
155. Frank Stanford to Alan Dugan, May 15 and 16, 1972, ADP.
156. Stanford to Dugan, May 15 and 16, 1972, ADP.
157. Bond, interview.
158. Stanford to Dugan, May 15 and 16, 1972, ADP.

## NINE

1. Frank Stanford to Alan Dugan, January 13, 1972, ADP.
2. Frank Stanford to Irv Broughton, February 18, 1972, *LPD*.
3. Frank Stanford to Alan Dugan, February 1, 1972, ADP; Frank Stanford to Alan Dugan, February 14, 1972, ADP. One thinks of Whitman's claim that "what I tell I tell for precisely what it is."
4. Frank Stanford to Alan Dugan, March 1, 1972, ADP; Frank Stanford to Alan Dugan, March 3, 1972, ADP.
5. Frank Stanford to William L. Fox, October 1972, *LPD*.
6. Frank Stanford to Irv Broughton, February 18, 1972, *LPD*.
7. Frank Stanford to Alan Dugan, August 1, 1974, ADP.
8. Frank Stanford to Broughton, February 18, 1972, *LPD*.
9. Frank Stanford to Alan Dugan, October 31–November 1, 1972, ADP.
10. Frank Stanford to Broughton, February 18, 1972, *LPD*.
11. Claude Arnaud, *Jean Cocteau: A Life* (New Haven, CT: Yale University Press, 2016), 13.
12. Derek Malcolm, "Creature Comforts: Derek Malcolm's 100 Greatest Movies. Number 24: *Beauty and the Beast*," Guardian (UK), June 30, 1999, https://www.theguardian.com/culture/1999/jul/01/artsfeatures1.
13. Lorenzo Thomas, "Finders, Losers: Frank Stanford's Song of the South," *Sun & Moon: A Journal of Literature and Art*, no. 8 (Fall 1979): 8.
14. Hortense Powdermaker, *After Freedom: A Cultural Study in the Deep South* (1939; repr., Madison: University of Wisconsin Press, 1993), 364.
15. LeRoi Jones (Amiri Baraka), *Blues People: Negro Music in White America* (1963; repr., New York: Harper Perennial, 1999), 188.
16. Frank Stanford, "With the Approach of the Oak the Axeman Quakes," in *Fifty Contemporary Poets: The Creative Process*, ed. Alberta Turner (New York: David McKay, 1977), 300.
17. Pier Paolo Pasolini, *Roman Poems*, trans. Lawrence Ferlinghetti and Francesca Valente (San Francisco: City Lights Books, 2005), 9.
18. Frank Stanford to Broughton, February 18, 1972, *LPD*.
19. Stanford, "With the Approach of the Oak," 303.
20. Irving Broughton, "Playing the Child: Frank Stanford's *The Pump*," *Ironwood 17* 9, no. 1 (Spring 1981): 116.
21. Frank Stanford to John McKernan, June 14, 1971, LFS.

22. Frank Stanford to Irv Broughton, February 10, 1971, *LPD*.
23. Frank Stanford to Alan Dugan, May 9, 1972, *LPD*.
24. Frank Stanford, "Breads and Rolls," *Northwest Arkansas Times* (Fayetteville, AR), Friday, April 26, 1972.
25. William L. Fox to Frank Stanford, September 25, 1972, LFS.
26. Frank Stanford to Eleanor Bender, July 10, 1972, *LPD*.
27. Irv Broughton, in discussion with the author, August 7, 2023, Spokane, WA.
28. Frank Stanford to Bender, July 10, 1972, *LPD*.
29. Frank Stanford to Bill Willett, July 9, 1972, LFS.
30. Frank Stanford to William L. Fox, June 19, 1972, *LPD*.
31. Frank Stanford to Alan Dugan, June 16, 1972, ADP.
32. Frank Stanford to Alan Dugan, May 15–16, 1972, ADP.
33. Frank Stanford to Willett, July 9, 1972, LFS.
34. Frank Stanford to Bender, July 10, 1972, *LPD*.
35. Frank Stanford to Bill Willett, ca. late September 1972, *LPD*.
36. Frank Stanford to Willett, July 9, 1972, LFS.
37. Frank Stanford to Willett, July 9, 1972, LFS.
38. Frank Stanford to Bender, July 10, 1972, *LPD*.
39. Frank Stanford to Bill Willett, ca. 1972, *LPD*.
40. Frank Stanford to Bender, July 10, 1972, *LPD*.
41. Frank Stanford to Alan Dugan, May 22, 1972, ADP.
42. Frank Stanford to Bender, July 10, 1972, *LPD*.
43. Frank Stanford to Willett, July 9, 1972, LFS.
44. Frank Stanford to William L. Fox, December 24, 1972, LFS.
45. Frank Stanford to David Walker, February 12, 1974, *LPD*.
46. Frank Stanford to Willett, ca. late September 1972, LFS.
47. Frank Stanford to Fox, December 24, 1972, LFS.
48. Frank Stanford to Dugan, February 14, 1972, ADP; Frank Stanford to Dugan, March 1, 1972, ADP; and Frank Stanford to Dugan, May 9, 1972, ADP.
49. Frank Stanford to Alan Dugan, May 10, 1972, ADP.
50. Frank Stanford to Irv Broughton, dated "May Day," *LPD*; Cher Ross [Cheryl Campbell], in discussion with the author, December 20, 2023.
51. Leon Stokesbury to A. P. Walton, email, February 23, 2015, shared with the author by A. P. Walton.
52. Frank Stanford to Dugan, May 15–16, 1972, ADP.
53. Frank Stanford to Theodore Solotaroff, May 15, 1972, *LPD*.
54. Frank Stanford to Alan Dugan, May 21–22, 1972, ADP.
55. Frank Stanford, "The Buried Sword," "Keeping the Lords Night Watch," "The Actresses at Night," and "The Paramour," *Iowa Review* 3, no. 3 (Summer 1972): 22–24.
56. Frank Stanford to Willett, July 9, 1972, LFS.
57. Frank Stanford to Alan Dugan, May 26, 1972, ADP.
58. Frank Stanford to Irv Broughton, Arkansas State Hospital, Little Rock, AR, ca. June 2–12, 1972, LFS.
59. Frank Stanford to Dugan, May 26, 1972, ADP.
60. Frank Stanford to Dugan, May 26, 1972, ADP.

61. Frank Stanford to Alan Dugan, May 27, 1972, ADP.
62. Frank Stanford to Irv Broughton, early June 1972, LFS.
63. Frank Stanford to Dugan, May 26, 1972, ADP.
64. Frank Stanford to Irv Broughton, June 1972, LFS.
65. Frank Stanford to Dugan, May 26, 1972, ADP. While ten thousand pages does seem like an exaggeration, it's worth remembering that Frank's output was often nonstop and obsessive. Steve Stern recalls seeing and reading from tons of stories in Frank's collection after his death, many of them hundreds of pages long. Stern, a novelist, said much of it was quite good. A. P. Walton to Leon Stokesbury, email, March 3, 2015, shared with the author by A. P. Walton. Still, Leon Stokesbury believes that the "talk about unpublished books may be a myth spread by Frank and also Carolyn." Leon Stokesbury to A. P. Walton, email, March 3, 2015, shared with the author by A. P. Walton.
66. Frank Stanford, "List of Ashes," n.d., private collection of Irv Broughton, accessed August 7, 2023, Spokane, WA.
67. John Keats, *Endymion*, preface, first page, enclosed with Stanford to Dugan, May 26, 1972, ADP.
68. Frank Stanford to Cheryl Campbell, July 5, 1972, *LPD*.
69. Stanford, "List of Ashes," n.d., private collection of Irv Broughton.
70. Linda Stanford to Alan Dugan, June 4, 1972, ADP.
71. Frank Stanford to Dugan, May 27, 1972, ADP.
72. Nicholas Fuhrmann, in discussion with the author, August 9, 2019, Subiaco, AR.
73. Admission and Discharge Records, Social Service Report, Arkansas State Hospital, case history 105913, private collection of Carrie Prysock, accessed May 3, 2020.
74. Linda Mencin Bond, interview by A. P. Walton, January–July 2014, shared with the author on November 23, 2020.
75. Frank Stanford to Walker, February 12, 1974, *LPD*.
76. Fuhrmann, discussion.
77. Admission and Discharge Records, Arkansas State Hospital, case history 105913, private collection of Carrie Prysock.
78. Nicholas Fuhrmann to Ata Moharreri, email, n.d., shared with the author in September 2021; Admission and Discharge Records, Arkansas State Hospital, case history 105913, private collection of Carrie Prysock.
79. Fuhrmann, "Frank Stanford."
80. Linda Stanford to Dugan, June 4, 1972, ADP.
81. Frank Stanford to Dugan, June 16, 1972, ADP.
82. Frank Stanford to Bender, July 10, 1972, *LPD*.
83. Nicholas Fuhrmann, "Frank Stanford: Like Rain Falling and Night Falling," unpublished manuscript, n.d., shared with the author by Ata Moharreri, May 2023.
84. Frank Stanford to Willett, July 9, 1972, LFS.
85. Admission and Discharge Records, Arkansas State Hospital, case history 105913, private collection of Carrie Prysock.
86. Frank Stanford to Bill Willett, September 15, 1972, *LPD*.

87. Frank Stanford to Willett, September 15, 1972, *LPD*.
88. Frank Stanford, *What about This: Collected Poems of Frank Stanford*, ed. Michael Wiegers (Port Townsend, WA: Copper Canyon, 2015), 118.
89. Stanford, *What about This*, 117–41.
90. Stanford, *What about This*, 117–41.
91. Admission and Discharge Records, Arkansas State Hospital, case history 105913, private collection of Carrie Prysock.
92. Admission and Discharge Records, Arkansas State Hospital, case history 105913, private collection of Carrie Prysock.
93. Admission and Discharge Records, Arkansas State Hospital, case history 105913, private collection of Carrie Prysock.
94. Admission and Discharge Records, Arkansas State Hospital, case history 105913, private collection of Carrie Prysock.
95. Linda Stanford to Dugan, June 4, 1972, ADP.
96. Alan Dugan to Frank Stanford, June 8, 1972, FSP.
97. Dugan to Frank Stanford, June 8, 1972, FSP.
98. Frank Stanford to Fox, June 19, 1972, *LPD*.
99. Frank Stanford to Cheryl Campbell, July 10, 1972, private collection of Cher Ross [Cheryl Campbell].
100. Quoted in Dugan to Frank Stanford, June 8, 1972, FSP.
101. David Walker to Frank Stanford, July 25, 1972, GCSC.
102. Frank Stanford to Bender, July 10, 1972, *LPD*.
103. Frank Stanford to Irv Broughton, early June 1972, *LPD*.
104. Frank Stanford, interview by Irv Broughton, 1973–1974, FSP.
105. Frank Stanford to Willett, July 9, 1972, LFS.
106. Frank Stanford to Broughton, early June 1972, *LPD*.
107. Frank Stanford to Broughton, early June 1972, *LPD*.
108. Frank Stanford to Alan Dugan and Judith Shahn, July 24, 1974, FSP; Fuhrmann to Moharreri, n.d., shared with the author in September 2021.
109. Frank Stanford to Fox, June 19, 1972, LFS.
110. Advertisements, *Periscope* (Subiaco Academy, Subiaco, AR), n.d.
111. Frank Stanford to Dugan, June 16, 1972, ADP.
112. Frank Stanford to Bender, July 10, 1972, *LPD*.
113. Frank Stanford to Irv Broughton, July 20, 1972, *LPD*.
114. Frank Stanford to Willett, July 9, 1972, LFS.
115. Mari Andrejco Bath, in discussion with the author, September 4, 2023.
116. Frank Stanford to Bender, July 10, 1972, *LPD*.
117. Frank Stanford to Alan Dugan, July 5, 1972, ADP.
118. Frank Stanford to Bender, July 10, 1972, *LPD*.
119. Frank Stanford to Alan Dugan, ca. July 1972, ADP.
120. Frank Stanford to Campbell, July 5, 1972, *LPD*.
121. Frank Stanford to Campbell, July 5, 1972, *LPD*.
122. Frank Stanford to Campbell, July 5, 1972, *LPD*.
123. Frank Stanford to Bender, July 10, 1972, *LPD*.
124. Frank Stanford to Willett, July 9, 1972, LFS.
125. Frank Stanford to Dugan, ca. July 1972, ADP.

126. Frank Stanford to Campbell, July 5, 1972, *LPD*.
127. Frank Stanford to Campbell, July 10, 1972, private collection of Cher Ross.
128. Frank Stanford to Broughton, July 20, 1972, *LPD*.
129. Frank Stanford to Cheryl Campbell, ca. July 29, 1972, private collection of Cher Ross [Cheryl Campbell].
130. Broughton, discussion, August 7, 2023.
131. Frank Stanford to Bender, July 10, 1972, *LPD*.
132. Frank Stanford to David Walker, February 12, 1974, *LPD*.
133. Frank Stanford to Irv Broughton, July 22, 1972, *LPD*.
134. Frank Stanford to Broughton, July 20, 1972, *LPD*.
135. Irv Broughton, text message to author, June 4, 2024.
136. James Babij, "Footsteps of the Artist," written account of the road trip, May 7, 2020, shared with the author on May 7, 2020.
137. Babij, "Footsteps of the Artist."
138. Frank Stanford to Irv Broughton, September 21, 1971, *LPD*.
139. Irv Broughton to Frank Stanford, October 1971, FSP.
140. Frank Stanford to Irv Broughton, February 8, 1972, private collection of Irv Broughton, accessed August 7, 2023, Spokane, WA.
141. Bobby Broughton's copy of Frank Stanford, *The Singing Knives* (Seattle: Mill Mountain, 1971), shared with the author by Irv Broughton on August 6, 2024.
142. David Walker to Frank Stanford, March 24, 1974, GCSC.
143. Willard A. Lockwood to Irv Broughton, March 8, 1973, private collection of Irv Broughton, accessed August 7, 2023, Spokane, WA.
144. Broughton, discussion, August 7, 2023.
145. Babij, "Footsteps of the Artist."
146. Leo Lensing, in discussion with the author, February 4, 2023.
147. Babij, "Footsteps of the Artist." This was likely Brother's Jerry's "museum," which Frank discusses in the film *It Wasn't a Dream: It Was a Flood*.
148. Fox to Frank Stanford, September 25, 1972, FSP.
149. Frank Stanford to Campbell, July 10, 1972, private collection of Cher Ross.
150. Babij, "Footsteps of the Artist."
151. Broughton, discussion, August 7, 2023.
152. Babij, "Footsteps of the Artist."
153. Frank Stanford to Alan Dugan, August 7, 1972, ADP.
154. Frank Stanford to Alan Dugan, ca. mid-August 1972, ADP.
155. Frank Stanford to John McKernan, July 27, 1974, *LPD*.
156. Frank Stanford to Michael Cuddihy, September 1974, MCIP; Frank Stanford to Malcolm Cowley, August 1, 1974, *LPD*. But he added to Cowley, in the same letter, that "I respected them."
157. Stanford, interview, FSP.
158. Frank Stanford to Cowley, August 1, 1974, *LPD*.
159. Babij, "Footsteps of the Artist."
160. Frank Stanford to Richard Eberhart, December 28–30, 1972, *LPD*.
161. Babij, "Footsteps of the Artist."

162. Richard Eberhart, "Frank Stanford," *Ironwood 17* 9, no. 1 (Spring 1981): 137. These remarks echo what Eberhart wrote to Irv Broughton in August 1978: "The news of Frank's death shocked me as it must have you. I remember him here so well, how silent he was for a day or so but then loosened up well." Eberhart to Broughton, August 5, 1978, private collection of Irv Broughton, accessed June 17, 2024.
163. Frank Stanford to Dugan, ca. mid-August 1972, ADP.
164. Frank Stanford to Dugan, August 7, 1972, ADP.
165. Babij, "Footsteps of the Artist."
166. Frank Stanford to Bill Willett, August 11, 1972, *LPD*.
167. Babij, "Footsteps of the Artist."
168. Broughton, discussion, August 7, 2023.
169. Frank Stanford to Richard Eberhart, December 28–30, 1972, LFS.
170. Stanford, interview, FSP.
171. Broughton, discussion, August 7, 2023.
172. Stanford, interview, private collection of Irv Broughton.
173. Frank Stanford to Campbell, August 10, 1972, private collection of Cher Ross. As for the Robert Lowell reference, see his poem "Skunk Hour," Poetry Foundation, accessed November 4, 2024, https://www.poetryfoundation.org/poems/47694/skunk-hour.
174. Frank Stanford to Alan Dugan, ca. mid-August 1973, ADP.
175. Frank Stanford to Irv Broughton, June 18, 1971, LFS.
176. Stanford, interview, private collection of Irv Broughton.
177. Babij, "Footsteps of the Artist."
178. Frank Stanford, *Hidden Water: From the Frank Stanford Archives*, ed. Michael Wiegers and Chet Weise (Nashville: Third Man Books, 2015), 150.
179. Broughton, discussion, August 7, 2023.
180. See Irv Broughton and Frank Stanford, *It Wasn't a Dream: It Was a Flood* (1974), 16 mm film, posted August 22, 2019, YouTube video, 26:19, https://www.youtube.com/watch?v=aPS1tXOvoC8, at 3:51–4:00.
181. Frank Stanford to Willett, August 11, 1972, *LPD*.
182. Frank Stanford to Campbell, August 10, 1972, private collection of Cher Ross.
183. Stanford, *Hidden Water*, 150–51; Frank Stanford to Fox, December 24, 1972, LFS.
184. Frank Stanford to Campbell, August 10, 1972, private collection of Cher Ross.
185. Frank Stanford to Fox, December 24, 1972, LFS.
186. Irv Broughton, ed., *The Writer's Mind: Interviews with American Authors* (Fayetteville: University of Arkansas Press, 1990), 3:128.
187. Broughton, discussion, August 7, 2023.
188. Irv Broughton, in discussion with the author, September 21, 2020.
189. Frank Stanford to Alan Dugan, October 1972, ADP.
190. Frank Stanford to Dugan, ca. mid-August 1972, ADP.
191. Broughton, discussion, August 7, 2023.
192. Ross, discussion, December 20, 2023.

193. Frank Stanford to Bill Willett, late August 1972, *LPD*.
194. Frank Stanford to Irv Broughton, ca. late September 1972, *LPD*.
195. Broughton, discussion, September 21, 2020.
196. Frank Stanford to Jim Babij, ca. mid-August 1972, *LPD*.
197. Babij, "Footsteps of the Artist."
198. Frank Stanford to Eberhart, December 28–30, 1972, *LPD*.
199. Frank Stanford to Cheryl Campbell, November 13, 1972, *LPD*.
200. Frank Stanford to Alan Dugan, ca. mid-August 1973, ADP.
201. Frank Stanford to William L. Fox, July 20, 1972, *LPD*.
202. Stanford, interview, private collection of Irv Broughton.
203. Ross, discussion, September 18, 2023.
204. Christopher Thompson, in discussion with the author, August 2023.
205. Frank Stanford to Cheryl Campbell, December 18, 1972, private collection of Cher Ross [Cheryl Campbell].
206. Frank Stanford to Bill Willett, September 13, 1972, LFS.
207. A. P. Walton, text message to author, December 11, 2023. Cheryl worked for a company called Rapidata.
208. Frank Stanford to Willett, September 13, 1972, LFS.
209. Frank Stanford to Alan Dugan, early October 1972, ADP.
210. Frank Stanford to Willett, September 13, 1972, LFS.
211. Frank Stanford to Campbell, December 18, 1972, private collection of Cher Ross.
212. Frank Stanford to Willett, September 13, 1972, LFS.
213. Frank Stanford to Alan Dugan, early October 1972, ADP.
214. Frank Stanford to Campbell, December 18, 1972, private collection of Cher Ross.
215. Frank Stanford to Bill Willett, September 14, 1972, *LPD*.
216. Frank Stanford to Alan Dugan, early October 1972, ADP.
217. Frank Stanford to Willett, September 14, 1972, *LPD*.
218. Frank Stanford to Willett, September 13, 1972, LFS.
219. Ross, discussion, September 18, 2023.
220. Frank Stanford to Irv Broughton, late September 1972, *LPD*.
221. Frank Stanford to Campbell, December 18, 1972, private collection of Cher Ross.
222. Frank Stanford to Willett, September 14, 1972, *LPD*.
223. Frank Stanford to Dugan, early October 1972, ADP.
224. Admission and Discharge Records, Arkansas State Hospital, case history 105913, private collection of Carrie Prysock.
225. Edward Hirsch, introduction to *Complete Poems and Selected Letters of John Keats*, by John Keats (New York: Modern Library, 2001), xxii.
226. Albert Camus, *Notebooks, 1942–1951* (New York: Paragon House, 1991), 96.
227. Frank Stanford to Willett, September 14, 1972, *LPD*.
228. Frank Stanford to Willett, ca. September 15, 1972, *LPD*.
229. Frank Stanford to Willett, ca. September 15, 1972, *LPD*.

230. Frank Stanford to Bill Willett, September 15, 1972, in Frank Stanford and Bill Willett, "Correspondence from Frank Stanford to Bill Willett, with Commentary by Bill Willett," ed. Matthew Henriksen, *Fulcrum: An Annual of Poetry and Aesthetics*, no. 7 (2011): 414.
231. Stanford, interview, private collection of Irv Broughton.
232. Frank Stanford to Willett, ca. September 15, 1972, *LPD*.
233. Frank Stanford to Dugan, early October 1972, ADP.
234. Frank Stanford, "I foxed them alright," n.d., GCSC.
235. Frank Stanford to Willett, ca. September 15, 1972, *LPD*; Ross, discussion, September 18, 2023.
236. Frank Stanford to Willett, ca. September 15, 1972, *LPD*.
237. Frank Stanford to Broughton, ca. late September 1972, *LPD*.
238. Frank Stanford to Willett, ca. September 15, 1972, *LPD*.
239. Cheryl Campbell to Bill Willett, September 19, 1972, private collection of Bill Willett; ellipses in original.
240. Campbell to Willett, September 19, 1972, private collection of Bill Willett.
241. Frank Stanford to Alan Dugan, October 1972, ADP.
242. Frank Stanford to Alan Dugan, early October 1972, *LPD*; Frank Stanford to Bill Willett, ca. September 15, 1972, LFS.
243. Frank Stanford to Willett, ca. September 15, 1972, *LPD*.
244. Frank Stanford to Dugan, early October 1972, ADP.
245. Frank Stanford to Dugan, early October 1972, ADP.
246. Frank Stanford to William L. Fox, January 1, 1974, *LPD*.
247. Frank Stanford to Broughton, July 22, 1972, *LPD*.
248. Frank Stanford to Willett, ca. September 15, 1972, *LPD*.
249. Frank Stanford to Alan Dugan, early October 1972, *LPD*.
250. Ross, discussion, December 20, 2023.
251. Frank Stanford to Campbell, December 18, 1972, private collection of Cher Ross.
252. Frank Stanford to Dugan, early October 1972, ADP.
253. Frank Stanford to Campbell, December 18, 1972, private collection of Cher Ross.
254. Frank Stanford to Malcolm Cowley, December 24, 1972, *LPD*.
255. Frank Stanford to Broughton, July 22, 1972, *LPD*.
256. Jane Garner, in discussion with the author, July 19, 2023; Walter Craig, email message to author, August 4, 2023.
257. Frank Stanford to Alan Dugan, late October 1972, ADP.
258. Frank Stanford to Irv Broughton, n.d., private collection of Irv Broughton, accessed August 7, 2023, Spokane, WA.
259. Frank Stanford, handwritten note at the bottom of a page of a typed fragment of Frank Stanford, "Blue Yodel of poets of times past," private collection of Irv Broughton, accessed August 7, 2023, Spokane, WA.
260. Frank Stanford, fragment of "Blue Yodel of poets of time past," private collection of Irv Broughton, accessed August 7, 2023, Spokane, WA.

261. Frank Stanford to Broughton, ca. late September 1972, *LPD*.
262. Frank Stanford to Eleanor Bender, fall 1972, *LPD*.
263. "As soon as I have (we have) something other than the fifth floor of the monastery and the monk's cabin on the lake . . ." he wrote in a letter to Cheryl. Frank Stanford to Cheryl Campbell, November 7, 1972, private collection of Cher Ross [Cheryl Campbell].
264. Frank Stanford to Alan Dugan, October 31, 1972, ADP; Frank Stanford to Alan Dugan, October 1972, ADP.
265. Frank Stanford to Campbell, November 7, 1972, private collection of Cher Ross.
266. Frank Stanford to Alan Dugan, December 2, 1972, ADP. It is worth noting here that when Greta Garbo saw Cocteau's *Beauty and the Beast*, she yelled, "Give me back my beautiful beast" when the spell was broken and the beast became a prince. I learned this from Sigrid Nunez's brilliant *The Friend* (New York: Riverhead Books, 2018), 123.
267. Frank Stanford to Campbell, November 7, 1972, private collection of Cher Ross.
268. Eberhart, "Frank Stanford," 137.
269. Frank Stanford to Campbell, November 7, 1972, private collection of Cher Ross.
270. Nicholas Fuhrmann to Frank and Ginny Stanford, October 23, 1974, GCSC.
271. Frank Stanford to Dugan, December 2, 1972, ADP.
272. Frank Stanford to Campbell, November 7, 1972, private collection of Cher Ross.
273. Frank Stanford to Dugan, October 31, 1972, ADP.
274. Frank Stanford to Alan Dugan, ca. late October 1972, ADP.
275. Frank Stanford to Campbell, November 7, 1972, private collection of Cher Ross.
276. Frank Stanford to Dugan, October 16, 1972, ADP.
277. Frank Stanford to Dugan, October 16, 1972, ADP.
278. Frank Stanford to Irv Broughton, June 1972, *LPD*.
279. Frank Stanford to Dugan, early October 1972, ADP. n

**TEN**

1. Frank Stanford to Irv Broughton, ca. late September 1972, *LPD*.
2. Frank Stanford to Bill Willett, September 13, 1972, FSP.
3. Alan Dugan to Frank Stanford, 1972, FSP.
4. "Frank was definitely a movie person back then," Bill Willett recalled. In discussion with the author, October 19, 2019, Mountain Home, AR.
5. Bill Lavender, in discussion with the author, December 14, 2021; Ralph Adamo, in discussion with the author, December 20, 2020, New Orleans, LA.
6. Bill Lavender, text message to author, December 12, 2023.
7. R. S. Gwynn, Deborah Luster, Ralph Adamo, John Biguenet, and Steve Stern, in discussion with the author, January 18, 2020, New Orleans, LA.
8. Frank Stanford to *Massachusetts Review*, March 1, 1971, *LPD*.
9. Frank Stanford to Irv Broughton, February 18, 1972, *LPD*.
10. Frank Stanford to Michael Cuddihy, August 28, 1973, MCIP.
11. Frank Stanford to Irv Broughton, February 1, 1972, LFS.

12. Frank Stanford to Bill Willett, October 7, 1971, LFS. The friend was Robert Carter.
13. James Whitehead, "One Poem from *You*," unpublished essay, n.d. This essay was commissioned by Michael Cuddihy for *Ironwood 17*, the issue in which a significant portion is a dedication to Frank Stanford, with essays by poets about Frank's work. Cuddihy chose not to run Whitehead's essay, because of "all the ambivalence, the innuendoes." It would have left Frank, he said, "turning over in his grave." "One poem from *You*" is included in Michael Cuddihy to Carolyn Wright, ca. 1979–80, LRPR.
14. Frank Stanford to Irv Broughton, ca. July 1972, LFS.
15. Frank Stanford, interview by Irv Broughton, n.d., private collection of Irv Broughton, accessed August 7, 2023, Spokane, WA. In the summer of 1974 Nan Talese wrote to Frank about his essays on poets in the cinema, saying that she would love to see them and help Frank get an agent. Nan Talese to Frank Stanford, July 30, 1974, FSP.
16. Frank Stanford to Irv Broughton, December 31, 1972, *LPD*.
17. Frank Stanford, "Snatches from a Wandering Interview on Film and Poetry," interview by Irving Broughton, *Ironwood 17* 9, no. 1 (Spring 1981): 155.
18. Ginny Crouch Stanford to Michael Cuddihy, n.d., MCIP.
19. Irv Broughton, in discussion with the author, August 7, 2023, Spokane, WA.
20. Nicholas Fuhrmann, "Frank Stanford: Like Rain Falling and Night Falling," unpublished manuscript, n.d., shared with the author by Ata Moharreri, May 2023.
21. Frank Stanford to Father Herbert, n.d., Dorothy Stanford file, SAA.
22. Frank Stanford to Irv Broughton, December 28, 1972 (postmark), LFS.
23. Frank Stanford to Cheryl Campbell, November 7, 1972, private collection of Cher Ross [Cheryl Campbell].
24. Frank Stanford to Irv Broughton, ca. late September 1972, *LPD*.
25. Fuhrmann, "Frank Stanford."
26. Frank Stanford to Irv Broughton, ca. late September 1972, *LPD*.
27. Frank Stanford to Alan Dugan, early October 1972, LFS.
28. Eric Horsting to Frank Stanford, January 26, 1973, FSP.
29. Frank Stanford to Michael Cuddihy, May 30, 1974, MCIP.
30. Frank Stanford, "Frank Stanford," interview by Irv Broughton, *The Writer's Mind: Interviews with American Authors*, ed. Irv Broughton (Fayetteville: University of Arkansas Press, 1990), 3:306.
31. Frank Stanford, "With the Approach of the Oak," 300.
32. Frank Stanford to Richard Eberhart, December 27–31, 1972, *LPD*.
33. Frank Stanford to Alan Dugan, July 24, 1974, ADP.
34. Gwynn, Luster, Adamo, Biguenet, and Stern, discussion.
35. William L. Fox to Frank Stanford, December 19, 1973, LFS.
36. Frank Stanford to Eleanor Bender, December 4, 1972, *LPD*.
37. Frank Stanford to Cheryl Campbell, December 12, 1972, private collection of Cher Ross [Cheryl Campbell].
38. Frank Stanford, "If found, please return to:," Notebook 1, 1972–75, GCSC.

39. Frank Stanford to Alan Dugan, ca. late October 1972, ADP.
40. Cheryl Campbell to Frank Stanford, November 1, 1972, private collection of Irv Broughton, accessed August 7, 2023, Spokane, WA.
41. Frank Stanford to Cheryl Campbell, November 13, 1972, *LPD*.
42. Frank Stanford to Cheryl Campbell, December 2, 1972, private collection of Cher Ross [Cheryl Campbell].
43. Frank Stanford to Campbell, December 2, 1972, private collection of Cher Ross.
44. Frank Stanford to Cheryl Campbell, December 18, 1972, private collection of Cher Ross [Cheryl Campbell].
45. Frank Stanford to Campbell, December 18, 1972, private collection of Cher Ross.
46. Frank Stanford to Campbell, December 18, 1972, private collection of Cher Ross.
47. Frank Stanford to Campbell, December 18, 1972, private collection of Cher Ross.
48. David Zimmerman, in discussion with the author, August 10, 2023, Eureka Springs, AR.
49. Barbara Scott, in discussion with the author, July 28, 2023.
50. Scott, discussion.
51. Willett, discussion; Ginny Stanford, email message to author, November 17, 2019. On the New Orleans Hotel: Located on Spring Street, it was called by the local paper a "hostelry." When Frank lived there, it had just been sold by Leonard and Russell Bjorkman to Mrs. Barbara Scott. The place had six apartments and thirty guest rooms. Originally built in 1892. Scott, discussion.
52. Frank Stanford to Broughton, December 28, 1972 (postmark), LFS.
53. Frank Stanford to Irv Broughton, ca. mid-February 1973, LFS.
54. Crescent Dragonwagon, in discussion with the author, August 23, 2023.
55. Frank Stanford to Alan Dugan, January 9–12, 1973, postcard series, *LPD*.
56. Frank Stanford to Alan Dugan, January 12, 1973, ADP.
57. Frank Stanford to Carolyn Gilbert, January 7–12, 1973, *LPD*.
58. Frank Stanford to Broughton, ca. mid-February 1973, LFS.
59. Clarke Freeman, in discussion with the author, August 9, 2023, Eureka Springs, AR.
60. Frank Stanford to Gilbert, January 7–12, 1973, *LPD*.
61. Frank Stanford to Broughton, ca. late January / early February 1973, LFS.
62. Frank Stanford to Irv Broughton, February 22, 1973, LFS.
63. Dragonwagon, discussion. Dragonwagon recalled how she worked occasionally in the Crescent Hotel washing dishes for cash.
64. Frank Stanford to Gilbert, January 7–12, 1973, *LPD*.
65. Frank Stanford, "In the Wet Fields," n.d., Prose Fragments, FSP.
66. Frank Stanford to William L. Fox, n.d., West Coast Poetry Review Records, John Hay Library, Brown University (hereafter cited as WCPRR).
67. Frank Stanford, Prose Fragments, FSP.
68. Frank Stanford to Mr. and Mrs. Cowley, August 1, 1974, LFS.
69. Frank Stanford to David Walker, February 12, 1974, *LPD*.

70. Frank Stanford, Prose Fragments, FSP.
71. Frank Stanford to Campbell, December 18, 1972, private collection of Cher Ross.
72. Dragonwagon, discussion.
73. Frank Stanford to Irv Broughton, late January / early February 1973, *LPD*.
74. Frank Stanford to Irv Broughton, late January / early February 1973, LFS.
75. Frank Stanford to Gilbert, January 7–12, 1973, *LPD*.
76. Frank Stanford to Alan Dugan, January 12, 1973, postcard series, FSP.
77. Willett, discussion.
78. Frank Stanford to Gilbert, January 7–12, 1973, *LPD*; emphasis added.
79. Frank Stanford to Alan Dugan, January 9–12, 1973, postcard series, *LPD*.
80. Frank Stanford to Cheryl Campbell, January 15, 1973 (postmark), private collection of Cher Ross [Cheryl Campbell].
81. Linda Mencin Bond, interview by A. P. Walton, January–July 2014, shared with the author on November 23, 2020.
82. Stanford, "Wandering Interview," interview, 153.
83. Willett, discussion.
84. "He brought the movies to [the University of] Arkansas," classmate R. S. Gwynn recalled, "several times a week." Gwynn, Luster, Adamo, Biguenet, and Stern, discussion.
85. R. S. Gwynn, in discussion with the author, January 4, 2022, New Orleans, LA.
86. Frank Stanford to Alan Dugan, June 25, 1973, ADP.
87. Frank Stanford to Dugan, June 25, 1973, ADP; Frank Stanford to George Garrett, ca. winter 1973, *LPD*.
88. Broughton, discussion. "Send Janus address," Frank wrote to Irv on February 1, 1973. Frank Stanford to Irv Broughton, February 1, 1973, LFS.
89. Bill Willett, "Dream of the Alluvial Field: An Interview with Bill Willett," interview by Peter J. Moore, *Rain Taxi* 13, no. 3 (Fall 2008): 39
90. Frank Stanford to Irv Broughton, February 27, 1973, private collection of Irv Broughton, accessed August 6, 2023.
91. Zimmerman, discussion.
92. Gwynn, Luster, Adamo, Biguenet, and Stern, discussion.
93. Frank Stanford and Bill Willett, "Correspondence from Frank Stanford to Bill Willett, with Commentary by Bill Willett," ed. Matthew Henriksen, *Fulcrum: An Annual of Poetry and Aesthetics*, no. 7 (2011): 412.
94. Willett, "Dream of the Alluvial Field," interview, 39.
95. Frank Stanford to Michael Cuddihy, August 30, 1974, MCIP.
96. Frank Stanford to Walker, February 12, 1974, *LPD*.
97. Willett, discussion; Ginny Stanford, email message to the author, November 17, 2021.
98. Frank Stanford to David Walker, February 12, 1974, *LPD*.
99. Frank Stanford to Campbell, December 18, 1972, private collection of Cher Ross.
100. Frank Stanford to Ginny Stanford and C. D. Wright, May 21, 1978, FSP.
101. Frank mentioned the idea of living on a farm, possibly with Cheryl, in letters written to Cheryl in August 1972 and January 1973. Frank Stanford

to Cheryl Campbell, August 11, 1972, *LPD*; Frank Stanford to Campbell, January 15, 1973, private collection of Cher Ross.
102. Frank Stanford to Gilbert, January 7–12, 1973, *LPD*. It's possible that, right after arriving in Eureka Springs, he might have tried to spend a couple of months with his uncle Jimmy Lee in Greenville, working on his farm to earn some cash. He mentioned in an early 1973 letter to Irv that he was "on this farm until early spring" but then also noted to his grandmother how "the only other thing I wanted was to work for Uncle Jimmy, and I muffed that." Frank Stanford to Irv Broughton, January 12, 1972, *LPD*.
103. Frank Stanford to Gilbert, January 7–12, 1973, *LPD*.
104. Frank Stanford to Campbell, January 15, 1973, private collection of Cher Ross.
105. Frank Stanford to Gilbert, January 7–12, 1973, *LPD*.
106. Irv Broughton to Frank Stanford, [January or February 1973?], FSP.
107. The Morris family to Frank Stanford, December 6, 1973, GCSC.
108. Gwynn, Luster, Adamo, Biguenet, and Stern, discussion. For "amnesia Frank" I also relied on a conversation with Tracye Wear, April 25, 2024, who immediately called him "amnesia Frank" without prompting.
109. See Carolina Soraggi-Frez et al., "Disentangling Working Memory Functioning in Mood States of Bipolar Disorder: A Systematic Review," Frontiers in Psychology 8 (April 26, 2017), https://pmc.ncbi.nlm.nih.gov/articles/PMC5405335/.
110. Frank Stanford to Walker, February 12, 1974, *LPD*.
111. Frank Stanford to Broughton, February 27, 1973, LFS.
112. Admission and Discharge Records, Arkansas State Hospital, case history 105913, p. 7, private collection of Carrie Prysock, accessed May 3, 2020.
113. Frank Stanford to John McKernan, July 13, 1971, LFS.
114. Frank Stanford to Walker, February 12, 1974, *LPD*.
115. Zimmerman, discussion.
116. Frank Stanford to Fox, n.d., WCPRR.
117. Frank Stanford to Alan Dugan, January 9–12, 1973, postcard series, *LPD*.
118. Frank Stanford to Alan Dugan, October 12, 1973, ADP.
119. Frank Stanford to Alan Dugan, March 1973, ADP.
120. Zimmerman, discussion.
121. Willett, discussion.
122. Frank Stanford to Alan Dugan, January 9–12, 1973, postcard series, *LPD*.
123. Frank Stanford to Irv Broughton, February 27, 1973, private collection of Irv Broughton, accessed August 7, 2023, Spokane, WA.
124. Frank Stanford to gran, n.d., private collection of Carrie Prysock.
125. Frank Stanford to Broughton, late January / early February 1973, *LPD*.
126. Frank Stanford to Irv Broughton, February 27, 1973, LFS.
127. Frank Stanford to George Garrett, ca. January 7–12, 1973, *LPD*.
128. Lawrence Ferlinghetti to Frank Stanford, January 3, 1973, FSP.
129. Frank Stanford to Irv Broughton, [January–February 1973?], LFS.
130. Frank Stanford to William L. Fox, ca. January 9–12, 1973, LFS.
131. Frank Stanford to Irv Broughton, ca. mid-January 1973, LFS.
132. Freeman, discussion, August 9, 2023.

133. Zimmerman, discussion.
134. Dragonwagon, discussion.
135. Clarke Freeman, in discussion with the author, June 23, 2023.
136. Freeman, discussion, August 9, 2023.
137. Dragonwagon, discussion.
138. Frank Stanford to Dugan, June 25, 1973, ADP.
139. Freeman, discussion, August 9, 2023.
140. Ginny Stanford, email message to the author, November 17, 2020.
141. A. P. Walton, email message to the author, July 6, 2023.
142. Freeman, discussion, June 23, 2023.
143. C. D. Wright, preface to *The Battlefield Where the Moon Says I Love You*, by Frank Stanford (Barrington, RI: Lost Roads Publishers, 2000), third page of the preface (unnumbered).
144. Frank Stanford to Irv Broughton, March 11, 1973, *LPD*; Frank Stanford to Irv Broughton, ca. late January / early February 1973, *LPD*.
145. Frank Stanford to David Walker, April 1, 1974, *LPD*.
146. Frank Stanford, "With the Approach of the Oak," 238.
147. Frank Stanford to Alan Dugan, October 16, 1972, ADP.
148. Frank Stanford to Irv Broughton, ca. mid-February 1973, *LPD*.
149. Frank Stanford to Dugan, October 16, 1972, ADP.
150. Frank Stanford to Eberhart, December 27–31, 1972, *LPD*.
151. Stanford and Willett, "Frank Stanford to Bill Willett," 412.
152. Frank Stanford to Irv Broughton, n.d., private collection of Irv Broughton, accessed August 7, 2023, Spokane, WA.
153. Frank Stanford to Garrett, ca. January 7–12, 1973, *LPD*.
154. Frank Stanford to Dugan, October 16, 1972, ADP.
155. Stanford, "Wandering Interview," interview, 154.
156. Frank Stanford, interview by Irv Broughton, 1973–1974, FSP.
157. Frank Stanford, "With the Approach of the Oak," 236.
158. Frank Stanford to Irv Broughton, July 17–18, 1974, FSP.
159. Frank Stanford to Dugan, October 16, 1972, ADP.
160. Frank Stanford, *What about This: Collected Poems of Frank Stanford*, ed. Michael Wiegers (Port Townsend, WA: Copper Canyon, 2015), 728.
161. Frank Stanford to Irv Broughton, ca. late January / early February 1973, *LPD*.
162. Frank Stanford to Dugan, October 16, 1972, ADP.
163. Stanford, "Wandering Interview," interview, 153.
164. James Babij to Frank Stanford, n.d., FSP.
165. James Babij to Frank Stanford, September 14, 1972, FSP.
166. Frank Stanford to Dugan, October 16, 1972, ADP.
167. James Babij to Frank Stanford, July 2, 1973, FSP.
168. James Babij to Frank Stanford, February 16, 1973, FSP; Lord Byron, "English Bards and Scottish Reviewers," in *Lord Byron: Selected Poems*, ed. Susan J. Wolfson and Peter J. Manning (New York: Penguin Books, 1996), 22.
169. Babij to Frank Stanford, February 16, 1973, FSP.
170. Babij to Frank Stanford, July 2, 1973, FSP.
171. Babij to Frank Stanford, July 2, 1973, FSP.

172. See Frank Stanford, Notebook 2, GCSC.
173. Frank Stanford to Irv Broughton, December 23, 1972, LFS.
174. Frank Stanford to Broughton, December 31, 1972, *LPD*.
175. Frank Stanford to Irv Broughton, November 17, 1972, LFS.
176. Irv Broughton to Frank Stanford, [January–February 1973], FSP.
177. Irv Broughton to Frank Stanford, n.d., FSP.
178. Irv Broughton to Frank Stanford, [January–February 1973], FSP.
179. Broughton, discussion.
180. Frank Stanford to Irv Broughton, [January–February 1973?], LFS.
181. Irv Broughton to Frank Stanford, February 8, 1973, FSP. Broughton would later write a novel about Dorothy and the levee camps called *The Levees that Break in My Heart* (self-pub., Open Look Books, 2016).
182. Broughton to Frank Stanford, February 8, 1973, FSP. The cinema issue never ran.
183. Irv Broughton to Frank Stanford, [February–May?] 1973, cache of Frank Stanford letters, Whitmore Rare Books, Pasadena, CA. My copy was obtained from a posting of the collection by Whitmore Rare Books on AbeBooks.
184. Irv Broughton to Frank Stanford, May 15, 1973 (postmark), FSP.
185. Frank Stanford, Handwritten Notes, FSP.
186. Ginny Stanford, email message to author, November 16, 2020. Ginny's parents' primary residence was in Fort Scott, Kansas, but they went to their house in Neosho on weekends. Frank Stanford to Alan Dugan, July 1, 1974, ADP.
187. Ginny Stanford, email message to author, November 16, 2020.
188. Ginny Stanford, email message to author, November 16, 2020.
189. Ginny Stanford, "Requiem: A Fragment," *New Orleans Review* 20, no. 3/4 (1994): 159.
190. Frank Stanford, interview, 1973–74.
191. Ginny Stanford, "Requiem: A Fragment," 159.
192. Ginny Stanford, email message to author, November 16, 2020.
193. Ginny Stanford, "Requiem: A Fragment," 160.
194. Ginny Stanford, email message to author, November 17, 2020.
195. Frank Stanford to Irv Broughton, December 30, 1972, LFS. One hundred eighty pounds was normal for him.
196. Frank Stanford to Broughton, March 11, 1973, *LPD*.
197. Frank Stanford to Cheryl Campbell, January 1, 1973 (or December 31, 1972), private collection of Cher Ross [Cheryl Campbell], shared with the author by A. P. Walton on December 14, 2023.
198. Bill Willett, text message to author, December 17, 2023.
199. Cher Ross [Cheryl Campbell], in discussion with A. P. Walton, December 2023. "Frank needed women who could support him," Cheryl, who could not support him, observed.
200. Frank Stanford, Notebook 2, GCSC.
201. Frank Stanford to Irv Broughton, March 14, 1973, *LPD*.
202. A. P. Walton, email message to author, June 22, 2023.
203. Ginny Stanford, email message to author, November 16, 2020.

204. Ginny Stanford, email message to author, November 17, 2020.
205. Alan Dugan to Frank Stanford, June 27, 1973, in *Hidden Water: From the Frank Stanford Archives*, by Frank Stanford, ed. Michael Wiegers and Chet Weise (Nashville: Third Man Books, 2015), 179.
206. Frank Stanford to Alan Dugan, June 23, 1973, ADP.
207. Frank Stanford to Irv Broughton, June 11, 1973, *LPD*.
208. Frank Stanford to Dugan, June 25, 1973, ADP.
209. Frank Stanford to Broughton, June 11, 1973, *LPD*.
210. Ginny Stanford, "Requiem: A Fragment," 164. The Mozart quotation is taken from Matthew Aucoin, "Alone in Paradise," *New York Review of Books*, March 7, 2024, https://www.nybooks.com/articles/2024/03/07/alone-in-paradise-picture-a-day-like-this/.
211. Frank Stanford to Dugan, June 25, 1973, ADP.
212. Ginny Stanford, email message to author, November 17, 2020.
213. Frank Stanford to Broughton, June 11, 1973, *LPD*.
214. Frank Stanford to Dugan, June 23, 1973, ADP.
215. Cher Ross [Cheryl Campbell], in discussion with the author, December 20, 2023.
216. Frank Stanford to Cheryl Campbell, May 15, 1973, private collection of Cher Ross [Cheryl Campbell], shared with the author on December 14, 2023.
217. Ross, discussion.
218. Ross, discussion.
219. Ginny Stanford, email message to author, November 17, 2020.
220. Frank Stanford to Alan Dugan, March 14, 1974, ADP.
221. Ginny Stanford, email message to author, November 16, 2020.
222. Frank Stanford to Michael Cuddihy, April 1974, MCIP.
223. Ginny Stanford, email message to author, November 17, 2020.
224. Frank Stanford to Walker, February 12, 1974, *LPD*.
225. Ginny Stanford, email message to author, November 16, 2020; A. P. Walton, in discussion with the author, June 17, 2023.
226. Frank Stanford to Alan Dugan, January 22, 1974, ADP.
227. Frank Stanford to Walker, February 12, 1974, *LPD*.
228. Frank Stanford, Handwritten Notes, FSP.
229. Ginny Stanford, email message to author, November 18, 2020.
230. Broughton, discussion.
231. Ginny Stanford, "Requiem: A Fragment," 151.
232. Frank Stanford to Irv Broughton, June 11, 1973, *LPD*.
233. Irv Broughton, interview by John Erwin (director and producer of *You*, a documentary film on the life and work of Frank Stanford), n.d., transcript, shared with the author in July 2023.
234. Ginny Stanford, email message to author, November 16, 2020.
235. Broughton, interview.
236. Frank Stanford to Irv Broughton, May 8, 1974, *LPD*.
237. Broughton, discussion.
238. Broughton, discussion. There was only one scene that Irv filmed with a sound camera, one he borrowed—an "ancient sound camera": It was a few seconds of Frank and Jimbo Reynolds sitting outside of Sherman's talking about dreams.

239. Irv Broughton to Frank Stanford, April 8, 1974, FSP.
240. Broughton to Frank Stanford, April 8, 1974, FSP.
241. Ginny Stanford, "Requiem: A Fragment," 153.
242. Irv Broughton to Frank Stanford, [spring 1974?], FSP.
243. Broughton to Frank Stanford, April 8, 1974, FSP.
244. Broughton to Frank Stanford, April 8, 1974, FSP; Irv Broughton to Frank Stanford, [spring 1974?], FSP.
245. Broughton to Frank Stanford, [spring 1974?], FSP.
246. Irv Broughton to Frank Stanford, [spring 1974?], FSP.
247. Broughton, discussion.
248. Irv Broughton to Frank Stanford, [spring 1974?], FSP.
249. Eleanor Bender to Frank Stanford, October 18, 1973, FSP. The poems never ran in *Open Places*, but two of them appeared in *Ladies from Hell* (1974). Bender was not alone in her opinion of Frank's unevenness. Ira Sadoff, editor at *Antioch Review*, said that Frank was "a talented but somewhat erratic poet." Email message to author, December 17, 2019.
250. Frank Stanford, *What about This*, 131.
251. Pier Paolo Pasolini, *Roman Poems*, trans. Lawrence Ferlinghetti and Francesca Valente (San Francisco: City Lights Books, 2005), 23.
252. Frank Stanford, *What about This*, 131.
253. Frank Stanford, *What about This*, 131.
254. Frank Stanford, *What about This*, 131.
255. Frank Stanford, excerpt of "Blue Yodel of poets of times past," *Boston Phoenix*, December 18, 1973.
256. Frank Stanford, *What about This*, 277.
257. Frank Stanford, *What about This*, 133.
258. A. P. Walton, "Toward Innumerable Futures: Frank Stanford & Origins," (master's thesis, Lund University, 2015), 57.
259. C. D. Wright, "Frank Stanford," in *The Before Columbus Foundation Poetry Anthology: Selections from the American Book Awards, 1980–1990*, ed. J. J. Phillips et al. (New York: W. W. Norton, 1992), 340.
260. Frank Stanford to Michael Cuddihy, "Last Day of Summer" [1973?], MCIP.
261. Michael Cuddihy, *Try Ironwood: An Editor Remembers* (Boston: Rowan Tree, 1990), 3, 5, 7, 22, 27, 34, 40. *Kayak* was an experimental literary journal. It is ironic that, despite frequent phone calls and a voluminous correspondence, Cuddihy—who lived in Tucson—and Frank never met in person.
262. Frank Stanford to Michael Cuddihy, April 1974, MCIP. Frank quotes Cuddihy saying, "I'm harder on you" back to him in this letter.
263. Cuddihy, *Try Ironwood*, 42.
264. Cuddihy, *Try Ironwood*, 42.
265. Michael Cuddihy to Frank Stanford, n.d., FSP.
266. Michael Cuddihy to Frank Stanford, [late 1973 before Dec 15?], FSP.
267. Frank Stanford to Michael Cuddihy, December 15, 1973, MCIP. Frank had not published in *Esquire*.
268. Frank Stanford to Alan Dugan, October 13, 1973, ADP.

269. Ginny Stanford, email message to author, November 16, 2020.
270. Ginny Stanford, email message to author, November 16, 2020.

## ELEVEN

1. Unless otherwise noted, this opening section relies on one letter: Frank Stanford to David Walker, February 12, 1974, *LPD*.
2. Ellipsis in original.
3. Frank Stanford, interview by Irv Broughton, 1973–74, FSP.
4. David Walker to Frank Stanford, March 1, 1974, FSP.
5. Frank Stanford to Irv Broughton, July 7–12, 1974, LFS.
6. Frank Stanford to Michael Cuddihy, April 1974, MCIP.
7. Judy Culbreth to Francis Gildart, January 11, 1973, FSP; Frank Stanford, *Hidden Water: From the Frank Stanford Archives*, ed. Michael Wiegers and Chet Weise (Nashville: Third Man Books, 2015), 132–33.
8. Frank Stanford, *Hidden Water*, 132–33.
9. A. Sobin to Frank Stanford, June 15, 1974, FSP.
10. Eric Horsting to Frank Stanford, March 4, 1973, FSP.
11. Arthur Vogelsang to Frank Stanford, June 10, 1974, FSP; Arthur Vogelsang to Frank Stanford, July 23, 1974, FSP.
12. Vogelsang to Frank Stanford, June 10, 1974, FSP.
13. Arthur Vogelsang to Frank Stanford, August 6, 1974, FSP.
14. Arthur Vogelsang to Frank Stanford, September 27, 1974, FSP.
15. "What about This," and "They Really Do," *American Poetry Review* 4, no. 2 (March/April 1975): 7.
16. Stuart Friebert to Frank Stanford, n.d., FSP.
17. Frank Stanford to Michael Cuddihy, May 22, 1974, MCIP.
18. Frank Stanford to Michael Cuddihy, May 1, 1974, MCIP.
19. Frank Stanford to Michael Cuddihy, April 1974, MCIP.
20. Frank Stanford to Michael Cuddihy, November 12, 1974, MCIP; Michael Cuddihy to Frank Stanford, May 14, 1974, FSP.
21. Michael Cuddihy to Frank Stanford, May 14, 1974, FSP.
22. Michael Cuddihy to Frank Stanford, March 10, 1975, FSP.
23. Michael Cuddihy to Frank Stanford, May 14, 1974, FSP.
24. Admission and Discharge Records, Social Service Report, Arkansas State Hospital, case history 105913, private collection of Carrie Prysock, accessed May 3, 2020.
25. Frank Stanford to Michael Cuddihy, late July 1974, MCIP.
26. C. D. Wright to Pamela Steward, n.d., CDWP.
27. A. P. Walton, text message to author, November 20, 2023. Walton noted that this book was delayed beyond its publication year just as *The Singing Knives* had been.
28. Frank Stanford, *Ladies from Hell* (Seattle: Mill Mountain, 1974), 9. Although it is unclear where Ginny saw the photo, a more recent print of it can be found in Eudora Welty, *Photographs* (Jackson: University of Mississippi Press, 1989), 15.

29. David Walker to Frank Stanford, June 18, 1975, FSP.
30. William Stafford to Frank Stanford, June 16, 1975, FSP.
31. Frank Stanford, *Ladies from Hell*, 26–27.
32. Irv Broughton and Frank Stanford, *It Wasn't a Dream: It Was a Flood* (1974), 16 mm film, posted August 22, 2019, YouTube video, 26:19, https://www.youtube.com/watch?v=aPS1tXOvoC8&t=315s, at 11:10–12:10.
33. Frank Stanford, *Ladies from Hell*, 12.
34. Frank Stanford to Ralph Adamo, February 20, 1978, *LPD*.
35. Frank Stanford to Alan Dugan, January 22, 1974, ADP.
36. Frank Stanford to Alan Dugan, May 20, 1974, ADP.
37. Frank Stanford, *What about This: Collected Poems of Frank Stanford*, ed. Michael Wiegers (Port Townsend, WA: Copper Canyon, 2015), 119.
38. Frank Stanford, *What about This*, 121.
39. Frank Stanford, *What about This*, 132.
40. Frank Stanford, *What about This*, 133.
41. Frank Stanford, *What about This*, 124.
42. Frank Stanford, *What about This*, 122.
43. Frank Stanford, *What about This*, 125.
44. Thomas Lux, handwritten notes for an article he was writing on Frank Stanford's death, in the possession of Jennifer Lux, Thomas Lux's widow. I found it at her Atlanta home in the summer of 2021. The article was published in *FIELD* 20 (Spring 1979): 50.
45. Ginny Stanford writes in an untitled, unpublished manuscript written in the early 1990s and shared with Ralph Adamo that Frank "showed her how to make the rows like he learned in Mississippi" and that "he taught her to plant in the hill not the furrow." Account of Frank's final day, unpublished manuscript, [early 1990s], shared with the author by Ralph Adamo on April 19, 2024.
46. Frank Stanford to David Walker, March 1974, FSP.
47. Handwritten Notes, FSP.
48. Note on envelope with Joan Fargason return address, GCSC.
49. Ginny Stanford, account of Frank's final day, unpublished manuscript, [early 1990s].
50. Frank Stanford to Alan Dugan, March 1, 1975, ADP.
51. Frank Stanford to David Walker, March 1974, GCSC.
52. Frank Stanford to Michael Cuddihy, April 1974, MCIP.
53. Frank Stanford to Alan Dugan, March 14, 1974, ADP.
54. Frank Stanford to Dugan, March 14, 1974, ADP.
55. Stanford, interview. He said, "I've got deer and skunks in my garden right now, but I won't kill them. I won't kill an animal."
56. Ginny Stanford, "Requiem: A Fragment," *New Orleans Review* 20, no. 3/4 (1994): 153.
57. Ginny Stanford, "Requiem: A Fragment," 154.
58. Frank Stanford to Dugan, May 20, 1974, ADP.
59. Frank Stanford to Alan Dugan, July 1, 1974, ADP; Frank Stanford to Michael Cuddihy, July 1, 1974, MCIP.

60. Frank Stanford to Dugan, January 22, 1974, ADP.
61. Frank Stanford to Michael Cuddihy, April 1974, MCIP.
62. Frank Stanford to Dugan, March 1, 1975, ADP.
63. Frank Stanford, *What about This*, 147–68.
64. Frank Stanford, *What about This*, 158, 167.
65. Frank Stanford, *What about This*, 168.
66. Frank Stanford to Dugan, March 14, 1974, ADP; Frank Stanford to Michael Cuddihy, September 1974, MCIP.
67. Frank Stanford to Alan Dugan, December 26, 1974, ADP.
68. Frank Stanford to Irv Broughton, November 20, 1973, *LPD*.
69. Stanford, interview.
70. Admission and Discharge Records, Social Service Report, Arkansas State Hospital, case history 105913, private collection of Carrie Prysock, accessed May 3, 2020.
71. Stanford, interview.
72. Frank Stanford to Dugan, January 22, 1974, ADP.
73. Frank Stanford to Alan Dugan, November 18, 1974, ADP.
74. Frank Stanford to Dugan, March 1, 1975, ADP.
75. R. S. Gwynn, email message to author, June 16, 2023.
76. Frank Stanford to Michael Cuddihy, March 15, 1975, MCIP.
77. Stanford, interview.
78. Frank Stanford to Dugan, January 22, 1974, ADP.
79. Frank Stanford to Alan Dugan, March 14, 1974, ADP.
80. Frank Stanford to Dugan, March 14, 1974, ADP.
81. Frank Stanford to Dugan, May 20, 1974, ADP.
82. Frank Stanford to Michael Cuddihy, March 1, 1975, MCIP.
83. Frank Stanford, *What about This*, 321.
84. Frank Stanford to Cuddihy, July 1, 1974, MCIP.
85. Frank Stanford to Walker, February 12, 1974, *LPD*.
86. Frank Stanford to Alan Dugan, May 20, 1974, ADP; Frank Stanford to Cuddihy, April 1, 1974, MCIP; Frank Stanford to Alan Dugan, December 26, 1974, ADP; and Frank Stanford to Michael Cuddihy, November 12, 1974, MCIP.
87. Frank Stanford to Michael Cuddihy, April 1974, MCIP.
88. Michael Cuddihy to Frank Stanford, May 8, 1974, FSP.
89. Frank Stanford, "Essential Expenditures Down to the Bare Minimum We Have to Make Each Month," private collection of Irv Broughton, accessed August 7, 2023.
90. Frank Stanford to Dugan, July 1, 1974, ADP.
91. Frank Stanford to Alan Dugan, March 26, 1975, ADP.
92. Frank Stanford to Irv Broughton, August 5, [1973], private collection of Irv Broughton, accessed August 7, 2023, Spokane, WA.
93. Frank Stanford to Dugan, September 20, 1974, ADP.
94. Stanford, interview.
95. Frank Stanford to Alan Dugan, August 1, 1974, ADP.
96. Stanford, interview.
97. Frank Stanford to Dugan, August 1, 1974, ADP.

98. Joan Williams to Ginny Stanford, June 27, 1978, GCSC; Joan Williams, interview by Irv Broughton, n.d., shared with the author on June 1, 2024; and Irv Broughton, in discussion with the author, June 18, 2024.
99. Frank Stanford to Dugan, July 1, 1974, ADP.
100. Frank Stanford to Dugan, August 1, 1974, ADP.
101. Frank Stanford to Cuddihy, April 1974, MCIP.
102. Frank Stanford to Dugan, July 1, 1974, ADP.
103. Frank Stanford to Dugan, July 1, 1974, ADP.
104. Frank Stanford to Malcolm Cowley, August 1, 1974, *LPD*. There is some evidence that the victim was beaten, and a .357 Magnum revolver was involved.
105. Frank Stanford to Cuddihy, April 1, 1974, MCIP.
106. Frank Stanford to Dugan, August 1, 1974, ADP.
107. Frank Stanford to Michael Cuddihy, [January 1975?], MCIP.
108. Stanford, interview.
109. Stanford, interview.
110. Frank Stanford to Dugan, July 1, 1974; Frank Stanford to Dugan, August 1, 1974, ADP; and Frank Stanford to Michael Cuddihy, September 10, 1974, MCIP.
111. Stanford, interview. Stanford declared to Irv that he was opposed to cockfighting.
112. Frank Stanford to Alan Dugan, September 1974, ADP.
113. Frank Stanford to Michael Cuddihy, August 6, 1974, MCIP.
114. Frank Stanford to Cuddihy, September 10, 1974, MCIP; ellipsis in original.
115. Frank Stanford to Cuddihy, August 6, 1974, MCIP.
116. Frank Stanford, unpublished poetry fragment, n.d., Poetry Fragments, FSP.
117. Frank Stanford to Cuddihy, November 12, 1974, MCIP.
118. Frank Stanford to Dugan, August 1, 1974, ADP.
119. Frank Stanford to Cuddihy, August 6, 1974, MCIP.
120. Frank Stanford to David Walker, February 1974, GCSC.
121. Frank Stanford to Dugan, August 1, 1974, ADP.
122. Frank Stanford to Cuddihy, August 6, 1974, MCIP.
123. R. S. Gwynn, Deborah Luster, Ralph Adamo, John Biguenet, and Steve Stern, in discussion with the author, January 18, 2020, New Orleans, LA.
124. Stephen Stepanchev, *American Poetry Since 1945* (New York: Harper & Row, 1965), 118.
125. Frank Stanford to Michael Cuddihy, May 30, 1974, MCIP.
126. Frank Stanford to Michael Cuddihy, December 30, 1974, LFS.
127. Frank Stanford to Cuddihy, December 30, 1974, LFS.
128. Cuddihy to Frank Stanford, March 10, 1975, MCIP.
129. Stanford, interview.
130. David Walker to Frank Stanford, March 21, 1974, FSP.
131. These scenes are listed in an undated letter that Frank sent to James Babij, and Babij sent them back in James Babij to Frank Stanford, July 1974, FSP.
132. Jim Babij to Frank Stanford, July 31, 1974, FSP.
133. Frank Stanford to Irv Broughton, July 20, 1972, LFS.
134. Frank Stanford, "With the Approach of the Oak the Axeman Quakes," in *What about This: Collected Poems of Frank Stanford*, ed. Michael Wiegers

(Port Townsend, WA: Copper Canyon, 2015), 236.
135. Frank Stanford to Cuddihy, May 30, 1974, MCIP.
136. Frank Stanford to Dugan, May 20, 1974, ADP.
137. "To Quarry or Not to Quarry," n.d., GCSC.
138. Frank Stanford to Dugan, May 20, 1974, ADP.
139. Frank Stanford to "Mr. Ferlinghetti," May 20, 1974, *LPD*.
140. Allen Ginsberg to Frank Stanford, June 9, 1974, FSP.
141. Nicholas Fuhrmann to Frank and Ginny Stanford, October 23, 1974, GCSC.
142. Frank Stanford, "In the Wet Fields," n.d., Prose Fragments, FSP.
143. Frank Stanford to Alan Dugan, August 24, 1974, ADP.
144. Babij to Frank Stanford, July 31, 1974, FSP.
145. Nicholas Fuhrmann, "Frank Stanford: Like Rain Falling and Night Falling," unpublished manuscript, n.d., shared with the author by Ata Moharreri, May 2023.
146. Frank Stanford to Dugan, August 24, 1974, ADP; Frank Stanford, "In the Wet Fields," n.d., FSP.
147. Frank Stanford to Dugan, July 24, 1974, ADP.
148. Fuhrmann, "Frank Stanford."
149. Frank Stanford, "With the Approach of the Oak," 236.
150. Fuhrmann, "Frank Stanford."
151. Frank Stanford, "With the Approach of the Oak," 236.
152. Frank Stanford, "With the Approach of the Oak," 236.
153. Frank Stanford, *What about This*, 289.
154. Lorenzo Thomas, "Finders, Losers: Frank Stanford's Song of the South," *Alsop Review* (2001).
155. Frank Stanford, *What about This*, 290.
156. Frank Stanford, *What about This*, 291.
157. Ginny Stanford, email message to author, November 17, 2021.
158. Cher Ross [Cheryl Campbell], text message to A. P. Walton, September 20, 2023; Cher Ross [Cheryl Campbell], in discussion with the author, December 20, 2023.
159. Frank Stanford to Cuddihy, December 30, 1974, MCIP; Frank Stanford to Irv Broughton, July 22, 1972, *LPD*; and Frank Stanford to Michael Cuddihy, July 21, 1972, MCIP.
160. Ginny Stanford, email message to author, November 17, 2021.
161. Frank Stanford to Cuddihy, September 10, 1974, MCIP.
162. Irv Broughton to Frank Stanford, n.d., FSP.
163. Frank Stanford to Irv Broughton, July 12, 1974, *LPD*; Frank Stanford to Cowley, August 1, 1974, *LPD*.
164. Irv Broughton, in discussion with the author, July 6, 2021.
165. Frank Stanford to Broughton, July 12, 1974, *LPD*.
166. Irv Broughton, in discussion with the author, August 7, 2023, Spokane, WA.
167. Frank Stanford to Cuddihy, September 10, 1974, MCIP.
168. Irv Broughton, in discussion with the author, October 24, 2019.
169. Brochure for the premiere screening of *It Wasn't a Dream: It Was a Flood*, private collection of Irv Broughton, accessed August 7, 2023.

170. See John Keats, *Complete Poems and Selected Letters of John Keats*, ed. Edward Hirsch (New York: Modern Library, 2001), 61.
171. Frank Stanford to Irv Broughton, ca. 1972, LFS.
172. Frank Stanford to Irv Broughton, ca. July 1972, LFS.
173. Alan Dugan to Frank Stanford, May 12, 1972, FSP.
174. Frank Stanford to Irv Broughton, ca. July 1972, LFS.
175. Frank Stanford to David Walker, April 1, 1974, *LPD*. It should be noted that Frank may never have sent those 375 pages.
176. Frank Stanford to Walker, April 1, 1974, *LPD*. Irv Broughton owns a letter Anthony Hecht sent to Frank in 1971 praising *The Singing Knives*.
177. C. D. Wright, "A Note on *The Battlefield Where the Moon Says I Love You*," *Ironwood 17* 9, no. 1 (Spring 1981): 157.
178. David Walker to Frank Stanford, May 1974, FSP.
179. Frank Stanford to Dugan, August 1, 1974, ADP.
180. Frank Stanford to Michael Cuddihy, July 18, 1974, MCIP.
181. Michael Cuddihy, *Try Ironwood: An Editor Remembers* (Boston: Rowan Tree, 1990), 42.
182. Thomas Lux to Frank Stanford, October 24, [1974?], GCSC.
183. William Packard to Frank Stanford, n.d., GCSC.
184. Frank Stanford to Cuddihy, April 1, 1974, MCIP.
185. Frank Stanford to Dugan, August 1, 1974, ADP.
186. "Rules and Terms: The Walt Whitman Award," FSP.
187. Frank Stanford to Alan Dugan, September 1974, LFS.
188. Academy of American Poets to Frank Stanford, November 16, 1974, FSP.
189. Frank Stanford to Dugan, November 18, 1974, ADP.
190. Alan Dugan to Jeffrey Mitchell, December 21, 1974, FSP.
191. Frank Stanford to Dugan, December 26, 1974, ADP.
192. Frank Stanford to Cuddihy, September 10, 1974, MCIP.
193. Marjorie Finnell, quoted in Frank Stanford to Dugan, August 1, 1974, ADP.
194. Marjorie Finnell to Frank Stanford, December 24, 1974, FSP.
195. Stanley Kunitz to Alan Dugan, August 9, 1971, ADP.
196. Frank Stanford to Alan Dugan, September 1974, ADP.
197. Frank Stanford to Dugan, March 26, 1975, ADP.
198. Stanley Kunitz to Frank Stanford, n.d., FSP.
199. Frank Stanford to Dugan, March 26, 1975, ADP.
200. Frank Stanford to Cuddihy, March 23, 1975, MCIP.
201. Frank Stanford to Cuddihy, September 10, 1974, MCIP.
202. Frank Stanford to Cuddihy, late July 1974, MCIP.
203. Vogelsang to Frank Stanford, July 23, 1974, FSP.
204. Frank Stanford to Dugan, March 1, 1975, ADP.
205. Frank Stanford, Notebook 2, GCSC.
206. Frank Stanford to Irv Broughton, February 1973, LFS.
207. Frank Stanford to Alan Dugan, September 1974, LFS.
208. C. D. Wright to Pamela Stewart, n.d., CDWP.
209. Frank Stanford, "A Past: Wintered Like a Circus," *Iowa Review* 5, no. 3 (Summer 1974): 39–54. David Hayman was fiction editor.

210. Frank Stanford to Cuddihy, March 23, 1975, MCIP.
211. Frank Stanford to Dugan, January 22, 1974, ADP.
212. *Atlantic Monthly* to Frank Stanford, January 30, 1975, GCSC.
213. Nan Talese to Frank Stanford, January 17, 1975, GCSC.
214. This was for the Houghton Mifflin Literary Fellowship.
215. Frank Stanford, submission to the Houghton Mifflin Literary Fellowship, n.d., GCSC.
216. Ruth B. Saunders to Frank Stanford, March 5, 1975, FSP.
217. T. Coraghessan Boyle to Frank Stanford, September 30, [1974], FSP.
218. Frank Stanford to Dugan, September 20, 1974," LFS.
219. Frank Stanford to Michael Cuddihy, August 28, 1974, MCIP.
220. Some of this chronology is explained in Julie Schwartz to Frank Stanford, November 5, [1974], FSP.
221. Julie Schwartz to Frank Stanford, August 19, [1974], FSP.
222. Frank Stanford to Cuddihy, August 28, 1974, MCIP.
223. Frank Stanford to Cuddihy, August 6, 1974, MCIP.
224. Gordon Lish to Frank Stanford, November 10, 1974, GCSC.
225. Gordon Lish to Frank Stanford, November 25, 1974, GCSC.
226. Frank Stanford to Dugan, November 18, 1974, ADP.
227. Frank Stanford to Michael Cuddihy, January 25, 1975, MCIP.
228. Gordon Lish to Frank Stanford, October 30, 1974, GCSC.
229. Gordon Lish to Frank Stanford, January 16, 1975, GCSC.
230. Gordon Lish to Frank Stanford, December 30, 1974, GCSC.
231. Lish to Frank Stanford, January 16, 1975, GCSC.
232. Frank Stanford to Gordon Lish, January 20, 1975, GCSC
233. Gordon Lish to Frank Stanford, February 3, 1975, GCSC. Heller's note is included in Lish's correspondence to Frank.
234. Gordon Lish to Frank Stanford, January 31, 1975, GCSC.
235. Gordon Lish to Frank Stanford, February 28, 1975, GCSC.
236. Frank Stanford to Gordon Lish, February 13, 1975, FSP.
237. Gordon Lish to Frank Stanford, April 18, 1975, GCSC.
238. Frank Stanford, *What about This*, 432.
239. John Biguenet, Ralph Adamo, Steve Stern, Deborah Luster, and R. S. Gwynn, in discussion with the author, January 20, 2020, New Orleans, LA.
240. Ira Sadoff to Frank Stanford, February 14, 1975, FSP.
241. Ted Solotaroff to Frank Stanford, March 21, 1975, FSP. He added, "It might be best if you send one story at a time."
242. Frank Stanford to John McKernan, ca. late summer or early fall 1977, *LPD*.
243. C. D. Wright to Carl Launius, n.d., CDWP.
244. C. D. Wright to Pamela Stewart, n.d., CDWP.
245. Frank Stanford to John McKernan, April 1, 1974, *LPD*.
246. Frank Stanford to Michael and Mary Cuddihy, November 9, 1976, *LPD*.
247. Frank Stanford to Dugan, August 1, 1974, ADP.
248. Frank Stanford to McKernan, ca. late summer or early fall 1977, *LPD*.
249. Frank Stanford to Michael Cuddihy, January 1975, MCIP.
250. Frank Stanford to Cuddihy, November 12, 1974, MCIP.

251. Frank Stanford to Mike and Mary Cuddihy, November 21, 1977, MCIP.
252. Frank Stanford to John McKernan, June 4, 1974, *LPD*.
253. Frank Stanford to Dugan, March 1, 1975, ADP.
254. Frank Stanford to Donald Justice, October 19, 1971, *LPD*.
255. Frank Stanford to Eleanor Bender, November 10, 1971, LFS.
256. Frank Stanford, *What about This*, 312.
257. Frank Stanford, *What about This*, 316.
258. Frank Stanford, *What about This*, 330.
259. Frank Stanford, *What about This*, 331.
260. Frank Stanford to Cuddihy, March 23, 1975, MCIP.
261. C. D. Wright to Carl Launius, April 25, 1986, CDWP.

**TWELVE**

1. Frank Stanford to Michael Cuddihy, late September 1974, MCIP.
2. Frank Stanford to Michael Cuddihy, July 18, 1974, MCIP.
3. Frank Stanford, interview by Irv Broughton, 1973–74, FSP.
4. Frank Stanford to Michael Cuddihy, September 1974, MCIP.
5. Admission and Discharge Records, Social Service Report, Arkansas State Hospital, case history 105913, p. 7, private collection of Carrie Prysock, accessed May 3, 2020.
6. Frank Stanford to Michael Cuddihy, September 10, 1974, MCIP.
7. Ginny Stanford, email message to author, November 17, 2020.
8. Ginny Stanford, "Requiem: A Fragment," *New Orleans Review* 20, no. 3/4 (1994): 152.
9. Frank Stanford to Michael Cuddihy, August 6, 1974, MCIP.
10. Ginny Stanford, "Requiem: A Fragment," 152–53.
11. Frank Stanford to Michael Cuddihy, November 12, 1974, MCIP.
12. Steve Stern, "Surveying the Boundaries: An Appreciation of Frank Stanford," in "10 Great Neglected Poets of the 20th Century," special millennial issue, *Asheville Poetry Review* 7, no. 1 (Spring/Summer 2000): 223.
13. Stanford, interview.
14. Frank Stanford to Alan Dugan, July 24, 1974, ADP.
15. Ginny Stanford, email message to author, November 16, 2020.
16. Frank Stanford to Alan Dugan, December 26, 1974, ADP.
17. Ginny Stanford, email message to author, November 20, 2020.
18. Frank Stanford to Michael Cuddihy, late September 1974, MCIP.
19. Stanford, interview.
20. Frank Stanford to Alan Dugan, January 22, 1974, ADP.
21. Frank Stanford to Alan Dugan, September 20, 1974, ADP.
22. Frank Stanford to Michael Cuddihy, late September 1974, MCIP.
23. Ginny Stanford, email message to author, November 20, 2020. This desk is currently owned by Carrie Prysock, Frank Stanford's niece.
24. C. D. Wright, "A Note on *The Battlefield Where the Moon Says I Love You*," *Ironwood 17* 9, no. 1 (Spring 1981): 157.

25. Ginny Stanford, email message to author, November 17, 2020.
26. Ginny Stanford, email message to author, November 17, 2020.
27. Ginny Stanford, "Death in the Cool Evening," in *Saltwater, Sweetwater: Women Write from California's North Coast* (Forestville, CA: Floreant, 1998), 27–32.
28. Composition book, notebook 5, GCSC.
29. Composition book, Busch Notebook, GCSC.
30. Frank Stanford to Irv Broughton, n.d., private collection of Irv Broughton, accessed August 7, 2023, Spokane, WA.
31. Frank Stanford to Alan Dugan, August 1974, ADP.
32. Composition book, Busch Notebook, GCSC.
33. Frank Stanford to Alan Dugan, August 1974, ADP.
34. Frank Stanford to Michael Cuddihy, late September 1974, MCIP.
35. R. S. Gwynn, Deborah Luster, Ralph Adamo, John Biguenet, and Steve Stern, in discussion with the author, January 18, 2020, New Orleans, LA.
36. Frank Stanford to Alan Dugan, July 1, 1974, ADP.
37. Frank Stanford to Cuddihy, November 12, 1974, MCIP.
38. Frank Stanford to Cuddihy, November 12, 1974, MCIP.
39. Frank Stanford to Alan Dugan, July 24, 1974, ADP.
40. Frank Stanford to Irv Broughton, August 5, [1973], private collection of Irv Broughton, accessed August 7, 2023, Spokane, WA.
41. Frank Stanford to Dugan, January 22, 1974, ADP.
42. Frank Stanford to Alan Dugan, May 20, 1974, ADP.
43. Frank Stanford to John McKernan, March 17, 1975, *LPD*.
44. Frank Stanford to Alan Dugan, July 1974, ADP.
45. Frank Stanford to Cuddihy, August 6, 1974, MCIP.
46. Frank Stanford to Dugan, July 1, 1974, ADP.
47. Frank Stanford to Alan Dugan, March 14, 1974, ADP.
48. Frank Stanford to Dugan, July 1, 1974, ADP.
49. Frank Stanford to Dugan, July 24, 1974, ADP.
50. Frank Stanford to Alan Dugan, August 1, 1974, ADP.
51. Michael Cuddihy to Frank Stanford, March 10, 1975, FSP.
52. Frank Stanford to Alan Dugan, November 18, 1974, ADP.
53. Judith Shahn to Frank Stanford, n.d., enclosed in Alan Dugan to Frank Stanford, December 2, 1974, FSP.
54. Frank Stanford to Dugan, December 26, 1974, ADP.
55. Frank Stanford to Michael Cuddihy, March 15, 1975, MCIP.
56. "Former Neoshoan Wins Art Award," *Neosho Daily News*, March 6, 1975.
57. Composition book, notebook 5, GCSC.
58. Frank Stanford to Alan Dugan, March 1, 1975, ADP.
59. Frank Stanford to Irv Broughton, June 18, 1971, LFS.
60. Frank Stanford to Dugan, July 24, 1974, ADP.
61. Frank Stanford to Dugan, July 24, 1974, ADP.
62. Ginny Stanford, "Requiem: A Fragment," 163.
63. Ginny Stanford, "Requiem: A Fragment," 163–64.
64. Ginny Stanford, email message to author, August 1, 2023.

65. Frank Stanford to Broughton, June 18, 1971, LFS.
66. Richard Leo Johnson, in discussion with the author, August 5, 2022, Savannah, GA.
67. Frank Stanford to Alan Dugan, January 1, 1974, ADP.
68. Frank Stanford to *Partisan Review*, March 8, 1971, LFS.
69. John Biguenet, in discussion with the author, October 22, 2019.
70. Frank Stanford, unpublished fragment, n.d., Prose Fragments, FSP.
71. Rodney Jones, in discussion with the author, July 18, 2023, New Orleans, LA.
72. Biguenet, discussion.
73. Frank Stanford, *What about This: Collected Poems of Frank Stanford*, ed. Michael Wiegers (Port Townsend, WA: Copper Canyon, 2015), 444.
74. Frank Stanford, *What about This*, 465.
75. Thomas Johnson to Frank Stanford, April 11, 1974, FSP.
76. *Stinktree* 4 (Spring 1975): 1–20.
77. Thomas Johnson to Frank Stanford, April [illegible], 1975, FSP.
78. Frank Stanford to Alan Dugan, August 24, 1974, ADP.
79. Frank Stanford, "In the Wet Fields," n.d., Prose Fragments, FSP.
80. Frank Stanford to Fr. Jerome Kodell, ca. late winter 1975, LFS.
81. Adrian Martin, "In Search of Mystery," *Screening the Past*, no. 36 (June 2013), http://www.screeningthepast.com/issue-36-classics-reruns/in-search-of-mystery/.
82. Frank Stanford to Michael Cuddihy, March 23, 1975, MCIP.
83. Frank Stanford to Cuddihy, March 15, 1975, MCIP; Frank Stanford to Cuddihy, March 23, 1975, MCIP.
84. Fr. Jerome Kodell, email message to author, July 20, 2023. It's even possible that Frank never mailed the letter he wrote to Father Jerome about the Bertolucci translations in the first place (and got an initial translation of the poem that appeared in *Stinktree* from elsewhere): "Unfortunately, I never did receive that letter and the first time I had any awareness of it was when I saw it in that collection," Father Jerome wrote. "I wonder whether he mailed it. Anyway, it hasn't shown up and I didn't know about the translation request."
85. Frank Stanford to Fr. Jerome Kodell, ca. late winter, 1975, LFS.
86. Thomas Lux to Frank Stanford, April 15, [1975], GCSC.
87. Frank Stanford to Cuddihy, March 23, 1975, MCIP.
88. Tom Whalen, in discussion with the author, July 18, 2023.
89. Irv Broughton, in discussion with the author, August 7, 2023, Spokane, WA.
90. Frank Stanford to Irv Broughton, n.d., private collection of Irv Broughton, accessed August 7, 2023, Spokane, WA.
91. Frank Stanford to Cuddihy, March 23, 1975, MCIP.
92. Frank Stanford to Cuddihy, November 12, 1974, MCIP.
93. Frank Stanford to Michael Cuddihy, January 1975, MCIP.
94. Frank Stanford to Allen Ginsberg and Peter Orlovsky, November 23, [1969], in *Hidden Water: From the Frank Stanford Archives*, by Frank Stanford, ed. Michael Wiegers and Chet Weise (Nashville: Third Man Books, 2015), 185.

95. Frank Stanford, *"Buckdancer's Choice,* by James Dickey," n.d., uncatalogued papers of James Whitehead, Special Collections, University of Arkansas Libraries.
96. Frank Stanford, *"Driving to Biloxi,* by Edgar Simmons," May 19, 1969, uncatalogued papers of James Whitehead, Special Collections, University of Arkansas Libraries.
97. Frank Stanford to Dugan, August 1, 1974, ADP.
98. Frank Stanford to Dugan, December 26, 1974, ADP. Willie Morris, who was born and raised in Mississippi, was the author of the highly acclaimed memoir *North Towards Home,* about his pilgrimage to New York and his adaptation to life as an editor at *Harper's.*
99. Frank Stanford to Irv Broughton, n.d., private collection of Irv Broughton, accessed August 7, 2023, Spokane, WA.
100. Frank Stanford to Irv Broughton, n.d., private collection of Irv Broughton, accessed August 7, 2023, Spokane, WA.
101. Pier Paolo Pasolini, *Roman Poems,* trans. Lawrence Ferlinghetti and Francesca Valente (San Francisco: City Lights Books, 1986), 9.
102. Frank Stanford to Dugan, August 1, 1974, ADP.
103. Frank Stanford to Cuddihy, August 6, 1974, MCIP.
104. Frank Stanford to Dugan, August 1, 1974, ADP.
105. Frank Stanford to David Walker, February 12, 1974, *LPD.*
106. Stanford, interview.
107. Frank Stanford to Cuddihy, August 6, 1974, MCIP.
108. Frank Stanford to Cuddihy, March 23, 1975, MCIP.
109. Frank Stanford to Cuddihy, July 18, 1974, MCIP.
110. Frank Stanford to Michael Cuddihy, January 1975, MCIP.
111. Frank Stanford to Cuddihy, March 23, 1975, MCIP.
112. Frank Stanford to Cuddihy, November 12, 1974, MCIP.
113. Frank Stanford to Cuddihy, March 23, 1975, MCIP.
114. Frank Stanford, untitled essay, Prose Fragments, FSP.
115. Stanford, interview.
116. C. D. Wright to Michael Cuddihy, 1981, MCIP.
117. Irv Broughton, interview by John Erwin (director and producer of *You,* a documentary film on the life and work of Frank Stanford), n.d., transcript, shared with the author in July 2023.
118. Frank Stanford to Irv Broughton, May 24, 1974, private collection of Irv Broughton, accessed August 7, 2023, Spokane, WA.
119. Frank Stanford to Irv Broughton, November 20, 1973, *LPD.*
120. Frank Stanford to Broughton, May 24, 1974, private collection of Irv Broughton.
121. Frank Stanford to Irv Broughton, December 4, 1974, LFS.
122. Frank Stanford to Irv Broughton, July 1, 1974, LFS.
123. Ginny Stanford to A. P. Walton, email, ca. summer 2023, shared with the author by A. P. Walton.

124. Frank Stanford to Irv Broughton, July 12, 1974, LFS.
125. Frank Stanford to Irv Broughton, July 12, 1974, FSP.
126. Frank Stanford to Irv Broughton, June 22 or 29, 1975, LFS.
127. Broughton, discussion.
128. Frank Stanford to Irv Broughton, August 5, [1973], private collection of Irv Broughton, accessed August 7, 2023, Spokane, WA.
129. Frank Stanford to Irv Broughton, ca. late March [March 26?] 1975, LFS.
130. Ralph Adamo, interview by John Erwin (director and producer of *You*, a documentary film on the life and work of Frank Stanford), n.d., transcript, shared with the author in July 2023.
131. Frank Stanford, *What about This: Collected Poems of Frank Stanford*, ed. Michael Wiegers (Port Townsend, WA: Copper Canyon, 2015), 63–112.
132. Frank Stanford, *What about This*, 104.
133. Frank Stanford, *What about This*, 108–9.
134. Frank Stanford, *What about This*, 87.
135. Frank Stanford, *What about This*, 95.
136. Frank Stanford, *What about This*, 101.
137. Frank Stanford, *What about This*, 90.
138. Frank Stanford, *What about This*, 91.
139. Frank Stanford to Irv Broughton, late spring / early summer 1975, LFS.
140. Frank Stanford, *What about This*, 190.
141. Frank Stanford, *What about This*, 177.
142. Frank Stanford, *What about This*, 175.
143. Murray Shugars, "What the Moon Says."
144. Frank Stanford, *What about This*, 180.
145. Frank Stanford, *What about This*, 174.
146. Frank Stanford to Broughton, August 5, [1973], private collection of Irv Broughton.
147. Frank Stanford to Broughton, May 24, 1974, private collection of Irv Broughton.
148. Frank Stanford to Irv Broughton, [August 1974], private collection of Irv Broughton, accessed August 7, 2023, Spokane, WA.
149. Frank Stanford to John McKernan, December 1, 1974, *LPD*.
150. Receipt, Overstreet Printing Company, June 11, 1975, LRPR.
151. Receipt, Overstreet Printing Company, August 1, 1975, LRPR.
152. Frank Stanford to Irv Broughton, January 20, 1974, private collection of Irv Broughton, accessed August 7, 2023, Spokane, WA.
153. Frank Stanford to Irv Broughton, ca. late January / early February 1973, *LPD*.
154. Frank Stanford to Irv Broughton, May 1, 1974, private collection of Irv Broughton, accessed August 7, 2023, Spokane, WA.
155. Frank Stanford to John McKernan, February 1, 1974, LFS.
156. Frank Stanford to Irv Broughton, ca. June 1973, LFS.
157. Frank Stanford to Irv Broughton, n.d., private collection of Irv Broughton, accessed August 7, 2023, Spokane, WA.
158. Stanford, interview.
159. Frank Stanford to Broughton, December 4, 1974, LFS.

160. Frank Stanford to Cuddihy, March 15, 1975, MCIP.
161. Leon Stokesbury to Frank Stanford, August 25, 1975 (postmark), FSP.
162. Stanford, interview.
163. Frank Stanford to Michael Cuddihy, ca. late September 1974, MCIP.
164. Frank Stanford to Cuddihy, March 23, 1975, MCIP.
165. Frank Stanford to Broughton, December 4, 1974, LFS.
166. Frank Stanford, *What about This*, 307.
167. Frank Stanford to Irv Broughton, March 4, 1971, private collection of Irv Broughton, accessed August 7, 2023, Spokane, WA.
168. Frank Stanford to Irv Broughton, February 8, 1972, LFS.
169. Frank Stanford to Broughton, March 4, 1971, private collection of Irv Broughton.
170. Frank Stanford to Irv Broughton, late spring / early summer 1975, LFS.
171. Receipt, Overstreet Printing Company, August 21, 1975, LRPR.
172. Quoted in Irv Broughton, *Surveying: Poems by Irv Broughton* (n.p.: A Lost Roads Book, 1974). I am grateful to Ralph Adamo for sharing his copy with me.
173. Frank Stanford to Irv Broughton, July 12, 1974, LFS.
174. Frank Stanford to Cuddihy, March 15, 1975, MCIP.
175. Frank Stanford to Irv Broughton, June 13, [1975], private collection of Irv Broughton, accessed August 7, 2023, Spokane, WA.
176. Frank Stanford to John McKernan, ca. late fall 1974, LFS.
177. Frank Stanford to Michael Cuddihy, September 1974, MCIP.
178. Frank Stanford to Michael Cuddihy, September 1974, MCIP.
179. Phyllis Morris to Frank Stanford, June 16, 1975, FSP.
180. John Morris to Frank Stanford, n.d., FSP.
181. Phyllis Morris to Frank Stanford, January 9, 1976, GCSC.
182. Receipt, Overstreet Printing Company, October 27, 1975, LRPR. Frank used the turkey hunter as his printer and Overstreet Printing Company to do the glossy cover and binding.
183. This was verified in a copy of John S. Morris, *Bean Street* (Rogers, AR: Lost Roads, 1975) loaned to the author by Ralph Adamo.
184. Irv Broughton to Frank Stanford, October 1, 1975, private collection of Irv Broughton, accessed August 7, 2023, Spokane, WA.
185. Phyllis Morris to Frank Stanford, January 9, 1976, GCSC.
186. John Moffitt to John and Phyllis Morris, February 5, 1976, FSP.
187. NEA grant application, LRPR. The expenses for C. D. Wright's *Alla Breve Loving* were paid for by an NEA grant.
188. Bill Harrison to Frank Stanford, September 27, 1975, GCSC. In an undated interview by Murray Shugars, C. D. Wright suggests that the party might have been after a reading on campus by William Stafford. Transcript, CDWP.
189. Wright, interview.
190. Wright, interview.
191. Wright, interview.
192. Wright, interview.
193. C. D. Wright to Carl Launnius, April 25, 1986, CDWP.

**THIRTEEN**

1. Margalit Fox, "C. D. Wright, Poet of the Ozarks and Beyond, Dies at 67," *New York Times*, January 6, 2016; Jennifer Steinorth, email message to author, December 23, 2023.
2. Ralph Adamo, in discussion with the author, September 19, 2019, New Orleans, LA.
3. Forrest Gander, in discussion with the author, August 4, 2023, San Francisco, CA.
4. Gander, discussion.
5. Adamo, discussion, September 19, 2019.
6. Gander, discussion.
7. Frank Stanford to Ginny Stanford and C. D. Wright, May 21, 1978, *LPD*.
8. Ralph Adamo, in discussion with the author, December 18, 2020, New Orleans, LA.
9. Frank Stanford to Ginny Stanford and C. D. Wright, May 21, 1978, LFS.
10. C. D. Wright, preface to *The Battlefield Where the Moon Says I Love You*, by Frank Stanford (Barrington, RI: Lost Roads Publishers, 2000), first page of the preface (unnumbered).
11. Frank Stanford, interview by Irv Broughton, 1973–74, FSP.
12. Wright, preface to Frank Stanford, *Battlefield*, fourth page of the preface (unnumbered).
13. Wright, preface to Frank Stanford, *Battlefield*, first page of the preface (unnumbered). Forrest Gander elaborated on her reaction: "She finds this motherfucker who's living in her landscape, writing about her landscape in ways she never imagined. And it really took her." Gander, discussion.
14. Deborah Luster, in discussion with the author, March 2, 2023, New Orleans, LA.
15. Wright, preface to Frank Stanford, *Battlefield*, second page (unnumbered).
16. C. D. Wright to Carl Launius, April 25, 1986, CDWP. In this letter she says she thinks they lived on "West St.," but with more confidence in a 1997 letter to Brett Long, she says it was "Watson St." C. D. Wright to Brett Long, n.d., CDWP.
17. Frank submitted "Directions from a Madman" to *Poetry Now*, which in a letter dated November 30, 1975, rejected it for being too long. FSP.
18. Frank Stanford, *What about This: Collected Poems of Frank Stanford*, ed. Michael Wiegers (Port Townsend, WA: Copper Canyon, 2015), 202.
19. Merideth Boswell, email message to author, April 18, 2022.
20. Wright, interview.
21. Gander, discussion.
22. David Reich, in discussion with the author, December 3, 2019.
23. John McKernan to C. D. Wright, May 13, 1977, LRPR.
24. Michael Cuddihy to C. D. Wright, October 27, 1979, LRPR. Wright would have her poems appear in *Ironwood 9* (Spring 1977) and *Ironwood 12* (Fall 1978).
25. Luster, discussion, March 2, 2023.
26. C. D. Wright to Michael Cuddihy, August 11, 1978, LRPR.

27. Gander, discussion.
28. Ginny Stanford, "*Requiem*: A Fragment," *New Orleans Review* 20, no. 3/4 (1994): 154.
29. Ginny Stanford, "*Requiem*: A Fragment," 153.
30. Ginny Stanford, email message to author, August 1, 2023.
31. Ginny Stanford, "Requiem: A Fragment," 150.
32. Receipt, House of Books, Aug 31, 1976, LRPR.
33. Reich, discussion.
34. Steve Stern, "Surveying the Boundaries: An Appreciation of Frank Stanford," in "10 Great Neglected Poets of the 20th Century," special millennial issue, *Asheville Poetry Review* 7, no. 1 (Spring/Summer 2000): 224. Stern wrote further: "He showed us his poems as a kind of evidence, as if, on some ordinate survey of Arkansas or the soul, he'd located a spot equidistant from heaven and hell."
35. Deborah Luster, in discussion with the author, October 2019; R. S. Gwynn, Deborah Luster, Ralph Adamo, John Biguenet, and Steve Stern, in discussion with the author, January 18, 2020, New Orleans, LA; and Ralph Adamo, in discussion with the author, December 20, 2020, New Orleans, LA.
36. Stern, "Surveying the Boundaries," 223.
37. Bill Willett, interview by John Erwin (director and producer of *You*, a documentary film on the life and work of Frank Stanford), n.d., transcript, shared with the author on July 12, 2023.
38. Steve Stern, in discussion with the author, September 20, 2023.
39. Gwynn, Luster, Adamo, Biguenet, and Stern, discussion; Adamo, discussion, December 20, 2020.
40. Adamo, discussion, September 19, 2019.
41. Richard Leo Johnson, in discussion with the author, August 5, 2022, Savannah, GA.
42. Stern, discussion, September 20, 2023.
43. Johnson, discussion.
44. Frank Stanford to Ginny Stanford and C. D. Wright, May 21, 1978, GCSC.
45. Frank Stanford, poetry fragment, n.d., Handwritten Notes, FSP.
46. Frank Stanford, *What about This*, 328.
47. Gwynn, Luster, Adamo, Biguenet, and Stern, discussion; Adamo, discussion, December 20, 2020.
48. Frank Stanford to Michael and Mary Cuddihy, November 9, 1976, *LPD*.
49. Frank Stanford, interview.
50. Ginny Stanford, "Death in the Cool Evening," *Portable Plateau* 1, no. 1 (1997).
51. "Agreement of Lease," Sept 28, 1976, LRPR.
52. C. D. Wright to the Cuddihys, late June / early July 1978, CDWP.
53. Adamo, discussion, September 19, 2019.
54. Ginny Stanford, "Requiem: A Fragment," 154.
55. C. D. Wright to Brent Long, May 22, 1997, CDWP. It does, however, seem likely that Frank moved many of his belongings into the house in Liberal.
56. Gander, discussion.
57. Johnson, discussion.
58. Irv Broughton, in discussion with the author, August 7, 2023, Spokane, WA.

59. Stern, discussion, September 20, 2023; Ralph Adamo, text message exchange with author, September 26, 2023.
60. Johnson, discussion.
61. Gander, discussion.
62. Kathy Thompson, in discussion with the author, March 9, 2023.
63. Stern, discussion, September 20, 2023.
64. Margaret Salassi, in discussion with the author, October 19, 2019. Salassi's son cut C. D. and Frank's yard. For all their differences, there was at least one way that Frank behaved similarly with these women. He asked them the same question when he woke up in the morning sexually aroused: "Would you like your morning cock?" Anonymous source, in discussion with the author, n.d. This discussion was conducted in confidence, and the name of the source is withheld by mutual agreement.
65. Jessica Slote, in discussion with the author, July 12, 2023.
66. Leslie Parr, in discussion with the author, July 27, 2023.
67. Gwynn, Luster, Adamo, Biguenet, and Stern, discussion; Adamo, discussion, December 20, 2020.
68. Thompson, discussion.
69. Johnson, discussion.
70. Stern, discussion, September 20, 2023.
71. Frank Stanford to Bill Willett, ca. September 14, 1972, LFS.
72. Thompson, discussion.
73. Steve Stern, in discussion with the author, September 9, 2019.
74. Gwynn, Luster, Adamo, Biguenet, and Stern, discussion.
75. Deborah Luster, in discussion with the author, September 29, 2019.
76. Boswell, email message to author, April 18, 2022.
77. Frank Stanford to Ginny Stanford and C. D. Wright, May 21, 1978, GCSC.
78. Kathy Walton, in discussion with the author, July 28, 2022, Fort Worth, TX.
79. Ginny Stanford, "Requiem: A Fragment," 152.
80. Slote, discussion.
81. Wright to Launius, April 25, 1986, CDWP.
82. Frank Stanford to Don Kemp, October 6, 1974, LFS.
83. Wright to Launius, April 25, 1986, CDWP.
84. Luster, discussion, September 29, 2019.
85. John Stoss, in discussion with the author, December 13, 2019, Salinas, CA.
86. Bruun Whitehead, in discussion with the author, June 10, 2021.
87. C. D. Wright, "Frank Stanford of the Mulberry Family: An Arkansas Epilogue," *Conjunctions* 29 (1997): 298.
88. Don L. Kemp to "Dear Client," September 20, 1976, FSP.
89. Frank Stanford to Michael and Mary Cuddihy, November 9, 1976, *LPD*.
90. "Precision International EDM (Beetle 500)," National Museum of American History, Smithsonian Institution, accessed December 16, 2024, https://americanhistory.si.edu/collections/search/object/nmah_748797.
91. R. S. Gwynn, email message to author, September 21, 2023.
92. Sales Order 2627, Trion Company, August 18, 1977, FSP; Frank Stanford to John McKernan, June 4, 1974, *LPD*.

93. Frank Stanford to Kemp, October 6, 1974, LFS.
94. Steve Stern, discussion, September 20, 2023.
95. C. D. Wright, Notebooks, September 24, 1978, CDWP.
96. Deborah Luster, in discussion with the author, March 3, 2023, New Orleans, LA.
97. Wright to Launius, April 25, 1986, CDWP.
98. C. D. Wright, Notebooks, September 29, 1978, CDWP.
99. C. D. Wright, "Frank Stanford of the Mulberry Family," 298.
100. Ginny Stanford, "Requiem: A Fragment," 154, 159.
101. Wright, interview.
102. "Publication Report and Cost of Manufacture Report," Mill Mountain Press, March 12, 1976, CDWP.
103. Frank Stanford to Irv and Connie Broughton, June 20, 1976, *LPD*.
104. "Sales Report for *Alla Breve Loving*," Mill Mountain Press, CDWP.
105. Frank Stanford to Irv and Connie Broughton, June 20, 1976, *LPD*.
106. C. D. Wright to Nicholas Fuhrmann, February 13, 1979, CDWP.
107. C. D. Wright to Fuhrmann, February 13, 1979, CDWP.
108. Frank Stanford to Irv and Connie Broughton, June 20, 1976, *LPD*.
109. Frank Stanford to Michael and Mary Cuddihy, November 9, 1976, *LPD*.
110. *The Battlefield* was jointly published by Lost Roads and Mill Mountain.
111. This image was important enough to Frank for him to have Ginny paint his portrait in front of her rendition of it. See Ginny Stanford, "Death in the Cool Evening," 28.
112. Frank Stanford, *What about This*, 223.
113. Frank Stanford, *What about This*, 229–30.
114. Frank Stanford, *What about This*, 232.
115. Frank Stanford, *What about This*, 202–5.
116. Frank Stanford, *What about This*, 209–14.
117. Frank Stanford, *What about This*, 209–14.
118. Frank Stanford, *What about This*, 234.
119. A document in the Frank Stanford Papers at the Beinecke breaks the book into nine sections and notes that there is only one copy of the first seven.
120. Frank Stanford to Irv and Connie Broughton, June 20, 1976, *LPD*.
121. Forrest Gander, "Note," in Frank Stanford, *Battlefield*, first page of "Note" (unnumbered).
122. Frank Stanford to Irv and Connie Broughton, June 20, 1976, *LPD*.
123. Wright, preface to Frank Stanford, *Battlefield*, first page one of preface (unnumbered).
124. Estimate for Mill Mountain Press for *The Battlefield Where the Moon Says I Love You*, September 1, 1976, LRPR.
125. Bill of receipt from Overstreet Quality Printing Products to Frank Stanford, August 15, 1977, LRPR.
126. Leonard Randolph to Frank Stanford, May 20, 1977 (crossed out and stamped with August 16, 1977), LRPR. On Lost Roads' joining with Mill Mountain to publish *The Battlefield*, see Frank Stanford to Michael and Mary Cuddihy, November 9, 1976, *LPD*.

127. Frank Stanford to John McKernan, ca. fall 1977, *LPD*.
128. This information comes from an unlikely but reliable source. In 2020 I purchased a copy of *The Battlefield*—with the 1977 copyright—from a bookseller in Atlanta, Georgia, my hometown. I was thrilled to learn that on the inside cover Forrest Gander had inscribed a long message to one John Field, explaining the provenance of the book, the details of the typesetting, and other facts about the book's publication.
129. Frank Stanford to John McKernan, ca. fall 1977, LFS.
130. Frank Stanford to Michael and Mary Cuddihy, June 15, 1977, MCIP.
131. A. P. Walton, text message to the author, November 6, 2023.
132. Frank Stanford to Michael and Mary Cuddihy, June 15, 1977, MCIP.
133. Frank Stanford to Fred Overstreet, ca. spring 1977, FSP.
134. Frank Stanford to Michael and Mary Cuddihy, June 15, 1977, MCIP.
135. Adamo, discussion, September 19, 2019.
136. Leon Stokesbury to A. P. Walton, email, February 3, 2015, shared with the author by A. P. Walton.
137. D. Nolan to "Dear Reader," January 1, 1978, LRPR.
138. Frank Stanford, draft of promotional copy for *The Battlefield Where the Moon Says I Love You*, n.d., miscellaneous papers, LRPR.
139. There were never any hardbound copies printed.
140. Frank Stanford, draft of promotional copy for *The Battlefield Where the Moon Says I Love You*, n.d., miscellaneous papers, LRPR.
141. Frank Stanford to Ralph Adamo, December 20, 1976, LRPR.
142. Frank Stanford to Irv and Connie Broughton, June 20, 1976, *LPD*.
143. Frank Stanford to John McKernan, ca. summer or fall 1970, *LPD*.
144. Frank Stanford to Michael and Mary Cuddihy, November 9, 1976, *LPD*. On valuing Stoss's work alongside C. D.'s, see Frank Stanford to Irv and Connie Broughton, June 20, 1976, *LPD*.
145. Frank Stanford to Alan Dugan, March 29, 1976, ADP.
146. Frank Stanford, *What about This*, 344–45.
147. Frank Stanford to Irv Broughton, October 20, 1976, LFS.
148. Frank Stanford to Irv Broughton, October 18, 1976, LFS.
149. Ralph Adamo, in discussion with the author, June 3, 2023, New Orleans, LA.
150. Frank Stanford to Ralph Adamo, March 27, 1976, LRPR.
151. Frank Stanford to Ralph Adamo, July 15, 1976, LRPR.
152. Alberta Turner to Frank Stanford, June 26, 1976, LRPR.
153. C. D. Wright to Michael Cuddihy, ca. early fall 1978, CDWP. Cuddihy published this manuscript with Copper Canyon Press in 1980 under the title *Celebrations*.
154. C. D. Wright to Michael Cuddihy, July 12, 1978, CDWP.
155. This copy is in the possession of Leo Lensing. It was shared with the author on September 8, 2023. Frank's comment was to Ralph Adamo in a letter dated October 20, 1976, *LPD*.
156. John Stoss to Everette Maddox and Rodney Jones, n.d., LRPR. That blank space is in the original.
157. Rodney Jones, text message to author, August 2023.

158. Steve Stern, in discussion with the author, September 5, 2019.
159. Gwynn, Luster, Adamo, Biguenet, and Stern, discussion.
160. Frank Stanford, Project Grant Application, National Endowment for the Arts, LRPR.
161. Gwynn, Luster, Adamo, Biguenet, and Stern, discussion. Deborah Luster, who had lived with Durbin for a couple of years, insisted that this would have never happened, if only because Reed, who had a history of mental illness, would "kill me first."
162. Frank Stanford to Ralph Adamo, December 20, 1976, *LPD*. Adamo had suggested *A Woman to Keep the Moon Away* among other titles, while Stanford insisted on *Sadness at the Private University*.
163. Frank Stanford to Michael and Mary Cuddihy, November 9, 1976, *LPD*.
164. Frank Stanford to Mr. Motter, September 20, 1976, LFS.
165. NEA Literature Program Application, application #A11961–77, submitted February 15, 1977, LRPR.
166. Frank Stanford to Leonard Randolph, August 15, 1977, LRPR.
167. Ralph Adamo, text message to author, October 15, 2023. "I imagine that Whitehead introduced them," Adamo said. "Maybe after talking Frank up to her."
168. Ellen Gilchrist, in discussion with the author, October 7, 2021, Ocean Springs, MS.
169. Ellen Gilchrist to Miller Williams, n.d., MWP.
170. Bill Lavender, in discussion with the author, December 14, 2021, New Orleans, LA.
171. Adamo, discussion, December 20, 2020.
172. Lavender, discussion.
173. Gwynn, Luster, Adamo, Biguenet, and Stern, discussion.
174. Slote, discussion.
175. Gilchrist, discussion, October 7, 2021.
176. Gilchrist, discussion, October 7, 2021.
177. Gilchrist, discussion, October 7, 2021.
178. Ellen Gilchrist to Miller Williams, n.d., MWP.
179. Frank Stanford to Ellen Gilchrist, January 17, 1977, *LPD*.
180. Ellen Gilchrist to Frank Stanford and C. D. Wright, August 30, 1977, LRPR.
181. Frank Stanford to John McKernan, March 15, 1977, LRPR.
182. Frank Stanford to "Six Authors," April 1, 1977, *LPD*.
183. Frank Stanford to "Six Authors," May 1, 1977, LRPR. Strangely, he inquired, "Can anyone give me the name of that tabloid like the *Rolling Stone* & *Village Voice* in the Boston area; there are 165 colleges within 75 miles of Boston." Strange because Frank had published several times in the magazine he was asking about: the *Boston Phoenix*.
184. Frank Stanford to "Six Authors," June 1, 1977, LRPR.
185. Fred Overstreet to "To Whom It May Concern," May 3, 1977, LRPR.
186. Frank Stanford to Fred Overstreet, ca. early May, 1977, LRPR.
187. Frank Stanford to Leonard Randolph, May 15, 1977, LRPR.
188. Frank Stanford to Michael and Mary Cuddihy, June 15, 1977, MCIP.

189. Frank wrote to Irv in late spring or summer 1975: "They are thinking of selling out of all of their equipment in the printing business after our jobs are over. They do have some fairly good equipment. I'd like maybe to get the hand press they have at least. Don't know what they're asking. Their goddam lawsuits are what is holding things up." Stanford to Broughton, late spring / early summer 1975, LFS.
190. Ernie Wright to C. D. Wright, November 15, 1977, CDWP. Frank mentions in an October 20, 1976, letter to Ralph Adamo that C. D. "is buying a lot of printing equipment and soon will be in the business of duplicating words." This claim seems hard to square with Frank's June 1977 claim that they had just recently bought a bunch of printing equipment. Perhaps this was a case of Frank putting the cart before the horse in that they were discussing the purchase of such equipment but it did not really happen until the falling out with Overstreet in the spring of 1977. The installment notes on the $2,000 grant and $3000 loan from Ernie Wright are dated March 29, 1977. It is unclear why these notes were made separately. Both Frank and C. D. signed both.
191. Frank Stanford to Michael and Mary Cuddihy, June 15, 1977, MCIP.
192. Henderson v. State, 255 Ark. 870, 503 S.W.2d 889 (1974).
193. Kathy Walton, discussion.
194. Adamo, discussion, December 20, 2020.
195. Ralph Adamo, interview by John Erwin (director and producer of *You*, a documentary film on the life and work of Frank Stanford), n.d., transcript, shared with the author in July 2023. A clothesline strung between the garage and the main house was where the printed pages of the six poets' books were hung to dry.
196. Frank Stanford to Michael and Mary Cuddihy, June 15, 1977, MCIP.
197. Frank Stanford to Michael and Mary Cuddihy, June 15, 1977, MCIP.
198. Frank Stanford to Louis Gallo, June 22, 1977, LRPR.
199. White River Printers (Frank Stanford) to Dear Editors, November 1, 1977, LRPR.
200. Frank Stanford to John McKernan, ca. late summer or early fall 1977, LRPR.
201. Adamo, interview by Erwin.
202. Adamo, text message to author, October 15, 20. On July 12, 1978, C. D. wrote to Michael Cuddihy, regarding Lost Roads, that "our first obligation is to distribute the six books from the first series and *The Battlefield*," suggesting that, indeed, that few books were sent out before Frank's death. Wright to Cuddihy, CDWP.
203. Ernie Wright to C. D. Wright, November 15, 1977, CDWP.
204. C. D. Wright, Notebooks, September 12, 1978, CDWP.
205. Frank Stanford to Michael and Mary Cuddihy, November 9, 1976, *LPD*.
206. Frank Stanford to Alan Dugan, ca. late 1977, ADP.
207. Frank Stanford to Dugan, ca. late 1977, ADP.
208. Michael Cuddihy to C. D. Wright, October 29, 1979 (postmark), CDWP.
209. Scrap of paper, n.d., LRPR.
210. This handwritten document, which consisted of notes in preparation for an article Lux was writing on Frank's death, is in the possession of Jennifer

Lux, Tom Lux's widow. I found it at her Atlanta home in the summer of 2021. A published version is Thomas Lux, "'Brother Leo Told Me the Bell Was Ringing': On Frank Stanford," *FIELD* 20 (Spring 1979): 49.
211. C. D. Wright to Pamela Stewart, n.d., CDWP.
212. Gander, discussion.
213. Gilchrist to Frank Stanford and C. D. Wright, August 30, 1977, LRPR.
214. Frank Stanford to Ginny Stanford and C. D. Wright, May 21, 1978, GCSC. To this line, he added, "but this meant death for me."
215. Newspaper clipping, private collection of Carrie Prysock, daughter of Ruth Rogers, sister of Frank Stanford, accessed April 26, 2020, Dallas, TX.
216. Frank Stanford to Ginny Stanford and C. D. Wright, May 21, 1978, GCSC.
217. Ellen Gilchrist to Miller Williams, November 15, 1976, MWP.
218. Résumé of Ginny Stanford (through 1992), SAA.
219. Ellen Gilchrist to Miller Williams, January 26, 1977, MWP.
220. Ellen Gilchrist to Miller Williams, May 12, 1977, MWP.
221. Gilchrist to Williams, May 12, 1977, MWP.
222. David Young to Frank Stanford, May 20, 1977, FSP. While Frank took pride in ushering C. D. into her own "real world," the same could not be said about some of the other authors with whom he worked. "Everyone has contributed to Stoss's legend," he wrote to Ralph Adamo, "but no one has taught him how to write. I know I can't teach him." Likewise, Frank found himself having to praise and promote Ellen's poems. C. D. observed somewhat frustratedly that Frank "would have let her print her book however she wanted it." But Frank told Ralph that working on Ellen's book was "my least favorite thing." See Frank Stanford to Ralph Adamo, February 20, 1978, *LPD*; Adamo, discussion, June 3, 2023.
223. Louis Gallo and David Hershkovits, eds., *Barataria Review* 1, no. 1 (1974): first page (unnumbered).
224. Ellen Gilchrist to Miller Williams, n.d., MWP.
225. Ellen Gilchrist to Miller Williams, n.d., MWP.
226. Ellen Gilchrist to Miller Williams, n.d., MWP.
227. Luster, discussion, March 2, 2023; Steve Allen, in discussion with the author, April 20, 2024, New Orleans, LA.
228. Frank Stanford to Ginny Stanford and C. D. Wright, May 21, 1978, GCSC.
229. Louis Gallo, in discussion with the author, October 5, 2019.
230. Ellen Gilchrist, in discussion with the author, December 9, 2019.
231. C. D. Wright, Notebooks, September 19, 1978, CDWP.
232. C. D. Wright, Notebooks, October 7, 1978, CDWP.
233. Ginny Stanford, "Requiem: A Fragment," 155.
234. Ginny Stanford, "Requiem: A Fragment," 155.
235. Frank Stanford to Ginny Stanford and C. D. Wright, May 21, 1978, GCSC.
236. Ginny Stanford, "Death in the Cool Evening," 155.
237. Gander, discussion.
238. Frank Stanford to John McKernan, ca. late summer / early fall 1977, *LPD*.
239. Frank Stanford to Ginny Stanford and C. D. Wright, May 21, 1978, GCSC.
240. Frank Stanford to Ginny Stanford and C. D. Wright, ca. June 3, 1978, GCSC.

241. Frank Stanford to Ginny Stanford and C. D. Wright, ca. June 3, 1978, GCSC.
242. Michael Cuddihy, *Try Ironwood: An Editor Remembers* (Boston: Rowan Tree, 1990), 109.
243. Frank Stanford to Michael and Mary Cuddihy, November 9, 1976, *LPD*.
244. Cuddihy, *Try Ironwood*, 75.
245. Frank Stanford to Michael and Mary Cuddihy, November 9, 1976, *LPD*.
246. A notable exception is "Death and the Arkansas River," an earlier version of which appeared in *Constant Stranger* (1976) and which was, as we have seen, written in 1974–75; the other is "Blue Yodel a Prairie," which ran in the May 1, 1973, edition of the *Boston Phoenix*.
247. Cuddihy, *Try Ironwood*, 108.
248. Frank Stanford, *What about This*, 256.
249. Frank Stanford, *What about This*, 254.
250. Frank Stanford, *What about This*, 254.
251. Frank Stanford, *What about This*, 258.
252. Frank Stanford, *What about This*, 254.
253. Frank Stanford, *What about This*, 253.
254. Frank Stanford, *What about This*, 268, 292.
255. Frank Stanford, *What about This*, 284.
256. Frank Stanford, *What about This*, 259.
257. Frank Stanford, *What about This*, 261, 284.
258. Frank Stanford to Ginny Stanford and C. D. Wright, May 21, 1978, GCSC.
259. Frank Stanford to Ginny Stanford and C. D. Wright, ca. June 3, 1978, GCSC.
260. Ginny Stanford, "Requiem: A Fragment," 155.

**FOURTEEN**

1. Frank Stanford, *Hidden Water: From the Frank Stanford Archives*, ed. Michael Wiegers and Chet Weise (Nashville: Third Man Books, 2015), 94.
2. Frank Stanford, "No One Need Whistle," n.d., notebook 1, GCSC.
3. Frank Stanford, *What about This: Collected Poems of Frank Stanford*, ed. Michael Wiegers (Port Townsend, WA: Copper Canyon, 2015), 92.
4. Frank Stanford, n.d., Poetry Fragments, FSP.
5. Frank Stanford, n.d., Handwritten Notes, FSP.
6. Frank Stanford, *Hidden Water*, 93–94.
7. C. D. Wright, Notebooks, n.d., CDWP.
8. Thomas Lux, "Elegy for Frank Stanford," in *New and Selected Poems, 1975–1995* (New York: Houghton Mifflin, 1997), 36.
9. Frank Stanford to Ralph Adamo, February 20, 1978, LFS.
10. Justin Caldwell, in discussion with the author, February 6, 202. My copy of *The Sleeping Porch* does not show Caldwell's age. But Caldwell is probably remembering the information included in the galley proofs that Frank gave to him in the spring of 1978. C. D. very likely resolved the problem by removing his birth date in the final revision before it went to the printer.
11. Frank Stanford to Ellen Gilchrist, February 1, 1978, LFS.

12. Ellen Gilchrist to John Clarence Laughlin, February 25, 1978, Historic New Orleans Collection, Williams Research Center, New Orleans.
13. Frank Stanford to Michael Cuddihy, March 20, 1978, MCIP.
14. Ellen Gilchrist, "Visual Poems: Clarence, a Celebration," in *Haunter of Ruins: The Photography of Clarence John Laughlin*, ed. John H. Lawrence and Patricia Brady (New York: Bulfinch, 1997), 29.
15. A. J. Meek, *Clarence John Laughlin: Prophet without Honor* (Jackson: University of Mississippi Press, 2007), 10–17.
16. Frank Stanford to Richard Leo Johnson, February 15, 1978, LFS.
17. Frank Stanford to Richard Albertine, February 15, 1978, LFS.
18. Frank Stanford to Adamo, February 20, 1978, LFS.
19. "We will be out of town as of the 17th," Frank wrote to John Johnson on January 15, 1978, in connection to a surveying job. On January 25, Frank wrote to Johnson, "I just returned to Fayetteville." Frank Stanford to John Johnson, January 15, 1978, LRPR; Frank Stanford to John Johnson, January 25, 1978, LRPR.
20. Ellen Gilchrist to Miller Williams, n.d., MWP.
21. Frank Stanford to Ginny Stanford and C. D. Wright, May 21, 1978, GCSC.
22. Deborah Luster, in discussion with the author, September 29, 2019.
23. Ellen Gilchrist, in discussion with the author, November 21, 2021, Ocean Springs, MS.
24. Given how they coordinated their plans to see each other during Frank's last weeks in New Orleans in May, it is fairly clear that part of the reason Frank went to New Orleans was to see her.
25. Barbara Scott, in discussion with the author, July 28, 2023.
26. Leslie Parr, in discussion with the author, July 27, 2023.
27. Scott, discussion.
28. Ellen Gilchrist, in discussion with the author, October 7, 2019, Ocean Springs, MS; Ralph Adamo, in discussion with the author, September 19, 2019, New Orleans, LA.
29. Ralph Adamo, in discussion with the author, August 2023, New Orleans, LA.
30. Kay DuVernet to C. D. Wright and Forrest Gander, June 9, no year, CDWP.
31. Ralph Adamo, email message to author, July 13, 2023.
32. Ralph Adamo, text message to author, October 29, 2023.
33. Frank Stanford to Judge Wright, March 6, 1978, LFS.
34. Frank Stanford to Judge Wright, "Monday Afternoon," LFS.
35. Frank Stanford to Judge Wright, "Monday Afternoon," LFS.
36. Lease Authorization, Surveyor's Leasing Company, to lessee Frank Stanford, signed April 7, 1978, FSP.
37. Frank Stanford to Dorothy Stanford and Carolyn Gilbert, April 16, 1978, FSP.
38. Ernie Wright to C. D. Wright, November 15, 1977, CDWP. See Installment notes for $2,000 and $3,000, signed March 29, 1977, LRPR.
39. The financial details summarized in this paragraph were compiled from receipts, bank statements, copies of checks, bills, and invoices that are dispersed throughout the LRPR.

40. D. Nolan to Frank Graziano, February 15, 1978, LRPR.
41. D. Nolan to Alan Dugan, February 20, 1978, LRPR.
42. Frank Stanford to Karl Elder, February 15, 1978, LRPR.
43. Frank Stanford to Dorothy Stanford and Carolyn Gilbert, April 16, 1978, FSP.
44. C. D. Wright, Notebooks, November 1, 1978, CDWP.
45. I first saw this painting, owned by Ralph Adamo, on October 28, 2023, in New Orleans.
46. Frank Stanford to Ginny Stanford and C. D. Wright, May 21, 1978, GCSC.
47. Frank Stanford to Ginny Stanford and C. D. Wright, May 21, 1978, GCSC.
48. Frank Stanford to Ginny Stanford and C. D. Wright, May 21, 1978, GCSC.
49. Frank Stanford to Ginny Stanford and C. D. Wright, May 21, 1978, GCSC; Deborah Luster, in discussion with the author, March 3, 2023, New Orleans, LA.
50. Frank Stanford to Ginny Stanford and C. D. Wright, May 21, 1978, GCSC.
51. Robert Trussell, "Frank Stanford: A Poet's Dreams, Death and Legacy," *Stage & Scream in Kansas City* (blog), January 16, 2012, https://kansascitytheater.wordpress.com/2012/01/16/frank-stanford-a-poets-dreams-death-and-legacy/.
52. Frank Stanford to Ginny Stanford and C. D. Wright, May 21, 1978, GCSC.
53. Frank Stanford to Ginny Stanford and C. D. Wright, May 21, 1978, GCSC.
54. Ralph Adamo, in discussion with the author, October 28, 2023, New Orleans, LA.
55. Merideth Boswell, email message to author, February 25, 2020.
56. Boswell, email message to author, February 25, 2020. This painting of Merideth is owned by Ellen Gilchrist and was used for the cover of her novel *Drunk with Love*.
57. Frank Stanford to Bill Willett, September 14, 1972, FSP.
58. Frank Stanford to Ginny Stanford and C. D. Wright, May 21, 1978, GCSC. In a notebook entry after Frank's death, C. D. returned the gesture, writing "Frank Stanford" up and down the page. C. D. Wright, Notebooks, September 29, 1978, CDWP.
59. Frank Stanford to Ginny Stanford and C. D. Wright, May 21, 1978. FSP.
60. Ralph Adamo, in discussion with the author, September 6, 2019, New Orleans, LA. The issue was followed up on and confirmed in a text message from Adamo to me on October 30, 2023, and, again, in another conversation in New Orleans on December 18, 2023, and finally in an email from Adamo on May 31, 2024.
61. Frank Stanford to Ginny Stanford and C. D. Wright, May 21, 1978, GCSC. Forrest Gander, in our August 4, 2023, conversation, noted how at one point C. D. "froze up" when she and Frank were making love and that this was a moment of recognition she never forgot.
62. Frank Stanford to Ginny Stanford and C. D. Wright, June 3, 1978, GCSC.
63. Frank Stanford to Ginny Stanford and C. D. Wright, May 21, 1978, GCSC.
64. Adamo, discussion, September 19, 2019.
65. Frank Stanford to Dorothy Stanford, May 12, 1978, FSP.

66. Irv Broughton, draft of an autobiography, unpublished manuscript, n.d., shared with the author on June 18, 2024.
67. Luster, discussion, March 3, 2023; "May 18, 1978 Weather History in New Orleans," Weather Spark, Cedar Lake Ventures, accessed January 5, 2025, https://weatherspark.com/h/d/11799/1978/5/18/Historical-Weather-on-Thursday-May-18-1978-in-New-Orleans-Louisiana-United-States#Figures-Temperature.
68. Ginny Stanford, "Death in the Cool Evening," in *Saltwater, Sweetwater: Women Write from California's North Coast*, ed. Barbara L. Baer and Maureen Anne Jennings (Forestville, CA: Floreant, 1998), 5. In Ginny Stanford, "Dreams Leave Their Hindtracks," unpublished manuscript, 1996, 2, shared with the author by Ralph Adamo. Ginny wrote, "He died before I had time to finish the portrait."
69. A. P. Walton, "Toward Innumerable Futures: Frank Stanford & Origins," (master's thesis, Lund University, 2015), 15. Walton reports that Ginny found the letters, not that Frank intentionally made them easy to find.
70. Ginny Stanford, "Dreams Leave Their Hindtracks," 3.
71. Frank Stanford to Ginny Stanford and C. D. Wright, June 3, 1978, FSP.
72. Frank Stanford to Ginny Stanford and C. D. Wright, May 21, 1978, GCSC.
73. C. D. Wright, Notebooks, September 24, 1978, CDWP.
74. Frank Stanford, "The Will of Frank Stanford," May 22, 1978, FSP.
75. Frank Stanford to Ginny Stanford and C. D. Wright, June 3, 1978, FSP.
76. Frank Stanford to Ginny Stanford and C. D. Wright, June 3, 1978, FSP.
77. Ralph Adamo to John Stoss, June 2, 2978, private collection of Ralph Adamo, accessed in November 2019.
78. Frank Stanford to Ginny Stanford and C. D. Wright, June 3, 1978, FSP.
79. Adamo, discussion, September 6, 2019.
80. Frank Stanford to Ginny Stanford and C. D. Wright, June 3, 1978, FSP.
81. Frank Stanford to Dorothy Stanford, May 31, 1978, GCSC.
82. Frank Stanford to Ralph Adamo, May 31, 1978, shared the author by Ralph Adamo.

## CODA

1. Irv Broughton and Frank Stanford, *It Wasn't a Dream: It Was a Flood* (1974), 16 mm film, posted August 22, 2019, YouTube video, 26:19, https://www.youtube.com/watch?v=aPS1tXOvoC8&t=315s, at 18:52–55.
2. C. D. Wright to Pamela Stewart, n.d. [after June 1978], CDWP.

# *Index*

Page numbers in italics refer to illustrations. Names enclosed in single quotes refer to characters (real or fictional) that appear in Frank Stanford's poems. Except for *The Battlefield Where the Moon Says I Love You* and *It Wasn't a Dream: It Was a Flood*, which can be found as main headings, all works by Stanford appear under BOOKS or POEMS.

## Abbreviations

**TB:** *The Battlefield Where the Moon Says I Love You*
**FS:** Francis Gildart (Frank) Stanford
**Dorothy:** Dorothy Gilbert Stanford
**CD:** Carolyn Davis (C. D.) Wright
**GS:** Virginia (Ginny) Crouch Stanford
**Frank Sr.:** Albert Francis Stanford

## A

Abraham, Rufus, 182–83, 442
*Abraham's Knife*, 182
Adamo, Ralph: about, 208; *Barataria*, editor of, 469, 474; on Broughton publishing FS, 219; and *Carolyn Wright readies herself for another evening* (GS painting), 496; on CD/FS/GS love triangle, 449; on CD's disinterest in being a lawyer, 441; on Dugan's reaction to FS, 215; on FS drawing on childhood in poems, 428; FS seeks opinion of, 487; on FS's disinterest in recognition, 378; on FS's last days, 503; on FS's poetry, xvi, xxii, xxiv; on FS's support to GS, 406; on FS's theme of the marginalized, xxxiii; on Gilchrist and Kullman, 465, 490; on legend/myth of FS, 199, 204–5; and MFA program, 200, 209, 216; on Mount Sequoyah, 230; *Sadness at the Private University*, published, 469; TB, receives bound copy of, 459; on Whitehead's reaction to FS, 192
Adelle (FS girlfriend), 112
*Aggressive Ways of the Casual Stranger, The* (Waldrop), 218, 222
Agrarianism, xxxiv–xxxv, xxxvii, 82, 195, 197, 200, 206–7, 284
Albertine, Richard, 469, 484, 486–87
*Aldebaran Review*, 252

Alexander, Edna (first wife of Frank Sr.), 21, 26
"Algonquin Round Table of Fayetteville," 191
Ali, Muhammad, 172, 228, 414, 502
Alighieri, Dante, 67, 71
All Saints' Episcopal Church, 121
*Alla Breve Loving* (Wright), 441, 453–54
"Alla Breve Loving" (Wright thesis), 441, 453
Allen, Steve, 475
Alquié, Ferdinand, 160
Alter, Carl, 6, 17
Alter, Dorothy Gilbert. *See* Stanford, Dorothy Gilbert
Alter, Francis Gildart. *See* Stanford, Francis Gildart (Frank)
Altman, Robert, 97
Alvarez, Julia, 202
"Always Looking for a Safe Place" (Stoss), 194, 199
American Academy of Poets, 389
American Federation of Labor, 28
*American Poetry Review*, xxx, 360, 391
Anderson, Sherwood, 408
Anderson, Walter, 197
Antioch Press, 308, 360, 395
*Antioch Review*, 360, 395
Apollinaire, 267
Arion, 149
*Ark River Review*, 360, 395
Arkansas Coast Guard Auxiliary, 145
Arkansas River, 381. *See also* Stanford, Francis Gildart (Frank), POEMS: "Death and the Arkansas River"
Arkansas State Hospital, 273, 278, 295, 310, 362. *See also under* Fuhrmann, Nicholas; Stanford, Francis Gildart (Frank), LIFE; Stanford, Francis Gildart (Frank), PERSONALITY
*Arkansas Weekly*, 80
*As I Lay Dying* (Faulkner), 110, 236
Astral Project (band), 491
*Atlantic Monthly*, 392
Atlantic Records, 266
Auden, W. H., 221

1034 Audubon Drive (Memphis, TN), 67
Audubon Park (neighborhood in Memphis), 49
*Autograph Poetry in the English Language: Facsimiles of Original Manuscripts from the Fourteenth to the Twentieth Centuries*, 403
"Automatic Co-Pilot" (Stanford script), 309, 416–17

**B**

Babij, James (Jim): about, 283–84; and film project with FS, 330–32; on FS, 284, 287–88, 292; on FS's commitment to artistic integrity, 331–32, 379–80; on FS's screenplay, 379–80; New England, road trip to, 286–89; on *The Singing Knives*, 285; mentioned, 356, 381
*Baby Doll* (film), 242, 244
'Baby Gauge,' 33, 36, 42, 57, 93, 149, 235, 237, 375
Baby Gauge (friend), 33, 35, 40, 90, 92, 149, 170, 375
Bach, J. S., 329, 346
Bad Fred. *See* McCuistion, Fred
Bankhead, Dan, 74
Banks, Richard Kenneth: about, 224–26, 322, 323, 344; illness and death, 396–97; in *It Wasn't a Dream: It Was a Flood*, 335, 343, 344, 345, 385; and 'Sylvester Martingale,' inspiration for, 324–27; mentioned, 337–38, 340, 352, 405, 409. *See also* 'Sylvester Martingale'; Stanford, Francis Gildart (Frank), LIFE: Banks, Richard
*Barataria*, 466, 469, 474–75, 488, 500
Barker, Miss, 50, 58, 60
Bartholomew (Subiaco monk), 138
baseball. *See under* Memphis; Stanford, Francis Gildart (Frank), LIFE; *The Battlefield Where the Moon Says I Love You*
"Basement Blues, The" (song), 179
Bates, Daisy, 80–81

# INDEX

*The Battlefield Where the Moon Says I Love You*: about, xix–xx; adolescent sexual desire, theme of, 110–11; adoption in, 61, 108; Agrarianism, treatment of, 82–83; analysis of "cavalry" passage, xxi–xxii; Antioch Press, submits to, 308; and the "astronomer," 65–66, 157, 182; autobiographical nature of, 50–52, 59–61, 68, 237, 308, 310; baseball as signifier of injustice, 74–76; Blacks in film, 241–45; Blake, William in, 328; blames for breakup of marriage, 277; body form, expressions of, 111; Bushido in, 130; and Camille (FS girlfriend), 112, 155; carnivals and fairs in, 76–80; 'Charlie B.' in, 29, 37–38, 56, 62–63, 65–66, 70, 175, 239–45, 429; childhood innocence and memory, theme of, 237, 257–58; 'Claude Ricks' in, 237; Cocteau in, 347; compared to *Shade*, 429; compared to *Ulysses*, xx, xxii; compared to Whitman, xxix; composition history of, xix, 108–9, 147, 226, 234–35, 268, 271–72, 308–9, 322, 373, 387, 429, 442, 454, 471; connection to "myths" of FS, xix; considered "finished," 404; death, theme of, 484; dream states in, 177, 240, 309; and Elvis Presley, 68, 71; film, influence of, 309–10; films in, 316, 325–26; fishing references in, 94; 'Five Spoke' and, 79–80; 'Francis' (*see* 'Francis Gildart'); freedom ride scene, 442; FS claims to have burned, 271; and FS, transitions on race, 70–71; FS's concepts and goals for, 264; FS's description of, xx; human dignity and, 235; idiom, language, and dialect in, xx–xxii, 98, 157, 235, 324–26; interiority of, xxii; and Jimmy Lee, 35, 37–38, 44, 68, 71, 73–74, 86, 96–98, 108–9, 155, 183, 196–98, 235, 240–41, 243–45, 316, 428; language of Black society as link between levee past and tavern present, 176; levee camps in, 29–37, 66, 237, 442; and manuscript, destruction of, 271; memory and dreams, themes of, 19x, 52–53, 161–62, 310, 363; Memphis and the Blues in, 69–71, 238–40; Memphis, treatment of ("Shadow History"), 68–83; Mountain Home, not mentioned in, 89–90; musical influences of, xx–xxi; New York City in, 221; occult and transcendence in, 118; Old English influences of, xx–xxi; older women, theme of, 111; orphanage motif in, 175; own thoughts on, 276–77; pages of, lost from *Rêve* (boat), 289; 'Pantagruel' and, 77–78, 183, 534n118; public obscurity of, xxiii–xxiv; publication, attempts at, 386–90; publication of, 457–60, 471; publisher's exploitation of poets in, 221; racial injustice, theme of, 235, 237–38, 244; racial unity, theme of, 240–41; reactions of Blacks and Whites to films, 241–45; recognition as masterpiece, xix; and relationship to "St. Francis and the Wolf," 264, 267, 429; 'Rufus Abraham' in, 182–83; segregation, theme of, 57; self-referential treatment of himself as a boy, 109–10; sexual encounters in, 111–12; and southern Black vernacular in, 181–83, 235; Sputnik Monroe and, 81–82; Sunset Drive Inn scene, 241–46; 'Sylvester' in, xxxi, 53, 76, 157, 176–77, 183, 235, 239, 324–27, 352; 'Tangle Eye' in, 56, 238, 240; time, themes of, 53, 257–58; utopianism and, 442; and "value of silence" in, 167; warrior culture, theme of, 246; as window on FS at Mount Sequoyah, 246

Baudelaire, 45

Baxter Laboratories, 89

Baxter Theater, 112, 305

Beal, Endia, xxxviii
Beale Street, 70, 72, 78
*Bean Street* (Morris), 438–39, 460, 468
Beaver Lake, 225–26, 233, 248, 320, 341, 363, 367, 404, 448. *See also* Rogers, AR
Beckett, Samuel, 371
Bell and Howell (movie camera), 330, 334, 386
Bellerophon, 272
Bender, Eleanor: FS rejects publishing offers from, 219–20; FS's poems, interest in, 218–19; on FS's talent, 346–47; mentioned, 208, 209, 222, 235, 253, 267–68, 274, 279, 282
Benjamin, Walter, 45
*Beowulf*, xx, 128, 138, 183–84, 259, 388, 416
Bergman, Ingmar, 305, 306, 317, 328, 425
Berlin, Isaiah, 66
Berry, Wendell, 213, 217
Berryman, John, xvi, 52, 363, 387
Bertolucci, Bernardo, 306, 382, 411, 413–14, 417–19, 424–25
*Best of Eddie Harris, The* (album), 339
'Beth,' 112–13
"Big boy," 165
"Big Boy Leaves Home" (Wright), 165
"Big Time" Sonny Morris, 186, 229, 248
Biguenet, John: about, 106; on FS's breach with MFA program, 207, 209; on FS's deep knowledge of literature, 106, 562n168; on FS's knowledge and interest in film, 306, 310, 412, 415; on FS's personality, 562n168; on FS's poetry, 197; on FS's use of language, 182; and Hollins Conference, 212, 306; mentioned, 200
Bilbo, Senator Theodore G., 43
'Billy the Jew,' 141
Bishop, Elizabeth, 333–34, 455
Black Americans for Democracy (BAD), xxx, xxxvi–xxxvii, 10, 171–72, 236
Black Angel. *See* 'Sylvester Martingale'

Blake, William, 145, 159, 185, 296, 327–28, 335, 406, 418, 422, 442
*Blessing of the Fleet, The* (Broughton), 461
"Blind Lemon" Jefferson (bluesman), 240
*Blind Man with a Pistol* (Himes), 179
the Blues: lyrics, sensual character of, 15–16; Parchman Farm, and, 14–15; and race, 70; in TB, 70
"Blues Before Sunrise" (song), 239
Bly, Robert, 160, 266, 270, 321, 415, 422
Bobby Bland (bluesman), 70, 240
'BoBo Washington,' 37, 94, 98, 183, 235, 429
Boccaccio, Giovanni, 106
Bond, Blair, 224, 509
Book League of America, 105
Borges, Jorge Luis, 316, 415
'Born in the Camp with Six Toes,' 33, 36, 149, 185, 429
Born in the Camp with Six Toes (childhood friend), 33, 149, 170, 237
*Boston Phoenix* (newspaper), 346
Boswell, Merideth, 450, 496
the bottoms (Fayetteville neighborhood). *See* Sherman's Tavern
Bowen, Ezra, 64
Boyle, Kay, 333
Boyle, T. Coraghessan, 392
"Branches of Water or Desire, The" (Dugan), 216
Bread Loaf, xxiv
Breton, André, 411
Brockman, Eliot, 337, 340–41, 352
Brooks, Jim, 157
Broughton, Irving: about, xxiv, 213, 332; creative control, allows FS, 219–20; on Dorothy, 56, 105; and films with FS, 306, 332–34 (*see also It Wasn't a Dream: It Was a Flood*); on FS and dreams, 160; FS poems published by, 213; on FS's double lives, 453; on FS's inexperience with film camera, 386; on FS's personality, 562n168; on FS's poetry, 213; on FS's writing habits, 158; on GS, 448;

## INDEX

and loyalty to FS, xxvii, 215, 220,
303, 332, 336, 362, 425, 434, 458,
562n183; New England, road trip
to, 284–90, 291, 292; poetry of, 437;
professional struggles of, 332–33.
*See also* Mill Mountain Press; *Mill Mountain Review*
Brown, Darrell, 172
Brown, Sterling, xxxvii, 165
*Brown v. Board of Education* (1954), xxxii, 42, 44, 57
Brust, John, 213
221 Buchanan St (Fayetteville), 157–58, 162–63, 170–73, 232, 236, 300
*Buckdancer's Choice* (Dickey), 420
Bull Shoals Lake, 92
Buñuel, Luis, 306, 318, 411
*Burden of Southern History, The* (Woodward), xxx
Burns, Robert, 299, 321
Burton, Sir Richard, 106
Busch, AR, 337, 341. *See also under* Stanford, Francis Gildart (Frank), LIFE
Bushido, 125, 128–30, 132, 139, 151, 180
*Bushido: The Soul of Japan* (Nitobe), 129
Butler, Jack, 191–93, 203, 210
*Byron in Italy* (Quennell), 50, 253
Byron, Lady, 258
Byron, Lord, 50, 258–59

**C**

Calabash Pottery Collective, 450
Caldwell, Justin, 424, 484–85
Camille (FS girlfriend), 112, 155
Camp, Burt, 426–27, 433, 437, 464, 468. *See also* Elk Ranch Printing
Camp Subiaco, 280
Campbell, Cheryl (*née* Crites, later Ross, Cher): about, 227, 230, 339; on breakups with FS, 298–300, 338–39; in Eureka Springs, 247; FS, affair with, 227–28, 230–32, 247, 268–69, 282–83, 292–98; on FS, love for, 311; on FS's creativity, 384;

on FS's drinking, 233, 247, 339; in FS's poems, 348, 456; on FS's probing interest in her, 231; on FS's writing habits, 232; Mencin, and discovery of Campbell's affair, 247; in New York City, 282–83, 312–13; pregnancy and miscarriage, 247. *See also under* Stanford, Francis Gildart (Frank), LIFE
Campbell, Gene, 32
Camus, Albert, 295
*Canterbury Tales, The* (Chaucer), 141
Cape Cod, MA, 291
Cape Rosier, ME, 288, 290–91
Carné, Marcel, 317, 341, 380
carnivals and fairs. *See* Cotton Carnival; Cotton Makers' Jubilee; Mid-South Fair
*Carolyn Wright Readies herself for another evening* (GS painting), 494–96
Carpenter, Bill, 32
Carr, Bobby Joe, 169
Carroll County, AR, 322
Carter, Hodding, 7–9, 43
Carter, Robert, 335
Cash, W. J., 195
*Catcher in the Rye, The* (Salinger), 138
Catholicism, 122, 135
Cervantes, Miguel de, 106
Cézanne, Paul, 407
Chagall, Marc, 102, 408
Chappell, Fred, 213
Char, René, 159
Charles, Ray, 71
'Charlie B.' *See under The Battlefield Where the Moon Says I Love You*
Charlie B. *See* Lemon, Charlie Bolivar (Charlie B.)
Chaucer, Geoffrey, xx, 103, 128, 138, 184, 392, 416
Checchio, Michael, 420
Cheryl. *See* Campbell, Cheryl
Chesterton, G. K., 253
*Childe Harold's Pilgrimage* (Byron), 50

*Children of Paradise* (Carné), 341
*Choice*, 395
*Chosen Few* (Rhodes), 179
Christ of the Ozarks, 210
City Lights Books, 321
Cleveland, MS, 74, 300
Clover Hill, MS, 374
Cocteau, Jean. *See under* Stanford, Francis Gildart (Frank), CREATIVE LIFE; *Singing Knives, The*; *The Battlefield Where the Moon Says I Love You*
Coleman, Frank (cousin of FS): on Dorothy's love for FS, 55–56; on Frank Sr.'s love for FS, 56; FS, physical description of, 56; and FS, youthful intimacy with, 61–62, 112; on FS's adoption, 60; on FS's happiness as child, 96; on FS's popularity, 59; on Lake Norfork home, 87; on levee life, 30–35, 43–44; on life at Lake Norfork, 96; on race in Stanford household, 63, 87; on Stanford sense of privilege, 87
Coleridge, Samuel Taylor, 138, 311, 422, 444
Coltrane, John, 240
Columbia County, xvi, 25
*Commercial Appeal* (newspaper), 80
*Complete Poems* (Lawrence), 279
Confederacy, 75, 78, 130, 131, 154, 172, 173, 197
Conrad, Joseph, 106, 215, 253
*Contemporary American Poets, The*, 199
Cooney, Camillus, 142
Coover, Robert, 252, 393
Copper Canyon Press, xvii
Cotton Carnival, 76–79, 149
Cotton Makers' Jubilee, 76, 78–79
Country Road 109 (Busch, AR), 337
Couperin, François, 67
Coury House, 123, 186, 273, 308
Cowley, Malcolm, xxvi, 287, 291–92, 300, 315, 321, 356, 375, 380, 388, 392
Cranfield Boat Dock, 92
Crites, Cheryl. *See* Campbell, Cheryl

Cuddihy, Mary, 350, 459
Cuddihy, Michael: about, 350–51; advises FS to pivot to new work, 379; "Bark" manuscript submitted to Lost Roads Publishers, 462, 486; on CD's poetry, 444, 478, 485; on concern for FS's mental health, 477; and *Crib Death*, origins of, 477; FS asks advice of, 390–91; FS, friendship with, 361, 390–91, 423; on FS's poetry, 351, 361–62, 379, 388, 478; on FS's sensitivity to criticism, 362; on GS's art, 408; on obscurity of FS, xxiv; urges FS to focus on writing, 372. *See also Ironwood*; Stanford, Francis Gildart (Frank), LIFE
Culbreth, Judy, 359

**D**

Dalí, Salvador, 318
Dallas Nine, 409
'Dark,' 53, 76, 240, 428–29
Dartmouth College, 287
Davidson, Donald, 195, 493
Davis, Miles, 240
Davis, Richard P., 19
Daye, Hippolyte, 407
De Maupassant, Guy, 317
Dean, James, 241
Deaton, Randy, 157
*Decameron* (Boccacio), 253
Deep Image (school), 422
Deep South, 16, 25, 130, 134, 150, 183, 242, 469
Deidre: affair with, 298–300; in FS poems, 456; mentioned, 307, 313, 315, 356, 357, 456, 489
Delius, Frederick, 358
*Deliverance* (Dickey), 330
DeQuincey, Thomas, 316
Dickens, Charles, 106
Dickey, James, 161, 212, 254, 270, 316, 321, 330, 420–21
Dickinson, Emily, 318, 474
Dickson Street (Fayetteville, AR), 156, 163, 165, 203, 225–26, 454, 488

INDEX 619

Dillard, Annie, 213
Dillard, R. H. W., 211
Dixie Hummingbirds, 71, 240
"Dixie" (song), 171, 172
Dobie Red, 15
Doby, Larry, 74
*Don Quixote* (Cervantes), 253
Dostoyevsky, Fyodor, 253
Dr. Ball (psychiatrist), 233
Dr. Snow (family physician), 146
Dr. Tichenor's Antiseptic, 75
Dragonwagon, Crescent, 314–15, 322
Drayton, Michael, 253
Dreyer, Carl Theodor, 318, 327–28, 335
Driver, AR, 26, 64
*Driving to Biloxi* (Simmons), 421
Dugan, Alan: drunkenness of, 215–16; FS, advises against 'academic' style, 254, 255; FS, as creative mentor to, 253–54; FS as genius, xvi, 216; FS, has trust of, 252, 254; FS, loses touch with, 471; FS, supports publishing efforts of, 226–27, 253–64; on FS's marriage to Mencin, 247; on FS's mental health, 278; on FS's poetry, xxii–xxiv, 215, 216, 254, 255; MFA program, visits, 215–17; MFA student poetry, savages, 216
'Durett, O. Z.,' 35–36, 44, 63, 235, 432
Durrett, O. Z. (Stanford household worker), 35, *36*, *39*, 40, 44, 62–63, 170
DuVernet, Kay, ix, xi, 489, *490*, 501–4
Dylan, Bob, 163

**E**
Earl of Sandwich, xvi, 91, 175
East Lafayette Street (Fayetteville, AR), 200
312 East Rock Street (Sherman's Tavern), 166
Eberhart, Richard: about, 287; on Broughton's poetry, 437; on FS's personality, 287, 521n101; on FS's poetry, 205; and FS's visit to Cape Rosier, 288–89, *291*; on news of FS's death, 575n162; mentioned, xxiv, 290, 327, 333, 356, 390, 392, 424

*Edge of Campus: A Journal of the Black Experience at the University of Arkansas, The* (Morgan), 172
"Elegy Written in a Country Churchyard" (Gray), 141
Eliot, George, 138
Eliot, T. S., 142, 441
Elk Ranch Printing, 0–190, 426, 464, 468. *See also* Camp, Burt; Lost Roads Publishers
Ellison, Ralph, xxxvii, 10, 212
Emery Memorial Home, 3, 6, 61, 90, 179
Emma. *See* Spriggs, Emma (Stanford household worker)
Empire State Building, 293
Empty Space Theater, 386
*Endymion* (Keats), 272, 386
*Esquire*, 352, 392–95, 399, 404, 424
Eureka Springs: about, 313–16; FS in, 247, 313–39, 425, 464; FS writes short fiction in, 391; FS's girlfriends in, 449–50; mentioned, 210, 269, 340, 342–43, 347, 349, 352, 356, 359, 365, 376, 396, 402, 426, 451, 461, 489. *See also* Banks, Richard Kenneth; Camp, Burt; Campbell, Cheryl; DuVernet, Kay; Stanford, Francis Gildart (Frank), LIFE: Eureka Springs
Eureka Springs Theater, 317–18
*Evergreen Review*, 213
*Exhibitionist, The* (Slavitt), 212
"Exil" (Follain), 412, 416

**F**
Fats Domino, 73
Faulkner, William: FS as compared to, xvii, xxvi, xxxii–xxxiv, xxxvi, 391; FS's ambitions towards, xvi, 103; FS's knowledge of, 64–65, 103, 138, 253, 254; mentioned, 42, 110, 220, 291, 317, 408
Fayetteville, AR: about, xxxvi, 154; and civil rights/racism, 165–69, 171–72, 180; as FS's Oxford and Salem, xxvi; FS's reputation in, 398, 445–46. *See also* Mount Sequoyah; Sherman's Tavern; UARK Master of Fine Arts program (MFA)

Fazenda, Louise, 67
Fellini, Federico, 305, 317-18, 439
Ferlinghetti, Lawrence, xvi, 321, 380, 416
"Fern Hill" (Thomas), 104
*FIELD: Contemporary Poetry and Poetics*, 360-61, 395, 459, 474
Finnell, Marjorie, 389-90
Finney, Nikky, xxxviii
Finton, William, 122
Firestone (company), 4, 6, 17-19, 31, 123
Fisher Body Company, 186
Fitzgerald, Ella, 240
'Five Spoke,' 79-80, 98, 235
Fletcher, Gary, 59
Fletcher, John Gould, 287
"Floating Troupe of the Unnaturals, The" (fictional troupe), 77
Flood of 1927, xxxii, 14, 16, 24, 26-29
Follain, Jean, 217, 411-13, 415-16
Foote, Shelby, 7-9, 212
Forché, Carolyn, 390
Ford, Jesse Hill, 220, 322, 336
Fort Hays State University, 191
Fort Smith, AR, 122, 133, 163-64, 165, 189, 305
Fort Smith Art Center Competition, 409
Fort Smith Northside High School, 127-28
*Four Seasons, The* (Vivaldi), 339
Fox, William L., on TB, 310, 388
'Francis Gildart': on adoption and orphans, 61, 175, 182; adventures of, xxiii, 240-46; as alter ego for FS, xx, xxix, xxxii, 327; on the astronomer, 65-67, 71, 157, 182; on authenticity/phoniness, 221; on avoiding "show of learning," 104, 106-7, 141; on baseball, 74-76; on biracial world, 90; on carnivals, 76-80; as champion of marginalized, xxix; and Charlie B., 29; on childhood black friends, 33-34; on childhood in Memphis, 49-51, 54, 57, 62-63, 69; on disinterest in education, 58-59; dreams and dream sequences of, 117-18, 162, 239-40, 258, 309; on Elvis, 68; on everyday experience vs. book learning, 157-58; on films, 316, 325-26; and the freedom ride scene, 442-43; on identity, 174, 176-78; on images, 330; on Jimmy Lee, 98, 316; language and expressiveness of, xx-xxi, xxiii, xxxi, 98, 182-84, 325-26; on levee life, 30-35, 37-38, 40-41, 56, 66; on memories and childhood, 52-54, 94, 257-58; on music, 70-73, 238-39; on observation and listening, 167; on Old South heritage, 8-9, 11-12, 23-24; and the oppressed, xxxii, 42, 57, 70, 237-38, 240-46, 324-25, 429; on Ozark nature, 87-88, 94-95; on promiscuity, 268; on racist press, 80-81; on reality of surreal south, 161-62; on Sputnik Monroe, 81-82; on Sylvester, 53, 76, 157, 176, 177, 239, 324-26; on warrior culture, 130. *See also The Battlefield Where the Moon Says I Love You*
Francis Gildart (FS pseudonym), 359-60
Francis, Saint, xiv, 106, 179, 347, 500
Franklin, Beverly, 99, 102, 112
Frayser (neighborhood in Memphis), 49, 57
Friebert, Stuart, 360-61
Friendship House, 132
Frost, Robert, 202, 221, 290, 319, 424
Fugitives, xxxv, xxxvii, 287. *See also* Agrarianism
Fuhrmann, Nicholas: about, 95, 135, 142-43, 500, 543n31; as boxing coach, 125; Dorothy as Southern Belle, 123; on Dorothy's influence on FS, 105-6; on FS as "furious, angry wild beast," 153; on FS's aloofness, 103; and FS's and Mencin's wedding, officiates at, 246, 248; on FS's athleticism, 124; and FS's

change to withdrawn and introverted, 163; on FS's conversion to Catholicism, 122; on FS's disinterest in money, 186, 249, 318; on FS's disinterest in team sports, 124; on FS's film-making, 382; on FS's introversion, 143; on FS's karate, 116; on FS's knowledge of adoption, 174; on FS's marriage to Mencin, 247–48; on FS's maturity, 145; on FS's mental health, 273; and FS's nervous breakdown, 273–74, 277; on FS's physicality, 155, 308; on FS's racism, 133; on FS's reaction to being an orphan, 175; on FS's reaction to Wiederkehr drowning, 382; on FS's reading habits, 138–39, 147; on FS's spiritualism, 134, 135; on FS's subtle double life, 146; on FS's support to *Rock Quarry*, 380–81; on FS's writing habits, 233–34; and manliness of poetry, 142–43; as mentor to FS, 141–43, 302; on monks' love of FS, 137; mentioned, 149, 157, 184, 194, 204, 280, 301, 302, 305, 454, 499–500, 502, 509

Fuller, B. A. G., 106

## G

Gage, Lawrence (father of Baby Gauge), 35
Gaines, Ernest J., xxxiii, 511
Gallo, Louis, 469, 474–75
Gambier, OH, 286
Gander, Forrest (husband of CD), 441, 444, 448, 457, 472, 490, 513
Garbo, Greta, 301, 303
Garman, Dean, 427
Garrett, George, 148, 211–13, 317, 321, 328, 506
General Motors, 186
George's Majestic Lounge, 156, 167, 169, 488
"Get on the Good Foot" (song), 346
Gilbert, Judson "Judd" Malcolm (father of Dorothy), 10, 12–14

Gilchrist, Ellen: about, 465–66; and *Barataria*, 469, 474, 488; on FS as beautiful, 465; FS, praise for, xvi; GS, champion and mentor to, 473–74; on GS's art, 474; on Kullman (husband), 490–91; Lost Roads Publishers, benefactor of, 464, 466, 475; money as entree to literary world, 474; New Orleans, social life in, 488, 491; mentioned, ix, xi, 470, 472, 486, 502. *See also* Lost Roads Publishers

Gildart, Carolyn Beatrice (mother of Dorothy), 6, 10, 91
*Gilgamesh*, 138
Ginsberg, Allen: on FS's poetry, xvi, 211; visit to UARK MFA, 210–11; mentioned, xix, 52, 191, 220, 229, 252, 270, 321, 380, 390, 420
Godard, Jean-Luc, 305, 318
*Goldfinch & Son* (Stern), 463
Goldwyn, Sam, Jr., 212
Golgotha, xxi
Gordon, Robert, 70, 172, 393–94
Graceland, 67
Gragg, Sara, 105, 336
Graham, Martha, 138, 293
Great Flood of 1913, 26
Great Migration, 26, 442
Great Mississippi Flood of 1927. *See* Flood of 1927
Green Acres (Dorothy's farm in Greenville), 5–6, 9–10, 17–18, 20
Greene, Graham, 138
Greene, Omar, 126–27, 142
Greenland, AR, 230
Greenville, MS: literary character of, 7–10; and race, 7–10, 12, 27, 62, 69, 88. *See also* Green Acres (Dorothy's farm in Greenville); Stanford, Dorothy Gilbert; Stanford, Francis Gildart (Frank), LIFE
Greer Real Estate (surveying client), 491
"Greta Garbo of the Ozarks" (FS girlfriend), 301–2

Griesemer, Kevin, 127
Griffith, D. W., 316
*Gris Gris*, 487
Gwynn, R. S. "Sam": on CD/FS/GS love triangle, 446; on Dugan, 215–16; on Fayetteville, xxvi; on FS and Mencin, 249; on FS and Pasolini, 317; on FS as surveyor, 249–51; on FS as Whitehead protégé, 199; on FS in MFA, 194, 204, 207–8; on FS's admiration for Mishima, 259; on FS's diverse childhood, 83; on FS's friendship with Jimbo, 165; on FS's reading habits, 106; on Hollis Conference, 213; on shared language of poor southerners, 182; on Sherman's Tavern, 236; on UARK MFA, 191–93, 195, 201, 204, 236; on Whitehead, 190, 195; on Williams, 200

**H**

*Hallelujah* (film), 242, 244, 246
Hanover, NH, 262, 287
Harris, Nancy, 202
Harris, Vernie, 157
Harrison, AR, 322, 323, 439, 441, 443, 465
Harrison, Bill, 190, 192, 194, 200, 212–13, 439
Harrison, Jim, 97
Hawkins, Emmett, 126, 132–34
Hawthorne, Nathaniel, xxvi, 253
Hayes, Terrance, xvi
Hayman, David, 392–93
Hecht, Anthony, 388, 390
Heller, Anne Conover, 394
Hemingway, Ernest, 138
Henriksen, Matt, 173, 514
Herbert (Subiaco monk), 123, 307
Hess, Carole (cousin of FS): on FS water-skiing, 95; on FS's charisma, 56; on FS's personality, 95–96; on seeing Elvis, 68; on Stanford life in Memphis, 54–56; mentioned, 59, 61
Hesse, Hermann, 253
Hi-Hat (bar), 320, 322, 339–40, 347, 402
Hide-Away (restaurant), 19

Himes, Chester, 179
hinkty (or hincty), 179, 181
Hirsch, Edward, 54, 295
*History of Philosophy, A* (Fuller), 106
Hoffman, Daniel, 290–91
Hogue, Alexandre, 409
Holbrook, Hal, 305
Hollins Conference on Creative Writing and Cinema, 211–13, 219, 412, 419
The Hollow (Fayetteville neighborhood). *See* Sherman's Tavern
Hooker, John Lee, 14, 72, 85, 240, 339
Hopkins, Gerard Manley, xi, 138
Horsting, Eric, 308, 360
Horton, Walter (bluesman, "Tangle Eye"), 15, 238
Houghton Mifflin, 392
House, Dick: on FS's disinterest in classes, 157, 158; on FS's erratic outbursts, 162; on FS's friendships with Sherman's Tavern men, 170, 171; on Mountain Home and race, 88–89
House of Books (now Dickson St. Bookshop), 445, 454
House, Son (bluesman), 28, 72, 240
Howard, Richard, xvi, 59, 252, 387–88
"Howl" (Ginsberg), 211"
Hughes, Charles, 72
Hughes, Langston, xxxvii, 10, 179, 339
Hugo, Victor, 77, 106, 183, 317
Hume, David, 66
Hurston, Zora Neale, xxvii, xxx

**I**

"I Sing the Body Electric" (Whitman), 111
"I Write in a Peculiar Mood Unworthy of the Trust" (Whitehead), 190
*I'll Take My Stand*, xxxv, 82
*Inferno* (Dante), 67, 71
*Iowa Review*, 270, 352, 361, 392–93
Iowa Writers' Workshop, 190
*Ironwood*, 104, 350–52, 361–62, 418, 420, 423, 435, 444, 477. *See also* Cuddihy, Michael
*Isle of the Dead* (Rachmaninoff), 329
*It Came from Memphis* (Gordon), 70

*It Wasn't a Dream: It Was a Flood* (film): Broughton directs remotely, 344–46; child coffin scene, 381–82; as levee camp documentary, 342, 374–75; origins of, 113, 324, 333–35; production and filming of, 290, 341–46, 380, *381*, 385; screenings of, 386, 439; soundtrack of, 346; mentioned, 137, 342, 348, 358, 363, 373, 404, 413, 432, 435, 439

**J**

705 Jackson Drive (Rogers, AR), x–xii, 447–49, 459, 468, 470, 484, 492, 500
Jackson, Mahalia, 71
Jackson, Mose, 35, 37
Jaeger, Werner, 66
'James Jefferson,' 206
James, Skip, 240
Jefferson, Lemon Henry "Blind Lemon" (bluesman), 240
*Jericho: The South Beheld* (Shuptrine and Dickey), 421
Jerry (Subiaco monk), 137, 406
Jimbo. *See* Reynolds, Willie E. (Jimbo)
'Jimmy Lee': in "The Blood Brothers," 96–97; in "The Singing Knives," 96–97. *See also* Lee, Jimmy; *The Battlefield Where the Moon Says I Love You*: and Jimmy Lee
Johns, Jasper, 197
Johnson, Larry, 202–3, 207, 210, 212–13, 233
Johnson, Robert, 67, 71, 240, 321
Johnson, T. Geronimo, xxxviii
Jones, Douglas C., 447
Jones, LeRoi, 265
Jones, Rodney, 205, 462
Jones, Tayari, xxxviii
Joy Motel (Eagle Springs, AR), 322
Joyce, James, xx, xxii, 75
Judge's Award (Northwest Film & Video Festival), 386
Judo Society, 125
Jung, Carl, 253
Justice, Donald, 45, 148, 211, 217, 220, 392, 397

**K**

Kael, Pauline, 305
Kafka, Franz, 106, 253, 502
Kant, Immanuel, 66
Kearney, Jack, 172
Keats, John, xviii, 102, 106, 138, 141, 142, 159, 253, 272–73, 284, 295, 296, 297, 349, 352, 386
Kemp, Christner, and Associates, 249, 251. *See also* Kemp, Don; surveying, FS and
Kemp, Don, 249, 251, 450–52, 491
Kenan, Randall, xxxviii
Kimple, Ben, 441
King, Albert, 70
King, B. B., 70, 239
*King Kong* (film), 326–27
King, Martin Luther Jr., 80, 171, 172
King Snakes (fictional team), 74–76
Kinnell, Galway, 287
the Klan, 8
Klimt, Gustav, 407
Knöpff, Fernand, 407
1157 Knox Avenue (North Memphis, TN), 49
Kodell, Jerome, 120–21, 126, 132, 135, 513, 596n84
Kooser, Ted, 361
Koran, 253
Kullman, Frederick (husband of Gilchrist), 465, 490
Kunitz, Stanley, 255, 390
Kurosawa, 306

**L**

*La belle et la bête* (film), 265, 306, 397
*Lady Chatterley's Lover* (Lawrence), 106
Lake Dardanelle, 124, 280, 282, 302, 329, 380–82
Lake Norfork: about, 85, 91–93; mentioned, 95–96, 99, 134, 145, 280, 464. *See also* Mallard Point; Mountain Home, AR; Stanford, Francis Gildart (Frank), LIFE, life at; Stanford, Dorothy Gilbert: Lake Norfork
"Lake Norfork Fishing Letter, The," 92–93
Lake Providence, LA, 132

*Land Surveyor's Daughter, The*
  (Gilchrist), 460, 466, 470, 485, 500
Lane, Freddy, 134
*Lanterns on the Levee* (Percy), 9
*Laughing to Keep from Crying*
  (Hughes), 179
Laughlin, Clarence John, 404, 470,
  484–86
Launius, Carl, 90, 117, 171
Laura (Stanford household worker),
  55, 89, 92
Lavender, Bill, 193, 305
Lawrence, D. H., 253, 279
Leadbelly, 240, 346, 432
*Leaves of Grass* (Whitman), xix, 235
LeBlanc, Joseph, 163–64
Lee, Elise (wife of Jimmy Lee), 95
Lee, James (cousin of Dorothy), 64
Lee, Jimmy (cousin of FS), 37–38, 96,
  109, 155
Lee, Robert E., 8, 132
Lemon, Charlie Bolivar (Charlie B.):
  about, 29, 35, 44, 62–63; and racial
  oppression of, 89–90; as source
  for 'Charlie B.,' 29; mentioned, 66,
  265. *See also under The Battlefield
  Where the Moon Says I Love You*
Lensing, Leo: on FS and boxing, 125;
  on FS's care for dress/appearance,
  124, 143; on FS's infatuation with
  Old South, 132; mentioned, 146, 508
*Let Us Now Praise Famous Men* (Agee,
  Evans), 421
*Letters to a Young Poet* (Rilke), 31, 45
"Levee Camp Holler" (song), 346
"Levee Camp Man Blues" (song), 32
levee camp (Snow Lake, AR): about,
  xxxi–xxxii, xxxv, 21, 22, 32, 34; Black
  labor, oppression of, 26–28; chil-
  dren integrated, 33–34; harsh con-
  ditions of, 31; idiom and language
  of, xx, xxiii, xxxvii, 66; laborers,
  34–35; and race, 42; recollected by
  Stanford Black help, 44; Stanfords
  at, xxxi–xxxii, 29–47; violence and
  prostitution in, 31–32. *See also The
  Battlefield Where the Moon Says I
  Love You*; Stanford, Albert Franklin;
  Stanford, Dorothy Gilbert; Stanford,
  Francis Gildart (Frank), CREATIVE
  LIFE; Stanford, Francis Gildart
  (Frank), LIFE; Stanford, Francis
  Gildart (Frank), POEMS
levee system, xxxi–xxxii, xxxv, 4–5,
  12–13
*Levees that Break in My Heart, The*
  (Broughton), 342
Levine, Philip, 213
Lewis, Furry, 238
Lewis, Jerry Lee, 70, 96
Lewis, Raymond Jr. (father of Ray
  Baby), 35
Liberal, MO, xxv, 402–3, 447, 452, 473,
  477, 482, 497, 500–501
*Lid & Spoon* (Turner), 462
Lightnin' Hopkins, xi, 138
Lincoln, Abraham, 13, 132
Lincoln (car), 44, 45, 87
Lish, Gordon, 393–95, 418
Liston, Sonny, xviii, 100, 183
Little, John, 212
Little Piney River, 319
*Little Review*, 179, 208, 252, 444
Little Rock, AR, xi, 126, 133, 164, 210,
  260, 273, 278–79, 339, 473
Logan, John, 396
Lomax, Alan, 14–15, 26, 28. *See also*
  the Blues; Parchman Farm
Lomax, John, 14–15
Lorca, Federico García, 293, 411, 436
Lorde, Audre, 174
Lost Cause, xxix, xxxiv, 8, 78, 130, 132
Lost Roads Publishers: and Albertine,
  487; *Arkansas Bench Stone*, publi-
  cation of, 427; authors solicited for
  submissions, 460–61; and "Bark"
  (Cuddihy), 486; and *The Battlefield
  Where the Moon Says I Love You*,
  386–90, 457–59, 471; *Bean Street*
  (Morris), publication of, 438; *The
  Blessing of the Fleet* (Broughton),
  publication of, 461; Broughton on,

436; Camp, Burt and, 426–27; challenges of running, 427–28, 437–38, 453, 457–58, 460–70, 484–85, 487, 492–93, 607n222; Elk Ranch Printing and, 426; Ernest Wright investment in, 468; and FS's editing process for submissions, 436; FS's life, effect on, 452, 472; Gilchrist investment in, 464, 466, 474–75, 485–86, 504; *The Land Surveyor's Daughter* (Gilchrist), publication of, 466, 485–86; origins of, 389, 399, 425, 435–36, 447–48; and photography books, 486–87; *Shade*, publication of, 427; *The Sleeping Porch* (Caldwell), publication of, 485; *SURVEYING: Poems by Irv Broughton*, publication of, 437; *Terrorism*, publication of, 474; mentioned, xvi, 447, 448, 449, 450, 451, 453, 473, 476, 488, 500, 502. *See also* Broughton, Irving; White River Printers; Wright, Carolyn Davis (C. D.)
Louise Joseph (Catholic Sister), 118
Louise (sister of Dorothy), 86
"Love Song of J. Alfred Prufrock, The" (Eliot), 142
Lowell, Robert, 52, 253, 412, 455
Lowrence, Charles, 27–28, 30, 64, 179, 527n26, 527n29. *See also* Parchman Farm
Loyola University, 200
Luster, Deborah: on CD/FS/GS love triangle, 446; on CD's personality, 475; on CD's poetry, 444; on CD's reaction to FS poetry, 443; on FS and Lucinda Williams, 488; on FS's charisma and reputation, 445; on FS's promiscuity, 450; on Sherman's Tavern, 166; on working surveys, 451; mentioned, 493, 509
Lux, Bill, *131*, 143, 163
Lux, Thomas, xvi, 361, 365, 388, 392, 418, 472, 484, 508
Lyon, MS, 28
Lytle, Andrew Nelson, xxxv, 318

## M

McAuley, James, 212
McBee, Montgomery Kurt, 75
McCarthy, Cormac, xxix
McCormick, Chandra, xxxviii
McCoy, F. M., 28, 240
McCuistion, Fred, 99, 156, 236, 451
McCullers, Carson, 195
McElduff, David, 35
McGraw Hill, 393
*Machines Always Existed* (Stoss), 487
McKernan, John: on CD's poetry, 444; on FS as best of his generation, xvii
McMillen, Neil R., 8
McMurtry, Larry, 212
Maddos, Everette, 462, 474, 488, 503
Maggio, Ron, 125–27
Mahler, Gustav, 282, 314, 333, 338, 366, 406
Main Street Bar, 320, 322
Mallard Point, 86, 90, 92, 95, 107–8, 123, 145–46, 149. *See also* Lake Norfork; Mountain Home, AR
Mallard Point Road, 86
Mallarmé, Stéphane, 267
'Mama Covoe.' *See* Spriggs, Emma (Stanford household worker)
Mamoulian, Rouben, 306
Manchester, William, 212
Maple Leaf Bar, 488
Maple Street Book Shop, 488
Markham Hill, 230
Marlowe, Christopher, 253
Martin, Fiddlin' Joe, 28
Martin's Stadium, 73
Marx brothers, 309
Marx, Karl, 106, 309, 414, 422
*Massachusetts Review*, 227
Matisse, Henri, 407
Matthews, William, 213, 252, 361
Mattie (childhood friend of Dorothy), 11
"May Day May Day May Day" (letter), 270, 276, 278, 321, 355, 362
Maynard, Snake, 377
"Megan" (FS lover), 450
Melrose High, 79

Melville, Herman, xix, 106, 253
*Memoirs from the House of the Dead* (Dostoyevsky), 253
Memphis: baseball and race, 73–76, 534n113; carnivals and fairs, racial aspects of, 76–90; character of, 51–52; FS's life in, 49–82; the press, racism of, 80–81; race in, 52, 62–83. *See also The Battlefield Where the Moon Says I Love You*; Stanford, Francis Gildart (Frank), CREATIVE LIFE; Stanford, Francis Gildart (Frank), LIFE; Stanford, Francis Gildart (Frank), POEMS
Memphis Red Sox, 73–75
Memphis Slim, 240
Mencin, Adolph (Linda Mencin's father), 320
Mencin, Linda (first wife of FS, *now* Bond): about, 224, 225–26, 228–29; champions FS's ideals, 226, 231; discovers FS's affair with Campbell, 247; divorce, files for, 283; on FS and alcohol, 233; on FS and Dorothy, 273; and FS relationship with, 225–35, 246–49, 260–61, 268–70; and FS wedding, 246–48, 268; on FS's interest in film, 316; and FS's nervous breakdown, 164, 273–74, 276–77; on FS's physical beauty, 228; in FS's poems, 456; and FS's poor treatment of, 268–70, 276–77, 350; on FS's thoughts of suicide, 260, 273; on FS's writing habits, 231–32, 234, 235; pregnancy and abortion, 247, 248; Stokesbury, affair with, 248; mentioned, xxv, 236, 246, 278, 286, 299, 311, 313, 320, 338, 340, 355, 357, 369, 373, 405, 410, 439, 443, 447, 450, 501. *See also under* Campbell, Cheryl; Fuhrmann, Nicholas; Stanford, Francis Gildart (Frank), LIFE; Stanford, Francis Gildart (Frank), POEMS
Meredith, William, 389
Merrill, James, 252

Merton, Thomas, 115, 139, 147–48, 150, 184–85, 272, 274, 289, 351, 382. *See also under* Stanford, Francis Gildart (Frank), CREATIVE LIFE
Merwin, W. S., 252, 270, 361, 415
MFA. *See* UARK Master of Fine Arts program (MFA)
Michelangelo, ix, 504
Mid-South Fair, 76–77, 79
Mill, John Stuart, xvii, 67
Mill Mountain Press: about, xxvii; *Alla Breve Loving* (Wright), publication of, 453; *Constant Stranger*, publication of, 455; *Field Talk*, publication of, 367; *Ladies from Hell*, publication of, 274; *The Singing Knives*, publication of, xxvii, 222, 252, 284, 425; TB, co-publication of, 458; mentioned, 213, 218–19, 362, 376, 388, 390, 398, 427, 453–54. *See also* Broughton, Irving
*Mill Mountain Review*, 205, 213, 214, 220, 252, 334, 407, 426–27, 468
Miller, Clyde, 241, 243
Miller, Jordan, 202
Mills, Keith, 226
Millsaps College, 190, 465
Milton, John, 138, 185
Mimms, Wolfgang, 348
Mingus, Charles, 240
Mishima, Yukio, 253, 258–60, 273, 411, 414–16
Mississippi Delta, xviii, xxxi, 7, 11, 27, 46, 64, 70, 246, 442
Mississippi Valley Flood Control Branch, 26
Mitchell, Jeffrey, 389
*Moby-Dick* (Melville), xix, 63, 185
Modigliani, Amedeo, 102, 408
Monie, Bill: on FS, 125, 127–28, 130, 132–34, 139
Monk, Thelonious, 240, 379, 403, 433
Monroe, Sputnik, 81–82
Moore, Brian, 212
Moore, Carl, 170
Morgan, Gordon D., 173

Morgan, Sherman: about, 167; civil rights, champion of, 168; courage of, 169; mentioned, xi, 167, 170, 171, 235, 237, 246, 265, 322, 375, 429. *See also* Sherman's Tavern
Morris, John S., 216, 424, 435, 438, 460, 463–64
Morris, Willie, 422
Mound Bayou, 150, 177, 238, 429, 442
Mount Sequoyah: about, 229–30; mentioned, xxv, 166, 204, 223, 231, 233, 235, 246–48, 260, 263, 272, 355, 362, 447. *See also under* Mencin, Linda; Stanford, Francis Gildart (Frank), LIFE
Mountain Home, AR: about, 85–88; Charlie B., oppressed in, 89; and community's disapproval of FS's Black associations in Fayetteville, 171; Laura (Stanford household worker), oppressed in, 89; unhelpful as source of material to FS, 90; as unwelcoming to Blacks, 88–90. *See also* Lake Norfork; Mallard Point; Stanford, Dorothy Gilbert; Stanford, Francis Gildart (Frank), LIFE; Stanford, Francis Gildart (Frank), POEMS
Mountain Home High School, 89, 101, 121
Mountain Home Junior High School, 57, 87, 98, 100–101
Mr. Charlie. *See* Lowrence, Charles
Mr. Cholly. *See* Lowrence, Charles
Muddy Waters, 240
"Mumbles." *See* Horton, Walter (bluesman, "Tangle Eye")
Murray, Albert, xxxvii
Myles, Eileen, xvi, xxx

# N

Nakayama, Shozaburo, 160, 424
*Nation*, 227, 252
National Association for the Advancement of Colored People, 28
National Endowment for the Arts (NEA) grants, 436, 438–39, 453, 458, 462, 463, 464, 466, 467, 470, 485, 502. *See also* Broughton, Irving; Lost Roads Publishers
Neal Hunting Lodge, 41
Nearing, Scott, 290, 319, 365
Negro Leagues, 73–75
Nelson, Nils, 423
Neosho, MO, 335, 341, 435, 451–52
Neruda, Pablo, xvi, 160
Nevius, Davilee, 100
*New American Review*, 213, 252, 271
New Orleans. *See* Gilchrist, Ellen; Stanford, Francis Gildart (Frank), LIFE
New Orleans Hotel (Eureka Springs, AR), 247, 313, 315, 316, 319, 320, 328, 336, 339, 356, 489, 580n51. *See also* Campbell, Cheryl; DuVernet, Kay; Stanford, Francis Gildart (Frank), LIFE
*New Orleans Review*, 200
New York City, NY: Campbell in, 282–83, 312–13; Deidre in, 299; in FS's poems, 221, 298, 456–57. *See also* Stanford, Francis Gildart (Frank), LIFE
*New York Quarterly*, 346, 350, 388–89
*New Yorker*, 191
"Nigger Richard." *See* Banks, Richard Kenneth
"Niggertown," 323
*9 Flags: Cherokee Trail of Tears, Battle of Pea Ridge*, 426
Nitobe, Inazo, 129
Nolan, Deborah. *See* Luster, Deborah
North Lindell Avenue (Fayetteville), 227, 233–34, 260, 447
North Memphis, 49
North Mississippi, xx, xxxvii
Northwest Arkansas, xvi, xviii, xxvi, 215, 265, 376, 451, 500
Northwest Film & Video Festival, 386

# O

1118 Oak Ridge Drive (Memphis), 49, 57, 59, 65

O'Connor, Flannery, xxiii, xxv, xxix, xxxvi, 87, 138, 160, 195, 357, 382
*Often in Different Landscapes* (Stokesbury), 462
Old Leland Road (Greenville), 5
Old Main (UARK building), 164, 172, 190, 211, 216
*Old Powder Man* (Williams), 64, 374
Old South, xxviii, 17, 21, 24, 78, 82, 130–32, 151, 154, 181, 195
Olsen, Tillie, 213
"On a Professional Couple in a Side Show" (Dugan), 255
"One Finger Zen" (Stanford, unpublished), 502
*One Time, One Place* (Welty), 353
*Open Places* (journal), 148, 217–18, 227, 251, 253, 267, 346–47
Oppen, George, 377, 423
Orlovsky, Peter, 210, 229
Ouachita Mountains, the, 170, 302
Our Lady of Sorrows Elementary, 57
Overstreet, Fred, 459, 467
Overstreet Printing Company, 427, 433, 437, 453–54, 457–59, 463, 467–68. *See also* Lost Roads Publishers; Mill Mountain Press
Oxford, MS, xxvi, xxxvi, 64, 434
Oyama, Masutatasu, 128
O. Z. *See* Durrett, O. Z.
Ozark Mountains, xvi, xxvi, xxxvi, 85–87, 91, 103, 210–11, 313–14, 317, 335, 347, 369, 409, 426, 447. *See also* "Greta Garbo of the Ozarks" (FS girlfriend); "Last Panther in the Ozarks, The" (unpublished)
Ozarks Merit Award, 473
Ozarks National Forest, 135, 210

**P**

Packard, William, 388, 390
*Paideia* (Jaeger), 66
'Pantagruel, Count Hugo,' 77–78, 183, 534n118
Parchman Farm: about, 10–16; and the Blues, 15–17; mentioned, 35, 44, 70, 238. *See also* Stanford, Dorothy Gilbert
Parker, Charlie, 240
Parmenides, 267
Parra, Nicanor, 200, 411, 416
*Partisan Review*, 52, 207, 227, 252
Pasolini, Pier Paolo. *See under* Stanford, Francis Gildart (Frank), CREATIVE LIFE
Pass Christian, xi, 504
Peabody Hotel, 20, 23, 42, 49, 55, 59, 64, 68, 70, 79, 88, 169, 240
Pendergrast, Martin, 126–28, 139, 143, 145, 147, 260
Percy, Walker, 306, 333–34
Percy, William Alexander, 7–9, 27, 428
*Periscope*, 124–25, 127, 140, 145–46
Perkins, Carl, 70
Pessoa, Fernando, xvii
Phillips, Adam, 87
Phillips, Billy, 50, 59
Phillips, Jerry, 81
Phillips, Sam, 70, 72, 81
*Philosophy of Surrealism, The* (Alquié), 160
Pilcher, Gregory, 142
Pilgrim Jubilee Singers, 71
Pine Log, GA, 25
Pink Palace (planetarium), 59, 68
Plath, Sylvia, 97, 252
Plymell, Charles, 217, 219
Poe, Edgar Allan, 253
*Poetry Now*, 396
*Poets on Street Corners: Portraits of Fifteen Russian Poets*, 259
Powdermaker, Hortense, 265
*Prairie Schooner*, 361
Precision International, 452
Presley, Elvis, 67–72, 74–75
Prévert, Jacques, 306, 411, 417
*Preview*, 199, 205, 208, 252
*Preview: Eight Poets*, 208, 438, 458
Price, Zelma, 5
Proust, Marcel, 52, 317
Provincetown, MA, 205
Prysock, Carrie (niece of FS), 511–12

Prytania Theatre, 496
Purcell, Henry, 339

## Q
Quennell, Peter, 253

## R
Rabelais, François, 67
Rachmaninoff, 329
RACISM, 1
*Ramblin' on My Mind* (album), 489
Random House, 218–20
Ransom, John Crowe, xxxv, 97, 195, 284, 286–87, 356, 392
'Ray Baby,' 37–38, 429
Ray Baby (childhood friend), 33, 35, 235
Raymond (Subiaco monk), 35, 122, 455
Reed, Ishmael, xxx
Reed, Jimmy, 38, 198, 240
*Rêve* (boat), *288*, 289
Rexroth, Kenneth, 147
Reynolds, Willie E. (Jimbo): about, 165; civil rights, champion of, 168; FS's friendship with, 165, *166*, 167–70, 235–37, 375, 404, 407, 442, 471; mentioned, 179, 235–37, 246, 265, 322, 406, 429. *See also* Sherman's Tavern
Rhodes, Hari, 65, 179
Rich, Adrienne, 361
Richton, MS, 3, 6, 61, 227
Ricks, Claude: about, 168; civil rights movement, leader of, 168–70; mentioned, 235–37, 246, 265, 322, 375, 429. *See also* Sherman's Tavern
Ricks, Deborah, 169
Rilke, Rainer Maria, 29, 31, 45, 115
Rimbaud, xix, 107, 265, 267, 284, 355
Ro-Ark (printing company), 427
Roaring River Fish Hatchery, 320
Robinson, Jackie, 74
*Rock Quarry*, 380–81
Rogers, AR. *See under* Stanford, Francis Gildart (Frank), LIFE
Rogers Humane Society, 341
Roger's Rec (bar), 156
Rollins, Sonny, 240

*Room Rented by a Single Woman* (Wright), 461, 468
Rosedale, MS, 32
Ross, Cher. *See* Campbell, Cheryl
Ross, RaMell, xxxviii
Rossellini, Roberto, 306
Rossetti, Dante Gabriel, 253, 327, 418. *See also* "Dante Gabriel Rossetti with His Head on the Virginal"
Rosy's Jazz Club, 488, 501, 503
Rousseau, Jean-Jacques, 317
Rucker, R. D., 171–72
Ryūnosuke, Akutagawa, 67

## S
Sadie (levee camp worker), 40, 71
*Sadness at the Private University* (Adamo), 461, 468
Saint Louis, 186–87, 189
Sanders, Pharoah, 240, 502
Saunders, Joe, 140, 142, 145
Saunders, Ruth B., 392
Schluterman, Benno, 123
Schmitt, Jude, 381
Schwartz, Julie, 393
Scott, Barbara, 489
Scully, Hazel, 6
Sears (company), 17–18, 31, 123
"Season of the Witch" (song), 201
Seawood, James, 170–72, 236
*Seventeen*, 359–60, 389
Shakespeare, William, 58, 138
Shelley, Percy Bysshe, 106, 253, 296–97, 327
Sheridan, AR, 171
Sherman, William Tecumseh, 7, 13, 25, 132
Sherman's Tavern: about, 165, *166*, 180; and accepting of FS, 168–69; appeal of to FS, 167; civil rights focus of, 167–68; interracial character of, 180. *See also* Morgan, Sherman; Reynolds, Willie E. (Jimbo); Ricks, Claude; Stanford, Francis Gildart (Frank), CREATIVE LIFE; Stanford, Francis Gildart (Frank), LIFE; Stanford, Francis Gildart (Frank), POEMS

Sherwood Junior High School, 57
Sho-Nuff, 94, 343
Shugars, Murray, 52, 128, 191, 432, 483, 509
Shuptrine, Hubert, 421
Silliphant, Stirling, 220
Silver Maple Resort, 92
Simic, Charles, 361
Simmons, Edward, 421
Simon & Schuster, 392
*Sir Gawain and the Green Knight*, xx, 128, 138, 180
'Six Toes.' *See* 'Born in the Camp with Six Toes'
115 Skyline Drive (Mount Sequoyah), 229–30
Slavitt, David, 212, 220
*Sleeping Porch, The* (Caldwell), 485
Slote, Jessica, 450, 465
Smith, Bessie, 233, 317
Smith, Dorothy Margaret (birth mother of FS), 3
Snodgrass, W. D., 217
Snow Lake. *See* levee camp (Snow Lake, AR)
Snow Lake Elementary, 57
Snyder, Gary, 217
Sobin, A. G., 360
"Song of Myself" (Whitman), 483
"Song of the Earth, The" (Mahler), 282
Sophocles, 253
southern exceptionalism, xxxiv–xxxvi, 82
Southern Renaissance, xxxvi, xxxviii
Spearmon, Neal, 157, 300–301
Spider Creek, AR, 337
*Spirit of the Dead Watching* (Gaugin), 455, 501
*Sports Illustrated*, 64, 125
'Spriggs, Emma,' 29, 32, 62, 428, 432
Spriggs, Emma (Stanford household worker, 29, 31, 35, 44, 237
St. Joseph Hospital, 29
St. Peter the Fisherman, 95
St. Peter's Chair (rock formation), 308, 311
St. Scholastica Monastery, 122
Stafford, William, 45, 154, 361, 363, 423

Stanford, Albert Franklin (Frank Sr.) (adoptive father of FS): about, xxxi, 7, 20, 21, 25–26; Black labor, exploitation of, 26–28; death of, 36, 46, 118, 121; and dream of FS playing football, 57, 100; as father, 54–55; in FS poems, 432–33; levee camps and, xxxii, 29–31, 35, 38–41; O. Z., support for, 63–64; poor health of, 31, 85–86, 90, 100; retires, 85–86; mentioned, 64–65, 67, 70, 99, 118, 122, 177, 300. *See also* levee camp (Snow Lake, AR); Stanford, Francis Gildart (Frank), LIFE
Stanford Contracting, 26
Stanford, Dorothy Gilbert (Dorothy) (née Gilbert, *then* Alter, *then* Stanford): ability to make plans and take action, 123; about, 3; Alter, marriage to, 17; cooking skills remembered, 19; desire for FS to join fraternity, 154; disapproval of FS leaving fraternity, 156; financial problems of, 248; Frank Sr. death, impact of, 118, 121–24; and Frank Sr. marriage, 20–21; on Frank Sr.'s dream of FS playing football, 100; on Frank Sr.'s family background, 25; FS, adoption of, 3, 5–6, 18, 90, 180; on FS as child, 29–30; FS as favored child, 55–56; on FS as genius, 58–59; FS, financial support to at UARK, 157; FS, withdraws financial support to, 186; on FS's athleticism and sports, 56–57, 86, 122–24; on FS's biological mother, race of, 180; and FS's erratic behavior and emotional health, 146, 163, 273, 307; on FS's interest in religion, lie of, 122; FS's lifestyle, disapproval of, 307; on FS's poetry, 58; on FS's popularity, 86; on FS's reading habits, 104; on FS's rejection of Catholicism, 135; and FS's writing ambitions, encouragement of, 105–6; "Gildart" name, importance of, 6–7; "Green

Acres," purchases, 5; Greenville in, 4, 7–9, 17–19; on Joan Williams, 64; Lake Norfork/Mountain Home, move to, 44, 85–86; levee camps, business connection to, 4; levee camps, role at, 31, 34; and Lost Cause, 130–31; Mattie (childhood friend), 11; and Old South heritage, 3–4, 7–8, 54, 61; and Old South heritage, myth of, 88, 99–100, 123; Parchman Farm and, 11–17; and race, 9–14; and Ruth's relationship, 122, 499; *The Singing Knives*, reaction to, 285, 307; single mother as, 3, 18–19; Subiaco, creativity in FS and Ruth admittance to, 121–23; Subiaco monks describe as 'Southern Belle,' 123; Subiaco, takes job at (Coury House), 123; working career of, 4–5, 17–20, 123; writings of, 17–18
Stanford, Edna (*née* Alexander, first wife of Frank Sr.), 21, 26
Stanford, Francis Gildart (Frank), BOOKS:
*Ark River Review*, 360, 395
*Arkansas Bench Stone*: analysis of, 177, 375, 427–28, 431–33, 445; Frank Sr. in, 432–33; levee camps in, 432; Mill Mountain Press, published by, 431, 433; poems in, 177, 375, 427–28, 431–33, 445; mentioned, 46, 177, 375, 427–28, 431–33, 445
"Black Patch, The" (Stanford play), 272
"Blackberry Tales, The" (unpublished), 392–93
*Children at the Point of Death*, 46
*Constant Stranger*: analysis of, 454–57; death, theme of, 455; Mill Mountain Press, published by, 454–55; mentioned, 383, 428, 434, 443, 457–58, 467, 501
*Crib Death*: dark tone of, xvii, 362, 477–78; dreams in, 478; FS on, 488; origins of, 477; poems in, 362, 368, 383–84, 478; mentioned, 398, 434, 471, 477–79, 488, 502
*Field Talk*, 147, 178, 338, 358, 367, 373, 431, 433
"Flour the Dead Man Brings to the Wedding" (unpublished), 395
"In the Midst" (short fiction), 394–95
*Ladies from Hell*: analysis of, 274–76, 363–65; critical reviews of, 362–63; dreams in, 363–64; and GS, in collaboration with, 362; Mill Mountain Press publishes, 362, 433; origin of, 363, 433; poems in, 363; mentioned, 147, 338, 358, 445
"Last Panther in the Ozarks, The" (unpublished), 395
"Naegling" (unpublished), 259
*Shade*: analysis of, 427–31, 433; childhood and adolescence, themes of, 7, 430, 433; levee camps in, 429; Lost Roads Publishers, published by, 433; poems in, 35, 46, 76, 93, 430; and Sherman's Tavern influence on, 429; mentioned, 147, 358, 445
*Singing Knives, The*: civil rights and oppression in, 431; and Cocteau, 430–31; critical reception to, 285; levee camps in, 430; publication of, 218, 222, 252, 254, 284; Wesleyan University, submitted to and rejected, 285; youthful vibrancy of, xvii; mentioned, 38, 93, 96, 99, 209, 213, 307, 361–62, 374, 397, 412, 425, 427–28, 432–34, 445, 464, 466
"Tancredi's Light" (short fiction), 394
*Those Fools Who Try to Write Books but Not That Russian* (unpublished short fiction), 35
*What about This: Collected Poems of Frank Stanford* (ed. Wiegers), xvii
*You*, 90, 183, 371, 398–99, 404, 428, 436, 461

Stanford, Francis Gildart (Frank), CREATIVE LIFE: adoption as connection to levee life, 175; on adoption as emancipation from past, 174, 179; adoption, impact of knowledge of, 61, 91, 173, 174; on adulthood's negative affect on creativity, 257; aesthetic mission of, xxvii; agrarian romance motifs and, 97; Agrarians and Fugitives, rejection of, xxxv, 82–83; antiestablishmentism and, 220; artist residencies, disinterest in, xxiv; artistic integrity and, 221–22, 332; the astronomer and, 65–67, 157; awards and fellowships, disinterest in, xxvii; beauty, capturing, 296–97; Bender, missed opportunity of, 222, 279; Black childhood friends and, 33–41; Black language and idiom and, 66; and Blake, 327–28, 442; the Blues, influence of, 71–73; Broughton, expresses thanks to, 434; Broughton, meets, 213; on Broughton's poetry, 437; burnout, signs of, 378; Bushido and, 128–29; carnivals and fairs as symbols of Old South racism, 78; carnivals and fairs in poems, 149, 153; and Charlie B., 63; childhood memories, unfiltered, need for, 256, 263, 265–66, 397–99; on Cocteau, 256, 264–66, 357; Cocteau, influence on FS, 347, 348; commercial success, new ambition for, 389–91, 433; commercialization, disdain for, 221, 410, 421–25, 434; conformity, disdain for, 191–92, 212–13, 220; contemporary poetry, ignorance of, 115, 308, 419; "contributor's" notes and bios of, 157, 213, 252, 256, 270, 360, 459–60; on Cowley, 291; creative control and, 217–18, 331, 360, 387; on dangers of literary theory, 267; on destroying own work, 271–72; on Dickey, 330; Donald Justice, comments made to, 217; on Dreyer, 327–28; Dugan's opinion, trust in, 252–53; eccentrics and marginalized, theme of, 264–66, 314–15, 370–71, 377; elitism in publishing, disdain for, 220, 289, 387; Elvis, influences of, 72; *Esquire* magazine and, 393–96; on experience as foundation for poetry, 295–96; faith in own poetry, xvi–xxv; and Faulkner, xvii, 64–65, 104, 110, 197, 220, 254; film and Cocteau, 327, 332, 386; on film and music, 329; on film and poetry, merging of, 306, 309–10, 326, 327–29, 363; film, ideas for images in, 328–29, 334–35; film, interest in, 280, 305–6, 309, 316–18; film, non-commercial viability of, 379–80; film, project ideas with Broughton, 333; film projects with Babij, 330–32, 379–80; fishing as inspiration, 93–94; on "flowing intensity" of good poets, 423; Frank Sr.'s influence on, 46–47; on Frost, 221, 290; FS on own reasons for leaving MFA, 209–10; FS's admiration for Yesenin, 259–60; Fuhrmann as intellectual mentor, 141–43; on Garrett, 148; Ginsberg and, 210–11, 321; history manifested in poetry, 52–54; at Hollins Conference on Creative Writing and Cinema, 211–13; on identity and art, 279; ignores own poetry to champion CD, 454; on importance of dating his poetry, 108–9, 350; "improvisations" on translated poems, 411–13; on interiority of poetry, 102–3; isolation from poetry networks and society, need for, 256; Japanese warrior tradition, influences of, 128–30; on John Crowe Ransom, 287; on John Stoss, 460–61, 463; on karate, influence of, 116–17; on Keats, 272; on Lake Norfork, importance of, 85,

87; on language, importance of to poetry, 297; on levee camp culture, immortality of, 183; levee camp language vs. Memphis language, dichotomy of, 66; levee camp vs. Memphis lives, 49, 58, 66, 82–83; levee camps, inspiration of, 29–41, 44–47; on Lish, Gordon, 395; literary criticism, talent for, 419–24, 435, 463; literary influences, breadth of, xvii–xix, 66, 104, 106–7, 128, 138, 195, 253; literary/poetic ambitions of, xxvii, 103–4; literary talents, protectiveness of, 103–4, 107; literature/books, access to, 104–5, 140; lived experience vs. book learning, 157, 324; on loss of muse, 396–97; and manliness of poetry, 142; 'mannerly' southern writing, disdain for, 264; memorization of literature, talent for, 139, 141–42; memory and dreams, themes of, 52–53, 265–66, 275, 297, 363–64, 373–74, 478; Memphis, inspiration from, 52; mentor, need for, 220; on Merton, 147–48, 185; Merton, influence of, 150, 184–85; and Mishima suicide, 258–59, 273; on Morris, 438; natural world, importance of, 87–88; on Nearing, Scott, 290; own comparisons to literary heroes, xvi; on own intensity of writing, 159; own reaction to Dugan's admiration, 216–17; on own reading habits, 106–7; on own writing habits, 107, 147, 231, 232, 395; Pasolini's influence on FS, xxix, 266, 297, 305–6, 317, 347, 363, 382, 411, 413–14, 417, 419, 422–24; poems, lost in movie theater, 298; on poetry as identity, 502; on poetry as self-destructive, 260–61, 276–78; poetry, earliest, 108–9, 115, 148, 256, 271; poetry establishment, disdain for, xxiv–xxvi, 210, 219; poetry muse, loss of, 374–76,

377–78, 396–99, 478–79; poetry obsession as source of life of turmoil, 271; and poetry/prose "fragments," xxv, 52, 105, 107–8, 110–11, 137, 158, 160, 221, 290, 315, 378, 415, 447; praise from contemporaries, xvi–xvii, 194–95, 210–12; prolific output of, xvii, 571n65; publishes in *American Poetry Review*, 360; publishes in *Antioch Review*, 360; publishes in *Ark River Review*, 360; publishes in *FIELD: Contemporary Poetry and Poetics*, 360–61; publishes in *Iowa Review*, 361; publishes in *Ironwood*, 361; publishes in *Prairie Schooner*, 361; publishes in *Seventeen*, 359; publishing and printing, knowledge of, 425–26; on Ralph Adamo, 461–62; reading habits of, xviii, 66–67, 103–6, 116, 138–40, 155; on self, 254, 312; on self-isolation and doubt, 256–57; Sherman's Tavern and Fayetteville Black culture, influences of, 180, 183, 235–37; Sherman's Tavern and rejection of Old South heritage, 179; Sherman's Tavern friends, as connection to muse of poetry, 375–76; short fiction of, 391–96; simple living, artistic need for, xxv, 311, 319, 402; on "small " magazines, 435; "southerphiles," disdain for, 299; Subiaco, and FS's knowledge of literature, 141–42; Subiaco and literary identity, 137; Subiaco as refuge, 310–11, 380; Subiaco, flaunts talent at, 140; Subiaco library, as source of literature, 140; on Subiaco monk's openness to his poetry, 137; Subiaco, reciting poetry at, 139; Subiaco students on FS's poems, 139; surrealism, interest in, 160; surrealism of South as reality, 161, 324–26, 329–30; surrealist, on being characterized as one, 160–61, 551n42;

Stanford, Francis Gildart (Frank), CREATIVE LIFE *(continued)*: surveying, thinks about poetry during, 227, 250–51; trancelike states necessary for poetry composition, 118, 159–60, 233–34, 250, 256, 263; UARK MFA, as springboard to publishing, 191–92, 205; UARK MFA, break from, 207–9; UARK MFA exposes FS to known poets, 210; UARK MFA, poems submitted to, 195; UARK MFA, recruited to, 192; UARK MFA, reputation in, 194; UARK MFA, scorn for/hostility towards, 208, 209, 231–32, 235–36, 252; on voices and images in poetry, 54; on watching films, 305; white myths, rejection of, 24; Whitehead's admiration of, 199; and Wilbur, Richard, 291; workshops, disdain for, 419; world literature, precocious knowledge of, 103, 106, 421; writing habits of, xvii, 86, 107–9, 138, 139–40, 155, 157, 158–59, 162, 226, 231–32, 233–34, 253, 257, 260, 263, 274, 313, 337, 352–53, 355, 358, 371–72, 373, 395, 397–98, 403–4; on writing in secrecy, 107–8, 115; Zora Neale Hurston Award bestowed on, xxx

Stanford, Francis Gildart (Frank), LIFE: about, xv, xvi, xxxi–xxxii, 22, *31*, *281*; adopted, 3; adoption, knowledge of, 10, 60–61, 90, 108, 173, 307, 495; on adulthood and creativity, 256, 397–99, 472; adulthood, difficulties with, 225, 228, 246, 255–56, 261, 476; affairs of *(see* Boswell, Merideth; Campbell, Cheryl; Deidre; DuVernet, Kay; Thompson, Elizabeth; Walton, Kathy; Wright, Carolyn Davis [C. D.]); affairs of, unnamed woman, 315; "all 3 of us loving" strategy, 494–99; "all women," concept of, 294–96, 449–50; amnesia of, 312, 319; at Arkansas State Hospital, 273–80; on art and relationships, 443, 476–77, 494–96; and the "astronomer," 65; athleticism of, 73, 124; on Babij, friendship with, 292; and baking, 267; Banks, Richard, death of, 396–97; Banks, Richard, friendship with, 322–26, 340; Black culture and society, re-immersement in, 155, 166–73; Blues album collection of, 240; the Blues and, 16–17; and boating accident/severed leg, 113; Broughton support for, 332–33; burnout of, 472; in Busch, AR, 336–40; at Camp Subiaco, 280–81; Campbell and, 227–28, 230–32, 247–48, 268–69, 282–83, 292, 311, 338–39; on Campbell, feelings for, 268–69, 282–83, 311–12, 336, 338; Campbell, FS ends affair with, 247; in Cape Rosier, ME, 288–90; carnivals, fascination with, 76–80; Catholicism, conversion to, 121–22; on CD and GS, love for, 498–99; on CD and GS reactions to threesome fantasies, 498; CD, affair with, xii, 439, 441, 443–44, 446–53, 475, 477, 485; CD, meets, 439; CD, mentor and champion of, 444, 453–54, 473–74, 487–88; Claude Ricks, friendship with, 168–69, 236; Coleman and Hess, importance of to FS, 59–60; Coleman, as brother to, 50; Coleman, youthful intimacy with, 61–62, 112; cooking and, 339–40; correspondence of, 472; correspondence wanes, 471, 472; Cuddihy and, 351–52, 361–62, 379; deceit and lies of, x; and domesticity of, 230; on Dorothy, 307, 403, 504; on Dorothy, calming/putting at ease, 499; double lives of, x, 103, 227, 230–31, 247, 339, 445–50, 476–77, 479; Dugan, visits in Truro, 292; on DuVernet, 503; in Eureka Springs, 313–39; on Eureka Springs, own happiness in, 320–21; and Eureka Springs Theater, 317–18; films, watching in New York City, 297–98, 456; financial strains, xxvi, 157, 186, 227, 248–49, 491–93; Frank Sr., respect and admiration for, xxxii, 46, 90, 118; Frank Sr.'s death, reaction to, 118–19; Fuhrmann, as mentor, 124–25, 134, 141, 500; Fuhrmann and, 95, 499–500; and gardening/self-sufficiency, 365, 366, 367; "Gildart" name, importance of, 6–7; Greenville, MS and, 61, 69, 85, 86, 96, 112, 130, 155, 161, 227, 281; on GS as artist, 338, 409, 473; GS, champion and mentor for, 338, 352, 404–11, 434–35, 473–74; GS/FS, scheme to meld relationships ("all 3 of us loving"), 494–99; on GS, loss of, 493; GS, relationship with, 335–53, 410–11, 445–46; Hawkins, Emmett, harassment of, 132–34; health issues of, 312, 320, 369, 476; and hunting, 40–41; on idea of becoming a priest, 136; intelligence of, 58–59; Jimbo Reynolds, friendship with, 164–65, 166, 404; and Jimmy Lee relationship, 96; and karate/martial arts, 116–17; at Lake Dardanelle, 280–81; Lake Norfork, AR, fishing and boating, 28, 92–95; Lake Norfork, AR, life at, 86–119; Lake Norfork, AR, move to, 85; Lake Norfork, AR, waterskiing at, 94–95, 121, 280; levee camp childhood, xxxi–xxxii, 24–47, 56; levee camp, fishing at, 93; levee camp life, Fayetteville racial injustice evokes memories of, 170; levee camp life, importance of, 82–83; levee camp living conditions, 30; loses touch with poets and friends, 470–71; on love for Dorothy, 500; Mallard Point home, described, 86; "May Day May Day May Day" letter, 270; Memphis, baseball and, 73–76; Memphis household, and race, 62–64, 88; Memphis, life in, 49–50, 51, 54–55, 60, 62–83, 88; Memphis, music and, 71–73; Mencin and, 225, 228–30, 246–48; on Mencin as 'all women,' 296; on Mencin, feelings for, 296; Mencin, files for divorce, 283; on Mencin, marriage to, 246; on Mencin separation, 260–61, 270; Mencin, wedding ceremony described, 248; mixed-race ancestry, FS's exploration of, 176, 179–80, 555n161; money, disinterest in, 249, 318–19, 487; Morgan, friendship with, 168–69; Mount Sequoyah, retreat to, 223, 229–30; in Mountain Home, AR, 44, 62, 91–118; nervous breakdown of, 260–61, 267–73; New England, road trip to, 284–87, 288, 289–90, 291, 292; New Orleans, travels to, 488–91, 493, 495–96, 500–504; in New York City, 283; on New York City, 283; in New York City, 292–94; on New York City, 293–94; in New York City, 297–300, 309–13, 327; on New York City, xxiv, 356; Northwest AR, importance as home base, xxvi; on NW Arkansas, life in, 356–57; occult and altered reality/transcendence, interest in, 117–18; Old South heritage, distancing from, 154, 170, 173–74, 184; Old South heritage, myth of, 7, 91; on own burnout, 472; own death, foreshadowing of, 480–81, 484; on own diet, 401, 476; on own double lives/deceit, 475–76; on own history/recent past, 352, 355–57; on own nervous breakdown, 355; on own relationships with Blacks, 170; on own talents as poet, 321; "paint-the-lover" strategy, 495–96; Parchman Farm, influences of, 16–17; physical descriptions of, x, 56, 62, 124–27, 164, 186, 192, 194, 228, 335–36; Pink Palace planetarium and, 61; politics and, 229;

Stanford, Francis Gildart (Frank), LIFE *(continued)*: and Presley, Elvis, 67–68; racism and Old South identity, embraces, 130, *131*, 132–34, 545n88; and religion, 121–22, 134–36; Rogers, AR, domestic life in, xxv, 341–53, 358, 365, 368–69, 372, 402–4; Rogers, AR, finances in, 369; sadness and fear, xi; school and grades, disinterest in, xxii, 57, 100, 138, 142, 157, 158, 189; schoolboy reputation as poet, 99; on seeing the ocean, 288–89; and Sherman's Tavern, 166–73, 235, 375, *376*; Sherman's Tavern, acceptance in, 169–70; Sherman's Tavern and language, 167, 235–36; Shermans' Tavern appeal of, 167; Snow Lake, teaches public school in, 44; on Spearmon suicide, 300–301; and spiritualism, 134–36; sports, childhood, 56; Stokesbury affair with Mencin, reaction to, 248; on Stokesbury stealing material, 209; at Subiaco, 121–51, 280, 300–303, 307–13, 380–83, 499–500; Subiaco, acceptance to, 122–23; Subiaco boxing team and, 125; Subiaco football team and, 124; Subiaco, grades at, 138; Subiaco judo club and, 125, *126*, 127–28, 130; Subiaco monks, affection for, 281; Subiaco monks, FS's admiration for, 136–37, 285–86, 308, 356, 357, 403; Subiaco monks, impact on FS, 134–37; Subiaco monks, teaches water-skiing to, 121–22; Subiaco student drowns, 382–83; Subiaco, visits, 380–83; suicide attempt by drowning, 282; suicide of, xii, xv; on surveying, 358, 370, 371; as surveyor, xxvi–xxvii, 227, 249–51, 267, 337, 352, 365, 369, *370*, 389; team sports, disinterest in, 100–101; UARK, acceptance to, 150–51; and UARK Black activists (Moore, Seawood, Rucker), 170–71; UARK, business program, withdraws from, 186; UARK classes and grades, 157–58, 188; UARK, joins fraternity and is business major, 154; UARK MFA program, 191–223; UARK MFA program, scorn for, 192; UARK, racism at, 171–72; UARK, withdraws from, 189; and unnamed cuckolded husband, 269–70; Vietnam draft, mental health as reason for deferment, 164; wage job in St. Louis, 186–87; "What is Frank looking for?," ix, 499, 504; will, writes, 491, 502; Willet, friendship with, 154; and Williams, Joan, 64–65; and Zen Buddhism, 128. *See also* Lost Roads Publishers; White River Press

Stanford, Francis Gildart (Frank), PERSONALITY: on own alcohol/drinking, 233–34, 255, 263, 297–98, 340, 406; on acceptance of own infidelity, 299, 313; and alcohol/drinking, 115, 202, 226, 233–34, 251, 255, 263, 269, 281, 292, 297–98, 300, 320, 340, 371, 401, 476; alcohol use, psychiatric report on, 401–2; appearance and dress, care of, 102, 124, 143, 156, 164; on Arkansas State Hospital, 279, 280, 356; and avoidance of confrontation, 101, 155, 307, 495; and avoidance of reality, x, xii, 495, 502–3; on beauty, capturing for poetry, 296–97; brilliance of, 140, 318; as champion of poets and artists, xi, xvi, 380–81, 399, 404, 420–21, 424, 434, 444, 467, 473; charisma of, xvi, 100, 124, 194, 210, 212, 228–29, 231, 284, 318, 445; childhood curiosity and, 29–30; on concept of "all women," 295–96, 443, 449–50, 497; death, obsession with, xv, 296; deceitfulness and lies of, ix, xv, 99, 227–28, 247, 352, 445–48;

despair of, 271–72; destruction of works as romantic/dramatic gesture, 272; as detached observer, 142; Dr. Joseph LeBlanc, sees, 163; dreaminess and aloofness of, 103, 138–39, 144, 232–33, 259–60, 286; emotional stability, concerns for, 163, 228; erratic and unpredictable behavior of, 117, 139, 144, 146, 163, 202–6, 250–51, 270; escaping, skills at, ix, 299, 300; friendships, lack of close, 145–46; as 'genius loner,' 207; on guilt/remorse for ruining lives, 268, 269–70, 282; itinerancy, habit of, 156; judo and, xv, 56, 117–18, 125, 126, 127–28, 130, 140, 203, 228, 230, 233, 248, 425, 464; kindness of, 98, 101, 126, 146, 189, 380, 399; leadership qualities of, 425, 464; maturity of, 145; mercurial and intense character of, xvi; non-committal nature of, 297; non-conformist attitudes of, 100; on own cruelty towards women in, 350; on own lies and deceit, 494; on own mental state, 270, 273–74, 279–80, 292–93; on own promiscuity, 299, 312–13; on own sensitivity and self-consciousness, 277–78; pain/cruelty inflicted on others, 268, 269, 271, 273, 278, 282, 294, 298, 350; pilfering books and, 140–41; popularity of, 59–60, 100, 102, 124, 138, 144, 250; promiscuity of, 112, 226, 251, 268, 269, 290, 294, 312–13, 315, 449–50, 496; psychiatric report on FS, 276–78; as quiet, moody, 194; schizophrenia, possible diagnosis of, 164; schoolmates, assessment of, 140; secrecy, inclination towards, 91, 103–4; self-aggrandizing attitudes of, 208; self-mythologizing of, 108, 252, 287, 350, 445–46, 484, 485; sensitivity concerning criticism, 155, 253–55, 276, 351; sobriety and, 339, 356, 476;

social manner, awkward, 145, 203; suicide, thoughts of and about, 164, 228, 258–60, 273, 282, 300–301, 478, 483, 497, 502; withdrawn, introverted nature, change to, 163
Stanford, Francis Gildart (Frank), POEMS:
"22 Poems," 213
adoption, theme in, 177–78
and Agrarianism, 206–7, 287
"Albino, The," 94, 205
"Allegory of Death and Night," 371
astronomy, theme of, 61
autobiographical nature of, 50, 57–58, 149, 276, 350
"Bass, The," 94
"Becoming the Unicorn," 218
"Belladonna," 255
Bender, interest in FS poems, 218, 346–47
"Bequeath," 218
"Black Cat Crossed the Road I Was Born On, A," 455
"Black Ship, The," 272
Black vernacular as common language of southern culture, 181–84, 325
"Blood Brothers, The": fishing references in, 93; levee camps in, 37–38; levee life, as lived experience, 149; midget motif in, 149; origins of, 148
"Blue Yodel a Prairie," 349
"Blue Yodel of poets of times past, 300, 346, 348
"Blue Yodel of the Desperado," 456
"Blue Yodel of the Wayfaring Stranger," 276, 347, 363
"Blue Yodel of Those Who Were Always Telling Me," 93, 113
Blue Yodel poems, 113, 115, 300
body form, expressions of, 111, 149–50
Bushido in, 128–30
"Cape, The," 483
character of, xvii–xviii, xix, 195–96

Stanford, Francis Gildart (Frank), POEMS *(continued)*:
childhood memories and innocence, theme of, 87, 115, 198, 237, 374
"Circle of Lorca," 436
connection of levee life and Sherman's Tavern, 178–79, 185, 375
"Dante Gabriel Rossetti with His Head on the Virginal," 347–48
dead children, theme of, 479–80
"Death and the Arkansas River," 239, 362, 383–84, 455
"Death in the Cool Evening," 346, 350, 363–64, 389
death, theme of, xviii, 196, 273, 348, 364, 368, 383–84, 478
"Delainey's Tale," 392
"Directions from a Madman," 443
"Do Tell," 364
double lives in, 479
"Dreaming with My Friend Mona," 105
"Dreams, The," 23, 40, 70
"Early Times in a Mississippi Liquor Store," 205–6
"Elegy For My Father, 1883–1963," 205
"Eleven Dark Women," 272
"Eleven Nocturnal Koans," 149–50
"Everybody Who Is Dead," 398
extended literary analysis of, 197–99, 205–7, 237–46, 274–76, 324–26, 347–50, 363–65, 383–85, 428–33
"Fair Trial," 431
"Farewell," 132, 274
fervent following of, xix, xxviii
"Field Hands on Plantation Night," 429
"Fire Left by Travellers," 178, 362, 368
fishing references in, 93, 94
"Flies on Shit," 208
"Fragment 293," 111
FS on own poetry, 13, 115, 153, 207, 253, 263, 321
gardening, theme in, 367–68
"Gospel Bird, The," 196, 205, 252, 306
"Gray Man," 155

growing reputation of, 199, 251–52, 255
GS in, 349
"Handling Paper with Cold Hands," 258
"He Was Talking to Himself about Butterflies," 359
"Hearse on the Other Side of the Canvas, The," 76
"Hidden Water," 361
"History of John Stoss," 461
"Holy Night," 205
human dignity in, xxix–xxx
"Humming This Song . . .," 347
"If She Lives in the Hills," 364
imagined world vs. reality, theme of, xxxiii, 326, 327
"In the Wet Fields," 221
injustice, themes of, xxix–xxx, 80–81
"Intruder, The," 412
"Inventory," 432
"Island," 432
"Kata at Dawn on the Cliff by the Lake," 116
"Kite, The," 179
lack of affectation and artifice, importance of, 115–16, 147, 153
"Lament of the Land Surveyor," 432
"Lap," 29
"Lay," 32
"Leer," 430
levee camps in, 40, 205, 364, 373–74, 429, 442
"Lies, The," 174
"Linger," 41, 274–75
literary canon, place in, xxviii
"Living," 195, 198
"Lullaby to a Child Who They Say Will Not Make It through the Night," 367
Maine experience in poems, 290
"Man Born in the Forest, A," 46
marginalized and downtrodden voices, themes of, xxviii–xxx, 76–80, 149, 153–54, 183

INDEX

maturity of FS's poetry, 116, 150, 205
mechanized urbanity, theme of, 206
Mencin in, 274, 456
"Mind Reader, The": autobiographical nature of, 109; Baby Gauge in, 42; Bushido in, 128; as earliest poetic composition, 109; FS on, xxv; Jimmy Lee in, 98; karate in, 117; marginalized, human dignity of, xxix; publication of, 252; race in, 42–43; secrecy of early poems, 115; mentioned, 57, 63, 90, 98, 109
mistreatment of women, theme of, 350
"Monk's Dog," 433
"Moon, The," 185, 271, 460
moon, theme of, 478–79
Mountain Home/Lake Norfork in poems, 113–15, 118, 430
"Mouths Full of Spit," 432
"My Hands Were Warm," 112
"Narcissus and Achilles," 218, 254
"Nautilus," 351
New York City in, 221, 298, 456–57
obligation to honor myth of heritage, 178
orphans, motif of, 175
own burnout in, 480
"Paramor, The," 274
"Partner," 368
"Past: Wintered Like a Circus, A," 392
"Pasture Dream," 364
Peabody Hotel in, 23–24
physicality and Karate in, 116
"Picture Show Next Door to the Stamp Store in Downtown Memphis, The," 195, 205–6, 212
"Poem," 218
poetry and film, merging of, 348–49
poetry, UARK MFA reactions to, 196–98
poets and editors on FS's poetry, 387–88
"Politicians, The," 205
"Professors, The," 205
public obscurity of, xxiv, xxviii

"Pump, The," 195, 197–98
racial justice/equality, themes of, xxix, 81–82, 196
regional character of, xvii
"River is Some Time to Kill without Warning, The," 368
"Rooms," 361
"Search Party," 398
on short poems, 148
"Silence the Thicket the Sniffing, The," 431
"Singing Knives, The"; Dugan on, 255; fishing references in, 93–94; FS on, 254; mentioned, 38, 96, 195. *See also* Stanford, Francis Gildart (Frank), BOOKS
"Slow Rag of the Yearbook," 93, 429–30
small details, importance of, 75
"Smoking Grapevine" unpublished, 395
"Smoking Mirrors, The," 94
"Snake Doctors, The," 253, 306
"Soaking Wet," 360
"Solitude of Historical Analysis, The," 205, 254
sound, as basis for language, 184
"Source," 398
and southern Blues, xxx
"Soybeans," 46
"Sphinx, The," 58
"St. Francis and the Wolf": FS on its relationship to TB, 264, 267; Jimmy Lee as "the Wolf," 108; origins of, 108–9, 139, 147, 180, 235, 264, 271, 355; relationship to TB, 235, 264, 387; revised to reflect emancipated identity, 185–86; sends to Fox and Dugan, 267–68, 286; mentioned, 113, 186, 260, 355, 387, 397, 429
"Strange Roads before Light," 478
"Strappado," 217
submissions to literary journals/magazines, 195–96, 360–61
"Sudden Opera," 274, 361
suicide, theme of, 483–84
"Suspect," 274

Stanford, Francis Gildart (Frank), POEMS *(continued)*:
"Swimming Towards Women," 259, 416
"Taking Your Life," 478
"Tapsticks," 253, 306
"Transcendence of Janus, The," 209, 284, 317
transformation of ordinary to transcendent, 114–15
"Truth, The," 395
"Tryst," 430
"Twilight," 363–64
"Unbelievable Nightgown, The," 360
as unclassifiable and raw, 148, 195
universal nature of, xviii, 97–98, 264–66, 419
use of repetition in, xxi
"Visitors of Night, The," 375
"What about This," 360
"Where We Slept Together," 274
"whereness" of his language, xxiii
"Will," 61, 177–78
"Wishing My Wife Had One Leg," 195, 205, 208, 217, 254
"With the Approach of the Oak the Axeman Quakes," 239, 329, 385
"Woman Driving a Stake into the Ground at Midnight, A," 478–80
"Women Singing When Their Husbands are Gone," 274, 351
Zen Buddhism in, 149–50
Stanford, James Cosby (father of Frank Sr.), 25
Stanford, John F. (nephew of Frank Sr.), 32, 64
Stanford, Ruth (Ruthie) *(later* Rogers, adoptive sister of FS):
about, xxxi, 39, 122; acceptance at St. Scholastica Monastery, 122–23; childhood of, 21, 39, 55, 59–67; conversion to Catholicism, 122, 135; and Dorothy, relationship with, 55, 56, 154, 499; on Dorothy's myth of Old South heritage, 88; and Dorothy's use of racist language, 532n39; on Frank Sr., 55; on FS, 56, 112, 116; on FS at Lake Norfork, 92–94; on FS's knowledge of adoption, 173, 174; on Greenville racism, 8; on Jimbo Reynolds, 167; on Jimmy Lee, 96; on levee life, 30, 33–34, 40; on Mountain Home, 88, 91; on Stanford's Memphis household, 50, 63–64; on surprise of move to Lake Norfork, 86; mentioned, xxxi, 29, 30, 45, 60, 61, 62, 67, 68, 98, 102, 105, 109, 118, 187, 189. *See also* levee camp (Snow Lake, AR)

Stanford, Virginia Crouch (Ginny) (*née* Crouch, second wife of FS): about, 336, 400i 448; Adamo, affair with, 498; art career of, 352–53, 362, 376, 408–9, 433, 437, 473–74; on Banks, Richard, 323; on Camp, Burt, 426; *Carolyn Wright readies herself for another evening*, 494, 496; and CD/FS/GS love triangle, x, 443–49, 452, 475, 477–78, 484, 493–99, 503; and CD meet, 501; on confrontation with FS, xi–xii, 501–2; describes meeting FS, 335; discovers CD's letters, 501; on discovery of CD affair, 495, 501; divorce, files for, xi; on FS, xii–xiii, 335, 481; on FS giving art 'assignments,' 338, 385, 405–6, 413–14, 500–501; on FS's affair with CD, x, 445, 448, 453, 476; on FS's bourgeois life, 402; on FS's championing of GS's art, 352, 399, 404–10, 473; on FS's creativity, 306, 384, 385; on FS's hostility to MFA program, 209; on FS's knowledge of film, 306; on FS's lies, 448; in FS's poems, 349, 478; on FS's poetry, 411; on FS's suicide, xii; on FS's writing habits, 337–38, 353, 403–4; and gardening, 365–67; and Gilchrist, Ellen, 466, 473; growing success of, 473–74; intimate images of FS and, 414–15; and *It Wasn't a Dream: It was a Flood*, 341–43,

345–46, 385; life with FS, 336–39, 340, 341, 352–53, 365–72, 401–4, *414*, 492; married, 358; "paint-the-lover" strategy and, 494–96; personality of, 448; and SHERMAN'S project, 376; mentioned, xxv, 347, 350, 355, 357–58, 369, 377, 380, 381, 396, 399, 420, 423, 425, 434, 435, 439, 451, 469, 486, 488, 492, 499. *See also* Stanford, Francis Gildart (Frank), LIFE; Wright, Carolyn Davis (C. D.)
Stanton, Maura, 390
Starlight Drive-In, 112, 305
Staten Island, NY, 282–83, 292–93, 298, 330
Stax Records, 266
Steinbeck, John, 138
Stern, Steve: on CD, 448; on CD/FS/GS love triangle, 446, 447, 449; on FS's deep knowledge and understanding of literature, 106; on FS's merging of reality and imagination, 162; on FS's personality, 318, 445–46, 449, 450, 463; on FS's poetry, 601n34; on FS's promiscuity, 450; on FS's writing habits, 158; on GS, 448; and Lost Roads Publishers, 463; mentioned, 395, 465
Stevenson, Robert Louis, 106
Stewart, W. D. "Bama," 15, 346
*Stinktree*, 416–18
Stokesbury, Leon: about, 191, 194, 199; on Dugan's admiration for FS, 216; on Dugan's visit to UARK MFA, 215–16; on FS driving off Mencin, 270; on FS's following, xix; on FS's personality, 159, 210; on FS's poetry, xxiv, xxix, 25, 194, 199, 235; on Lost Roads Publishers, 435; Lost Roads Publishers and, 435, 462; Mencin, affair with, 248; surveying and, 251; on TB, publication of, 459; mentioned, 192, 195, 205, 207, 208, 209, 220, 235. *See also under* Stanford, Francis Gildart (Frank), LIFE
Stoss, John: about, 191; on FS and his poetry, 194–95, 198, 199, 203, 207, 211; and Lost Roads Publishers, 460, 462, 466, 474, 487, 492; on Miller, 200–201; on surveying, 249, 451; on UARK MFA program, 193, 203; mentioned, 208, 424, 435, 503. *See also under* Stanford, Francis Gildart (Frank), CREATIVE LIFE
Strawberry (FS girlfriend), 315, 450
Subiaco Academy: about, xxvii, 95, 119, 121, 138, 140, 284, *301*, 303; civil rights and equality, promotion of, 132–33, 150; judo program and, 125–30. *See also* Hawkins, Emmett; Fuhrmann, Nicholas; Stanford, Dorothy Gilbert; Stanford, Francis Gildart (Frank), LIFE
*Sundays and Cybéle* (film), 234
Sunset Drive Inn, 241
"Surveying" (Broughton), 461, 468
surveying, FS and: CD as helper, 451; business arrangement with Kemp, 450–51; contested Greer Real Estate job, 491–92; as convenient cover for double-life, 451–52; equipment purchases for, 452, 464–65, 491; income used to support Lost Roads Publishers, 451; use of friends as field labor, 451, 491. *See also under* Stanford, Francis Gildart (Frank), LIFE
*SURVEYING: Poems by Irv Broughton*, 437
Suzuki, Daisetz, 129
'Sylvester Martingale,' 157, 176–77, 183, 235, 239, 324–27, 352. *See also* Banks, Richard Kenneth; *The Battlefield Where the Moon Says I Love You*; 'Francis Gildart'
Szalapski, James, 335
Szondi, Peter, 45

**T**

Taff, Evaline (mother of Frank Sr.), 25
Talese, Nan, 218, 392
Tangle Eye (Bluesman). *See* Horton, Walter (bluesman, "Tangle Eye")
'Tangle Eye' (Tang), 56, 235, 238, 240–45, 375, 429, 442
*Tansy*, 205, 252

Tate, Allen, xxxv, 97, 195
Tate, James, 217
Tau Kappa Epsilon, 154, 156
Taylor and Taylor (company), 40
Taylor, Bruce, 193, 195, 200, 215–16; on Miller Williams, 559n89
Tekes. *See* Tau Kappa Epsilon
*Terrorism* (Wright), 470, 474
"the bottoms" (Fayetteville neighborhood). *See* Sherman's Tavern
"The Hollow" (Fayetteville neighborhood). *See* Sherman's Tavern
Thomas, Dylan, 104, 421
Thomas, Lorenzo, xix, 265, 383
Thomas, Lowell, 253
Thomas, R. S., 221, 421
Thomas, Rufus, 70, 72, 78
Thompson, Clive, 293
Thompson, Elizabeth, 293, 312
Thompson, Kathy, 448
Thompson, Semon, 165–69
Three Way, TN, 300
Tichenor, George H., 75
Till, Emmett, 238
"Tin Cup" (Fayetteville neighborhood). *See* Sherman's Tavern
Tobias, Brother, 382
Trethewey, Natasha, xxxviii
Truffaut, François, 306
Truro, MA, 215, 278, 291–92
Turgenev, Ivan, 106
Turner, Alberta, 361, 462
Twain, Mark, xxix, 253
8475 Twin Coves Road (Rogers, AR), 341
Tyner, McCoy, 240

**U**

UARK Master of Fine Arts program (MFA): about, 190–91; combative teaching methods of, 192–93; Dugan visits, 215–17; focus on Southern traditions, 195, 200; freewheeling social atmosphere of, 199–200, 202; Ginsberg visits, 210–11; harsh treatment for bad poetry, 193–94; manly and masculine nature of, 190, 193, 202, 485; student's acceptance of value of program, 193–94; successes of, 191; and Whitehead, 190–91. *See also under* Adamo, Ralph; Biguenet, John; Dugan, Alan; Ginsberg, Allen; Gwynn, R. S. "Sam"; Stanford, Francis Gildart (Frank), LIFE; Stokesbury, Leon; Stoss, John; Whitehead, James Tillotson (Jim)
UARK Theatre, 203, 226, 305
*Ulysses* (Joyce), xx, xxii, 75
Undercliff Road (Cape Rosier, ME), 290
Union Gallery (Fayetteville), 473
University of Arkansas (UARK). *See* Fayetteville, AR; Stanford, Francis Gildart (Frank), LIFE; UARK Master of Fine Arts program (MFA)
University of Mississippi, 150
University of Pittsburgh Press, 462
Upton, Lee, xix, 160
Uptown (New Orleans), ix, 490

**V**

Valéry, Paul, 159
Vallejo, César, 160, 197, 363
Van Ostad, Adrian, 407
Vance, Rupert, 27
Vardaman, James K., 12
Vaughan, Bruce, 352
Vaughan, Mary, 352
Vermeer, Johannes, 102, 407, 424
Vernacular Black English (VBE), 181
Vico, Giambattista, 53, 103, 177
*Victory over Japan* (Gilchrist), 465
Vidacovich, Johnny, 491
Villon, François, 67, 272
'Vine, Crawling,' 77
Vivaldi, Antonio, 339
Vogelpohl, Herbert, 307
Vogelsang, Arthur, 360, 391

**W**

Wagner, Richard, 305
Wagon Wheel (bar), 320
Waldron, AR, 25
Waldrop, Rosmarie, 218, 222

Walker, David: about, 355; advises FS on film, other arts, 379; on FS's mental state, 278–79; on FS's poetry, 285, 362, 388; on FS's recounting of recent past, 357–58
Wallis, Hal, 67
Walt Whitman Award, 389
Walton, A. P.: on autobiographical nature of FS poetry, 50; FS, research on, 508–9; on FS's adoption, 173; on FS's poetry, xvii–xviii; on FS's talent vs. obscurity, xxiii–xxiv
Walton, Kathy: FS, affair with, 232, 268, 450; on White River Printers, 468; mentioned, 212, 229
Ward, Bob, 180, 195, 199, 202
Ward, Jesmyn, xxxviii
Warren County, 25
Warren, Robert Penn, xxxvi, 97, 195
Washington, DC, xxvi, 229, 300, 328
Washington, BoBo (childhood friend), 33, 90, 94, 98, 170, 237, 375
Washington County, MS, 6
Washington State, xxvii, 343
*WCPR*, 396
WDIA, 63, 72–73
"Wealth of Knowing, The" (Pasolini), 347
519 Webster Street (New Orleans, LA), ix
Weigl, Bruce, 361, 493
Wellfleet, MA, 291
Welty, Eudora, xxxvi, 306, 333–34, 353, 362, 404, 465
Wesleyan University Press, 285, 391
*West Coast Poetry Review*, 252, 264, 267, 278, 321
*West Coast Review*, 177, 251
West Frayser Elementary School, 57
Whalen, Tom, 164, 172, 419, 488
White, Minor, 469, 487
White River, 91–92, 231, 337–38, 342
White River Basin, 91
White River Lodge, 337, 340
White River Printers: about, 468–69, 488, 493; Ernest Wright investments in, 468, 469, 470. *See also* Lost Roads Publishers
Whitehead, Bruun, 451
Whitehead, Gen, 200, 203
Whitehead, James Tillotson (Jim): about, 190, 200; on FS's brilliance, xvii, 192; on FS's love of film, 306; on FS's poetry, 195–96, 198–99; FS's suicide, hears of, xii; insults Ginsberg, 211; "manly" style of, 190–91; recruits FS to MFA program, 192, 194; mentioned, 193, 200–201, 205, 207, 212–13, 220, 225, 419–20, 439, 465. *See also* UARK Master of Fine Arts program (MFA)
Whitman, Walt, xix, xxi–xxiii, xxix, 111, 114, 128, 182, 235, 253, 332, 389–90, 422, 483
Whitney, Ira, 314
"Whoa, Back, Buck" (song), 346
Wiederkehr, Mark, 382–84
Wilbur, Richard, 212–13, 291, 319, 356, 390, 392
Willett, Bill: about, 152; on accessibility of FS poems, xviii, 101, 155; and 'Billy the Jew,' 141; on CD/FS/GS love triangle, 446; on Eureka Springs Theater, 318; on friendship with FS, 154; on FS and levee camp kids, 170; on FS and the draft, 164; on FS and women, 350; on FS as surveyor, 568n114; on FS at Sherman's Tavern, 168–69; on FS's alcohol/drinking, 115, 155–56, 320; on FS's ambition to be Faulkner, 103–4; on FS's avoidance of conflict, 155, 410; on FS's behavior at preinduction exam, 164; on FS's care for appearance and dress, 102; on FS's competitiveness, 101; on FS's conversion to Catholicism, 122; on FS's disinterest in grades/school, 99; on FS's erratic behavior, 162, 163, 204; on FS's (false) heritage, 91; on FS's girlfriends, 112; on FS's interest in film, 305, 316–17, 578n4; on FS's karate, 116–18; on FS's knowledge of adoption, 90, 173, 175; on FS's popularity, 100; on FS's thoughts of suicide, 260;

Willett, Bill *(continued)*: on FS's writing habits, 107, 158–59; on Lake Norfork water-skiing accident, 112–13; on race in Mountain Home, 88–90; on Seawood and Moore, 170; on time at fraternity, 155–56
Willett, Kenny, 100
*William Blake's Illustrations to the Grave*, 296, 328
Williams, Bo (son of Joan Williams), 94, 98
Williams, Hank, 71, 200, 428
Williams, Joan: on Frank Sr.'s failing health, 86, 90; as friend of the Stanfords, 64–65; on FS's athleticism, 73; on FS's interior self, 102; on FS's kindness, 98–99; on FS's knowledge of adoption, 90; on FS's reading habits, 104; on life at Lake Norfork, 94; mentioned, 21, 68, 104, 105, 122, 254, 333, 343, 374
Williams, Jordan, 202
Williams, Karyn (sister of Lucinda), 488
Williams, Lucinda: FS on, 516n12; FS's influence on, 488–89; on impact of FS poems, xix; on love for FS, xi; mentioned, 201–2, 490
Williams, Matt (son of Joan Williams), 94, 98, 173, 507, 514
Williams, Miller: about, 200, *201*, 559n89; teaching style of, 201–2; mentioned, 181, 190, 212, 220, 416, 463, 465–66, 473–74, 488
Williams, Tennessee, 305
Williams, William Carlos, 197, 408
*With Lawrence in Arabia* (Thomas), 253
WLAC, 72
"the Wolf." *See* 'Jimmy Lee'
Wolfe, Thomas, xxxvi, 253
"Wolfman." *See* 'Jimmy Lee'
Wood, John, 190–92, 203, 210–11, 319, 408
Woods, Clyde, xxxvii, 16, 24, 46
Woodward, C. Vann, xxx, xxxiii–xxxvi, 42
Wordsworth, William, 138, 444

Wright, Aline (CD's mother), 441
Wright, Carolyn Davis (C. D.): about, 440, 440–41, 443–44, 448; discovers FS married to GS, xxx; and end of CD/FS/GS love triangle, 500–503; FS, affair with, xii, 439, 441, 443–44, 446–53, 475–77, 485; on FS as gifted, 148; on FS as mentor, 454, 472–73; on FS as surveyor, 451; in FS poems, 478–79; on FS's adoption, 174; on FS's appearance, 186; on FS's burnout, 472; on FS's charisma, xvi; on FS's commitment to changing, 399; on FS's deceit regarding GS, 447–48, 452, 477–78; on FS's interest in carnivals and fairs, 77, 149; on FS's lack of domesticity, 230; on FS's memory for literature, 142; on FS's poetry, xviii, xxii–xxiii, 221, 362, 443, 506; on FS's reading and grasp of literature, 106, 128; on FS's regionality/provincialism, xxvii; on FS's view of poetry publishing, 425; on FS's writing habits, 107, 395; and Gilchrist, 473, 485–86; on GS's discovery of CD affair, x, 501; and GS's relationship, x, 494–98, 500–501; on Jimmy Lee, 96; on loss of FS's love, 475–76; and Lost Roads Publishers, 448, 460–64, 466–70, 472, 484–88, 492–93; on meeting FS, 99–100, 441–42; personality of, 448, 475; poetry of, 444, 453–54, 461, 474; poetry similar to FS's, 444; on Sherman's Tavern, 167; on TB, xxx, 50, 162, 182, 238, 388, 392, 443; TB, helps publication of, 457–59; on women and FS's poetry, 350; mentioned, 209, 488, 490, 492, 493, 494, 499, 500, 501
Wright, Ernest (CD's father), 441, 468–70, 491–92
Wright, Franz, xvi, 361, 379
Wright, James, xxiv, 160, 361, 416, 423
Wright, Richard, xxxvii, 165
WRP. *See* White River Printers

**Y**
Yaddo, xxiv, 291, 321
Yale Series of Younger Poets Award,
　215, 390
Yates, Richard, 212
Yeats, William Butler, 162, 185, 202
Yesenin, Sergei, 259–60, 416
Yoknapatawpha County (fictional), 110
Young, David, 361, 474
Young, Dean, 196–97
Young, Kevin, xxxviii, 10, 27
Yvette (FS girlfriend), 171

**Z**
Zen Buddhism, 128–29, 132, 148–50,
　185, 191, 502
*Zen Buddhism and Its Influence on
　Japanese Culture* (Suzuki), 129
Zimmerman, David, 318
Zolotow, Ellen (Crescent Dragonwagon),
　314–15, 322

www.ingramcontent.com/pod-product-compliance
Lightning Source LLC
Chambersburg PA
CBHW021846230426
43671CB00006B/284